CITY OF BURBANK

Public Library

.OCT 1 9 1995

NOTE DATE DUE

EACH BORROWER is required to sign an application and is responsible for books drawn in his name.

FINES are charged for each book kept overtime (including Sundays and Holidays.)

WARPATHS

BY THE SAME AUTHOR

Politics of Colonial Policy

Guerillas and Grenadiers

Atlantic Merchant-apothecary

The English Atlantic, 1675–1740

Betrayals: Fort William Henry and the "Massacre"

WARPATHS

Invasions of North America

IAN K. STEELE

New York   Oxford

OXFORD UNIVERSITY PRESS

1994

Oxford University Press

Oxford   New York   Toronto
Delhi   Bombay   Calcutta   Madras   Karachi
Kuala Lumpur   Singapore   Hong Kong   Tokyo
Nairobi   Dar es Salaam   Cape Town
Melbourne   Auckland   Madrid

and associated companies in
Berlin   Ibadan

Published by Oxford University Press, Inc.,
200 Madison Avenue, New York, New York 10016

Oxford is a registered trademark of Oxford University Press

Library of Congress Cataloging-in-Publication Data
Steele, Ian Kenneth.
Warpaths : invasions of North America / Ian K. Steele.
p. cm.   Includes bibliographical references and index.
ISBN 0-19-508222-2
ISBN 0-19-508223-0 (paper)
1. Indians of North America—Wars—1600–1750.
2. Indians of North America—First contact with Europeans.
3. Indians of North America—History—Sources.
4. Ethnohistory—United States.
5. Europe—Colonies—America—Administration.
I. Title   E82.S74   1994   973—dc20   93-42276

9   8   7   6   5   4   3   2   1

Printed in the United States of America
on acid free paper

Dedicated to W. J. Eccles

Teacher and Exemplar

PREFACE

This is an invitation to rethink a major aspect of early North American history by bringing together two scholarly fields that do not usually interact. One is the fashionable, if sometimes shrill and sanctimonious, field of ethnohistory, which is developing so quickly that any attempt at accessible synthesis is bound to be premature and incomplete. Ethnohistory has rightly restored the Amerindian to North American history and "discovered" the invasions of the continent. The other field is the less fashionable, sometimes case-hardened and myopic, study of "the colonial wars." Military history can measure the capacity to gather and use allies, warriors, food, weapons, and ideologies in conflicts that make some essential comparisons horribly obvious; cultural relativity offers no comfort to those defeated in battle. Drawing on both military and ethnohistorical perspectives, this brief study tries to reach beyond the racism evident in many accounts about victims, criminals, or heroes—accounts that are either myopic or antidotal.

Warfare, between states or between peoples, deserves to be neither celebrated nor forgotten. Colonial North American history was not created in peace and interrupted by war; wars, rumors of war, and costs of war affected every generation of Amerindians and colonists. It is disturbing to recognize that modern North America was established amid such violence, but this sobering realization is better than accepting sanitized myths that make modern levels of violence seem like moral degeneration from some peaceful colonial or pre-colonial Arcadia. It is a small comfort to notice that neither Amerindians nor Europeans were ever racist enough before 1765 to put aside pre-existing enmities and unite against the strangers.

The boundaries of a story are one clue to its purpose. Beginning in 1513 seems obvious, though less common than the Anglocentric 1585 or 1607, or the attempt to bypass almost all the inter-racial violence of "discovery and settlement" by pretending that the "colonial wars" began in 1689 and ended in 1760. Part I describes and compares five diverse centers of interaction between Amerindians and Europeans in the crucial initial phase that included meeting, fighting, tolerating, cooperating, or incorporating each other into their own pre-existing conflicts. Part II examines the Anglo-French inter-colonial wars, including the consequences of both war and peace for Amerindians. This was the period when flintlocks became the common weapon in warfare that mixed incompatible martial values, methods, and objectives. The length of this struggle indicates a balance of violence between the colonial competitors and an Amerindian interest in perpetuating the contest. The climax of the story, Part III, involves the changes attending the arrival of substantial numbers of European regulars, changing the ways of war once again. These changes led to British victory in the European invasion of colonial North America, and an equally unprecedented negotiated peace after the Amerindian War of 1763 to 1765. It should not be surprising that the end of this story bristles with new beginnings.

The naming of people and places cannot be entirely value-free. "Amerindian" is a term that overcomes some erroneous stereotypes and is a better description than Columbus's lie that he had met the people of India. Amerindian tribal groups are, for ready identification, ascribed their anglicized names. The Ojibwa are not called by the corrupted name "Chippewa" or by their eighteenth-century name, the "Sauteux." The Iroquois in Canada are called the "Caughnawaga," after their major settlement. The terms "Spanish," "English," and "Dutch" refer to the language groups, and to designate all subjects of specific European monarchies or republics. "French" refers to the language group and, in contexts that are obvious, to natives of France. "British" here refers to natives of Britain. Britain's North American colonists came to be called "Americans" by about 1740. Most places of habitation or fortification are given the names assigned by their possessors at the time, but geographical features are given their modern names.

In surveying this general topic, I have been uncommonly indebted to the authors whose works are cited in the notes. My colleagues George Emery and J.C.M. Ogelsby gave me the benefit of their expert reading of parts of this book. Ken Steele designed the maps, and Herta Steele processed every word in ways my computer cannot. Thanks for this help comes with the required waiver that all rights, and especially wrongs, remain the exclusive property of the author.

London, Ontario   I. K. S.
August 1993

CONTENTS

FIGURES

MAPS

WARPATHS

Chapter 1

ARMS IN ARCADIA
1513–1565

The North America of 1513 was, and unfortunately remains, a world of extremely potent legends. The early European intruders transplanted their alluring myths of cities of gold and fountains of youth. Some Amerindians reinforced those hopes either to please their visitors or to encourage troublesome intruders to hurry elsewhere. Descendants of North America's European invaders came to prefer another, more practical, legend. This legend came to be called the "history" of a continent deemed empty in 1513, a continent about to be "discovered," "explored," and "settled" by Europeans who thereby converted a worthless wilderness into a rich and fruitful world. Native inhabitants were too easily categorized as irritating fauna and viewed as minor obstacles to progress.

Although this traditional settler legend has finally been challenged, it is rapidly being replaced by the enthusiastic revival of yet another equally ancient and dubious legend. North America of 1513 is increasingly being seen as a bountiful paradise thought to have given as many as 18 million people a life of health, plenty, and peace. This North American Arcadia is seen as having been polluted and destroyed by European invaders bringing alien diseases, ecologically disruptive plants and animals, insatiable materialism, and deadly war. Legends are seldom as idle or harmless as they appear, and challenging the legends about North America at the time of European contact is as illuminating as it is difficult.

America north of the Rio Grande was, in 1513, a complex universe whose unnumbered inhabitants lived in some five hundred distinct and competing tribal and language groups, whose ancestors had invaded the continent by land or water from northern Asia more than twenty-five thousand years earlier. No one then, or now, could count their number in 1513; estimates range from 1 million to 18 million, but, on this issue, it is by no means safe to assume that the truth lies in the middle.[1] North America can be regarded as having been lightly populated when compared with the concentration of peoples in Europe or in the rich Central American empires of the Aztecs and the Mayans, where tens of millions lived in complex hierarchical civilizations. Nonetheless, north and east of the mountains and deserts of what would be called Mexico and Texas lived numerous cultures of corn planters and hunters, some organized into sophisticated empires, paramount chiefdoms, and confederations of tens of thousands of people. There were, of course, no Indians. *Los Indios,* a lie invented by Columbus, quickly became a dismissive European stereotype and would take centuries to become a broader identity for those it initially misrepresented.[2] The Natchez of the lower Mississippi; the Creek and Cherokee of the lower Appalachians; the Apalachee, Calusa, and Timucua of the Florida peninsula; the Cofitachiqui and Powhatan of the Atlantic coastal plain; and the Delaware, Iroquois, Huron, Narragansett, Massachusetts, and Wampanoag of the northern woodlands were among the major concentrations of people who would continue to contend with competing Amerindian powers while they met European invaders in the century after 1513 (Map 1).

Europeans, from a smaller and more fractious universe of some 60 million people, joined only by their disintegrating links as Christians, thought the North American continent did not exist at all in 1513. Both Christopher Columbus (1492, 1493, 1498, 1502) and John Cabot (1497, 1498) had insisted that the islands they visited were outposts of the fabled mainlands of Asia, and investors in exploration continued to hope that this was so.

Prefiguring the invasion of the Americas, Europe's belligerent westward oceanic expansion had already overrun a series of eastern Atlantic islands that were located, fought over with indigenous and European competitors, and settled by the victors. The Iberian powers of Portugal and Spain led this Atlantic expansion. The Portuguese had established colonies of fishermen, wine producers, and sugar planters in the Azores, Madeira, and Cape Verde Islands. Portugal, a pioneer of Atlantic navigation, was initially a serious contender in the European scramble for new worlds to the west. Portuguese and Spanish piratical raids on each other's bases in the Canary Islands had become part of a full-scale war between 1475 and 1479, in which the Portuguese allied with the Guanches inhabitants of those islands against Castilian Spanish colonists. Westward exploration from these island bases was not a priority in the next decade.

After Columbus's successful Caribbean voyage of 1492, Portugal threatened to send a powerful expedition in the same direction. The Castilian and Portuguese monarchs signed a treaty at Tordesillas in 1494, which established a longitudinal demarcation line some nine hundred miles west of the Cape Verde Islands. The powers recognized the exclusive rights to exploration, trade, and conquest in their generous respective spheres. The Iberian courts had appropriated and divided

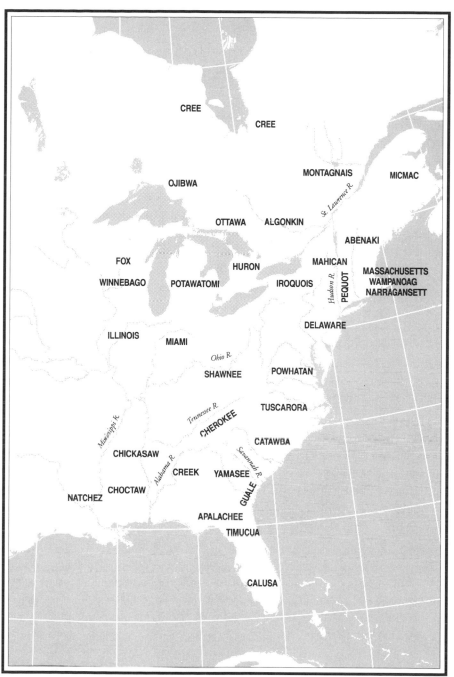

©1993 Ian K. Steele

Map 1. Major peoples of eastern North America, ca. 1513.

all the worlds they might still find, without any agreement with other rivals.

Although it was vague, since accurate longitudinal readings would not become possible for another 250 years, the Tordesillas line was immensely significant for Portuguese expansion. England's King Henry VII, who had earlier declined participation in Columbus's "enterprise," was among the first to challenge that line. John Cabot, following the oceanic navigation of Bristol fishermen and merchants, sailed to the Gulf of St. Lawrence region (1497, 1498). The Portuguese court sent the Corte-Real brothers out from the Azores to test the location of the line in the Northwest Atlantic in 1500 and again in 1501, and a Portuguese fishing colony was established on Cape Breton Island (1520–1525). However, rapid Portuguese acquisitions in Brazil, Angola, the Indian Ocean, and the China Sea caused their enthusiasm for the Treaty of Tordesillas to rise and that for North America to fall. They continued to fish the Grand Banks, but North America's main value to the Portuguese was to block European rivals from direct access to the Portuguese trading world in Asia.

Castile, numbering some 8 million people, was the kingdom that actually led Europe into America, and Castile had been created by war. Inspired by chivalric traditions and fortified by faith, soldiers had won wealth, status, and royal applause by continuing the age-old plundering of towns and herds along the Islamic frontier within Spain. The 781-year-long Christian drive to oust Islam from Spain was finally completed in 1492. As would be the case in America, the military expeditions had been financed and led by *hidalgos*, whose royal license often granted those "who went before" *(adelantados)* the right to govern seized territory, aided by unpaid volunteers operating from fortified strongholds called *presidios*. Armored mounted lancers were the essence of these raiding parties, with lances and swords reinforced by infantry using pikes and crossbows if the intention was to hold conquests against counterattack.

Castile's martial and religious *reconquista* mentality was exported to North Africa, the Canary Islands, and the Americas. Spanish incursions into the austere lands of North Africa did not produce sufficient booty to encourage further ventures southward. The Canaries represented brutal success that lured ambitious Castilians westward, but native Guanches on some of the Canary Islands resisted conquest for nearly two centuries. The methods of later imperial rivalries were already evident when Portugal supported those Guanches against Castilian colonists during the War of the Castilian Succession (1475–1479).[3] Castilians did not conquer the island of Palma until 1492 and took Tenerife the following year. All four of Christopher Columbus's American voyages proceeded via these newly subdued Canary Islands, and the Spanish easily, and brutally, conquered the peaceable Arawak peoples of the major Caribbean islands of Hispaniola (1494), Puerto Rico (1509), Jamaica (1509), and Cuba (1511).

 Although North America was always peripheral to Spain's empire, Spain pioneered Europe's encounter with North America's people. In much of the Gulf and the southeastern Atlantic region, which the Spanish called *La Florida*, contact was synonymous with invasion. Encounters between 1513 and 1565 illuminate essential features of both civilizations, and severely test all the competing myths about the relative martial, economic, and biological strengths of the societies that collided there.

Juan Ponce de León (1460–1521) accompanied Columbus on his 1493 voyage, when he founded the town of Isabella on Hispaniola. Ponce de León was prominent in the conquest of the eastern region of that island, where he became a leading settler in an area producing food with forced Arawak labor. His slaves, many of whom had been taken in raids on neighboring Caribbean islands, indicated that there was gold on the island of Puerto Rico. In 1509 Ponce de León led a successful invasion, taking that island from its remaining Arawak cultivators, serving briefly as governor, and quickly accumulating wealth from alluvial gold recovered by Arawak slaves. By 1512 the gold had become scarce, and most of the Amerindian laborers had died from overwork or European diseases, repeating the tragic pattern of horrendous depopulation already witnessed in Hispaniola. That year, enticed either by the need for new lands and laborers or by Arawak tales of gold, Ponce de León financed and organized the royally approved expedition to explore what was thought to be the "island of Bimini."

Ponce de León's three well equipped vessels sailed north from Puerto Rico, dropping anchor south of modern St. Augustine, Florida, in March 1513. On entering their first Timucua village, the Spanish met armed resistance and withdrew. Another fight erupted when the expedition landed again to take on wood and water, and the Spanish retreated to the sea. Keeping within the inshore countercurrent after discovering the Gulf Stream, they scouted south to the tip of Florida and up the west coast, perhaps as far as San Carlos Bay, where they intended to clean and recaulk one of the ships. When some eighty canoes full of Calusa archers with shields approached, the Spaniards attacked. Pursuing the Calusa ashore, the Spanish broke up canoes and captured women but, once again, had to withdraw in the face of fierce opposition. Perhaps earlier encounters with Spanish slavers and traders had already angered the Timucua and Calusa, or hostility had been promoted by encounters with other intruders. In any case, these societies were certainly martial enough to drive off the Spanish with bows and arrows.[4]

The Spanish visited San Carlos Bay again in 1517, when Hernández de Córdoba's three-vessel fleet stopped for water while returning from a failed Central American campaign against the Mayans. Antonio de Alaminos, who had been a pilot with Ponce de León, directed them into the familiar bay on Florida's southern Gulf coast. Although wary and well armed, the landing party of twenty was soon routed by the Calusa.

> They had very long bows and good arrows and lances and some weapons like swords, and they were clad in deerskins and were very big men. They came straight on and let fly their arrows and at once wounded six of us.[5]

Superior Spanish swords prevailed at close quarters, but neither muskets nor crossbows[6] were effective against the more numerous Calusa.

Ponce de León returned to San Carlos Bay in 1521 with two hundred well-armed men, bringing missionaries, livestock, and seeds for a settlement that would have been strategically located to assist ships homeward bound to Spain. There was the predictable fight with the Calusa shortly after the Spaniards landed, and the intruders were defeated and driven off once more. Calusa and Timucua warriors displayed well-developed martial skills in repulsing experienced *conquistadores;* both Ponce de León and Hernández de Córdoba died of wounds inflicted by the Calusa.

Having provoked ferocious resistance to their slaving and finding no visible treasure on the Gulf coast of Florida, it is not surprising that the next Spanish venture from a Caribbean base would be farther north on the Atlantic coast. Lucas Vásquez d'Ayllón, a judge and member of the governing Audiencia of Santo Domingo, was also a wealthy sugar planter and mill owner. He invested in a 1520 exploratory voyage toward the Carolina coast, and in another the following year led by Pedro de Quxós to the idyllic "land of Chicora" (Winyah Bay, South Carolina). There Quxós exchanged gifts, explored the area, then entrapped some sixty Guale to be sold as slaves, making the voyage profitable. Ayllón formally denounced Quxós and supported a court order to return the slaves to their native land.[7]

Returning to Spain and taking along a precocious captive who learned Spanish and was baptized Francisco Chicora, Ayllón publicized the merits of the bountiful, peaceful "New Andalucia." He received a royal license in 1523 that offered him a trading monopoly, a large personal estate, and the option of establishing forts and settlements in Chicora at his own cost. In 1525 Ayllón sent Quxós, commanding two caravels and crews totaling sixty men, to return most of the Guale captives. Preparations for Ayllón also included acquiring interpreters from three language groups that the "Chicoran" interpreters did not understand: Muskogean from the Savannah River area, Timucuan from St. Helena, and Algonquian from north of Cape Fear.[8] Quxós exchanged gifts with the trusting Guale and effectively scouted the coasts from St. Helena to Chesapeake Bay, setting up stone crosses claiming the area for Charles V, king of Spain and Hapsburg emperor. Christian claims of religious superiority were again conveniently translated into royal claims to lands of non-Christians.

In 1526 Ayllón led an expedition of six ships, carrying five hundred men, plus about a hundred wives and children, African slaves, and Dominican monks, to start a colony on the Georgia or South Carolina coast. This was not an army like the five hundred soldiers, fourteen cannon, and sixteen horses with which Hernán Cortés had conquered the fractious and fabulous Aztec empire in 1521. Nevertheless, the Ayllón expedition included some soldier-adventurers with experience in both worlds, artillery, and eighty-nine horses. He took a supply of cassava bread and corn to sustain the colonists until a food supply could be found, and he also brought cattle. Although piloted by the able Pedro de Quxós, making his third voyage to Chicora, the intended site was missed and the flagship was wrecked, with most of the supplies lost while landing. Despite being outwitted and deserted by their "Chicora" interpreters, the Spanish established San Miguel de Gualdape in Winyah Bay near the mouth of the Pee Dee River (Map 2).

Although they were excellent archers, the Guale of Chicora, a southern branch of the Creek people, did not resist the settlement. Their own lives involved seasonal hunting, fishing, and gathering, as well as occasional migration to clear new fields for growing corn, beans, and pumpkins. They could not sustain the Spanish, and food shortages soon became a serious problem because of the lost ship, the lateness of the season, and poor soils. Ayllón and a majority of the colonists soon died of locally endemic malaria, to which they had little immunity. Dissension within the Spanish colony also led to killings, as well as some conflict with the Guale. Within three months the colony was abandoned, with only one-quarter of the original expedition surviving, and these 150 were near starvation.[9] *La Florida* was proving to be as hard on Spanish ambitions as North Africa had been.

Spanish interest in North America, like that of the rest of Europe, was revived once the astounding wealth of the Central American Aztec empire became clear. Spanish officialdom soon sought to control the fortunate renegade Cortés, and venturers like Pánfilo de Narváez wanted to find "other Mexicos." Narváez had become wealthy in the conquests of Hispaniola, Jamaica, and Cuba, where he had gained a reputation as particularly brutal and untrustworthy. Ambitious to duplicate the success of his rival Cortés and to curb Cortés's empire on the north, Narváez launched his own major expedition. Armed with a perpetual royal grant to the entire northern Gulf coast and its unlimited hinterlands, but required by a new royal order to give fair treatment to native peoples, Narváez sailed directly from Spain in June 1527 with a force of six hundred volunteers in five ships.[10]

Although a third of the men deserted in the West Indies and half the horses died during passage, the expedition seemed promising enough

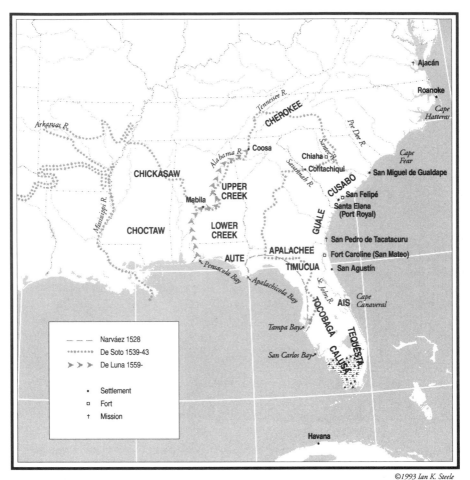

©1993 Ian K. Steele

Map 2. *La Florida* to 1575.

once it reached Florida. The landing was safely beyond the territory of the Calusa, who had thwarted Ponce de León and Córdoba, and relations with the inhabitants began cautiously. An officer of the expedition was landed on an island, where he traded with the Timucua for fish and venison. Some forty thousand Timucua, divided into two rival confederations and some fifteen distinct tribes, are thought to have lived in numerous sizable villages across north central Florida, sustained by farming, hunting, and fishing.[11] It is not known what these particular villagers knew of the Timucuan encounter with Ponce de León fifteen years earlier, but their approach was also cautious.

What we know of the disastrous Narváez invasion of Florida comes from the memoirs of Alvar Nuñez Cabeza de Vaca, one of only four known to have survived the expedition.[12] The day after the initial trading, Narváez landed as many men as the ship's boats could hold. They found the Timucua village, which included one dwelling that could accommodate more than three hundred people, entirely evacuated. If the Timucua had planned to encourage the Spaniards to re-embark by offering no hospitality, the plan failed, for "amid some fish nets we found a gold rattle." The next day, Narváez landed the rest of his men and the forty-two surviving horses, and ceremonially claimed the country for Charles V. The following day, some villagers approached; although there were no interpreters and little comprehension, Cabeza de Vaca was sure that "their many signs and threats left little doubt that they were bidding us to go."[13]

After scouting, and unwisely sending his fleet to an inadequately known rendezvous farther north, Narváez marched his three hundred remaining men to Tampa Bay without discovering any of the cornfields they had presumed would be a source of provisions. The Spanish captured four Amerindians, showed them corn, and were taken to a small field of green corn near a village. These surprised Timucua offered no resistance to the invaders, even when the Franciscan commissary ordered the burning of the revered remains of their ancestors. The villagers did offer the usual refrain that whatever interested the intruders, particularly gold, could be found in abundance in the land of their rivals, in this case the powerful Apalachee to the north.

As the Spanish moved northward, they found the country without people, settlements, or food. After fifteen days on ships' rations, they saw some two hundred Timucua approaching them with what the Spanish regarded as menacing gestures. The Spanish attacked, reportedly without inflicting any casualties but again taking a few prisoners, who led them to precious edible corn and guided them on toward "Apalachen." The Spanish marched northward for another month "without seeing a native who would let us catch up to him."[14] The Timucua could regard their strategy as successful; despite the destruction of some revered objects and the loss of some grain, the intruders had been moved along without reported loss of life on either side.

Approaching the Apalachicola River, the Spanish were met by Dulchanchellin, a chieftain accompanied by a large retinue including musicians playing reed flutes. He was carried on a man's back, which appeared ludicrous to the Spanish who equated status with horsemanship and were themselves mounted on the first horses ever seen in the area. After an hour of exchanging gifts and gestures, which may not have conveyed much more than did the mutually incomprehensible words, the Spanish believed Dulchanchellin to be an enemy of the Apalachee. He led the expedition to his village and fed them, but when they awoke, the Spaniards found themselves alone in the village.

As the Spaniards proceeded, they saw that they were being shadowed by Amerindians. Since this army was recruited in Spain rather than the Spanish Caribbean, the men wore hot, heavy breast- and back plates as well as metal helmets. The tired and hungry Spaniards, many with open wounds caused by the chafing of armor that to date seemed unnecessary, recorded relief as they reached their first major objective, the Apalachee village they called Apalachen.

Narváez ordered an entirely unprovoked surprise attack. Ten horsemen and fifty infantry fell upon the village of forty small thatched huts nestled defensively in a clearing between lakes. The attack met no resistance, as the men were not in the village. Apalachee bowmen soon retaliated, skirmishing from the cover of nearby swamps and tall cornfields. From scouting forays and from prisoners, the Spanish learned that, though they were in the biggest village of the Apalachee, there were no riches. The only treasures had been corn, deerskins, roughly woven cloth, and corn-grinding bowls. After three weeks of sporadic fighting, resulting in the death of an Aztec prince accompanying the expedition and in the frequent wounding of armored men and horses, Narváez became increasingly interested in prisoners' reports about Aute, nine days to the southwest.

After an uneventful first day in which no inhabitants were seen, the expedition was chest deep in a lake when it was attacked by bowmen who wounded several men and horses. These unidentified warriors, likely Apalachee, harried the marching Spaniards, then disappeared when a counterattack was launched. Successes lured the warriors to challenge the Spaniards in an open area, but mounted Spanish lancers chased them off, killing two. For the next eight days, the wary Spaniards saw no one.

As the Spaniards approached Aute, near the mouth of the Apalachicola, they came under random attack. A prominent *hidalgo* was killed by an unseen adversary whose arrow found the space between helmet and body armor. The Aute, who were allies of the Apalachee, had evacuated and burned their village before the Narváez expedition arrived, though some food was found. Narváez and about a third of the Spanish infantry soon came down with malaria, and the encampment endured night attack. The cavalry plotted to desert what was now a doomed venture, but accepted a plan to build boats with which the whole expedition could escape.

Lessons learned from the military encounter with Florida bowmen are evident in the boat building. Armored horses, a major Spanish advantage against astonished Aztec and Inca infantry, had seldom been effective in the swamps and bush of this region, and the prized horses were now needed for food. To get iron for boat construction, armorers reworked not only stirrups and spurs, but also the metal-tipped arrows for the crossbows. Spanish crossbows had failed to compete with Amerindian longbows that were six to seven feet long, thick as a man's arm, and very accurate at two hundred yards.[15] Although Spanish armor had been effective against most arrows encountered on three continents, these Aute arrows penetrated six inches of wood, and even Spanish breast- and back plates. Ten Spaniards were killed while foraging. "We found their bodies pierced all the way through, although some of them wore good armor."[16] Some flint arrowheads shattered against armor, producing wounding shards. Cabeza de Vaca's tragic story of the 250 who escaped from this "Bay of Horses," is an extraordinary postscript to the fourth failed Spanish invasion of Florida. Only 4 of the 250 eventually made their way to Mexico City.

The attempt to match Cortés's looting was, of course, futile in societies that had limited experience with metals, no fascination with those the Europeans called precious, and a social organization that extracted limited tribute from members or neighbors. Cortés had demonstrated that an unpromising coast might mask a rich civilization available to invaders who undertook an *entrada,* a persistent armed exploration of the interior. Ayllón and Narváez had tested that method in *La Florida.* Its inhabitants defended themselves so effectively as to cause massive Spanish losses from privation, disease, and native weapons.

Although the Narváez disaster and the failure of the Ayllón venture quelled Spanish interest in *La Florida,* the phenomenal success of Francisco Pizarro's invasion of Peru (1531–1533) revived hopes that forbidding lands could lead to unimaginable wealth. What could be impossible when the ruler of a mountainous empire could pay a ransom of a roomful of gold? Hernando De Soto, Pizarro's chief military adviser, had been among the mere 168 men who, through force, extortion, and the exploitation of Inca factions, seized control of that empire. De Soto, a fifteen-year veteran of American warfare, took an impressive fortune home to Spain but was soon prepared to gamble it in search of even more in the hinterlands of *La Florida.*

Emperor Charles V gave De Soto the vacated rights of both Ayllón and Narváez as well as the governorship of Cuba and appointed him lifetime salaried *adelantado* of whichever six-hundred-mile stretch of newly discovered coast and interior he might choose. Although the grant included the commendable orders of 1526 concerning the fair treatment of natives, the mood of the venture was better reflected by a royal levy of one-half of all looted grave-goods, rather than the usual one-fifth of valuables.[17]

De Soto's expedition was a remarkably well-equipped, persistent, and brutal military reconnaissance of much of *La Florida.* The 330 infantry and nearly 270 cavalry who landed in or near Tampa Bay in May 1539 included a number of officers and men who had fought with De Soto in Central and South America. The cavalry consisted of lancers and swordsmen. Although the infantry had crossbows and arquebuses, swords and shields were more common. Understandably, the Spanish infantry preferred close combat in groups rather than a long-range exchange of projectiles with enemies who vastly outnumbered them.

Muskets were not the predominant weapons in De Soto's army, for good reason. The heavy early matchlock muskets misfired half the time even in good weather, could not be used in the rain, and always revealed the musketeer's position because he had to carry a lighted, pungent-smelling wick. The advantages of this weapon over the crossbow were its irresistible penetrating power at comparable range, the possibility of firing several small deadly musket balls at once, and the comparative ease of becoming competent at its use. For the last of these reasons, the musket would replace the crossbow in Spanish *La Florida* by around 1550, long before it did so in Europe.[18]

De Soto's army came directly from Spain, bringing traditional European armor of varying quality. Some of those having American military experience exchanged the hot and heavy metal breast- and back plates for the lighter Aztec armor of quilted cotton covered with leather.[19] Such armor protected Spaniards from arrows, but would not protect Amerindians from muskets. The army was also accompanied by large ferocious dogs, trained as "dogs of war."

Food was the primary wealth of most North American societies, and as the troubles of the Narváez expedition had emphasized, corn was the vital golden fuel of the invaders, even if it was not their primary objective. De Soto used his position as governor of Cuba to move that island's capital from Santiago to the new port of Havana, which lay across the channel from Florida. There he assembled massive provisions for his six hundred men and three hundred horses, the largest Spanish force to invade Florida. Nine vessels carried the men, horses, a large herd of pigs, provisions, and equipment. The prolific Spanish pigs, ancestors of the southern "razorback," had to be driven by a herder;[20] the rest of the provisions, equipment, and supplies had to be carried. Ominously, iron collars and chains for some three hundred bearers were among the weighty supplies; the men on horseback were ready for a land where man was the only beast of burden.

Despite provisions, it became evident upon arrival that the men, horses, and even pigs were to subsist mainly on donated or stolen Amerindian corn. De Soto insisted on tribute paid in food, and he did not hesitate to be extortionate. The approach, already used by both Cortés and Pizarro, was to capture the most powerful native leaders and hold them as long as the expedition was in their territory, demanding food, bearers, concubines, and guides into the territory of the next tribe. Although some of the fertile fields yielded two or even three crops a year, the continuing presence of De Soto's force was a terrible burden on the food supply. The four communities where the expedition wintered (Apalachee, Chickasa, Autiamque on the Arkansas River, and Aminoya on the Mississippi) were chosen because of their stores of food, but it seems safe to assume that famine came in the wake of each De Soto visitation.

De Soto presumed conflict. His lancers killed two of the first inquisitive Amerindians they saw, and his men established their campsites with a surrounding clearing extending a bowshot in all directions. There were numerous attacks on individual Spaniards, as well as fatal skirmishes, but major confrontations were few, given the intruders' vicious tyrannies over large and well-organized communities.

The only major battle of the expedition occurred at the Choctaw town of Mabila (Selma, Alabama). De Soto's seekers of treasure had been met, with considerable ceremony, by Chief Tascaloosa. Promptly captured by the Spanish, in keeping with their routine extortion, he agreed to lead them to his town of Mabila, where the Spaniards would be given the bearers and concubines they demanded. The sizable town was surrounded by a newly repaired fifteen-foot palisade of sturdy logs, plastered with mud to retard burning. De Soto and his mounted advance guard entered Mabila boldly and were seated and entertained by a dance in the central square. When Chief Tascaloosa escaped his Spanish guards, his bowmen immediately attacked. With numerous men killed, and De Soto among the wounded, the Spanish were driven from the town. They left behind equipment, some weapons, and all the loot of the expedition to date. In the flush of initial victory the Tascaloosa charged after the fleeing Spanish. Spanish cavalry seemed to join the retreat, luring the defenders farther from their protecting walls. The horsemen then turned and attacked, lancing a number of warriors before they could regain safety. Regrouped and reinforced, Spanish foot companies attacked simultaneously from several positions. Although "the Indians fought with so great spirit that they drove us outside again and again," the stockade was breached and the buildings were torched. The Spanish cavalry commanded the whole perimeter of the town, driving back those trying to escape the flames. By Spanish accounts, at least 2500 defenders died in Mabila, compared with only 20 Spaniards killed and 150 wounded. Horses, and especially the Aztec armor, had been of great advantage to the Spanish. One horseman, who had covered De Soto's escape from the town, pulled twenty arrows from his leather coat. The Tascaloosa chiefdom collapsed in the wake of this battle and the attending introduction of European diseases, though Mabilian would remain the traders' language of the lower south.[21]

De Soto's expedition spent twenty-five days recovering from wounds and burning neighboring villages, then changed course abruptly from a march south toward the Gulf coast to a northwesterly course into the interior. Although the entire route of De Soto's treasure hunt was often like that of an erratic tornado, this reversal of direction owed much to the resistance of the Tascaloosa at Mabila. Although his army would suffer more severe losses when the Chickasaw attacked and burned his winter camp in northeastern Mississippi in March 1541, Mabila was De Soto's only major battle.[22]

In their persistent search for treasure and their interim need for massive supplies of food, De Soto's soldiers ranged across the American southeast from Georgia to Texas (see Map 2). The survival of the force for more than four years indicates that it had overcome some of the problems of food and armor that had ruined the Narváez expedition. Yet De Soto's methods could serve only his treasure-hunting ambitions; control over these fruitful lands and numerous peoples was beyond De Soto's resources or purpose. De Soto's hunt for a bullion-oriented civilization led him west of the Mississippi, where he became ill and died in 1542. The survivors, half of the original force, fled down the Mississippi in brigantines they had constructed. They were being pursued by the arrows and large war canoes of Quigualtam, a powerful chiefdom of the lower Mississippi. A parting taunt shouted from a canoe, as translated by an Amerindian slave with the Spaniards, was: "If we possessed such large canoes as yours . . . we would follow you to your land and conquer it, for we too are men like yourselves."[23]

If Narváez had proven that Florida contained no other Mexico, De Soto proved that the vast *La Florida* included no other Peru. While De Soto scoured the southeastern section of North America, Francisco Vázquez de Coronado, with a force of three hundred Spanish horsemen and eight hundred native Mexican infantry, hunted vainly in the southwest for the mythical Seven Cities of Gold (1540–1542). These failures brought a temporary halt to "exploration and discovery" throughout these frontiers.

By the early 1540s, the Dominicans finally convinced Charles V that his overlordship of native societies was legitimate only if it was requested, and that would be likely only after they had become Christian. Luis Cáncer de Barbastro was an experienced Dominican missionary in Guatemala and a close follower of Father Bartolomé de Las Casas, the most famous and influential critic of the Spanish *conquistadores*. Cáncer set off to preach to the Florida Amerindians, ignoring the legacy of hate left by the Narváez and De Soto expeditions. Under direct sponsorship of the viceroy of New Spain, Cáncer and his small unarmed party sailed from Vera Cruz in 1549, landing on Timucuan territory at Tampa Bay. Despite initial gifts and courtesies, and interpreter-slaves present on both sides, the Timucua soon killed two of the visitors, including Cáncer. These peaceful and well-intended "first Catholic martyrs" had come too late, victims of the hate provoked by the Spanish quest for wealth in Florida.[24]

The great Spanish discoveries of treasure in the 1540s were elsewhere, in the exceedingly rich silver mountains of Potosí in modern Bolivia (1545) and Zacatecas in the lands of the ferocious Chichimeca of what became north-central Mexico (1546). There, over the next half century, Spain's soldiers and friars would develop the techniques of "pacification" by mission and presidio that would be exported more successfully northward.[25]

Spaniards had not been the only Europeans anxious to imitate the success of Cortés or to share in the proceeds. French privateers had captured two Spanish ships laden with the looted treasures of Monte-zuma's palace in 1523. Rivalry between Hapsburg Emperor Charles V (1500–1558), who was also king of Spain, and French King Francis I (1494–1547) had already launched the Hapsburg–Valois Wars in Europe (1521–1559). France's first official expedition to North America had sailed in 1524, backed by Florentine merchants in Lyon and led by Florentine navigator Giovanni da Verrazano, who scouted the coasts between the Carolinas and Nova Scotia searching in vain for rich trade or a passage to Asia. The Spanish responded the next year by sending the Portuguese navigator Esteban Gómez, who scouted the North American coast from northern Florida to Cape Cod. England's Henry VIII also showed interest in North America in the wake of the success of Cortés and the claims staked by Verrazano. Henry sponsored John Rut's 1527 exploration of the coast between Labrador and Florida, fol-lowed by armed reconnaissance that made his the first foreign Euro-pean vessel to enter Santo Domingo harbor (1527–1528). Jacques Car-tier's first two voyages (1534, 1535–1536) claimed the St. Lawrence River for France, but subsequent French attempts to found a colony at Cap Rouge lasted for only a few months. French and English rivals had failed to find gold, silver, or civilizations comparable to the Aztec, Inca, or Mayan cultures and had also failed to find a passage to Asia's wealth.

To Spain's European rivals, the wealth of America appeared to be the wealth that could be taken from the Spanish. As Spain's treasure fleets became better protected from the 1540s, French privateering harassment of Spanish American settlements intensified, climaxing in the capture, ransom, and complete burning of Havana in 1555.[26] War with France and several expensive shipwrecks on the Florida coasts prompted Philip II (1527–1598), king of Spain from 1555, to order his viceroy of New Spain to protect the treasure route with a settlement on Florida's east coast.

The last of the great *entrada* into Florida, led by a veteran officer of Coronado's expedition, Tristán de Luna y Arellano, was intended to be a settlement completely funded by the Spanish crown. To be more accessible to Spanish authority in Mexico City and safer from French privateers, Viceroy Luis de Velasco proposed an initial base on the northeast Gulf coast, to be linked by road across the peninsula to a settlement at Santa Elena, a port familiar to the 1526 Ayllón colony.

De Luna's fleet of thirteen ships finally left Mexico's port of San Juan de Ulua in June 1559, with five hundred soldiers, including numerous veterans of De Soto's *entrada*, and one thousand settlers, including fam-ilies of Tlaxcalan Amerindians from Mexico who were firm allies of the Spanish. Some 240 horses were sent, and more than 100 muskets.[27] Pensacola Bay was chosen as the landing site, where the expedition was crippled within a week by a ferocious hurricane. Only three ships remained afloat, most of the food was ruined, and some colonists were drowned. The local area could not feed such a large group, so most of them were led inland toward Mabila, the prosperous Choctaw town that De Soto had ruined. Although the Choctaw had rebuilt their towns, these were smaller than previously and their tribute areas much reduced. The inhabitants were also understandably prone to desert their towns at the approach of the Spanish, without leaving any food.

By the end of the winter, the Spanish intruders were starving. An advance party, led by Mateo del Sauz and including several De Soto veterans plus a Coosa woman they had earlier enslaved, traveled up the Alabama River to the eight Creek towns of the paramount chief of Coosa. Although food was supplied in sufficient quantities to send some back to the main party, the Spanish did not find Coosa as they had remembered it. The population was smaller, less prosperous, and relocated, probably due to famine and diseases linked to the De Soto expedition. Broader cultural consequences were already evident. Complex hierarchical settlements, including temple mounds and elaborate palisades, were no longer being built. Decorative crafts were in decline, and some European manufactures began to be prominent among grave-goods.[28] Former tributary tribes had also rebelled, including the neighboring Napochies. Sauz provided twenty-five cavalry and twenty-five infantry to accompany three hundred Coosa in a punitive raid that subjected these "rebels" to their former overlords and provided the Spanish with a stock of Napochie corn.

Viceroy Velasco, informed of the state of the expedition by dissidents who had returned to Mexico, sent additional supplies, ordered the settling of the Coosa area as a Spanish base, and replaced de Luna as commander. However, the proposed settlement had become merely another failed expedition. Three lesser efforts to establish a Spanish presence on the Atlantic coast between 1560 and 1563 also failed. Antonio Velázquez's accidental discovery of Chesapeake Bay, in 1561, was not immediately pursued, nor were attempts at settlement.[29]

The Peace of Cateau-Cambrésis of 1559 had brought the Hapsburg–Valois Wars to a close even before de Luna sailed to Florida. However, negotiations had failed to provide any agreement on access to American waters. America was informally acknowledged to be a permanent war zone; there was to be "no Peace beyond the Line."

Philip II of Spain (r. 1555–1598) had excellent reasons for excluding the New World from the formal Cateau-Cambrésis treaty. Spanish claims to exclusive rights in America were thereby maintained at a time when America was becoming a major royal resource. The silver production of Mexico and Peru had grown remarkably, constituting an average of 20 percent of Philip's revenues. This bullion was seen by all as the foundation of Spanish power in Europe, paying major armies directly, funding dissidents in rival countries, and backing Spanish government borrowing on a scale that transformed European military contests.

Spanish American bullion had a greater impact on European rivalries than would any other colonial commodity, and it immediately became the target of pirates, privateers, and expeditions sponsored by Spain's royal competitors. However, Philip's advisers had inherited and perfected a convoy system that proved a formidable defense for the treasure fleets. Two well-defended fleets, averaging approximately sixty ships, left Seville's port of St. Lúcar each year for the Canaries and the Caribbean. The spring fleet, the *flota*, sailed for Mexico City's port of Vera Cruz, and the late summer fleet, *galeones*, stopped at the Panama isthmus port of Nombre de Dios before wintering at better-protected Cartagena. The *galeones* began their return in the spring, timed to meet the Peruvian silver that was being carried by ship and mule caravan from Panama to Nombre de Dios. The *galeones* and *flota* met at Havana and sailed in early autumn for Spain. The major attraction of North America during the rest of the sixteenth century was as a base from which to attack these riches, and Spanish assertions of monopoly there and in the Caribbean were predicated on defending these fleets. Florida, and the neighboring southern Atlantic coast of North America, was acquiring European strategic importance.

The European conquest of North America had failed between 1513 and 1562. Aside from peripheral visits and fishing camps, the deliberate efforts to conquer had focused on well-financed Spanish expeditions to *La Florida*. The Calusa, Timucua, Apalachee, Choctaw, and Chickasaw proved ferocious against seasoned Spanish conquerors who came with the supposed advantages of steel swords, crossbows, muskets, armor, horses, war dogs, and a crusading warrior mentality. Spanish raiders, shipwrecked sailors, and prisoners taken by the Amerindians unknowingly spread European microbes in societies that were not immune to them. Outbreaks of imported disease occurred, but there is no evidence that a "virgin land pandemic" swept through Florida in the first half century of contact. It should also be noted that disease was not an exclusively Spanish weapon. Both the Spanish settlement of Ayllón and the Narváez expedition were decimated by local malaria, to which they were not immune.

Comparatively speaking, the natives of peninsular Florida had won; Spanish avarice exceeded anything the Amerindians of Florida could provide. Unlike the complete disruption of the Tascaloosa chiefdom, the Spanish recorded little immediate death, dislocation, or disease among their hosts in Florida. Expecting tribute, rather than trade or land, the Spanish left little behind them that was technologically or culturally disruptive. Guns, which had not been particularly effective, were not sold to any Amerindians. Working for the Spanish temporarily as bearers proved less onerous than working in the mines of Hispaniola, where the Arawak had been obliterated in less than half the time the Spanish had spent trying to establish a permanent base in Florida.

The Spanish *entrada* had proven that no fabulous extractable wealth had been accumulated in the region, that slave raiding there was extremely dangerous, and that the whole area was not worth the costs of conquest. As long as the ferocious Calusa and Timucua could be counted on to drive off all European approaches, thereby forming what amounted to an unintended defensive buffer for the treasure fleets, the Spanish could suffer the loss of an occasional ship and crew in the area. In Chicora, however, the Spanish failure had not been due to Guale resistance, and French adventurers would soon exploit the comparative hospitality of the Guale.

Part I

BASES FOR INVASION
1565–1684

Permanent European bases in North America represented a significant revolution in the continent's human relations and were not simply heralds of other changes to come. A trading ship or a nine-hundred-man *entrada* had been an imposing display of the organized resources of the Europeans but, like all natural disasters, was only temporary. Stray Europeans, and the children they sired, had been incorporated into the tribal life of the Timucua, Apalache, or Guale villages, and pigs had become a valued new food source and trade item. In these brief preliminary encounters, few native leaders had been able to use the transient Spaniards effectively in their own more important and persistent intertribal rivalries, except to direct the Spaniards toward their enemies. European visitors had the initiative, but lacked the knowledge and resources to profit much from tribal weaknesses, intertribal enmities, or Amerindian resentments at mistreatment by other Europeans.

Although not presumed permanent by anyone at the time, European bases transformed the position of Europeans in Amerindian diplomacy, warfare, economy, and culture. Successful Amerindian leaders came to include Europeans among their allies and enemies, and came to fathom and profit from some of the insatiable appetites of European consumers on both sides of the Atlantic. Fortified European bases, like supply ships permanently at anchor, were deceptively small in representing the people and resources behind them. They could defend new settlers from the consequences of their aggression, offer sanctuary to Amerindian renegades and malcontents, and affect the terms of trade by intimidation, as well as offering the advantages of secret storage of durable supplies amid societies that did not all have substantial food reserves.[1]

These trading centers gradually transformed the life of those Amerindians attracted to them for copper kettles, blankets, clothing, and, particularly after about 1650, firearms, ammunition, and gunpowder. Amerindians varied in their views of these opportunities, but many individuals and communities appear to have adjusted pragmatically to these new conditions. Trade in skins enhanced the value of hunting versus farming in the many Amerindian societies that combined both activities. Competition for beaver pelts, and for deerskins, forced migration on those who exhausted the available supply of their traditional hunting grounds. This shift to hunting, together with an increase in war and diplomacy, enhanced the relative importance of the male warrior-hunter over the female farmers, weavers, and potters, though grain remained essential to the hunt and dressing skins became vital to the trade. Rivalry over access to new metal-edged weapons provoked some intertribal wars and increased casualties. Flintlock muskets, rather than matchlocks, had advantages for war and hunting that proved irresistible to Amerindians, creating dependence on European weapons, repairs, ammunition, and gunpowder. Alternative European sources for these trade goods gave some Amerindian societies advantages throughout this period, but the cost of trade dependence would be made clear repeatedly.[2]

European bases also traded European diseases. The people composing the new European colonies were from a variety of disease environments, each with its own prevailing deadly diseases and limited natural immunities. Within some of these new settlements, Europeans, Africans, and Americans died in great numbers as they shared the diseases of three continents without being able to share immunities. Periodic shiploads of new migrants or supplies reinforced the colonies of both humans and microbes. European imperial and colonial armies could be entirely immobilized by disease. The devastation of the Narváez and Ayllón expeditions, as well as many early deaths in Jamestown, were caused by local malaria.

Unknowingly, these colonial bases also became incubators for the even more devastating invasions of European and African microbes into Amerindian populations that were entirely without immunities to most of these diseases. Coosa may have been the first well-documented disaster, but the Powhatan, Iroquois, Huron, and Wampanoag were among the many victims. The most potent weapon in the invasion of North America was not the gun, the horse, the Bible, or European "civilization." It was pestilence, feared by all and understood by none, that carried off untold tens of thousands with a bias that favored the Europeans. Despite the substantial immigration of Europeans, the total population of eastern North America declined throughout the period 1565 to 1675, and likely continued to fall for another half century.[3]

Permanent North American settlements were also part of a European diplomatic calculus. Extravagant Iberian claims to much of the planet, supported by papal donation and the Treaty of Tordesillas (1494), had never been accepted by the French or the English. All European maritime powers had made claims on the basis of so-called rights of discovery that were not dismissed as inherently absurd by fellow Europeans, but such pretensions were vague, vast, and conflicting. Ayllón's stone crosses claiming Chicora for Spain, like Ribault's stone columns of 1562 appropriating parts of the same coast for France, indicated unenforceable pretensions. The only European claims that were recognized by other Europeans and by Amerindians were ultimately martial, summarized and sanitized as "effective occupation." For a century after the founding of San Agustín, America remained diplomatically "behind God's back." Unrestrained and brutal European rivalries in America encouraged spasmodic piracies, unaffected by peace made in Europe. Some bases, like Fort Caroline and Mount Desert Island, were permanently destroyed. Many more, including San Agustín, Québec, New York, and Albany, were severely disrupted by maritime attacks. Most European bases in North America were forced to divert a high proportion of limited public resources to defense against possible seaborne attack.

Despite these conflicts, this crucial century of North American history was dominated by the interaction of Amerindians with one another and with the invading Europeans, rather than by European imperial or inter-colonial rivalries. This meeting of Amerindians and Europeans, often becoming violent, will be illustrated by examining five European bases successfully established between 1565 and 1624. Considered in the order of their founding, these are the Spanish fortress town of San Agustín (1565), the English settler beachhead among the Powhatan at Jamestown (1607), the French colony at Québec (1608), the English puritan community at Plymouth (1620), and the Dutch trading outpost of Fort Orange (Albany, 1624), which was all but hostage to the Iroquois. Each collided with a different Amerindian world, and each had a different population and purpose. The generous space of at least a week's travel between these centers serves both to remind us that early European rivalries in North America could be deadly and to allow their early stories to be considered as distinct invasions. The social and military history of all these European bases, from their foundations through the first three-quarters of the seventeenth century, was overwhelmingly about a variety of ways of "settling with the Amerindians."

Chapter 2

SPANISH SAN AGUSTÍN
1565–1672

San Agustín represented a military model of a European invader's base. The Peace of Cateau-Cambrésis (1559) and the eruption of religiously oriented civil wars in France (1559–1589) had initially led Spain's Philip II to discount warnings that French Calvinist Huguenots were planning a settlement in North America, intended as both a refuge and a privateering base. Nonetheless, the first permanent Spanish settlement in North America was initiated and sustained with support from the Spanish crown, anxious to defend its treasure fleets from these aggressive European rivals. The character of the venture would be affected by its founder and greatly influenced by missionary ambitions, but San Agustín would be established and maintained because it prevented European rivals from building privateering bases on that Florida coast.

French Admiral Gaspard de Coligny (1519–1572), a Huguenot leader who had invested in earlier American buccaneering and colonizing voyages, sent out a crown-approved preliminary expedition in the spring of 1562, under experienced navigators Jean Ribault (ca. 1520–1565) and an unknown renegade Portuguese pilot.[1] Two ships carrying 150 men, including 75 soldiers, made a landfall in Saturiba Timucua territory near modern Jacksonville and erected a stone column claiming the land for France. Ribault's party, with René Goulaine de Laudonnière as second in command, then coasted northward until they found the spacious harbor in Guale territory where Ayllón and Villafañe had tried to establish Santa Elena. Here they erected another stone column defining French claims and built a small wooden earthwork fort (Port Royal, South Carolina) and a house for the twenty-six men left behind as garrison. Losing their supplies in a fire, the garrison was sustained for a year only by food provided by friendly Guale. The Guale lived by hunting, fishing, and farming in villages of what would become coastal Georgia. Like those of their relatives, the Creek, each Guale village was led by a hereditary headman, or *mico*. Despite support from a friendly *mico*, the French fort failed because of its own brutal dissensions, and most survivors sailed for France in a makeshift sloop that the Guale were happy to help build. One Guilliaume Rouffi stayed behind, married into a Guale clan, and learned their language. In the spring of 1564, the Spanish burned the abandoned French fort and removed both the stone column and Rouffi, who would become useful to them as an interpreter.[2]

The first Huguenot settlement in Florida had self-destructed, but another soon followed. A court-approved French Huguenot fleet under Laudonnière, carrying three hundred sailors, soldiers, and colonists, arrived in June 1564. Like its predecessor, this expedition's landfall was in Saturiba territory near the St. John River, but this time a triangular Fort Caroline was built there (Jacksonville, Florida). Some two hundred men and two women stayed behind with Laudonnière when their fleet sailed for France late in July. This location was, even more obviously than Port Royal, a direct challenge to all Spanish shipping bound homeward from the Americas.

The French were initially well received by local Timucua chiefs who promptly drew them into intertribal warfare. These "settlers" did not plant crops, but traded for precious metals and built ships. Within six months, more than a third of the garrison had "stolen" newly built ships to raid the Spanish Caribbean. Their plunder, and their own capture, confirmed the worst Spanish suspicions about the purpose of the settlement. Internal dissent, outright war with the disillusioned neighboring Timucua, and resulting famine threatened Fort Caroline long before the Spanish could. Abandonment was narrowly averted by the arrival of Jean Ribault's large relief squadron of seven vessels carrying provisions and reinforcements of soldiers and colonists.

The Spanish response emerged gradually, but proved decisive. Pedro Menéndez de Avilés, a capable and experienced commander of the Indies fleets, was asked by Philip II to report on *La Florida* and on the best way to respond to the challenge of Ribault's first colony. Menéndez recommended three royally funded settlements on the Atlantic coast from Santa Elena north to Newfoundland, to be sustained by sugar and cattle production. However, in March 1565 he accepted the position of *adelantado,* meaning he would spend his own fortune in the area in return for extensive trade, land, and political privileges. Yet this was no mere *entrada;* settlement and defense had clear priority over exploration. Little was said of the native inhabitants, who apparently were to be drawn to the Spanish interest by missionaries. When Philip II heard, at the end of that month, of the second Huguenot colony, the newest Spanish venture to Florida was transformed. His terms for Menéndez became more generous, and the focus was on the very unpromising Florida Atlantic coast, which the Spanish had come to regard as worthless. The expedition became a joint venture with the crown, with an urgent preliminary task of routing the French. Unknowingly, the parsimonious Philip II was launching a project that would, over the next three years, consume more than one-fifth of the entire military budget of his global empire.[3]

Menéndez's five-vessel advance squadron, comprising less than a third of his total expedition, had failed in its race to beat Ribault to Florida. The Menéndez squadron reached the Fort Caroline area late in August 1565 with some eight hundred people aboard, including five hundred royal soldiers of varying levels of training, about two hundred sailors, and a hundred others, including colonists and the families of twenty-six soldiers. Menéndez's night attack drove off the four larger French ships anchored outside the river, but the five hundred French soldiers already landed prevented a direct attack on the fort. A Spanish force that could easily have overwhelmed the wintering French garrison, or prevailed if positioned between Fort Caroline and Ribault's reinforcements, could not challenge the reinforced and better protected French defenders. Menéndez withdrew southward some forty miles and went ashore to claim the country and formally establish the city of San Agustín.

Whatever he made of the European antics, the local Timucua village headman, Chief Seloy, saw nothing sinister in having the Spaniards fortify part of his village against the increasingly unwelcome French; Spaniards had come and gone before. Meanwhile, rival Timucua reported to the French at Fort Caroline of the Spanish landing and defenses. Fort Caroline was left with fewer than 250 defenders as Ribault launched a maritime attack intended to catch the Spanish unloading supplies. Acting on Timucua information and exploiting a prolonged storm that scattered Ribault's fleet and relaxed vigilance at Fort Caroline, Menéndez led his five hundred troops overland to attack the fort on its weaker landward side. One hundred and thirty-two Frenchmen were killed in the dawn attack, forty-five escaped, and about fifty Huguenot women and children were spared. The captured fort, well supplied and armed, became Fort San Mateo. Most of Ribault's fleet was wrecked along the shoreline south of San Agustín, and those who survived these disasters and attacks by local Ais tribesmen were forced to surrender unconditionally to Menéndez.

The ferocity of Reformation warfare was displayed clearly. The Spaniards summarily executed at least 111 prisoners as heretics and spared only 17. Another group, including Ribault, surrendered two weeks later and received similar treatment. Early in November, a remnant French group near Cape Canaveral, who had tried to fortify themselves with earthworks and salvaged ship cannon, fled to the woods at the approach of overwhelming Spanish force. About seventy-five surrendered when offered their lives, a civility Menéndez felt he could afford since the French threat had ended.[4]

Menéndez and Philip II had been forced to establish a Spanish presence along the least fruitful Atlantic coast of Florida. A French settlement of any kind would have given legitimacy to armed French maritime presence throughout the Spanish Caribbean, for ships could be blown to strange places "by the stress of weather." Failed Spanish ventures had proven conclusively that the sandy soils and pine barrens of the south Atlantic coast could not sustain substantial Amerindian or European settlement, yet defense of the treasure fleets required a base at San Agustín rather than exploring the richer and more promising lands north of Santa Elena, or the great bay that Velázquez had found north of Cape Hatteras.

Menéndez used three groups to invade Florida; soldiers, settlers, and missionaries all competed for Amerindian labor that was the only wealth of the area. Circumstances had ensured that military considerations initially received priority. By the end of 1565, the fort at San Agustín symbolized the recent Spanish victory, but it was a precarious and poorly placed toehold on a vast continent that Menéndez wanted to exploit for himself and his king. In the spring of 1566, he took a small force, with Guilliaume Rouffi as interpreter, north up the coast. Visiting the Guale people and leaving Spanish hostages to replace Cusabo prisoners whom the Guale had taken in war, Menéndez then took the Cusabo captives north to their home, assuring himself of a friendly reception in what would become his northern anchor-port of Santa Elena. On Parris Island, where the French had built Charlesfort in 1562, the Spanish built Fort San Felipe. They mounted six cannon and garrisoned it with 160 men, although disease, famine-provoked mutiny, and desertion reduced this garrison to a mere 25 by summer.[5] Although San Felipe, San Mateo, and San Agustín were his main bases, Menéndez established seven other short-lived shoreline garrisons that ranged around the Florida peninsula from the Guale to the Tocobaga, a Timucua people of the St. Mary's River on the Gulf of Mexico coast. Theoretically, all the bases were located so that fifteen hundred soldiers could be supplied readily by sea. Actually, some of them were established because of a shortage of supplies and an official assumption that garrisons of twenty to a hundred would be fed by tribute from peoples who would soon learn the cost of allowing the Spaniards ashore. The newly founded Guale mission of San Pedro de Tacatacuru (Cumberland Island, Georgia) was the only one of the smaller bases that lasted beyond the summer of 1569. Although one Jesuit, four civilians, and eleven soldiers had been killed at Tacatacura by then, the garrison was reinforced as an intermediate base between Santa Elena and San Agustín, and the mission lasted until 1689.[6]

It was the same shortage of supplies that prompted Menéndez's major exploration. When reinforcements arrived in the summer of 1566, Menéndez initially assigned Captain Juan Pardo and three hundred soldiers to the dwindling northern garrison at San Felipe. Pardo was sent inland twice, with more than a hundred men, to extract food tribute and "to discover and conquer the interior country from there to

Mexico."[7] In 1567 Pardo followed an Amerindian trail to Cofitachiqui on the Savannah River, as De Soto had done twenty-seven years earlier, and established a blockhouse at the foot of the Alleghenies before returning to Santa Elena. Aggressive Sergeant Hernando Moyano de Morales, left in charge of some thirty men at this temporary base, became involved in intertribal politics. Joining Amerindian armies, he fought in two wars within a few months, helped to burn several villages, and claimed to have killed fifteen hundred Chisca before building a fort at Chiaha (near Columbus, Georgia). By the fall of 1567, many inland peoples had supposedly accepted their Spanish overlords, and six garrisons were set up inland from San Felipe. However, by the following spring, all garrisons were overrun by angered Amerindians.[8]

Menéndez's garrisons had been too large and persistent an imposition on the limited resources of their Amerindian neighbors, yet too small to control the predictable resistance. Soldiers who were disappointed with this "new Mexico," or desperate for food, committed brutalities that the Amerindians avenged. When trying to house men with the unwilling *cacique* of Escamacu in 1576, Moyano de Morales, now a lieutenant, and his twenty-one musketeers were tricked into snuffing the matches that lit their muskets; only one escaped with his life.[9] As Amerindian retribution spread, San Felipe was momentarily abandoned and was promptly burned by the Cusabo.

Menéndez's string of failed coastal garrisons bequeathed no impressive fortifications, but they marked places where Spain's European enemies might gain wary allies. In 1568, for instance, a French privateer gained Timucua assistance in destroying San Mateo and exacting his revenge for the fate of the Huguenot venturers by hanging all the captured Spanish. However, a French attempt to reoccupy the same area ended in shipwreck and Guale and Cusabo conquest of their small fort. More than a hundred Frenchmen were dispersed as prisoners among neighboring tribes. When the Spanish rebuilt San Felipe, recovering those potentially dangerous Frenchmen became a major diplomatic objective.[10]

The military character of Spanish Florida would be shaped considerably by direct royal control after Menéndez's death in 1574, by mounting Amerindian resistance, and particularly by the coming of an Anglo-Spanish war in 1585. Walter Ralegh had sent a scouting expedition to the Carolina Outer Banks and Chesapeake Bay in 1584, and attempted a colony on Roanoke Island. Francis Drake, the knighted English buccaneer, attacked and burned San Agustín in 1586 on his way to visit Roanoke. The Spanish response to these intrusions was to evacuate Santa Elena and San Marcos in 1587. The military government of Florida, supported by a royal budget for three hundred men, henceforth became centered on San Agustín.

Settlers, who ultimately would prove to be the most effective conquerors of North America, were by far the weakest of the three elements of Menéndez's invasion of *La Florida*. Of the 2646 original Spanish soldiers and settlers, only 26 were married and accompanied by family, and very few unmarried Spanish women arrived in the colony. Spanish agriculture and diet did not migrate well. The 273 who settled near Fort San Felipe, for instance, found that their wheat was unsuitable, and the feeble crops were lost to flooding and voracious small animals.[11] The emerging creole culture of San Agustín was Amerindian in the kitchen, although Spanish in the *presidio* and the church.

The third element of Menéndez's empire was to be the missionaries to the Amerindians. Whatever is claimed for the effectiveness of the alliance between the military and the missions in Spanish imperialism, the relationship was poor in Menéndez's *La Florida*. The missionaries were paid from the royal military budget, to the endless laments of the governors, who in turn expected the missionaries to assist in extracting tribute of corn or labor from the Amerindians. The missionaries sought to be free of the soldiery, whom they regarded as poor examples of Christian life and provokers of hostility that was then vented on the defenseless missionaries.

Three Jesuits joined the Menéndez venture in 1566, at the request of both the *adelantado* and the king. Evangelizing among the ferocious and suspicious Carlos, Tocobaga (Safety Harbor), and Tequesta (Miami), they encountered well-defended gods and customs, and the Jesuits were discouraged even before Spanish soldiers provoked vengeance that destroyed these missions along with the garrisons. By 1568 the Jesuits, like Menéndez and his settlers, had shifted their attention northeast to Guale and Santa Elena without improved results.

The final Jesuit initiative came in 1570. Menéndez had longed to extend his province to the Bahía de Santa María (Chesapeake Bay), following the Spanish discovery of it in 1561. The Jesuits, who undertook to establish a mission in Bahía de Santa María, counted on the help of an Algonquian convert, Don Luis de Velasco, and insisted that no corrupting soldiers be allowed to accompany the group. The eight Jesuit priests and a boy initially seemed magical enough to have revived the presumed-dead Paquiquineo, alias Don Luis, but their value soon fell. Don Luis had no religious authority as a chief's son and no wish to forfeit his tribal status, so he abandoned the Jesuits soon after they landed on the banks of the James River in September 1570. Five months later, he led the warriors who killed the entire Jesuit party except for the boy, who had found refuge in a nearby village. In 1572 Menéndez, now captain-general of Spain's royal armada, visited Bahía de Santa María on his way home to Spain. The Spanish recovered the surviving boy, learned what had happened, but failed to find Don Luis. After avenging themselves by killing twenty in combat and hanging fourteen Amerindians said to have been involved in the killings, Menéndez and the Jesuits left *La Florida*.[12]

In the face of Amerindian hostility and European buccaneering, diminishing Spanish influence prompted the Spanish Council of the Indies to send Franciscan missionaries to the province. A group arrived in 1577 to establish the Nombre de Dios and San Sebastian missions among the Timucuan-speaking on the outskirts of San Agustín itself. The Franciscans established missions in Guale in 1594, reasserting Spanish claims and reporting considerable success until 1597, when five of the six missionaries were killed in a widespread nativist revolt led by Juanillo. He was a Christian Guale chief whom the missionaries attempted to bar from his hereditary tribal position as *mico* because he persisted in traditional polygamy. After punitive expeditions by the Spanish and their Christian Guale supporters, the Franciscans renewed their efforts among the Guale in 1601. The missions enjoyed eight decades of religious success that changed a seminomadic people into farmers in the none-too-rich soils of coastal Georgia. Missions among the Western Timucua Potano community began in 1606. In the next twenty-seven years, the missions spread to cover all of Timucua territory, altering their politics and religion without significantly disrupting their material culture.[13]

Florida tribes showed a growing interest in missions at the turn of the seventeenth century. This interest may have owed much to the courage and persistence of the missionaries, but it accelerated as rival tribes saw security advantages in being allied with the Spanish. Given their limited military resources, the Spanish were also anxious to claim easy overlordship by arranging peace between tribes. A contending faction within a tribe could also use Spanish endorsement to strengthen its own internal position. The Spanish wisely resisted the first Apalachee invitations to establish a mission in 1608, rightly suspecting that tribal power was then too unstable for the friars' safety.[14]

The Apalachee missions, finally started in 1633, illustrate this form of Spanish presence and influence effectively. The Apalachee were primarily an agricultural people numbering about thirty-five thousand, whose crops of corn, squash, and beans flourished in the rich red clay soils of northwestern Florida. Unlike many indigenous peoples, both Apalachee men and women had worked their fields before Spanish contact. Apalachee corn surpluses and hogs were sold to San Agustín for years, increasing Spanish interest. These farming people could embrace Christianity with a minimum of social and economic disruption, and the missionaries reinforced the Apalachee way of life by teaching them double-cropping. The missionaries had changed their approach in order to succeed, and both sides accepted the "two republics," the Apalachee village power structures and the Spanish missions; by the 1640s, a fifth of the village chiefs were Christian.[15] The principal mission, San Luis de Talimali (Tallahassee), was in the town of the pre-eminent chief. A small port was developed to ship grain to Cuba and

San Agustín, and a few soldiers arrived to oversee work on the governor's own wheat farm there. Increased calls for Apalachee farm labor, and especially the despised work as bearers, caused grievances.

Traditionalist Apalachee attacked the missions in 1647, burning seven churches and monasteries and killing three of the friars as well as the recently established deputy governor and his family. The limits of Spanish power were evident in the response. The "rebels" were first checked by a force of thirty-one Spanish soldiers and five hundred Timucua allies who fought a day-long indecisive battle. The number of the "rebels" is not known, but thirty Spanish matchlocks firing an average of ninety times each had failed to decide the battle. It was Christian Apalachee, supported by a mere twenty-one Spanish soldiers and sixty Timucua, who eventually defeated their rivals and turned thirty-eight of them over to the Spanish for punishment. Typically, the Spanish missionaries and the soldiers exchanged accusations about the cause of what was essentially an Apalachee civil war. The victory of the Christian faction was soon complete, with numerous conversions and prompt rebuilding of the missions.[16] As reparation for the destruction, the Apalachee unwisely agreed to a levy of labor that came to be demanded every year, for porterage and construction locally and in San Agustín.

The Apalachee missions expanded through the next generation, but three challenges appeared. Total population fell to merely a third of the 1630 estimates, numbering only ten thousand by 1670. These large losses are thought to have been caused by epidemics of European diseases, probably imported by Apalachee laborers returning from the burdensome work at San Agustín. The missions of Apalachee were also threatened by a 1670 decision to allow Spanish settlers into the area. These farmers and ranchers extracted forced labor from the Apalachee community and used violence to disrupt and monopolize the profitable hog trade to San Agustín. An even greater challenge was the settlement of Carolina that year by Barbadian planters and slavers. Over the next generation, these English colonists would arm, join, and finance ferocious Creek slaving expeditions against the Spanish missions, eventually destroying all missions beyond the protection of San Agustín itself.

The missions of *La Florida* had served their own primary purpose. When the archbishop of Santiago de Cuba visited this northern frontier of his diocese in 1675, with its thirty-six missions and 40 friars, he confirmed 13,152 Christian Amerindians in a territory with only 1500 Spanish.[17] With settled agricultural people like the Apalachee, the missions brought some new crops, better hoes, but little initial change in life's cycles. Missions required more adaptation by the seminomadic Guale and Timucua, but eventually the Franciscans prevailed. Among the ferocious Calusa, Tequesta, Giacata, and Ais of the everglades and sandy barrens of southern Florida, the missions failed as repeatedly and completely as had the early garrisons. Society, geography, and early Spanish slaving all contributed to keeping those coasts dangerous to nearly all Europeans.

The military had occasionally helped the missionaries by garrisoning a few soldiers, but mainly by retaliating for "outrages." The missions were less helpful to the military, for the missionaries laid special claims to extensive territories and peoples, and objected to a pious Spanish king against the very presence of the military and the settlers.[18] The very success of the missions consumed part of the military budget directly. Expensive punitive expeditions were also required whenever a Christianized faction lost power or friars were threatened or martyred. Although the missions remained a relatively inexpensive form of "effective occupation," they spread the paltry Spanish military resources thinly in areas that did not otherwise need protecting from European rivals. When faced, after 1670, with the military challenge of the Carolina slavers and their well-armed Creek allies, aided by disgruntled mission Amerindians, the missions proved entirely indefensible.

 Through two centuries, the forts that succeeded one another at San Agustín were the symbols and centers of Spanish military presence in *La Florida*. Originally chosen by an ambitious naval officer as a defensible temporary supply base for a personal empire, the fort began in a small Timucua village on a peninsula with very limited agricultural land, surrounded and defended by dunes, swamps, and waterways. An undefended adjoining settlement grew from a few soldiers' huts to a town of 3104 by 1763. San Agustín became an amalgam of Spanish public institutions and Timucua and Guale domestic patterns. Marriages in San Agustín were overwhelmingly between Spanish men and Amerindian women, gradually mixing and binding the cultures at the domestic level.[19]

Nine wooden forts succeeded one another during San Agustín's first century; all included artillery, and all were intended primarily to thwart European maritime invasion. Six of the nine forts fell to hurricanes, floods, and especially rot. The first fort, a triangular palisade built with the encouragement of the Timucua villagers of Seloy in 1565, was the only one destroyed by the Timucua, who burned it entirely the following spring, as the climax to very strained relations that had included a number of murders. The third fort, triangular like its predecessors to protect a single battery most economically, was destroyed in a mutiny of part of the garrison in 1570.[20]

The only San Agustín fort to fall due to European cannon fire was the sixth, still under construction when Sir Francis Drake's twenty-three ships and two thousand men attacked in 1586. A hexagonal palisade had been completed, and the garrison of 150 could supplement small arms with thirteen or fourteen functioning brass cannon. The defense against such odds was the standard one used in all smaller coastal towns throughout the Spanish Caribbean. Women, children, and the thirty black slaves, sent from Cuba to help with the fortifications, were promptly evacuated to the woods. The tiny garrison held for two days, then escaped to the woods at night. The Timucua made a sortie against the English, without much success. The attackers completely destroyed the fort and town over the next four days, taking the treasury as well as cannon and supplies to Roanoke, but leaving the germs of what would become a deadly typhus epidemic. Governor Pedro Menéndez Marqués began rebuilding immediately with the help of local Amerindians.[21]

Nature's assaults came close to obliterating San Agustín in 1599. The September hurricane and attending floods demolished and carried away part of the fort and extensively damaged the town, which, despite epidemics in 1570, 1586, and 1592, was home to 400 people, in addition to the garrison of 225. The rebuilt town of some 120 palmetto-roofed dwellings, and the surviving Franciscan priory, were all destroyed in a disastrous fire later that same year. At this juncture, there was a thorough royal inquiry into the Franciscan plea that San Agustín be abandoned as a waste of royal funds and a hurtful labor tax on the Christian Amerindians whom the fort could not defend. When rebuilding began in 1604, it was done with the ravages of nature in mind. There were masonry foundations, one wall was of stone, and the others were shot-proof double palisades; the five feet between the palisades were filled with earth from digging the moat. This fort survived for nearly fifty years, though it was sustained against decay only by extensive and regular repair by black slaves and by Timucua and Apalachee workers who occasionally rebelled against paying tribute in such labor.[22]

When San Agustín was attacked again, by the English pirate Robert Searles in 1668, the anchorage was protected by the last of the wooden forts, featuring four bastions and twenty mounted cannon. Amerindian revolt against forced labor had halted extensive repairs to the already decayed structure, and the unpaid and poorly supplied garrison was below 130 men. Searles had captured the long-awaited supply ship, with which he surprised the settlement. The night attack was by men armed with flintlock muskets, while the defenders had matchlocks that were ignited by a lighted match cord, which betrayed their positions.[23] Sixty Spaniards were killed in the attack on the town, whose inhabitants fled to the fort or the woods. Searles did not besiege the fort, allowing Governor Francisco de la Guerra y de la Vega to fulfill his oath of office easily, for all commanders were required to defend the fort, not the town, to the death.[24]

The massive stone Castillo de San Marcos, started in 1672 and substantially completed by 1687, was built at precisely the right time, despite the laments of earlier governors and later historians (Figure 1). The wooden forts had usually been adequate for their paltry martial challenges during the previous century and were even seen as unnec-

Figure 1. Castillo de San Marcos, San Agustín. (Courtesy of National Park Service, Harpers Ferry, West Virginia)

essary extravagances by the Franciscans and by the Amerindians who were forced to work on them. Searles, who had failed to take the wooden fort in 1668, may have prompted a gradual replacement of the garrison's matchlock muskets with flintlocks, but he did not prompt the vast Spanish investment in the building and garrisoning of the new stone fort.[25] Enemies capture, rather than burn, undermanned strategic stone forts, not only depriving the vanquished, but adding to the conquerors' strength. When the Spanish government decided to build the Castillo, it automatically endorsed a permanent garrison of three companies of infantry, one company of cavalry, and one of artillery, totaling 355 men. San Agustín's future was assured.

It was sustained English aggression near the treasure routes that prompted the building of the Castillo. There had been small English settlements in the Bahamas from 1646, and Spanish Jamaica was conquered by the English in 1655. English from Barbados were frequenting the Guale coast in the 1660s, starting a colony on Cape Fear River in 1666. By the Treaty of Madrid (1670), Spain was reluctantly forced to accept the existence of the new English colony of South Carolina.

The Castillo de San Marcos was designed by Ignacio Daza, an accomplished military engineer who had recently redesigned Havana's defenses. The square parade, which could protect the whole town's population of about a thousand, was bounded by massive masonry walls of local coquina stone, cornered with excellent bastions designed to allow the fifty mounted cannon a wide field of fire and to protect rooms and powder magazines beneath. Although the bastions were the defensive core of the fort, it was also surrounded by a sea-water moat and an earth and stone counterscarp beyond. The main doorway was protected by a drawbridge and a triangular masonry "ravelin" beyond the moat.

The Castillo and San Agustín grew as the uneconomic empire of *La Florida* collapsed before the Carolina slavers. Loyal Guale, Timucua, and Apalachee refugees would resettle near the shelter of its guns, as did runaway slaves from Carolina. Christian Amerindians in these new mission villages found subsistence in return for building the fortress and joined the vast majority of the town who depended on the military for their livelihoods. Between 1675 and 1763, with the missions a mere shadow of their former power, the Spanish empire in Florida returned to its original aim: defense of the shipping routes from Spanish Central America. Of the five North American bases considered here, San Agustín was the only one built for military purposes.

Castillo de San Marcos, the continent's first great European fortress, built to the best seventeenth-century standards, successfully withstood English sieges in 1702, 1728 and 1740, as well as three centuries of weather.[26] When Florida was eventually exchanged for British-conquered Havana in 1763, more than 3000 people, including 350 slaves, 79 free blacks and mulattos, but only 83 surviving Christian Amerindians, were forced to abandon unconquered San Agustín.

Chapter 3

ENGLISH JAMESTOWN AND THE POWHATAN 1607–1677

Two new and expanding empires, Powhatan and English, collided in the hardwood and pine forests and in the vital cornfields west of Chesapeake Bay. Both societies were agrarian; controlling land was more important than appropriating the labor or the souls of their rivals. Erroneously assuming that one could dominate, each attempted to obliterate the other. After a lifetime of intermittent conflict, one nearly succeeded.

During the quarter century before 1607, the Pamunkey chief Powhatan had become the paramount chief of most of the thirty Algonquian-speaking tribes in what would eventually become Virginia. Powhatan's accumulation of power may have been assisted by disruptive epidemics, but was based on his outstanding military and diplomatic skills and on solidarity prompted by threats from the Siouan-speaking Monacan and Manahoac to the west, the Iroquoian-speaking neighbors to both the north and the south, and the few alien Europeans invading from the east (Map 3). Powhatan's relatives and lieutenants acted as the *werowances* in each subject town and region, gathering taxes and tribute in corn, furs, and cold-hammered copper. Eventually, Powhatan led some fourteen thousand people, including thirty-two hundred warriors equipped with long bows, clubs, and wooden swords, as well as small protective bark shields. Stone weapons and tools were scarce in this land of deep alluvial soils, with consequences for trade and war with the English.[1]

The Amerindians of the Chesapeake had previously encountered Europeans, although Powhatan's personal experiences are not known. The Spaniard Antonio Velázquez had commanded a ship that accidentally entered Chesapeake Bay in 1561, causing a major epidemic and carrying away Paquiquineo, a leading chief's son whom the Spanish later called Don Luis de Velasco. This Christian convert, who likely was a distant relative of Powhatan's, had returned from Spain in 1570 and re-established his tribal status by leading the warriors who killed the missionaries. Menéndez's visit of retribution in 1572, the year Pow-

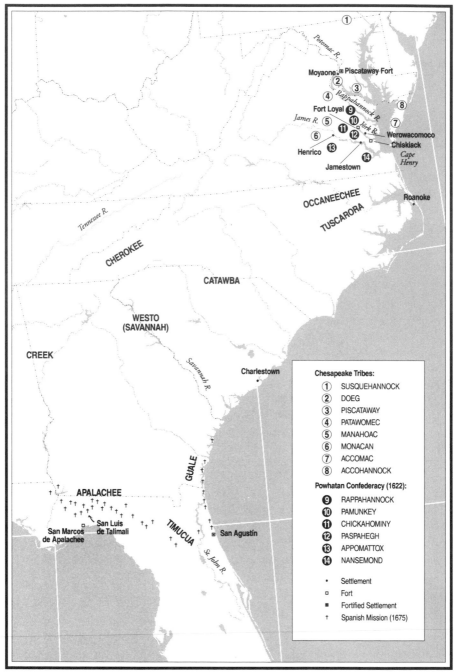

Chesapeake Tribes:

① SUSQUEHANNOCK
② DOEG
③ PISCATAWAY
④ PATAWOMEC
⑤ MANAHOAC
⑥ MONACAN
⑦ ACCOMAC
⑧ ACCOHANNOCK

Powhatan Confederacy (1622):

⑨ RAPPAHANNOCK
⑩ PAMUNKEY
⑪ CHICKAHOMINY
⑫ PASPAHEGH
⑬ APPOMATTOX
⑭ NANSEMOND

• Settlement
▫ Fort
▪ Fortified Settlement
† Spanish Mission (1675)

©1993 Ian K. Steele

Map 3. The southeast to 1676.

hatan began his rise to power, could only have reinforced hostility toward Europeans. The other major European initiative in the region had been the English colony among the Roanoke (1584–1590), where relations deteriorated completely from excellent beginnings. English from the Roanoke settlement visited the Chesapeake tribe, Algonquians of the Cape Henry area who were still semi-independent of Powhatan. It seems likely that some English survivors of the "lost" Roanoke colony were absorbed by these Chesapeake. As the Virginia Company of London was launching its new colony into the heart of Powhatan's territory, Powhatan completely annihilated the Chesapeake and any English who may have lived among them. Powhatan, the powerful leader of the most integrated of all the eastern Algonquian tribes, was confident that he could use or destroy the mere 104 English whose three small ships arrived in the James River in the spring of 1607.[2]

The newly founded Virginia Company of London had sent the leaders of their private, profit-seeking venture out with ambitious, aggressive, and revealing instructions that made clashes with Powhatan unavoidable. A fortified base was to be established far enough up some great river to command a trading hinterland and to escape Spanish attack. The all-male settlers, with very few trained soldiers or husbandmen, were to be divided into three crews: one to fortify and defend, one to plant crops, and a third to explore a passage to Asia. Not only was there no mention of negotiating with the inhabitants about land use, but conflict with the "naturals" was presumed. The company advised its appointees to trade for local grain, which might grow better than imported seed, and to do so before the Amerindians realized that the English intended to stay. Although the fort was to be as much as a hundred miles up river, the instructions insisted:

> [Y]ou must in no case suffer any of the native people of the country to inhabit between you and the sea coast; for . . . they will grow discontented with your habitation, and be ready to guide and assist any nation that shall come to invade you.

Nothing was mentioned about how the coast was to be cleared of inhabitants, and this impractical tyranny was initially ignored. Although the Virginia Company assumed both Amerindian hostility and weakness, the colonists were warned that their only protection was an exaggerated Amerindian fear of their firearms. Amerindians should never be allowed to handle muskets and should see only the very best marksmen fire. For additional bluff, the Amerindians were never to see the English sick or dying, which would reveal that they were not indestructible, "but common men."[3]

The English, like other Europeans, shared the misguided belief that their methods of agriculture were inherently superior. People from more crowded Europe lavished enormous amounts of human and animal labor to maximize the yield per acre. Amerindians of the less populated eastern American woodlands were lavish with land in order to maximize the yield per day of work. In a patch of forest already dense enough to eliminate competing grasses, Amerindians girdled and later burned trees, planting seed in the rich ashes to gain excellent crops of the corn, squash, and beans that sustained them. Whenever the ash fertilizer became depleted, a new area had to be burned. Since this method worked well only in fully timbered areas, former fields were best left for a generation in which to reforest. This ideal rotation of fields required a great deal of land, but more frequent rotation required much more labor to dig grass roots. The ideal was not always possible, even before 1500, and intertribal rivalries included this desire for sufficient land. Less successful tribes, and particularly the women who planted and tended crops, were condemned to more field work. What looked like agricultural "civilization" to Europeans was seen as slavery behind oxen to Amerindians. What looked like criminally idle land (and people) to arriving Englishmen was valued as fallow land by resident Amerindians.[4]

Confrontations in Virginia were inevitable. The confidence of the English invaders went far beyond their ships, or their matchlock muskets, or their view of agriculture. Protestant England had survived Elizabeth's long war with mighty Spain (1585–1603), though knighted Elizabethans, like Martin Frobisher, Humphrey Gilbert, and Walter Ralegh, had all failed in North America. After a generation of plundering Spain's America, Elizabethans had learned to organize oceanic expeditions, to navigate in open seas, and to develop new markets for exotic products. England's predatory gentry had re-established armed dominance over Catholic Ireland by 1601, after savage wars that had too much influence on English military and colonizing methods in North America. English Protestantism also gained dynastic and diplomatic security by the accession of Scotland's King James VI (1567–1625) as England's King James I (1603–1625). Powhatan could feel confident that the people of his growing empire outnumbered the greedy intruders by at least 140 to 1. When Powhatan sent his priest-councilor Uttamatomakkin to England, he optimistically asked for a count of all English. The English, from an expanding society with more than two hundred times the population of the entire Powhatan empire, were quite confident that their society possessed complete religious, political, economic, technical, and military superiority over those they were about to meet. Such confident general assumptions met unsettling realities in Chesapeake Bay.[5]

There was some good sense as well as good fortune in the English landing on the Jamestown peninsula, despite massive fatalities from dysentery, salt poisoning, malaria, and typhoid that would be linked to its unhealthy swamps and tidal waters.[6] This deep anchorage, where ships were "moored to the Trees in six fathom water," was forty miles up the James River, hidden from the Spanish, and partially defended by water and swamp from Powhatan's subjects, some of whom had already wounded two of the scouting English even before the expedition had landed. The arrivals promptly began cutting timber in this Powhatan wasteland to build a simple triangular fort, the same design used in the 1560s by the French and Spanish for speedy fortification of Florida beachheads.[7]

Powhatan had his lieutenants gather preliminary information about these few, womanless, strangers who were beginning to fortify a worthless, swampy little peninsula. While one of his sons was exchanging hospitality and trinkets with Captain Christopher Newport's exploratory expedition near the falls of the James River on May 26, a raiding party of more than two hundred warriors from five Powhatan tribes tested the defenses of the unfinished James Fort. Two of the surprised English were killed and twelve to fifteen were wounded before musket fire and ships' cannon forced the attackers, who had even more casualties, to retreat. The fort was hurriedly completed, with a fifteen-foot palisade and at least a dozen platform-mounted cannon in three modest "half-moon" bastions. However, security inside was contrasted by insecurity outside, evident in fatal attacks on those who went out, even to "doe naturall necessity."[8] The English ships retaliated by bombarding Amerindian villages along both banks of the James River, returning with some stolen corn and prisoners.

After regaining control of the vital waterways once the English ships sailed homeward from their James River outpost in June, Powhatan dominated the military and diplomatic situation. The English survivors did not initially grasp that both their kind hosts and their attackers were subjects of Powhatan, who was weighing the advantages of either killing the English or using them and their muskets against his much more serious Siouan enemies. The English were left largely to their own inadequate devices through a summer of scarce supplies and devastating diseases, from which nearly half the inhabitants of the fort died. Powhatan then renewed contact with gifts of food, presuming that acceptance implied English dependence, and with resumption of his monopoly trade of corn for English copper.

Both empires sought to impose their dominance by diplomacy. Captain John Smith, the most vigorous and effective of the remaining English leaders, explored possible links with the Chickahominy, an Algonquian tribe that remained fairly independent in the heart of Powhatan territory. Smith was captured by a large hunting party headed by Powhatan's brother and eventual successor, Opechancanough. Powhatan studied Smith carefully, adopted him, and likely appointed this frightened and uncomprehending new relative as his *werowance* for the new subsidiary white tribe.[9] Peace and trade were offered the intruders, whose tribute was to be two cannon, a grindstone, and military aid against Powhatan's enemies.

The English tried to reverse this relationship a year later, when Captain Newport sought to crown Powhatan in what the English took to be his submission as a vassal of James I. Powhatan refused to come to Jamestown, and elaborate gifts were then shipped for a ceremony at his capital, Werowacomoco on the York River. Although persuaded to wear the alien scarlet cloak and new shoes, Powhatan resolutely refused to kneel to be crowned. Captain Newport, a one-armed former privateer, even had trouble getting the much taller Powhatan to bend enough to place the crown on his head. For the emperor, these strange new vassals had brought him traditional presents of clothing, including a headdress, and his gracious response was to give them his old mantle and shoes.[10]

Peace and trade between Powhatan and the small, sickly English community lasted for little more than a year. Copper from beyond the Siouan-dominated piedmont had been an expensive ornamental luxury and a durable form of wealth that Powhatan used to hire allied warriors and reward priests and *werowances*. The Virginia Company, very anxious to find what it considered precious metals, was soon trading comparatively cheap English copper for Powhatan corn. Poor recruiting, factious leaders, and ill health were among the reasons the colonists did not raise nearly enough food for themselves. The company strengthened Powhatan's trading position by deciding that it was cheaper to buy corn from him rather than to ship foodstuffs from England. Predictably, the value of the copper fell as Powhatan acquired more, and the value of corn rose as the English consumed more. The English tried to improve their trading position by purchasing corn directly from families of the Chickahominy, but the additional supply of English copper soon lowered its value further.

The surviving Jamestown colonists became desperate even before fire destroyed the settlement and much of its palisade early in 1609. Powhatan's corn prices and demands for gifts were escalating; he had already acquired three hundred iron hatchets and fifty swords, and now proposed to trade corn only for muskets. After the English approached his Monacan enemies in November 1608, Powhatan understandably halted the corn trade entirely. Smith drew on his military experience against the Turks for solutions, leading raids to extort corn from *werowances*. One raid on a Pamunkey village would return to haunt Anglo-Powhatan relations, for in this case Smith held a loaded pistol to the head of Opechancanough, until he was ransomed with boatloads of corn. Smith prudently began to train some colonists to fight in the woods, while hungry English defectors were teaching the Powhatan how to use their stolen muskets.

The English inadvertently launched the first Anglo-Powhatan war in August 1609. An English fleet brought reinforcements and new snaphance muskets, but it also brought inadequate provisions and disappointing news that the new deputy governor, Sir Thomas Gates, was shipwrecked and stranded on Bermuda, where he remained for a year.

Because of famine and sickness at Jamestown in the summer of 1609, yeoman-born Captain John Smith dispersed the new arrivals and accompanying higher-born political rivals to outposts along the James River, where they were to be "self-sufficient." One party of a hundred, whose emissaries to the Nansemond tribe were tortured and executed, responded by burning villages and robbing graves. Within weeks, half of this group was killed in retaliation. Another party of 120 went up the James, where Smith forced Amerindians to "sell" him a complete and defensible village of huts and ripening cornfields. Within two months, the Powhatan had killed nearly half of these English intruders, and also killed another party of thirty-three by ruse and ambush. Powhatan then moved to encircle and starve Jamestown, to which nearly all the English survivors had retreated. This "starving time" brought death to more than half of the 220 besieged that winter and induced some wretched survivors to commit the only reported cases of cannibalism in the area. When Gates finally arrived from newly claimed Bermuda the following June, he was so shocked he immediately ordered abandonment of defeated Virginia.

Just as Jamestown was being abandoned, a reinforcing squadron of three English vessels arrived, robbing Powhatan of his clear and complete victory. The Virginia Company, which had lost 350 people and £20,000 in three years, had become rechartered, revitalized, better informed, and more aggressive. The colony was now instructed to ally with Powhatan's enemies, who were far enough away to limit occasions for friction.[11] Colonists were now promised land at the end of their seven-year term with the company, presumably Powhatan land. Governor Thomas West, Lord De La Warr, brought 100 veteran soldiers among the 150 new colonists, and his deputies, Gates and Sir Thomas Dale, introduced ferocious military discipline that would last for five years in the embattled settlement. Both the Virginia Company and Powhatan were transforming an English commercial colony into a garrison: all adult males were militiamen, and all had the need and duty to buy, repair, and practice using muskets.

Five expeditions out of Jamestown in 1610 indiscriminately killed scores of Powhatan's subjects, burned villages, and confiscated crops. Particularly vicious was the exterminating raid against the Paspahegh, a small Powhatan tribe mustering forty warriors whose lands included Jamestown. Seventy English attackers burned the main village, stole ripe grain, and killed more than sixty-five people, including the *werowance*'s children who had been taken captive, thrown overboard, and then shot.[12]

Retaliation by the Powhatan was less effective than previously. One twenty-man English garrison at a blockhouse near Jamestown was annihilated the following summer, but a second siege of Jamestown aborted when three hundred more veteran soldiers arrived in supply ships. That summer, for the first time, English musketeers wore heavy armor that proved effective against the Nansemond bowmen of the lower James River. Armor was much more effective in Virginia than similar equipment had been for the Spanish in Florida because the Powhatan had fewer stone arrowheads, which could penetrate armor or cause serious injury when shattering against it. Systematic English attacks on cornfields, called "feed fights," became strategic to both sides, and the Powhatan were forced to defend those fields in open combat, a battle milieu familiar to the armored English musketeers.[13]

As the fighting became more lethal, the Powhatan became more cautious. The new English fortification up the James River at Henrico (Richmond) was not effectively resisted, nor were English raids on Appomattox villages in the vicinity. In the next two years fighting abated, for neither side had the resources for a decisive battle. The English had more success diplomatically, as Captain Samuel Argall formed trading alliances with the Accomac and Accohannock of the Eastern Shore and restored good relations with the Patawomec on the Potomac. In return for protection against Powhatan, the Patawomec *werowance* Japazaws assisted Argall in capturing Powhatan's favorite daughter, Pocahontas, in March 1613. Over the next year, Powhatan returned seven colonial deserters and some broken muskets, but would not pay the huge ransom in corn that was demanded for his daughter, nor would he surrender his functional muskets.

The climax and conclusion of the first Anglo-Powhatan war came in the spring of 1614. Under pressure from the company in London for decisive action, Dale took 150 English soldiers and the captive Pocahontas into the York River core of Powhatan's empire to deliver an ultimatum. On the way up the York River, a shower of arrows was answered with swift retaliation on the nearest village, killing six warriors and burning forty lodges. When the English disembarked amid hundreds of Pamunkey warriors in the heart of Powhatan's territory, his power was palpable despite his absence. Neither side fired. After two days of threats and ignored deadlines for a response from the absent Powhatan, the English suddenly reimbarked and returned to Jamestown unmolested. There the war ended, not with a truce or capitulation on either side, but with Powhatan accepting the marriage of his daughter, now the Anglican prisoner-princess Pocahontas, to a prominent English colonist who had recently begun experimenting with Powhatan tobacco as an export crop. Both empires attended this Jamestown wedding, one of only three Anglo-Powhatan marriages known to have occurred in the seventeenth century. Both empires claimed victory as peace broke out.[14]

Peace brought a repudiation of the military regime by both the colonists and their employer, the Virginia Company. The English inhabitants, numbering 350 by 1616, gradually emerged from their enforced military life on the palisaded little peninsulas at Jamestown and Henrico. The company, which had not made any money in a decade, reorganized yet again, this time as a land company offering migrants free land on arrival. After a poor Powhatan corn crop, the better-supplied English were even selling some corn to the Powhatan and Chickahominy.[15] In 1617 the first tobacco crop was sent to what proved to be a good market in England. By 1619 the colony was allowed a legislative assembly, the House of Burgesses, to attract and control settlers who were no longer company employees. Over the next three unhealthy years, some 3570 migrants arrived, although by the spring of 1622 the entire surviving English population consisted of only 1240.

Although it seems probable that attempted cultural integration and increasing English land hunger soured relations with the Powhatan, direct evidence is rather limited. Dozens of Powhatan families had come to live within the English settlements, trade resumed, funds for an Indian college were collected by the company in England, and a policy of fair treatment and cultural integration was declared. By 1616 the English were confidently instructing some Powhatan warriors in the use of muskets, and Kissarourr may have been the first Amerindian anywhere to own a snaphance, an innovative musket with flint on steel ignition. This musket instruction was Opechancanough's price for allowing any Christian instruction.[16] Increasing peacetime contact and integration between these societies likely produced friction; between 1617 and 1619, it definitely produced the first epidemic to hit the Powhatan in the decade since the English began arriving to die at their sickly Jamestown. It is noteworthy that the Powhatan, who may have suffered virgin land epidemics in the sixteenth century, had no major population losses due to epidemics during the seventeenth century.

By 1622 the land-hungry English had claimed most of the excellent waterfront along the James River, interfering with Powhatan access to fields, reed-gathering areas, and the waterway itself. However, tobacco-inspired land competition was just beginning; the largest crop of tobacco exported to England thus far could have been grown on less than three hundred acres.[17]

Relations had begun to deteriorate even before the elderly Powhatan died in 1618, as the capable Opechancanough gained power. He had tricked the English into a wrongful attack on the Chickahominy in 1616, in which thirty to forty had been slain; then he used the incident to draw that tribe under direct Powhatan protection and control.[18] Opechancanough had long-standing personal resentments, aggravated by the growing waves of invading English. Although many of them died soon after arrival, the influx of armable adult males between 1619 and 1622 had equaled the total number of Powhatan warriors. A nervous Governor George Yeardley paid an English renegade living with Opechancanough to steal the "feathers" from the firing mechanisms of Powhatan muskets, thereby disabling them. The muskets were brought to the English for repair and not returned.[19] English provocation of the Powhatan was denounced at the inaugural meeting of the Virginia

House of Burgesses in 1619, and the gathering also imposed the death penalty on anyone selling muskets to Amerindians.

Relations were further strained after the apparently random murder of Morgan, an English trader invited on a trading venture in the fall of 1621 by the famous Powhatan war captain Nemattanew. Nemattanew was familiar with muskets and was also an inspirational leader. He reportedly claimed immortality and inspired fellow warriors with the discovery of a body oil that supposedly resisted musket shot. Within days of Morgan's departure, Nemattanew appeared at the trader's store wearing Morgan's hat and announcing his death. In an ensuing argument, one of Morgan's servants shot and killed Nemattanew. Opechancanough immediately threatened revenge, then appeared to be deterred by English counterthreats.[20]

Surprise was essential for Powhatan victory over the heavily armed English, and Opechancanough orchestrated a long-planned, devastating surprise. On the morning of March 22, 1622, hundreds of Powhatan men visited the English farms and settlements scattered for eighty miles along the meandering James and Appomattox rivers. The unsuspecting English, including the relatively few women and children among them, were then attacked in a bid to exterminate all these intruders. Powhatan warriors did not usually kill women and children, but the English, like the Chesapeake tribe, were now treated differently.[21] Despite warnings by a Christian Powhatan, 347 of the 1240 English colonists were slaughtered that day, and a few others in the following days. Opechancanough's subsequent strategy was Powhatan, not European: he expected his enemies to learn from this single ferocious blow and to withdraw.

Instead, the shocked English survivors gathered in eight defensible strongholds along the James, where they were soon subjected to martial law, very short rations, and siege. For a second time in thirteen years, the Powhatan seemed poised to eradicate the English invaders. Hundreds of the English would die of starvation and disease within their defenses or in attempting to return to plant fields. Sorties of up to three hundred heavily armed and armored men attacked Nansemond, Chickahominy, and Pamunkey villages, but they had invariably been emptied of people, food, and valuables. As summer advanced, the raids became effective, shifting to equally undefended Amerindian cornfields, giving the English the harvest. The Powhatan confederacy would suffer food shortages over the next year.[22] Warriors now carried an additional burden; as the English raided the best cornfields of the Powhatan empire, warriors had to clear new ones in safer places.

Despite aid from London and ten major raids in the first year of the war, the English remained entirely thwarted in avenging their initial casualties. A massive shipment of muskets and obsolete armor from the Tower of London, and the Virginia Company's own muskets, helped in developing a thoroughly armed, if cumbersome and unruly, white militia. The Patawomec, English allies and guides in the search for new Amerindian cornfields, had more than thirty killed when they were mistakenly attacked by the English. The colonists' anxiety grew after their best woodsman and Patawomec-raised interpreter, Henry Spelman, and twenty-two heavily armed companions were ambushed in April 1623 on a grain-buying trip up the Potomac River. Besides losing the men, the English lost muskets, powder, shot, armor, and swords.[23]

The English resorted to duplicity. At peace talks the following month in Opechancanough's territory, the English murdered two hundred Pamunkey by serving them poisoned wine, then practiced their first reported scalping on another fifty Pamunkey killed in an ambush. The London leaders of the now bankrupt Virginia Company objected to the poisoned wine, but the colonists were just beginning their vengeance.[24] In November 1623, the Virginia militia expanded its range and made new enemies by attacking and burning Moyaone, the stockaded Potomac town of the Piscataway.[25]

The only major battle of the war occurred in July 1624, when a rather small expedition of sixty armored Englishmen sailed up the York River to the center of the Powhatan empire, to confiscate corn in the fields. Hoping to overwhelm so small a party, the Pamunkey decided to stand and fight. In a battle that lasted two days, massed snaphances fired by musketeers in heavy armor proved unbeatable. By this time, snaphances had come to be the most common muskets of the English in Virginia.[26] Eight hundred Pamunkey and other Powhatan warriors displayed remarkable courage and took many casualties, while no English were killed and their sixteen wounded were safely evacuated after the corn-fields were stripped of enough corn to feed four thousand for a year.[27]

Opechancanough's strategem had ultimately failed. Rather than sig-naling the end of the English invasion, the massacre became the justi-fication that clarified and accelerated the process. For the remaining years of the war, the English routinely raided Amerindian villages and cornfields, curtailed only by their own preoccupation with tobacco planting, by serious gunpowder shortages, and by clever Amerindian relocation of these crucial fields. The massacre had completed the destruction of the failing Virginia Company of London, and the deci-sion not to grant any monopoly thereafter threw this growing trade open to all royal subjects. There were few local changes as Virginia became England's first royal colony in 1624, directly under King James. The war apparently ended late in 1632 in a fragile English truce with both the Powhatan and the Chickahominy, although it was violated repeatedly on both sides for the next dozen years.

The cultures now became almost completely separate, with pali-sades, dangerous no-man's-lands, and persistent hatred between them. The English built a six-mile-long palisade from Jamestown to a fort at Chiskiack on the York River, excluding Amerindians from about 300,000 acres of the peninsula. In 1632 the English militia was ordered to bring muskets to church and practice military drills after the Sunday service. After 1634, the gentry militia commanders in each of Virginia's eight counties could order attacks on neighboring Amerindians almost at will. Some Amerindian captives were now enslaved, but more often sold abroad rather than kept for field work on tobacco lands that had once been their cornfields. Within a year, another power of the new militia was revealed when they "arrested" and expelled their own royal governor, John Harvey, for challenging the validity of land claims and negotiating the truce with Opechancanough.[28]

The founding of Maryland in 1634, and the spirited rivalry between these Chesapeake Bay colonies for the fur trade northward, may have misled the Powhatan into thinking this would divide the intruders. The trade, which thrived in this area for only a generation, illustrated the difference that economics could make to the invasion of North America. In the fur trade, Amerindian trappers and customers were active, and often armed, participants in the ambitions of the Europeans. In the tobacco cultivation that came to dominate this area, the crop was grown on lands from which the Amerindians had been expelled. By 1640 the English were claiming lands north of the York River, two years later they were staking lands on the Rappahannock, and by 1643 they were settling along the Potomac. The Powhatan were being pushed west and north, into the boundaries of their ancient enemies. The Virginia House of Burgesses displayed its own fears, and aggravated tensions further, by passing a new law that not only forbade the sale, gift, or loan of guns to Amerindians, but also allowed any white settler to confiscate guns from any Amerindian.[29]

By 1644, when the nearly hundred-year-old Opechancanough again decided to drive out the English, the relative power of the two groups had been radically changed. The English invasion had continued relentlessly, spurred by the rapidly expanding consumption of tobacco in northern Europe. Chesapeake tobacco exports had multiplied twenty-six times in twenty years, exceeding 3 million pounds by 1638. Virginia's English population was now over fourteen thousand, with a heavy predominance of immigrant adult males who made the militia larger than usual for that population.[30] Although Powhatan population figures are unreliable, that society had suffered severely from disease, famine, and war in the forty years since they, too, had numbered about fourteen thousand.

The Powhatan response to this unrelenting English invasion of their territory was again to reject and resist. Although the coordinated Powhatan attack of April 18, 1644, killed nearly five hundred, more than had died in 1622, the single blow struck only the areas west of the palisade and on the southern frontiers of white settlement.

The English retaliation, organized by Governor William Berkeley before he hurried back to an England disintegrating into civil war, was predictably fierce. Two of the three attacks were on the James River, one against the surviving Nansemond of the lower river, and the other west from ravaged Henrico and Charles counties to distract the Powhatan from the main English assault up the York River against Opechancanough's Pamunkey. Three hundred armored musketeers burned Pamunkey villages and destroyed crops, but could find few Pamunkey or Chickahominy. These deserted lands were promptly "claimed" by four forts built the following spring to link the enlarged frontier from the falls of the Appomattox and James to the head of the York River. At the last of these, Fort Loyal, the English lured the Powhatan to peace talks, then attacked the party of emissaries as they arrived. Some were killed or captured, but most of the party, including Opechancanough, escaped. By this time, the colonists were routinely selling Amerindian prisoners of war into slavery in the West Indies.[31]

Neither raids nor ruses had broken the Powhatan, and English frustration was compounded by the high costs of garrisoning their new forts. In 1645 the colony raised a force of paid volunteer "rangers" who contracted to defend the colony for a year, thereby introducing specialized forces that the developing tobacco economy was expected to support. In the spring of 1646, the Virginia House of Burgesses decided to postpone other raiding and to send a force of sixty militiamen to assassinate or capture Opechancanough. Berkeley and a group of horsemen joined the pursuit and captured the aged and feeble paramount chief as he was being carried on a litter. The prisoner, carried to Jamestown prison, was subsequently murdered by one of the guards.

The Powhatan empire died with Opechancanough, though Necotowance became the new titular leader. He accepted a peace treaty in October 1646 that ceded the lands south of the York and promised to return all "negroes and guns." The treaty also forbade Amerindians any access to the ceded lands on pain of death, confined trading to specific forts, and required an annual tribute of twenty beaverskins to demonstrate that the Pamunkey's own lands were now held under the king of England. By 1650 the Amerindians of Virginia had been assigned to reservations at the rate of fifty acres per bowman. This arrangement might have been adequate for a plowman, but not for a hunter.

The English colony had developed from dependence on the Powhatan before 1622, to racial apartheid by 1644, and then to complete dominance over the next thirty years. By 1675 Virginia contained approximately 44,000 people: about 2500 African slaves, some 3500 Amerindians, and about 38,000 Europeans, the largest concentration of European immigrants and descendants anywhere in North America. Although these population figures were unknown then, and are only rough estimates now, it is hard to appreciate subsequent white fears of annihilation.

By 1675 tobacco had not only transformed the Chesapeake tidewater area, but also linked it increasingly to Europe; more than 17 million pounds of tobacco had been exported to England from Chesapeake Bay during 1672. Thousands of European indentured servants migrated to tend tobacco along with the few African slaves then in the colony. More than a hundred ships each year came to freight tobacco, delivering European commodities cheaply. Europeans by the tens of thousands smoked or chewed the increasingly accessible narcotic weed, but production could be expanded even more easily than consumption, and the general trend in tobacco prices was downward. European governments taxed tobacco heavily, making smuggling or disruption of that trade a significant policy matter.[32]

After English revolutionary forces had overthrown and finally beheaded King Charles I in 1649, some English colonies, including Virginia, refused to acknowledge the new regime or its laws monopolizing major colonial trades. It would be the English navy that first brought effective maritime power against Virginia. The first English naval squadron to cross the Atlantic in half a century forced the surrender of royalist governments in Barbados, Antigua, Bermuda, Virginia, and Maryland. Royal governors, including William Berkeley of Virginia, were replaced, and the authority of Parliament was acknowledged.

As the tobacco trade grew, so did the threat of attack from European rivals. Initial fears of Spanish eradication of the colony proved unwarranted; there had been nothing more serious than a Spanish reconnaissance ship in 1611, which carried off a James River pilot. English legislation, to ensure that English colonial sugar and tobacco were shipped and marketed by the English, provoked the first of three Anglo-Dutch wars (1652–1654, 1665–1667, 1672–1674). War was an extension of trade rivalry used by the uncompetitive English and French to force the more efficient Dutch to increase spending on convoys, forts, and marine insurance, thereby weakening their comparative price advantage. Although the actual fighting was confined to European waters, the first war disrupted the English tobacco trade, which normally found re-export markets in the Netherlands. In the second war, a single Dutch privateer took a couple of prizes within Chesapake Bay in 1666, but the real threat came from a five-ship Dutch squadron under Admiral Abraham Crijnsen that arrived in the James River the following June. After surprising and burning the only English frigate in the area, the squadron went on to capture a dozen or more tobacco ships and destroy five or six others. Governor Berkeley, who had been reinstated by the restored King Charles II in 1660, attempted a counterattack with some twelve hundred militia handling hastily mounted cannon aboard tobacco ships, but they proved too late to confront the Dutch.

This humiliation prompted better preparedness. When a nine-vessel Dutch squadron entered Chesapeake Bay in July 1673, it was challenged by two English frigates, six armed merchantmen, and modest shore batteries, as well as a militia of fifteen hundred horse, twenty-five hundred "able men with snaphances," and more than three thousand other militia. This Dutch fleet destroyed eleven merchantmen before leaving the bay and successfully retaking the colony of New

York. It is also noteworthy that, for the first time in thirty-five years, Virginia counties spent public money buying flintlock muskets. These arrived too late for the last Dutch war, but were in time to arm hundreds in Bacon's Rebellion (1675–1676).[33]

Although the incidents of the last two Anglo-Dutch wars indicate the increasing integration of North America into Europe's economic, diplomatic, and military calculations, it was Virginia–Amerindian tensions that provoked the next serious explosion, Bacon's Rebellion. The English had long since broken the power of the Powhatan empire, but had not inherited it. They had continued to expand their settlements, but the English were not the only contenders for the power vacuum they had created in destroying the buffer that had both limited and insulated them. Local Rappahannock who clashed with encroaching planters had been cowed by the militia in 1655, but a greater threat appeared the following year. Suddenly between six and seven hundred unfamiliar Amerindians, referred to as "Richahecrians," established themselves in the land above the falls of the James River. The Virginia assembly ordered a militia colonel, Edward Hill, to take a hundred of his men, and what proved to be an equal number of Pamunkey, to warn the strangers off "without makeing warr if it may be." Hill had five Richahecrian chiefs treacherously murdered when they came to negotiate, provoking a pitched battle in which most of the Pamunkey, including Necotowance, were killed. The entire Virginia militia fled in panic. Although the well-armed Richahecrian moved away as mysteriously as they had arrived, the inexperienced Virginia militia had disgraced itself in the colony's first serious battle in thirty years. It is noteworthy that there is no evidence of armor being used here; Amerindians now had muskets in quantity, and Virginia colonists had lost a significant advantage [34]

The Westo, loosely amalgamated refugees and renegades from a variety of tribes between Virginia and Florida, represented a new type of Amerindian group created in the wake of white invasion. From a base on the Savannah River, this small tribe raided Guale and Cusabo communities to their south and east, as well as Cherokee and Creek tribes to their west, taking captives and plunder. The Westo traded these Amerindian slaves for guns with increasingly venturesome Virginia traders and, after 1674, with the very competitive traders of the new English colony of Carolina. Themselves a product of displacement, the Westo were forcing migrations as far away as the Apalachee and Timucua settlements of Florida by 1680. The Westo blocked Carolinian access to direct trade with the more numerous Creek and Cherokee beyond. By arming a larger group of Algonquian Shawnee migrants from west of the mountains who became the Savannah tribe, the Carolinians provoked a war that gave them a buffer of powerful Savannah allies, Westo slaves to sell in the West Indies, and access to a trade in Amerindian slaves and deerskins with the Creek and Cherokee that quite overwhelmed their comparatively poorly placed Virginia competitors. This classic pattern of guns for slaves followed by enslaving the slavers, familiar in English and French dominance in West Africa and parts of North America, was used to eliminate virtually all the Westo and later to destroy the Savannah in their turn.[35]

The Richahecrian were a frightening visitation on Virginia's exposed western fringe, and the Westo represented profitable trade to the southwest for a few Virginians and troubling firearms proliferation for the rest, but it was the Iroquoian Susquehannock from the north who were more serious contenders for power in the Potomac Valley. These aggressive fur traders lived in a defensible town of about six thousand on the Susquehanna River. Powerful rivals and relatives of the Five Nations of the Iroquois to their north, the well-positioned Susquehannock had been early allies of the French (1615) and of the short-lived New Sweden colony (1638–1655), later becoming major fur traders with the English of Maryland. Dominating their region early in the century, the Susquehannock invaded the valley of the Delaware and fought a deadly but inconclusive war with the Mohawk for direct access to Dutch traders. Susquehannock terrorizing of the smaller Piscataway tribe, tributary to the Maryland government, led to an indecisive war with that colony in the 1640s, during which the Susquehannock were thoroughly rearmed by the Swedes. After 1652 Maryland authorities drew closer to the Susquehannock, in peace, trade, and alliance, recognizing them as the only effective buffer against raids by the Five Nations down the notorious "warriors' path."[36]

Having secured their southern flank and armament supply, the Susquehannock launched a generation-long war against all the Five Nations except the Mohawk. Successful Susquehannock raids would help bring the Five Nations to make peace with New France in 1667, and sectors of these harassed tribes migrated to safety on the northern shore of Lake Ontario. Initial counterstrikes against the Susquehannock failed completely. A massive Five Nations army besieged the Susquehannock fort in 1663, but met complete defiance, reinforced by Swedish cannon and Maryland gunners. The Susquehannock contemptuously tortured and burned an entire legation of twenty-five who came to negotiate during the siege. Three years later, another attacking Five Nations army was completely destroyed. Susquehannock security was suddenly undermined, most likely by a major defeat by the Five Nations. Maryland officials, although anxious for peace with the Five Nations in order to appropriate land and trade in the Delaware Valley, gave the Susquehannock refurbished Piscataway Fort, which these Europeans had built on the Potomac in the 1640s.[37]

In moving to the Virginia–Maryland border region, the Susquehannock moved into an explosive situation. Frontier settlers and militias were increasingly nervous about vulnerability to unknown Amerindian raiders, and they became aggressive toward familiar Amerindians who had lost their value as buffers or provisioners but occupied valuable fields and were suspected of aiding unknown attackers. The English frontier farmers were also angry with governments that showed more concern for peace and their monopoly trade with the Amerindians than for the safety of English settlers. Virginia's Governor Berkeley, whose martial concerns had centered on defending the colony from Dutch naval invasion, saw the frontiersmen as unscrupulous. They might well provoke an Amerindian war in order to secure land and slaves, thus drawing the whole colony into the human and fiscal consequences.

The spark was ignited in July 1675 by the Doeg, a small tribe on the Maryland side of the Potomac who were now a close neighbor of the Susquehannock. Angry with Thomas Mathew, a wealthy Virginia planter who reportedly refused to pay for goods received, the Doeg took hogs from one of Mathew's plantations. The English pursued, killing several of the tribe and recovering the hogs; in revenge, a Doeg war party killed one of Mathew's herdsmen. Two Virginia militia captains then led thirty of their men across the Potomac into Maryland. While one group terrorized a Doeg settlement, killing ten, the other militiamen attacked a nearby cabin, killing fourteen before discovering that these were Susquehannock, erstwhile English allies. Once again, Virginians had displayed surprising, or feigned, difficulty distinguishing between Amerindian friend and enemy. Maryland protests against both the invasion and the killing of innocent Amerindians were soon forgotten amid the cries of victims of a wave of Amerindian attacks on the frontiers of both colonies.[38]

Virginia militia officers John Washington and Isaac Allerton exceeded their orders in calling out 500 Virginia militia and securing 250 Maryland soldiers to help them make "a full and thorough inquisition" into the raids and murders. Without provocation, these white militia promptly attacked a hundred Susquehannock warriors caught, with their families, within their fortified compound at the old Piscataway Fort. Although they outnumbered the defenders by at least seven to one, the militia chose to starve the defenders rather than storm their ably defended earthen fort, complete with cannon, bastions, and ditch, to which had been added a strong exterior stockade (Figure 2). Five Susquehannock negotiators were treacherously killed, but in a number of well-executed night sorties, the Susquehannock killed or wounded fifty of the poorly disciplined militia. One night, after seven weeks of siege, all the Susquehannock escaped, killing another ten militiamen. The Susquehannock had expertly used a European fort and weapons and defended themselves honorably and bravely by the martial standards of either civilization. Their opponents had been impetuous, treacherous, cowardly, and negligent, but thought they had won after burning the deserted fort. However, they had provoked war without gaining booty and, by scattering the Susquehannock had exposed

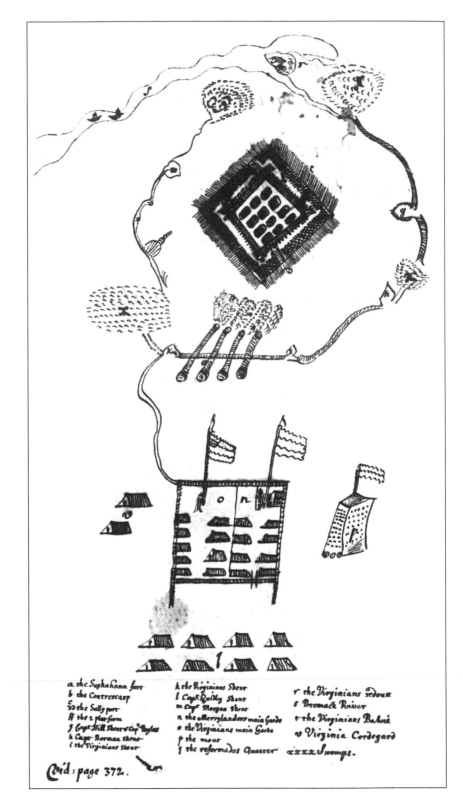

a the Sufkahana fort k the Virginians Shent r the Virginians redoux
b the Contrescarp l Capt. Quilby Shent s Potomack River
cc the Sally port m Capt. Morgan Shent t the Virginians Bahni
ff the 2 platform n the Merrylanders main Garde w Virginia Cordegard
g Capt. Hill Shent & Cap. Boylan o the Virginians main Garde xxxx Swompts.
h Capt. Borman shent p the moat
i the Virginians Shent q the reformados Quaever

Vid: page 372.

their homes not only to predictable retribution, but also to attacks by now unopposed northern raiders. By March 1676, Amerindian raids had killed nearly three hundred colonists.[39]

As Virginia's frontiers caught fire, terrified settlers called for their government's help, gathered in clusters for defense, accused local Amerindians of involvement, and lashed out at whatever Amerindian groups were at hand. Some Amerindians, recognizing the danger, fled for their own safety, thereby encouraging frightened whites to presume guilt. Governor Berkeley, furious about the unauthorized campaign against the Susquehannock, countermanded his own initially aggressive response and convinced the assembly to focus on building and garrisoning a series of nine frontier forts. Berkeley's forts could challenge hostile Amerindians, monitor unruly frontiersmen, and protect tribes attempting to live in peace with the colonists. Berkeley's policy might have been prudent considering the feasibility of attacking the dispersed Susquehannock, or it might have been sensible because he received a Susquehannock peace offer. This contained the admission that the Susquehannock had avenged the betrayal of their five chiefs by killing ten Englishmen for each of them. While Berkeley could not condone this, he did insist that any further militia expeditions were to be cleared with him first.[40]

Whatever the merits of Berkeley's forts, they were resented in much of the colony and were unworkable on the frontier. Those English who had best been able to appropriate Amerindian land, borrow English capital, and control the labor of English indentured servants and African slaves had established themselves as a new and unpopular planter elite around the governor. Falling tobacco prices forced many smaller planters to sell their land, and crippling taxes would rise even further to finance the new forts. Berkeley himself wrote of the trouble of governing "a People wher six parts of seaven at least are Poore Endebted Discontented and Armed."[41] For those fearing Amerindian attack, especially a universal Amerindian uprising as was rumored after news arrived of the outbreak of King Philip's War in New England, the Virginia forts would be no protection, and the governor's prohibition on immediate pursuit only increased vulnerability.

Nathaniel Bacon, a young, prosperous, well-connected planter of Henrico County and a member of the Virginia Council, emerged as a leader who would attack Amerindians in defiance of the aged Governor Berkeley. In the autumn of 1675, Bacon had illegally seized several Appomattox, falsely accusing them of stealing corn; he was rebuked by Berkeley. In April 1676, Bacon, who had no militia rank but expected Berkeley to commission him, offered to lead volunteers against the

Figure 2. *(facing)* Susquehannock Fort on the Potomac, ca. 1675. (Courtesy of the Public Record Office, Kew [CO 5/1371, fol. 186])

Amerindian threat after his commission was refused. Bacon's two-hundred-man party spent a futile week hunting for the Susquehannock, then visited the Occaneechee, a small tribe whose easily located island fort in the Roanoke River controlled a crucial ford for Virginia's trade to the interior. The Occaneechee had refused to help two groups of Susquehannock who were fortifying themselves in the vicinity and had even sent runners to inform the English. Bacon's hungry force was fed, and the Occaneechee also offered to attack the rival Susquehannock traders on behalf of their guests. This was readily agreed to and was carried out successfully. Some thirty Susquehannock were killed, and an impressive booty of furs and prisoners was gathered. Some, if not all, of the prisoners were turned over to Bacon, who tortured and killed them. Then Bacon's volunteers turned on their hosts. In what may have begun as a squabble over furs, twelve of Bacon's men were killed and fifty Occaneechee were either killed or captured. Bacon was regarded as a conquering hero when he returned from this squalid "campaign."[42]

The challenge to Berkeley now became more direct. In mid-May, Berkeley had denounced Bacon, removed him from the council, and called the first election in fourteen years. When the "victorious" Bacon refused to apologize, he and his supporters were declared rebels. Nonetheless, Bacon was elected to the new assembly and came to Jamestown in a sloop with fifty armed supporters. Promptly tricked and captured, Bacon was made to confess, then pardoned and restored to the council. Berkeley also promised him a military commission. Bacon went home, and the new assembly passed a number of reforms and developed an Amerindian policy that emphasized Berkeley's distinction between friendly and hostile Amerindians. The assembly even heard Cockacoeske, queen of the Pamunkey, give a dignified speech defending her people's limited support of the government during the Susquehannock war. Berkeley's strategy of garrisoned forts, however, was replaced by one thousand well-paid troops, who were also entitled to booty, including Amerindian prisoners who automatically became slaves for life.[43]

When he returned to Jamestown on June 22 with five hundred men, Bacon gained his commission against the Amerindians at gunpoint. He also received assembly support to transform his men into the colony's Amerindian-enslaving army. Bacon then directed the campaign, not against frontier enemies, but against the colony's tributary tribe, the Pamunkey. Berkeley again declared Bacon a rebel, but had trouble gathering support and fled briefly to the Eastern Shore. Bacon plundered and captured the Pamunkey who had sought refuge in the Dragon Swamp, gaining supporters as he paraded his forty-five captives. In Bacon's brief siege of Jamestown in September, he and his three hundred supporters were greatly outnumbered by Berkeley's defenders within the strong palisade. On the third day of the siege, Berkeley ordered unenthusiastic militia to attack Bacon's position in trenches behind an *abattis;* twelve died in the failed attempt. As Bacon brought cannon to bear on the palisade, and paraded the families of Berkeley's supporters as well as the captured Pamunkey, Berkeley's troops deserted. On September 19, Bacon's men entered abandoned Jamestown and burned it to the ground. Rebel confidence weakened in the next month, then was shattered by the sudden illness and death of Bacon. The following January, Berkeley and his supporters, aided by captains of well-armed tobacco ships, defeated those who still resisted, executed rebel leaders, confiscated their property, and extended the terms of service of all servants who had joined Bacon.[44]

There had been two aspects to Bacon's Rebellion, each with distinct consequences. The first aspect was a race war against Amerindians by frightened and avaricious frontiersmen whose purpose often seemed to be the elimination of their Amerindian neighbors. The enslavement and sale abroad of Virginia Amerindian prisoners, occurring earlier but formally authorized by the assembly of 1676, now became standing policy. The accompanying confiscation and sale of all Amerindian lands to pay for the "war" was halted by the Treaty of Middle Plantation (1677), and reservations were confirmed.[45]

Although the unruly militia's intentions failed to translate into Amerindian casualties comparable to colonists killed in the winter raids of 1675/1676, the English invasion of Virginia was essentially completed. The ambushed Occaneechee were destroyed by Bacon's treachery, thereby opening Virginia's direct trade with the Cherokee by way of the Occaneechee Trail. The Susquehannock were dispersed after the siege and were hounded by colonists and Amerindian rivals, and their remnants were incorporated by the Five Nations before 1680, when war between them and the allies of New France resumed. The Five Nations became stronger both by rebuilding their warrior numbers and by absorbing the Susquehannock sphere, including influence over the Delaware and control of the "warrior path" to the south. Some of these Susquehannock would avenge themselves on Virginia by raiding down that "warrior path" as members of the Five Nations. However, the Five Nations were not a major threat to Virginia, as they were then forging a mutually beneficial alliance with the English at Albany. The Pamunkey survived the rebellion as a subsidiary reservation tribe of fewer than two thousand, and an embarrassed Virginia government even granted Queen Cockacoeske what proved to be uncollectable tribute from both the Chickahominy and the Rappahannock, in partial compensation for Bacon's plundering.[46]

The second aspect of the uprising was the rebellion against the governor of Virginia and King Charles II. A three-person commission of inquiry, including newly appointed Lieutenant-Governor Herbert Jeffreys, arrived from England early in 1677. Their authority was backed by a fourteen-vessel fleet carrying one thousand English regular troops who, like the commissioners, arrived too late to end the rebellion but helped limit retribution by Berkeley and his party. Berkeley was replaced, as he had previously requested, and died in England before being able to defend his conduct. Virginia's emerging elite had split during the rebellion, but would not allow their own factional strife to foster social revolt again. The commissioners, responding to popular complaints as well as royal directives, cut the powers of the unrepentant assembly. The Virginia militia, which had twice ousted a royal governor considered too friendly to Amerindians, was dangerous to government when well armed. It was replaced by a paid force of mounted troopers, who were reinforced by a new "bourgeois militia" that was nearly as exclusive and politically safe as England's.[47] Such a militia would reinforce the internal authority of a developing gentry oligarchy and would not challenge that authority. For the next three-quarters of a century, Virginia was successful in defending itself only because it did not need much defending, against either Amerindians or Europeans. When Virginia finally provoked war in the Ohio in 1753, the help of British regulars was needed promptly.

Bacon's Rebellion against England's king accelerated and justified transformations in colonial administration already under way in London. The cash-strapped government of Charles II extended royal power to protect the substantial customs revenues on tobacco and sugar imported into England. The new Privy Council committee, known as the Lords of Trade, increased bureaucratic and legal control of all colonial governors and assemblies. A plan to have all Virginia laws drafted in London had to be abandoned, but a perpetual tax on exported tobacco provided the governors with considerable revenues independent of the assembly. The Powhatan had destroyed the Virginia Company; the Susquehannock and their English opponents destroyed Berkeley's political fiefdom. Royalists and Baconians used the opportunity to convert Virginia into a model royal province.[48]

 Ironically, the burning of Jamestown by Bacon's militia supporters in 1676 was as clear a symbol of the colony's strength as the building of Castillo de San Marcos marked the weakness of Spanish Florida. Jamestown had begun as a wretched fortified base within an overwhelming Powhatan empire. By 1640 English control expanded to a palisaded peninsula between the James and York rivers, and then exploded beyond all palisading in the next thirty years. Unlike the Castillo de San Marcos, Jamestown had never been needed against Europeans and was no longer needed against Amerindians. Like the burning of the deserted Piscataway Fort, but unlike the ferocious burning of the people and palisades of Paspahegh or Moyaone by earlier militias, empty Jamestown was burned in defiance of unconquered enemies who had escaped. Although a government house, prison, and church were rebuilt after 1678, the settlement never recovered. After another fire in 1698, the capital was moved to a healthier site at Williamsburg.

Chapter 4

FRENCH QUÉBEC
1608–1682

Québec, and its relationship with Amerindians, was shaped by its founding as a fur traders' strategic monopoly base. Its agriculture was essentially for subsistence, unlike Virginia's; its fortress, which ultimately fell, never represented a metropolitan presence as completely as did Castillo de San Marcos. In exploring French–Amerindian relations, it is helpful to begin by comparing the earlier experiences of Jacques Cartier (1534–1543) with those of Samuel de Champlain at Québec (1608).

It was fish that first drew Europeans to the Gulf of St. Lawrence, and most fishermen required nothing from the Amerindians and resented the presence of European colonists. The northern arc of rich Atlantic fisheries lured fifteenth-century Europeans to the Shetland and Faeroe Islands and on to Iceland, Greenland, the Grand Banks of Newfoundland, and the gulfs of St. Lawrence and Maine. Although little is recoverable from those whose silence protected their prosperity, an annual concourse of Portuguese, Spanish, English, French, and Basque fishermen is known to have begun off Newfoundland about the time of John Cabot's voyage from Bristol in 1497. The major Grand Banks fishery was offshore, where large cod were salted down aboard ships early in the year and hurried to Europe's Lenten markets. The French and Portuguese, who had the best sources of salt, were dominant here. The inshore fishery was for smaller cod, dried on shore to produce a less salty and more expensive commodity. This "dry" fishery would lead to direct competition for shore space and to spasmodic trade with Newfoundland's Beothuk people, who were neither numerous, prosperous, nor particularly dangerous.

The French had been trading and raiding in the Americas from the opening of the sixteenth century, and Verrazano's 1524 voyage had claimed the entire Atlantic seaboard between Spanish Florida and what was briefly Portuguese Cape Breton Island (1520–1525). Since Verrazano had found neither wealthy civilizations nor a passage to the Orient, Francis I of France directed the first crown-financed exploratory voyage toward the Gulf of St. Lawrence. Jacques Cartier's two sixty-ton ships were sent out in 1534 to see what could be found farther north. The ships entered the Gulf of St. Lawrence from the north, coasted down the barren western shore of Newfoundland, and explored Chaleur Bay. There they met Micmac (Souriquois), whose persistent attempts to trade furs, despite French indifference and hostility, indicated that other Europeans had previously traded with this widespread coastal tribe of about forty-five hundred. Coasting farther along the Gaspé Peninsula, Cartier met the populous Laurentian Iroquois, who dominated the river valley. He planted several massive wooden crosses to guide sailors and to claim land for France in the same ineffectual way that Ayllón's stone crosses had done for Spain in Chicora. Cartier returned to France with two sons of the Iroquois chief Donnacona as captives; he had found no riches, no passage to Asia, only more fish and poor people with a few furs of little relative value. While Cartier was in France, Donnacona's Iroquois were defeated in a battle with the Micmac, perhaps over access to European trade goods at Gaspé.[1]

Cartier was commissioned to return to the Gulf of St. Lawrence even before his two Iroquois captives had learned enough of the language to lure the French into another expedition that would take them home. Domagaya and Taignoagny promoted French exploration just as captive-interpreters Francisco Chicora and Don Luis de Velasco did in Spain. Cartier returned with three ships and 110 men to discover, and be told by his Iroquoian passengers, that Anticosti was an island in a great river that came from the southwest. Following it, they reached Donnacona's unpalisaded village of Stadacona, on the commanding heights that later became Québec. Despite Donnacona's protests, Cartier explored up river as far as the larger, heavily stockaded Iroquois town of Hochelaga, the future site of Montréal. In the meantime, Cartier's men palisaded a camp, complete with artillery, just north of Stadacona. The fort represented Francis I's belief in "effective occupation," but it also reflected deteriorating local relations. Donnacona wanted control of the French trade in the area, resented Cartier's excursion up river, and had learned enough from his sons about French prices and preferences to deprive Cartier of the lucrative trade terms that fostered and funded so much of early European expansion. Wintering near Stadacona was hard on the Breton sailors, but scurvy was even worse; twenty-five died, and nearly all the eighty-five survivors were incapacitated. Scurvy had also afflicted the Iroquois, and Cartier eventually was given their white-cedar-tea treatment without revealing that his force was helpless.

In the spring of 1536, when many of his men had recovered, Cartier intervened in a power struggle within the Iroquois community. Cartier pretended to support the increasingly unsympathetic Donnacona, while assisting his rival, Agona. Donnacona, Domagaya, and Taignoagny were all tricked and captured by Cartier, who took them into exile in France, where they died. French alienation of the Iroquois had begun.

War, royal financial restraints, and court intrigue in France delayed Cartier's third voyage, by which time the search for treasure and a route to Asia were subordinate to establishing a colony. Cartier took five ships, some fifteen hundred people, livestock, and a two years' supply of food to the St. Lawrence in 1541. A fortified settlement was attempted at Cape Diamond, above Stadacona, but the thin surviving evidence suggests that the Iroquois besieged the settlement and killed at least thirty-five. Cartier spent one winter here, and the colony's new "lieutenant-general," Jean-François de La Rocque, seigneur de Roberval, spent the next, but the colony did not take root, and all survivors were repatriated by 1543.[2] Scurvy had struck again, "Canadian diamonds" proved to be quartz, and the limited potential of the area was completely negated by Laurentian Iroquois hostility. They had ousted armored settlers equipped with cannon and matchlock; another early-sixteenth-century invasion of North America had failed miserably.

Renewed French interest in colonizing America shifted far to the south, with Admiral Coligny's attempts to settle Huguenots at Rio de Janeiro (1555–1560) and then Florida (1562–1565). Both were destroyed by prompt Iberian military response. French religious dissenters had been prominent in these efforts, and the same religious division reinforced antimonarchical groups in the intermittent French Wars of Religion (1559–1589), which precluded further colonization. It was 1598 before the next French colonization was attempted in America. Lieutenant-General Mesgouez de La Roche, with power over all French-claimed lands from Acadia to Labrador and from Newfoundland to Hochelaga, took two hundred men and fifty women to found a colony on uninhabited Sable Island, in a rich fishing area some eighty-six miles east of Nova Scotia. Little is known of this settlement during the next five years, except that there were murders and mass desertions. In 1603 the eleven surviving inhabitants were taken back to France; a colony on this barren outpost of North America had failed without interference from either Amerindians or other Europeans.[3]

The long-standing claims and ambitions of the French crown in North America required permanent occupation, which the crown could not afford. In 1603, to accomplish this goal and reward a distinguished loyal soldier, Henry IV granted a ten-year trade monopoly and the post of lieutenant-general "of the coasts, lands and confines of Acadia, Canada and other places in New France" to Pierre du Gua, sieur de Monts. His post had some elements of a Spanish *adelantado*, but de Monts promptly organized a trading company to raise capital for colonization, displaying some features used by the English Virginia Company organized just three years later. Attempts to monopolize the fur trade could now finance colonization of New France because fur, especially beaver, was becoming increasingly fashionable and valuable to European hatters.

With his associate, the soldier, cartographer, and journal-keeper Samuel de Champlain, de Monts visited Tadoussac on the St. Lawrence, but was unimpressed. In 1604 de Monts sent three fur-trading vessels to Tadoussac, then the center of the seasonal fur trade with the Montagnais but, accompanied by Champlain, took his two colonizing vessels to the Bay of Fundy. For security, they decided to settle on Ile Sainte-Croix in Passamaquoddy Bay. A dozen houses, a chapel, and outbuildings were grouped within a partial palisade to create a fortlike structure, defended by cannon, but by the end of the long winter, half of the thirty-man contingent had died of scurvy. The following spring, Champlain, guided by the Micmac chief, Panounias, and his Abenaki wife, traveled the coast occupied by her tribe and visited other tribes to the south as far as Cape Cod without finding an alternative site for a fur-trading settlement. Instead, the colony moved across the bay to the previously scouted Annapolis Basin, founding Port Royal in 1605 on lands de Monts had already granted to his lieutenant, Jean de Biencourt de Poutrincourt. Reinforcements came from France, grain was grown, and a gristmill was built. However, scurvy claimed victims in each of the next two winters, and the best furs were being acquired along these open coasts by uncontrollable "illegal" traders. A party led by Poutrincourt, exploring west of Cape Cod in 1606, tried to overawe the large Wampanoag village of Monomoy with guns, swords, and yet another large cross erected for navigational and spiritual, if not diplomatic, guidance. In reaction, the Wampanoag killed four of a five-man shore party, tore down the cross, and jeered the retreating French. Poutrincourt had confirmed Champlain's suspicion that French purposes were better served farther north.

Port Royal was more than a promising French outpost; it was also part of the growing power of the adaptable local Micmac sagamore, Henri Membertou, the first Amerindian baptized in New France. Like other Micmac in the area, Membertou's band of about a hundred was increasingly occupied with hunting furs for the European trade. Being host to the French brought trading and martial advantages, and French grain supplies for the lean late-winter months. Micmac–Abenaki rivalry, which the French tried unsuccessfully to stop, resulted in the deaths of several Micmac in 1606, including Panounias. Membertou led a coalition of Micmac bands, who displayed their new imported power in an avenging raid on the Abenaki village of Chouacoet in June 1607. The Abenaki attempted to defend themselves with a few French knives, but relied primarily on bows, bone-tipped arrows, wooden clubs, and shields. The attacking Micmac had metal spears, daggers, cutlasses, and metal arrowheads, as well as a few French muskets. Ten Abenaki were promptly killed, and the rest fled. Membertou's triumphant Micmac were expanding their own as well as French power, and strengthening their terms of trade with farmers on the northern edge of corn cultivation.[4]

De Monts' trade monopoly was canceled in 1607, and the French were driven from the Bay of Fundy over the next seven years. Port Royal was reoccupied after 1610, but was overshadowed by attempts to found a French Jesuit missionary colony on Mount Desert Island in Penobscot Bay in 1612. This unfortified camp was promptly captured and destroyed by Captain Samuel Argall and sixty soldiers of the fourteen-gun Virginia Company ship *Treasurer,* which carried fifteen French prisoners to Virginia. Argall would return again the next year to burn Port Royal.[5] Although the English and French were at peace in Europe, and though there were only forty-five French and some three hundred English living on the whole North American continent, their inter-colonial rivalry was already fierce.

 De Monts' Acadian colony failed because he could not enforce his fur-trading monopoly; he hoped to do better with a one-year extension of his trading monopoly for the upper St. Lawrence. In 1608 Samuel de Champlain, in his first independent command for de Monts, took three ships from France to Tadoussac, only to find Basque traders using firearms to resist the monopoly. Champlain went on up the St. Lawrence to what had been the Iroquois town of Stadacona when Cartier had visited three-quarters of a century earlier.

The site was now uninhabited. The St. Lawrence Valley was surprisingly vacant above Tadoussac, for the Iroquois had mysteriously disappeared from the entire St. Lawrence Valley and the few Algonquian speaking inhabitants were nomadic hunters. It is not clear what combination of factors caused the Laurentian Iroquois to disappear. They may have died of epidemic diseases introduced by European fishermen, migrated south to the center of their culture, fought among themselves, or lost a war to the Mohawk or to a wide-ranging alliance of Montagnais, Maliseet, Algonquin, Micmac, and Huron. Whatever had happened, Champlain certainly benefited from the existing inter-tribal alliance that gave him peaceful access to a large fur hinterland and Amerindians anxious for help in excluding the Iroquois. The nomadic hunters of the immediate area supplied excellent furs, and the French could settle a comparatively empty no-man's-land without conquest, purchase, or treaty.[6]

Despite good relations with neighboring peoples, strengthened by French promises to join them in war, Champlain's habitation at Québec was more compact and defensible than the earlier ones at Ile Sainte-Croix and Port Royal. At Québec, three substantial buildings huddled together, linked by a second-floor gallery, and protected by cannon, a wall, a moat with drawbridge, and a palisade. Champlain's Québec was built to challenge French or other European trading rivals seeking access to the upper St. Lawrence. The greatest enemy was still scurvy, as Champlain did not know the treatment Cartier had learned from the Iroquois. Of the twenty-eight men left at Québec during the winter of 1608/1609, only eight survived scurvy and dysentery.

Over the next six years, Champlain's new Amerindian allies used him as an effective secret weapon. Champlain's promise to join the Montagnais, Algonquin, and Huron in war against the Five Nations was fulfilled after French reinforcements arrived the following May. The French were supporting Huron anger over Five Nation violation of a recent truce, and an ages-old feud that was given new ferocity as the Mohawk fought for access to the French axes and knives that were becoming available to their northern enemies. By Champlain's account, the expedition of more than three hundred Amerindians and ten French faltered as it entered the River of the Iroquois (Richelieu River) looking for the Mohawk, the easternmost of the Five Nations of the Iroquois Confederacy (Oneida, Onondaga, Cayuga, and Seneca ranged west from there to Niagara). Only sixty Montagnais and Huron, plus three French, including Champlain, proceeded by canoe up to the lake that bears his name. Each evening the Amerindians barricaded their camp on the landward side, scouted the area, practiced martial drills that intrigued Champlain, and discussed strategy. As they proceeded farther up the lake, the war party traveled only at night. Late in the evening of July 29, 1609, the invaders spotted a party of two hundred Mohawk on the lake near the eventual site of Fort St. Frédéric.

The ensuing Battle of Lake Champlain is rightly studied as a display of Amerindian warfare before contact and, like the battle at Chouacoet, a demonstration of the impact of firearms on that warfare. The Mohawk landed and built a barricade, using what Champlain described as poor-quality iron and stone axes. Champlain's companions spent the night in their canoes, anchored together offshore. After sending a legation to confirm Mohawk willingness to fight in the morning, both sides spent the night singing songs and shouting insults. Champlain and his allies landed unopposed in the morning, and the Mohawk came out of their barricade to fight. According to plan, the French remained hidden behind the Montagnais and Huron warriors until they were within thirty yards of the Mohawk, still without any arrows being shot. Champlain, supposedly the first white man seen by these Mohawk, then stepped forward and fired his overloaded matchlock arquebus at the three Mohawk chiefs. The Mohawk arrow-proof shields of wood and woven cotton proved worthless against musket balls; two chiefs were killed immediately, and the third was mortally wounded. As another French musketeer fired, the Mohawk fled with Huron and Algonquin in pursuit. When the skirmish had ended, Champlain's allies had reportedly killed numerous Mohawk and taken a dozen prisoners, while suffering fifteen wounded. In the subsequent victory celebration, one of the prisoners was subjected to the traditional Huron torture unto death. Although torture was common enough in France for treason, heresy, or witchcraft, Champlain became outraged at this cruelty to a prisoner of war and was finally allowed to shoot the victim.[7]

It is difficult to know the extent to which Champlain Europeanized what he saw and inflated his own importance in an incident that was to be used to claim the area for his king. The impact of firearms was never as dramatic again on that frontier; within five weeks, Henry Hudson was sailing up the river that bears his name, to within eighty miles of the recent battle, to begin a Dutch fur trade that eventually brought guns to the Mohawk. Champlain had established a diplomatic and military position that was to change little over the rest of the century. Although this involvement would be regretted often in the seventeenth century, and has been debated since, Champlain had little choice. A tiny band of French strangers, anxious to explore and trade, were tested in the martial gestures that Amerindians required of those who claimed to be their friends. Champlain thought he had achieved his objective, for the Montagnais promised to take him up their Saguenay River to the great salt sea (Hudson Bay), and the Algonquin said they would take him up their Ottawa River route to the great lakes of Huron country.

However, Champlain's Amerindian allies protected their intermediary role in trade again in 1610, arguing that his travels should come only after another campaign against the Mohawk. Champlain's allies launched this second campaign without waiting for him and his four French companions. Some two hundred Algonquin and Huron warriors discovered a party of about one hundred Mohawk on the lower Richelieu River. The outnumbered Mohawk managed to build a strong, circular barricade and defended it effectively. When the French finally arrived, delayed by their cumbersome pikeman's armor, they fired into the enclosure, and a passing group of French fur traders added their arquebuses to the next barrage. After pulling down part of the barricade with ropes, the allies attacked, killing all but fifteen, who were taken prisoner.[8]

The honor of the Algonquin and Huron was restored, and the strength of their new ally was confirmed; there were no raids into Five Nation territory during the next five years. Champlain, who had been wounded in the ear and neck by a well-placed Mohawk arrow, received more promises to guide him into the interior. The Mohawk, who numbered only five thousand and were simultaneously at war with the Susquehannock to their south, could not afford such heavy losses. The Mohawk would not raid the St. Lawrence Valley again for a generation. Since they were gaining some access to Dutch trade goods on the Hudson River, the Mohawk had less need to raid to the north.[9]

Five years later, with Champlain still pressing reluctant allies to guide him farther into the country, the Huron finally welcomed Champlain, apparently to draw him into another scheme against the Five Nations. He and the newly arrived Récollet missionary, Father Joseph Le Caron, were taken to Huronia, where between twenty thousand and thirty thousand Huron of four nations lived in fortified towns and villages south of Georgian Bay, raising the corn, squash, and beans that characterized Amerindian agriculture. As major suppliers of corn to the more nomadic northern Algonquian in return for skins, dried meat, and European goods, the Huron had become the dominant traders and diplomats of the Great Lakes region, where Huron was the language of commerce. Champlain roused Huron suspicions by visiting the tobacco-growing Neutrals and the Ottawa of southwestern Ontario, as well as by asking about the Nipissing.

From a very reliable subsistence base, the Huron had elaborated a warrior culture shared with others in the Iroquoian language group. Although neither the Huron nor the Five Nations of the Iroquois were as well equipped with the new iron-edged weapons as were the coastal Algonquian allies of the French by 1615, the Huron Confederacy was easily the most powerful military force in the alliance, able to muster between five thousand and seven thousand warriors.

Champlain's curiosity and ambition were only heightened by what he learned in Huronia of the peoples, lands, and waters to the west and the north, but his hosts emphasized yet another campaign against the Five Nations. Susquehannock from the south, currently at war with the Five Nations, had urged the Huron to join them. The Huron were most interested in attacking the Onondaga and Oneida, who had been disrupting Huron trading convoys heading to Québec along the Ottawa River. Involving the French not only brought the helpful French muskets, but also reinforced a Franco-Iroquoian enmity that prevented trade. The Huron attack route, across Lake Ontario, led to a large unidentifiable, fortified Onondaga or Oneida town. Four concentric thirty-foot palisades of large tree trunks carried galleried ramparts from which defenders shot arrows and threw stones. There were even special wooden water gutters to quench enemy-set fires.

Champlain, who presumed that his experience and equipment entitled him to command rather than to serve as an alien volunteer, wanted to breach the walls and destroy the town. He did not function well with the Huron, who did not accept his authority and wanted only to threaten the town in order to lure defenders into gladiatorial combat. Champlain could neither order nor pursuade the Huron to undertake a direct and rather suicidal assault on the walls. He was allowed two concessions to what were ancient European methods, *mantelets* and a *cavalier*. The first were movable wooden screens that allowed attackers to approach the walls in safety. The second was a sheathed wooden platform, built high and close enough to the town walls to allow a few French musketeers to deny defenders access to their galleries. After two leading Huron headmen were injured by arrows, the attack evaporated. Champlain's harangues, if understood, were ignored, though it was agreed that an attack would be resumed if the promised five hundred Susquehannock arrived within a few days, which they did not. The Five Nations attempted sorties, but retreated in obvious fear of the French matchlock muskets. Although the Huron went home satisfied with the casualties inflicted and the prisoners taken, and the Five Nations counted their dead and continued to fear French guns, some historians have mistakenly joined Champlain in regarding the battle as a failed siege and therefore a Five Nation victory.[10]

A handful of French fur traders, led by a man anxious to explore, had earned their Amerindian alliance. The jealousies of the Montagnais and Algonquin, who were anxious to remain exclusive middlemen in the French trade with their neighbors, had been overcome less by French insistence on direct trade than by gratitude for the sudden advantage that the French musketeers had given them all against the Five Nations. Having served their allies, the French gained more than furs and promises. Champlain successfully insisted that allies avoid separate peace with the Five Nations, particularly fearing that the Huron could be drawn into trade southward. Amerindian diplomacy through grand intertribal conferences under French auspices began with the Mohawk peace settlement of 1624.[11] The power of New France would depend on brokering Amerindian alliances against the Mohawk, then against English colonists, and eventually against the British army.

Despite very good relations with neighboring Amerindians, the settlement at Québec remained precarious throughout its first two decades. The French fur monopolies that were expected to support the colony proved unenforceable, underfunded, unsympathetic to settlement, and short-lived. During numerous winters spent in France, Champlain publicized the colony, encouraged merchant support, and solicited help from the crown and the church. Yet by 1628 the results were still disappointing. Québec's population still ranged between sixty and eighty-one, mostly male, living in a small cluster of wooden buildings with a small wooden fort on the heights above. Less than seventeen acres were under cultivation by a community still overwhelmingly dependent on French supply ships for food.[12]

A Catholic religious revival under way in France gave the colony needed support. The Jesuits re-entered the North American mission field by sending a vanguard of eight priests to Québec by 1626. A new initiative by King Louis XIII's first minister, Armand Jean du Plessis, duc de Richelieu, seemed particularly promising. This worldly cardinal favored overseas expansion for economic and dynastic, as well as religious reasons. Through the new Company of One Hundred Associates, noblemen, clergy, officeholders, and merchants provided capital that was as much a religious charity as an investment. The company was granted a fifteen-year monopoly of all trade except fishing, a perpetual monopoly on the fur trade, and the right to grant seigneurial lands to settlers. In return, the company was expected to subsidize the missions, to defend the colony, and to bring four thousand settlers in the next fifteen years.

The plans of Cardinal Richelieu, the Company of One Hundred, the Jesuits, and the colony were all thwarted by an Anglo-French war that began with a failed English attempt to aid French Huguenots, besieged in La Rochelle by the French royal army commanded by none other than Cardinal Richelieu himself. At the outbreak of hostilities, Gervase Kirke, an English merchant living in France, formed a company that obtained an English royal commission to capture Québec. Kirke's three French-born sons sailed three English privateers into the St. Lawrence in 1628. At Tadoussac, they were welcomed by the Montagnais as alternative suppliers, and they went on to demand the surrender of Québec. Champlain refused, expecting the new company's first fleet of settlers and supplies at any moment. The Kirke fleet withdrew down river without attacking, only to discover the expected fleet of five vessels with four hundred settlers and supplies. After a day of cannonfire, the better-armed English forced the whole French relief squadron to surrender, and they took their prisoners and prizes, including nineteen fishing vessels, away to England. This defeat left the Québec trade in tatters, its Amerindian alliance strained, and its colonists starving. The next year, the first fleet to come up the river was again that of the Kirkes, returning with three ships and two hundred men. Without gunpowder or match for his muskets, and also short of food, Champlain had no choice but to surrender.

Most of the French were repatriated, though some remained to work for the English; the ninety Europeans wintering in Québec in 1629/1630 were more than had done so previously. In the next year, Québec shipped a record thirty thousand pelts to Europe. Reorganized as the Anglo-Scotch Company, the Kirkes' backers not only had conquered and occupied Québec profitably, but also had brought English settlers in 1629 to recently captured Port Royal in Acadia, as well as sixty Scots who were promptly ousted from their attempted settlement on Cape Breton Island. Although Québec had been captured after peace had been declared in Europe, the village was not returned to the French for two years.[13]

The forty-three French who repossessed Québec in 1632 were starting again, though some things were very different from 1608. Fort St. Louis remained on the bluff, repaired by the English soldiers, and there was usable cleared farmland, though the English had destroyed or severely damaged most of the buildings. Three Jesuits were among the vanguard of resettlement, representing the order that would have exclusive spiritual control over the colony and the missions during a generation that was visibly more religious than its predecessor in France and New France. The twenty land grants made to the order, the heroic Jesuit missions in Huronia, the coming of the Ursuline nuns and nursing sisters (1639), and the founding of Montréal by a powerful Catholic secret society, the Company of the Holy-Sacrament (1642), were all manifestations of uncommon religious zeal. The same was true of the *Jesuit Relations* (1632–1673), reports from the missions that were published annually in Paris to encourage financial support from the devout.

The fur trade had continued to thrive without the French, who had lost much by their absence. The Montagnais had traded with the English for muskets and would continue to trade with any interlopers who came to Tadoussac.[14] The Algonquin of the Ottawa River had used the recent opportunity to close the river to all European traders and Huron canoemen, resuming the benefits of their position as middlemen.

Historians have been irrationally embarrassed by Amerindian economic interests evident in the fur trade of the north and the deerskin trade of the south. Earlier portrayals of naive Amerindian victims of underpriced furs and overpriced European goods have rightly been superseded by more plausible accounts of discerning Amerindian customers able to demand exactly the kind of kettles, blankets, knives, or guns they wanted. They acquired many of these goods in order to share them within their communities, to multiply the value of grave-goods astronomically, to offer impressive and exotic diplomatic tokens, or to defend their communities. Amerindians were not "economic men" or accumulating capitalists; the fur trade even strengthened traditional clan leaders who distributed the proceeds of the trade. Their communitarian values deserve respect and celebration, but prestige and reputation were, and still are, powerful motives for acquiring things; Amerindians seeking those personal objectives could be as interested as anyone else in material goods. Overtrapping of the beaver in the northeast and destruction of the deer in the south resulted from the perceived needs of both Europeans and Amerindians.[15]

One vital change that occurred during the French absence was the return of Mohawk raiders to the St. Lawrence Valley. The "Wars of the Iroquois" are discussed in Chapter 6, but their destruction of the Huron–French alliance deserves consideration here. Conditions had changed since the Mohawk had contested the St. Lawrence area in 1608. The Mohawk used their 1624 peace with the Huron–French alliance to defeat the Mahican and win direct access to the Dutch trade at Fort Orange (Albany). The Algonquin had chosen the losing side in that struggle, hoping for access to competitive Dutch trade goods. The Mohawk were now seeking retribution against the Algonquin and other old enemies, as well as alternative trade in the St. Lawrence Valley. A few Algonquin and Mohawk were prepared to consider intertribal peace in return for exchanging access to their European traders, but the Europeans assumed that Amerindian allies of their European enemies, were automatically their enemies, and helped to make it so. Champlain, returning in 1633 as "commander" in New France with a population of only one hundred, nonetheless called for the destruction of the Mohawk by invasion. Failed negotiations in 1635 inaugurated thirty years of intermittent Mohawk war against the French and their allies.[16]

The mighty Huron, the essential power-base of the initial Huron–French alliance, proved unable to resist the Five Nations. Jesuits who came to Huronia and Huron who came to trade at Québec spread epidemics of European diseases in 1634/1635, 1636/1637, and 1639/1640. Whether they had previously numbered twenty thousand or thirty thousand, by 1640 there were only ten thousand Huron. Although the Jesuits were blamed for the epidemics, Huron conversions to Christianity increased greatly with improved Jesuit linguistic competence, with their displays of courage in martyrdom, and with French inducements in trade and diplomacy. After 1640, for instance, Christianized Huron could buy French muskets. The Christian Huron became a revolutionary faction dividing families, clans, towns, and the confederacy. By 1649 nearly half the Huron were Christian, in addition to those baptized just before dying. Traditionalists were much more interested in peace and trade with the Five Nations, particularly the Onondaga, than were the understandably pro-French Christians and their Jesuit priests. When the final attack came, the dispirited traditionalists disintegrated into those seeking to join the hostile Five Nations, those fleeing to preserve their ways among other tribes, and those accepting Christianity in desperation.[17]

Minor blood feuds between the Huron and the Five Nations had continued throughout the period of the epidemics, with the Huron usually attacking Five Nation settlements and hunting parties, and those retaliating with ambushes along the Ottawa River trade route. In 1642 the raids escalated, as the Seneca destroyed a Huron frontier village, and the Mohawk made the Ottawa River route impassable. The French sent twenty soldiers to winter in Huronia in 1644 and help bring the furs to a colony economically dependent on them. Two peace conferences at Montréal in 1645, which marked the first European adoption of the Iroquoian diplomatic rituals that would become the standard for intercultural conferences throughout the northeast, appeared to settle matters. However, after promising to trade some furs with the Five Nations, the Huron sent their entire unmolested fur fleet of the next year to the French.

Seneca and Mohawk began recruiting their fellow Iroquois for war, not to capture the Huron trading network, but to destroy it. Early in 1648, the Mohawk slaughtered a Huron legation to the Onondaga, and a Seneca war party equipped with firearms destroyed the well-fortified Huron frontier town of Teanaostaiaé. Of its two thousand inhabitants, three hundred were killed, and seven hundred were taken captive, predominantly women and children. The Huron may have had more guns than their enemy, but at that time most of them were with a trading convoy bound for Montréal, a convoy that destroyed a Mohawk ambush that month by using superior musketry tactics.[18]

In March 1649, a thousand Seneca and Mohawk succeeded in an unprecedented, off-season, night attack on well-fortified Taenhatentaron (St. Ignace). Although a ferocious fight for nearby Saint Louis was eventually won by the Five Nations, the resistance deterred them from proceeding to the main mission town of Saint Marie. The Huron, who had not been able to plant and tend crops in 1648, were already starving when these attacks began. They burned their own villages and abandoned their indefensible fields, dividing into smaller clan groups. The majority, nearly six thousand, followed earlier refugees to nearby Christian Island, where they were joined by Jesuit survivors and where they built a stone fort. Lack of food in the winter and spring prompted numerous expeditions back to their homeland, where Five Nation armies defeated the weakened Huron. By the late summer of 1651, Christian Island was also abandoned and some six hundred Huron migrated to Québec.

Archeologically and anthropologically, the Huron can be regarded as exterminated in 1649 because their sites were abandoned and their cultural structures were destroyed. Historically, however, many of these people survived the calamity. Several thousand Huron, including Christians, survived as individuals adopted into the Five Nations tribes. A few migrated south to join the Susquehannock and the Catawba, and many more joined the Iroquoian-speaking Neutral, Petun, and Erie—all of whom would be dispersed in turn by the Five Nations before 1654. Huron refugees moved to the hunting grounds of the Ohio or fled to the marginal corn areas of the upper Great Lakes, where some amalgamated with the Petun to become a separate group known as the Wyandot. In this *pays d'en haut*, these and later refugees also lived in multitribal villages, effectively creating a new culture. Only six hundred Huron kept their name, eventually becoming the Huron of Lorette and the Huron of Detroit.[19]

The dispersal of the Huron was a cultural catastrophe with widespread consequences. While some of the surviving Huron hated the French, most would support them against the Five Nations and, later, against the English. The strength of Huron clan ties would prompt numerous small remigrations that permanently affected the power of both the Five Nations and the French. The Seneca, who had adopted more than five hundred Huron and established an entirely Huron town of Gandougarae, became noticeably pro-French for a century. The more neutral Onondaga, who also included numerous Huron, experimented with a Jesuit mission (1656–1658) and had a respected Catholic spokesman for the entire Iroquois Confederacy in Daniel Garacontié. The Mohawk had incorporated even more Huron and were torn apart by the migration of the Catholic Mohawk to the Canadian mission of Caughnawaga a generation later. By 1687 that settlement included a hundred warriors, suggesting at least four hundred people, and that number would triple in the next half century.[20] Traditionalists came to dominate the remaining Mohawk villages, making them particularly anti-French. The clan loyalties of the Mohawk Caughnawaga would limit the strategy of both the Mohawk and the French thereafter. Dispersal of the Huron had also exposed their Algonquin allies to Mohawk attack, causing them to disperse for a generation and then settle closer to the French.[21] Canada's trade and diplomacy was in disarray, its dominant military ally and buffer against the Five Nations was gone, and its minuscule settlements were vulnerable to the now hegemonic power of the northeast: the Five Nations.[22]

Dispersal of the Huron made New France more vulnerable to Mohawk attack, though the French settlement had been threatened spasmodically by the Mohawk from 1635. The financially exhausted Company of One Hundred Associates, unable to bring the required settlers, had granted *seigneuries* to lesser noblemen who did. By 1640 the colony numbered 356 people: 116 women and 240 men. Farming in New France, for local consumption and trade to the Amerindians, was further encouraged by the 1649 dispersal of the grain-supplying Huron. As settlement spread in characteristic strip farms fronting along the St. Lawrence near the three centers of Québec, Trois Rivières (1634), and Montréal (1642), isolated farmsteads became increasingly vulnerable to minor Mohawk raids. Aside from the Jesuits, all the men had to learn something of firearms and woodland warfare, though few were designated as soldiers. The floundering fur trade had been opened to all inhabitants in 1645, but was disrupted further by the Five Nation–Huron war.

In renewed raiding against New France after 1650, the Mohawk showed special interest in capturing remnant Huron living near Québec. A series of attacks on Montréal, Trois Rivières, and Québec in 1651 and 1652 brought numerous deaths, destructive fires, and widespread terror, which prompted the formal beginnings of a local militia. In response to one raid on Trois Rivières, the town's governor rashly led fifty men, including ten Amerindians, in pursuit. Eleven, including the governor, were killed and eight others captured. The following summer, Trois Rivières was effectively under Mohawk siege. Rivalries, between the Mohawk and the Onondaga over Huron adoptees and over trade with the French, led to what the French regarded as heaven-sent peace negotiations in 1653.[23] The battered little colony even agreed not to challenge the Mohawk as they continued to harass Huron, Algonquin, and Ottawa, who either lived nearby or attempted to bring furs to Montréal.

Direct Mohawk raids against the French resumed in 1659, and the languishing fur trade was strangled. The following May, seventeen

Montréal volunteers led by the garrison's commander, Dollard des Ormeaux, joined forty Huron and four Algonquin led by Huron chief Annaotaha on their annual expedition to ambush wintering Five Nation hunters at the portage of Long Sault on the Ottawa River. However, an army of nearly eight hundred Onondaga, Oneida, and Mohawk soon besieged these well-armed would-be raiders in a fortification the Algonquin had built the previous year. At Annaotaha's suggestion, the small-arms battle was suspended for talks; twenty-four of the besieged Huron decided to join the adopted Huron among the attackers. To Annaotaha's disgust, the angered French fired in violation of the truce, thereby dooming the rest of the besieged. The Five Nations now used *mantelets* to protect those attempting to breach the palisade. When the fort was finally overwhelmed, only five French and four Huron were still alive, and they were subsequently tortured to death. The week-long fight distracted the Five Nation army from other targets, but their loss of about twenty warriors ensured escalation of the conflict.[24]

During 1661, thirty-eight French settlers were killed and sixty-one captured in Five Nation raids, making it the colony's worst year for casualties. Québec itself, no longer on the frontier, had twenty-one killed and six captured. Peace negotiations began with the Seneca, Onondaga, and Cayuga, who were preoccupied by an intensifying war with the Susquehannock. The Mohawk, hit by another smallpox epidemic and martial reverses at the hands of the Mahican and the Ottawa, mounted smaller and less frequent raids on Montréal after 1662. In addition, the colony's cries for military and financial help from the French crown, conveyed by the colony's governors, bishop, and the Jesuit order, were finally being heard. Young King Louis XIV (1638–1715), whose fifty-four years of personal leadership of the French government began in 1661, had his leading economic adviser, Jean-Baptiste Colbert, develop a new plan for the colonies. Expansion of an economically interdependent empire became a ministerial concern, including the growth of productive colonial populations and of the merchant fleet.[25]

When the crown took direct control of Canada from the defunct Company of New France, safety of the colonists was recognized as a precondition for growth. The government was organized along rather military lines, with a veteran soldier in command as governor-general, supported by local governors in Acadia, Montréal, and Trois Rivières. A royal *intendant* controlled matters of justice, finance, and civil administration. Governor Daniel de Rémy de Courcelle and *intendant* Jean Talon arrived in 1665, as did nearly twelve hundred French regulars under Lieutenant-General Alexandre de Prouville, marquis de Tracy. The twelve companies of the veteran Carignan-Salières Regiment, which had just become the first French regiment to be entirely armed with the new flintlock muskets, constituted most of these regulars. This imported regiment of a thousand transformed the military balance immediately and temporarily increased the little colony's population of 3035 by nearly 40 percent. They also permanently imprinted a military tone to royal government, introduced social and economic opportunities that usually accompany the military, and strengthened the defenses, while overflowing the accommodations of Québec, Trois Rivières, and Montréal.

The French offensive of 1665 to 1667 against the Mohawk, the primary purpose of the troops, revealed a clash of military cultures. The French immediately built three palisaded forts on the Richelieu–Lake Champlain frontier, the primary Mohawk invasion route. While these could not prevent raids, the outposts housed troops nearer the enemy, served as bases for patrols and supply points for subsequent offensives, and provided diversionary targets. The troops and these forts were among the reasons why all the Five Nations, except the Mohawk, made peace with New France by the end of 1665.

Contrary to both local advice and European practice, Tracy and Courcelle decided on a winter attack on the Mohawk. Of the six hundred men sent out in January 1666, all but seventy were regulars, without either snowshoes or experience in a Canadian winter. The Algonquin guides, who were also expected to provide meat, were not accustomed to European military scheduling and were not with Courcelle's army as it left Montréal. For three weeks, the army fought a losing battle against storms, four feet of snow, false trails, and frigid temperatures that killed more than three hundred. The survivors emerged from the forest to attack cabins that proved to be the outskirts of the new Dutch settlement of Schenectady (1661), in what had recently become English-controlled New York. Thirty well-armed Mohawk, who happened to be trading in the town, skirmished effectively from cover. The outnumbered Mohawk and outmaneuvered French inflicted comparable casualties, about ten, before the mayor of Schenectady apprised Courcelle of his whereabouts. The mayor became victualer for the embarrassed French, helping them to prepare for their return journey. Luckily, no one at the scene knew that England and France had been at war in Europe for a month. The Algonquin finally arrived, providing the French with fresh meat and advice on survival during their two-week journey home. The disastrous venture had squandered the lives of perhaps four hundred soldiers in a frightful demonstration of ignorant careerism, followed by a predictable attempt to blame the Algonquin. When applauding the relative military unity and efficiency of New France, in comparison with the disunited English colonies, it is worth remembering that the authoritarian governance of New France also made misguided fiascos like this possible.[26]

The Mohawk alternated peace talks and raids, prompting Tracy and Courcelle to mount a stronger campaign against them. Thirteen hundred men, consisting of six hundred regulars, a hundred Algonquin and Huron, and six hundred Canadians, set out for the Mohawk villages early in October 1666. Advancing from what were now five French forts along the Richelieu route, this canoe-borne army reached the first Mohawk village in just thirteen days, but did not catch the Mohawk. The four palisaded and bastioned Mohawk towns had been hastily deserted, and the French burned these settlements and destroyed the stored food. The Mohawk would suffer some privation because of this raid, and the French formally claimed the area by right of conquest, but the military strength of the Mohawk remained unaffected. Nevertheless, inhabitants of New France took heart from their "victory," and the Mohawk decision not to contest the invasion by this large well-armed force was the beginning of the peace they made with New France and its Amerindian allies the following July. The Mohawk had been moved, but not defeated, by a display of French royal power.[27]

Both the Mohawk and the French knew that this peace was not won by the military prowess of the colonists of New France. As the Carignan-Salières Regiment completed its assignment, the soldiers were officially encouraged to settle in New France, and at least 446 took their discharge and did so. In 1668 some 360 other discharged regulars arrived from France, also to settle with royal encouragement. That same year, Colbert ordered all adult male settlers to become soldiers in an effective militia. The militia captains acquired civil functions within the parishes, providing the *intendant* with a network of assistants and informants who were neither noblemen nor clergy. This armed and unpaid militia, stiffened with retired regulars, showed none of the rebelliousness of the Virginians, but became a central part of the authoritarian military culture of a small colony in the shadow of the Five Nations. In 1669 Colbert took the defense of New France a step farther by instituting six companies of *troupes de la marine*, consisting of three hundred "colonial regulars" recruited in France, paid by the court, and trained and led by officers who had settled in the colony. These colonial regulars were a significant military and financial support throughout the history of New France.[28]

This peace with the Five Nations lasted for sixteen years, providing an opportunity to develop the Canadian colony and to claim a vast empire. These two ambitions were often in very direct conflict. Colbert's plan for a concentrated, agriculturally self-sufficient, and economically diversified colony was launched with royal funding. As minister of marine, he was particularly interested in promoting shipbuilding and the production of timber, pitch, and tar for a French navy that was uncomfortably dependent on Baltic sources. Sponsored migration of soldiers, settlers, marriageable women, and indentured servants was used to build the population of a colony that had numbered only 3035 in 1663 to 10,977 by 1685. There was little immigration thereafter, though the population doubled every generation. The

French government also wanted Amerindians Christianized, married to Frenchmen, and incorporated into the colony; the Amerindians found the first of these options the most appealing. The Jesuit missionaries who were allowed into Iroquoia with the peace of 1667 were soon luring converts to Canada. The mission settlements fringing the colony already counted more than 180 warriors, or more than 700 people, in 1687. The wheat-centered agricultural colony of Canada became nearly self-sufficient, with small surpluses for export in the best years but the need for imported French food in the poorer crop years that might be expected twice a decade.[29] Colbert's initiatives generally lasted only as long as major crown funding for shipbuilding, lumbering, and fisheries.

Private investors were attracted to the more profitable fur trade that supported a compact colony, but made it impossible to contain. The French government's Compagnie de l'Occident held a monopoly on the export of beaver pelts and moose hides, but paid generous fixed prices for as many of these as traders gathered. Taxes on fur exports were also the major source of government revenues within the virtually untaxed colony. Peace with the Five Nations and the seemingly unlimited market for fur drew hundreds of young men into the *pays d'en haut* to trade for furs. By 1671 the Ottawa fur convoys had ceased to come to Montréal, for the furs had all been bought up country by the French. Vainly attempting to make the colony defensible and compact, to keep the colonists at home, and to encourage the Amerindians to bring in their own furs, the government even outlawed all the *coureurs de bois*, said to number as many as six hundred in 1679. These measures failed because of widespread connivance, including that of Louis de Baude, comte de Frontenac, an ardent expansionist who was governor-general from 1672 to 1682 and again from 1689 to 1698.[30]

Peace with the Five Nations had finally converted the St. Lawrence–Great Lakes network into a usable waterway to the heart of the continent. French missionaries and traders usually had competing purposes, but both were extending French influence into Iroquoia, the upper Great Lakes, Hudson Bay, and the Ohio and Mississippi valleys before Fort Cataraqui was built on Lake Ontario to dominate this exploding Canadian fur trade. English traders, organized as the chartered Hudson's Bay Company the same year that the Jesuit explorer Jacques Marquette founded the French mission at Michilimackinac (1670), returned to that bay to compete for the prime beaver pelts of the Cree just as the French began approaching the same peoples via Lake Superior and the Saguenay–Rupert river route. Before long, firearms were central to this trade. Between 1670 and 1689, the Hudson's Bay Company traded 10,100 flintlock fusils to the Cree, who were also buying French flintlock muskets. The Cree consolidated their territory and began harassing the English Hudson Bay posts as early as 1680. The Ojibwa, with the same suppliers of muskets, were attempting to drive their traditional rivals, the Fox and the Sioux, away from the upper Great Lakes access to firearms.[31]

René-Robert Cavelier de La Salle (1643–1687) became seigneur of Cataraqui in 1675, renaming it Fort Frontenac after the governor who was his partner in monopolizing the fur trade of the Mississippi Valley. A chain of trading posts was established from Niagara (1676) and St. Joseph (1679), to Fort Crèvecoeur (1680), Fort St. Louis (1683), and Fort Prud-homme (1682). In the spring of 1682, La Salle reached the mouth of the Mississippi with a party that included thirty-three Frenchmen and thirty-one Amerindian men, women, and children. Here, two thousand miles from Québec, La Salle confidently made trading alliances and tried to establish a colony in Spanish-claimed Texas. Spanish authorities sent out a total of eleven expeditions before finding the ruins of the settlement, which had been destroyed by local Karankawa tribesmen.[32] The reach of New France was swift and light, but fragile, like the birch-bark canoes they had adopted from the Algonquin and Huron.

Although the Spanish and English would attempt some countermeasures against this explosion of French trading posts and missions, it was the Five Nations who terminated the expansion by ending their peace with New France and its allies. A series of wars that began with a Five Nation attack on the great Illinois town of Kaskaskias in 1680 would eventually merge with the first Anglo-French colonial war. Colbert died in 1683, having failed to restrain an overextended religious and trading empire that he knew would prove expensive and difficult to defend.

Québec and New France owed more to the Amerindians than did the Virginians or the Spanish of San Agustín. New France had begun with a remarkably wide alliance of diverse Amerindians, who were necessary partners in the fur trade long before they became souls to be saved. It was easier to cooperate with nomadic Amerindian hunters and trappers, who moved with the game and avoided the traumatic epidemics and "feed fights" that often marked confrontations between Europeans and Amerindian farmers. Yet New France was also fundamentally shaped by Five Nation enemies whom it could not defeat. Five Nations hostility crippled early French and Canadian fur-trading companies, as surely as the Powhatan had ruined the Virginia Company. As with Virginia, New France became a royal colony because of war against Amerindians, but the social and military results were very different. Five Nations attacks had prompted French royal intervention to defend, fund, develop, and control the colony on a scale unprecedented in North America. The Five Nations, for reasons that are elaborated later, survived disease and war to remain a threat to New France, thereby reinforcing the military aspects of royal power, colonial acceptance of a disciplined militia, and the need for colonial regulars who were eventually officered by the colony's elite.

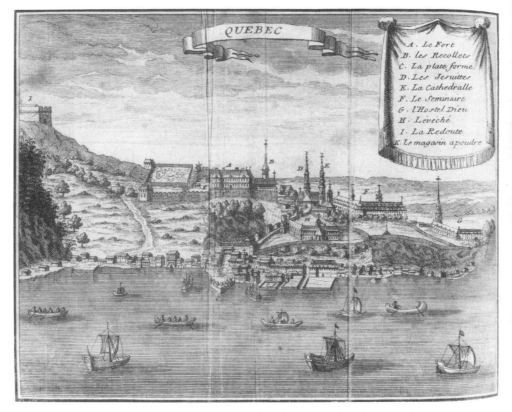

Figure 3. Québec, ca. 1722. From Claude-Charles Le Roy de La Potherie, *Histoire de l'Amérique septentrionale* (Paris, 1722). (Courtesy of Clements Library, University of Michigan)

By 1683 the geography of the town of Québec clearly reflected its history. On the 250-foot cliffs of Cape Diamond stood Fort St. Louis, with the governor's residence and nearby council house, featuring cannons that controlled traffic on the St. Lawrence River. The government shared this eminence with the spired stone churches, the cathedral, and convents of the religious orders that had been so dominant a generation earlier. Down the steep road was the lower town of warehouses, shops, and stone houses of substantial merchants, and the wooden houses of other merchants, clerks, artisans, and laborers (Figure 3). By 1687 eleven hundred people lived in Québec, with several hundred Amerindian converts at the nearby missions of Sillery and Lorette. However, Québec now had only one-tenth of the population of New France, separated by seventy forested miles from up river Trois Rivières, and as far again from Montréal. Montréal dominated the fur trade and was, with a population of

1205, now the largest town. San Agustín had become an impressive defensive bastion of a retreating frontier by this time. Jamestown had been bypassed in Virginia tobacco expansion. Québec by 1683 was a busy little administrative and commercial town superbly positioned both to regulate contact between France and New France and to protect a vast interior empire from maritime challengers.

Chapter 5

PLYMOUTH, NEW ENGLAND, AND THE WAMPANOAG 1620–1677

The English invasion of what came to be called New England was different from the establishment of San Agustín, Jamestown, and Québec in ways that are instructive. A symbiosis developed fairly quickly between the weakened Wampanoag and the few Plymouth settlers, who were not called on to participate in intertribal war. Serious contest between these farming peoples was postponed for half a century, though the massive invasion of English into Massachusetts Bay and the Connecticut River brought bitter conflicts in the general vicinity. When war finally did start between the Wampanoag and Plymouth settlers, it was between well-acquainted opponents, all armed with flintlocks. The resulting slaughter and destruction exceeded that of any previous inter-racial war in North America and heralded the horrors of the inter-colonial wars to come.

The Wampanoag (Pokanoket) of Cape Cod, their allies, and their rivals to the north along the Gulf of Maine and to the west into Long Island Sound had sporadic encounters with European fishermen and explorers during the century of trading that preceded the Pilgrims' landing at Plymouth. Verrazano, trading in 1524, had been delighted with the welcoming Narragansett, who enthusiastically exchanged decorative items with him, but he found that the Abenaki of Casco Bay already had experiences that caused them to insist that Europeans stay in their ships and trade only useful metal items, exchanged only by rope.[1] The next three-quarters of a century of trading with Europeans brought some new tools, new intensity to some intertribal rivalry, and skirmishes and kidnappings by the intruding mariners, but brought no substantial threat to Amerindian peoples.

Corn sustained the Wampanoag and the other major Amerindian populations of southern New England from the Saco River Valley to the Connecticut, as it had since its introduction about A.D. 1000. By 1600 the Wampanoag were more numerous than the Powhatan, numbering more than 21,000 of a total of about 135,000 Algonquian-speaking people thought to be living in this farming region. The Wampanoag, Massachusetts, Pawtucket, Narragansett, and Mohegan-Pequot people were approximately ten times as numerous per square mile as the hostile Eastern Abenaki and Micmac hunters living farther north.

Wampanoag women grew the precious grain, as well as beans and squash, but neither they nor their neighbors established matrilineal lines of descent like those of the Huron or Five Nations women farmers. Farming was semimigratory, and new fields were opened by burning trees and underbrush and were fertilized regularly with fish and the burning of cornstalks. The English, who valued saving their own women from field work, were reluctant to appreciate the efficiencies of Wampanoag (or Powhatan) agriculture.[2]

Wampanoag men grew tobacco, hunted, traded surplus grain to northern hunter-gatherers, negotiated alliances, and defended their people and crops. The growing value of the fur trade and the disruptive wars of the seventeenth century would intensify the importance of these riskier male functions. Winter villages were protected by palisades and by clubs, tomahawks, spears, and the excellent long bows with quartz or bone-tipped arrows. Warriors' bark shields became as obsolete here as elsewhere with the arrival of European muskets. Strong Wampanoag clan leaders like Massasoit could unite related bands against the rival Narragansett, sometimes in alliance with the Massachusetts to the north. However, individual kinship bands, often confined to a single village or river valley, were the effective units of organization throughout the entire region. These decentralized groups had been able to deal with sixteenth-century European fishermen-traders, but now faced a second, and very different, wave of European invasion.[3]

The French, Dutch, and English came to southern New England regularly after 1600. The French fished and exchanged hardware for furs with the Micmac and Abenaki, and these tribes in turn traded some French goods to their southern neighbors for corn. While the French explored the entire coast, their sphere of influence did not reach south beyond these hunters and trappers of prime furs. The French mission colony in Penobscot Bay was destroyed by the English in 1612, as were the French Acadian posts the following year, but John Smith claimed that the French had all the trade of the Gulf of Maine coast when he was there in 1614.

The Dutch trade on the Hudson was also developing quickly, in the wake of Hudson's initial voyage and the Dutch truce with Spain (1609–1621). There were at least five Dutch ships trading on that river in 1614, one of which initiated trade in Long Island Sound with the Pequot, Mohegan, Narragansett, and the Wampanoag of Buzzard's Bay, described as "sturdy and fairly tall. They are somewhat shy, however, since they are not accustomed to trade with strangers." The Dutch also traded up the Connecticut River that year, meeting the Mahican.[4]

French and Dutch visitors were primarily trading for furs in southern

New England; the English initiatives were different and more ominous. Even before the Anglo-Spanish peace of 1604 ended English privateering in Spanish American waters, English ships were scouting the New England shore. A 1602 expedition coasted from Maine to Cape Cod, trading from a fortified campsite and gathering sassafras roots, prized in Europe as a treatment for syphilis. Minor "thefts" by Amerindians provoked hostility that forced the English to leave. The next year, another expedition built a sturdy palisaded trading camp in Wampanoag territory at Cape Cod. Again relations soured, and the English loosed mastiffs and fired muskets at some 140 angry Nauset or Wampanoag warriors before abandoning their fort.

English attention shifted to the Abenaki lands farther north with George Waymouth's voyage to the Kennebec River in 1605. A season of trading ended when Waymouth kidnapped five Abenaki and took them to England, apparently to become guides and interpreters. In this strategy, the English were imitating Spanish and French methods. These Abenaki were turned over to Sir Ferdinando Gorges, commander of the fort at Plymouth, England, and an enthusiastic member of the new Virginia Company's Plymouth investors. Granted a thousand square miles around any settlement they created between 38°N (modern Washington, D.C.) and 45°N (entry to the Bay of Fundy), the Plymouth group sent two ships out immediately. One had a disastrous voyage, ending with the disabled vessel and its crew, including two of the kidnapped Abenaki, captured as interlopers in the Spanish West Indies. The other vessel fulfilled expectations, returning the captured Pemaquid River sagamore Tahanedo to his people, trading and surveying successfully, and returning to encourage the launch of a colony the next year.[5]

George Popham and Raleigh Gilbert, former privateers and chartered Virginia Company members, brought 120 men, including one of the captured Abenaki, Skidwarres, to establish the Sagadohoc colony on the Kennebec River in August 1607, three months after their Virginia associates had landed at Jamestown. Defense against possible French attacks quickly became a consuming priority. The colonists built a major up-to-date earthenwork fort, mounting eight cannon and boasting a trench, drawbridge, watergate, magazine, storehouse, church, and thirteen other buildings within its palisade. Food shortages became critical because grain was difficult to purchase locally and because the *Gift of God* and its crew remained at the colony until December in anticipation of a French attack. Forty-five men, already divided into rival factions before a calamitous fire and the death of George Popham, were left to winter uncomfortably at Sagadohoc.[6]

One of the underlying reasons why these well-funded colonists insisted on leaving on next summer's supply ship was their mismanaged relations with the local Abenaki. The colony had begun within two months of the Abenaki defeat at Chouacoet, and the Abenaki desperately wanted weapons with which to avenge themselves on the French-equipped Micmac. Despite the urgings of both Skidwarres and Tahanedo, the English colonists ignored repeated overtures of the most prestigious Penobscot Abenaki sachem, Bashaba. The English also angered their Abenaki neighbors; all trade was suspended, and several minor skirmishes occurred at the fort, killing at least eleven colonists. The English had bungled their opportunity to establish influence with the Abenaki, who soon resumed negotiations with both the French and the Micmac. Aside from a small trading post at Pemaquid, the only other English presence on this coast were now visiting fishermen. English colonizers had learned the risks of trying to settle north of the ample cornfields of New England.[7]

Colonizers remained convinced that their kidnapping of Amerindians as diplomats was a successful strategy and would try the same approach several times over the next seven years. The persistent Ferdinando Gorges was again grooming captured Amerindians to facilitate development. His most promising and consequential candidate was Epenow, a Wampanoag sachem from the island later known as Martha's Vineyard, who was with Gorges from 1611 to 1614. Epenow, a tall, strong, and clever man who was displayed "up and downe London for money as a wonder," was predictably inclined to support English dreams of gold mines. Gorges sent him back home with a 1614 expedition to find such mines. As they approached the island, Epenow leaped overboard, as though signaling his people on shore to fire the barrage of arrows that wounded several sailors. The voyage proved completely futile for the English, though it was passage home for Epenow.[8]

Captain John Smith, the disgruntled former commander at Jamestown, now became the premier promoter of English settlement in New England. In 1614 he led a London-financed two-vessel expedition in search of gold and whales, but found himself fishing and trading along the coast of Maine. Smith's aggressive methods provoked disagreements with Amerindians, causing at least three minor skirmishes. Smith also busied himself with mapping the coastline, observing the land and its people, and developing a scheme for colonization. The large populations of southern New England led him to advocate an English fishing colony provisioned by Spanish-style tribute from local peoples, a method that he inaccurately claimed to have perfected with his Virginia "feed fights." Smith left a small crew to finish fishing and to market the cargo in Spain. They proceeded to supplement their income by capturing and attempting to sell into Spanish slavery twenty-seven Patuxet Wampanoag and neighboring Nauset. The English had come to Cape Cod as belligerent sassafras diggers and fur traders, as kidnappers, and as slavers. Although the English had poisoned their relations with the Wampanoag even more than those with the Abenaki, Smith went home to prepare his *Description of New England*

(1616), promoting New England colonization for the remaining fifteen years of his life.[9]

Between 1616 and 1618, a devastating "virgin soil epidemic," the inevitable companion of increasing contact with Europeans, raged through New England. Fully 90 percent of the Wampanoag died of an unidentified European disease, as did a comparable number of the Massachusetts and nearly as many Pawtucket and Eastern Abenaki. Dozens of known coastal villages along Massachusetts Bay were entirely abandoned. The epidemic did not reach the Narragansett to the west or the more dispersed Micmac hunters to the north. Now both these tribes were suddenly of formidable size to their shattered enemies. The Micmac resumed raiding to the south, and the esteemed Wampanoag sachem Massasoit was promptly forced to concede lands to the now overwhelming Narragansett. The epidemic also improved English chances to found a colony successfully in what was now an underpopulated area.[10]

Squanto, one of the Wampanoag captured in 1614 and intended for slavery in Spain, would inspire Ferdinando Gorges and his associates to sponsor two more voyages under Captain Thomas Dermer. Squanto had made his way from Spain to England and reached Newfoundland in 1617, where he met Dermer. Squanto's way home was to be by way of England yet again, for he returned with Dermer and became another Amerindian, like Epenow, promoting the glories of his homeland to Europeans in order to find passage home. In 1619 Squanto sailed home in Dermer's ship, gaining Dermer a friendly reception from the surviving Wampanoag. Squanto's own village had been destroyed by the epidemic, but he stayed to seek his relations and soon joined the band led by Massasoit.

Dermer continued down the southern New England coast without his interpreter and encountered what was now a characteristic hostility. At the Wampanoag village of Monomoy, where Poutrincourt had provoked an attack in 1606, Dermer was captured but escaped. At Martha's Vineyard, Dermer encountered a suspicious but civil Epenow. The ship was attacked again as it approached Long Island, and Dermer headed for England. He returned in 1620 to find the Wampanoag even more hostile because of recent murders by English sailors. He was captured again, but Squanto arrived to negotiate Dermer's release and to rejoin his crew. In a poorly recorded battle at Martha's Vineyard, Epenow and his followers killed most of the ship's crew. Dermer died later of his wounds, and Squanto became a distrusted prisoner of Epenow's Wampanoag band. The Wampanoag were not numerous in the summer of 1620, but they were still able to resist English intruders. Dermer's last warnings did not reach England until after Gorges's Council for New England had received a generous royal charter to much of North America and after the *Mayflower* had reached Cape Cod.[11]

The Pilgrims who migrated into the charged atmosphere of Cape

Cod were as prepared for hostility as their limited funds allowed. The group that undertook the voyage, dominated the colony, and eventually created its legends were a mere seventeen men, ten women, and fourteen children. These few families were radical Calvinist "separatists," who fled the East Midlands after 1607 and settled for a decade in more tolerant Leyden, Netherlands. Fear of local worldliness and of the factionalism that was destroying their associates in Amsterdam led a determined minority of this congregation to migrate to a more isolated refuge. Although their stay in Leyden coincided with the twelve-year truce in the Dutch war for independence, the Pilgrims were certainly not pacifists fleeing impending war. Some of them had even read Richard Hakluyt's accounts of Elizabethan voyages to America, which included frightful warnings about cannibals and Amerindian treachery.

Permission to settle within the grants of the Dutch West India Company, the Virginia Company of London, or the new Council for New England proved easy compared with obtaining the money to do so. Thomas Weston, a wealthy London ironmonger, led a group that eventually lent money on terms that would prove onerous. Weston also recruited additional poor migrants and servants (thirty-three men, ten women, and twenty children) in London, who were not religious dissenters and were dubbed "strangers" by Pilgrims who as easily called themselves "saints." Wrangling, waiting, and expensive repairs that put oversized masts into the misnamed *Speedwell*, which had brought the Pilgrims to Southampton, all left the migrants so strapped for funds that they were selling needed provisions to pay harbor clearance fees. They were in "great extremities, scarce having any butter, no oil, not a sole to mend a shoe, nor every man a sword to his side, wanting many muskets, much armoure, etc."[12] before they sailed in August 1620. Their situation worsened when they were forced to abandon the floundering *Speedwell* at Dartmouth and set out again, a month later, crammed into the *Mayflower*.

The Pilgrims had recruited one experienced English soldier, Myles Standish, whose snaphance musket, rapier sword, dagger, armor, and helmet represented the well-equipped European warrior of 1620. The other forty-nine men of the initial settlement were less completely armed. There were only four snaphances, the other muskets being the cheaper matchlocks, which would remain the predominant firearm in the colony for a decade; it would be 1645 before an entire Plymouth expedition was reportedly equipped with snaphances. Rapier swords were more numerous than muskets at Plymouth and were preferred over the heavier cutlasses for charging opponents after firing an initial volley from the hard-to-reload matchlocks. Standish may have been the only one equipped with complete armor: the corselet of hammered iron back- and breastplates, the helmet, and the tasses, thules, and gorgets that protected thighs, loins, and neck respectively. Despite their expense, weight, and discomfort in hot or cold weather, the group seems to have brought and used at least sixteen corselets. It would be a generation before these disappeared in favor of heavy leather or quilted coats; a transition that mirrored Spanish developments in America a century earlier. The Plymouth settlers brought no cannon of their own except the twelve guns of the 180-ton *Mayflower*, which remained with them through the first winter.[13]

From their first expeditions ashore, each led by Standish, the Pilgrims showed themselves ready to presume and provoke unfriendliness. On November 11, sixteen armored men took their primed muskets ashore on Cape Cod, but found neither Amerindians nor a settlement site. Four days later, a similar party went ashore at the neck of the cape. A small group of Wampanoag-related Nauset were seen in the distance, but the armored English were unable to catch them. The next day, still tracking the Amerindians, they dug up a large basket of corn, some of which they hauled away in a stolen kettle. This stolen Nauset corn too easily became God's providential assistance to his chosen people. Weeks later, the colonists returned to take more of the corn, totaling about ten bushels, and to ransack graves and empty huts. Amerindian corn was as vital to Pilgrim survival as it had been for most other intruders.

The colonists suspected trouble from the understandably angry Nauset, but these chose to remain invisible to the English for three weeks, then suddenly attacked a shore party that was breaking camp. The arrows were immediately answered by snaphances, until the cumbersome matchlocks could be readied. No one was hurt on either side, though the colonists claimed victory simply because the Amerindians "left the field." The next day, the Pilgrims, who had spent a precious month of late autumn roaming Cape Cod, suddenly chose to settle at the harbor that John Smith had called Plymouth, where Dermer had returned Squanto only the previous year.[14]

After their preliminary aggressions, it is not surprising that the English remained nervous and defensive at their new location. It was not initially evident why the extensive local cornfields were deserted. The smoke of distant field-burning also suggested numerous Amerindians who were never there when an armed English party investigated. The belligerent "saints and strangers" of Plymouth assumed that the invisible Amerindians were plotting some murderous attack. Guard duty on shore each night proved uneventful, but drained manpower and spirits. Fears mounted as Amerindians were occasionally seen observing the newcomers from a distance and as scurvy, pneumonia, and tuberculosis killed half of the colony and ship's crew by the end of the winter. Most colonists stayed aboard the *Mayflower*, since construction of huts on shore had all but ceased for lack of healthy workers and guards. In February, a dozen Amerindians were seen in the vicinity, prompting a meeting that readily elected Myles Standish as captain-general and accepted his authority in military matters. Four small cannon, the largest being a fifteen-hundred-pound minion, were promptly hauled from the *Mayflower* and mounted on a heavy wooden platform atop Fort Hill. These guns did not command either the harbor or the entire settlement, but were expected to dissuade the Amerindians temporarily. Within a year, a fort was built here, and, in 1622, a four-company militia was organized and a palisade was built around the entire settlement, apparently in fearful reaction to news of the Powhatan massacre of Virginia colonists.[15]

Although besieged by hunger and disease, as well as their own fears and projections, the survivors huddled in their Plymouth beachhead were not besieged by the Wampanoag. Massasoit did not have Powhatan's power or numbers, but similarly saw the English as potentially useful against his powerful enemies to the west, the Dutch-supplied Narragansett. Massasoit patiently gathered information from scouts and from two knowledgeable advisers, Squanto and Samoset. Squanto had been released by his rival Epenow, with or without the latter's informed warnings about the English. Samoset was an English-speaking Abenaki from Pemaquid, where Sir Francis Popham had been trading in the twelve years since the collapse of the Sagadohoc colony. Samoset made the first approach to Plymouth in March 1621, and a meeting with Massasoit was promptly arranged.

The Plymouth settlers, who could muster only twenty fit men, though these were all now well armed, formed an honor guard that could not intimidate the much taller and stronger sixty-man entourage that accompanied Massasoit. He and elected Plymouth governor, John Carver, negotiated a treaty that seemed to fulfil mutual objectives. The English were misled about Massasoit's power, assuming that he could command all the Wampanoag and impose compliance on neighboring tribes. The Pilgrims thought that Massasoit would be their Amerindian agent, and he thus gained some tribute-collecting power. Massasoit accepted being a "friend and ally" of King James, without imagining that the English would later fraudulently claim that he had thereby surrendered a sovereignty that had never been his. Other misunderstandings promptly became evident when a number of dissident Wampanoag sachems sought alliance with the Narragansett, who attacked Massasoit. The English colony at Plymouth protected him against the dissidents, and the renewed treaty expanded the Wampanoag signatories to include even Epenow of Martha's Vineyard. Whatever the misunderstandings and repeated violations, the agreement usually fulfilled its peaceful objectives for the remaining forty years of Massasoit's life.[16]

The survival of Plymouth began with the planting of corn, under Squanto's instructions, in the fields that had belonged to his kin, and with corn acquired as trade or tribute from surviving bands. Although more English immigrants were welcome strength for the tiny colony, they could also force everyone to half-rations, as when thirty-five settlers arrived on the *Fortune* in November 1621. Another subsistence crisis occurred two years later when ninety-three settlers arrived, consisting of twice as many "strangers" as "saints."

These difficulties were mild compared with the arrival of sixty "lusty" workmen sent by Weston in 1622 to develop a rival trading and fishing settlement at Wessagusset (Weymouth). Plymouth residents provided food and shelter for these unwelcome visitors for three months before they moved to their Boston Bay destination in the territory of the Massachusetts Amerindians. Soon there were predictable complaints from the Massachusetts about men stealing corn and furs, leaving none for trade with Plymouth. The Pilgrims also learned that some of these "rude fellows" were living with Massachusetts tribeswomen. When the Massachusetts refused to trade more corn to the fractious Wessagusset men and forced them to do manual labor in exchange for food, the disgruntled workers warned Plymouth of their intention to take corn by force.

This growing mutual suspicion was exploited by Massasoit, who claimed there was a Massachusetts conspiracy to exterminate the English and advised murder of the Massachusetts tribal leaders. Plymouth leaders were quick to believe the worst and acted accordingly. Standish took eight men to Wessagusset to assert control over the territory and to end the supposed Massachusetts conspiracy. His group treacherously murdered seven Massachusetts sachems over the next few days. Understandably outraged, the Massachusetts killed three Englishmen who were living with them. Standish had provoked the Massachusetts, then left the survivors at Wessagusset to face the consequences; the Wessagusset workers wisely chose to sail away. By these murders, both Massasoit and the Pilgrims extended their power and ended a rival settlement that threatened trade, peace, and the Pilgrim notion of armed social insulation between English and Amerindian.[17] However, Plymouth's modest fur trade promptly slumped, angering the London investors who expected payment in furs. Brutal domination, which came very easily to soldiers like John Smith and Myles Standish, was detrimental to trade with Amerindians.

As in all European settlements in North America, the people of Plymouth sought more than mere survival; they wanted something saleable in Europe, with which to repay debts, buy manufactured necessities, and prosper. Inevitably, these pursuits affected the life of the colonists and their Amerindian neighbors. A Plymouth fishing venture into the Gulf of Maine proved unprofitable, but by 1625 the Pilgrims had begun a lucrative exchange of Wampanoag or Plymouth corn for Abenaki furs. Eight leading "saints" and their London associates, known as the Undertakers, gained a six-year monopoly on Plymouth's fur trade in return for repaying the colony's existing public debt.

Two years later, Dutch traders introduced the Undertakers to another bonanza, the wampum trade. Wampum, beads cut from the white or purple shells of small whelks found along the coast from Cape Cod to New York, then drilled and threaded into decorative strings and belts, were highly prized by all Algonquians and Iroquoians. Although some wampum dates from before 1600, this very profitable new industry developed rapidly in the 1620s, using European tools and trading networks. At first, Plymouth traders found sales limited by Amerindian traditions that wampum was worn only by high-status sachems. Gradually, more Abenaki, Massachusetts, and Wampanoag "consumers" began wearing the growing supply of these status-giving beads, which soon became the inter-cultural currency.[18]

The thriving wampum market helped to refocus power in southern New England for the Europeans and the Amerindians. The Undertakers tacitly agreed to stay out of the Narragansett Bay trade in return for Dutch guarantees of wampum supply. Plymouth trade north of Cape Cod meant challenging, discrediting, or even deporting English rivals, like Thomas Morton of Mare Mount, with exaggerated charges of selling guns to Amerindians and of the "immorality" of living with them. The Plymouth Undertakers, badly overcharged by their London associates, quickly became uncompetitive compared with the new merchants who arrived in the flood of settlement centering on Boston after 1630.[19] The Undertakers now turned to contest control of this valuable trade on the southern New England coast, a trade that drew excellent furs from as far away as the Algonquians of Canada, who had no other source of wampum.

The wampum trade also affected relations among the Amerindians of southern New England. Heightening rivalry between the Pequot and their allies over the manufacture and sale of wampum gave the Plymouth Undertakers the chance to compete. In 1631 Plymouth traders established a palisaded trading post near Massasoit's village on Narragansett Bay. The Narragansett besieged the outpost early the next year, but suddenly made peace in order to join a new war to the west, helping Mohegan tributaries defy Pequot overlords. The Dutch, recognizing that their monopoly trade with the Pequot was now in danger, established the House of Good Hope (Hartford) and invited all to trade. Plymouth leaders responded boldly by establishing a trading post of their own a mile and a half above Good Hope on the Connecticut River.

In 1633 the rivalries on the Connecticut River were suddenly revolutionized by the same massive smallpox epidemic that devastated both the Five Nations and the Huron. The Pequot, thought to have numbered some thirteen thousand, were reduced to a mere three thousand.[20] The remnant Pequot tried to reassert their monopoly by attacking customers coming to trade at Good Hope in 1634. The Dutch retaliated brutally by capturing the paramount Pequot sachem, Tatobem, holding him for ransom in wampum, then killing him after receiving payment. Under his son, Sassacus, the few Pequot could not control their dissident sachems or tributary tribes, most of whom joined the Narragansett. These, once again, had not been as decimated as their neighbors by the epidemic. The opportunistic Mohegan sachem Uncas would vacillate between submission to Sassacus, his brother-in-law, and alliance with the powerful Narragansett.

The weakened and diplomatically isolated Pequot leaders turned, late in 1634, to the new English power, the colony of Massachusetts Bay, already four thousand strong. Sassacus sought to counter the Dutch by encouraging English traders and settlers and to gain a truce with the Narragansett. John Winthrop, the governor of Massachusetts, offered only to be at peace, to send some trade goods, and to arrange what proved a brief truce between the rival tribes. The price demanded for these services was high: four hundred fathoms (twenty-four hundred feet) of wampum, thirty otter skins, and title to the Connecticut River Valley, occupied by "River Indians" previously paying tribute to the Pequot. Within eighteen months, there were three villages of Massachusetts migrants in that fertile valley, totaling about eight hundred settlers. To control squatters and individuals buying land from local sachems, the Massachusetts authorities hurried to gain English confirmation of an old Ferdinando Gorges patent. Before the end of 1635, John Winthrop, Jr., was building Fort Saybrook at the mouth of the Connecticut River, aided by a professional military engineer, Lion Gardiner. The Pequot were already paying for dubious European assistance.

Plymouth's role in the region changed dramatically because of its inability to compete with Massachusetts Bay in the fur trade of either the Pequot or the Abenaki frontier. The Pilgrims had been the pioneers of what became a "Great Migration" of twenty thousand of England's "vexed and troubled" to New England between 1620 and 1640. From the founding of Massachusetts Bay by "nonseparating" Puritans in 1630, the husbandmen of Plymouth found an excellent market in Boston. Switching from corn to English grains and building herds of imported cattle, horses, and pigs that would transform the entire countryside, Plymouth farmers found profit in providing food, seed, and livestock for a growing Boston and for new arrivals anxious to establish farms in Massachusetts, Rhode Island, and Connecticut. From belligerent beginnings that made Massasoit's Wampanoag into clients, Plymouth's small community established an armed and segregated peace with their Wampanoag neighbors for the next four decades, buying additional unused Wampanoag land as needed. Plymouth was insulated by Massachusetts Bay and by Connecticut from the troublesome opportunities farther north and west; Plymouth bluntly refused to participate in the hostilities developing against the Pequot.[21]

English prejudice and guilt often prompted over-reaction to rumors of devilish Amerindian conspiracies. Massasoit had used this ploy to destroy Massachusetts sachems in 1622, and Uncas used it against his Pequot rivals in 1636. When Uncas reported that the Pequot were preparing for war, John Winthrop, Jr., now an authorized negotiator for the Massachusetts Bay colony as well as governor of Saybrook, presented the Pequot with a provoking ultimatum. He demanded that the Pequot make their tributary tribes turn over the murderers of a thoroughly disreputable English trader and pirate who had unwisely attempted to kidnap several Pequot for ransom. Winthrop also required the Pequot to pay a heavy tribute. It was no longer a question of whether there would be war against the weakened and isolated Pequot, but whether the settlers of Massachusetts Bay or those of the Connecticut River Valley would strike the first blow that let them claim sovereignty over the conquered land.[22]

Massachusetts attempted to strike first, and failed miserably. Captain John Endicott gathered ninety volunteers for what was to be a profitable punitive expedition against the Pequot and against the Amerindians of Block Island, accused of another recent murder of a prominent Massachusetts trader. The force, including a Netherlands-trained soldier and trainer of the Massachusetts militia, John Underhill, was commissioned to kill the men of the tribe, enslave the women and children as booty, and take possession of the island. They were then to challenge the Pequot on the mainland, who were to return the murderers, pay a thousand fathoms of wampum in damages, and provide children as hostages for good behavior. In the likely event that all these demands were not met, they were to use force. Well-armed and -armored, the expedition could not find the Amerindians of heavily wooded Block Island and rummaged in abandoned villages for nonexistent loot. Lieutenant Gardiner at Fort Saybrook was outraged when this gang disclosed its intended affront to the Pequot, leaving him to bear their understandable wrath once these Massachusetts volunteers had gone. The Pequot sachems met Endicott, stalled, then left the armored English waiting in an open field for a battle they did not know had been declined. Two alien military cultures, each carrying a different perception of valor and combat, failed to clash here. The Pequot vanished, and the invaders vented their frustration on an empty village and ripened cornfields.[23]

As Gardiner had predicted, the belligerence of the Massachusetts volunteers provoked trouble, including a nine-month Pequot siege of Fort Saybrook's twenty-man garrison. Nervous settlers at Wethersfield drove off the Pyquag band who had allowed these strangers to share their Connecticut Valley village for the previous year. With Pequot assistance, the Pyquag avenged themselves in April 1637 by killing nine Wethersfield farmers, including a woman and a child, and by capturing two girls. The girls were traded to the Dutch once it was discovered that they did not know how to make the gunpowder needed for the few Pequot muskets.[24]

It is revealing that the elders and magistrates of Massachusetts, when asked whether the Pyquag had violated the "law of nations" in this instance, said that the Pyquag were entirely justified in using force or fraud to inflict damage a hundred times worse than they received, and that they were not required to seek peaceable solutions first, provided they had complained.[25] This was the Puritan understanding of vengeance in a just war, apparently for Amerindians or themselves; Amerindian vengeance required less blood. For the Puritans, wrestling to unite their fears and ambitions with their beliefs, the Wethersfield attacks made vilification and their own justification easy. Massachusetts Bay, which had been convulsed with internal religious and political controversy, was now ready to answer the repeated pleas for help against the "devil's minions" besieging Fort Saybrook; however, Massachusetts was too late.

The Connecticut–Mohegan attack on the Pequot village on the Mystic River in May 1637 was the horrific climax of the Pequot War, detailed and symbolized in John Underhill's drawing (Figure 4). The Connecticut General Court mobilized ninety men under Captain John Mason, twenty of whom were replaced by members of the Saybrook garrison led by Underhill, together with some seventy of Uncas's Mohegan and tributaries. Rather than assaulting Sassacus's fortified village directly, as might be expected of Europeans, the attackers sailed forty miles farther east, gathered five hundred Narragansett reinforcements and guides, then marched back overland to surprise the other major Pequot village, five miles from Sassacus on the Mystic River. In taking this circuitous route, the invaders exposed Connecticut Valley farmsteads to the Pequot, but evaded the main Pequot forces and achieved complete surprise. Encircling the village with one ring of English armed with snaphances and a second ring of Amerindian allies, the English led the dawn attack. If the English initially planned to plunder and take captives, which historians dispute, the ferocious defense by 150 warriors and the prospect of assault by the approaching main Pequot force changed English tactics. Mason ordered the village burned and survivors killed. Some of the Amerindian allies left as they saw the plan develop; others stayed to watch, participate, or denounce the English for their unnecessary slaughter. Neither the burning of palisaded villages nor the slaughtering of women and children were regular parts of Amerindian or European military convention, but this form of total war had previously been used by Europeans at both Mabila and Paspahegh. The English had been frustrated and humiliated when the Pequot refused battle; Amerindian witnesses at Mystic Fort were "dreadfully Amazed" at this new English version of woodland war-

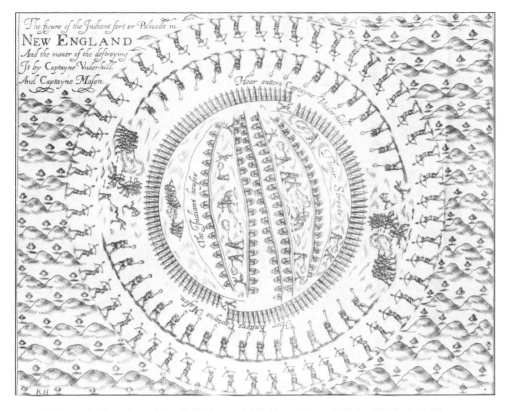

Figure 4. Attack on Mystic Village, 1637. From Captain John Underhill, *Newes from America* (London, 1638). (Courtesy of The Library Company of Philadelphia)

fare, using stealth and fire to annihilate a village. This outrage served initially as a warning, and eventually as an invitation to imitation.

Only five Pequot escaped what was a slaughter of approximately five hundred; two of the English were killed and twenty were wounded, as were twenty of their Amerindian allies. The substantial Pequot army arrived too late and was astonished and demoralized. More than two hundred surrendered to the Narragansett, but Massachusetts troops killed any adult male refugees they could find among them. Sassacus fled with a party of forty and sought sanctuary with the distant Mohawk, but they killed the entire group. Most survivors hid themselves among Uncas's Mohegan or joined the Narragansett. Although the Pequot were brutally smashed and thoroughly dispersed by 1638, between fifteen hundred and two thousand of them would be living in distinct villages again by 1675, when they joined the *English* side in King Philip's War.[26]

Connecticut won the scramble for Pequot territory, creating a confidence displayed in an arrogant motion of a Milford town meeting in 1640: "Voted, that the earth is the Lord's and the fulness thereof; voted, that the earth is given to the Saints; voted, we are the Saints."[27] Connecticut also elevated Uncas to power in return for his clientage. That year, he ceded all Mohegan and tributary lands that were not occupied, making the colony the guarantor of his lands while expanding the colony's boundaries and wampum tribute. The immediate growth of Connecticut farmland would not be on Pequot or Mohegan lands, but on those of smaller tributary bands. Connecticut and the Mohegan had repeated the pattern established by Plymouth and the Wampanoag, though the resulting peace was less secure because the old Pequot–Narragansett rivalry promptly became a Mohegan–Narragansett struggle.

The thirty thousand Narragansett still outnumbered all their neighbors and maintained an independence characteristic of an earlier period. Their great sachem, Miantonomi, was a close friend of Massachusetts dissident clergyman Roger Williams, now a trader and leader of the fractious little colony of Rhode Island, with a dispersed population of only a thousand. Promised the Pequot hunting grounds in return for supporting Massssachusetts Bay, Miantonomi found the lands pre-empted by Connecticut and its Mohegan allies after the war. New Puritan settlers invaded directly from England to found New Haven in 1637, buying land from local Amerindians without regard for Narragansett overlords. At the Treaty of Hartford (1638), Miantonomi saw Connecticut authorities pretend jurisdiction over him in return for granting him some surviving Pequot prisoners. The upstart Uncas also had Connecticut support in competing with the Narragansett for the loyalty of neighboring smaller bands. Tributary tribes of the Narragansett even began selling land directly to Massachusetts settlers after 1642, in violation of both Amerindian convention and agreement with the Massachusetts Bay authorities.

Sensing danger, Miantonomi sought to build on his Mohawk alliance to create a general Amerindian resistance movement. Speaking to the Montauk in the summer of 1642, Miantonomi reportedly warned:

> For so are we all Indians as the English are, and say brother to one another; so must we be one as they are, otherwise we shall all be gone shortly, for you know our fathers had plenty of deer and skins, our plains were full of deer, as also our woods, and of turkies, and our coves full of fish and fowl. But these English having gotten our land, they with scythes cut down the grass, and with axes fell the trees; their cows and horses eat the grass, and their hogs spoil our clam banks, and we shall all be starved.

He went on to claim that all Amerindians would rise on a prearranged day "and kill men, women, and children, but no cows, for they will serve to eat till our deer be increased again."[28] Miantonomi had English friends and had helped the English destroy the Pequot. He wisely did not mention the Mystic River village massacre in this speech or accuse the English of exterminating powerless Amerindian people who could easily have been adopted into other tribes after capture. His was an early, eloquent, and desperate invitation to a course seldom taken by Amerindians. Like existing European rivalries, those among Amerindians were ultimately too strong to make race war possible.

Despite his call for Amerindian solidarity, Miantonomi became involved in a tributary band's revenge against the Mohegan in 1643. Wearing a suit of armor lent by a well-meaning Rhode Island friend, he was easily captured by Uncas. In captivity, Miantonomi returned to his vision of a general Amerindian alliance, proposing one agreement to be marked by his marriage to Uncas's daughter, and hoping that his brother could extend the dynastic alliance by marrying the daughter of Wampanoag sachem Massasoit. Uncas resisted this invitation, accepted the ransom offered by the Narragansett, then treacherously turned Miantonomi over to the English.

Miantonomi was held by Connecticut authorities pending the first meeting of the new inter-colonial United Colonies of New England. The orthodox Puritans who led the Massachusetts Bay colony had witnessed a decade of rapid English colonial expansion and dispersal that took religious friends beyond their strict control. Expelled dissidents had established four communities in Narragansett territory and were seeking an English royal charter, while unreformed Anglicans were settling in what would become New Hampshire. Fellow Puritans had founded what were becoming rival colonies, Connecticut and New Haven, and nearby Plymouth ran an independent policy in religious and military matters that could compromise the security of the larger colony. England's descent into civil war (1642–1649), apparently along lines of religious conviction, likely inspired the Puritan inter-colonial agreement. The United Colonies of New England, named in conscious imitation of earlier Dutch rebels against Spain, was formed in May 1643 to defend the shared interests and beliefs of Massachusetts, Connecticut, Plymouth, and New Haven, which were "all in Church fellowship." Although there were civil functions, joint military and diplomatic action was the central purpose of the league. Six of the eight commissioners, two from each colony, had to authorize action, so opportunistic scrambling for Amerindian lands could be stalled by rival colonies. Citizen militia volunteers were to constitute the army that was provided, provisioned, and paid by the colonies in the proportion of their fighting male population, those between sixteen and sixty. The United Colonies functioned regularly, though not perfectly, until Connecticut absorbed New Haven in its new charter of 1662. The union would be revitalized to fight the war against the Wampanoag in 1675. Whatever the intended purposes of the league, its first and last significant acts concerned Amerindians.

At the first meeting of the United Colonies, in September 1643, the commissioners unjustly accused Miantonomi of having violated the Treaty of Hartford, which Massachusetts had previously refused to recognize. More plausibly, they argued that he had plotted against the English, which violated the treaty but was not a crime for an independent leader. Unable to execute Miantonomi, who was outside the jurisdiction of any of the colonies, the commissioners had Uncas execute him, with English witnesses to prove it had been done. The Narragansett promptly sought revenge against Uncas, but failed in their attempt to besiege a Mohegan village that Connecticut had helped fortify. In 1645 the United Colonies declared war on the Narragansett, prompting several threatened sachems to sign a humiliating treaty. Belligerent threats and fraudulent "purchases" of Narragansett lands continued, but the Narragansett used their Mohawk alliance, the Rhode Island–Massachusetts rivalry, and even the support of King Charles II to survive unconquered for another thirty years.[29]

Clashes between confident Puritan and resistant Algonquian civilizations were predictable, if not inevitable; peace, like that enjoyed by southern New England for thirty years after 1645, demands explanation. First, the "Great Migration" had come to an end with the outbreak of England's civil war. More people migrated back to England in the 1640s, either to fight for the Puritan cause or to enjoy its triumphs, than migrated the other way. The English population of New England more than doubled between 1640 and 1660, to over thirty-three thousand, but most of the additions were children born to families that had migrated earlier, children who would not need land for a generation.[30] The lands acquired through the Pequot War were not much in demand, nor was the farm produce that previously had been sold for cash to arriving migrants. When land was needed, it could be bought reasonably through those accommodating sachems, Uncas and Massasoit, whose power had been enhanced by association with the English.

A second restraint on the territorial aggressions of individual colonies was the diplomacy of the United Colonies of New England, which functioned effectively from 1643 to 1663. While representing Puritan dominance, it needed internal consensus and wanted no troublesome scrutiny from the "reigning" English Parliament. Connecticut and New Haven were encouraged to expand into Long Island and adjoining territories claimed by the Dutch, an activity that seemed more patriotic with the outbreak of the First Anglo-Dutch War (1652–1654). This European naval war came directly to New England with a three-vessel English squadron that arrived in Massachusetts in 1654 with orders to capture New Netherlands. Commanded by a former Massachusetts merchant, now a Cromwellian general-of-the-fleet, Robert Sedgwick, this squadron was carrying seventy soldiers and was strengthened by one hundred local volunteers, but it was stopped by news of the Anglo-Dutch Peace of Westminster. The forces at Boston were profitably diverted to violate peace with France by looting and conquering all three Acadian trading posts: Port Royal and the posts on the St. John and Penobscot rivers. Plymouth was poorly placed to benefit from these intrusions on either Dutch or French claims.[31]

Third, Amerindians and colonists needed each other more than usual, as producers, customers, workers, and even converts. The direct fur trade now meant less to Plymouth merchants than to other New England entrepreneurs, but the trade in European goods to neighboring Amerindians expanded. The wampum trade of the Narragansett with the Mohawk continued to flourish, yielding Mohawk furs that were exchanged for English manufactures. The Narragansett–Mohawk connection was also a major deterrent to New England aggression against the still independent Narragansett. The ties between Puritans and Amerindians were taken further with the modest success of English-funded Puritan missions after 1649, featuring the establishment of "praying towns" separate from either culture but modeled on the English in more than consumption. A mixture of economic interdependence and social segregation supported the precarious peace.

For Plymouth, as well as the other parts of New England, all three restraining conditions began to collapse after 1660. A new generation of locally born English sought more Amerindian land as agricultural exports developed to the West Indies. As the colonists and Wampanoag came into closer contact, irritating incidents involving stray livestock multiplied. Pilgrim elders who had negotiated with and respected Massasoit had died by 1657, as did Massasoit himself in 1661. His less-accommodating son Wamsutta promptly began selling land to outsiders and was soon rumored to be plotting against Plymouth. Taken to Plymouth at gunpoint to defend himself in 1662, Wamsutta fell ill and died. His brother Metacom, who had accepted the English name Philip, assumed the position of leading sachem. "King" Philip renewed the treaty with Plymouth, but decided not to sell any land for seven years.[32]

The English Restoration of Charles II also threatened Plymouth's diplomatic and legal position. Plymouth never had a legal charter and had based its land claims solely on its increasingly threadbare treaty with the Wampanoag. A new royal charter for Connecticut (1662) ominously annexed New Haven, and that for Rhode Island (1663) included land claimed by Plymouth, including Philip's own Wampanoag village of Sowams. Massachusetts was also encroaching from the north, asserting its 1629 charter. In 1664 four royal investigators arrived in Boston with three Royal Navy ships and three hundred soldiers, as part of their assignment to conquer New Amsterdam. These commissioners insisted that the disintegrating United Colonies was illegal, thereby aggravating the renewed competition for territory and treaties. Fraudulent claims on Narragansett lands were disallowed in a relished display of royal power against the local dominance of these embattled Puritan governments.

The third support for peace, the economic interdependence of the English, the Narragansett, and the Mohawk, also evaporated. The southern New England fur trade was exhausted, Mohawk trade shifted to the newly conquered English center at Albany, and the wampum trade had destroyed itself with overproduction. As Narragansett links with the Mohawk withered, they were replaced by closer ties with neighboring Algonquian-speaking tribes and those farther north, including the Abenaki. Improving relations between the Wampanoag and the Narragansett, and links with anti-Mohawk and pro-French tribes to the north, would lead to charges in 1664, 1667, and 1669 of an intertribal conspiracy to destroy the English. This Amerindian diplomatic revolution was preparing the way for later Algonquian cooperation against the English.[33]

Friction between the Wampanoag and Plymouth, which would ignite King Philip's War, intensified. To provide land for young farmers and to assert authority in the disputed lands bordering Rhode Island, the Plymouth General Court authorized the establishment of the town of Swansea in 1667, within four miles of Philip's village. Philip's unwillingness to sell land had been ignored, and relations became strained. In March 1671, Philip went beyond angry words to a defiant threat as he paraded armed warriors at Swansea. Brought to answer accusations in the Plymouth town of Taunton, Philip signed a humiliating treaty by which he agreed to surrender his muskets. He promptly appealed to Massachusetts, but a full meeting of the United Colonies commissioners in Plymouth that September confirmed most of the treaty. This time his fine for contemplating war was £100, which he more than paid for with a land sale, spending the balance on guns and gunpowder.[34]

Christian missions also caused tensions here, as elsewhere, though neither Pilgrim nor Puritan settlers showed much enthusiasm for them. For these Calvinists, who demanded literacy and familiarity with the Bible, the task of converting Amerindians was particularly daunting. New England missions, among the Wampanoag of Martha's Vineyard and the Massachusetts, did not begin until the 1640s. English donations and the Reverend John Eliot's efforts had established seven "praying towns" in Massachusetts by 1660, composed primarily of displaced Amerindians given a life near, but not in, Puritan society. By 1674 some eleven hundred Amerindians in fourteen such settlements were attempting the required Calvinist behavioral revolution. The lone Plymouth mission before 1675 was Richard Bourne's, thriving among the weakened Nauset tribe on Cape Cod. Although Massasoit and his successors may not have known of the dissension that Christian missions caused among the Apalachee, the Guale, the Huron, or the Mohawk, they were completely opposed to the introduction of Christianity among the Wampanoag. Ministers like John Cotton, Jr., and

Eliot increasingly ignored these prohibitions after 1667, and their Massachusetts Amerindian converts were urged to proselytize among the Wampanoag.[35]

 King Philip's War was triggered by the murder of a Massachusetts Amerindian convert, John Sassamon, who had studied briefly at Harvard, then left to become Philip's competent secretary and adviser in the 1660s. He returned to settle as minister in the Massachusetts praying town of Nemasket, undertaking the occasional diplomatic assignment to Philip's court on behalf of the English. After such a visit late in 1674, Sassamon reported to Plymouth that Philip was preparing for war. Sassamon was killed before reaching his home, and three Wampanoag, including a prominent adviser to Philip, were tried in Plymouth's town house and convicted of his murder. Within days of their execution in June 1675, armed Wampanoag were threatening Swansea and looting its evacuated houses, in the course of which a warrior was killed[36] (Figure 5).

Although repeatedly accused over a thirteen-year period of plotting the slaughter of the English, Philip did not plan the war that began in June 1675. Philip, who had never been a "king" like Powhatan, could not restrain the angered warriors. Philip found himself, with fewer than three hundred warriors and no confirmed allies, at war against three English colonies with combined militias of at least ten thousand men who had much better access to the flintlocks and gunpowder that were now essential to both sides.[37] Philip's strategic position was also too unfavorable to have been planned. His followers gathered at his home on Mount Hope peninsula before provoking hostilities in Swansea, at its neck, predictably bringing massive English forces to confine him to the peninsula and patrol the surrounding waters.

The English were not ready for war either, though initial responses seemed appropriate. English families evacuated Swansea, local men gathered in reinforced "garrison houses," and Plymouth's Governor Josias Winslow ordered some two hundred militia into Swansea, including Christian Amerindian scouts commanded by the adaptable Plymouth-born frontiersman Benjamin Church. Massachusetts sent negotiators to the Narragansett and the neighboring Nipmuck to ensure that they remained neutral. They also alerted Connecticut, sent a boatload of arms and ammunition to Plymouth, and raised two militia companies, one mounted, to go to Swansea. These combined forces swept through the peninsula at the end of June, but found it deserted. Rhode Island provided boat patrols to confine the Wampanoag, though they failed to do so.

Mobilization had not been slow, nor inter-colonial command particularly awkward, but conflicting objectives were already apparent. A Plymouth decision to build a fort on the abandoned peninsula was opposed by those, like Benjamin Church, who were anxious to pursue

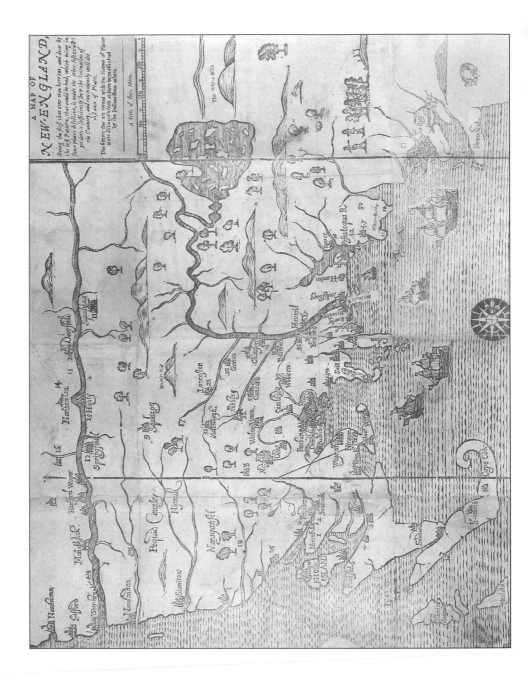

A MAP OF
NEW·ENGLAND,

Being the first that ever was here cut, and done by
the best Pattern, that could be had, which being in
some places defective, it made the other less exact:
yet doth it sufficiently show the Situation of
the Country, and conveniently well the
distance of Places.

The figures that are joyned with the Names of Places
are to distinguish such as have been assaulted
by the Indians from others.

A Scale of Fory Miles

Philip into Pocasset country to the east. The fort appealed to those who wanted to make sure Philip did not return to lands now deemed forfeit and to secure those conquered lands for Plymouth despite the claims of Rhode Island and Massachusetts.[38]

Massachusetts forces had been diverted to a similiar purpose, a belligerent visit to strengthen claims against the Narragansett. Suspicions survive that Plymouth–Massachusetts cooperation already included an agreement that the first would confiscate Wampanoag lands and the second would take those of the Narragansett.[39] A few Narragansett were already with Philip as private warriors, and the Narragansett were giving refuge to some Wampanoag women and children. Nonetheless, the Narragansett negotiators readily agreed to outrageous and unenforcable Massachusetts terms that went beyond neutrality to demand loyalty to the English and opposition to the Wampanoag. Connecticut also had designs on Narragansett lands, and the colony complicated matters further as it entered the war. It was anxious to keep peace with the Narragansett for the moment, because its forces were diverted to a brief boundary dispute with English New York's opportunistic governor, Edmund Andros. The English colonial authorities were all maneuvering, very prematurely, for another land scramble like the Pequot War.

Philip won initially by evading capture and organizing some of the numerous profitable raids conducted in 1675. He moved to the swampy Pocasset territory of a female sachem, Weetamoo, and organized effective raids against five Plymouth towns. Success brought valuable allies and imitators among the Nipmuck of Massachusetts and the River Indians of Connecticut. Since both Massachusetts and Plymouth had reacted to the outbreak of war by interning most of their Amerindian converts, it is not surprising that Philip also gained some early supporters from Nipmuck praying towns. Small parties of Narragansett even raided Providence, though Quaker-run Rhode Island stayed out of the war.

In the futile pursuit of Philip, Plymouth and Massachusetts militia invaded the Pocasset swamps, suffered casualties without inflicting any, then withdrew. War costs, the need to tend crops, and military ineffectiveness prompted the withdrawal of most Massachusetts troops and the building of yet another fort, this time on the Pocasset shore. All pretense that Philip was besieged within the vast swamps was gone by the end of July, when Philip's force disappeared northwest into Nipmuck territory. Uncas had joined Connecticut in this war, and a

Figure 5. (*facing*) Map of New England, 1677. Notice: 1. Mount Hope, 2. Swansea, 5. Seaconke or Rehoboth, 6. Pocasset, 21. Lancaster. This first map engraved in North America is from William Hubbard, *A Narrative of the Troubles with the Indians in New England* (Boston, 1677). (Courtesy of the Trustees of the Boston Public Library)

pursuing force of English and Mohegan skirmished with the Wampanoag, but could not penetrate another defended swamp. Over the next three months, Amerindian discontent fueled a massive war against vulnerable English frontier settlements in Plymouth, Massachusetts, and Connecticut, which were besieged, destroyed, or abandoned. Several English colonial patrols were ambushed and scattered by well-armed warriors who then melted into the surrounding forests.

Unable to respond to guerrilla warfare in kind, New England's usual reply was a massive conventional siege echoing the destruction of Mystic Fort in 1637. After ineffectively fighting in swamps during 1675, New Englanders recognized the advantages of a winter attack on a swampy stronghold. The United Colonies, finally roused to cooperation by sufficient losses, did not choose to attack Philip's winter quarters far to the west on the Hoosack River. That strategy was undertaken independently, and very effectively, by Mohawk encouraged by Governor Andros of New York. The United Colonies, for reasons that remain very suspicious, chose to attack the winter camp of the still neutral Narragansett, thereby provoking a thousand more warriors to join Philip in an even more extensive war. Narragansett failure to turn over Wampanoag refugees was simply a pretext; Narragansett land was definitely a prospect.

The United Colonies raised nearly a thousand troops for this Narragansett expedition. They were recruited from the militias and supplied and paid in the proportions of Massachusetts, 517; Connecticut, 315; and Plymouth, 158. Josias Winslow, Plymouth's native-born governor, was given command of the expedition, which also included 150 Mohegan and Pequot. Aware of the danger, the Narragansett were finishing a large palisaded fort, complete with firing platforms, blockhouses, and surrounding massive *abattis*. These winter quarters were in a secret location on an obscure island in the Great Swamp and were found only because a captured Narragansett agreed to guide the colonial army. Attacking an uncompleted gap in the defenses as soon as they arrived on December 19, 1675, the impetuous English soldiers were driven back with heavy losses. The second attack by a larger contingent made some progress against fierce resistance, but losses soon prompted an order to burn the fort. Unable to gain victory cheaply, the poorly supplied attackers burned food and shelter, which they needed, and killed valuable captives, whom they wanted. The United Colonies' casualties were 70 dead and about 150 wounded. Of the Narragansett, at least 48 warriors were wounded and 97 were killed, as were between 300 and 1000 women and children.[40] The outraged Narragansett survivors fled to join Philip, wintering among the Mahican (not Mohegan, see Map 4). A belated English pursuit of these Narragansett failed, ending in a long, hungry march and in the disbanding of Winslow's army in February 1676.

Philip and his allies were already beginning their most effective season of war with a ferocious Narragansett attack on the fifty-family town of Lancaster, Massachusetts, on February 10. The Narragansett, seeking revenge for their recent devastation, set fire to most of the town and killed more than fifty people. They also took twenty prisoners, including Mary Rowlandson, whose printed account of her eleven weeks in captivity and subsequent "redemption" became a persistent colonial best seller.[41] Soon thereafter, raiders burned the Massachusetts towns of Medfield, Weymouth, and Groton, though another attack on Northampton met effective resistance because reinforcements were there by chance. Other raids destroyed towns in Plymouth and Rhode Island in the south, as well as towns along the northeastern fringes of the Massachusetts settlement, indicating both careful deployment of Philip's two armies and local Amerindian initiative. On March 26, a patrol of sixty-five Plymouth militia and twenty allied Christian Amerindians was ambushed. Surrounded and outnumbered by Narragansett, the column was destroyed; only one of the Plymouth militiamen and eight of the Christian Amerindians survived. Two days later, the Plymouth town of Rehoboth was attacked and burned. As the Amerindians continued to triumph, frontier towns were abandoned by terrified refugees, crops were not planted, and three hundred Plymouth militia exhausted themselves trying to catch elusive enemies.

The demoralized English could devise no offense against these enemies, and inter-colonial cooperation all but ceased; Philip had effectively defeated the United Colonies of New England. Connecticut, which was not a prime target of the spring campaign, had some success conducting independent operations with Mohegan and Pequot support. Plymouth and Massachusetts leaders found morale so low, and attacks so widespread, that they could not raise an effective army at all that spring. Governors proclaimed days of religious humiliation, and ministers tried to explain the reasons for God's wrath and the moral reformations needed to placate him. Seeking comforting explanations amid these difficulties, Puritans readily concluded that God was upset with English avarice, the wearing of wigs, and the tolerance shown Quakers.[42]

The sudden collapse of this successful Amerindian war needs an explanation. A revealing incident occurred in May 1676, when hundreds of Amerindian families, including Sokoki Abenaki who were not in the war, gathered to catch and dry fish at Peskeompscut, twenty miles north of Hatfield on the Connecticut River. Some of the warriors confidently raided Hatfield's undefended cattle herd, driving the animals to their camp. No Connecticut force was mustered to follow the cattle or their tracks. Two days later, an English prisoner escaped from Peskeompscut to inform the Hatfield garrison commander, Captain William Turner, that there were comparatively few warriors among these Amerindians. This assurance prompted 150 men to undertake a mounted raid. In a dawn attack, the English infiltrated the sleeping

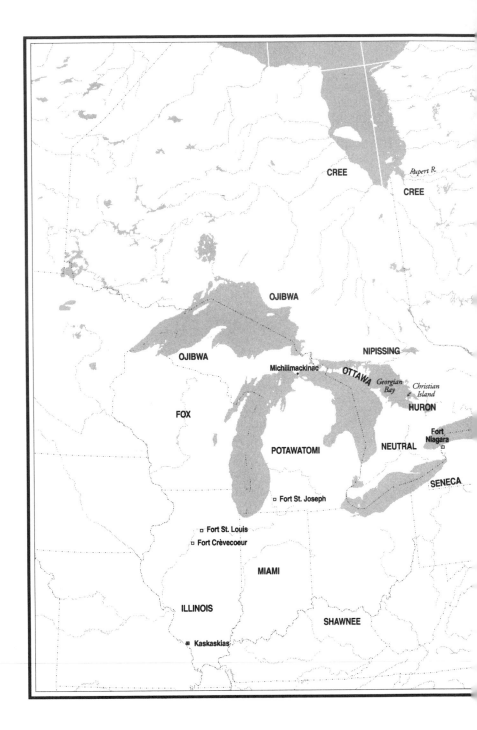

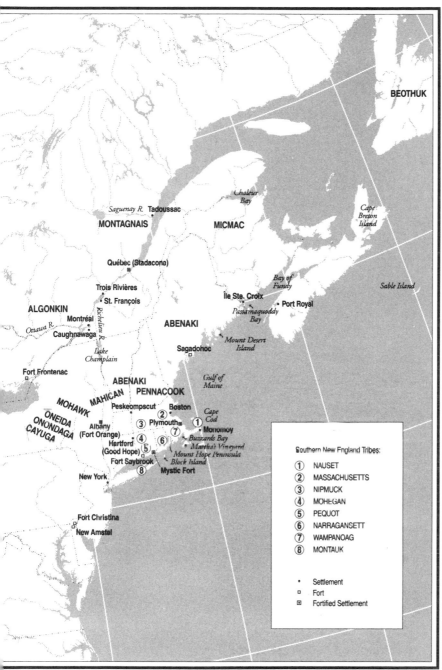

BEOTHUK

Chaleur
Bay

Cape
Breton
Island

Saguenay R. Tadoussac

MONTAGNAIS   MICMAC

Sable Island

Québec (Stadacona)

Trois Rivières   Bay of
                                   Funty
St. François   Île Ste. Croix
ALGONKIN   • Port Royal
        Montréal   Passamaquoddy
Ottawa R.   Bay
        Caughnawaga   ABENAKI
                                  Mount Desert
            Lake   Island
        Champlain   Sagadohoc
Fort Frontenac
                      Gulf of
        ABENAKI   Maine
MOHAWK MAHICAN PENNACOOK
ONEIDA   Peskeompscut Boston
ONONDAGA   Cape
CAYUGA   Albany   ③ Plymouth   Cod
          (Fort Orange)   ① Monomoy
                      ⑦
          Hartford ④ ⑥ Buzzards Bay
          (Good Hope) ⑤   Martha's Vineyard
          Fort Saybrook   Mount Hope Peninsula
                           Block Island
New York   ⑧ Mystic Fort

Fort Christina
New Amstel

Southern New England Tribes:

① NAUSET
② MASSACHUSETTS
③ NIPMUCK
④ MOHEGAN
⑤ PEQUOT
⑥ NARRAGANSETT
⑦ WAMPANOAG
⑧ MONTAUK

• Settlement
□ Fort
⊡ Fortified Settlement

©1993 Ian K. Steele

Map 4. The northeast to 1676.

camp and slaughtered an estimated one hundred to three hundred men, women, and children. The attackers also wrecked two forges used to repair guns and threw two great "pigs" of lead into the river. The Amerindians countered by ambushing the retreating colonials, killing thirty-nine, including Turner, in a single volley.[43]

Peskeompscut offers a glimpse of the Amerindian side of the war. Their traditional warfare was not an unending year-round struggle, and defeat was usually conceded before annihilation. However, out-dated European assumptions about total, dogged, continual war were being preserved on this frontier and imposed on the New England Algonquians. Driven away from the cornfields that subsisted them and forced to hunt in unfamiliar territory, the Narragansett and Wampa-noag refugee armies and their attending families suffered food short-ages. Raiding yielded fewer cattle and less grain as the war continued and English defenders strengthened their surviving garrison houses. The twenty-mile band of deserted and destroyed English frontier set-tlements in Plymouth and Massachusetts had become a foodless bar-rier, with the hungry, retreating English better able to find food than their now migratory enemies.

This was a war of flintlock muskets, lead, and gunpowder on both sides. The Hatfield raiders had found two operational forges, with which Amerindians attempted to maintain muskets. However, without an additional supply of at least one-fifth of a community's flintlocks each year, the total number of usable guns diminished. The Peskeomps-cut camp had sufficient ammunition and the lead to make more. There is no mention of finding gunpowder, though there was enough to shoot the retreating English. Gunpowder, which was all imported from Europe, was expensive, difficult and dangerous to store or transport, and worthless if it was shaken into dust or became even slightly damp. Redrying damp gunpowder was an extremely dangerous activity, even for especially equipped European powder mills.[44] Serviceable gunpow-der was increasingly scarce among the Amerindians. The French in Canada were not providing gunpowder during this war, though they would subsequently; the Dutch suppliers had been driven from New York for the last time in 1674. English-controlled Albany was accused of buying New England loot with weapons, ammunition, and gunpow-der early in the war, but both the booty and the trade dwindled. The renewed Mohawk attacks on New England tribes not only disrupted Philip's winter camp, but also kept his supporters away from Albany. Philip and his allies had not been entirely ready for war when it began and were under a weapons and ammunition embargo throughout this contest, which was much larger and longer than any they had previ-ously fought with firearms.

The Amerindian offensive peaked months after the only major English colonial "victory" at Great Swamp and faded without another comparable battle. In the summer of 1676, Plymouth and Massachusetts

organized small volunteer expeditions; these were landbound privateering ventures for loot and prisoners to be sold into slavery. Amerindian converts were recruited into these units, and captives and
deserters from Philip's forces assisted the English in an increasingly
successful hunt for poorly defended, hungry, and dispersed groups of
Amerindians. Connecticut militia and their Mohegan allies wantonly
slaughtered more people than they captured from two sizable bands
of Narragansett who were obviously short of food and gunpowder.[45]
A mixed Plymouth force of 150 English and 50 Amerindian volunteers
under Benjamin Church prospered in this anticlimactic phase. A Plymouth soldier wrote to his wife in mid-July that they "have killed and
taken upward on one hundred Indians but never an English slain nor
wounded only one or two bewildered in the woods and captured."[46]
On August 12, one such unit surprised the remnant of Philip's army
foraging back on Mount Hope peninsula. The fleeing sachem was shot
dead by a Christian Amerindian named Alderman.

Vengeance against the Wampanoag was relentless. Early in the war,
a group of neutral Wampanoag living near Dartmouth had voluntarily
presented themselves to the Plymouth authorities for protection, but
were promptly sold into slavery despite the protests of Benjamin
Church, who had negotiated with them. Prejudice also prompted the
confinement of converted Amerindians in both Plymouth and Massachusetts from the beginning of the war. Plymouth leaders had claimed,
primarily to neighboring colonies before 1661, to be the overlords of
the Wampanoag. Given these pretensions, Philip's rising could be
regarded as a rebellion rather than a war between sovereign enemies.
Europeans did not award their fragile "honors of war" to those they
regarded as defeated rebels. For decades, Philip's head was displayed
on a pike atop the new brick watchtower on Plymouth's Fort Hill. Philip's nine-year-old son escaped execution, but was sold into slavery in
Bermuda. Leading Wampanoag warriors who surrendered their entire
bands to Benjamin Church, who had promised that their lives would
be spared, were summarily killed amid public enthusiasm, and their
followers sold into slavery. The atmosphere was not unlike that in Marblehead, in neighboring Massachusetts, where a group of women beat
and stoned to death two Amerindian prisoners being escorted to jail.[47]
Of the estimated three thousand Amerindians killed in the war, at least
one-quarter were Wampanoag. All the captured, and many of those
who surrendered, were indiscriminately sold into slavery by their individual captors. Children under fourteen were sold into servitude
within the colony until they were twenty-four.[48] Wampanoag society
was entirely destroyed, and few survivors lived in Plymouth. The
aroused citizen armies of New England had once again come to define
victory as "extirpation," and this victory seemed their most complete.

Plymouth colony also paid heavily, though less severely than the
Wampanoag, for the war they had provoked and supposedly won. Of

the farming colony's fourteen towns, three had been completely burned, three extensively damaged, and two others somewhat damaged. Plymouth soldiers suffered twice the casualty rate of the other participating colonies; fully 8 percent of Plymouth's adult males, about one hundred of some thirteen hundred, were killed in the war. Very few of Plymouth's women and children were among the thousand English civilians killed in the entire war, and the war contributed to demographic change in Plymouth. Sex ratios became more equal, women married later, and families were smaller than those of the founding generation. To pay the colony's share of the military costs, taxes in surviving towns increased as much as sixfold at a time when the colony's five thousand people were struggling to rebuild their homes and livelihoods.[49] Philip's lands on Mount Hope peninsula were awarded to Plymouth and promptly sold to outside speculators to help the surviving Plymouth towns with the crushing war costs. King Philip had forced Plymouth into more war than it could afford.

The war inevitably promoted centralization in other ways besides taxation. Defense required coordination of forces and supplies between the remarkably independent towns of Plymouth, as did refugees, prisoners, and land distribution. The general courts of each New England colony gained power during the war, though the United Colonies mechanism could no longer command respect. King Philip's War, like Bacon's Rebellion in Virginia, also attracted the attention of ambitious English colonial administrators intent on closer management of the Empire. Tighter supervision began with an inspection (1676) by the combative English customs official Edward Randolph; developed further with the establishment of the authoritarian Dominion of New England (1686–1689), which combined all English colonies from New York east; and was stabilized with a reformed Massachusetts charter (1691) that included the colony of Plymouth, which had never been granted a charter. Collapsing under taxation for yet another major war and unable to afford the political lobbying needed to ward off this annexation, the colony of Plymouth became a rural Massachusetts county. Within that new county, the palisaded Puritan beachhead itself had become the agricultural town of Plymouth, dispersed over its ample 144-square-mile area.

After King Philip's War, the New England militia vastly outnumbered all potential opponents. Although this militia had not performed particularly effectively, it had "won" its climactic Amerindian war without the intervention of European regulars like the Carignan-Salières Regiment in New France and the English regulars who were still stiffening the authority of Governor Jeffreys in Virginia as he dismembered the colony's rebellious militia. The covenanted militias of New England had not revolted against their colonial governments, despite high losses. Subsequent short-term contracts for

New England's paid military volunteers may have reflected the "contract theory of government" and ensured local control of offensive strategy, but it also limited the painful commitments of not only the soldiers, but also their financially vulnerable governments. The militias of Plymouth, Connecticut, and Massachusetts continued to affect and reflect the comparatively egalitarian social, military, and political features of their communities. However, King Philip's War changed New England warfare. It created a new wilderness between New England towns and Amerindian refugee settlements, thereby separating future warfare more clearly into offensive expeditions by paid armies and local defense by the militia.

The Amerindians had lost much of southern New England by 1677, whatever revenge might be exacted thereafter. It had been an uncommon achievement for the Narragansett and Wampanoag to maintain most of their lands through 150 years of contact with Europeans and their diseases and weapons, and through a half century of colonial settlement. King Philip's War revealed the strengths and weaknesses of Amerindian societies that had adapted well to European invasion. The crucial, and quite unavoidable, military weakness was Amerindian dependence on European arms, ammunition, and gunpowder. The emerging Anglo-French struggle would mask that problem for much of the next eighty years, as the warring colonies vied for Amerindian support.

In its savage dispersal of Amerindians, New England planted the seeds for a century of retaliation much worse than the Susquehannock revenge on the Chesapeake colonies. Defeated New England Algonquian peoples migrated north and west to find refuge among the Mohegan, Mahican, Western Abenaki, and smaller tribes of the Hudson River. Others went north and east to live among, and influence, the harassed but still neutral Pennacook and Pigwacket Abenaki. Although Governor Andros of New York tried to attract refugees by granting asylum, most of the scattering New England Amerindians were entering the Canadian sphere of influence. Refugee bands, some multitribal and all anti-English, established themselves as hunters throughout the Green and White mountains. Many Western Abenaki moved farther north; some joined the Canadian mission communities at St. François and Sillery and continued to attract their displaced relatives. By 1687 there were seven hundred Abenaki at Sillery alone. New England had won a major war, but would face ninety years of revenge.[50]

Chapter 6

DUTCH FORT ORANGE (ALBANY) AND THE FIVE NATIONS 1624–1684

The Dutch invasion of North America offers numerous contrasts with that of other Europeans and is particularly intriguing because of the unique Dutch relationship with a major indigenous power, the Five Nations of the Iroquois. The Spanish could not save the Apalachee from extinction; the English succeeded in Virginia only by destroying the Powhatan. French fur traders were immediately drawn into Amerindian rivalries, yet could not save their valued Huron allies from defeat and dispersal by the Five Nations. In contrast, the Five Nations expanded as a military and economic power in the seventeenth century. Their success, even more than the effective resistance by the peoples of Spanish Florida in the first half of the sixteenth century, is a reminder that European invasions of North America were not automatically a disastrous parade of irresistable disease, alluring consumerism, and overwhelming martial superiority, though the Five Nations would face all these challenges.

The United Netherlands was the economic miracle of seventeenth-century Europe and an unlikely colonizing power. Although still in the middle of an eighty-year war for independence from Spain (1569–1648), this decentralized republic was already the leading commercial power in Europe by 1600. It consisted of seven rebel provinces of the Spanish Netherlands, led politically by Calvinist merchants and manufacturers. Economic opportunity, religious toleration, and refuge from the devastations of the Thirty Years' War (1618–1648) all drew immigrants, including the English Pilgrims, to the Netherlands. Population tripled to 3 million in the century after 1550, and the ordinary people of this burgher culture were the best fed and housed in Europe. The Dutch expanded their crowded land in this period by extending elaborate dikes that reclaimed more than 200,000 acres from the sea.[1]

Amsterdam, the last of Europe's great city-states, provided the majority of the taxes and the economic leadership of a federated state designed to benefit commerce. The city was a prototype of a prosperous plebeian consumer society, pioneering retail specialty shops that showcased the city's dominance in the global chocolate, coffee, fur, spice, sugar, tea, and tobacco trades. Amsterdam was also the entrepôt of western Europe's shipping, printing, banking, insurance, and cloth trade. Dutch seaborne commerce developed from dominance in the North Sea herring fishery to control of the Baltic trades in grain, timber, and naval stores, as well as the Arctic whaling industry. The Dutch dominated shipping on the Rhine and in the ports of western France, Spain, and Portugal. Dutch traders were also prominent in the Mediterranean, though their economically run *fluits* were lightly manned and therefore less defensible against corsairs than were the ships of their English and French commercial rivals. A powerful specialized fleet of war ships, funded by the state to provide convoy protection for Dutch private commerce, was an innovative if predictable merchant solution that revolutionized Europe's naval warfare.[2]

The Dutch fight for independence from Spain became a sporadic global war of raiding and trading, especially after the Spanish monarchy incorporated Portugal in 1580. The Dutch invaded the Portuguese Atlantic empire to become major participants in the slave trades to the Caribbean and Brazil. The Dutch East India Company (1602) captured much of the rich Portuguese trading empire in the Orient and quickly dominated Europe's oceanic commerce with the Far East, especially by monopolizing the production and marketing of Moluccan pepper. A global commercial empire of strategically located trading posts and convoyed merchant fleets served a Dutch people who had the highest standard of living in Europe.

As the Twelve Year Truce (1609–1621) with Spain drew to a close, the governing States General supported venturers urging a more systematic assault on Spain's American empire. The Dutch West India Company, founded as the truce expired, was given a monopoly of Dutch trade and settlement in West Africa and throughout the Americas. Lack of sufficient private investment forced the States General to provide capital and lend men-of-war to what became a branch of public wartime policy as much as a private trading company. A powerful Dutch squadron captured the rich Brazilian capital of San Salvador (Bahia) in 1624, and the diversion of massive Iberian resources to recover that city a year later would allow Dutch, English, and French intruders the opportunity to establish colonies in the eastern Caribbean. The most spectacular and unique Dutch maritime success was the capture of the entire Spanish treasure fleet, including all *flota* and *galeones* and 200,000 pounds of silver, off Cuba in 1628. This capture crippled the Spanish treasury and weakened its war effort in Europe, in addition to affording the Dutch West India Company investors a special 50 percent dividend. Subsequently, Spanish settlements and trade in the Caribbean were scourged by fleets of the Dutch West India Company and by Dutch privateers. The Dutch went on to capture several islands, including Curaçao and St. Eustatius, bases from which illicit trade with Spanish America flourished once persistent raiding became less profitable. It was in the midst of these exploits that the Dutch West India Company established peripheral trading centers at Fort Orange (Albany, New York, 1624), New Amsterdam (New York, 1626), and Fort Nassau (Gloucester, New Jersey, 1626) on the Delaware River.[3]

The Dutch did not need North America. Neither the prosperous, expanding Dutch society nor the profit-oriented Dutch West India Company was inclined to lavish capital, colonists, or soldiers on ventures to a relative economic wilderness. The Dutch were not among the fishing fleets off Newfoundland or Canso, preferring to buy from fishermen on those banks and bays whenever catches in European waters fell low enough to make the voyage profitable. The Dutch led the world in processing and marketing tobacco; they set its prices, sought to buy it in the Chesapeake, but did not develop significant tobacco colonies. The Dutch fur markets did not depend on North America either, as they were stocked by a large and profitable trade with Russia. Like Spain, the Netherlands found North America much less profitable than enterprises elsewhere.[4]

Dutch interest in North America began accidentally in 1609 when Henry Hudson, an English explorer in Dutch pay, tried to redeem his aborted northeasterly passage to the Orient by seeking a passage through North America. After scouting the entrances of both Chesapeake and Delaware bays, Hudson sailed up the Hudson River nearly as far as it was navigable by ocean-going vessels. There, in the vicinity of modern Albany, he traded profitably with the Mahican for beaver and otter pelts. The Mahican were a tribe of hunters and farmers, then numbering approximately sixty-four hundred. Dutch merchant ships arrived annually for this profitable trade until 1614, when a group of Amsterdam merchants called the New Netherlands Company gained a three-year trading monopoly. They constructed a fort on Castle Island, then a defensible, if flood-prone, island and now a part of Albany's western shore. This Fort Nassau measured a mere thirty-six by twenty-six feet and was protected by a stockade, a moat, two cannon, eleven muskets, and an equal number of traders. Both fort and monopoly ended in 1617, but successful clerk-cum-trader Jacob Elkens learned Mahican and Mohawk and stayed to become the leading European fur trader in the area over the next six years.[5]

After forcing Elkens out, the Dutch West India Company built Fort Orange (1624), on the west bank of the Hudson facing the ruins of Fort Nassau. Square Fort Orange was large, with palisaded walls each over five hundred feet in length, but it seldom housed as many as twenty-five traders and an equal number of the company's mercenary soldiers. Eight refugee families from the Spanish Netherlands were brought to provide labor and grow food for the fort, but they were relocated to Manhattan Island two years later for their own safety and that of the company's trading monopoly. From its beginning, Fort Orange was destined to change the distribution of power in the whole region, and particularly that of the Five Nations.

In 1624 the Iroquois Confederacy was roughly comparable to the fellow Iroquoian Huron Confederacy. Each was a league of as many as thirty thousand agricultural peoples, living in palisaded towns containing up to two thousand. Towns were moved at least once in a generation, as cornfields and ready sources of firewood became exhausted. The Five Nation towns, called "castles" by Europeans, had double or triple palisades and elaborate defenses, as Champlain had described a decade earlier. The Huron and the Five Nations shared the "mourning war" tradition. Female relatives of the recently deceased called on their men to ease their mourning by taking enemy prisoners. The prisoners were either adopted to replace the dead or tortured to death as part of completing the mourning process. It is noteworthy that the Five Nations, unlike the Huron, fought nearly all their wars without the help of allies outside their league.

The Five Nations, like the Huron, occupied strategic areas that were located far enough inland to avoid initial direct invasion by the Europeans. The Five Nations controlled the best route across the Appalachian Mountains barrier, the Mohawk River, and Finger Lakes region. Unlike the Huron, the Five Nations were not primarily traders, but used the waterways that flowed out of their region to hunt and raid over a vast area. The Hudson, Delaware, and Susquehanna rivers all invited Five Nations raiders downstream to the south. The Lake Champlain–Richelieu river route and the St. Lawrence invited the Five Nations downstream to the north, while the Allegheny–Ohio river system led downstream into the west as an alternative to the very accessible Great Lakes. A few European trade goods had already reached Iroquoia as early as 1615, from both Jamestown and Québec. In their search for prisoners or pelts, a search that accelerated with the coming of the Dutch, the Five Nations were superbly positioned.[6]

The Iroquois Confederacy was still developing in 1624. It had begun in the sixteenth century as a league of peace between five belligerent, though related, nations: the Seneca, Cayuga, Onondaga, Oneida, and Mohawk. Under this "tree of peace," each tribe, village, clan, and matrilineal family could more safely conduct its own affairs. Europeans exaggerated the political unity among the Five Nations through most of the seventeenth century. The confederacy's elaborate rituals promoted a broad cultural unity, but came to represent fairly unified diplomatic and military power only in response to inter-colonial European conflict toward the end of the century.

For the Five Nations, and especially the Mohawk, the establishment of Fort Orange was a major event in the quest for European weapons and edged tools. Until 1624, they had been at a disadvantage compared with Algonquian and Huron rivals to the north, which was made particularly clear in confrontations that included Champlain and his muskets. Mohawk raiding of Amerindians had proven more effective than trade in acquiring French iron axes and knives. Access to English goods from Virginia was also indirect, since the powerful Susquehannock were belligerent Iroquoian middlemen. Individual Mohawk had been trading with Dutch ships at Fort Nassau from as early as 1614, but did so only by passing through recognized Mahican territory on the west side of the Hudson. Dutch enthusiasm for the excellent furs, which the Mahican acquired from the north in exchange for Dutch-controlled wampum, was troubling for the Mohawk. A rumored Mahican–Algonquin–Huron alliance, with access to both French and Dutch sources of European goods, was a serious threat to the Mohawk. The Mohawk immediately made peace with their Huron and French enemies farther north in order to make war on the Mahican.

The Mohawk–Mahican War (1624–1628) was unquestionably prompted by trading concerns, though these might have been linked to Mohawk military, social, and even demographic fears. The Mohawk succeeded in driving the Mahican east and north of Fort Orange, thereby gaining direct access to the Dutch. The Dutch West India Company's strengthening monopoly of the trade on the upper Hudson was being matched by a growing Mohawk monopoly of access to those Dutch. The Dutch traders at Fort Orange recognized that Mohawk success would encumber trade, but were so powerless that they could only witness the process and evacuate families to the new Manhattan Island fort in 1626.

The weakness of the Dutch was made frightfully clear by the single Dutch attempt to intervene. Commissary Daniel van Krieckenbeeck, a senior trader who had been with the Dutch West India Company on the Hudson for five years, responded to a Mahican request for help in 1628. The Algonquian-speaking Mahican seemed likely to win and offered links to the hunters of the thicker furs of the north. Van Krieckenbeeck and six traders took muskets, but apparently no armor, and accompanied a Mahican war party. This venture proved to be the opposite of Champlain's successful intervention and subsequent prominence in a native alliance. Mohawk armed exclusively with bows and clubs ambushed the Mahican–Dutch war party. Van Krieckenbeeck and three of his companions were killed by arrows, and one of the dead Dutch was roasted and eaten by the victorious Mohawk warriors. Nonetheless, the mutually advantageous relations between the Mohawk and the Dutch were quickly restored. This Dutch defeat prompted extreme caution in Amerindian diplomacy that became characteristic of vulnerable Fort Orange thereafter.[7]

Although the Mohawk–Mahican War severely disrupted the fur trade with New England, trade at Fort Orange thrived. Some 5788 skins were purchased in 1625, 10,000 by 1628, and nearly 30,000 by 1633. There is very little evidence that guns were a part of this early trade with the Mohawk; metal hatchets, knives, hoes, and kettles were understandably prominent, as was wampum. Rapid expansion of the Mohawk trade at Fort Orange intensified trapping in Mohawk territory, which became depleted of furs by 1640. This expanding trade was increasingly dependent on Mohawk capture of Huron and Algonquin fur convoys bound down the Ottawa River to Québec. Significantly, the Mohawk preferred to attack these fur convoys rather than attack the returning shipments of French trade goods. Fort Orange was becoming a fairly comfortable Mohawk hostage, though one that would prosper only as the Mohawk prospered.[8]

The Mohawk were suddenly devastated by the massive smallpox epidemic that struck all the Five Nations and the New England Algonquians in 1633, and the Huron the following year. Of a population of some eighty-one hundred, only two thousand Mohawk survived this initial epidemic. The infection likely came from the small settlement started around Fort Orange in 1630 by Kiliaen van Rensselaer, an Amsterdam diamond merchant and a prominent director of the Dutch West India Company.[9] The terrible Mohawk losses, plus substantial losses among the neighboring tribes, reduced the entire Five Nations by at least half their numbers and provoked a ferocious cultural response. In keeping with the mourning war tradition, women demanded captives to replace their dead. The Five Nations and their northern enemies all suffered from epidemics in the 1630s, and the subsequent generation of intensifying intertribal warfare owed something to the need to rebuild populations.[10] Mohawk success at repopulation was vital to their tribal survival and to the prosperity of the Dutch traders at Fort Orange.

Dutch and Mohawk needs led them into a closer alliance. The diminished Mohawk faced new threats to their fur raiding after the French established both Montréal and Fort Richelieu in 1642. Sale of Dutch firearms to the Mohawk had certainly been a temptation that increased after the Dutch West India Company's monopoly on the fur trade at Rensselaerwyck had ended in 1639. Draconian punishment for gun traders, by both the company and the settlement, indicated that such trading had occurred. Suddenly, between 1643 and 1645, the Mohawk acquired as many as four hundred Dutch muskets, apparently with the approval of Governor Willem Kieft of New Netherlands.[11] Governor Kieft favored arming the Mohawk in order to use them in an entirely different world of Dutch–Indian relations, the contrasting if predictable world of inter-racial conflict on the lower Hudson River.

At the principal Dutch settlement of New Amsterdam (New York, 1626), relations with the small Amerindian tribes of farmers had begun with mutually beneficial food and land purchases, as well as fur trading. As the furs declined and Dutch farming increased, predictable tensions similar to those in Virginia developed between company, settlers, and Amerindians. The company was having financial difficulties, and

Kieft sought to offset local fortification costs and payments to some sixty company soldiers by taxing neighboring Amerindians "in peltries, maize or wampum." Spasmodic raiding and counter-raiding, particularly between harvest and planting, began in 1640. In February 1643, a party of eighty to ninety Mohawk, newly armed with muskets, came south and attacked several bands who had resisted paying tribute to Kieft. At least seventeen defenders, armed only with bows and arrows, were killed, and women and children were carried away for adoption into the Mohawk tribe. Hundreds of terrified refugees relocated in two camps closer to the Dutch. With Kieft's approval and considerable support from the settlers, Dutch soldiers and settlers surrounded and attacked both camps on a single night. In these attacks, between 80 and 120 Amerindians were killed without regard for age or sex, and 30 others were enslaved. Retaliatory raids increased through the year; by autumn, an estimated 1500 warriors from eleven small tribes in the vicinity intensified their raiding of outlying Dutch settlements. The Dutch colony could counter with only 60 soldiers and 250 male settlers, including 50 English from Long Island.

The well-armed but cumbersome colonial winter expeditions ransacked and burned deserted Amerindian villages, but seldom saw their inhabitants.[12] One important exception occurred in March 1644. Captain John Underhill, veteran of New England's Pequot War, led 130 men on a night attack against a major Tankiteke or Siwanoy village. Using tactics borrowed from the Pequot War, Underhill's musketeers encircled the village, killed an estimated 180 with initial gunfire, then set fire to the buildings and slaughtered those trying to escape. The Amerindians estimated that they lost some five hundred people in this unequal battle between bowmen and encircling armored musketeers; the Europeans had several wounded, but only one killed.[13] The martial advantage of massed and armored musketeers against those who could not flee had been proven once again. A thousand Amerindians died before the five-year war ended, and the colony of New Amsterdam was also diminished by death, emigration, and disruption of trade and farming.

Peace for New Amsterdam began at Fort Orange in July 1645, with a friendship treaty with both the Mohawk and the Mahican. A second treaty, signed in New Amsterdam at the end of the following month, brought peace with other tribes, mediated by the Mohawk.[14] The Mohawk would help the Dutch solve similar problems a decade later, but the immediate Mohawk preoccupation was raiding for captives and furs to the north.

The celebrated mid-century "Wars of the Iroquois" are too easily seen as a unified explosion of the Five Nations, shattering rivals to the north, west, and south. Internal Five Nation military cooperation was impressive, with headmen and warriors from any village in the confederacy able to participate in the initiatives of any tribe. However, there were powerful rivalries for captives, trade, and prestige, particularly among the three larger tribes, or "elder brothers": the Seneca, Onondaga, and Mohawk. The Seneca, "keepers of the western gate," had special advantages. Being farther inland, they had suffered less than the Mohawk in the epidemics of the 1630s, though they would be harder hit in the 1660s. They were best positioned to expand their lands, people, and fur sources westward in wars that would destroy, disperse, or incorporate their fellow Iroquoian Huron (1649), Petun (1650), Neutral (1651), Erie (1657), and, eventually, Susquehannock (1680). The Onondaga, "keepers of the council fire," were at the geographical, ritual, and prestigious center of the confederacy, somewhat insulated from both the threats and the opportunities available to the east or west, but concerned about frontiers to the north and south. The Mohawk, "keepers of the eastern gate," had power over the Five Nations access to Fort Orange and had the best supply of muskets, gunpowder, and ammunition. However, because their Amerindian neighbors were allied with Europeans and also supplied with firearms, Mohawk expansion was much more difficult.

The Mohawk used their Dutch muskets in larger and more frequent raids on Huron fur convoys after 1642, and four years later, both the Mohawk and the Seneca were recruiting among all the Five Nations for outright war against the Huron. In March 1649, the two tribes combined to deliver the crucial blow that prompted the disintegration of the Huron Confederacy. While the Seneca expanded westward in the wake of this triumph, the Mohawk focused on a northern war: against remnant Huron, particularly at Lorette (1651); against the exposed Algonquin, who were driven from the Ottawa Valley for a generation; and against New France. The Mohawk successfully separated the French from their allies for several years after the peace of 1653. Mohawk raids on the Huron, Algonquin, and Ottawa yielded prisoners for adoption and captured furs that helped push Fort Orange's exports to a record high of forty-six thousand beaver and otter pelts per year in 1656 and 1657. This Dutch trade with the Mohawk grew with mourning wars and with Mohawk need for Dutch guns, gunpowder, and lead.[15]

The Mohawk and the Dutch helped each other more directly in the renewed Five Nations contest with the Susquehannock to the south. This antagonism climaxed in a bloody but indecisive battle in 1652, from which the Mohawk are said to have returned with five hundred to six hundred captives.[16] A parallel Dutch rivalry with the Swedes, who had established a small trading colony at Fort Christina (1638) on the Delaware River and had armed the Susquehannock, escalated when the Swedes unwisely captured the nearby Dutch post of New Amstel (New Castle, Delaware, 1651) in 1654. Pieter Stuyvesant, who had replaced Kieft as director-general of New Netherlands, counterattacked the Swedes the following year with a force of seven ships and 317 soldiers, prompting a sensible Swedish surrender and causing the Susquehannock to develop their fateful connection with English Maryland.

While Stuyvesant and his army were busy on the Delaware, a war erupted in New Amsterdam itself, involving resentful local Hackensack and Wecquaesgeek tribes and others from as far away as the Esopus River Valley, halfway up the Hudson. Fifty settlers were killed and a hundred prisoners were taken in what was apparently an unplanned massacre. Outlying Dutch plantations were abandoned, as was the new Dutch settlement of Esopus (Kingston, New York, 1652), resented by the neighboring River Indians. Three years later, it became a scene of violence when settlers returned. Stuyvesant tried to restrain these Dutch and protect them in a garrisoned village, but the settlers soon provoked a brief siege by five hundred warriors in 1659, and there were other major incidents in 1661 and 1663. Although the Dutch eventually won peace (1664) by repeatedly burning Amerindian crops and villages, they twice asked the Mohawk to "advise" the other Amerindians, and helped the Mohawk mount an attack on these determined opponents after Stuyvesant had isolated them diplomatically. The attack was half-hearted, however, as the Mohawk were once more preoccupied with war against New France.[17]

By the time war with New France resumed in 1659, the Mohawk had lost their firearms advantage over their Amerindian enemies. Their raids against New France peaked in 1661, and the Mohawk suffered defeats at the hands of both Mahican and Ottawa in 1662. In 1663 they failed to overpower the English-armed Western Abenaki (1663), and other Five Nation armies failed against the Susquehannock and Delaware. The Mohawk expanded their raiding range to include attacks against the Algonquians of New England. In 1664 they entirely destroyed the Pocumtuck, who had occupied the site of what would soon be the vulnerable English frontier town of Deerfield, Massachusetts (1669).[18] These wars with the New England Algonquians, which provoked retaliatory raids on Mohawk towns, would continue for another decade, but the Mohawk prudently avoided confronting the better-armed French, Canadian, Algonquin, and Huron army that invaded and burned all four Mohawk towns in 1666. The towns were due for their periodic migration, and the Mohawk rebuilt a little closer to the Dutch.[19]

Although they were the most in need of it by 1667, the Mohawk were the last of the Five Nations to make peace with New France. The Mohawk had adopted so many prisoners of war that they were a minority in their own towns. Increasing casualties in musket battles and recurring epidemics had made it hard to maintain the post-epidemic population of about two thousand, even before the emigration of Christian Mohawks to Canada.[20]

The Dutch of New Netherlands also had demographic limitations that were aggravated by Amerindian war and became more troubling as the Anglo-Dutch rivalry escalated in Europe and America. The Netherlands of this "Golden Age" was attracting immigration, not promoting emigration to marginal American wildernesses. Stuyvesant's entire colony numbered only four thousand by 1650, and about one-third of these were unruly English settlers linked to twenty-three thousand more farther to the east in New England. Although Stuyvesant sought Amerindian alliance against the English, as well as English alliance against the Amerindians, he achieved neither.

Stuyvesant negotiated his way through the First Anglo-Dutch War (1652–1654) with little direct loss, though Captain Underhill led an unsuccessful English revolt on Long Island, then led the capture of the House of Good Hope (Hartford, 1632) on the Connecticut River.[21] The Sedgwick squadron, which reached Boston too late to attack New Netherlands before peace arrived, was a more ominous threat that evaporated into piratical raids on French Acadian bases. Belligerent English naval power, which also captured Spanish Jamaica before declaring war (1655–1660), was one threat to New Netherlands; New Englanders' ambitions on the Connecticut River and Long Island were another.

The Second Anglo-Dutch War (1665–1667) included America more directly than had any previous European contest. Maritime commercial rivalries had led to incidents in the Baltic, West Africa, and the East Indies. In 1664 the English government of restored King Charles II (r. 1660–1685) initiated hostilities with predatory raids on Dutch colonies during a time of peace. One naval squadron captured most of the Dutch slaving forts and numerous ships along the West African coast. Another squadron of three men-of-war and three hundred soldiers was sent under Major Richard Nicolls to take New Netherlands. The financially embarrassed Dutch West India Company had heard of the preparations, but told Stuyvesant that the squadron's only purpose was to discipline New England. When the fleet reached New Amsterdam in August 1664, Stuyvesant had only 150 soldiers to defend a dilapidated fort and a town vulnerable to naval bombardment. The burgher militia of some 250 men flatly refused to fight against the English fleet. Stuyvesant surrendered without firing a single shot. Sir George Cartwright sailed up the Hudson to Fort Orange, which also surrendered readily to those who controlled the river and who agreed to continue that settlement's monopoly of the fur trade. The Five Nations promptly signed a treaty that promised both continued trade and alliance. New Amsterdam became New York, and Fort Orange became Albany, named for the English king's younger brother, the duke of York and Albany, who had already been granted the conquest as a personal proprietary colony.[22]

The tiny Dutch West India Company garrison on the Delaware River at New Amstel offered the only resistance to English confiscation. Sir

Robert Carr arrived aboard the forty-gun HMS *Guinea*, accompanied by an armed merchant-vessel and more than one hundred English regulars. Following instructions from Nicolls, Carr persuaded most of the settlers to accept excellent surrender terms, thereby isolating the fort. Governor Alexander d'Hinoyossa refused to surrender the fourteen-gun wooden fort or his thirty-man garrison. After a brief naval barrage, the English quickly overran a fort built for protection against forces without cannon. The English soldiers and sailors then looted the fort, the Dutch West India Company storehouse, as well as the houses and farms of those who had not surrendered earlier. Three of the Dutch garrison were killed and ten wounded in the attack, which produced no English casualties. Carr, who appropriated and redistributed some choice lands, reportedly sold the Dutch garrison into servitude in Virginia.[23]

The Dutch proceeded to reclaim vital Atlantic commercial and colonial interests in response to this English aggression, but showed no interest in New York. Admiral Michiel Adriaanszoon De Ruyter (1607–1676) circled the North Atlantic in 1665, retaliating in West Africa, attacking Barbados, and raiding commerce in the Leeward Islands and at Newfoundland. A small Dutch privateering squadron later captured an eighteen-vessel English tobacco convoy on the James River in Virginia. The French joined the Dutch in 1666, capturing and looting the English West Indian colonies on St. Christopher's, Antigua, and Montserrat. The English court encountered political and fiscal difficulties in 1666, as well as the panic caused by the plague and the Great Fire of London. In 1667 they were unable to fit out their battle fleet, and the best of it was lost when the Dutch raided the Medway River dockyards in June 1667. The Peace of Breda was concluded a month later. The English returned the Dutch West Indian sugar island of Surinam, and the Dutch readily confirmed English possession of New York.

The Five Nations had been deeply disturbed by the English conquest of New Netherlands, despite assurances from the duke of York's governor, Richard Nicolls. Dependent on European weapons that allowed them to take captives and furs from a host of enemies, the Five Nations found themselves relying on the little-known and less liked English. The English of Maryland had armed the Susquehannock enemies of the Five Nations, and the English of Connecticut and Massachusetts had armed the Mahican and Abenaki enemies to the east. With both Swedish and Dutch traders eliminated, the only alternative supplier of guns, lead, and gunpowder was the French, with whom the Five Nations were once again at war.

Five Nations village councils and increasingly frequent intertribal meetings of village headmen gradually developed three alternative strategies, each of which would be tried in turn over the next generation. The first option was to make peace with the French and their allies, revolutionizing a traditional position. The second option was to rely on the Dutch traders who still dominated the fur trade in English Albany, assuming that interest and circumstance would preserve the existing rivalries between the regions and peoples. If Albany functioned as Fort Orange had done, there would be few Christian missionaries invading to foment faction in tribes still trying to integrate so many adoptees. The final option was to seek a more risky independent position between the English and the French, affording competitive trade with each. Although access to the trade of both Québec and Albany had been a Mohawk objective earlier, this option now drew the least support.[24]

Those leaders of the Five Nations who promoted the first option initially gained the largest following. The disruption at Fort Orange and the arrival of the Carignan-Salières Regiment in Canada led four of the Five Nations to make peace with New France by 1665, and the Mohawk accepted peace after the burning of their villages the following year. Although there were Mohawk supporters of this peace, the pro-French position lessened both Mohawk prestige within the league and the power they derived from controlling access to Albany. The Onondaga headmen, particularly the orator Daniel Garacontié, emerged as the leaders of Five Nation–French diplomacy.

The Jesuit missionaries, ousted from Iroquoia in 1658, returned as one of the terms of the French peace and as a traditional Iroquoian exchange of visitors between new friends. Garacontié, who had been instrumental earlier in inviting and protecting French missionaries and captives, smoothed the way for the Jesuits. The Jesuits were also welcomed back by Christians among the Five Nations, including some adopted Huron. As Five Nations martial fortunes faltered in the 1660s, the Jesuits also represented alternative "medicine" to interested Iroquois, and even those who were unimpressed saw the priests as hostages whose presence limited the likelihood of French duplicity. Prominent converts included the leading Mohawk chiefs Assendassé and Kryn (Togouiroui), as well as Garacontié, whose baptism in Québec in 1670 was celebrated with public festivities organized by his godfather, Governor Courcelle. The Jesuits had considerable success in the decade after 1668, baptizing some four thousand of the Five Nations. Although half of these were the less-demanding conversions of those near death, the others represented about 20 percent of the entire Five Nations and even more among the Mohawk.[25]

As in the case of the Huron, conversions divided the Five Nations, since the Jesuits had not reduced the social segregation they demanded of converts. In the late 1660s, a few Five Nations Christians began migrating closer to the French, and the Jesuits pursued another alternative somewhat like the New England "praying towns." Christian Amerindian communities were segregated from both their "heathen" tribesmen and those white sinners whose behavior mocked Christianity. The predominantly Mohawk mission of Caughnawaga (Kahnawake) grew into a community of some six hundred by 1682, while another fifty joined the Christian Huron at Lorette. Some 160 Amerindians, including Five Nations Iroquois, were at the Lac des Deux Montagnes (Oka) mission by 1680. These migrations were often led by women, who drew their kin and spread family connections in ways that would affect trade and war for generations. Also transformed were the Five Nations communities they left; those who were not favorably inclined to the French became more dominant in villages from which pro-French emigrants had departed.

The Five Nations were also growing closer to the French in another way in the decade 1665 to 1675. Under attack by the Susquehannock, a number of Seneca, Cayuga, and Oneida families migrated into the former Huron hunting grounds on the north shore of Lake Ontario. These *Iroquois du nord* established at least six villages by 1670, welcoming French fur traders and, initially, missionaries. These Five Nations hunters appeared to be building a new trade route to Montréal. However, they were upsetting Ottawa allies of New France and were also accused by the newly expansionist French of extending the trading territory of Albany.[26]

Count Frontenac, the fur-monopolizing new governor of New France, took four hundred men up the St. Lawrence to the Five Nations village of Cataraqui (Kingston, Ontario) for a conference in 1673, during which his men converted a choice campsite into palisaded Fort Cataraqui (Fort Frontenac). Frontenac's timing was most fortunate. The English and French were momentarily allies in a new war against the Dutch in Europe (1672–1674). Within days of the completion of Fort Frontenac, both New York and Albany surrendered to a Dutch fleet as readily as they had surrendered to the English a decade earlier. The resulting disruption of trade goods and prices at Albany made the new French fort valuable to the Five Nations during the year before an Anglo-Dutch peace returned New York to the English. The palisades and earthworks of Fort Frontenac gave substance to the new Franco–Five Nation ties, but this fort soon came to represent aggressive French competition in the rapidly developing fur trade farther west.[27]

Traditionalist Iroquois, some of whom became pro-English, gradually gained political dominance in the league's villages in the decade after 1674. These traditionalists favored Albany as the less intrusive source of now essential weapons, as they had seen the cultural disruption that the French missionaries had brought to the Huron and to the Five Nations themselves. The English at Albany showed as little interest in religious missions as had the Dutch. Naturally, the Mohawk saw special merit in this, the second option, since it strengthened their place in the league. The Albany traders, led by the accomplished friend of the Mohawk, Pieter Schuyler, gave every encouragement. The western tribes of the league were attracted to this position after the French built

Fort Niagara in 1676, and Franco-Iroquoian fur rivalry spread quickly up the Great Lakes to the Ohio and upper Mississippi valleys.

Five Nations ambitions fitted well with those of the duke of York's energetic and authoritarian new soldier-governor, Major Edmund Andros, who had arrived at New York with over a hundred garrison troops to reclaim the colony in October 1674. He secured the town of New York using the forty-six cannon of repaired Fort James and six hundred flintlocks to defend, as well as to intimidate, the town's fifteen hundred people, about twelve hundred of whom were Dutch. His assignment was to assert the duke's fulsome claims from the Delaware Valley to Maine, against Dutch, French, and English competitors. His ambition was to make New York dominant among the fractious English colonies.

The Amerindians of New England, the Chesapeake, and New York proved crucial to Andros's considerable success. King Philip's War in New England created one opportunity. Bacon's Rebellion, provoked by Susquehannock guerrilla war with Maryland and Virginia, eventually created another. The Five Nations of New York helped Andros, while helping themselves to arms, furs, and adoptees. By 1678 the Five Nations had some claim on all the lands they had raided, from Maine to Huronia, the Ohio, and the Carolinas. Thereafter, English authorities indulged all these pretensions because the English, in turn, claimed sovereignty over the Five Nations. The English would spend the next ninety years conquering most of this world claimed by their Five Nation allies.[28]

The New England war had spread to the upper Connecticut Valley by the autumn of 1675, and Philip's numerous Mahican allies traded loot for gunpowder at Albany before wintering in the vicinity. Andros, called *Corlaer* in honor of a beloved Dutch settler, supplied the Mohawk with guns, food, and clothing, as well as shelter at Albany for their families, in return for a Mohawk attack on Philip's winter camp on the Hoosack River. The attack scattered and demoralized the estimated twenty-one hundred warriors gathered there. Hundreds of these Algonquian fugitives accepted Andros's offer of asylum, from both the irate New Englanders and the aggressive Mohawk, in return for forfeiting Christian prisoners and settling on New York's unguarded eastern frontier. These refugees, and subsequent Mohawk raids against the Abenaki, were part of Andros's defense of the duke of York's claims in a war that had quickly become an English inter-colonial scramble for "conquered" Amerindian land. For the Mohawk and the rest of the Five Nations, this cooperation brought the defeat of the rival Mahican, victory over New England enemies, and security to the east, allowing more ambitious expansion westward supported by an arms supply that henceforth proved reliable and reasonably priced at Albany.[29]

The Five Nations and Andros also benefited from the disruption of the Susquehannock, first by Five Nations armies and then by Chesapeake colonial militias in the autumn of 1675. Andros attempted to lure the scattered remnants of this martial Iroquoian tribe to join "his" Mohawk. At Garacontié's insistence, the Susquehannock were absorbed into the Seneca and Onondaga tribes by 1680, and the latter claimed the Susquehanna Valley. These successful Five Nations bidders had apparently promised to assist the Susquehannock in revenge raids to the south in return for their participation in an Onondaga campaign against the Illinois. The Five Nations welcomed the destruction of another great enemy and the stabilization of their southern borders, as preliminary to initiatives against French expansion to the west. Andros did not succeed in having the Susquehannock join the Mohawk, but he was able to use his place in Five Nation diplomacy to advantage in dealing with the English colonies of the Chesapeake, as he had done with New England.[30] To acquire Susquehannock lands or negotiate an end to raids, Chesapeake officials were forced to meet with the Five Nations, and to do so exclusively through Andros at Albany.

With their eastern and southern frontiers relatively secure, with most of the *Iroquois du nord* back in Iroquoia, and with the adopted Susquehannock ready to prove themselves as Seneca and Onondaga warriors, the Five Nations moved toward confrontation with the new French trading empire in the west. French forts at Cataraqui (1673) and Niagara (1676) had been followed by La Salle's building of an armed merchant ship on Lake Erie (1679). Although the ship was soon lost, it displayed the potential strength of La Salle's entry into the carriage of furs from the Great Lakes hinterlands. Bypassing Amerindian carriers who had previously brokered the spread of arms to the Illinois and Sioux of the interior, La Salle's "explorations" included trading flintlocks for furs. The increasingly powerful Illinois, a loose confederation of a dozen tribes who had numbered approximately 10,500 in 1670, were migrating eastward, seeking furs and French weapons in what the Five Nations regarded as their Ohio Valley. The great Illinois village of Kaskaskias, for instance, had 74 dwellings in 1673, and 460 by the time La Salle visited in 1679.[31]

Some five hundred Five Nations Iroquois, including the newly acquired Susquehannock, attacked Kaskaskias in September 1680. Most of the Illinois warriors possessing flintlocks were absent, but the few hundred who remained parleyed and defended the town with bows and arrows long enough to allow its evacuation. La Salle's lieutenant, Henri Tonty, was trading there at the time; he was wounded while trying to negotiate with the attackers, but released when the Seneca realized he was French. The capture and destruction of the empty town was less rewarding than the attack on Illinois who were hunting in the vicinity, which yielded some furs, thirty scalps, and three hundred women and children as prisoners. The returning victors showed an uncharacteristic lack of discipline that has been attributed by some to frustration and by others to the limited acculturation of the Susque-hannock among them. The Five Nations attacked two small encampments of neutral Miami and then kept the prisoners as well as their substantial ransom of three thousand beaver pelts, thereby permanently damaging prospects of a useful alliance with these six thousand estranged relatives of the Illinois. Another major raid in 1682 brought a reported seven hundred Illinois prisoners into Iroquoia.

These raids did not disperse the Illinois, conquer the area, or expel the French. A large Five Nations army lost several hundred warriors in a battle with the Ojibwa and Fox in 1683. La Salle's Fort St. Louis of the Illinois was built in 1682, attracting trade, alliance, and the settlement of Illinois, Miami, and Shawnee. The Seneca besieged the fort in March 1684, but forty-six French and Amerindians held them off for six days, then drove the Seneca away with considerable losses and allowed most of their prisoners to escape. Hearing of the siege, but not its outcome, Governor Joseph-Antoine Le Febvre de La Barre of New France prepared a retaliatory expedition directly against the Seneca villages.

The Five Nations, who had lost several hundred of their numbers since 1679, were rethinking their strategy for countering the French.[32] As some Seneca went to meet La Barre's army, others joined their fellow Iroquois at Albany late in July for a major conference with the governor of New York, Thomas Dongan, and the governor of Virginia, who was seeking an end to sporadic attacks on Virginia colonists and Amerindians. Although England and France were at peace, and La Barre had solicited fellow Roman Catholic Dongan's neutrality, Dongan told La Barre that an attack on the Seneca was an invasion of the duke of York's territory. Dongan also presumptuously warned the Five Nations not to make any agreements without his approval. The Five Nations politely asserted their diplomatic freedom at the conference, voicing their doubts that copies of the duke of York's coat of arms, which Dongan had given them to mount at the entrances to their towns, would suffice to ward off the French. Dongan's empty pretensions only confirmed the Five Nations in their decision to negotiate once more with La Barre.[33]

The Onondaga delegation that outwitted La Barre at La Famine (Salmon River, New York) in September 1684 was led by the neutralist orator and diplomat Otreouti (Grangula). He was known as a ferocious raider against the French and had also been outraged by Dongan's claims. La Barre opened proceedings by threatening invasion. The Five Nations knew that his force of eleven hundred *troupes de la marine*, militia, and Amerindians had been entirely debilitated by an epidemic, and Otreouti dismissed La Barre's bluff. Surprisingly, La Barre then accepted Otreouti as mediator of the differences between the Seneca and the French (Figure 6). La Barre, who was unsympathetic to La Salle's western empire and anxious to profit from a trade based in Mon-

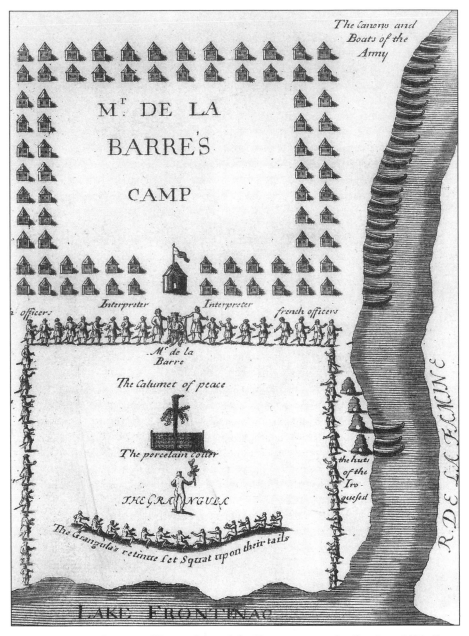

Figure 6. Otreouti (Grangula) and La Barre meet at La Famine, 1684. From Louis-Armand de Lom d'Arce, baron de Lahontan, *New Voyages to North America . . .* (London, 1703). (Courtesy of The Library Company of Philadelphia)

tréal, completely abandoned his Illinois allies to the Five Nations in return for Seneca compensation for direct attacks on the French. The Onondaga also offered a covenant chain between the French and themselves. Such Five Nations power, including both French and English allies, was politically and economically unacceptable in Montréal, Québec, and Paris, where La Barre was ridiculed and dismissed and his treaty was rejected as craven. Such a notion was also contrary to the real-estate ambitions of Dongan and the duke of York, who were not about to share the Five Nations world with the French. The road to Five Nations neutrality would be long and difficult, taking them through a fierce Franco-Iroquoian war that merged with the first Anglo-French inter-colonial war.[34]

The Five Nations had survived, adapted, and prospered in the seventeenth century, compared with other indigenous peoples of eastern North America. Warfare, to replace the dead with prisoners, had produced more dead, but martial success had nearly maintained population levels and the supply of captured pelts paid for weapons. The Five Nations were able to fight without allies, thereby avoiding some dependences, surprises, and disappointments. This approach made the comparatively unadventuresome Albany fur traders suitable as arms suppliers. Although both the Dutch and the English displayed their belligerence as land-hungry settlers farther down the Hudson, the Dutch of Albany had a symbiotic relationship with the Five Nations. The English *Corlaer*, for his own reasons, accepted the same role and supported increases in the range and size of Five Nations raids. All other English colonies, to defend themselves against these raids and New York territorial claims, were being drawn into Five Nations diplomacy centered in Albany.

 Albany was still a transplanted Dutch town in 1684. A total of 2144 were included in a 1687 census of the town and its hinterland, nearly a fifth of the population of the whole colony. Males (1166) outnumbered females (978) only slightly in this atypical "frontier town," and children matched adults in number. Only one household in twenty was non-Dutch European, and all the 157 black slaves lived on farms near the town. After the *stadhuis*, or city hall, bell announced that the town gates would be locked for the night, visiting Amerindians other than known Mohawk or Mahican, and sachems of other tribes, stayed in cabins provided by the town outside its palisaded walls. The town's substantial but unpretentious houses, mostly one-and-a-half story stone and brick, were huddled at the front of their lots to make a rather egalitarian and dense townscape[35] (Figure 7).

The merchants, or *handelaars*, appropriately provided the name of the main street that paralleled the Hudson and gave their burgher values to the town. The town's monopoly of the fur trade had been repeatedly secured and reinforced, most recently by Governor Andros in

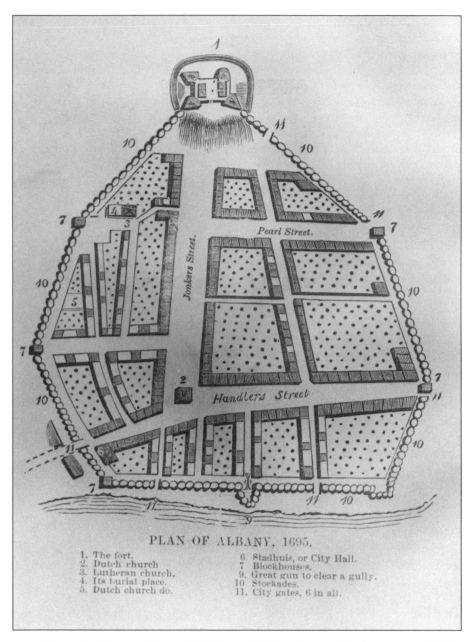

PLAN OF ALBANY, 1695.

1. The fort.
2. Dutch church
3. Lutheran church,
4. Its burial place.
5. Dutch church do.

6. Stadhuis, or City Hall.
7. Blockhouses.
9. Great gun to clear a gully.
10. Stockades.
11. City gates, 6 in all.

Figure 7. Plan of Albany, 1695. From William Barnes, *The Settlement and Early History of Albany* (Albany, N.Y., 1864). (Courtesy of Burton Historical Collection, Detroit Public Library)

1676. Only residents of the town could trade without paying discriminatory taxes, and all trading was to be done in the town during daylight. The *handelaars* had profited greatly during King Philip's War, which had disrupted their Connecticut competitors. Price advantages over French competitors for the Amerindian fur trade remained substantial, though the trade dwindled to a mere fourteen thousand pelts in 1687, as European markets for beaver deteriorated with the end of the vogue for beaver hats. Farming around Albany was beginning as an alternative to the fur trade, but was hampered by heavy soils, Amerindian ownership, and New York City's grain and flour export monopoly, which was the established quid pro quo for Albany's fur monopoly.[36]

Albany's substantial *stadhuis* proclaimed local priorities to arrivals entering by the busiest of the six town gates. Not only was this where local magistrates made and enforced trading ordinances, but it was also the site of English–Amerindian conferences. These meetings were conducted to the advantage of the Mohawk within the Five Nations, the New York government within the English colonies, and the town of Albany within New York. A group of young Dutch merchants, led by Pieter Schuyler, had its political and economic power confirmed as the "English" caretakers of the Five Nations alliance even before the town received its charter in 1686 and Schuyler became mayor. Mohawk was the language of these conferences, and all translators were non-English-speaking Dutch. Since English governors for the next half century suspected that the Dutch were exploiting this situation, they relied heavily on Robert Livingston, an ambitious Dutch-speaking Scot who was town clerk and secretary for Indian affairs from 1675 to 1722.[37]

Compared with the *stadhuis* or with the religious architecture of Québec, church buildings were not prominent in a town that did not emphasize religion in its Indian diplomacy. A small Lutheran chapel on the periphery of Albany reflected Dutch religious tolerance. Although the Calvinist Dutch Reformed church was adequate and centrally located, it faced up broad Jonkers Street to the fort dominating the hill.

Fort Albany stood on a hill some seven hundred feet above the Hudson, commanding, more than protecting, this twice-conquered Dutch town. Governor Andros had personally overseen the building of the fort in 1676, to replace decaying Fort Orange, which had been closer to the Hudson and better located to command the river. The new fort had four bastions capable of mounting twenty-four cannon, though only nine were in place in 1687. The defensive wooden palisade of the fort and the town appeared more Iroquoian than Dutch, and needed regular renewal because, in most locations, buried timbers rotted within a few years. The English garrison varied between twenty and one hundred men; there were muskets for forty of them in 1687. The garrison commander had joined the magistrates in governing Albany by 1684, but the fort was no longer the site of Amerindian conferences. However, the structure represented the military dominance that Andros and the duke of York had attempted to impose on the colony and the English empire.[38]

This paltry military presence, which the townspeople could regard as less intimidating than the Dutch West India Company troops of a generation earlier, was a reminder that this town and colony defended itself with hired mercenaries rather than a burgher militia. The English military officers were among the first importers of gentry values that would gradually supersede those of the town's merchants. The soldiers were also harbingers of Albany's profitable future as a military staging point, supply base, and headquarters in the Anglo-French wars that were about to begin.

Part II

COLONIES AND TRIBES
1687–1748

A new phase in the invasions of North America began as the Anglo-French contest for dominance developed. Elements of the earlier phase continued in frontier areas, often masked as aspects of this new and broader contest, but the Amerindian and European players were changing, as were the methods and objectives of war. An odd new balance of inter-colonial power emerged amid these convulsions.

Earlier approaches continued from new bases, including Charlestown, Mobile, Detroit, New Orleans, Savannah, and Halifax. Tribes of the Mississippi Valley and of the Great Plains now confronted the challenges of Europe's microbes, trade goods, religions, firearms, and farmers with the same range of responses and results evident earlier in the east. Some fought until nearly annihilated, like the Yamasee and Fox, or until achieving coexistence, like the Creek and Cherokee. Some tribes migrated and coalesced to form new powers like the Catawba Nation, strengthened surviving confederacies like the Five Nations, or joined mission communities like La Présentation. Amerindian communities long familiar with these challenges were still being changed by them.

Warfare for North America was being transformed during the last quarter of the seventeenth century. Amerindian peoples who had survived the virgin land epidemics were somewhat less vulnerable to disease, were experienced with European trade and diplomacy, and were increasingly armed with the same flintlocks, knives, and hatchets as their colonial neighbors. These Amerindian survivors formed a buffer, though not necessarily a friendly one, between European bases and the tribes still entering this new world of trade and war. The Anglo-French contest could bring new power and opportunities for Amerindians, while their growing dependence on European firearms and gunpowder was masked by the diplomatic courtship of powers with apparently inexhaustible supplies of both. Bounties on scalps and prisoners revived profitable hunting where game had become scarce; fighting as allies or mercenaries offered new sources of tribal income. Using French allies in attacking the English could enhance revenge, respect, and profit, though it could also bring death. The Anglo-French wars would prove better for many Amerindians than the wars that preceded them or the periods of "peace" that punctuated them.

Most colonial-born Europeans, who now constituted a majority of the expanding white populations in most colonies, were no longer fighting from fragile bases of settlement; they had developed some immunities to the diseases of their areas, and most communities were self-sufficient or even exporting food. Nonetheless, frontier towns and garrisons remained subject to Amerindian attacks reminiscent of earlier times, and garrison houses and militias were prepared in deadly earnest. The resources for the new wars were, however, drawn primarily from people who were seldom directly threatened. Increasingly, their wars involved expeditions and patrols by paid volunteers or voyages by sailors turned privateers. Marshaling these resources centralized political and economic power on a scale impossible earlier; colonies, and even empires, became functional in unprecedented ways.[1]

Why was the Anglo-French contest for North America so long, so intermittent, and so indecisive before 1748? One of the most obvious factors is that neither the British nor the French had been fighting in or for North America during these years. To these European powers, the North American theater was an insignificant sideshow to a much more vital and expensive European main event. A single battle around the little French village of Malplaquet in 1709 was fought by 190,000 men, more than participated in the entire Anglo-French struggle for North America. The duke of Marlborough, in charge of England's troops through most of the War of the Spanish Succession, was typical in opposing expeditions to the colonies. To his wife, Sarah, he confided:

> [I]t can end in nothing but a great expence and the ruining of those regiments. Besides, nothing can be done there [that] will forward the peace; and if we can be so fortunate as to force them here, we may have by one dash of a pen much more than any expeditions can give in many years.[2]

There was irony, and false hope, in the English colonial names for the three major wars of this period: King William's War (War of the League of Augsburg, 1689–1697), Queen Anne's War (War of the Spanish Succession, 1702–1713), and King George's War (War of the Austrian Succession, 1744–1748). Both kings had personal interests in Europe that ensured England's preoccupation with European wars, and Queen Anne could not alter these priorities. The North American wars were fought primarily by and for colonists and Amerindians; most major European interventions only confirmed Marlborough's judgment.

There were two times in each war when the imperial governments showed interest in the colonies. Each declaration of war provoked a race to exploit that news with a quickly assembled invasion of a particularly valuable sugar island in the West Indies, like the French conquest of the English portions of St. Kitt's in 1689 or the English retaliation in 1702. The other time when colonies attracted attention was during peace negotiations. Fighting in the colonies would not seriously jeopardize negotiations, and might yield a fortress or colony valuable enough to affect the nature of the peace. The English, who could not hope to gain much European territory from warfare, were particularly prone to this strategy.

The North American theater of war was usually insulated by the imperial navies, rather than invaded by them. Major North American trades were assigned modest escorts, and preferred colonies might be spared a naval "guard vessel," but naval resources for North American waters were usually very limited. Aside from occasional intervention in North American waters, fleets were firmly tied to wars of maneuver, blockade, and trade defense in European waters. Jean-Baptiste Colbert had very quickly built Louis XIV's navy from a mere 20 ships in 1661 to over 250 by 1677, so that the French navy matched the combined Anglo-Dutch navies.[3] Even when the French navy lost royal support, as it did after the defeat at La Hogue in May 1692, French privateers like Jean Bart, René Duguay-Trouin, and Pierre Le Moyne d'Iberville hired French men-of-war and forced massive deployments of their enemies' ships to defend maritime commerce in European waters. Although Britain finally established a naval base in the West Indies in the 1730s, the first North American naval base came with the founding of Halifax in 1749.

Although English North America's 200,000 settlers outnumbered the Canadians by nearly twenty to one in 1687, and the same ratio remained through the next half century of population growth, these odds were never relevant. Historians lament that the English colonies were too parochial and uncooperative to join and crush the Canadians, but this judgment is heavily weighted with hindsight. English colonies competed with one another for land, immigrants, Amerindian trade, and overseas markets, generating more occasions for conflict than did the far-off Canadians. Throughout this period, Pennsylvania, Maryland, and Virginia were all quite safe from New France, with the Appalachians still serving as defensive ramparts rather than obstacles to expansion. Southern English colonies fought an entirely separate war against Spanish Florida whenever Spain became an enemy in Europe. Even New York tacitly adopted the neutrality of the Five Nations when possible.

Massachusetts, New Hampshire, and Connecticut were the only English colonies regularly involved in inter-colonial war, usually provoked by Abenaki neighbors who used the wartime opportunity for revenge and for the profits of trading prisoners. The populations of these three colonies remained about eight times that of Canada, but that advantage was never translatable into paid volunteers sufficient to "extirpate" the Canadians, or into a political leadership comfortable with the fiscal and political cost of campaigning far from home for extended periods.

The Canadians had several significant military advantages. Canada was led by a governor-general who might squabble with the *intendant* or the bishop of Québec, but was able to command the government's manpower and resources without obstruction by power-hungry elected assemblies.[4] His budget included crown allowances for fortification and pay for the colony's regular *troupes de la marine*. Ultimately, his management was subject only to an annual review in Paris on an ex post facto basis. However, the general Canadian objective could never be more than survival. Every year of survival could be regarded as a year of victory, waiting for France to salvage matters with military victory in Europe and consistently adept peace negotiations.

Canada was also defended by geography. The Adirondacks, Green Mountains, and White Mountains helped protect the heart of Canada from its more numerous neighbors. These defenses had only three gates: the lower St. Lawrence, the Richelieu River–Lake Champlain waterway, and the upper St. Lawrence–Lake Ontario route. Winter defended these gates seasonally, and fortification made access costly for major invading forces on any of these routes, though small overland raids were harder to stop. These three approaches funneled all attacks to places where the defenses of New France could be gathered readily; these same funnels allowed Canadian raiders to surprise a wide variety of English colonial targets, especially via the Richelieu River.

Amerindians were so fundamental to the survival of Canada throughout this period that the contest cannot be viewed solely as intercolonial. Amerindian refugees and converts lived in missions that protected major Canadian towns from surprise attack and provided enthusiastic guerrilla warriors who set their own timetables of peace and war. As though it were a spasmodic continuation of King Philip's War, Canada's allies formed a force of unknowable size that terrified the New England frontier throughout this period. Eventually, the English feared that a network of well-armed Amerindian allies of Canada and of Louisiana was encircling English North America. Canada's allies also provided alternative targets for English colonial armies in war, and especially just after the Europeans made what was always a separate, imported peace. Amerindians, whether neutral or supporting Canada, had reason to prolong the contest indefinitely. Powerful independent tribes and regrouped refugees used these inter-colonial wars to push back the land-hungry English colonials; to build supplies of French arms, ammunition, and gunpowder; to adopt prisoners into their populations or trade them for profit; and to pursue war against Amerindian enemies with Canadian support that often included Canadian comrades-in-arms.

Amerindians, who had adapted their own warfare to paralyze European intruders, now provided arduous training for a corps of Canadian colonial regulars and traders who became guerrilla fighters. Guerrilla warfare, used here in a general sense, involved offensives by small groups able to "live off the land," strike hard at vital and vulnerable targets, enhance the impact of small operations by using terrifying brutality, then melt into the forest before they could be counterattacked. Amerindians had learned the hard way that they must defend nothing, not even stockaded settlements or cornfields. This type of warfare could immobilize much larger forces of colonial militia preoccupied with defending their farmsteads. The eventual flaw in Canadian guerrilla strategy was that ultimately the guerrillas, too, would defend their settlements. This kind of guerrilla warfare was usually inconclusive, except when surviving meant winning.

In attacking distant Amerindians, or French and Spanish positions defended by regular soldiers, New Englanders developed what became a new colonial approach to the military. All colonial assemblies eventually offered enlistment bounties, wages, provisions, the prospect of booty, and sometimes even weapons, clothes, and other inducements to volunteers willing to serve as soldiers outside their colony for a contractual period. Despite its risks, this opportunity could attract patriotic, adventurous, and cash-strapped young men of all races and occupations. When volunteers were not numerous enough, they were supplemented by draft, occasionally directed first at the imprisoned (New York, 1750s) and vagrants (Virginia, 1740, 1754), but usually allowing substantial citizens to pay a fine and hire a substitute. Some resulting colonial armies resembled European regulars in social composition and personal prospects, though enlistments were short term. When even more soldiers were required, as for the New England campaign of 1745 against Louisbourg or for the Seven Years' War, these armies came closer to being cross sections of their societies.[5]

These armies were controlled by the assemblies that raised them, appointed senior officers, and determined both the objectives and duration of the campaigns. Assemblies that normally faced imperial disapproval of their paper money issues were able to expand these instruments for the war effort. Favored army contractors became wealthy in economies that were distorted by war. The transatlantic staple trades in rice, tobacco, fish, and fur were disrupted by war, making additional wartime taxes more onerous in some colonies. Privateering flourished in the same periods, as did the provisions trades, with increased demand and reduced supply caused by frontier raids and absent workers. English colonial assemblies gained a power to make war that exceeded that of their royal governors, who had clearer authority over the few British regulars in some colonies, and over the militias that now busied themselves with night watches and slave patrols. War reduced internal political and religious faction, united Protestants against the alien Catholics, and integrated towns and counties into colonies.[6]

Colonial warfare, as exemplified by the expeditionary forces, tended increasingly toward European models.[7] North America was now thoroughly incorporated into Europe's expanding world of diplomacy, though this brought Europe's wars more promptly and fully than Europe's peace. English colonial expeditions were routinely organized to use superior numbers to besiege and conquer fortified enemy ports. Soldiers were drilled to achieve massed musket fire, in accordance with the imported military manuals. A farmer could be made into a regular foot soldier in weeks, whereas it would take years to train him in woodland war. At its most ambitious, the English colonial strategy involved using cannon to besiege the fortifications of Canada and Florida. Frontiersmen and Amerindian scouts were allowed to conduct raids, but were usually less effectively deployed in defense of settlements or armies.

Governors and colonial military officers also imported aspects of Europe's emerging "honors of war," with its comparatively humane conventions about sieges, surrenders, and the treatment of prisoners of war. Europeans fighting for North America no longer slaughtered one another after surrender or sold one another into servitude. These imported marks of "civilized" treatment were generally reserved for whites; Amerindian and black prisoners of the French or English were comparatively few and usually subject to sale. In this, as in strategy and tactics, the ways of colonial war depended on the perceived enemy.[8]

These inter-colonial wars would establish and repeat a pattern of conflict that reflected an unexpected balance of usable martial resources. These wars would also reveal the ongoing cooperation, confusion, and conflict between developing colonial and Amerindian warfare.

Despite the general Amerindian role as equalizers in these wars, they were not automatically drawn to alliance with New France. Canadian prospects in the 1680s depended on dealing effectively with the Five Nations, who had demonstrated a capacity to terrorize the St. Lawrence Valley and to disrupt Canada's newly claimed western fur-trading empire. In this contest, which merged with the first Anglo-French war, it was the Canadians who were forced to defend frontier farms and send expeditions to burn Amerindian towns. This was the immediate challenge for Jacques-René de Brisay, marquis de Denonville, the new governor-general who arrived in 1685 with orders to subdue the Five Nations by whatever means necessary.

Chapter 7

ESTABLISHING PATTERNS 1687–1701

The Five Nations and New France had collided in Illinois country before the summer of 1685, when the able and perceptive marquis de Denonville, hitherto brigadier and inspector-general of Louis XIV's dragoons, arrived at Québec. Although Denonville opposed expensive trading posts in the west, he recognized the western fur trade as central to the prosperity of the colony. This trade was being challenged by the English from two directions, Hudson Bay and New York. His solutions were direct and military. Newly arrived chevalier de Troyes and a force of thirty *troupes de la marine* and sixty Canadian volunteers traveled overland from Montréal to Hudson Bay in the early spring of 1686. They captured all three English trading posts on James Bay, left them garrisoned by forty Canadians under Pierre Le Moyne d'Iberville, and brought back fifty thousand beaver pelts.[1] Later that year, ministers at the French and English courts, which were at peace, signed a treaty of neutrality applicable only to their American possessions in the event of European war, but it curbed neither rivalries in North America nor the subsequent import of Europe's next war.

In New York, the contest between New France and the Five Nations, supported by Albany traders, was intensifying. Since La Barre's repudiated agreement of 1684, Five Nations parties had robbed Canadian traders in the *pays d'en haut*. By 1685 Albany traders, with expansionist Governor Dongan's support, had been guided by renegade Canadian *coureurs de bois* to the Michilimackinac trade with the Ottawa. Denonville proposed that Louis XIV either buy New York from James II, take it with a major naval squadron, or at least provide soldiers for simultaneous attacks on the Mohawk and the Seneca. As the Five Nations began diplomatic overtures to Canada's western allies and suppliers, Denonville decided on a well-prepared surprise attack on the Seneca.

Denonville's expedition was an impressive muster of 2722 men, representing much of the military and diplomatic strength of New France. He left Montréal in June 1687 with 832 uniformed *troupes de la marine;*

some 1030 militia, including 100 to escort convoys; and 300 Amerindians from the neighboring missions, including Abenaki and Caughnawaga. As planned, this army was joined by a contingent from the *pays d'en haut* of 160 *coureurs de bois* and nearly 400 Amerindian allies, predominantly Ottawa.[2] This western contingent also brought two parties of captured Albany traders, who were held in Montréal during the campaign, as were two hundred surprised *Iroquois du nord* detained as the French army reached the neighborhood of Fort Frontenac. Later Denonville unwisely followed royal orders and sent thirty-six of these detainees to France as galley slaves.

The orderly invasion of Seneca territory, with the *coureurs de bois* and Amerindians covering the advance, was contested only briefly. Some 750 Seneca, divided into two flanking parties, ambushed the van of the invading army in a ravine. The Caughnawaga were prominent in the ensuing fight, and the Seneca fled as terrified *troupes de la marine* were regrouped and sent forward as reinforcements. Reportedly, forty-five Seneca were killed and sixty were wounded; of Denonville's forces, eleven were killed and an equal number were wounded. From that point on, the campaign was reminiscent of the 1666 attack on the Mohawk, a war against cornfields, stored food, and deserted villages defended only by those ineffectual totems, the plaques bearing the arms of James II. An estimated 400,000 bushels of standing and dried corn were destroyed, and the most numerous Five Nations tribe was humiliated. Denonville had halted English intrusion into the western fur trade, demonstrated French power, built a garrisoned blockhouse at Niagara, and started a war.

In response, Five Nation war parties so effectively besieged Niagara and Fort Frontenac that their 240 soldiers could not venture out to hunt; they contracted scurvy from living exclusively on salted rations, and 180 of them were dead by spring. Five Nation attacks on the fringes of the St. Lawrence settlements were ferocious, though much less deadly than the epidemic of smallpox and measles that literally decimated the colony, killing over eleven hundred of the colony's eleven thousand inhabitants. Unable to obtain more than an additional three hundred *troupes de la marine* from France, on the verge of a major war, Denonville was forced to make peace with the Five Nations. Otreouti, the Onondaga neutralist, again led the Five Nation delegation, and again insisted that they were independent of the English and the French, but willing to befriend both. A provisional peace, including the promised return of the Five Nation prisoners from the French galleys, was to be ratified at a major conference in Montréal the following year.[3]

While Denonville's fragile truce with the Five Nations was achieved by a united and aggressive French colony, relations between Massachusetts Bay and the Abenaki were symptomatic of the political chaos into which the northern English colonies were descending. James II and his advisers showed a sensible grasp of the larger problems of building an empire in America, but the authoritarian shape of their solution proved disastrous. In 1686 the new Dominion of New England combined the English colonies of Massachusetts (including Maine), New Hampshire, Connecticut, and Rhode Island under a single royal governor, Sir Edmund Andros. Two years later, this dominion reached south as far as Pennsylvania and Delaware, combining more than 120,000 English colonials in a single government. However, with legislative assemblies suppressed, some religious sensibilities offended, and taxes raised, discontent against this "tyranny" was widespread.[4]

Isolated Abenaki attacks on the frontier of Massachusetts had continued after settlers violated a treaty of 1685, and New Englanders suspected that Baron Jean-Vincent d'Abbadie de St. Castin was the source of the trouble. St. Castin had come to Canada with the Carignan-Salières Regiment in 1665 as a thirteen-year-old ensign. When Acadia was returned to the French in 1670, the ensign was among those who repossessed the fort on the Penobscot River. St. Castin married the daughter of Penobscot chief Madokawando and rose to become a chief as well as a fur and gun trader. He became increasingly independent of French control, trading with the English and arming his fellow Abenaki. In 1687, while St. Castin took Abenaki warriors to join in Denonville's campaign against the Seneca, Andros authorized an attack on his home and storehouse at Pentagouet. The Abenaki of Saco, who had protested about damaged crops due to English cattle and who eventually killed a few, were targets of a Boston order to seize those suspected. Twenty Abenaki men, women, and children were captured as prisoners or hostages. Abenaki raiding escalated to open war in 1688, including the burning of New Dartmouth and Newtown. Andros felt forced to launch a punitive expedition though he was furious with the mismanagement that had destroyed the precarious peace. He led some three hundred Massachusetts volunteers to supplement his two companies of regulars and to garrison eleven new fortifications. Armed supply boats were used to launch quick strikes against Abenaki settlements, but negotiations had not been concluded when Andros's government collapsed.[5]

The startling news that England's King James II had been deposed by his son-in-law, William of Orange, reached Boston, garbled and belated, in April 1689. Leaders and militia in Boston and New York safely replayed the English revolution of 1688 by seizing control and imprisoning the detested Andros and his associates. Massachusetts militia deserted the northern frontier, regarding service there as one of Andros's numerous oppressions. Edward Randolph, one of the imprisoned officeholders, lamented the vulnerable military situation:

> The French have above four thousand good men about Canada, ready for any designe. I expect that upon the news of the Bostoners reassuming their old government (no care being taken for the out-towns and Prov-

inces) they will joyne with the Indians, and in a short time swallow and be masters of that part of the Countrey.

He went on to anticipate French damage to the trade and safety of the other colonies, "the prevention whereof was one chiefe ground of putting all those petty governments under one generall Governour."[6] With the Abenaki raiding on the Maine frontier, and with a precarious truce on the New York frontier, the English colonies learned that England, now led by William of Orange as William III, had joined the European war already being fought against France by the Hapsburg Empire and William of Orange's Netherlands. In Albany, Mayor Pieter Schuyler proclaimed William and Mary as monarchs, but resisted New York's revolutionaries, led by Jacob Leisler, with the timely assistance of the Mohawk.

The Five Nations, who had not yet ratified their peace with New France, promptly exploited the news of this Anglo-French war. Otreouti had died after the 1688 negotiations with Denonville, and pro-English leaders regained ascendancy of an increasingly integrated, but factious, Iroquois Confederacy. The Mohawk Tahiadoris spoke confidently of the gigantic alliance of all their "Majesties Subjects from the Sinnekes Country quite to the Eastward as farr as any Christian Subjects of our great king lives and from thence Southward all along New England quite to Virginia."[7] The Five Nations, who had previously fought their wars without allies, were venturing into dangerous new diplomatic territory.

Continuing their own war with New France, the Five Nations delivered news of another war, declared in London in May 1689, to the unsuspecting farmers of Lachine. Some fifteen hundred Five Nations attacked the village at dawn on August 5, killing twenty-four *habitants* and more than forty soldiers. Several Christian Mohawk from nearby Caughnawaga were among the dead; this Mohawk civil war was a subtheme of the ensuing struggle. As many as ninety French were taken prisoner, more than forty of whom never returned, and fifty-six of some seventy-seven houses in the area were burned.[8] It was only after two more months of minor, and more equal, skirmishes that the delayed French fleet brought formal word of the larger war, and brought Frontenac for his second term as governor, together with the thirteen surviving *Iroquois du nord* from Louis XIV's galleys.

New France launched King William's War in a way that would become familiar. Despite grandiose schemes for a maritime attack on the city of New York and sensible plans to attack Albany, Frontenac decided on three separate winter raids on the New England and New York frontiers. The unified authority of New France could confirm vital Amerindian support promptly with such invitations to revenge and plunder. These raids exploited the revolutionary disruptions in the English colonies and used terror to reinforce the reluctance of those colonists to undertake operations far from their vulnerable homes. The February 1690 raid on Schenectady, New York, involved 114 Canadians, including Iberville, and 96 warriors from the missions, led by Kryn. The attackers silently entered the palisaded but undefended village at night and torched nearly all the houses, killing sixty and capturing twenty-seven. Of the twenty-one Mohawk in Schenectady, all but one were able, or were allowed, to escape; if Lachine was being repaid in kind, it was against Dutch settlers, not Five Nation villagers. After an efficent offensive, in which only two attackers were killed, the victorious army straggled back to Montréal with prisoners and loot, harassed by Five Nations who freed some captives and took nineteen prisoners of their own.[9] This Schenectady raid from Montréal was matched by smaller raids eastward from Trois Rivières and Québec. Twenty-five Canadians and an equal number of mission Amerindians surprised and burned Salmon Falls, New Hampshire, killing thirty-four and capturing fifty-four. Fort Casco (Falmouth, Maine) and Fort Loyal (Portland) were also burned before the end of May by a party of fifty Canadians and sixty Abenaki from Québec, reinforced by the Trois Rivières contingent and by local Abenaki led by Madokawando and St. Castin. These successful raids had unintended, if predictable, results. New England was roused to strike back, and the bitter political factions that had divided Albany from Leislerian Schenectady and New York were put in abeyance.

The New York revolutionary government of Jacob Leisler had craved military success to gain outside recognition. With powerful political enemies hurrying to the English court, Leisler had every incentive to avenge the destruction of Schenectady. When he had called for an intercolonial conference to plan the campaign, Massachusetts, Connecticut, and the soon-to-disappear government of Plymouth were the only colonies to send delegates.

New York's answer to the Schenectady raid proved no muster of that distracted colony's potential strength. New York's colonial population of nearly fourteen thousand should have been able to muster at least twenty-eight hundred men, and Leisler optimistically claimed that the Five Nations would provide two thousand more. When the army assembled, there were only 150 volunteers from the New York militias and 70 Five Nations, whose warriors were deterred by a smallpox outbreak among their western tribes and by another among the troops gathering at Albany.[10] The New Yorkers were joined by 135 Connecticut colonists and some 50 Mohegan, on condition that their anti-Leislerian leader, Fitz-John Winthrop, command the expedition. Winthrop once had a gentleman's role in the English army and had led the Connecticut militia in King Philip's War without seeing much action. The original plan was to attack with nearly three thousand men, forming one prong of the attack on Canada, while a New England fleet, commanded by William Phips, formed the other. Instead, Winthrop led a party of about four hundred as far as Lake Champlain, taking verbal shots at Leisler's government for inadequate manpower, supplies, and canoes. At Wood Creek, he discovered only enough canoes for half his party, and it was too late in the season to strip birches to build more. The canoes were manned by 149 volunteers, nearly all Amerindian, and supposedly led by twenty-two-year-old Captain John Schuyler, younger brother of the mayor of Albany. On August 23, 1690, they attacked the hamlet of La Prairie, killing six, taking nineteen prisoner, and setting houses, barns, and crops ablaze. They left, escaping a Canadian force of twelve hundred by barely two days, but their attack had been two months early (and too small) to draw troops from Québec toward Montréal while Phips attacked Québec. Mohawk and Mohegan raiders, accompanied by thirty colonials, had profitably avenged the destruction of Schenectady.[11]

New Yorkers attempted their only other major offensive the next year. Organization was comparatively smooth; Leisler had been deposed, tried, and executed by a royally appointed governor whose authority was now uncontested, and other colonies were not asked to participate. Some 146 Mohawk and Mahican warriors joined 266 Albany militia under Albany's former mayor, Pieter Schuyler. As a surprise attack on Canadian settlements, the operation failed, leaving the New Yorkers to fight their way home through bloody ambushes, skirmishes, and an intense hand-to-hand battle with a much larger Canadian force of *troupes de la marine* and militia. Thirty-seven of Schuyler's force were killed and thirty-one were wounded, while forty-five Canadians were killed and sixty were wounded.[12] Albany was thereafter garrisoned by 150 men, but New Yorkers would not return to the offensive again for a full eighteen years, when an imperial and inter-colonial expedition promised overwhelming manpower advantage.

New England's response to French frontier raids established a pattern for the next two wars. It might be thought that King Philip's War would have initiated New Englanders in woodland warfare useful against the Canadians and Amerindians. It is true that Benjamin Church made his reputation in 1675 and 1676 and would lead five village-burning expeditions against the Abenaki in the 1690s. Yet few New Englanders were trained in Church's methods, and the Amerindians, who might have been either buffers or trainers, were gone. Church pleaded in vain with his men not to light fires during a 1690 expedition, but was taunted as a coward. He acquired the growing Amerindian aversion to forts, telling the unappreciative Sir William Phips that they were "only nests for destruction." New England tried to defend itself with search parties, expensively manned frontier garrison houses, bounties on raising mastiffs, and £100 bounties on Amerindian scalps, but ultimately hoped to use its 13,279 militia in a more ambitious, more dramatic, and more conventional invasion of Canada.[13]

Sir William Phips, not Benjamin Church, was New England's leader of choice in 1690. One of twenty-six children of a gunsmith with land on the Maine frontier, William Phips's good fortune began when, as a young ship's carpenter in Boston, he met and married Martha, widow of a wealthy Boston merchant. Luck enabled him to salvage a fortune from a sunken Spanish treasure galleon in the Caribbean, and thereby obtain a knighthood as well as a portion of his £300,000 discovery. It was this "great adventurer, half crusader and half clown,"[14] who led the two most significant Massachusetts offensives of the war, the attack on Port Royal and the siege of Québec.

Attacking Port Royal and Québec was part of a strategy that Cotton Mather explained in a parable about predatory birds. New France provided the roosts for these villains, and "it was thought that the New-Englanders might very justly take this Occasion to Reduce those French Colonies under the English Government, and so at once take away from all the Rooks for ever, all that gave 'em any Advantage to Infest us."[15] Early in May 1690, as Massachusetts legates prepared for the opening of Leisler's inter-colonial conference that planned the invasion of Canada, Phips set sail with 736 men to capture Port Royal. This force, two-thirds of whom were conscripts, landed without opposition and challenged the fort. The Acadian governor, realizing that his decrepit fort had only a tenth of the manpower of the attackers and that none of his fourteen cannon were mounted, agreed to surrender. The fort was burned, and prisoners and booty were taken back to Boston. Aside from some pillaging contrary to the articles of surrender, the successful excursion was conducted according to the rules and goals of European warfare as described in the manuals. Taking this pathetic little fort did little to stop Abenaki raiders or French privateers, but it encouraged recruitment for New England's next expedition.

Phips had been away from Boston for a month and on his return was given command of a naval expedition that constituted the main force of an inter-colonial invasion of Canada. The simple conquest of Port Royal had cost Massachusetts £3,000, and the provisional government was particularly hard-pressed to outfit this second expedition. The English government had been asked for aid but none arrived, though the colonists waited until well past midsummer. Reluctant Boston merchants finally agreed to invest in the venture. The resulting little armada might have been large enough if its timing, and that of the overland party from Albany, had been perfect. Twenty-three hundred men, with supplies for three months, were put aboard thirty-two vessels, the largest of which would have been too small to sail in any European line of battle.[16]

Phips was less than lucky on this expedition; it took two months to reach Québec. Attempting to busy himself while his fleet bucked the prevailing westerlies or the sails hung limp, Phips landed repeatedly to claim deserted stretches of the south shore of the Gulf of St. Lawrence. Delay meant that an outbreak of smallpox devoured more men, and men devoured more provisions. The most fortunate thing that happened was that the fleet, without experienced pilots, navigated the treacherous St. Lawrence to Québec without mishap. As he finally reached Québec on October 16, 1690, Phips realized that the overland expedition from Albany had failed to divert any of the more than fifteen hundred defenders of this citadel, soon to be reinforced by more than five hundred Montréal militia. He knew that smallpox was still winnowing his forces, and he knew that the easterly winds of late autumn, which finally helped him sail to Québec, would make the trip home even more arduous and hungry. Ice also covered the streams at night, threatening to trap ships and crush the weak like peapods in a vise.

The daunting responsibility of the thirteen hundred men under Major John Walley, whom Phips had landed two miles below Québec, was to launch a conventional assault with "ammunition, provision, field pieces, shovels, spades, and other necessarys for the souldiers."[17] This force was harassed by Canadian scouting parties, "while the New England men taunted them as cowards who would never fight except under cover."[18] To reach the citadel, Walley's men would need to ford the St. Charles River, at one of two extremely well-defended locations, and would need to do so at low tide, after which there would be no retreat. Rather than using his cannons to disrupt the batteries and the troops defending the lower ford, Phips prematurely bombarded the citadel, expending his ammunition to little effect. Under heavy answering fire, "the admiral being, as they say, forced to leave their best cable and anchor behind him" withdrew out of range.[19] Mercifully, the ground attack had not yet been attempted by the weakened, undisciplined, and inadequate force. Walley described the confusion of re-embarkation, which may or may not have been ordered:

> [B]oats were like to be five times longer a loading than they needed. . . . I was forced to goe from boat to boat . . . for otherways some of the seamen would throw the souldiers overboard if they did not belong to them or the souldiers would have pressed into boats to have sunk them.[20]

Phip's amateurish expedition had been hopelessly undermanned for a conventional assault on a fortified position, usually requiring at least three times the number of attackers as defenders.

After all that calculation, effort, and prayer, Phips's failure was bitter and brutal. While the *Te Deum* was sung with fervor in Canadian churches, God seemed to be whipping New England's forces all the way home with winter storms. The Massachusetts government lost a thousand men to sickness and shipwreck as well as losing £40,000.

Pious Puritans saw the failure of the expedition as God's judgment, rather than human error, and searched for the sins that had caused God to abandon them.[21] This search formed part of the context for the hysteria of the 1692 Salem witch trials.

The Phips expedition may have convinced New Englanders that they should not attempt a comparable venture again without British support, but the only sizable British fleet to visit Boston during the entire war was hardly inspiring. Sir Francis Wheler's seventeen-vessel fleet limped into Boston in 1693 after a disastrous West Indian campaign. The fleet, having lost two-thirds of its forty-five hundred men to yellow fever before reaching Boston, promptly spread the only epidemic of that fatal disease ever to hit the town. Wheler arrived entirely unannounced, terribly undermanned, with his ships in pathetic condition, but he was trying to follow instructions to help New England attack Québec before making his way home to England. Phips understandably refused to join Wheler in an impromptu attack on Canada.[22]

The strenuous efforts of these first three years represented the type of war that the colonials found both possible and necessary. However, the three principal contenders found direct attack unprofitable, creating an illusion that the usable forces of English and French colonies were comparable and that European assistance was necessary for a decisive victory. New York had found fighting garrisons more expensive than terrorizing hamlets. Massachusetts had found the siege of Québec arduous, expensive, and disappointing. New France discovered that attacks launched against New York and Massachusetts provoked massive counter-attacks rather than the intended confusion and defensive preoccupations. While these contenders remained hostile, took defensive measures, and lamented to their respective imperial authorities about the immense burdens of war, direct inter-colonial conflict decreased, becoming largely a war against Amerindian enemies. New York enjoyed relative calm by failing to honor the obligations of the "covenant chain" with the Five Nations, who regretted this unprecedented alliance. Massachusetts focused on the Abenaki, while Canada directed efforts against the Five Nations and undertook peripheral maritime raids on English trading outposts at Newfoundland and Hudson Bay.

The Treaty of Ryswick brought the War of the League of Augsburg to a close in September 1697. North American issues may have received as much attention as they deserved in the broader context of the war, but that was scant. The general stalemate in the colonial war was tacitly recognized in the agreement to accept the status quo ante in North America. Acadia, which had been in English colonial hands for only a year, was officially restored to France. The treaty recognized the English reconquest of Newfoundland in 1697 and accepted English control of Hudson Bay, invalidating Canadian gains made there after the peace was signed at Ryswick. The next five years in Europe was a long truce, allowing combatants to gather strength for the next round of fighting.

As Amerindian orators later recognized, European colonists at war were like a pair of scissors. The two sharp blades appear to clash noisily, but actually cut the Amerindians between them.[23] Amerindians used inter-colonial war to gain support in avenging themselves against intruders, while colonists defending their troubled borders could claim patriotic pursuit of imperial war while deploying substantial resources to dispossess local Amerindians. Both the Massachusetts war with the Abenaki and the Canadian war with the Five Nations had established this pattern.

The second Abenaki war (1688–1699) with Massachusetts had begun before King William's War and continued after the Peace of Ryswick. Massachusetts officials consistently refused to admit that English settler provocations, rather than French influence, caused the war. Abenaki captured and burned Pemaquid early in August 1689, before New France was aware of war with England, and even before the Five Nation attack on Lachine. Abenaki who had migrated to Canada formed a significant component in the raiding parties of 1690, but were peripheral to the Abenaki's own war. Some four hundred Abenaki, with some Canadian aid, struck the Maine frontier at York and Wells early in 1692, killing fifty and taking a hundred prisoner, and Massachusetts responded with damaging raids on the food supplies of evacuated Penobscot and Kennebec villages. A fraudulent peace was negotiated between Sir William Phips and a handful of Abenaki chiefs in 1693, but never accepted by the majority of Abenaki. Oyster Bay (Durham, New Hampshire) was destroyed in 1694, and by the following year Abenaki raids had forced the abandonment of the Maine and New Hampshire frontiers, making raiding less profitable. French support for the independent Abenaki had been steady but minimal until August 1696, when Iberville's fleet arrived to help St. Castin's Abenaki strike the last significant blow of the war in the east, the conquest and destruction of the rebuilt stone Fort Pemaquid, poorly defended by a garrison of ninety-five with fifteen mounted cannon.

A group of Abenaki raided Haverhill, killing twenty-seven, capturing thirteen, and inviting a gruesome retaliation that became a New England folk legend. In March 1697, Hannah Dustin, about forty years of age and only five days "out of childbed," witnessed the callous killing of her crying newborn shortly after she was captured; the Abenaki were in a hurry to escape retaliation and killed those who could not keep up as well as those whose cries could locate the group. Hannah and the newborn's fifty-year-old nurse, widow Mary Neff, were marched a difficult 150 miles in a few days, then assigned to a family of two Abenaki warriors, three women, and seven children. After six weeks with this hunting family, Hannah convinced Mary and a boy named Samuel Lenorson, who had been captive for nineteen months, to slaughter the entire sleeping Abenaki family and then escape. Ten of the twelve Abenaki were hatcheted, one woman ran off severely wounded, and one child "scuttled away from this desolation." The captives then took the ten scalps and made their way home to a heroine's welcome. This tough-minded frontier matron was celebrated as God's instrument in a sermon by the Reverend Cotton Mather, though she did not become a full church member for another twenty-two years. She was honored with gifts and praise by the governor of Maryland and the General Assembly of Massachusetts, in addition to receiving her scalp bounties. Whether the instant public account of Hannah's story was used to shame men or inspire women, it was not used to promote feminine meekness.[24]

Although the Peace of Ryswick did not end the Abenaki raiding, the uncomprehending Massachusetts authorities insisted that the governor of New France had the power to stop these raids. This Eurocentric assumption that all Amerindians were subject peoples, rather than independent allies, was only one part of English misunderstanding of the Abenaki. Massachusetts authorities deluded themselves into claiming control over their own aggressive young men; Abenaki chiefs did not even pretend to have such control. Massachusetts did not get a grudging renewal of the 1693 treaty until 1699. English trade, not English victory, finally brought an interlude of peace. The Abenaki were seeking, but never found, a neutrality that would allow them to trade with the English and pray with the Jesuits.[25]

The Five Nations war with New France (1680–1701) also preceded, paralleled, and outlasted King William's War. Five Nations successes in the 1680s had climaxed with the Lachine raid, and New York proved a false ally in the war that followed. After the failure of the 1690 invasion of Canada and the losses in the 1691 raid from Albany, New York gave no practical support to its Five Nation allies. Fratricidal raids between the Five Nations and their kin in New France were particularly destructive and demoralizing. Mohawk warriors were fewer than half their earlier number, and the same was true of the Caughnawaga.[26] Canadian armies invaded and burned three Mohawk towns in 1693, reoccupied Fort Frontenac in 1695, and burned Onondaga and Oneida towns in 1696. In the spring of 1696, a larger party of Ottawa and Potawatomi attacked a Five Nation hunting party, killing as many as seventy and taking thirty prisoner. The European Peace of Ryswick allowed New France to give even more encouragement to Ottawa and Ojibwa allies to attack Five Nation hunting parties, even near Seneca villages.[27] In 1699 a major offensive against the Five Nations by a well-provisioned intertribal army of French allies killed at least seventy Onondaga and ninety Seneca, and comparable losses occurred the following year. The unopposed French construction of Detroit in 1701 symbolized the Five Nations' loss of the west. In the thirteen years after

1688, the Five Nations had lost nearly half of their 2150 warriors, who had been either killed or captured, or had migrated to Canadian mission villages. The "scissors" of European war were shredding the Iroquois Confederacy.

The Five Nations had discussed peace with New France, and with their Amerindian enemies, intermittently from 1693. Debates within the Iroquois Confederacy still involved three factions. The Anglophiles faced derision for the lack of English assistance and the blundering diplomacy of New York governors who insisted that the Five Nations were English subjects who could not exchange prisoners or discuss peace with a New France that was equally insistent on a separate peace. Since Ryswick brought neither peace nor the return of prisoners, the Francophiles became the more credible leaders, especially after Frontenac's death in November 1698. Teganissorens, the Onondaga successor to Otreouti as leader of the neutralists, gradually gained control of the negotiations and developed parallel treaties with the French and the English that would unite and insulate the Five Nations. Preliminaries of a peace with New France and a virtual Five Nation capitulation to the western tribes were negotiated in the summer of 1700, as was a renewal of the covenant chain with the English. The famous Montréal meeting of July 1701 brought some thirteen hundred representatives of thirty-one tribes allied with the French, together with the French and the Five Nations to ratify the "Great Peace" (Figure 8). Meanwhile, other Five Nations legates capped their negotiations at Albany with a gift for William III: sovereignty over a vast tract around the shores of Lakes Erie and Huron, reaching as far as Michilimackinac. This shrewd offer, of lands the Five Nations had won and lost again, was a gesture intended to establish favorable boundaries between European spheres of influence and to stake new claims to lost Five Nation hunting grounds.[28]

Even in desperate circumstances, the Five Nations managed to gain a neutrality that the Abenaki were never allowed. New France's victory was a measured one, though enough to justify claims that the French ultimately won King William's War. The Five Nations remained part of New France's buffer against the English colonies and a barrier to Canada's allies intent on direct trade with Albany. Moreover, the Five Nations were suitably humbled and were clear losers in the war for the momentarily depressed western fur trade. New France's victorious allies now securely occupied lands they had recently retaken from the Five Nations in the Ohio Valley and in what would become known as Ontario. By ending a difficult war, the Five Nations could now turn their attention southward, attempting to dominate the Delaware and to chasten traditional Cherokee and Catawba enemies. Although the longevity of Five Nation neutrality with New France was not immediately predictable, it served as a model of survival that would attract

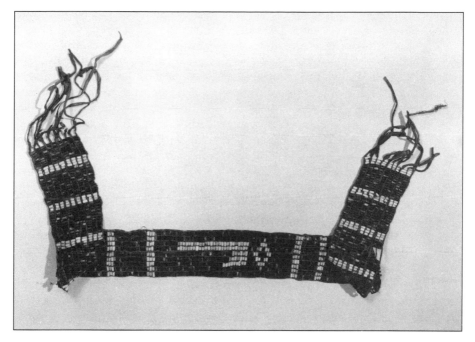

Figure 8. Wampum belt said to represent a clause from the "Great Peace" between the Five Nations and the French, 1701. (Courtesy of McCord Museum of Canadian History, Montreal)

Amerindians throughout the Anglo-French struggle, which in itself was made longer by this agreement.

The northern English colonies had failed to defend themselves and failed to execute their most ambitious offensives during this war. As the European war ended, the newly created English Board of Trade, the appointed commission to oversee the colonies, expressed disappointment:

> The King has subjects enough in those parts not only to defend themselves against any attack of French and Indians, but they are so crumbled into little governments and so disunited in their interests that they have hitherto afforded but little assistance to each other.

They went on, "It is almost incredible that the Governor of New York, in the middle of above 40,000 English . . . should say, as he does, that he has only the companies in the King's pay that he can rely on."[29] The English government solution, which proved too cumbersome to survive even this short peace, was to appoint Richard Coote, earl of Bellomont, simultaneously as governor of New Hampshire, Massachusetts, New York, and the New Jerseys, as well as commander of the militias of Rhode Island and Connecticut.

A pattern of inter-colonial warfare emerged, though this first Anglo-French war was braided into two pre-existing Amerindian–European conflicts that were made more equal because each Amerindian society had a fairly reliable supplier of European arms, ammunition, and gunpowder. As with the next two Anglo-French wars, the crowns told their colonies when to begin fighting each other, and New France initiated the fighting with major raids. In each war, New England responded energetically with a successful siege of a fort on the Nova Scotia peninsula, followed by a failed attack on Québec. New York's recurring contribution to the grand pincer strategy against Canada became even more pathetic without a repetition of the concurrent Five Nation–Canadian war of 1680 to 1701. Thereafter, minor raids masked, or confirmed, what became a customary stalemate. The English government, assuming that the colonists could manage their outnumbered opponents, provided only four undermanned, independent companies of regulars for New York, another for Newfoundland after 1696, and occasional shipments of ordnance or presents for Amerindian allies. Royal Navy vessels convoyed fleets of Virginia tobacco and New Hampshire masts. The navy also sent Sir Francis Wheler's fleet to Boston, an afterthought that became a macabre joke, and retook St. John's, Newfoundland in the final months of the war. French government involvement was also limited, though significant to New France. The French navy convoyed an annual fleet bringing supplies, presents for Amerindian allies, and both recruits and pay for as many as sixteen hundred *troupes de la marine*. The direct North American commitments of both crowns remained insufficient to upset what had become a local balance of violence. The Peace of Ryswick, like those of Utrecht and Aix-la-Chapelle, was a European announcement that halted direct inter-colonial fighting, allowing colonists to focus on Amerindian enemies. In this case, New England dealt with the Abenaki, and New France had forced the Five Nations to a settlement.

Chapter 8

RECURRING PATTERNS
1702–1748

European monarchs called North American colonists to arms against one another in 1702 and again in 1739 and 1744, renewing conflict between the English and French colonies in the north and formalizing a new theater in the south. The Spanish, English, and French contended for dominance over one another and for the trade and alliance of powerful Amerindian societies. The English from the days of Elizabeth I and Cromwell, had a predatory view of Spanish America as a rich victim rather than a competent enemy. The English, and English colonials were much more anxious to commence war against Spanish America than against New France. The English initiated hostilities in the south in 1702 and in 1739, but in other respects, the Anglo-Spanish contests followed the pattern characteristic of Anglo-French inter-colonial war in North America.

The related dynasties of western Europe had anticipated the dismemberment of the Spanish empire throughout the entire thirty-five-year reign of the sickly last Spanish Hapsburg, Carlos II (r. 1665–1700). Louis XIV of France, whose kingdom was bounded by Spanish territory on all land frontiers, had sought the Spanish inheritance by marrying the sister of Carlos, Maria Theresa. Louis had also attempted to negotiate with Carlos's father, and later with William III of England, to partition the Spanish empire. In addition, Louis had fought to acquire the Spanish Netherlands (1665–1668) and Spanish possessions in Italy. His rivals, led by William III, sought to curb France's hegemonic power in western Europe and to appropriate some of the vast, valuable Spanish possessions for themselves. After Carlos' death, for instance, English Vice-Admiral John Benbow's squadron, patroling the Caribbean in peacetime and shadowed by a French squadron, had secret orders to start war by capturing the Spanish treasure fleet.[1] The War of the Spanish Succession finally began, in Europe and America, in 1702.

When English colonials attacked Spanish Florida, their effort was fortunate enough to coalesce, like that against New France earlier, with

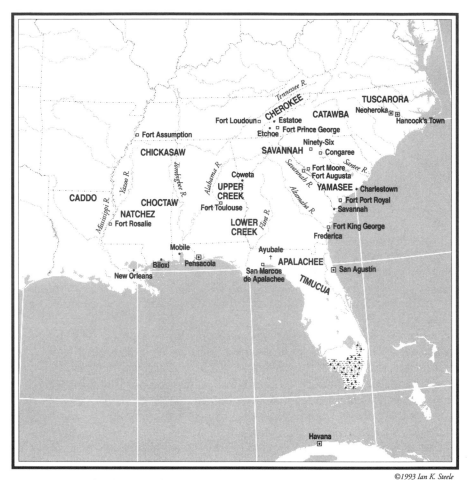

©1993 Ian K. Steele

Map 5. The disputed south, 1702–1763.

an existing struggle between their enemy and a powerful Amerindian confederacy, in this case the Creek (Map 5). In the last quarter of the seventeenth century, fifteen thousand Creek, composed of matrilineal clans within seven agrarian tribes, lived in sixty well-ordered villages on the upper reaches of the Flint, Chattahoochee, Scambia, and Alabama rivers. The rich soils, farmed by the women, yielded beans, sweet potatoes, and especially corn. As with the Iroquois, the men were responsible for the riskier tasks of hunting, warring, and trading. Creek warriors hunted the deer-filled hills reaching north toward the Cherokee-dominated Appalachians, and usually fought at least one of their neighbors: the more numerous Choctaw and the Chickasaw to the west, the Spanish-allied Guale and Apalachee to the south, and the bellicose

Westo and Savannah to the east, who were being supplied with guns by Carolina traders. Under these circumstances, the Creek had found it increasingly difficult to continue their traditional feuds. Although they proved as adept as the Five Nations of the Iroquois at incorporating prisoners, strangers, and remnant tribes, the Creek were under siege.

Seeking a European ally, the Creek first invited Spanish missionaries, two of whom arrived at the Lower Creek town of Apalachicola in 1681, accompanied by seven Spanish soldiers. This very successful mission quickly caused so much internal friction that, within a few months, the converts and the mission migrated south to the Apalachee frontier. In 1685 a large group of Carolina traders were allowed to travel the "Creek Path" to the Upper Creek center of Coweta, starting fifteen years of a trading monopoly that would arm the Creek with muskets paid for with deerskins, Apalachee horses, and Amerindian slaves. Spanish military expeditions initially tried to disrupt this threatening trade, but were forced to withdraw as the Creek became better armed. However, contact with the English brought epidemic disease; the Creek population fell by 40 percent to nine thousand during the 1690s. In the same decade, the Lower Creek trade with the Spanish-allied Apalachee became strained as the Apalachee demanded higher prices for their horses and payment in English guns. This dispute became open war in 1701, when Creek raids on Apalachee mission towns brought a vigorous defense by the Spanish.

Creek regional military superiority was challenged from another quarter. The ubiquitous Pierre Le Moyne d'Iberville had just founded the new French colony of Louisiana, with posts at Biloxi (1699) and Mobile (1701). The French immediately became the supplier of European arms to the Choctaw, who began retaliating against the Upper Creek for enslaving so many of their people in the previous fifteen years. The French also attempted to open negotiations and trade with the Creek, but were soon drawn into war against them. The Creek now had the same enemies as the Carolinians and needed their muskets, ammunition, and powder.[2]

In May 1702, before news of the English declaration of war against Spain and France had reached America, the Creek, backed by Carolinia traders, attacked and burned the Spanish Timucua mission at Santa Fe de Toloco and sold the captives to the Carolinians as slaves. An Apalachee retaliatory force of eight hundred, armed with bows and matchlocks and accompanied by several Spanish soldiers, was overwhelmed near the Flint River by a smaller force of flintlock-armed Lower Creek raiders, who reportedly killed or captured six hundred of these Apalachee.

The Carolinians had been disturbed by the founding of Louisiana and now feared a combined Franco-Spanish invasion exactly like that being proposed to the French government by Iberville. South Carolina was an English colony vulnerable to attack and revolt; thirty-eight hundred whites held twenty-eight hundred African slaves and were entirely outnumbered by some seventy-five hundred suspicious local Amerindians. Governor James Moore, an ambitious Irish immigrant planter, trader, and avaricious Amerindian slave-dealer, began a preemptive war against Florida as soon as official word of the war arrived in August 1702.[3]

The 1702 siege of San Agustín was an inglorious launch to a struggle for the trade and sovereignty of the entire southeast. Moore gathered five hundred Carolina volunteers on prospects of £10 per month and an equal share of the anticipated rich and easy booty. The assembly established its own standing committee to buy captives for resale at prices intended to cover war costs.[4] Three hundred Amerindians, mostly Yamasee, joined the volunteers aboard the fourteen small commandeered merchant vessels, better armed for defense against pirates than for attacking a major fortress. On its way south, part of this force raided remnant Spanish missions for slaves, but found the town of San Agustín completely deserted. Its fifteen hundred people and their animals had retreated into Castillo de San Marcos, ably defended by Governor José de Zúñiga, 250 soldiers with four months' provisions, and thirty-six mounted guns. Zúñiga sent for naval support from Cuba before the English had arrived; Moore apparently did not realize the inadequacy of his eight cannon until after he arrived, and he sent to Jamaica for mortars and exploding shells to destroy the crowded occupants of a fort he could not hope to take by breach and storm. After two futile months of one side creating trenches and *gabions*, the other sending sorties from the fort, and both sides watching supplies dwindle while waiting for ships from the south, the siege was abruptly ended by the arrival of Spanish men-of-war. Moore's force hastily destroyed eight of their own trapped ships, burned what they could of the town, and retreated. Both sides reported only a few deaths, but the siege proved expensive. The Spanish town took decades to recover from the destruction, and the English had been forced to abandon half their fleet and all their artillery. The South Carolina assembly, faced with costs that were more than four times its estimates, issued inflation-inducing paper money to stagger their repayment.[5]

Carolina's government had exhausted its financial resources in testing the strength of Castillo de San Marcos; from this point on, the war became one of Creek expansion. James Moore, superseded as governor and discredited as commander, sought his own revenge after the government declined to fund a new expedition in 1703. Moore, having recruited fifty Carolinians, joined about one thousand Lower Creek raiders for a massive attack on the missions of Apalachee in January 1704. Ayubale fell after fierce fighting in which the town was burned, four hundred Apalachee were killed, and the survivors were enslaved. A relief force of thirty Spanish and four hundred Apalachee lost nearly half its number in a failed counterattack. The inhabitants of five other towns either surrendered unconditionally or agreed to migrate to South Carolina. Moore returned home with at least one thousand slaves, and the Creek held others for later sale. After two additional Creek raids that summer, Apalachee country was virtually abandoned, its people dispersed as slaves or refugees heading northward to join the Lower Creek, eastward to San Agustín, or westward to Spanish Pensacola or French Mobile. Creek slave-raiding was a self-financing "English" offensive against which the Spanish proved entirely inadequate. Spanish and French privateers raided the outskirts of Charlestown in 1704 and 1706, but the Spanish mounted no effective counterattack. The Creek and the English thrived in alliance. With English trader encouragement and profit, the Upper Creek allied with the Chickasaw against the French-allied Choctaw; raided Spanish Pensacola in 1707 and 1708, taking everything but the fort; and, less successfully, attacked French Mobile in 1709. A few Carolinians accompanied fifteen hundred Lower Creek in 1711 under a powerful chief, Emperor Brims, in yet another attack on the Choctaw. Having won a war that increased their population, territory, and musketry, the Creek wisely consolidated their diplomatic and trading position between European rivals by making peace with the French of Louisiana in 1712, before the Europeans made their separate peace. Official Creek–Louisiana neutrality, like that between the Five Nations and New France, lasted until the end of the French regime.[6]

 On the northern Anglo-French frontier, Queen Anne's War had begun as a slow motion rerun of King William's War. Although Governor Joseph Dudley of Massachusetts sought a tacit neutrality on his vulnerable Abenaki borders, the new soldier-governor of New France, Philippe de Rigaud de Vaudreuil, sponsored raids to bolster his Abenaki alliances against both the attractions of English trade and the neutralist advice of Jesuit missionary Sébastien Rale. Fighting began belatedly in the summer of 1703, when Canadians and mission Abenaki from St. François lured Micmac and Abenaki into joining raids on Wells, York, Saco, Winter Harbor, and Casco (Map 6). The southernmost Androscoggin and Penobscot Abenaki, now deprived of New England trade and exposed to New England attack, followed Jesuit advice and migrated to Canada in 1704. Earlier that year, fifty Canadians and two hundred mission Amerindians had conducted a devastating raid on the frontier town of Deerfield, Massachusetts, in which three-fifths of the town's population of 250 was either killed or captured and half the town was burned.[7]

As well as sending forces with Colonel Benjamin Church to burn the Abenaki village and church at Norridgewock in 1705, the Massachusetts authorities again responded to French raids by resolving to conquer Port Royal and Québec. Although English assistance was sought,

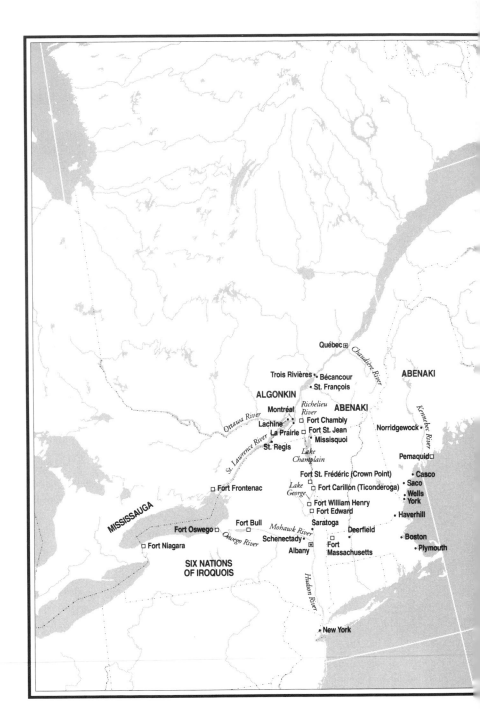

ABENAKI

Québec

Trois Rivières • Bécancour
• St. François

ALGONKIN

Montréal   Richelieu   ABENAKI
                River
Lachine   □ Fort Chambly
            □ Fort St. Jean
La Prairie • Missisquoi   Norridgewock •

St. Regis   Lake
            Champlain   Pemaquid □

            Fort St. Frédéric (Crown Point)   • Casco
□ Fort Frontenac   Lake   □ Fort Carillon (Ticonderoga)   • Saco
                    George   • Wells
                          □ Fort William Henry   • York
                          □ Fort Edward   • Haverhill
MISSISSAUGA
                    Fort Bull   Saratoga
        Fort Oswego □   Mohawk River   • Deerfield
                    Oswego River Schenectady •   • Boston
□ Fort Niagara   Albany   □   • Plymouth
                                   Fort
                                   Massachusetts

Ottawa River
St. Lawrence River
Chaudière River
Kennebec River
Hudson River

SIX NATIONS
OF IROQUOIS

• New York

156 ■

Map 6. The disputed east, 1688–1760.

©1993 Ian K. Steele

and waited for, Massachusetts finally launched two unsuccessful raids on Port Royal in 1707. Two years later, with a promise of help from England and New York, New England prepared for a re-enactment of the 1690 two-pronged attack on New France. The English ships were diverted to Portugal, aborting the North American expedition. In 1710, however, five Royal Navy vessels, carrying four hundred marines, supported four regiments of New England volunteers in the easy conquest of Port Royal and the other French settlements around the Bay of Fundy.[8]

British involvement in the North American war escalated further in 1711, when the Walker expedition was sent to capture Québec. This initiative was not to avenge Deerfield or to fulfill the broken promises of earlier ministries. A convulsion in English politics in 1710 brought leaders of Tory sentiment to power in Queen Anne's councils. These ministers wanted a hero of their own who might achieve a military victory to match the reputation that Lord Marlborough's victories had given the rival Whigs. They also were impatient with the length and cost of the war in continental Europe. Secretary of State Henry St. John, who now promoted the Walker expedition, argued that Britain had paid and suffered through a long European war in defense of the interests of other powers.

> [I]t is now high time to do something in particular for Britain, by which the enemy will receive as great and as essential a prejudice, as he has done by any of those operations the sole benefit whereof resulted to some of our confederates.[9]

With purposes like these, fourteen ships-of-the-line (all bigger than Phips's flagship) and thirty-one transports (there were only thirty-two vessels in Phips's entire fleet) were sent from Britain with fifty-three hundred troops, including seven of Marlborough's veteran regiments. The armada left Boston with a force of nearly sixty-five hundred men, while twenty-three hundred more advanced overland by the Lake Champlain route. Canada was being invaded by three times as many troops as in 1690, by a force numbering nearly half the total population of Canada. The ships took little more than three weeks to reach the mouth of the St. Lawrence River, but nine ships were wrecked there in fogs and gales, and nearly nine hundred men were lost. Although the fleet was still an overwhelming one, and though it was closer to Québec than Phips had been by the last week of August, a council of war judged it impractical to proceed. Again the Lord was thanked in Québec, but this time the New Englanders were not blaming themselves; they accused the British of frustrating a great design. New France's survival in 1711, as in 1690, was due to incompetence and misfortune. As Walker's squadron disappeared over the horizon, the war on this frontier effectively ended.

Despite achieving a stalemate against great odds, and at least a three-to-one advantage in terms of inflicted casualties, New France was punished in the Peace of Utrecht.[10] France ceded all claims to Newfoundland, except for fishing rights on the north shore. British control of Nova Scotia was accepted, and, even if boundaries were immediately in dispute, the main Acadian settlements clearly belonged to the British. Hudson Bay was recognized as British territory as well, though the limits of that claim were contested. France also agreed to a clause that implied British sovereignty over the Five Nations, weakening the accomplishment of New France's Great Treaty of 1701.

Marlborough had been right; a dash of the pen yielded a great deal more for Britain than its North American efforts warranted. In accordance with Henry St. John's priorities, Britain deserted its European allies to make a separate peace with the French, and France paid for a less punitive peace with colonial and commercial concessions to the British. New France paid Louis XIV's debts at the bargaining table in Utrecht.

Britain's diplomatic victories were primarily for itself, not for its colonies. The cession of Hudson Bay benefited a London-based trading company. British fishing interests tried desperately to monopolize the recently won Newfoundland fisheries at the expense of their New England rivals.[11] When Phips had taken Port Royal (Annapolis Royal) in 1690, the English government had been willing to incorporate Acadia into an expanding Massachusetts; when New England took the same place again in 1710, with British assistance, the conquest became the separate royal colony of Nova Scotia. However, Massachusetts used European attempts to draw an Anglo-French boundary to make unwarranted claims of sovereignty over some of the Eastern Abenaki. New York was the only British colony granted more at Utrecht than it had earned. Clause XV of the treaty began:

> The Subjects of France inhabiting Canada shall hereafter give no Hindrance or Molestation to the Five Nations or Cantons of Indians subject to the Dominion of Great Britain nor to the other natives of America who are Friends to the same.

This appropriation of the Five Nations blithely ignored their views, those of other tribes, and those of New France.[12] Britain's peace with Spain just as readily overlooked the devastation in Florida, merely confirming arrangements in the Treaty of Madrid (1670), while Britain acquired the strategic European naval bases of Gibraltar and Minorca, as well as limited access to the trade of Spanish America.

In the Anglo-Spanish struggle along the Carolina–Florida borderlands, prospects of European peace had only worsened the "scissors effect" of colonial war on Amerindians. Some seven thousand Tuscarora lived uneasily with the English colonists of Virginia and North Carolina, as well as with hostile Amerindian neighbors. Victims of a smallpox epidemic in 1707 and of Susquehannock–Seneca raids that lasted until 1710, the Tuscaroras' greatest danger now was from South Carolina traders and slave-raiders, and from North Carolina land developers. In September 1711, angry Tuscarora captured a surveying party laying out a new Swiss colony (New Bern, North Carolina), then launched well-coordinated raids on frontier farms, taking captives and killing some 120 colonists.

The predictable Carolinia response, particularly from South Carolina, was to employ the successful methods of their recent war. Weapons, clothing, and a share of the booty, including captives to be sold to Carolina slavers, were given to any Amerindians who were willing to attack the Tuscarora. In 1711 some five hundred warriors, "led" by thirty South Carolina volunteers, overwhelmed a Tuscarora town, after which much of the army evaporated with its rewards. An inconclusive siege of the Tuscarora stronghold of Hancock's Town ended with a negotiated peace that the colonial governments repudiated and "unruly" allies violated. In March 1713, the South Carolinians repeated their earlier strategy, with a larger and more unified force of eight hundred Creek, Cherokee, and Catawba, combined with one hundred South Carolina volunteers. This army soon burned and stormed the Tuscarora fortified town of Neoheroka, taking 192 scalps and enslaving 392. In this war, an estimated fourteen hundred Tuscarora were killed and about one thousand enslaved. Most of the tribal territory was confiscated, and survivors "scattered as the wind scatters the smoke." Between fifteen hundred and two thousand Tuscarora survivors fled north to join the Five Nations, transforming them into the Six Nations. Like the Susquehannock before them, the Tuscarora and their Six Nation confederates revived raids to the south, especially seeking revenge against the Catawba and Creek who had driven them from their homelands.[13]

 In western Europe, the Peace of Utrecht was truly a peace, not merely a recess in an exhausting war. General war did not return for twenty-seven years, evidence of the stability possible from a peace agreement that did not bring complete defeat or destruction to any of the main antagonists. Yet the peace was not self-perpetuating; the Anglo-French entente needed to be defended and survived only as long as it served the interests of both. For the British, the arrangement meant some security against French support of the rebellious Jacobites, who attracted significant support in 1715 and even in 1745. On the French side, the duc d'Orléans became sole regent for young Louis XV in 1715, in violation of the will of Louis XIV. In the face of considerable French and Spanish opposition, the duc d'Orléans needed peace with Britain. Despite this diplomatic accord, both powers realized that "to utilize peace in order to procure for ourselves all the advantages of a large trade is to wage war on our enemies."[14] The peace represented a balance of power that would eventually be disrupted by unequal economic growth, particularly in the colonial trades, and by Bourbon Spain's diplomatic migration from an aggressively independent foreign policy to an active alliance with France after 1733.

Was there an entente in North America to parallel the understanding between Britain and France in Europe? Hardly anyone who had fought before 1714 would be involved when the fighting resumed after 1739; these new combatants had been raised in a generation of comparative peace. The unprecedented length of formal colonial peace fostered sustained growth of almost all colonial settlements in North America, so that a continent that seemed spacious enough to afford reluctant coexistence in 1714 was too small to permit it to continue thirty years later.

Intense inter-colonial competition for land, trade, and Amerindian alliances led to intermittent fighting along numerous frontiers during the "peace." The eastern end of the Anglo-French frontier remained tense due to stubborn Acadian honesty about their continuing loyalties to France and to Catholicism, spasmodic Canadian and French machinations to regain Acadia, New Englanders' ambitions and suspicions, and British vacillation on requiring an oath of allegiance from these neutral Acadians. The trade of New France exploded into the Mississippi Valley heartland of the continent, drawing the French into numerous Amerindian wars. Tension was even greater on the southern frontiers, where the Peace of Utrecht had done nothing to define French, Spanish, or English spheres. Only enough of the Anglo-French entente was brought to North America to prevent open inter-colonial war, and imperial authorities themselves usually argued as though this was understood.[15] Peace also provided a special opportunity to increase control of Amerindian trade and diplomacy and to strengthen strategic fortifications and settlements. Like gladiators maneuvering for preliminary positions, the empires hesitated to do more than feint, lest a misplaced blow should cost balance, position, or perhaps the entire contest.

In the northeast, peace initially brought trade and reoccupation of abandoned frontier towns on both sides of the Abenaki–New England frontier, but subsequent "expansion" brought English settlers and conflict to the Kennebec River region by 1717. The Abenaki, including some who had returned from Canada after the peace, were divided on whether to allow the New England settlers into their lands, and Sébastien Rale, a missionary who had been there for nearly thirty years, now led the opposition. Early in 1722, New England raiders again burned Norridgewock, including Rale's church, in an attempt to capture the priest. A successful Abenaki revenge raid on the nearest English settlements prompted Massachusetts Governor Samuel Shute to declare the Abenaki rebels and traitors. Abenaki would now pay for the seemingly harmless rhetoric of British claims based on the terms of Utrecht; the Massachusetts government considered the Abenaki not sovereign enemies, but merely rebellious subjects. That government proceeded to offer exorbitant bounties of £100 for scalps of male Abenaki over twelve years of age and left the fighting of this nonwar to bands of private Massachusetts and New Hampshire bounty hunters. After two previous attempts to catch Father Rale, a third raid was made on Norridgewock in August 1724, leaving thirty killed and scalped, including the sixty-seven-year-old missionary. Predictably, English and French records of the incident are entirely irreconcilable, but 150 Norridgewock Abenaki promptly migrated to the Canadian missions of St. François and Bécancour.

What was dubbed Dummer's War on the Eastern Abenaki frontier was called Grey Lock's War (1723–1727) in the upper Connecticut Valley, where this elusive Western Abenaki chief managed a clever guerrilla war from Missisquoi and from the Green Mountains. The Eastern Abenaki and Canadian mission Abenaki finally made peace with Massachusetts in 1727, and Grey Lock's War evaporated without formal settlement. The Abenaki had remained, and even returned, after what had been another unsuccessful attempt to eliminate them, and New England governments now regulated trade through approved "truck houses" to limit disputes. The French had not actively supported the Abenaki beyond supplying them in "peacetime," but it was not for lack of interest in the Abenaki, the war, or the eastern frontier.[16] French construction of the expensive Louisbourg fortress, begun in 1720, was intended to restore Acadian and regional Amerindian loyalties, strengthen the French fisheries, replace lost Port Royal (Annapolis Royal) as a base for privateers, and act as a formidable barrier to New England maritime assaults on New France. Since Québec proved unable to provision Louisbourg, this fortress grew dependent on an illicit trade with New England.[17]

Peace was more secure on the Six Nations–New France frontier, though the French rebuilt Fort Niagara (from 1720) and built Fort St. Frédéric (1731), and New York responded with a rival trading post at Fort Oswego (1727). The Six Nations helped the peace, and themselves, by encouraging western nations to trade at Albany, but discouraging Albany traders from going west. New France nearly went to war over the construction of Fort Oswego, but was restrained by the French government to competing with subsidized prices and some imported English quality cloths that the Amerindians preferred. The fur trade of French forts farther west was leased to garrison commanders, encouraging them to exclude English colonial traders and to foster peace and trade among tribes.

The Peace of Utrecht gave New France the same freedom it gave New England to chastise, or even attempt to eliminate, troublesome Amerindians without much European interference. French relations with the Fox had been uneasy from their beginnings in the 1660s, but were thoroughly poisoned by an incident in 1712. Commandant Lamothe Cadillac had unwisely invited the Fox to settle at Detroit, and those who came in 1711 generated tension that erupted into intertribal war with their traditional enemies in the following year. When forced to choose sides, the French clearly favored their own Huron, Ottawa, and Potawatomi allies and did not protect the newcomers. The Fox surrendered, only to have an estimated one thousand warriors systematically butchered. From a fortified base at Green Bay, those Fox who had not migrated to Detroit took revenge on their Amerindian enemies and on the French. A French–Amerindian expedition against the Fox in 1715 disintegrated without even reaching Fox territory, due to an epidemic and drunkenness. The next year, some four hundred Canadians and four hundred Amerindians volunteered for what proved a more successful venture. The main Fox stronghold was besieged, and a profitable, if unenforceable, peace was negotiated by which the Fox were to repay the war costs of their conquerors. Payment was to be in furs and slaves, taken by going to war against unspecified distant tribes, then surrendered to replace the people slain by the Fox.[18]

By 1720 the Fox had renewed intermittent war against the Potawatomi, Miami, and Illinois, and also, by 1723, against the Ojibwa. New France lost much of its western fur trade during this disruption, and contemplated war against the Fox even before they killed eight Canadian traders heading for Dakota country in 1727. While Fox orators now called for an Amerindian confederacy against all Europeans, Fox warriors were raiding virtually all their neighboring tribes. In 1730 another major Franco-Amerindian army set out to destroy the diplomatically isolated Fox. The intended victims tried to migrate east to join the Seneca, but were forced to defend an improvised stockade against 1400 enemies, including 150 French. Of over eleven hundred Fox refugees, about five hundred were captured and distributed among the victors, four hundred were killed, and only two hundred escaped. The governor of New France, hoping "that this damnable nation will be totally extinguished," encouraged Amerindian allies to raid any remnants of the Fox. By 1738 the Fox, who had numbered ten thousand in 1666, were reduced to a few hundred scattered refugees being protected by tribes who were questioning French intentions. Although the French usually had an accommodating view of Amerindians, there were clear exceptions, even in the fur-trade economy.[19]

In comparison with the Abenaki and Six Nations, or even with the Fox, there was less peace in the lower Mississippi world of the Natchez. The French establishment of Louisiana was intended primarily to keep the English and Spanish away from the Mississippi, a task largely accomplished by Jean-Baptiste Le Moyne de Bienville in his various capacities, between 1701 and 1742. Dependent at first on Amerindians for food and protection, Louisiana quickly became a Choctaw ally, and an enemy of the English-supplied Chickasaw, as well as a competitor for the trade and friendship of the Natchez and the Creek. Links with the three thousand Natchez were demonstrated and strengthened by the building of the palisaded trading post at Fort Rosalie (1716), as were those with the Lower Creek by Fort Toulouse (1717). The hierarchical, sun-worshipping Natchez welcomed French goods, and even French tobacco farmers, but trade produced irritating dependence and the land-hunger of settlers generated Natchez resentment in the 1720s. The great Natchez war chief Serpent-Pique denounced trade dependence prophetically: "Before the arrival of the French, we were living as people who know how to survive with what they have; in place of this, today we are walking as slaves."[20] In the fall of 1729, the Natchez responded with violence to a French land fraud. The French colonial community around Natchez had consisted of 228 men, 80 women, 150 children, and 200 black slaves before the Natchez massacred nearly 300 and destroyed Fort Rosalie. The Natchez farmers fled northward, but were eventually attacked, captured, or dispersed by French and Choctaw forces. Some five hundred Natchez were sold into Caribbean slavery. Refugees fled to the Chickasaw or to the Cherokee; the Natchez, as a tribe, had been destroyed. Eighteenth-century French tobacco planters, quite like seventeenth-century Virginia ones, established a settlement base, encroached on Amerindian farmers, provoked conflict and paid heavily in a massacre that also bankrupted a chartered company, then destroyed a tribe caught without access to Spanish or English weapons or ammunition.[21]

Although the French dispersed the Fox and the Natchez as part of "expansion" during the Peace of Utrecht, the Chickasaw showed the possibilities for resistance by being better situated and better equipped. This bellicose tribe of hunters, who had battered De Soto's army in 1541, had numbered about five thousand in the 1680s when Carolina traders arrived to trade guns, cloth, and utensils for deerskins and Amerindian captives. From their fortified villages on pine ridges of the upper Yazoo and Tombigbee rivers, these Amerindian musketeers conducted slaving raids against their more numerous Choctaw neighbors and against tribes as far away as the Caddo and Illinois. The Louisiana–Choctaw alliance remained rather consistently opposed to the Chickasaw, and negotiated French agreements with the latter would disappoint both sides.

After the Chickasaw incorporated the Natchez refugees, who had good reason to attack French trade and settlements, Bienville and the French government decided to eliminate the Chickasaw. Large raids by unenthusiastic Choctaw, "led" by groups of Canadian and French officers, only burned cornfields. In 1736 Bienville planned an assault involving one army of more than four hundred Canadians, Illinois, and Wyandot from the north and another army of thirteen hundred from Louisiana, led by himself. The northern army was ambushed and destroyed, and nineteen were captured and tortured, disclosing the entire campaign plan. Bienville's own army of 700 Choctaw, 460

French, and 140 black slaves, organized as a separate black-officered company, were ambushed in turn and forced to retreat with a loss of more than a hundred.

Three years later, provided with massive French government support that included cannon, twenty-pound mortars with explosive shells, ten gunners, and a shipment of nearly four times the fifteen thousand pounds of gunpowder requested, Bienville tried again. This time, 1000 French soldiers and settlers and 300 blacks formed the core of Bienville's army, with 88 Canadians and 354 northern Amerindians meeting the force at newly built Fort Assumption for a winter campaign. The ox-drawn artillery could not proceed without expensive and time-consuming bridges and roads. By abandoning artillery, even if it had come halfway around the world, Bienville may have avoided a Braddock-like disaster. After defeating a volunteer advance party, the Chickasaw suddenly agreed to a negotiated end to the fighting. The Louisiana government had spent three times its annual budget and its army had spread disease throughout the lower Mississippi, but still failed to impress the Chickasaw opponents, the Choctaw allies, or the French court. The Chickasaw, who would later turn back another French expedition of annihilation, were confirmed in their trade alliance with the English.[22]

The aggressive instability that characterized North American frontiers during the thirty years after the Treaty of Utrecht was also obvious in the southern world of the Creek. The Yamasee, well-armed Savannah River relatives of the Creek, had allied with the Carolinians against the Apalachee in Queen Anne's War, and had been regarded by the English colonists as the most reliable allies in their war against the Tuscarora. However, unscrupulous Carolinia traders and planters increasingly manipulated Yamasee trading debts to confiscate land and enslave women and children. With Creek instigation, and perhaps some encouragement from Bienville, the Yamasee suddenly captured all Carolina traders in their territory on April 15, 1715, and immediately attacked South Carolina frontier settlements. Lower Creek and Catawba, who had benefited from a trade war they presumed would continue between Virginia and South Carolina, joined the growing anti-English Amerindian alliance that soon included Savannah (Shawnee), Guale, Cherokee, and several remnant tribes from the old chiefdom of Cofitachiqui. As the raids increased, approaching within twelve miles of Charlestown, colonists feared that their Amerindian and African slaves would "revolt" and join the raiders.

South Carolina was threatened with destruction and was poorly prepared to defend itself, given its predatory buccaneering style of warfare and its precarious internal order. In 1715 South Carolina contained 5500 Europeans enslaving 8650 Africans and irritating many of the 5100 Amerindians within the colony and thousands more nearby. The government asked Britain, New England, Virginia, and North Carolina for help. The militia, whose main function was internal social control, was unwilling to undertake expeditions, even within the colony. A hired force of one hundred mounted rangers was ambushed and scattered by the Yamasee. In desperation, a paid army of twelve hundred was raised, including five hundred blacks and one hundred friendly Amerindians. The South Carolina government even armed some slaves during this crisis. This army had little success against the Yamasee, but diplomacy was effective once it became clear that the Virginians would not trade arms or ammunition to be used against their fellow English in the Carolinas. The Catawba withdrew from the Yamasee alliance, and the Cherokee changed sides to aid South Carolina actively from early in 1716. By the following year, the Creek also withdrew from a war that would drag on intermittently for another eleven years, with the Yamasee and Guale still raiding from bases in Spanish Florida.

This Yamasee War, which came very close to becoming a race war, cast a very long shadow on the history of the southeast. The Yamasee became firm allies of the Spanish, giving San Agustín a new protective buffer composed of Apalachee, Guale, and numerous Lower Creek (eventually forming the Seminole), as well as escaped black slaves from Carolina. These warriors raided from villages near Fort San Marcos de Apalachee (1718) or from San Agustín. The French had been unable to become arms suppliers to the anti-English alliance, but gained from the disruption of English trade and the growth of anti-English feelings among Amerindians, particularly the Upper Creek. The displaced Shawnee moved north into Pennsylvania, then west into the upper Ohio and Mississippi valleys, carrying enduring enmity toward the English, the Cherokee, and the Catawba. The Lower Creek, led by Emperor Brims, tried to alternate friendship and hostility toward the English, Spanish, and French, in turn, while nursing a sense of betrayal by the Cherokee that would prompt the bitter Creek–Cherokee War (1716–1727).

English South Carolina was also transformed by the Yamasee War. Some four hundred settlers had been killed, a larger percentage of the population than were killed during King Philip's War in New England, trade was disrupted, and frontier areas were abandoned. Carolina traders became much more accommodating in the Amerindian trade that was now regulated by a government that built blockhouses at Fort Moore (1716), Port Royal (1716), Congaree (1718), and Fort King George (1721–1727) to control traders as well as defend frontiers. The British proprietors of the colony had been discredited by their failure to assist during the war, and by local coup, the colony offered itself directly to the British crown in 1719. Amerindian war had destroyed yet another colonial government.[23]

The Peace of Utrecht was used by colonists not only to fight Amerindians, but also to tolerate or encourage wars between tribes. The Six Nations allies of the British continued traditional raiding against other

British allies, the Catawba and the Cherokee. Iroquois "mourning war" was matched by Catawba "crying blood" practices to continue a long-distance limited war that trained young warriors of each group. For both the Catawba and the Cherokee, who were even more decentralized than the Six Nations, these wars promoted solidarity. The English in New York and in the Carolinas recognized these raids as occupying belligerent young warriors who might otherwise harass English settlers. It was only when the European peace ended that British and colonial officials sought to suspend these wars between their allies. The British orchestrated a peace between the Cherokee and the Six Nations in 1742 and again in 1757, and a Catawba–Iroquois peace in 1751. Only the British thought that these conferences brought effective peace; the sachems who negotiated realized that they could not speak for all warriors. British colonial cynicism would become evident again after the peace of 1763, when these intertribal wars were again actively encouraged.[24]

The Peace of Utrecht was also interrupted in Spanish North America whenever Spain was at war in Europe. England and France went to war against Spain between 1718 and 1721, putting Charlestown and San Agustín on guard. San Agustín privateers ranged as far north as New England to capture English ships. A major Spanish expedition of fourteen ships and fourteen hundred men assembled at Havana, intended against Charlestown, but was diverted to retake Pensacola, which Bienville had opportunistically captured by way of informing the local Spanish commander of the outbreak of war. The French and their Choctaw allies took Pensacola again, but it was restored to Spain in the peace settlement of 1721. The English and Spanish were again at war in 1727 and 1728, leading to an English naval blockade of Portobello, which deprived the Spanish government of its Central American silver fleet. The Carolinians took the opportunity to attack San Agustín; a force of a hundred colonial volunteers, led by Colonel John Palmer, and a hundred Amerindians invaded by land. They attacked the new outworks of Castillo de San Marcos with some success, but failed against the citadel. After burning the Yamasee mission village of Nombre de Dios, they retreated with fifteen captives.[25] By this time, Carolina gun traders had distributed flintlocks so thoroughly to Spanish and Amerindian customers that their own earlier military advantage was largely destroyed.

The Peace of Utrecht was not a peace for the Abenaki, Fox, Natchez, Chickasaw, or Yamasee, or for their opponents. Extensive French colonies increased their protection at key places by building major fortifications that would eventually prescribe a different kind of warfare. British colonies expanded in population and trade, colliding repeatedly with the French and Spanish spheres, particularly in the south. The Spanish insisted that the clearest European violation of the peace in North America was the founding of British Georgia in 1733, which was a confiscation of Florida's evacuated province of Guale. For the British, this government-funded colony offered humanitarian opportunity to poor English debtors and soldiers, and it was a defensive buffer for the valuable South Carolina plantations. By 1739 Georgia contained two thousand settlers, several fortifications, and a regiment of seven hundred Scottish Highlanders under the colony's founder, General James Oglethorpe. Georgia was not a major cause of the ensuing war, but a British preparation for it.

Wholesale English violations of trading restrictions in Spanish America during the 1730s had been met with excessive violence from Spanish privateers and *guarda costa*, including one minor incident in which Captain Robert Jenkins's ear was severed. Through the Convention of Pardo (1739), Robert Walpole's government negotiated compensation for Spanish confiscations, but Spain refused to pay in reaction to mounting British belligerence. British clamor for a predatory war against Spain overwhelmed Walpole's political resistance, and British naval squadrons in the Mediterranean and Caribbean were ordered to take Spanish prizes as compensation for the nonpayment. A mere six men-of-war under Walpole's bellicose parliamentary critic, Admiral Edward Vernon, captured the valued Spanish Caribbean port of Portobello in November 1739, inflaming British and colonial enthusiasm for the still undeclared War of Jenkins' Ear.

The British offensive against Spain in America, characteristically more reckless than conflicts with New France, began with another siege of San Agustín and an amphibious attack on Cartagena. Both of these imperial campaigns anticipated problems that would become clearer in British colonial America during the next war, as well as repeating some patterns of the earlier wars. Oglethorpe commanded the operation against Castillo de San Marcos, which had defeated Moore in 1702 and Palmer in 1728. The British gave Oglethorpe supplies, six Royal Navy frigates, two sloops, and command of the South Carolina and Georgia militias, in addition to his own Forty-second Regiment.

The South Carolina government, though anxious for success against San Agustín and sympathetic to Oglethorpe, promptly raised many of the objections that would plague subsequent imperial-colonial military relations and immediately altered his campaign. Oglethorpe, aware of previous experiences and current conditions, intended a long, patient siege to force capitulation by Governor Manuel de Montiano's famished garrison and civilians. Oglethorpe asked South Carolina for six hundred volunteers, eight hundred black "pioneers," one hundred rangers, and two thousand well-equipped Amerindians. The South Carolina government had just been severely shaken by the Stono slave rebellion of November 1739, when twenty English colonists had been killed by nearly one hundred armed slaves. They then attempted to escape to San Agustín, where sixty-six other escaped slaves already lived in the freedom promised by the Spanish. It had taken the South

Carolina militia and the well-paid local Amerindian recruits a month to suppress the uprising completely, and the government was unwilling to send blacks with Oglethorpe or to strip the colony of either effective militia or Amerindian forces. Also anxious to limit costs, the South Carolina legislature offered only four hundred volunteers, most hired from North Carolina, and five hundred well-equipped Cherokee and Creek. The legislature stipulated that the volunteers serve for only four months, remaining in their original units, and that their newly appointed officers be treated like regular officers of equal rank in councils of war. Any of that regiment's military offenses were to be tried and punished only by the South Carolinia regiment itself, rather than by regular courts-martial. Relations between Oglethorpe and the Carolina regiment were strained from the beginning and deteriorated further.[26]

South Carolina had forced Oglethorpe into a quick assault on San Agustín, with fewer men than he had requested for his less strenuous siege. His 1620 attackers had poor odds against an excellent fort defended by 750 Spanish troops. In April 1740, the Royal Navy squadron began blockading San Agustín, but heavily armed shallow-draft Spanish half-galleys prevented Oglethorpe's planned landing of men and artillery directly from the British ships. Driven back to his earlier idea of a siege, Oglethorpe was unable to develop a detailed plan that allowed artillery to be advanced over marshy approaches. British batteries could reach but not damage the fort, which was near the limit of their firing range. A courageous Spanish night sortie against a captured redoubt caused 122 British casualties. British morale was further eroded by disease and bickering, and especially by the arrival of seven Spanish supply ships that had evaded the blockade and replenished supplies for the two thousand people within the fort. The British forces now retreated, sharing recriminations, rather than anticipated booty. Captain Peter Warren of HMS *Squirrel* denounced "the ill-concerted and worse conducted attack on St. Augustine. I hope I shall never have any part in such an expedition again."[27]

The second major English initiative was the 1741 siege of Cartagena. Some thirty-six hundred "Americans," called such for the first time by British authorities who were paying, arming, and supplying them, enthusiastically accepted bounty money and joined with two regular army regiments and six experimental regiments of British marines in what they thought would be a buccaneering raid. Effective Spanish defense, strategic disputes between Admiral Vernon and General Thomas Wentworth, and an epidemic in the fleet respectively delayed, confused, and destroyed the expedition. More than half the expedition, including half of the Americans, died. Another transatlantic offensive against a strong fortification had revealed the axiomatic advantage of defense, and another grand design of British imperial cooperation, like the Walker expedition of 1711, had ended in disillusionment.

The Spanish made one major attempt to retaliate for the English attacks. San Agustín's Governor Montiano led a Spanish army of nineteen hundred regulars and militia in an attack on Georgia in 1742. Their naval artillery quickly overpowered Georgia's main coastal defense at St. Simon's Island, but two hundred Spaniards were killed in an ambush by Highlanders and Creek; that incident ended the advance on Oglethorpe's capital at Frederica. The expedition hastily withdrew to San Agustín, amid rumors of an approaching British squadron. In September 1742, a British squadron tried to enter San Agustín harbor, but was driven off by well-armed half-galleys. A major raid by two hundred Amerindians and a few Georgia volunteers, sometimes glorified as another Oglethorpe siege, ravaged the San Agustín vicinity the following March. Slave-raiding was apparently becoming more difficult, so both sides lost their taste for major offensives. A privateering war continued at sea, but San Agustín began to enjoy two decades of local peace (1743–1763), as its English rivals became entirely preoccupied with the French.[28]

The North American version of the War of the Austrian Succession, known as King George's War (1744–1748), was more like a replay of earlier Anglo-French contests than a preliminary for the climactic final struggle. As with the two earlier wars, European monarchs signaled the commencement of hostilities. Once again, the Europeans gave only spasmodic support in the colonial theater, and the colonists fought less than the full duration of Europe's war. In the hope of regaining Acadia, or at least obtaining supplies and a great quantity of fish as booty, the French governor of Louisbourg began hostilities by a successful expedition against Canso, Nova Scotia, in May 1744. A base for New England fishermen, Canso had little strategic importance except as a minor British military outpost that, if reinforced, might sever communications between Louisbourg and Acadia. After this initial success came failure in a more ambitious French attempt to take Annapolis Royal in July. A perceptive resident of Louisbourg, realizing that this Franco-Canadian raid on Canso provoked the New England attack on Louisbourg in 1745, complained:

> It was the interest of the people of New England to live at peace with us and they would undoubtedly have done so if we had not been so ill-advised as to disturb the security which they felt in regard to us. They expected that both sides would hold aloof from the cruel war that set Europe on fire, and that we, as well as they, should remain on the defensive only.[29]

The raid on Canso, like Frontenac's raids of 1690 or Vaudreuil's of 1703/1704, was an initial blow that prompted invasion. New Englanders were outraged, and Governor William Shirley of Massachusetts grasped this opportunity to improve his political support, and to reduce faction, by promoting an attack on Louisbourg.[30] The prevailing view was that a land attack would be very difficult, and French engineers had lavished most of their resources on the port's naval defense. Even so, the four thousand attacking New Englanders were pleasantly surprised to discover that they were safe from the big cannon of the Grand Battery. Once captured, these guns provided firepower against the citadel itself. The siege was conducted by New England paid volunteers led by "merchant prince" William Pepperrell. Lack of experience and discipline were apparent; nearly half the American casualties came from mishandled cannon.[31] The siege was a caricature of European warfare conducted with levity and recklessness, but fortune was with the New Englanders at Louisbourg.

Although the New Englanders considered the victory largely their own, they had received £11,000 from New York and Pennsylvania and had been supported by a British West Indian naval squadron under Commodore Peter Warren. By fortunate communications, Warren had been able to bring his squadron from the Leeward Islands to protect the landing of the colonial troops. Before the siege ended, Warren had twelve ships, totaling nearly six hundred guns, blockading Louisbourg and taking prizes that would make his personal fortune. French munitions for Louisbourg were captured and used against the city, and maritime communications and supply lines to New England were secured. Warren's squadron was sufficient because other British naval squadrons were blockading French naval ports.

The 1745 capture of Louisbourg was the British empire's first major success against New France, but British and Americans had complemented each other rather than cooperating closely to achieve victory. A Louisbourg resident commented: "So striking was the mutual independence of the land army and the fleet that they were always represented to us as of different nations."[32] As with the successful 1710 attack on Port Royal, the fleet only protected the army that took the citadel. This was not an amphibious operation. Ships' guns did not bombard Louisbourg, as had those of Phips when he failed to take Québec, or those of Vernon when he failed at Cartagena.

Conquest of Louisbourg was the most significant event of the American theater in King George's War, and reactions to it explain much of the rest of the war. New England and Britain were exuberant, though the secretary of state, Thomas Pelham-Holles, duke of Newcastle, was embarrassed by the conquest, which made the angry French court less willing to negotiate peace. Just as the Walker expedition had followed the capture of Port Royal, so a two-pronged invasion of Canada was planned for 1746, with the rendezvous for the forces at newly captured Louisbourg. When the British fleet and eight battalions failed to arrive, New Englanders could console themselves with the knowledge that the colonial troops raised in anticipation of the invasion were in British pay.

The fall of Louisbourg, and the British naval blockade of French ports, had cut off French presents and trade supplies for their Amerindian allies and customers of the upper Great Lakes, Ohio Valley, and Louisiana. This weakened French alliances, helped to provoke the anti-French Ohio Valley "Indian Conspiracy of 1747" and the Choctaw Revolt of 1746 to 1749, and diverted trade and friends to the English.[33]

While Britain schemed to build on the Louisbourg success, France tried to reverse it. In the spring of 1746, an armada of seventy-six sail, including ten ships-of-the-line, assembled at Rochefort. This massive fleet, under the duc d'Anville, escaped the British blockade of French ports, but its escape was the last good fortune for this ill-fated flotilla. Its three-month Atlantic passage featured ferocious storms, deadly calms, and epidemics that cost three thousand lives, including that of the commander. Like ghost ships, the tattered fleet went home from Nova Scotian waters without accomplishing anything; the death toll had been higher than that of the whole war in North America.

European schemes of 1746 also provoked feverish defensive measures in North America. New England troops, sent to Albany for the invasion of Canada, were hastily redeployed when rumors arrived of Anville's expected descent on either Louisbourg, Annapolis Royal, or Boston. Scores of Abenaki from St. François and Missisquoi raided with impunity throughout the war, driving settlers from Vermont, the upper Connecticut River Valley, and Massachusetts frontier settlements.[34] New France's defense forces against the 1746 invasion turned into offensive attacks that captured Fort Massachusetts and destroyed New York's frontier settlement at Saratoga. The governor of New France took initiatives in Acadia to offset the loss of Louisbourg, using Micmac and Abenaki allies to force cooperation from neutral Acadians. Captain Nicholas-Antoine Coulon de Villiers led 235 Canadians and 42 Malecite, Micmac, and Abenaki on a gruelling winter raid that surprised a New England garrison twice their number at Grand Pré, forcing their surrender. The capture of Louisbourg had done nothing to calm New England frontiers.

Taking Louisbourg brought other unpleasant consequences for Massachusetts. Whatever Anglo-American goodwill had come from the Louisbourg campaign was largely dispelled in Massachusetts by having the entire Massachusetts contingent stay as a garrison for Louisbourg for ten months and by the failure to attack Québec in 1746. A significant irritant for Boston was a new act of Parliament that excluded North American colonies from its ban on West Indian impressment of seamen without the consent of local governors and councils. Impressment was a brutal form of forced naval recruitment that occasionally produced riots in seaports throughout the British empire, often begun by deserters from the Royal Navy in danger of being identified and executed if forced aboard naval vessels. Boston sailors had violently resisted in 1741 and again just after the capture of Louisbourg when two merchant sailors were killed by a press gang from Admiral War-ren's fleet. A three-day riot, including hostage-taking and widespread vandalism, occurred late in 1747 against Admiral Charles Knowles's efforts to impress sailors for his undermanned fleet, from which scores had deserted in Boston. Frightened local authorities, who discovered that the town's militia refused to intervene, joined a chorus of local worthies who denounced the violence once it had ended. Although there were prophetic elements in Sam Adams's printed rhetoric about the natural right to resist tyranny, as well as ample evidence that reg-ular troops might be needed to keep order in Boston if its militia would not, this localized outburst against authority was neither uncommon nor revolutionary. Knowles was governor of captured Louisbourg, and his sizable fleet had been welcome while it monitored the fate of Anville's fleet. The Royal Navy's requirements were resented as part of the increasing price of war for Massachusetts, a war on a scale that was escaping local control and becoming inescapably imperial.[35]

North American issues were generally ignored in the European peace of Aix-la-Chapelle (1748), though colonial pawns were exchanged. Louisbourg, for all its importance and all the effort involved in its capture, was returned to France. Europeans tried, in the face of unprecedented colonial tensions, to keep this peace in North America. The earl of Holderness, British secretary of state, warned Massachusetts Governor Shirley as late as August 1753 of French schemes:

> But as it's His Majesty's determination not to be the agressor, I have the King's commands, most strictly to enjoin you, not to make use of the armed force under your direction, excepting within the undoubted limits of his Majesty's dominions[36]

Those "undoubted limits" were in more doubt than ever, as was con-firmed by the futile Anglo-French commission on North American boundaries. The Abenaki had not made peace and raided New England occasionally for prisoners and revenge. The British established a naval station and military colony at Halifax, Nova Scotia (1749), to balance Louisbourg, placate New England, and intimidate the Acadians. There was, once again, some ferocious fighting between Amerindians during this short peace. French-allied Ottawa attacked the Mississauga in 1749 as punishment for trading with the English, and the same enforcers destroyed the pro-English Miami town of Pickawillany in 1752. Louis-iana's new governor, Pierre de Rigaud de Vaudreuil, had seen the Choctaw alliance eroded by desperate wartime shortages of French trade goods, by invasions of English traders, and by Choctaw civil war.[37]

In some respects, King George's War had ended with a familiar rep-etition of what had become the essence of inter-colonial war in North America. Europeans announced the war, drained resources from huge populations to conduct massive campaigns every year in Europe, but paid little attention to colonists who, when imperial assistance came, had reason to wish it had not been given. New England colonies were provoked by Canadian raids into a major initial effort, but could not sustain the costs and enthusiasm needed for a decisive victory. A certain balance of irritants, and opportunistic "disciplining" of Amerindians, accompanied the peace. The building of Louisbourg, Niagara, and Fort St. Frédéric, the founding of Georgia, the San Agustín siege of 1740, Anville's armada of 1746, the Knowles Riot of 1747, and the British founding of Halifax were all, in retrospect, evidence of increasing European government investment in the North American contest. However, it was not yet entirely clear that the indecisive inter-colonial warfare for North America was about to be superseded.

Part III

EMPIRES, COLONIES, AND TRIBES 1748–1765

Three kinds of invasion were evident concurrently in North America in the middle of the eighteenth century. Some Amerindians in remoter parts of the Great Plains, in the Rockies, and in the Arctic tundra were still beginning their confrontation with permanent European bases, new diseases, and firearms. The second type of invasion: inter-colonial war, resumed between English and French traders, soldiers, and settlers, now fighting over a wider area with larger forces, and beyond the levels of economic and social exhaustion that had limited the first three Anglo-French wars. This intensification resulted from the meshing of inter-colonial war with the third type of invasion: the coming of European regular warfare to North America.

This new mixture of military assumptions, methods, and objectives was first displayed in the contest for the Ohio Valley after 1748, which introduced new Amerindian, colonial, and imperial contestants. New groups of Ohio Amerindians became involved in a war that could no longer be contained by the Appalachian Mountains and by the neutrality of a Six Nation confederacy at one end and a Creek confederacy at the other. Amerindian refugees and immigrants to the upper Ohio, predominantly Delaware, Shawnee, and Mingo, were suspicious of French and British ambitions and skeptical of their promises. Ohio villagers sought the security of a trade and price advantage of what had become necessary European goods, including arms and gunpowder. They were wary not only of encroachments by either European power, but also of Six Nation pretensions, which too easily became the power to sell Delaware lands. The bitter experiences of the Shawnee and the Delaware also indicated that English settlers with Amerindian allies were particularly dangerous to other Amerindian hunters and farmers. The coming Anglo-French war would attract a great number of warriors from various tribes who were anxious to fight for reputation, French gifts, and English booty, and to expel English colonial settlers from Amerindian lands. Although New France outfitted these raiders and claimed their victories, the Amerindians were largely fighting a parallel war of their own, which would resume without French support in 1763.[1]

Participation in the next Anglo-French war also expanded to include more of the 1.2 million British colonial settlers and slaves. The new Ohio frontier drew Virginia and Pennsylvania directly into the Anglo-French contest, nearly doubling the colonial taxpayers and potential soldiers on the English side. However, Virginia had social, political, and economic difficulty in organizing for war after two generations of peace. Although Pennsylvania may well have been able to feed an army of 100,000 in 1755, the Quaker-led government was incapacitated and replaced when war proved inescapable.[2] The concerns of these new participants were capable of rousing the British government to direct action, though this time inter-colonial war began before the imperial courts declared it. In a colony like Massachusetts, which had already faced the taxes, casualties, and tensions of escalating war in the 1740s, these disturbing problems intensified. Internal political and religious wranglings and problems of shrinking economic opportunity were largely suspended to fight for the survival of the English Protestant empire that was also their own.[3]

The North American strategic situation was also new, with the French now forced to protect extended exterior lines of communication from the Gulf of St. Lawrence to the Gulf of Mexico. Even in these vast wildernesses, the English could force their opponents to move resources along even longer, more exposed frontiers in response to alarms. The Appalachian barrier between empires was now being breached by the roads built by Washington (1754), Braddock (1755), and Forbes (1758), in addition to the long-contested Mohawk Valley and Lake Champlain routes. Increased inland fortification could be challenged only with siege cannon, requiring roads, bridges, and larger armies, theoretically favoring the more populous English over the Canadians, and favoring European regulars even more. Colonial population growth and expansion also encouraged conventional warfare, since the relative number of experienced frontiersmen declined, especially in British America.

The most important change was that both Britain and France lavished unprecedented military resources on this theater of their global war. The new scale of the conflict and the growing dominance of European regulars in its management and execution brought predictable collisions over the objectives, methods, and ethics of war, and also broke the inter-colonial stalemate. The European concepts of gladiatorial war, limited objectives, and negotiated settlements made possible a resolution of the long Anglo-French struggle for North America. After two hundred years of competing European invasions, a single imperial power finally triumphed, though for only fifteen troubled years.

This latest invasion of European power was invited, assisted, and witnessed by Amerindians and by colonists of each empire; their worlds were being changed in ways that became apparent only after the British victory. The Amerindian communities would face the consequences of these changes first, and many of those in the *pays d'en haut* fought the intruders. Amerindians reacted to this final invasion of colonial North America with an explosion of violence against British regulars occupying the western posts. The bizarre war of Amerindian sieges of British forts indicated how much had changed in the decade after Braddock's regulars had arrived. The Amerindian War of 1763 quickly became a stalemate and eventually ended in a precarious negotiated accommodation.

Chapter 9

INVADING THE OHIO
1748–1755

The upper Ohio country had long been a relatively uninhabited hunting area, claimed by the Six Nations by conquest, the British colonies by charter, the French crown by discovery, and various Amerindian tribes by occupancy. After 1701, refugees from a number of tribes began to settle in the area, led by Shawnee and Delaware migrants escaping British colonial encroachment east of the Appalachians. Other tribes drifted in from the west, including Mascoutens, Kickapoo, and Miami, moving closer to European suppliers. Some Iroquois also settled, becoming known as the Mingo, and resisted Six Nations pretensions to sovereignty over the residents. The French founding of Detroit (1701) attracted bands of Wyandot, Ottawa, Ojibwa, Potawatami, Fox, Miami, and other French allies whose settlements interposed between the Six Nations and the Ohio Valley.

New France had not shown much interest in the upper Ohio Valley before 1749, when it was formally put under the jurisdiction of Canada's governor. Although French explorers, missionaries, and traders had long traveled the Mississippi Valley, their preferred routes were through the Green Bay–Fox River waterway or down the Illinois River to the Mississippi (Map 7). New France's population had tripled since 1715, to some fifty-five thousand, but farmlands had expanded little beyond the Ottawa, Richelieu, and Chaudière valleys. By the mid-eighteenth century, the upper Ohio region was no longer yielding quantities of prime fur, so that the region's primary value was now reverted to the farmers, Amerindian or British American. For New France, this peripheral trading area now became vital in defending the entire western empire, once British Americans began proving that the Appalachians were no longer adequate defenses.

The fundamental links between trade and alliance had already been demonstrated by the Ohio Valley tribes when there was a shortage of French trade goods in the wake of the capture of Louisbourg in 1745. When suddenly deprived of gunpowder and ammunition, musket-using Amerindian hunters could starve, and warriors could fall victim

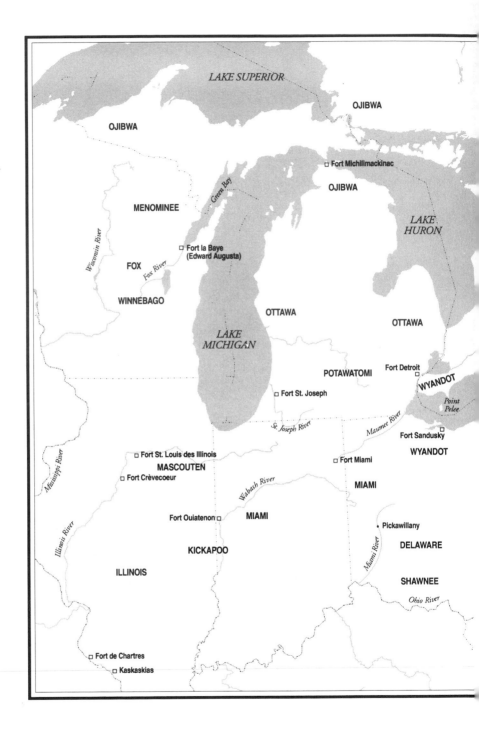

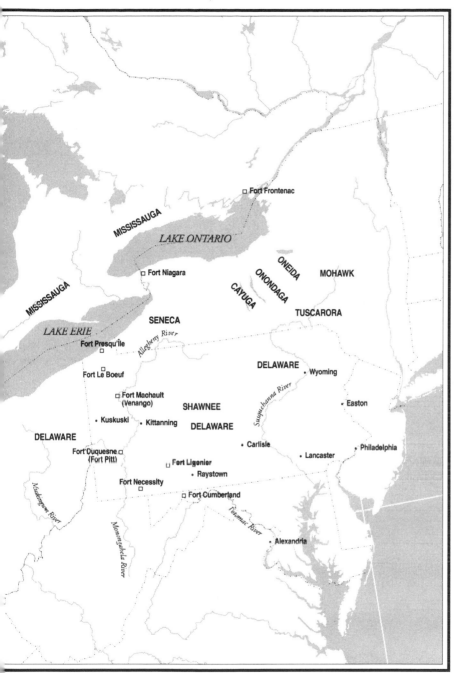

Map 7. The disputed west to 1765.

©1993 Ian K. Steele

to better-supplied enemies, or those still adept with bow and arrow. French-allied tribes turned to Pennsylvania traders who were breaking through the Appalachian Mountains barrier into the upper Ohio Valley. By 1747 there was a large intertribal conspiracy against the French, apparently under Six Nation auspices, involving Shawnee, Choctaw, and Creek. It also included fatal attacks on French fur convoys by Wyandot, Ottawa, and Ojibwa, as well as the ransacking of Fort Miami by Miami chief Memeskia (also known as La Demoiselle or Old Briton). Some of these groups migrated eastward to the Sandusky and Miami rivers, and formalized their new Pennsylvania connections with the Treaty of Lancaster (1748).[1] Although the "conspiracy" faded with the coming of French trade goods and military reinforcements, the French had been warned.

The English colonial invasion of the Ohio became more direct in 1749. The Pennsylvania traders returned in numbers and, led by interpreter George Croghan, based their very competitive trading at the Miami village of Pickawillany, attracting various tribes. This was the most imminent threat to the power and interests of French commanders, though the Virginians associated with the new Ohio Company of Virginia proved more aggressive intruders. This company's British government grant of 500,000 Ohio Valley acres was valid only if it built and maintained a fort at the forks of the Ohio and settled a hundred families on these lands within seven years. Theirs was the first of a series of competing land ventures that provoked rivalries among groups of speculators, among colonies, and between all intruders and Amerindians. Their first major obstacle, however, was French determination to exclude all English from the Ohio Valley.

Canada's four new governors between 1747 and 1755 and the new French minister of marine misjudged the Ohio Valley tribes. Chiefs were humiliated, subjection was demanded, and naked force replaced the familiar rituals of Amerindian–French negotiation. The first Canadian attempt to reinforce claims to the upper Ohio was a somewhat quixotic expedition of 1749, when veteran commander Pierre-Joseph Céleron de Blainville led 265 colonial regulars, militia, and Amerindians on an armed tour. He carried a number of lead plates to be posted or buried at strategic points, each proclaiming French sovereignty over the entire Ohio basin. Blainville's expedition forced out, momentarily, small groups of Pennsylvania traders and conducted rather strained conferences with Seneca, Delaware, Mingo, Shawnee, and Miami. These councils were openly hostile to the French, confirming the suspicion that, like the stone pillars and crosses two centuries earlier, the lead plates would be no substitute for occupation in the coming confrontation.[2]

Blainville's reception had been particularly poor at Pickawillany, strategically positioned to command French use of three excellent canoe routes from Lake Erie to the Mississippi. British colonial traders had helped the Miami, led by chief Memeskia, build a split-log palisade that also protected their own flourishing trade at Pickawillany. To Canada's leaders, still resenting the Miami attack of 1747, this English intrusion was intolerable. However, Blainville lacked the manpower and firearms advantage to force the Miami back to the Maumee River, as intended, and his larger expedition two years later was stalled at Detroit by reluctant allies. In June 1752, a Canadian-instigated war party of some 240 Ojibwa and Ottawa finally attacked Pickawillany. This surprise raid was led by Charles-Michel Mouet de Langlade, son of an Ottawa Amerindian and a French trader. As most of the Miami warriors were away hunting, the remaining fifteen, along with five traders, were able to resist for only a few hours. Memeskia was killed despite the terms of surrender, and his body, as well as the heart of an English trader, was boiled and eaten, symbolically completing the victory. Having looted and burned the traders' storehouses, the raiders hoisted the French flag over the fort and left with three English prisoners. Although the French flag would be replaced by a British one a few days later, Pickawillany had proved too dangerous for trade. Equally significant, a Miami call for assistance yielded nothing whatever from their Six Nation or Pennsylvania allies.[3]

Governor Ange Duquesne de Menneville, marquis Duquesne, took a more direct military initiative in 1753. Fifteen hundred *troupes de la marine* and Canadian militia built Fort Presqu'île and two more forts between it and the Allegheny River. They were accompanied by Seneca "hunters" who gave some Six Nation support to the venture at the same time as Mohawk were sounding alarms about the expedition to New York authorities. English traders found in the area were sent to Québec in chains. Local Amerindians, rebuffed when they insisted that the French leave, sent delegations to Virginia seeking help. In return, the Mingo "half-king" Scarouady privately agreed to allow the Virginians to establish a fort at the forks of the Ohio.[4] The governor of Virginia sent young George Washington, a struggling planter, militia officer, and fellow Ohio Company stockholder, to order the French to leave their newly built Fort Le Boeuf. The veteran Canadian explorer, interpreter, and soldier Jacques le Gardeur de Saint-Pierre politely but firmly refused.

At the end of 1753, Virginia's Governor Robert Dinwiddie received what proved to be fateful British permission to use force to eject the French from British-claimed territory in the Ohio. It was difficult to interest Virginians in fighting for speculators' lands "about two hundred miles back of our nearest mountains";[5] virtually no one volunteered for the new Virginia Regiment, and most of the 159 soldiers accompanying Washington and his few Mingo scouts in 1754 were destitute and reluctant draftees. On their way to the forks of the Ohio, they ambushed a small Canadian group sent to warn the Virginians away. Ensign Joseph Coulon de Villiers de Jumonville was among ten

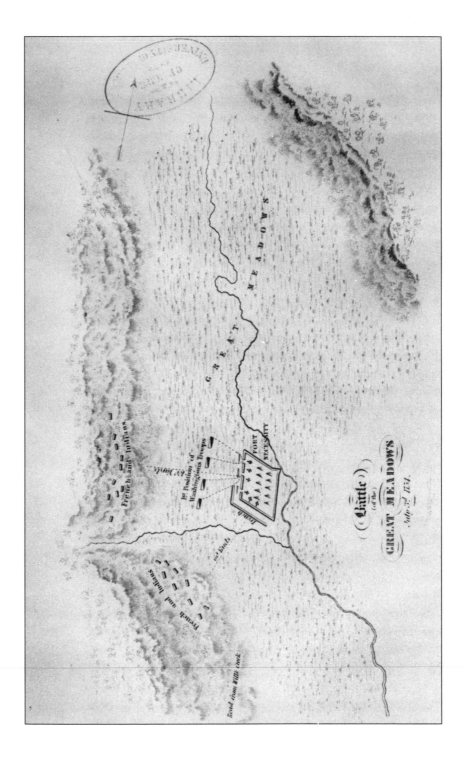

Battle of the
GREAT MEADOWS
July 3d 1754.

killed, and twenty-one were taken prisoner. The peacetime "assassination of Jumonville" eventually caused a diplomatic furor in Europe. More immediately, it provoked a larger force, of French, Canadian, and Amerindian warriors led by the ensign's brother, to go in pursuit of Washington.

Washington's reaction, in retreating to his aptly named supply base at Fort Necessity, displays the colonial confusion of guerrilla and regular warfare already evident in the ambush of Jumonville. These were not irregular frontiersmen using the new and expensive rifles, but undertrained conventional soldiers with muskets and bayonets. Their retreating to a small stockaded supply cabin, rather than scattering, was logical but conventional. On July 3, 1754, while the Virginians were digging entrenchments and fire pits in the mud outside their weak palisade, a force of five hundred French, Canadian, and mission Amerindians filtered into the nearby woods.[6] Judging the fort too weak, Washington formed his men into a firing line in front of it, to defend the fort that could not defend them (Figure 9). War whoops from the woods convinced the Virginians that this would not be a "civilized" contest, and they soon scrambled for the meager protection of the palisade. Fortunately for Washington and his men, this mixture of martial values ended in an honored formal surrender rather than in a massacre. All the surviving Virginians returned home, except two hostages intended to secure the return of the surviving prisoners taken from Jumonville's group. Building a fort and surrendering it actually proved a better claim to territory than a lead plate, for the attack was a well-documented act of war. French victory was symbolized by the capture and completion of another unfinished Virginia fort, renamed Fort Duquesne.

During that same summer of 1754, delegates from the seven English colonies north of Virginia met at Albany at the British government's request. Although best remembered for its plans for inter-colonial unity, the Albany Congress's main role was to provide men and money for inter-colonial defense and to placate the Six Nations. The pro-English Six Nations attending proved disappointingly few, and they were very upset with the English failure to match French initiatives in the Ohio and elsewhere and with English encroachment on Six Nation lands and mismanagement of trade. The thirty wagon loads of presents did not compensate for English inactivity. The congress gave more extensive consideration to proposals for an effective colonial union, endorsing a "general government," headed by a "president general."

Figure 9. *(facing)* Fort Necessity, 1754. What is here represented as walls were actually the trenches, the fort being an even smaller circular palisade protecting a storage cabin. From Jared Sparks, *Writings of Washington* (Boston, 1834–1837). (Courtesy of Hatcher Graduate Library, University of Michigan)

Persistent problems were addressed by the proposal to give this government exclusive power to declare war, make peace, raise and pay troops, build forts, equip ships, and regulate trade and diplomacy with Amerindians. In addition, this government would have the power to levy the necessary taxes. The proposal was not supported by the colonial or the imperial governments, all defending their own powers; cynics pointed out that this theoretical talk allowed delegates to avoid immediate appropriations for the defense of the northern frontier. The conference was aware that existing inter-colonial measures would be inadequate in the renewed conflict that was already beginning.

Virginians had initiated much more than they could accomplish. Amerindians had been provoked to raid in Pennsylvania, Maryland, and Virginia because of Virginia's unsuccessful attempt to claim the forks of the Ohio. South Carolina had been alienated by Virginia's attempt to recruit Creek and Catawba warriors without any reference to that government. Pennsylvania traders had been frightened with Virginia's aggressive entry into the Ohio, and more Pennsylvanians were disturbed with the attending loss of their Delaware friends. Virginians had struck a spark, with tacit British approval, in very dry tinder. Virginia did bring a population (231,000 in 1750) four times that of Canada into the already unequal colonial contest, but its real significance was as the premier English tobacco colony, important enough to draw unprecedented British support for its ambitions.

British ministers were reluctant to accept that New World events were drawing them into war. The duke of Newcastle, the central figure in the ministry in 1754, regarded the capture of Fort Necessity as one more French outrage, "and no war can be worse to this country, than the suffering [of] such insults as these."[7] He calculated that the French court would not go to war if the British confined themselves to taking "care of our rights and possessions in North America, by either building Forts on our boundaries to render theirs useless, or else by demolishing such as may have been clearly and notoriously built upon our ground."[8] The British stumbled into a tremendous commitment to the North American war. At first, Britain offered Virginia £13,000 plus three companies of regulars, already in New York and South Carolina, to man new forts. The figure was raised to £120,000 upon hearing that the French had taken and renamed Fort Duquesne. Newcastle was prepared to invest his entire budget surplus in this project, thereby avoiding direct parliamentary debate. With news of the fall of Fort Necessity, which arrived later, the British considered sending British officers to train Virginians. In the ensuing ministerial debate, William Augustus, duke of Cumberland, used his position as captain-general of the British army and favorite son of King George II to promote a more aggressive policy; two Irish regiments were sent to America at the end of 1754 under the experienced major-general of Cumberland's own regiment, Edward Braddock of the Coldstream Guards.[9]

The French ministry had been at least as reluctant as the British to anticipate war. Near the end of 1754, Governor Duquesne sent a list of grievances against his British neighbors, culminating in the assassination of Jumonville, and asked if he could presume that France would declare war. The minister of marine's reply was an unequivocal "No."[10] The French government's finances were not ready for war, though France had three times the population of Britain and ten times the army. However, France now had only half as large a navy, 57 ships-of-the-line facing Britain's 130, despite a mammoth rebuilding campaign that had left the service hopelessly in debt.[11] Despite superior naval architecture, which was to turn captured French vessels into British flagships, inferior numbers and budget problems dictated a defensive French naval strategy. The ensuing "great war of Empire" between these powers could be caricatured as a duel between an expert swimmer who could barely fence and an expert fencer who could barely swim. The British swimmer prefered to swim first and fight in America, whereas the French swordsman preferred to duel first in Europe and swim later. France drew Britain into Europe with threats of direct or indirect invasion from conquered ports in the Low Countries, with martial challenges to the British king's territory of Hanover, and with an attack on the British Mediterranean naval base at Minorca.

The campaign of 1755, while Europe still remained at peace, did not reflect Britain's naval advantages. In response to Braddock's 2 regiments dispatched for Virginia, France sent 6 of its 395 regular infantry regiments to Louisbourg and Canada in the summer of 1755. A British squadron, reinforced to nineteen men-of-war under Vice-Admiral Edward Boscawen, was sent to seize Admiral comte du Bois de La Motte's vulnerable sixteen-vessel fleet, which was too crowded with troops and equipment to mount most of its guns. "And in Case any opposition shall be made to your so doing, you will use the Means in your Power to take and destroy them."[12] Boscawen captured only two of the unsuspecting troop ships, and only ten of that fleet's seventy-eight companies of French regulars under Maréchal de camp Jean-Armand, baron de Dieskau. The British navy also failed to prevent the arrival of another thousand regulars with the marquis de Montcalm the following year.

Charges that France abandoned Canada are hard to sustain for the early part of the Seven Years' War. It is true that the French government, which had been investing in Canada's public fortresses and private fortunes for a generation, warned the Canadian governor in 1754 that the bills would not be paid and the colony would be abandoned if economies were not made.[13] Yet the French government took the risk of sending Dieskau's troops in 1755, Canada's largest reinforcement during the entire war. These regulars, who played an important part in the Lake George campaign that year, and the money that supported it, the fortresses, and every Canadian, Amerindian, and French defender of New France, represented France's substantial contribution to the defense of French North America. The failure of the British offensive of 1755 and the success of the Canadian offensive of 1756 to 1757 helped to postpone full realization of the new limits being imposed on French assistance.

In April 1755, the bustling, overcrowded Virginia frontier town of Alexandria was host to Braddock and his two encamped regiments. Braddock held a conference attended by the commander of Royal Navy vessels in North American waters; by the governors of Virginia, Maryland, Pennsylvania, New York, and Massachusetts; and by William Johnson, New York's intermediary to the Six Nations, who would soon be appointed to superintend English–Amerindian relations on the entire northern frontier.

Braddock revealed what London had decided was to be done, and the conference discussed how it was to be accomplished. The British government had targeted four French forts as clear encroachments on British territory: Fort Duquesne, Fort Niagara, Fort St. Frédéric, and Fort Beauséjour. The initial plan was to take each of these seriatim, perhaps pausing to negotiate between captures. In addition to Braddock's two regiments, totaling one thousand men to be supplemented by seven hundred American recruits, the two former North American regiments, those of William Shirley and William Pepperrell, were to be revived. No invasion of New France was contemplated; this was a peacetime operation to roll back the edges of France's American empire, presumably without war.[14] Since Massachusetts Bay Governor William Shirley had already been very active in raising his own regiment to attack Fort St. Frédéric and in organizing a campaign against Fort Beauséjour, the conference decided to accelerate the campaign by attacking all four targets at once.

Four very different Anglo-American armies were each intended to undertake a conventional European siege. The attack on Fort Duquesne involved British regulars, Americans recruited into the regulars, and draftees from southern colonial militias. Fort Niagara was to be taken by Americans joining two revived British regiments, assisted by Six Nation and New England volunteers. More New England and New York volunteers and Six Nations were to take Fort St. Frédéric. The fourth army, of New England volunteers and a small force of British regulars stationed in Nova Scotia, was to serve under British Colonel Robert Monckton in attacking Fort Beauséjour. These expeditions, manned and financed in different ways, should have provided the British government with ideal information for comparison and analysis.

Fort Duquesne was to be attacked by Braddock's two Irish regiments, reinforced in Britain to a total of one thousand men, plus some four hundred Virginia recruits. These regulars, supplemented by the British-paid independent companies of regulars transferred from New York and South Carolina, brought the total number of men drawing pay from the British treasury to sixteen hundred. Nearly one thousand colonial troops paid by the governments of Maryland, Virginia, and North Carolina brought the entire force to about twenty-five hundred men. Lieutenant-Governor Dinwiddie had promised a major force of Cherokee and Catawba auxilliaries, but South Carolina jealously guarded its customers and allies, and none arrived.[15]

After an impressive two-month effort, Braddock's advance force of 1450 marched into disaster on July 9, 1755, within a few miles of its destination. A counterforce of 637 Amerindians, together with 146 Canadian militia and 108 *troupes de la marine*, had been sent from Fort Duquesne to ambush the English. These Amerindians included Ottawa, Potawatomi, mission Huron and Abenaki from Canada, local Shawnee, as well as Delaware and Mingo warriors who had been English allies. Too late for their planned ambush, they suddenly encountered the British column on the woodland roadway. While the surprised *troupes de la marine* and the British van tried to form firing lines on a twelve-foot-wide road flanked with underbrush and trees, the Amerindians and Canadians melted into the surrounding cover on both sides of the road. From a hill commanding the road, from a ravine that crossed it, and from brush everywhere, a rain of musket fire destroyed Braddock's army. A better ambush could hardly have been planned. Of the 1450 in the advance force, 977 were either wounded or killed, including 60 of 86 officers and Braddock; of the 150 in the Virginia Regiment, there were 120 casualties. Their opponents reported a total of 16 wounded and 23 killed, including their Canadian "commander."[16]

Braddock's expedition failed for a variety of reasons. Dinwiddie bungled the recruitment of Amerindian scouts. The commander of the van, Lieutenant-Colonel Thomas Gage, failed to follow standard military procedure and scout the hill to the army's right and the road ahead, suggesting that careful scouting had been suspended once the army had forded the Monongahela River on July 7. The British were unable to push through the *troupes de la marine*, conventional soldiers who blocked the narrow road long enough to jumble the line of march of the British column. Unable to halt, Braddock's column plowed into itself amid the noise and confusion of musket fire from the wooded flanks, as Amerindians and Canadians applied the Amerindian crescent formation of "moving fire" used in both communal hunting and major battles.[17]

The commander-in-chief was ultimately responsible, especially since he did not survive to help distribute any of the blame. Braddock and his fellow officers were certainly familiar with guerrilla warfare analagous to that used by Amerindians, and had requested Amerindian auxilliaries. For more than a decade, European armies had utilized and fought Balkan pandours, Austrian and Dutch partisans, the French Regiment de Grassin, and Scottish Highlanders in the '45. All these opponents used irregular warfare, including raids, ambushes, and skirmishes from cover. Military manuals of the 1740s and 1750s, including those of Franz von Der Trenck, La Croix, Turpin, de Crissé, and Maurice, comte de Saxe, all discussed partisan combat, or *la petite guerre*. Although Braddock's library is not known, fellow officers Henry Bouquet, John Forbes, George Townshend, and James Wolfe were familiar with these works.[18]

Even after this disaster, it would have been possible to push on to Fort Duquesne with a good chance of success, but Colonel Thomas Dunbar made sure that all had been in vain by sending the humiliated army to its winter quarters in Pennsylvania in August. Although Braddock had British funding, there had been wrangles with colonial assemblies over routes, wagons, and supplies. Even though these disputes had little direct bearing on the military fiasco, they revealed the delays and restrictions that attended dependence on a variety of colonial assemblies.[19]

The expedition against Fort Niagara was quite different. William Shirley, an able English lawyer, ambitious politician, and successful governor of Massachusetts, succeeded Braddock as British commander-in-chief in America. His part in the 1755 operations, as agreed in Alexandria, was to attack Fort St. Frédéric, for which he had lobbied and recruited his own regiment, and Fort Niagara, which New Yorkers including William Johnson had wanted as Braddock's first objective. Shirley recruited Johnson to lead one of these projects, though for some reason he was given the Fort St. Frédéric assignment and Shirley took personal leadership of the Niagara campaign. This latter objective was a four-hundred-mile expedition that included transporting supplies down the treacherous Oswego River and constructing boats to convey the force up Lake Ontario.

There were immediate political problems with New York's Lieutenant-Governor James De Lancey, whose local connections were bypassed for army contracts and angered by the disruption of their illicit fur trade between Montréal and Albany. As chief executive of New York, De Lancey also resented having the governor of Massachusetts lead a military force through his jurisdiction. From quibbling over the use of New York cannon, the dispute escalated to complete non-cooperation.

A growing rift between Shirley and Johnson made matters worse. Both were competing for what proved to be scarce Six Nation support. Johnson made traditional offers of presents, supplies, and booty; Shirley tried to outbid him by offering wages and organizing the Six Nation volunteers into formal military companies. Johnson also tried to escape Shirley's formal control by obtaining a parallel commission from De Lancey. The competition became fierce between the two armies assembling at Albany, as they vied for Iroquois, cannon, wagons, and whaleboats.[20]

Although Shirley's twenty-five hundred men were wearing the king's uniform, they were untrained colonial troops of revived regiments, accompanied by five hundred New Jersey volunteers and about one hundred Six Nations. Politically inspired delays, the arduous journey west of Albany, and news of Braddock's defeat contributed to some eight hundred desertions by the time the force reached Fort Oswego. With twelve hundred opponents across the lake at Fort Frontenac, Shirley did not venture up the lake to Niagara; instead, he busied his men with repairs to the dilapidated fort. Shirley argued that a successful French attack on Oswego while his army was away at Fort Niagara would disrupt his line of communication, supply, and retreat. However, a disappointed British government, paying all the bills except the wages of the New Jersey Blues, listened to Shirley's critics from the Johnson–De Lancey faction that winter.

 The attack on Fort St. Frédéric was a colonial frontier expedition to an even greater degree than Shirley's operation. Not only were the troops American, but these volunteers were paid, supplied, and ultimately controlled by colonial assemblies. The force of thirty-five hundred was led by William Johnson, Irish pioneer, Mohawk sachem, and former fur trader. His force included veteran warrior-diplomat Theyanoguin (Chief Hendrick) and some three hundred other Six Nations. Here, more than anywhere in the major English expeditions of the war, one might expect a demonstration of woodland warfare, as far as circumstances would allow.

However, Johnson's assigned task was not one for woodland guerrilla fighters. Fort St. Frédéric was a major fortress that dominated the northern borderlands from its site at the narrows of Lake Champlain (Crown Point). Thick black limestone walls surrounded the four-story stone tower of this fort, which mounted forty cannon. Johnson's expedition included a siege train of sixteen cannon, some weighing nearly three tons. On reaching the upper end of navigation on the Hudson, some fifteen hundred men revived an old riverside road and built the supply base of Fort Edward. From there, the army cut a sixteen-mile road north to Lac St. Sacrament, which Johnson prematurely and patriotically renamed Lake George. It was already early September when the Six Nations joined Johnson's incomplete camp at the lake, still some fifty miles from their objective. Six Nation scouts prompted a change in priorities when they reported tracks of 150 to 200 French-allied Amerindians on September 3 and tracks of three major French units four days later.

The French fleet that Boscawen had so inadequately disrupted had delivered most of its troops to Québec in June, together with Baron Dieskau and the new governor-general of New France, the tough Canadian who had been governor of Louisiana, Pierre-François de Rigaud de Vaudreuil de Cavagnal, marquis de Vaudreuil. New France's defenders included two thousand French regulars, a similar number of *troupes de la marine*, about eight thousand Canadian militia, and unnumbered Amerindian allies who were not impressed with the European military methods and conventions that were becoming dominant. The embattled governor had arrived during Braddock's offensive; it was too late to reinforce Fort Duquesne or Fort Beauséjour, and a planned attack on Fort Oswego evaporated when erroneous reports suggested that Johnson was close to Fort St. Frédéric.

In mid-August, Baron Dieskau, who had fought with irregulars in Europe even before becoming a protégé of Maréchal de Saxe, was put in charge of stopping Johnson; if the defeat of Braddock showed how easily Europeans could forget, Dieskau's expedition showed how quickly a flexible European commander and his American opponents could adapt. On the march south, Dieskau's three thousand men moved quickly, with the seven hundred French regulars flanked by three hundred *troupes de la marine* and thirteen hundred militia. This army was screened by six hundred Amerindian scouts, half of whom were Caughnawaga who traveled regularly along this route to trade illicitly at Albany.

Dieskau decided to isolate Johnson by destroying his incomplete supply base at Fort Edward with a fast-moving irregular force of Amerindians (700), Canadian militia (600), and the grenadier companies of his European veterans (220). As his *corps d'élite* approached Fort Edward on September 7, Dieskau's excellent plan was destroyed by the adamant refusal of the Amerindians to attack the fort. The Caughnawaga, who had Six Nation relatives and trading contacts on the other side, convinced their fellow Amerindians not to attack an incomplete fort with one mounted cannon and lectured Dieskau on the "watershed theory" of boundaries, by which Fort Edward was in the British Hudson River watershed and Lac St. Sacrament (Lake George) was in the French Richelieu River system.

Although Dieskau's bold strategy was in tatters, he seemed to salvage the situation by convincing the Caughnawaga to join the attack on Johnson's camp at the other end of his new road. When Dieskau learned that a contingent of Johnson's army was coming down this road, he immediately agreed to prepare an ambush, with Amerindians and Canadians under cover, and the grenadiers blocking the road at the end of a wooded ravine four miles from Johnson's camp. Meanwhile, in the single-file formation that Iroquois used in moving large armies quickly over uncontested ground, Theyanoguin's Mohawk led a Massachusetts regiment into Dieskau's trap.[21] Although controversy continues about which Amerindian sprang the trap prematurely, it killed fifty New Englanders and forty Mohawk, including Theyanoguin. The terrified survivors rushed back to Johnson's camp, where logs, wagons, and whaleboats were dragged together to improvise a breastwork. Johnson's barricaded position included four of the large field guns, ably supervised by Johnson's engineer and sole organizational aide from the British regulars, Captain William Eyre.

Dieskau intended to accompany the retreating English and rush the encampment but was, once again, foiled by his cautious Amerindians. They had earlier preferred to attack a camp, rather than a fort, but were not now about to challenge Johnson's cannon. Dieskau's Amerindians had already participated in a victory that day, had taken scalps, and had suffered a few casualties of their own. Dieskau learned that Amerindian allies were different from European partisans.

Dieskau's final tactic against Johnson's larger well-protected force was another gamble that demonstrated a European professional's view of valor unto death. He ordered the grenadiers into a block, six men wide and thirty-six men deep, for a bayonet charge to capture Johnson's cannon. Their steadiness while sustaining one-third casualties won the admiration of their commander and their colonial adversaries, but Amerindians were understandably puzzled by this deliberate waste of life. The American militia fired effectively from behind their barricade, and Eyre's cannon "made Lanes, Streets and Alleys thro' their army."[22] Dieskau was wounded and captured at this point, though some of his troops had yet another sharp skirmish before the end of the day, besting English reinforcements from Fort Edward. Reported casualties in the three encounters, collectively known as the Battle of Lake George, totaled 331 dead, wounded, or missing on the English side, and 339 on the French. Although they had won the battlefield, Johnson's troops were in no mood to pursue the French army, which carried its wounded back to Fort St. Frédéric without interference.

The Battle of Lake George was full of ironies and confusion between guerrilla and regular warfare. A frontier trader and adopted Mohawk chief, who had absolutely no conventional military experience, struggled to conduct his campaign like a regular officer. A European-trained French general, in North America for only three months, adopted Amerindian ambush techniques successfully. A veteran Mohawk warrior was among forty who died after failing to scout adequately. American volunteers and Mohawk defended a makeshift breastwork against attack by bayonet-wielding French regulars, rather than scattering to fight a guerrilla war in the woods. Dieskau, in defeat, had stopped Johnson's offensive.

The aftermath of the battle revealed other incongruities of this new type of war. The Mohawk went home to bury their dead and stayed there, as instructed by their influential women elders; the Six Nations would not return to scout for British armies for four years, making the development of Robert Rogers' Rangers an urgent necessity. Johnson discretely sent the Mohawk several French prisoners to take the names and places of their slain warriors in condolence ceremonies. He insisted that General Shirley was to hear nothing of this violation of European honors of war, meanwhile making extraordinary efforts to save and accommodate his noble prisoner, Baron Dieskau. Johnson's "victorious" troops, staffed by elected officers, refused to proceed farther against Fort St. Frédéric, to the consternation of Shirley and the supporting legislatures. The American provincials had won the battle site, but were forced to build and garrison Fort William Henry because the road they had just built from Albany would let the French invade much more quickly than Johnson's army had been able to travel. The no-man's-land between opposing forts was shrinking; by the end of 1755, Governor Vaudreuil would finish that process by building Fort Carillon (Ticonderoga) just beyond the other end of Lake George.[23]

 Nova Scotia was the weakest British possession in North America in 1755. The new British base at Halifax (1749) could not yet compete with Louisbourg, and the French had defined Nova Scotia by building Forts Beauséjour and Gaspereau on the isthmus of Chignecto. Beauséjour was a substantial stone fortress that defended overland winter communications between Louisbourg and Québec and indicated French concern for the Acadians, who were the other military weakness of Nova Scotia. Nova Scotia in 1755 contained twenty thousand Acadians, twenty-five hundred new German immigrants, and about twenty-five hundred English. For forty years since the Peace of Utrecht, the British government had compromised each time the Acadians refused an unqualified oath of allegiance. The British Board of Trade advised the colony's governor in 1753:

> The bringing [of] the French inhabitants to take the oath is certainly a very desirable thing, and the sooner they are brought to it the better; but it would be highly imprudent to disgust them by forcing it upon them at an improper time, and when they are quiet and at peace.[24]

One might wonder what time would be proper if not a time of quiet and peace. Britain preferred to have disloyal subjects rather than give loyal ones to Louisbourg or Canada.

Lieutenant-Governor Charles Lawrence of Nova Scotia, a major in the British regulars, joined his friend William Shirley in planning what became the fourth objective of the British offensive of 1755, to rid Chignecto of French influence. Colonel Robert Monckton led some 2000 New England volunteers and 270 British regulars from the Halifax garrison in the siege of Fort Beauséjour. The flotilla from Boston surprised the French and landed without opposition, having had considerable assistance from a traitorous French officer, Thomas Pichon. The fort surrendered before the siege had properly begun, and Fort Gaspereau promptly capitulated without a shot being fired. This most successful and least arduous part of the English 1755 offensive, and the only one that avoided wilderness marches, had been financed and led by the British and manned largely by New England volunteers.[25]

This swift military success helped prompt a drastic measure that was an admission of political failure, the expulsion of the Acadians. With the French forts conquered, nearly twenty-three hundred troops at his disposal, and conflict with France increasing, Lawrence decided that the "proper" time had come to impose an unconditional oath on the Acadians. The Acadians had heard this kind of blustering before, and each time the governors retreated when Acadians refused to consider bearing arms against the French. This time, however, Lawrence ordered Monckton's force to oversee the expulsion of all Acadians unwilling to take the oath. More than half the Acadians, those who could not flee, were expelled without being given the status of prisoners of war and were sent to hostile British American colonies. Expulsion of civilians was not part of European martial conduct in the eighteenth century, though there were many refugees. Lawrence was certainly not condemned by the British authorities; he became governor of Nova Scotia later that year and was promoted to brigadier-general after two more years. Britain conquered Acadia in 1755, but not the Acadians. The "solution" imposed on the Acadians, the first French wards of the British crown in North America, would encourage Canadians to fight even harder in the next five years.

 While the Americans fought, the British paid for the generally unsuccessful English offensive of 1755. The four major operations involved some eleven thousand men, about ninety-four hundred of whom were either Americans recruited into British regiments, American volunteers, or Amerindians. Britain assumed all the costs of the two most expensive expeditions, those under Braddock and Shirley. Colonial assemblies paid all expenses connected with Johnson's expedition, but the British Parliament granted them "a bounty and recompense" of £120,000 in 1756. Robert Monckton's expedition, manned almost entirely by colonials, was entirely financed by Britain. In addition to paying expenses, the British paid the wages of six thousand of the eleven thousand soldiers in the field, and the costs of naval fleets and convoys.[26]

In reflecting on the year's efforts, the British government decided to send a new commander with more power and more regulars. The duke of Cumberland urged that the base of operations be moved to Albany and chose John Campbell, fourth earl of Loudoun, as commander-in-chief. Colonial governors and assemblies had delayed and politicized what commanders regarded as crucial military operations; Loudoun was assigned greater powers than his predecessors, and matters of provisions and supply, which had become so tortured in the De Lancey–Shirley feud, were henceforth organized from Britain.[27]

The British decision to employ more regulars seemed to defy some of the most obvious evidence of the 1755 campaign. Braddock's destroyed army consisted mainly of regulars; the only successful operation had been predominantly the work of New England volunteer regiments. However, Americans had done most of the fighting in this unsuccessful year, and British military leaders undoubtedly preferred explanations that emphasized the limitations of the "provincials." Peter Wraxall, a regular officer with Johnson's expedition, complained to the British secretary of state:

> The Officers of this Army with very few Exceptions are utter Strangers to Military Life and most of them in no Respect superior to the Men they are put over. . . . The Men are raw Country Men. They are flattered with an easy & a speedy Conquest; All Arts were used to hide future Difficulties and Dangers from them, and the whole Undertaking in all it's Circumstances smoothed over.[28]

Officers who were elected by their men had proved to be their political representatives rather than their commanders, which was anathema in Europe's authoritarian professional armies. The 1755 English campaign had made clear that American volunteers and recruits, though few Amerindians, accepted the military methods and objectives proposed by Braddock and the British government. Having imposed the objectives of conventional war, the British government had little trouble convincing itself that those with experience and training in European warfare should be superior to those without it. In 1756 the British sent an additional thousand regulars and established four battalions of regulars in America, named the Royal Americans, who were to be trained, disciplined, and led by European officers. The increased commitment of regulars also owed something to the pride and prejudices of a British army anxious to vindicate itself after Braddock's defeat.

Regardless of how much reflection and reorganization was needed in the English war effort, the process took too long. When Loudoun finally reached New York in July 1756, he immediately became entangled in debilitating arguments with colonial military officers and with assemblies. Military officers argued about their rank, and assemblies argued to retain their customary power over individual expeditionary forces, which were very nearly separate armies. Long before that wrangling began, the Franco-Canadian and Amerindian forces had seized the military initiative. They would dictate the shape of the war for the next two years.

Chapter 10

VAUDREUIL'S OFFENSIVE 1756–1757

The defeats of the English in North America between 1755 and 1757 were accomplished by a unique and surprisingly effective mixture of Amerindian and European warfare. If the campaigns of Washington, Dieskau, and Johnson displayed a confusing medley of regular and irregular warfare, Vaudreuil's offensive demonstrated how complementary these methods could be.

Governor Pierre de Rigaud de Vaudreuil, son of an earlier governor and the only Canadian-born governor of New France, had been an ensign in the *troupes de la marine* from the age of ten. He had joined an abortive attack on the Fox tribe in 1727 and ably governed the weak and undersupplied colony of Louisiana during a tangle of Amerindian diplomacy and war between 1743 to 1752. This vain, self-important, fifty-seven-year-old administrator, with a strong prejudice in favor of native-born Canadians, returned to Québec as governor-general in June 1755, aboard the same ship that carried Dieskau.[1] Although he arrived amid the fear and confusion of a country under attack by four armies, Vaudreuil supervised a remarkably effective war between 1755 and 1757. He could soon describe the failed attacks of Johnson, Shirley, and Braddock as Canadian successes. In his reports to the French ministry, he lost no opportunity to celebrate the fighting capacity of Canadians, routinely appropriating the accomplishments of Amerindians and French regulars. For Vaudreuil, attack was the only defense possible for New France. The three major elements of Vaudreuil's counterattack were the raids out of Fort Duquesne, the 1756 capture of Fort Oswego, and the siege of Fort William Henry the following year.

As Colonel Thomas Dunbar led the retreating survivors of Braddock's disaster, the Delaware and Shawnee of the Ohio launched a major war of their own against the frontier settlements of Pennsylvania, Maryland, and Virginia. The Ohio Amerindians seized the opportunity to defend their world against the invasive Europeans and to gather scalps, provisions, and loot as allies of the French. A mission Iroquois had argued the previous year:

Brethren, are you ignorant of the difference between our Father [the French] and the English? Go and see the forts our father has created, and you will see that the land beneath their walls is still hunting ground, having fixed himself in those places we frequent only to supply our wants; whilst the English, on the contrary, no sooner get possession of a country than the game is forced to leave; the trees fall down before them, the earth becomes bare.[2]

Others, including the old Ohio Delaware sachem Ackowanothio, saw little difference between the French invasion of 1753 and Braddock's, but needed French assistance to drive out the more numerous English, confident that thereafter "we can drive away the French when we please."[3] The French alliance flourished, encouraged by the recent profitable victory and Amerindian wartime requirements for arms, ammunition, and gunpowder. Captain Jean-Daniel Dumas of the *troupes de la marine*, who had been prominent in the defeat of Braddock, handled diplomacy and supply from Fort Duquesne.

The Ohio Amerindian war against outer settlements of the English colonial frontiers was terrifyingly successful. The Moravian Amerindian mission at Gnadenhütten was burned by Delaware that fall, killing ten missionaries and dispersing two hundred Amerindian converts. By the spring of 1756, an estimated seven hundred colonists had been killed or captured, and by the autumn the total was three thousand, along with massive destruction of frontier property from Pennsylvania to South Carolina. More than two thousand raiders, including adventurous warriors from the upper Great Lakes, Canadians, and Ohio Valley residents, ranged hundreds of miles beyond dozens of new British colonial forts.[4] Pennsylvania was politically convulsed by these raids, which soon destroyed its Quaker government. Quaker assemblymen, who had long and justifiably argued that their insulated colony's best defense was its enlightened Amerindian policy, were forced to deal with attacks that could no longer be blamed on the provocations of non-Quaker frontiersmen. Quaker assemblymen withdrew from politics as Pennsylvania went to war; Amerindians had defeated yet another colonial government.[5] "Colonel" Benjamin Franklin supervised the construction of forts at crucial passes in western Pennsylvania, and in September 1756, a Pennsylvania militia patrol conducted the most effective retaliation of this war when it surprised and burned the Ohio Delaware village of Kittanning; the accompanying explosions of gunpowder confirmed and ended the village's role as a staging point for raids to the east. By 1758 Virginia was maintaining twenty-seven forts between the Blue Ridge and Allegheny mountains, at costs that had tripled in as many years.[6] These wooden forts could not prevent attacks and could occasionally be targets; Fort Granville was burned in August 1756, and the entire garrison killed or taken prisoner.

The Ohio war served Vaudreuil's purposes well. The guerrilla raids caused Virginia and Maryland to defend their own frontiers, keeping them out of the war to the north until 1758. Washington led a Virginia regiment that attempted to resist raids and calm fears of possible slave uprisings. Once drawn into the war, Pennsylvania was also preoccupied with border defense. Vaudreuil took credit for planning and funding this campaign of terror, and applauded the Canadians who participated in this *petite guerre*.

 The Ohio war displayed successful woodland guerrilla warfare, but the Oswego campaign of 1756 showed the value of those techniques as an adjunct to European-style siege warfare. Oswego (1728), like many North American forts, began as a trading post and was therefore situated conveniently at the mouth of a river. Fortification had escalated with the Anglo-French struggle, but the fort was still in a river valley where it could be commanded by higher ground on both sides. In the year before the siege, Shirley's army strengthened the fort and built subsidiary forts on the higher ground.[7] Three weak forts, however, did not make a strong one.

For Vaudreuil, who had originally planned an attack on Fort Oswego upon his arrival in 1755, this was a major target. During the winter of 1755/1756, two small Canadian–Amerindian scouting parties were sent to the Oswego vicinity, each returning with two prisoners for questioning. One of the two groups also managed to burn sixty boats used to supply the fort via the Mohawk–Oswego waterway. At the end of March 1756, a force of 166 Canadians, 136 mission Amerindians, and 60 regulars trekked over two hundred miles on snowshoes to capture and destroy Fort Bull, which defended the portage between the Mohawk and Oswego rivers. In storming the little fort, the raiders lost four men, but killed sixty and took thirty prisoner, then detonated the fort with its large stock of powder, destroying ammunition and provisions intended for Oswego, as well as wagons, horses, and river boats.[8] One major convoy of river boats arrived at Oswego in July, after fighting its way through an ambush eight miles from the fort. These raids added to the misery of the eighteen hundred Americans garrisoned at Fort Oswego, victims of a preliminary siege net that was in place for more than six months.

Effective combination of irregular and regular warfare was evident throughout the siege at Oswego in August 1756. The new commander of the French regulars in New France, Louis-Joseph de Montcalm, was a cautious strategist, unlike the unfortunate Dieskau. Montcalm found the target attractive in the context of maneuver-conscious European campaigning. As the British forces concentrated at Albany for a push north, Montcalm supported an attack on Oswego to divert some British troops westward up the Mohawk River. Montcalm's expedition consisted of 1500 Canadian militia, 1300 French regulars, 137 *troupes de la marine*, and 260 Amerindians. Forty Menominee and twenty-two

Ojibwa had come from the *pays d'en haut,* and the rest of the Amerindians were Abenaki, Algonquin, Iroquois, and Nipissing from the mission villages around Montréal.[9] Vaudreuil's audacious brother, François-Pierre de Rigaud de Vaudreuil, led the vanguard of militia and Amerindians that quickly cut communications between the three forts, took one of the two new outforts, and harassed the main garrison with musket fire and war whoops. Montcalm's first battery took the expected three days to prepare for firing, and an early shot killed the English commander; the white flag was run up by noon, to Montcalm's clear disappointment. He wrote to the French minister of war apologizing for the rashness of this attack of thirty-two hundred against an eighteen-hundred-man garrison, a siege that succeeded so quickly it failed to draw any British soldiers west from Albany. Montcalm hoped to be considered a careful commander and promised to "conduct myself on different principles."[10] His irregulars shortened his siege, and Amerindians shocked the French by killing at least thirty wounded prisoners after the surrender. The rest of the garrison, 1520 men and 120 women and children, were taken to Canada as prisoners of war. This European convention, customary after a poor defense, proved unhelpful. Canada was about to suffer another crop failure, making it difficult to feed its civilians, militia, and regular troops, not to mention its prisoners of war.

In the conduct of the Oswego campaign, there had been some tensions between Canadians and regulars, but few serious problems. However, Montcalm was becoming increasingly uncomfortable. Coded passages of his November letter to the minister of war dismissed Vaudreuil as a leader ignorant in warfare and described the governor's plans for the next year as a difficult siege of Fort William Henry and an impossible one of Fort Edward. Montcalm would have preferred another diversion to draw troops from Albany, only this time to Acadia. A letter from Vaudreuil did not detail his plans, but appealed to the French court for additional provisions and eighteen hundred men, unless the British were sending more.[11]

The French ministry's reaction to Vaudreuil's request was to send only eighteen hundred reinforcements, though it was clear that the British were sending eight thousand regulars. If the British regulars were intended for Louisbourg or Québec, as the French ministerial sophists claimed, Vaudreuil would not need more troops for the New York frontier. If the British reinforcements were intended for New York, Vaudreuil could draw all his resources together for a stand at Fort St. Frédéric. After agreeing with Vaudreuil that maintaining a successful offensive was the ideal strategy, the ministry suggested that a defensive focus might be more appropriate for 1757. The economies of the smaller forces needed for defense obviously made Montcalm's defensive preferences attractive to a ministry preoccupied with an expensive European war. Vaudreuil was reminded that French government expenses in New France had recently risen eightfold, and the accumulated debt of the "colonial chest" was 14 million livres. It was noted that, since the Canadian crops of 1756 had failed, any additional soldiers would require even larger shipments of grain, causing more transportation difficulties and more expense.[12] France had no more troops to spare for North America and was urging a defensive colonial posture until French victories in Europe won a favorable peace.

Vaudreuil was not deterred; what he had done to Oswego in 1756 he intended to do to Fort William Henry in 1757. Four circumstances, however, conspired to make the task more difficult.[13] Fort William Henry (1755) was located only sixteen miles along a good road from what was now a solid supply base at Fort Edward. This location allowed easy communication and reinforcement from the British troop concentrations at Albany and made this link much more difficult for Vaudreuil's raiders to disrupt. Second, the corner-bastioned earthwork of Fort William Henry—the political accomplishment of William Johnson and the engineering success of Captain William Eyre—was fireproof and nearly cannonproof. Pine logs were used for the outside and inside walls, cross-braced, and filled with sand from digging the exterior ditch, forming thirty-foot-thick walls that rose ten feet before narrowing to create well-protected cannon platforms and parapets (Figure 10). Third, French operations were limited by Canadian grain shortages that were becoming severe and persistent; in that sense, New France was besieged for the final four years of the struggle. Finally, the rift between Montcalm and Vaudreuil was widening, affecting planning and cooperation.

The strength of Fort William Henry and its well-tended cannon was demonstrated in March 1757, when Rigaud took a superbly equipped guerrilla force of 650 Canadian militia, 300 *troupes de la marine*, 300 Amerindians, and 250 French regulars to attack the garrison of only 474 British regulars and colonial rangers. Failing to surprise Captain Eyre's garrison, Rigaud and his men spent four days burning boats, storehouses, and other outbuildings. Vaudreuil, who apparently gave no written instructions, reported his brother's exploits as a clever spoiling raid that would delay any major British offensive for lack of boats. Montcalm, who had given Vaudreuil a comparable plan to be executed by a smaller force of regulars, hinted to French authorities that Rigaud should have been able to take the fort. Captain Eyre, naturally, saw the event as a siege that his garrison and fort had successfully frustrated.[14] Whatever had been intended for Rigaud's force, it had contributed to the defensive British posture on that frontier, while Loudoun attempted an unsuccessful campaign against Louisbourg.

Vaudreuil assembled an astonishing multicultural army in the summer of 1757. A thousand warriors from the *pays d'en haut* eventually came as far as fifteen hundred miles to join the attack on Fort William Henry, hundreds more decided to follow the promising warpaths out

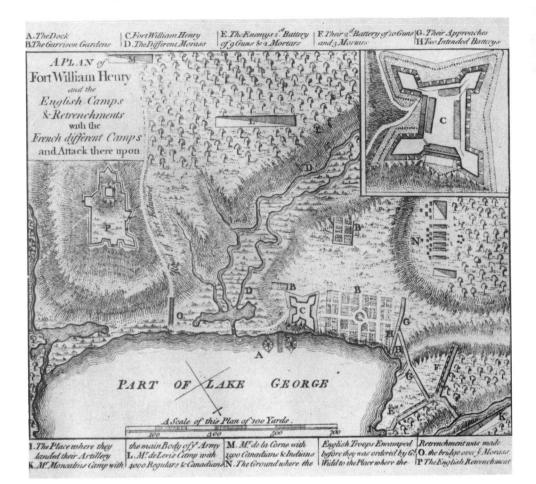

A.The Dock | C.Fort William Henry | E.The Enemys 1.st Battery | F.Their 2.d Battery of 10 Guns | G.Their Approaches
B.The Garrison Gardens | D.The Different Morass | of 9 Guns & 2 Mortars | and 3 Mortars | H.Two Intended Batterys

I.The Place where they landed their Artillery | the main Body of y.e Army | M.M.r de la Corne with 2500 Canadians & Indians | English Troops Encamped before they was ordered by G.l Widd to the Place where the | Retrenchment was made
K.M.r Moncalms Camp with | L.M.r de Levis Camp with 4000 Regulars & Canadians | N.The Ground where the | | O.the bridge over y.e Morass. P The English Retrenchment

Figure 10. Siege of Fort William Henry, 1757. From Ann Rocque, *A Set of Plans and Forts in America* (London, 1765). (Courtesy of the Metropolitan Toronto Reference Library)

of Fort Duquesne, and still others came as far as Detroit but turned back because of rumors of smallpox in New France.[15] Those who arrived at Montréal for the Fort William Henry campaign came without priests and some even without translators; most were from New France's economic but not its cultural hinterland. Some 337 Ottawa, nearly 300 Ojibwa, 129 Menominee, 88 Potawatomi, 48 Winnebago, a few Sauk and Iowa, and even a handful of Fox, Miami, and Delaware brought generations of rivalries into this army. Montcalm could only hope to influence these Amerindians through a mere dozen Canadian officers and interpreters, and these "officers attached to the Indians" could communicate with some warriors only through Amerindian interpreters.[16] This assemblage of unpaid allies was drawn by tales of Braddock and Oswego, seeking coup, plunder, and a chance for retribution on the English, while expecting to be well armed and well fed by Vaudreuil. The arrival of these strangers in Montréal early in July hastened the launch of the campaign. The rest of Montcalm's army of nearly 8000 included 800 "domiciled" Abenaki, Algonquin, Caughnawaga, and Nipissing warriors attended by missionaries anxious about "bad" influences on their catechumens; 2570 regular *troupes de terre*; 2546 Canadian militia; and 526 *troupes de la marine* brigaded inappropriately like a regular regiment.

The Amerindians were extremely effective in scouting and raiding ahead of Montcalm's troops, and also won a significant victory of their own on Lake George on July 24. The British commander at Fort William Henry, Lieutenant-Colonel George Monro, unable to gain any reliable information about his opponents, sent a major scouting expedition of 350 men from the New Jersey and New York regiments down Lake George in twenty-two whaleboats, to capture prisoners and information. Fewer than one hundred of the men, and only four of the boats, returned safely after a dawn ambush off Sabbath Day Point by about six hundred Amerindians from the *pays d'en haut*. Once the victorious Amerindians felt their canoe battle was won, they took more than 150 survivors prisoner. Like Dieskau's allies two years earlier, they regarded one bloody engagement as enough, and they intended to take their prisoners home. Even with accomplished negotiators, and the promise of more prisoners, Montcalm lost two hundred warriors who considered their campaign completed. Their battle ensured that the French would not be challenged further on the waters of Lake George.

The ruin of this scouting expedition prompted General Daniel Webb, commanding the area in Loudoun's absence, to visit Fort William Henry and prepare a defensive strategy. It was decided that some two thousand troops were appropriate to defend Fort William Henry. Since the fort could hold only five hundred men, most were stationed in a new breastwork on the defensible site of Johnson's 1755 camp, to the east of the fort. Webb returned to Fort Edward and sent a thousand men north to the threatened fort, bringing its garrison to 2372.

The French siege, which began the morning of August 3, was a textbook operation. Brigadier François-Gaston de Lévis led nearly three thousand Amerindians and Canadians overland to encircle Fort William Henry, severing its communications with Fort Edward. The main French force spent the first three days of the siege establishing its camp out of cannon range to the northwest, building a road, and positioning the first battery of artillery. Most of the casualties during this period resulted from skirmishes between Amerindians and those in the entrenched English camp. When a second French battery was completed two days later, a total of seventeen cannon, two mortars, and two howitzers were firing on a fort that was increasingly outgunned as more of its own artillery became disabled. As the siege progressed, one of the greatest dangers inside the fort was its own cannon, exploding from metal fatigue or from loading overheated cannon with standard measures of gunpowder. By August 9, the French regulars and Canadian militia were preparing to open a third battery of nine cannon within only 150 yards of the fort. Deprived of sleep for five days and left with few functional cannon, the garrison surrendered. Montcalm, impressed with their bravery, offered them the latest version of the European honors of war. They were to be allowed to march back to Fort Edward, keep their muskets and private belongings, and be accompanied by beating drums and flying colors, as well as one of their own brass cannon. In return, the garrison became "parolees" who agreed not to fight the French or their allies for eighteen months, and Monro was to arrange the return of all French, Canadian, and Amerindian prisoners. Montcalm explained the generous agreement to a council of chiefs, who reportedly approved terms that clearly deprived their warriors of promised scalps and booty.

The price of mixing irregular and regular war in this wilderness was about to be paid. Montcalm, fearing some repeat of the killing of prisoners at Oswego, posted guards in the English camp, from which he had excluded Amerindians for the night. He connived, unsuccessfully, to slip the English prisoners away under cover of darkness. The next morning, as the English prepared for the sixteen-mile march to Fort Edward, Amerindians returned to the camp in search of plunder. Acceptable plunder might include anything that was neither the private property of an English soldier nor the ammunition, stores of war, or provisions, which had been reserved for the French. The first targets were the horses to pull the single retrieved cannon, kettles, and the massive baggage of some of the officers. As the British regulars began to move out with their small French escort, warriors within the camp killed and scalped seventeen wounded. Other warriors dragged away Amerindians who had been in the American colonial forces, as well as black soldiers and servants. As some of these captives were paraded as trophies in the nearby camps flanking the road to Fort Edward, more of the sixteen hundred warriors raced to capture proof of their share in a great victory. The war whoop was sounded as the warriors charged to claim packs, guns, money, and clothes. Those who resisted were summarily killed. Of 2456 people attacked, at least 69 died in the "massacre," and the fate of another 115 remains unknown.

The "massacre" lasted for only a few moments, and then became a chase for prisoners. The French commanders tried to protect the English by bargaining, by harboring those who escaped, and even by confiscating them from their captors. A few more English were killed by Amerindians who chose to take scalps rather than surrender prisoners. Montcalm's allies were disgusted with him, and most left immediately for home, with or without prisoners, effectively ending the campaign. Montcalm blamed the victims for the incident, promised to recover and return those taken by the Amerindians, and presumed that the conditions of the surrender were still in force. Vaudreuil redeemed more than two hundred prisoners at Montréal, each at a cost of thirty bottles of brandy and 130 livres of goods. The Amerindians, unlike the Canadians, had managed some personal reward despite Montcalm's alien surrender terms. Abbé Picquet recorded one warrior's comment:

> I make war for plunder, scalps, and prisoners. You are satisfied with a fort, and you let your enemy and mine live. I do not want to keep such bad meat for tomorrow. When I kill it, it can no longer attack me.[17]

Amerindians from the far west returned home angry and carrying smallpox; they would not return in comparable numbers to aid New France again.

Nine months later, after most of the parolees recovered by the Canadian government had been returned, the new British commander-in-chief, General Jeffrey Amherst, declared the capitulation terms null and void. The Fort William Henry incident echoed through the war, leading Amherst to deny the honors of war to the French at Louisbourg (1758) and Montréal (1760) and encouraging his disastrous anti-Amerindian policies, which prompted Robert Rogers's raid on St. François (1759) and helped provoke the Amerindian War (1763–1765).

Vaudreuil's offensive had ended abruptly, despite orders that Montcalm proceed to take Fort Edward. Montcalm had opposed that assignment, was now without his massive scouting force, and claimed a shortage of provisions as an excuse that fit well with the Canadians' concern to get home for the harvest. The campaign closed with Montcalm and Vaudreuil writing damning letters about each other to the French ministry.[18]

The coherence of Vaudreuil's strategy, and the capable use of limited resources, are easily lost by approaching these simply as English "years of defeat." The raids out of Fort Duquesne continued to deflect the resources of Virginia, Pennsylvania, and Maryland, though they would not deflect the British regulars assembling on the Hudson, as they were not paid by colonial taxpayers. The first two major sieges of the North American war showed the successful combination of Amerindian, colonial, and imperial troops on an unprecedented scale.

New France's war was, however, about to shift to the defensive. The following year, Montcalm would read the challenge of the British regulars as decisive:

> It is no longer the time when a few scalps, or the burning [of] a few houses is any advantage or even an object. Petty means, petty ideas, petty Councils about details are now dangerous, and waste material and time.

He advocated retreating from the Ohio, Lake Ontario, and Lake Champlain in order to defend Québec and Montréal. Vaudreuil insisted on "contesting the ground on our frontiers inch by inch with the enemy."[19] Although the French ministry formally gave Montcalm command over Vaudreuil in military matters only in February 1759, Vaudreuil's preferred approach had been less evident after the raid that destroyed the Mohawk Valley settlement of German Flats in the fall of 1757. It is doubtful whether a continuation of Vaudreuil's methods could have saved New France, but his strategy had certainly postponed its fall.

Chapter 11

THE BRITISH IMPERIAL VICTORY 1758–1763

The course of the great European war for North America changed abruptly in the summer of 1758. The triumphal *Te Deum* of the Catholic churches of New France and Old were replaced by equally triumphal bells of victory ringing from the Protestant church towers of New England and Old. This migration of grace or fortune deserves examination, for it allowed the English to recover and maintain the military initiative thereafter.

There was nothing original about British strategy in North America; it was a rerun of Braddock's diffuse, four-pronged approach of 1755, despite the fact that wartime operations were no longer confined to French prewar "encroachments." The general British plan for 1758, drafted by Lord Loudoun, targeted Louisbourg, Fort Carillon, Fort Frontenac, and Fort Duquesne. Loudoun's 1757 attack on Louisbourg had failed prematurely, leaving an army wintering in Halifax. Loudoun had intended to reinforce these regulars with Americans for road building and support, but the new secretary of state, William Pitt, made this 1758 siege into his showcase operation, trusting the fighting almost exclusively to British regulars. Loudoun had planned a two-pronged attack on Montréal, with the first advance against Fort Frontenac, to draw French troops from the Lake Champlain forts, which were then to be attacked by a force of British regulars. Pitt dropped the Fort Frontenac campaign, which was carried out by local initiative, and he increased the proportion of Americans in the army on the Lake George–Lake Champlain frontier. Pitt's tampering with the Fort Duquesne operation caused delays, but no basic changes in that part of the plan.[1]

The major difference between British operations in 1755 and 1758 was that three of the four earlier campaigns had failed, and three of the four later ones succeeded. There is no single reason for the difference, but four factors deserve particular notice: political leadership, military funding, soldiers, and fleets. William Pitt's appointment as Britain's secretary of state for the southern department, and as effective prime minister, had begun a minor revolution in government in the summer of 1757.[2] A vicious parliamentary critic of his predecessors' conduct of the war, this arrogant, eloquent, and ambitious administrator came to power with public support but no party; a political opponent commented acidly that Pitt "wanted friends for places, more than places for his friends."[3] King George II and Pitt's chief colleagues, the duke of Newcastle and the earl of Hardwicke, disliked Pitt and worked with him only of necessity. However, Pitt charmed a heavily taxed public, reassured government suppliers and debt holders, and supported armed forces with enough resources to win. Charismatic patriotism had come to power, and it began the destruction of the comfortable Whig politics of the previous generation.

Pitt changed the top military administrators, and new appointees found their authority circumscribed by this aggressive secretary of state who dominated military planning. The duke of Cumberland withdrew from public life after his spring campaign of 1757 ended in the humiliating Convention of Kloster-Zeven, which his father repudiated. Field Marshal John Ligonier replaced Cumberland as captain-general of the British army, providing Pitt with an able, vigorous, and cooperative seventy-eight-year-old professional assistant.[4] In replacing Lord Loudoun as commander-in-chief in North America, Pitt significantly reduced the power of that position. Loudoun had been granted more authority than Braddock in order to facilitate united military action on the part of what had proved to be very resistant English colonial governments. Pitt assumed direct control of negotiations with the colonial assemblies, issued extensive and detailed instructions to Loudoun's replacement, Major-General James Abercromby, and gave fulsome instructions for independent campaigns led by Major-General Jeffrey Amherst and Brigadier-General John Forbes. Although most of the decisions that Pitt conveyed were made with his cabinet colleagues, especially Lord Anson at the Admiralty and the duke of Newcastle at the Treasury, Pitt was able to monopolize the management of Britain's war. By the end of 1757, the detailed British planning of the North American war had migrated across the Atlantic to London, linked by as many as five mail packet boats a month.

Money fights even more effectively than it talks, and Pitt sold Britain a very expensive war. Parliament voted £10 million for the war in 1758, financed half by taxes and nearly half by borrowing at a confident 3.5 percent.[5] Pitt did not win a European war in America or an American war in Germany, as he once claimed, but greatly increased Britain's commitment to both wars. The bill for fighting in North America also increased sharply, averaging nearly £1 million a year, spent mostly on the army. This economic transfusion for disrupted colonial economies momentarily eliminated their balance-of-payment deficits with Britain. Pitt introduced a "subsidy plan," a requisition system that offered full reimbursement of most colonial assistance beyond levy money and pay. Colonial assemblies responded to this invitation to earn sterling with prompt and expensive levies of men, supplies, and services. Colonial governments would emerge from the war in improved fiscal condition; Britain's reimbursement totaled £1,544,830, representing approximately half the colonial war expenses.[6] Money could make the fractious and cumbersome first British empire work with surprising efficiency.

The troops fighting Britain's war in North America in 1758 were also different. Of the eleven thousand involved in British operations in 1755, one-seventh had been British regulars; this proportion changed to more than half of those involved in the 1758 offensives. British recruiters had increasing difficulty competing with colonial governments offering huge enlistment bounties for men who were then used in volunteer forces for defense within their own colonies. Yet an estimated eleven thousand colonials enlisted in the British regulars in the course of the war, accepting the longer enlistment, lower pay, and legendary harsh discipline. British interest in expanding the regulars came from officers' observations that colonial volunteers were more expensive than British regulars, less reliable under fire, and prone to "desert" even before their eight-month enlistment contracts expired. Regulars in North American winter garrisons could also be moved more quickly in the spring to exploit the advantages that an earlier thaw gave New France's enemies farther south. By contrast, English colonial troops had to be voted in legislatures after the objectives had been decided; then the volunteers had to be recruited and mustered after spring planting, and they were always subject to colonial administrations sensitive to frontier raids and willing to divert troops to defensive efforts. Colonial rangers had established an excellent reputation with the British army, becoming regulars active in winter garrison and woodland operations, as well as raiding to gather information. The British army recruited Americans into the regulars by the thousands, notably into the four battalions of the Royal American Regiment and the Shirley and Pepperrell regiments, as well as the rangers. Loudoun also decided to introduce light infantry units into regular regiments, and by the summer of 1758, all regiments were trained to deal with ambushes, with the ten best marksmen in each battalion using rifles rather than muskets. One officer commented that spring:

> The art of War is much changed and improved here. I suppose by the end of the summer it will have undergone a total Revolution. . . . The Highlanders have put on breeches. . . . Swords and sashes are degraded, and many have taken up the Hatchet and wear Tomahawks.[7]

Loudoun not only had improved the regulars, but also reorganized supply and created the innovative army transport service that was a prerequisite for their wilderness campaigns.

British prejudice was less against Americans as soldiers than against colonial government armies, with elected officers, lax discipline, and contracts so short as to limit operations. These colonial volunteer reg-iments also expanded and improved with experience and the promise of British financial assistance. Massachusetts raised an average of more than forty-six hundred soldiers a year in this war, and Virginia's new policy of a substantial enlistment bounty promptly filled two regiments in a colony that had not been able to raise even one before 1758. Although the colonial regiments expanded, they did so less rapidly than the regulars, either imported from Britain or recruited in America.[8]

As to the last of the four factors of change, the British navy was more heavily involved in American operations in 1758 than had been pos-sible three years earlier. Between 1755 and 1758, annual British naval expenditures doubled to the unprecedented level of nearly £4 million. By 1758 the British fleet included 239 commissioned ships, another 25 in reserve, and 49 under construction. This navy included 98 ships-of-the-line, against which the French had 72. The British fleet that brought the regulars to North America also brought its own gunpower, man-power, and tactical mobility, especially to the amphibious assaults on Louisbourg and Québec. The British naval blockade of French ports was never entirely successful, but 1757 had seen the last major "escapes" of French support squadrons for Louisbourg and Canada. The British navy's clear success would come between the spring of 1758 and the end of 1759, when the French navy lost nearly half its fighting strength. By the following year, France had only 50 battleships to face Britain's 107.[9]

 Of the four British targets for 1758, the siege of Louisbourg was a direct and uncomplicated use of Britain's military and naval power, without intervening wilderness. The fortress was stronger than when New Englanders had captured it in 1745, for the shore of Gabarus Bay, where the earlier attackers had landed, was now protected by an effective line of entrenchments. The strength that Louisbourg could muster, and the effort France was still willing to expend to defend it, had been illustrated in 1757. Loudoun wanted to bypass Louisbourg in favor of a bold assault on Québec to break what was becoming a fortified stalemate along the Lake George–Lake Cham-plain frontier. Pitt, like more conventional military planners, preferred a preliminary siege of Louisbourg, but left both the decision and the onus with Loudoun. By mid-July 1757, he had a force of nearly fifteen thousand and a fleet of seventeen ships-of-the-line, a comparable num-ber of smaller vessels, and a fleet of transports. Although his force in 1757 was four times as large as the one that had taken Louisbourg in 1745, Loudoun decided to abort the operation. The deterrent was a comparable French fleet, led by eighteen ships-of-the-line; by daring and devious means, three French squadrons had escaped the British blockade of French ports and assembled at Louisbourg as the most powerful fleet gathered in North America to date, commanded by

Admiral La Motte. He did not bring his fleet out of the harbor to fight Loudoun, and Loudoun withdrew without challenging Louisbourg.[10] According to their detractors, both leaders were cowards, but both can be defended as respecting the military assumption that one does not risk massive government resources without a clear prospect of victory.

In 1758, however, British blockades of French Mediterranean and Atlantic ports kept all but six French ships from reaching Louisbourg, too few to prevent this attack. The British fleet included twenty-three ships-of-the-line and sixteen smaller vessels, mounting 1842 guns, plus a hundred transports. The shoreline of Gabarus Bay now displayed thirty defending cannon mounted strategically and more than twenty-three hundred French regulars entrenched behind a twenty-foot *abattis*.[11] The *abattis*, a version of which was used as early as 1676 by both Nathaniel Bacon and the Narragansett, assisted the outnumbered French in 1758 at both Louisbourg and Fort Carillon, serving as an eighteenth-century equivalent of barbed wire. These massive tangles of freshly cut trees with sharpened branches, too green to burn and too enmeshed to move, were intended to thwart a conventional frontal assault.

The British assault landing on June 8, 1758, was the first of its kind. Aware of the entrenchments, the British had considered alternatives and had practiced landing troops quickly from the ships' boats. The minutes while vulnerable soldiers waded from boat to beach had to be minimized, and the number who could be landed simultaneously had to be maximized. Although the 1745 landing had allowed a healthy separation between the landing force and the fleet, the 1758 attempt demanded their closest cooperation. There were heavy swells as well as French musket and cannon fire from behind strong protection, and even ambitious young leaders like Brigadier-General James Wolfe were prepared to call off the attempt. Then Wolfe noticed that a boatload of resourceful infantry had found a "neck of rocks" that allowed them to land protected from French fire. Gaining the entrenchment above required a bloody bayonet charge, but the entire operation had been salvaged by the perceptiveness of an unknown soldier or sailor.

Once the thirteen thousand British regulars were ashore, and the surprised and confused defenders of the outworks had withdrawn to the fort, the heroics were with the French. Governor Augustin de Drucour's garrison was outnumbered three to one by an aggressor with plans to take Louisbourg and Québec in a single season. In the face of mounting losses, limited supplies, and appeals from the residents that he surrender, Drucour held out until the end of July. Drucour kept Amherst from Québec in 1758. Major-General Jeffrey Amherst had conducted a careful but unimaginative attack in this and subsequent campaigns, lengthening the struggle for New France.

The British failure of 1758 was the attack on Fort Carillon (Ticonderoga) that July, and Montcalm's surprising victory proved to be not only over Abercromby, but also over his colleague Vaudreuil. Mutual distrust and conflict with Vaudreuil over strategy might have cost more than it did, but goes far to explain why Montcalm found himself with no more than thirty-five hundred men to resist a force of fifteen thousand. The lack of Amerindian scouts, who could also have raided to disrupt Abercromby's advance, was due less to Vaudreuil than to Montcalm's handling of the "massacre" at Fort William Henry the previous summer.[12] Although only three years old, Fort Carillon was difficult to defend. Montcalm's chief engineer had warned him: "Were I entrusted with the siege of it, I should require only six mortars and two cannon."[13] The cannon would have been placed atop nearby Mount Defiance, entirely dominating a fort that had been located to intercept smaller water-borne expeditions and facilitate supply. Montcalm, like Washington at Fort Necessity, was unwilling to trust the fort to defend his army, so he prepared his army to defend the fort; the sixteen mission Amerindians present could see that Europeans regarded forts as more precious than lives. Entrenchments were dug across the only possible path of direct assault, a quarter of a mile from the rocky outcrop on which the fort stood. Earth, logs, and sandbags strengthened the entrenchment, and an *abattis* was built beyond them. Montcalm's scouts were ordered to give only token resistance and gather information; advance forces were to withdraw into the defense works as the enemy approached. Given such odds, these cautious tactics were entirely appropriate and represented, in miniature, Montcalm's overall strategy for New France.

Abercromby's attack proved precisely the kind for which Montcalm had prepared, and he conducted an excellent defense against odds of more than four to one. However, the grossly inflated accounts of British casualties reported by Montcalm and his lieutenants, in which 464 dead became 3000, were part of a ploy that succeeded in strengthening the political position of Montcalm and the French against Vaudreuil and the Canadians. By the end of the month, Montcalm's closest aide, Louis Antoine de Bougainville, enthusiastically noted the change in New France:

> Now war is established here on the European basis. Projects for the campaign, for armies, for artillery, for sieges, for battles. It no longer is a matter of making a raid, but of conquering or being conquered. What a revolution! What a change! . . . [T]ownsmen, bankers, merchants, officers, bishops, parish priests, Jesuits, all plan this [war], speak of it, discuss it, pronounce on it.[14]

This 1758 military revolution in New France tended in the opposite direction from that noted in the same year in the British army in North America.

Abercromby has too easily been dismissed as criminally responsible for the disastrous attack on Fort Carillon on July 8, 1758. A British captain, Charles Lee, who would become a patriot general in the American Revolution, fumed that use of cannon on Mount Defiance "must have occur'd to any blockhead who was not absolutely so far sunk in Idiotism as to be oblig'd to wear a bib and bells."[15] Cannon fire would certainly have made the entrenchments untenable and could have opened roads through the *abattis*. However, Abercromby was in a hurry. All French and Canadian prisoners, interrogated separately before the battle, agreed there were six thousand troops with Montcalm and three thousand reinforcements coming under the talented Chevalier François-Gaston Lévis. Abercromby knew that Lévis had a large independent command and found the reports plausible. More significant, Abercromby hurried because his scouts on Mount Defiance reported that Montcalm's defenses were incomplete and could be taken if attacked at once. With hindsight, it is obvious that Abercromby should have waited a few days for his cannon to be positioned or should have marched around Montcalm's entrenched troops and on down Lake Champlain, isolating Fort Carillon from reinforcements and supplies. Abercromby ordered an attack in line formation, instead of the more likely column attack that an equally hurried Dieskau had tried at the other end of Lake George in 1755. The frontal assault continued long after casualties confirmed that Abercromby's scouts had been wrong. He was not brilliant or imaginative, but he was not a candidate for "a bib and bells." One historian has even argued that most of the English colonial forces with Abercromby were little more than horrified observers, and the actual British assault force, of only seven thousand regulars, incurred no ignominy in failing to overpower an entrenched force half their number.[16]

To salvage something from his ruined campaign, Abercromby violated Pitt's instructions and authorized an expedition from Albany against Fort Frontenac. Lieutenant-Colonel John Bradstreet led a force of thirty-six hundred, which was somewhat larger than Shirley's army had been in 1755, though also with primarily colonial Americans in British pay. Secrecy about Bradstreet's destination was uncommonly effective, even within his force, and pro-Canadian Six Nations declined to alert Vaudreuil about the passing army. Fort Frontenac was a better target than Fort Niagara had been. A reinforced Fort Frontenac had prevented Shirley from sailing from Oswego to Niagara three years earlier, but in 1758 Fort Frontenac was very vulnerable to surprise attack in its weakened condition. Bradstreet's army was neither temperamentally nor logistically equipped for a long siege, and it made good use of the undermanned fort's weaknesses. The garrison of seventy surrendered before Bradstreet's cannon had exhausted their twenty-four-hour supply of ammunition.[17] However, the attack on Fort Frontenac had been a raid into untenable territory, and the fort was burned, as was the French Lake Ontario fleet. Montcalm, who thought Fort Frontenac "in truth was good for nothing," was nonetheless happy to blame Vaudreuil for its loss.[18] For Abercromby, the destruction of Fort Frontenac helped, but did not offset, the Fort Carillon disaster.

The campaign against Fort Duquesne was a point of honor with the British army, but by 1758 it had limited strategic intent, except as a way to involve Virginia and Pennsylvania directly in the war. Like Braddock previously, Brigadier-General John Forbes had trouble finding wagons and raising colonial troops to build a road through the wilderness to Fort Duquesne. Braddock had lacked Amerindian support because of inter-colonial politics; Forbes lost his five hundred Cherokee and Catawba warriors due to boredom during the tedious construction. For all their similarities, the two attempts were quite different. While Braddock had built a road as quickly as possible to move his twenty-five hundred men and cannon, Forbes moved an army of nearly seven thousand in order to build a secure road to Fort Duquesne. Forbes's road was shorter, better planned, better built, and better defended; this road favored Pennsylvania with excellent access to the Ohio as surely as Braddock's had favored Virginia. The 193-mile road west from Fort Bedford (Raystown, Pennsylvania) was laid out to avoid the difficulties with forage, supply, and flooding encountered by Braddock. Using his own experience in suppressing the Scottish '45, as well as Turpin de Crissé's new *Essai sur l'art de la guerre*, Forbes built a supply road marked by defensible stockades and forts no more than forty miles apart.

When Forbes and his army finally approached their objective, their first encounter was disastrous. On September 11, Major James Grant and a mixed force of eight hundred Highlanders, Royal Americans, and colonial volunteers were sent forward to scout Fort Duquesne and take prisoners. One English patrol became lost in the woods, and a second was overwhelmed by French and Amerindians from the alerted garrison at Fort Duquesne, then numbering seventeen hundred. At least 275, primarily Highlanders and Virginians, were killed or captured in the confusing woodland battle, while the French reported only 8 killed and as many wounded. However, the English forts along the road remained secure; a French and Amerindian attack on the entrenched camp at Fort Ligonier a month later was effectively repulsed.

Forbes's road was more important to the disparate Amerindians of the upper Ohio Valley than it was to the English and led, figuratively, to the Treaty of Easton (1758). Despite grievances against the English that had made Ohio Delaware, Shawnee, and Mingo warriors prominent in raids against English frontier settlements for three years, some leaders of these tribes also wanted the French ousted from Fort Duquesne. Now there were prospects that English cannon would accomplish that task. Moravian missionary Christian Frederick Post, Quaker intermediaries, and Teedyuscung's Susquehanna Delaware, who had made peace with Pennsylvania a year earlier, all helped arrange Anglo-Amerindian negotiations. More than five hundred representatives of fifteen tribes, though primarily Six Nations and Susquehanna Delaware, gathered at Easton in October 1758 to meet with Pennsylvania Governor William Denny, his entire council, New Jersey Governor Francis Bernard, and Colonel Henry Bouquet representing the ill Forbes. The Six Nations and Delaware sparred over relations between themselves and over the right to represent the Ohio Amerindians, a few of whom were also present. The Amerindians agreed to withdraw support from the French, in return for cancellation of a fraudulent sale of Delaware lands to the Pennsylvania proprietors by the Six Nations, plus assurances that the British would withdraw from the forks of the Ohio. The agreement was carried to the Ohio towns by a delegation that included Post and both Six Nations and Delaware representatives, each seeking to extend its authority over the tribes and multitribal villages of the upper Ohio. Six days before Forbes occupied Fort Duquesne, the British flag had already replaced the French at the major Ohio Amerindian town of Kuskuski.[19]

The French garrison at Fort Duquesne was desperately short of provisions, since its supplies had been captured or destroyed in the fall of Fort Frontenac. Commandant François-Marie Le Marchand de Ligneris, who had been decorated for his part in the defeat of Braddock, saw his Amerindian allies leaving to go "hunting," and he could no longer provision his garrison. The Louisiana and Illinois militia reinforcements, with some of the fort's cannon, were sent down the Ohio. Canadian troops were posted to Detroit or Montréal. The remaining three hundred Canadians, aware that Forbes's army was advancing, detonated Fort Duquesne and took salvaged cannon and supplies to reinforce Fort Machault (Venango) for the winter.[20]

The Anglo-American offensive of 1758 had demonstrated how fortune favors the biggest armies. Franco-Canadian forces had received little reinforcement since 1756, when they totaled four thousand plus militia, and there had been severe loss of Amerindian support. The English, who had fielded eleven thousand men in 1755, were using forty-four thousand in 1758. Britain's naval blockade of French ports had strengthened, and a realistic French minister of marine could only lament:

> To send succors in divisions is to run the risk of losing all in detail; to send them together, is to expose ourselves to a general action and to lose all at once.[21]

Unable to send more troops, the ministry could only advise that women and old men of New France work the fields while all the able bodied males were mobilized.[22] By the end of 1758, English success seemed assured; the pessimistic Montcalm assumed that embattled Canada would fall in the next one or two campaigns.[23] All that could save New France was peace, which the Pitt–Newcastle ministry was not planning.

The British offensive of 1759 built on the previous year's victories and focused resources for a decisive attack on the heart of New France. Amherst was to follow the classic strategy of 1690, 1711, and 1746, an overland invasion down the Lake Champlain route combined with a maritime attack up the St. Lawrence River. With Fort Frontenac and Fort Duquesne gone, Fort Niagara became even more valuable to the French, and more vulnerable to an English attack. For the fourth year in a row, Albany was profiting as the staging point for two campaigning English armies.

The Six Nations of the Iroquois, most of whom had remained neutral throughout the war, began to change their minds in the wake of the destruction of Fort Duquesne. By early 1759, the Six Nations told the English that they now stood "ready to join and revenge both Your Blood and ours upon the French."[24] The Seneca, who had long resented the presence of French Fort Niagara on their territory, were particularly interested in having Amherst do for them what Forbes seemed to have done for the Delaware and Shawnee at the forks of the Ohio.

Amherst finally decided, early in May 1759, to undertake the siege of Fort Niagara, assigning the command to newly arrived Brigadier-General John Prideaux. A thousand New York provincial troops and Royal Americans were to rebuild and garrison Fort Oswego, while two thousand regulars and nearly one thousand Six Nations surprised Captain Pierre Pouchot and the garrison at Fort Niagara on July 7. Here, as in the attack on Fort Frontenac the previous year, no Six Nations informed the French of English troop movements on the Mohawk–Oswego waterway. Pouchot had just reduced his garrison by sending reinforcements to Fort Machault, where Ligneris was assembling a force, including Amerindians from the upper Great Lakes, to attack Fort Pitt (Fort Duquesne). Left with a total of only 486 regulars, *troupes de la marine*, and militia, as well as about 30 Amerindians, Pouchot now sent to Ligneris for help.

One of the most revealing aspects of Amerindian participation in the Seven Years' War became clear at Fort Niagara. Two Six Nation legates were admitted into Fort Niagara, where they and several Seneca, Mississauga, Ottawa, and Potawatomi discussed the misfortune of Amerindians fighting one another. They also learned of the impending relief force expected from Fort Machault. After the legates returned to the camp, all the Six Nations suddenly decided that they were withdrawing from the siege and establishing a camp nearby at La Belle Famille. As the English siege progressed, Pouchot learned that Ligneris was approaching with six hundred French and Canadians and one thousand Amerindians from the *pays d'en haut*. However, after discussions with the Six Nations, all but the thirty Amerindians with Pouchot refrained from the contest. Ever since the "Bloody Morning Scout" of September 1755, Amerindians had rather successfully avoided killing one another while fighting the white man's war. Most Amerindian participation was intended to destroy the English in a parallel war, not pit Amerindians against one another. The thirty Amerindians with Pouchot may have been reason enough for the Six Nations to withdraw, and their diplomacy prompted a massive "desertion" of Ligneris' Amerindian companions, who had paddled the length of Lake Erie to attack the English.

The rest of Ligneris' force, including a number of Canadian *troupes de la marine* officers with decades of experience in woodland warfare, were warned on their way to the fort that the British were waiting for them near La Belle Famille. Five hundred British regulars and one hundred New York provincials, protected by logs and an *abattis*, accepted the initial fire from the confident French and Canadians, then fired seven quick volleys on command to shatter the advance. As the British regulars charged after the fleeing French, the Six Nations joined in pursuit of scalps and prisoners; more than two hundred French were killed and at least one hundred captured. Apparently Six Nations warriors also killed a few Amerindians from the Ohio Valley, which strained relations for years. Although Pouchot held out for two more days, he had no choice but to surrender the garrison as prisoners of war. The thirty Amerindians who had fought with the French were allowed to go free.[25]

The Battle of the Plains of Abraham has often been regarded as the decisive climax of the long Anglo-French contest. In a dramatic sense, this view has merit. A British fleet of 141 warships and transports delivered nearly nine thousand troops to Québec before the end of June. Montcalm, with a total of fifteen thousand regulars and militia, plus nearly a thousand mission Amerindians, had prepared the citadel and environs so effectively that General Wolfe was unable to find a landing anywhere on the north shore of the St. Lawrence for more than two months. From the British-controlled south shore, forty British cannon pounded the city mercilessly, and Wolfe ordered a ferocious campaign of terror against the farmers of this same shore, but Montcalm could not be lured from his defenses. Early in August, British vessels began braving Québec's batteries to slip up the river, forcing Montcalm to detach a force of three thousand to shadow their activities. However, it was another month before Wolfe's brigadiers convinced him to attempt a landing above the city that could cut Montcalm's supply lines and might draw him out to fight. With his supplies, time, and hope running out, Wolfe planned a risky night landing that required his regulars to scale a 150-foot cliff at Anse de Foulon, overpower French pickets, and assemble for a battle on the Plains of Abraham, from which there was no retreat. Montcalm regarded this British move up river as

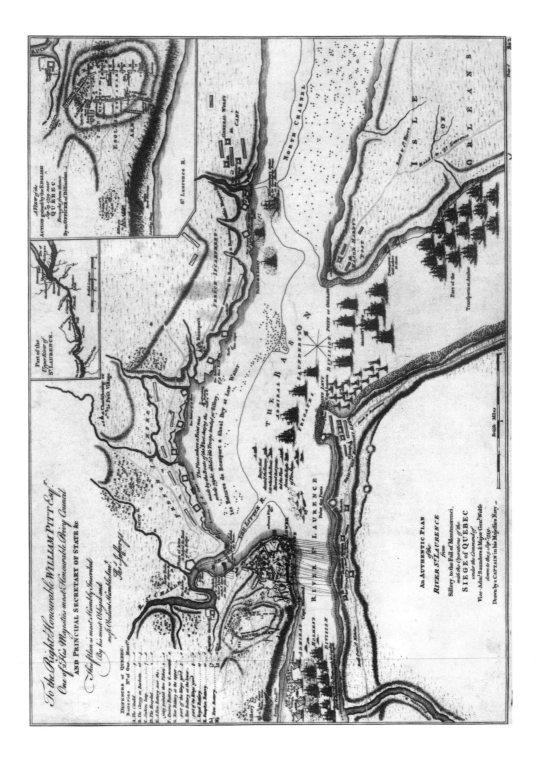

just one more of dozens of feints, but by daybreak of September 13, 1759, Wolfe had assembled forty-four hundred men within a thousand yards of the walls of Québec (Figure 11).

Montcalm acted with uncharacteristic haste, apparently on the same mistaken assumption that had proven disastrous for Dieskau at Lake George and Abercromby at Fort Carillon: the assumption that the enemy was not yet prepared for battle. Having assembled only forty-five hundred French regulars and Canadian militia and without waiting for sufficient field cannon or reinforcements that would have at least doubled his force, Montcalm ordered an attack in three columns. These columns were disrupted by shot from a pair of well-placed brass field cannon, which British sailors had managed to haul up the cliff, and by disciplined volleys from Wolfe's six battalions of regulars, who then charged with bayonets and claymores. When the half-hour battle was over, the British controlled the Plains of Abraham and the French controlled the town. Each side had inflicted casualties of nearly 15 percent (658 English casualties and 644 French); Wolfe was among the dead and Montcalm among the dying. Before dying four days later, Montcalm surrendered the city to Wolfe's successor.[26] New France's first permanent settlement, which had long been associated with complete victory in the minds of New Englanders who remembered the failures of Phips and Walker, had finally been taken.

For all its drama and poignancy, it is possible to challenge the decisiveness of this battle, and one alternative is to regard it as a *coup de grâce* in a contest already won. The French government assumed that New France was already lost. No help of consequence was sent to Canada, and the planned French invasion of England was a most unlikely diversion. If the French navy could not elude the much stronger British fleet in the spacious Atlantic or the Gulf of St. Lawrence, and if the French government presumed naval defeat in the event of an encounter, how could a French amphibious landing be attempted in what was, by then, a very English Channel? Pitt was right in refusing to be panicked by rumors of invasion, and Boscawen's defeat of a sizable French squadron off Portugal's Lagos Bay in August ended all speculation.

Most interested Amerindians, like the French, had already decided that New France was lost. Only three hundred Amerindians from the *pays d'en haut* were defending Québec in 1759, and half of those were Cree who had not been involved previously. Forbes's road to Fort Duquesne had convinced the Ohio tribes to make peace and the Six Nations to end neutrality. Those who were not yet convinced had learned during the spring and summer of 1759 that it was very difficult

Figure 11. *(facing)* Siege of Québec, 1759. From Thomas Jefferys, "Plan of . . . Operations of the Siege of Quebec." (Courtesy of the National Archives of Canada, Ottawa)

to disrupt this road.[27] Amerindian diplomacy throughout the siege of Fort Niagara indicated both a growing sense of fellowship between Amerindians allied with either European power and a calculated willingness to attack the French as part of positioning themselves with the anticipated victors.

New France was shriveling rapidly in 1759. Both ends of its St. Lawrence lifeline had been cut. Fort Carillon and Fort St. Frédéric were also abandoned in July and August in the face of Amherst's eight-thousand-man army, which slowly but relentlessly destroyed this southern extension of New France as Forbes's methodical invasion had done in the west. The defenders of New France were already isolated and vastly outnumbered in August 1759; whether Wolfe's army wintered in Québec or Louisbourg was incidental. One might argue that Wolfe could not conquer Canada because it was already beaten.

It is also arguable that New France was not beaten until long after the fall of Québec. Disparity in casualties was minor, and, regardless of the confusion of the French retreat, the Franco-Canadian army was neither captured, reduced, nor separated from its supply bases farther up the St. Lawrence. The second battle for the citadel of Québec, the Battle of Sainte-Foy, on April 28, 1760, was the crucial battle. Lévis, who had inherited Montcalm's command, led an army of nearly seven thousand, more than half regulars, against Brigadier-General James Murray's winter garrison at Québec of fewer than thirty-nine hundred. Murray decided to counterattack, with even less reason than had prompted Montcalm into the same error the previous September. The resulting battle was bloodier than the earlier one, and Lévis' victory was more obvious than Wolfe's. Murray recorded his casualties at 1104; Lévis, at 833.[28] Murray's army had abandoned its field guns in retreating into the Québec citadel, where it remained besieged by a French army that was itself desperately short of gunpowder. When the first ships arrived in the second week of May, they proved to be British; the besiegers became the besieged.

Lévis' success had depended on the arrival of a French squadron with the requested four thousand reinforcements and supplies. The British naval victory at Quiberon Bay in Brittany, in November 1759, had crippled the French navy's ability to deliver what meager assistance was intended. The lone frigate *Machault* and five merchant vessels sailed out of Bordeaux in April 1760, carrying only a tenth of the troops and a fifth of the supplies Lévis had requested. The vessels were soon scattered by the British navy, then two were captured and one was sunk in the Gulf of St. Lawrence. The three surviving vessels, and several small prizes they had taken, sailed into the Restigouche River from the Bay of Chaleur. While a messenger went overland to find Vaudreuil, the mouth of the river was made defensible by the remaining two hundred French regulars, who mounted shore batteries to protect a chain boom they had laid across the river. These determined defenders were entirely outgunned by a British squadron sent after them from Louisbourg and were forced to burn the *Machault* and the other vessels, except one containing the English sailors from the captured prizes. The last French reinforcements then scattered after trying in vain to hide the salvaged stores of war. The loss of this pathetic final French assistance in July 1760 indicated the extent to which British operations in New France had become "a leisurely march to a foregone conclusion."[29]

It was evident that most Canadians and Amerindians considered the war lost by the time Murray began moving his twenty-two hundred men toward Montréal in July. Resisting civilians were met with a more discriminating violence than Wolfe had instigated the previous summer.[30] Many of Lévis' regulars also regarded the war as forfeit; 548 of them were listed as deserters, and another 122 were absent from their regiments.[31] With only two thousand regulars, fewer than a thousand militia, and inadequate provisions, guns, and ammunition, Lévis could do little to defend Montréal. Amherst was concentrating some seventeen thousand troops on that city, bringing his army down the St. Lawrence, while Murray's force sailed unopposed up the river and Lieutenant-Colonel William Haviland brought another army down the now defenseless Richelieu River. The approaches were well coordinated, and all three English armies arrived at Montréal within forty-eight hours of one another.

Despite the impossible situation, Lévis was prepared to continue fighting when Amherst refused to grant the French full honors of war because of the "shocking cruelties" in the French-supported Amerindian war. Vaudreuil, who had sponsored the effective mixture of regular and irregular warfare, rejected Lévis' position and signed the terms on September 8, 1760. An infuriated Lévis could only withhold symbols from the British; French regimental colors were ceremonially burned, and Lévis broke his own sword.[32] Although Vaudreuil did not value the finer points of European military etiquette, he had witnessed the triumph of European warfare and the negotiated conclusion that had been made possible.

 The Seven Years' War had been another invasion of North America. The Anglo-French struggle for North America had involved two related, but distinct, contests: the fight over the kind of weapons, methods, and rules within each contending army, and the duel itself. North Americans' pride in the ways of their New World has supported the assumption that in warfare, as in much else, the adaptable people of the New World were superior to the history-laden people of the Old World. The defeat of Braddock and Dieskau can be misrepresented as evidence for this superiority. However, in the climax of the imperial struggle, the Europeans came and imposed their kind of warfare on the wilderness. Guerrilla tactics had already found a place in European warfare, but had lost their strategic function for imperial and colonial, though not yet for Amerindian, contestants. The eclipse of guerrilla warfare followed from the stouter forts erected between 1714 and 1740, which occasionally interfered with the easiest water transport of raiding parties, but neither stopped these raids nor fell to them. Larger armies using cannon were needed to take these forts, and larger armies needed secure supply lines for water or road transport. Forts had engendered siege warfare and more forts.

In the Anglo-American army, there had been relatively little struggle over adoption of the essentials of mid-eighteenth-century European war. Siege warfare had been the essence of New England offensives since King Philip's War, and colonial regiments showed no inclination to abandon forts for woodland warfare with Amerindians. To utilize American manpower advantages, with a minimum of training for most recruits, European conventional warfare had clear advantages. The large increase of British regulars after 1755, as well as British control of the campaigns, ensured complete acceptance of European military conventions. Colonial rangers were well-paid and well-respected specialists, some of whom were incorporated into the British army; their main assignment was to provide a protective screen for regulars in wilderness situations, a task that was incompatible with guerrilla warfare. Although Amerindian alliances that neutralized opponents were important for the English, Amerindian allies apparently were not.

The Franco-Canadian situation was entirely different. Amerindian warriors and their acclimatized Canadian companions vastly outnumbered those Americans adept at woodland warfare. Governor Vaudreuil's experience made him committed to the full use of guerrillas. Even on the defense, he saw the harrying of communication lines and the attacking of outposts and frontier settlements as winning time. Montcalm insisted on a tighter, conventional defense, and his success at Carillon confirmed the French court's predilections. Vaudreuil's strategy could not have saved New France, and he accepted what could only be a conventional defense of Québec. Winning a little time was no solution; the British were committed to victory in North America, and there was little that could be done to save Canada. New France did not fall because of absolutism, Catholicism, feudalism, paternalism, or factionalism. New France fell to a much bigger army.

The conquest of 1760, like all military conquests, was only an interim solution; the negotiated peace that would confirm this redistribution of power was still more than two years away. The death of George II, on October 25, 1760, proved decisive in beginning negotiations for a peace. He prized his native Hanover, had personally led its armies, and was as aggressive about continental peace demands as William Pitt was about colonial ones. By contrast, young George III was anxious to extricate his native England from his grandfather's European entanglements and from the Whig ministers associated with that war. The pursuit of peace by the twenty-two-year-old king was supported by his confidant and former tutor, the earl of Bute, by popular opinion, and by advisers concerned about the phenomenal growth of war debt.

During 1761, victorious British armies and navies continued to impound France's empire in America, the West Indies, West Africa, and India, giving British diplomats additional assets with which to negotiate a favorable peace. They captured Belle-Ile-en-Mer, on France's Atlantic coast; added Dominica to the already captured premier sugar island of Guadeloupe (1759) in the French West Indies; and helped the East India Company army take the main French base in India at Pondicherry. Pitt and the more skillful French foreign minister, Étienne François, comte de Stainville, duc de Choiseul, could not agree on the terms of peace. While Pitt was accused of warmongering by the war-weary British, Choiseul was finalizing a Spanish alliance to improve France's negotiating position. Pitt called for an immediate declaration of war against Spain and resigned when his colleagues and the king refused.

Nonetheless, Britain declared war on Spain three months later, creating additional targets for the triumphant British military in 1762. They successfully besieged the major remaining French sugar island of Martinique and added the French-occupied West Indian islands of St. Lucia, Grenada, and St. Vincent. Although a French squadron captured St. John's, Newfoundland, in the summer, it capitulated in September to a stronger British relief force. A battalion of British regulars and a miscellany of other recruits gathered at Madras, India, from which they sailed to surprise, besiege, and capture Manila, the capital of the Spanish Philippine Islands.

The greatest British success of 1762, the capture of Havana by a combined force of fifteen thousand, marginally involved British North American troops. Amherst was ordered to contribute four thousand soldiers from his North American command, regulars if necessary, but half provincial troops if they could be raised without revealing the target. It is significant that, despite memories of Cartegena, all four colonial governments that were approached (New Jersey, Rhode Island, Connecticut, and New York) sent the required troops for an unspecified campaign outside North America. New York's assembly had some difficulty, but found the required 553 volunteers by raising the enlistment bounty from £10 to £12. The resulting North American contingents were delayed by shipwreck on the Cuban coast and by an encounter with a French squadron. They arrived to witness the British regulars storming El Morro and to participate in the final days of skirmishing before Havana surrendered. Although helping to garrison the conquered city for only two months, the American provincials joined the British regulars in losing nearly half their men to disease.[33]

Americans who volunteered to fight King George's imperial battles outside North America in 1762, like the estimated eleven thousand colonials who overlooked the draconian discipline of the British regulars to enlist with them during the course of the war, did so for reasons now impossible to recover.[34] Those risking their lives might wish to believe in their altruistic loyalties rather than their selfish interests. It seems likely that many of these soldiers, and many of the thousands of Americans who volunteered for the colonial regiments in this war, had easily "stacked" their loyalties to community, colony, religion, and king. Puritan New Light or Old, Presbyterians, Baptists, Quakers, and Anglicans had all prayed, they thought successfully, for the victory of King George's Protestant empire. Benjamin Franklin rejoiced at the imperial conquest of Canada "not merely as I am a colonist, but as I am a Briton."[35] Americans revealed more British patriotism than ever before in celebrating the accession of George III, British victories in New France, the West Indies, and Europe, as well as the Peace of Paris. The city of New York, having raised enough money by public subscription, erected a two-ton gilt equestrian statue of George III, portrayed as a Roman emperor, as well as one of William Pitt.[36]

France lost the war but won the peace. Choiseul had made it clear as early as February 1760 that France was willing to cede all of Canada except Louisbourg, and Pitt had immediately ensured that the fortress was detonated that year. The anxious new British negotiators found the string of British victories of 1762 so embarrassing that Choiseul was able to minimize their significance. There was much debate then, and since, about why British negotiators settled for a half-continent of snow and bush rather than rich West Indian islands of sugar. British West Indian sugar planters, who were not anxious to see the more productive French islands adding cheap sugar to Britain's markets, agreed with the majority of Americans in calling for the choice of Canada. The short answer is that the unprofitable colony of Canada was what the French were prepared to offer as they salvaged their profitable maritime empire of slaves, sugar, and fish. The restoration of Havana in exchange for Florida gave Britain yet another revenue-draining annex of empire in exchange for a vital node in Spain's American empire.[37] Britain had conducted a war that humiliated France, then made a peace that alienated allies but did not limit France's power to seek revenge.

The "Great War for Empire" and the peace that ended it integrated eastern North America into the British empire more thoroughly and more completely than ever before. The invasion of British troops had overwhelming American support, the attending invasion of British government money was even more welcome, and the defeat of New France and the retention of all of North America east of the Mississippi River sent some eloquent American publicists into raptures like those of the Reverend Thomas Barnard of Salem, Massachusetts:

Safe from the Enemy of the Wilderness, safe from the griping Hand of arbitrary Sway and cruel Superstition; Here shall be the late founded Seat of Peace and Freedom. Here shall our indulgent Mother, who has most generously rescued and protected us, be served and honoured by growing Numbers, with all Duty, Love and Gratitude, till Time shall be no more.[38]

Expectations of both the British and the Americans were too high. Seventy-five hundred British troops remained in North America after the peace, initially causing more concern among Amerindians than among Americans. The British government had accumulated a total war debt of £137 million, with interest payments alone consuming more than 60 percent of the annual peacetime budget; they expected grateful Americans to help with the costs of the army. Massachusetts was the colony that had spent the most on the war (£818,000) and had resorted to unprecedented excise and stamp taxes until Pitt's "subsidy policy" improved finances after 1758; Massachusetts received £352,000 of these costs back from the British government.[39] While the people of Massachusetts could think they had contributed enough, the British sought ways to distribute some of their fiscal pain to colonies that had benefited from the war.

The war had solved some problems, postponed others, and created new ones. The postwar economic slump caused unemployment, aggravated by the end of good wages for thousands of Americans who had been soldiers. The peace that removed France and Spain from eastern North America made British ministries confident that they could impose their will on British Americans and gave Americans more confidence to resist. The oldest contest ended on July 20, 1763, when the British flag was hoisted at the Castillo de San Marcos, making the first permanent European base in North America the last to submit to a triumphant British empire. Unlike the Spanish, the vast majority of the sixty thousand Canadians accepted an alien king and stayed in the land of their birth. They were treated with the consideration necessary to hold a defeated people thought capable of revolt. The undefeated Amerindians of the *pays d'en haut* would receive less consideration and would quickly launch the war that concluded the colonial phase of the European invasion of eastern North America.

Chapter 12

DIFFERENT DRUMMERS
1759–1765

The last major European invasion of Amerindian colonial America was the intrusion into the Ohio Valley, which had triggered the climactic last Anglo-French struggle and been fundamentally altered by the war's outcome. The Ohio Delaware had voiced suspicion of the Europeans from the early 1750s:

> [W]hy do you come to fight in the Land that God has given us. . . . Why don't you and the French fight in the old Country, and on the Sea? Why do you come to fight on our Land? This makes every Body believe you want to take the Land from us, by force and settle it.[1]

Amerindians who had survived the initial waves of European diseases, who lived by firearms, and who thoroughly understood the threat of European farmers were trying to preserve their land and their way of life by shrewdly exploiting rivalries between the European imperial powers, as well as those between the Six Nations and the Susquehanna Delaware.

The Ohio Amerindians were also cooperating comparatively well across tribal and linguistic lines, and most of them spoke related Algonquian languages. The French alliance had brought chiefs and warriors together at conferences and on campaigns, arbitrated some intertribal differences, and introduced a religion that created additional fraternal connections. Intertribal links were even closer among the Amerindians of the upper Ohio Valley, where some villages were multitribal, shared by Shawnee, Delaware, and Mingo. The Shawnee and Delaware also shared grievances against the English who had taken their lands east of the mountains through war or chicanery. A call to unite in defense of a threatened Amerindian way of life would find special resonance here.

At the end of 1758, there were some prospects of holding the English invaders to the east of the Appalachians. In the recent years of French victory, Shawnee, Delaware, and Mingo inhabitants, accompanied by Canadian, Ojibwa, Ottawa, and Potawatomi allies, had pushed back the frontiers of English settlement on the eastern side of the Appalachians. Given continued Anglo-French rivalry, such guerrilla raids would have established a tidal pattern of wartime ebb and peacetime flow of English settlement, like that long familiar on the New England frontier. The calculated withdrawal of Amerindian support for Fort Duquesne, negotiated in return for British promises to withdraw beyond the mountains, initially appeared as a shrewd decision that resulted in the burning of Fort Duquesne in November 1758. With the Iroquois, Cherokee, and Creek confederacies to hold back the English where the Appalachians did not, the Ohio Amerindians had prospects of preserving what Europeans were coming to call "Indian country."

Months before it became apparent to other Amerindians of eastern North America, those of the upper Ohio were facing the prospect of a complete British victory over the French. The hurtful "scissors" of inter-colonial war were almost a happy memory compared with a possible end to imperial rivalries; even the inconclusive European Peace of Utrecht had brought complete destruction to the Yamasee, Natchez, and Fox. The Ohio Amerindians faced several disturbing questions between 1760 and 1763. What would happen to Amerindians who had fought beside the French and Canadians? Who would control unscrupulous British traders selling cloth, hardware, and alcohol without diplomatic restraints or European competitors? What would stop the unending hordes of land-hungry European farmers who had already consumed the Atlantic coastal plain? What would prevent war between unruly English frontiersmen who hated the Amerindians and unruly young braves who hated the English? Finally, would war against a monopoly supplier of guns and gunpowder merely invite the sad fate of King Philip's Wampanoag?

Some questions were answered by three developments in the year after the fall of Fort Duquesne. General Forbes immediately established a garrison of two hundred at Fort Pitt commanded by Colonel Henry Bouquet. When shocked Delaware chiefs insisted that the soldiers withdraw as agreed at Easton, they were met with denial of any such agreement by George Croghan, translator and land speculator, and by Bouquet's unconvincing assurance that the fort was to protect Amerindian land and English traders.[2] With twice as large a French garrison still at Fort Machault, the British decision had been a military precaution. Aware of this, Ohio Delaware negotiators attempted to convince the French to withdraw, as a preliminary to having the British do likewise. It was only after the fall of Fort Niagara in July 1759, prompted by the withdrawal of support by the Amerindians of the *pays d'en haut*, that the French left Fort Machault. The British, however, remained at Fort Pitt.

The second event that carried ominous messages for Amerindians was Rogers's raid on the Abenaki mission village of St. François. In agreeing to the raid, General Amherst endorsed an attack that was explicitly for revenge, without strategic significance beyond promoting Amerindian insecurity, and oblivious to the value of Amerindian neutrality in the recent British successes at Fort Duquesne and Fort Niagara. Robert Rogers led 141 of his rangers, who were under regular army pay and discipline, in torching the entire village in a dawn raid in October 1759. Estimates of Abenaki and ranger casualties vary enormously, from 30 to 250, but it was evident to all that the village was entirely destroyed. Those who escaped were taken in by the new Iroquois mission village of St. Regis (1755), where they lived for several years.[3] The raid was conducted in wartime and was analogous to the earlier Pennsylvania destruction of Kittanning, but it indicated one way in which the English might deal with Amerindian allies of New France. There was also something disturbing in Amherst's choice of Rogers as the emissary to take news of the fall of New France to the former French posts of the *pays d'en haut* in the fall of 1760 and spring of 1761.[4]

The third and much more serious development, confirming Amherst's callous attitude to Amerindians as well as displaying British regulars' strategy in war with Amerindians, was the Cherokee War of 1759 to 1761.[5] About ten thousand Cherokee hunters and farmers lived in some forty towns in the valleys of the southern Appalachians. Although pro-French and neutral factions existed, the Cherokee had long been British allies. South Carolina farmers and hunters had been encroaching on Cherokee hunting lands during the 1750s. Serious trouble started when a few of the 450 Cherokee warriors, returning from assisting the Forbes expedition, threatened a number of Virginia farmers, stole goods and horses, and skirmished with Virginia militiamen in the summer of 1758. Several Virginians and at least seventeen Cherokee were killed in these encounters, prompting revenge by some Cherokee of the Lower, Middle, and Overhill Towns as well as by some Virginians. Isolated murders of Cherokee were also fostered by Virginia's scalp bounty of £50, equivalent to a year's income for many farmers. Some rangers, militia, and bounty hunters were prepared to kill allied Cherokee and offer their scalps as those of the enemy Delaware or Shawnee, whose raids had prompted the bounty.

After months of sporadic killings in Virginia and along the Carolina–Cherokee frontier, Governor William Lyttelton of South Carolina prohibited arms and gunpowder sales to the Cherokee in August 1759. In the internal arguments among the Cherokee headmen, the aggressive were asked, since they were prepared to fight the English, whether "they found a mountain of powder? Had their women learned to make clothes and their men to make knives?"[6] Cherokee access to gunpowder, which the English controlled because of naval blockades of French sources, was recognized as a serious concern of the Cherokee and the English throughout the ensuing war.

The central issue for the English of South Carolina and elsewhere, on this and many other occasions, was the delivery of Amerindian "murderers" for punishment by the English. This issue was simple justice from the English perspective, but intrusive and disruptive domination in the eyes of the Cherokee. English justice not only created political difficulties within the tribes because of its death penalty, but also was incomprehensible to many Amerindians because it offered no compensation other than vengeance to relatives of the initial victims. Cherokee anxious to restore amicable relations drew on their own inter-clan and intertribal tradition to suggest seriously that each Cherokee murderer of an English person be required to bring in a French scalp or prisoner as recompense. Understandably, this notion was dismissed out of hand by Charlestown authorities.

The English, intent on disciplining the Cherokee, invaded their country in each of the three summers of the war. Each army had different forces, limitations, and results. Governor Lyttelton gained assembly support for an army of fifteen hundred men to force the Cherokee to turn over murderers, but funding for the operation was limited to the last three months of 1759. A Cherokee peace legation came to Charlestown just as final preparations for the expedition were being made in October, but Lyttelton took them hostage. His army of colonial volunteers and one company of regulars arrived, with his twenty-eight hostages, at Fort Prince George on December 9, leaving him only three weeks before his funding and most of his army evaporated. The pro-British Cherokee chief, Attakullaculla (Little Carpenter), who was fighting the French to prevent war with the English, arrived ten days later for talks that also included the Cherokee diplomats being held hostage. Lyttelton demanded that twenty-four unnamed Cherokee "murderers" be delivered to him if the Cherokee wanted the release of the hostages and the departure of his army. Negotiations were awkward, but six Cherokee chiefs, including Attakullaculla, signed a treaty agreeing that twenty-two of the hostages would be held in Fort Prince George until the chiefs could deliver the remaining twenty-two Cherokee murderers of colonists. As an inducement, Lyttelton then displayed the presents that would be distributed once the murderers had been received, gifts that included several cases of muskets, three tons of gunpowder, and proportionate ammunition. Neither the prospect of these presents, the release of six hostages, nor Lyttelton's promise of renewed trade could make this agreement palatable to most Cherokee.

Lyttelton's army retired from Fort Prince George at the end of December, just as his funding expired, to receive the misplaced applause of Charlestown. The expedition had done nothing but provoke the Cherokee and bring a smallpox epidemic to the fort. The garrison at Fort Prince George, under Lieutenant Richard Coytmore, was to guard the twenty-two prominent Cherokee hostages and three tons of prized gunpowder, and to negotiate with the Cherokee who were thoroughly angered by the hostage-taking, the invading army, and Lyttelton's treaty. In less than three weeks, a party of more than seventy

Cherokee with concealed weapons attempted to turn the delivery of "murderers" into a surprise attack on the garrison. At the same time, raiding parties were killing English traders residing in Cherokee towns and settlers in the Carolina backcountry. In mid-February, Cherokee diplomats lured Coytmore out of his fort for a parley, then fatally wounded him; the angry garrison then killed all twenty-two of the remaining Cherokee hostages. Cherokee raiders killed scores of settlers on the frontiers, pushing white settlement back as much as a hundred miles. Lyttelton petitioned General Amherst for regulars to campaign against the Cherokee, and he asked Virginia for a force to relieve isolated Fort Loudoun, among the Overhill Cherokee.[7]

War in North America was changing again. Amherst responded quickly to Lyttelton's request, ordering more than thirteen hundred Highlanders and Royal Scots from New York to Charlestown under the command of Colonel Archibald Montgomery and Major James Grant. British regulars were about to begin unprecedented campaigns of direct war against major Amerindian forces. Unlike earlier confrontations, such as those of De Soto and Courville, these soldiers faced Amerindians armed with comparable weapons and aware of European rivalries, in addition to being familiar with the rugged terrain. The regulars were not limited to three-month contracts like Lyttelton's volunteers, and Amherst was afraid that the wealthy colony of South Carolina would not contribute much to its own defense as long as the regulars were available. He made it clear that Montgomery's forces were expected back in the north for the campaign against New France that summer, and the transport ships that delivered these troops were to wait for them at Charlestown.

Montgomery's regulars were in South Carolina by early April 1760, early enough to be literally waiting for the grass to grow in the upcountry so that their horses and cattle could forage. The army's thirteen hundred regulars had knowledgeable assistance from nearly three hundred rangers, forty picked men from the provincial forces, nearly fifty Catawba warriors, and a dozen guides. Entering Cherokee territory, they set up tents as a ruse, then marched twenty-five miles under cover of darkness to attack the Cherokee town of Estatoe. However, the town of two hundred dwellings was virtually deserted when the troops attacked it at dawn. After looting and burning, the army hurried on to burn three more Cherokee towns without meeting any resistance. Although there were few warriors among the sixty to eighty killed or the forty taken prisoner, Montgomery's Highlanders had "chastised" the Lower Cherokee Towns.

Montgomery now went to Fort Prince George, where Ensign Alexander Milne was holding Cherokee hostages he had tricked with a pretended parley, hostages who may have been the reason Montgomery's army was not attacked earlier. Three of these hostages were sent home with a message to return all white prisoners and to instruct

Attakullaculla to come for talks. The Middle and Overhill Towns were threatened with attack if the terms were not met. Montgomery's deadline expired without any response from the furious but confident Cherokee; Montgomery's ultimatum forced him into a mountain campaign supplied entirely by pack horse. Eighteen miles from their next target, the rangers were fired on from dense brush. When the Cherokee attacked what appeared to be a disorganized group, they suddenly met a rebuilt line of musket fire, forcing them back into the thicket. The regulars took losses, but drove the Cherokee from their cover, then moved on to the completely deserted town of Etchoe. In this campaign, seventeen of the British were killed and sixty-six wounded, and there were a number of additional casualties among the rangers; an estimated fifty Cherokee were killed.

Having "won" this remote field of battle, Montgomery decided to return to Charlestown and New York with the regulars, satisfied that they had done what Amherst expected in the time available. Montgomery felt that peace could not be negotiated because of Milne's "ungentlemanly" hostage-taking, which deterred the Cherokee from approaching the fort. For their part, the Cherokee had seen no significance in yielding the worthless thicket. They had killed many of their enemies, had proved that Montgomery's threat to burn the Middle and Overhill Towns was idle posturing, and had cause to celebrate the retreat of the British as a great Cherokee victory.[8]

Although the Cherokee "victory" against Montgomery's regulars could be the subject of cross-cultural debate, the Cherokee conquest of Fort Loudoun could not. This fort, garrisoned by a hundred regulars and a hundred South Carolina provincial troops, had been built in 1756 with British and South Carolina funds to forestall the French from building there. During this war, it had become a detested intrusion deep in Overhill Cherokee territory, separated from the support of Fort Prince George by two hundred difficult miles. On short rations since the spring because local corn was scarce, Fort Loudoun came under complete siege early in June when the Cherokee wives and mistresses of the garrison, who routinely bought food for the soldiers, were prevented from returning to the fort. With Montgomery's campaign at an end, the Virginians stalled fifty miles away, and the fort's food supplies completely exhausted, the garrison negotiated a surrender on August 7. The Cherokee agreed to terms that would allow the English garrison to march to the nearest English fort, carrying their arms and a few rounds of ammunition; the Cherokee prize was the half ton of gunpowder that remained in the fort after the English had filled their powder horns. Two days later, the retreating English column was attacked and all officers except Captain John Stuart were killed, as well as twenty-five soldiers and three women. All survivors were taken prisoner. Cherokee military success, displayed to visiting Amerindians by a dance of two hundred English prisoners, could not now be disputed.[9]

Although buoyed by the capture of Fort Loudoun, more Cherokee became interested in peace after August 1760. The Middle Towns, crowded with refugees from the Lower Towns and anticipating a winter of food and gunpowder shortages, opened preliminary talks with South Carolina's new governor, William Bull. Attakullaculla purchased Captain Stuart and smuggled him to the Virginia army camp, where a truce was arranged and peace terms were discussed. Oconostota, the Great Warrior of the Cherokee, declared a truce that allowed the English to resupply Fort Prince George twice and to remove its extra tons of gunpowder. Lachlan McIntosh, a former commander of that fort who had been popular with the Cherokee, replaced the hated Ensign Milne. Despite several small Cherokee raids in the spring of 1761, the Cherokee released 113 prisoners and discussed ransoming or exchanging others.

Peace talks with the Cherokee were not popular either in Charlestown or with the British army, where revenge was demanded. By March 1761, Governor Bull was particularly anxious to accelerate the ransom of prisoners because they might be killed once the Cherokee discovered English plans for the coming summer. Major James Grant returned to lead an army of more than twenty-eight hundred into Cherokee country. Half his forces were regulars, plus nearly seven hundred Carolina volunteers, four hundred rangers, and a comparable number of Amerindian auxilliaries who were Catawba, Chickasaw, and Mohawk. Grant was convinced that most of the Cherokee wanted peace, but Amherst dismissed this observation out of hand and insisted that the Cherokee must be punished. The army protected its vital train of six hundred packhorses from a major ambush in a gorge on the road to Etchoe, then went on to burn five deserted Middle Towns and to destroy crops and peach trees, newly introduced from Carolina. Taking all the regulars and a new "Indian Corps" of Mohawk and Stockbridge rangers, Grant crossed the mile-high Cowee Range to attack the Overhill Cherokee. In thirty-three days, Grant's force destroyed a total of fifteen towns and an estimated fourteen hundred acres of corn. The surprisingly limited Cherokee resistance may have been due to a shortage of gunpowder. Whatever the reason, the war faction lost its remaining credibility among the Cherokee, now crowded into the undamaged westernmost towns.

This destruction had been unnecessary, except to convince the English that Cherokee peace initiatives were not merely devices to spy on or stall an invading army. In extensive separate negotiations with South Carolina and Virginia, the Cherokee, who had not been defeated even though they had been harassed, won a moderate peace that was ratified in December 1761. The Cherokee returned captured Fort Loudoun and accepted the right of the English to build other forts. Both sides were to return all prisoners and punish with death those who murdered people of the other culture. A line of demarcation between the English and the Cherokee was drawn forty miles east of Fort Prince George. The Cherokee negotiators declined the usual presents of clothing offered at the end of the formal signing, preferring gunpowder for hunting.[10]

One of the most striking features of this war was the complete failure of the Cherokee to gain allies. Despite the best efforts of a small anti-British group of Creek, that tribe refused Cherokee advances throughout the war. The Chickasaw, who had often been allies of the Cherokee against the French and their Amerindian allies, resisted Cherokee overtures; more than twenty Chickasaw accompanied Grant. The Ottawa visited the Cherokee in the spring of 1759, but offered no help against the British. The Ohio Shawnee, who were also former French allies now drawing closer to the Cherokee, were not interested in helping either. Early in 1760, the Cherokee sent a request north to the Shawnee, Ottawa, and Wyandot without success. They also sent a legation and English prisoners south to the French at Fort Toulouse. This overture was answered by a French visit to the Cherokee that fall, but neither the French nor their allies were willing to help. Late in 1760, the Illinois and their allies refused a French invitation to aid the Cherokee to "drive the English into the great Water."[11] In the spring of 1761, the Overhill Cherokee sent delegates to the Seneca in search of a wider coalition against the land-hungry whites. Although the Chenussio Seneca, who resented the British presence at Fort Niagara, sent a war belt to the Ohio Amerindians calling for a simultaneous attack on British posts by all neighboring tribes, it was received with skepticism. The only Six Nations warriors involved in the Cherokee War were the Mohawk serving with Grant's army. The Detroit Huron claimed even to have attacked the Cherokee later in 1761. In the light of the events of the next few years, it is surprising that the Cherokee were as unable to find allies as the Pequot and Fox had been when fighting Europeans.[12]

The Amerindians of the Ohio Valley had reason and occasion to learn from the Cherokee War. Amherst urged William Johnson to use his judgment in spreading news of the British destruction of towns and crops and of hungry Cherokee refugees.[13] Amerindians would also hear from Cherokee ambassadors and messengers of the ruses that nearly took Fort Prince George, of the successful siege of Fort Loudoun, of British armies unable to force the Cherokee into battle, and of Amerindian military survival for three years without a significant European supplier of muskets, lead, or gunpowder. They also could see that British regulars were deployed to punish and take revenge on Amerindians who were at war with colonial Americans. Amherst's contempt for Amerindians may not yet have been obvious in the Ohio Valley, but it was clear enough in the colonies. When he heard of the fall of Fort Loudoun, Amherst noted that this was the first time royal troops had surrendered to Amerindians and that the garrison "must be blameable for doing so." Amherst had not learned another obvious lesson from the Cherokee War, that isolated frontier forts were at the mercy of neighboring Amerindians.[14]

Origins of the Amerindian War of 1763 to 1765, too often called Pontiac's War, are difficult to determine and are subject to much scholarly debate. Perhaps a greater puzzle is that, despite plans as early as those of Miantonomi of the Narragansett, this first extensive Amerindian war came only after two centuries of localized tribal or confederacy resistance and accommodation to European presence. King Philip's War had come too late to save the New England Algonquians, too early to gain French support, and both Mohawk and Mohegan made significant contributions to that English victory. The Anglo-French wars had provided a covert vehicle for much Amerindian resistance against the English during the seventy years prior to 1760. The Yamasee War of 1715 had begun as a broad intertribal reaction to the English, but disintegrated as the English detached the Catawba and the Cherokee. The end of the Anglo-French contest forced Amerindians of the Ohio and Great Lakes region to make major adjustments. The war of 1763 to 1765 shared much with earlier wars against the Europeans, but it developed from new Amerindian perspectives, new specific grievances, intertribal encouragements, as well as a triggering event. Each of these elements demand brief mention.

A cluster of new Amerindian spiritual and cultural ideas are known to have gained currency in the Susquehanna Valley and Ohio country from the Delaware dispersal of the late 1730s. A number of Delaware prophets and reformers gained followings beyond their villages and tribes. All insisted that the sufferings of Amerindians derived from the Master of Life's anger with their dependence on European goods, guns, and alcohol. Spiritual power could be recaptured only through ritual purgings, gradual withdrawal from trade with Europeans, and training of the young in the liberating skills of their ancestors. These visions were not mere nostalgia, for they revolutionized some basic features of Amerindian spirituality and reached beyond the tribal preoccupations of the traditionalists to embrace all Amerindians. Several of these prophets are known to have preached of a "separate creation" of Amerindians, Europeans, and Africans, each given different paths to salvation. Some of these prophets, like the Munsee Delaware Papoonan, were determined pacifists. Others, like a Wyoming Valley Delaware prophetess, challenged both the tribal leaders and their Six Nations "overlords." Still other prophets, including the famous "Delaware Prophet" Neolin, became the spiritual inspiration for those determined to fight the English. Neolin's message had reached as far west as the Illinois country by 1763, and a leader of the Detroit Ottawa, Pontiac, was among those who followed him.[15]

Although these nativist ideas had considerable power of their own, their rapid spread after 1760 was assisted by mounting uncertainties and by accumulating grievances as the English occupied the former

French forts of the *pays d'en haut*. As soon as they felt confident enough of their victory, English military leaders had begun demanding, as a prerequisite of peace, the return of all European prisoners still in Amerindian hands, as had been done with the Cherokee. Although Amerindian diplomacy often included the exchange of a few recently taken prisoners as part of peacemaking, the custom of adopting prisoners meant that they became permanent members of Amerindian communities. There was very little trade in prisoners on the Ohio, unlike the New England frontier, where selling wartime captives provided the Abenaki with income, the Canadians with labor, and the New England captives with hope of redemption by their families, parishes, or governments. Acquiring people, to strengthen one's group and weaken one's rivals, was one purpose of Amerindian war. Some women prisoners married and raised families within the Ohio villages, and those taken prisoner as children came to regard their Amerindian villages as their only homes. After returning prisoners who wanted to rejoin the English, the Shawnee and Delaware were reluctant to disrupt families in order to appease imperious alien commanders who would not even ransom the prisoners or consider them as part of a gift exchange. The British continued to insist, causing the Ohio Amerindians to wonder whether the British wanted all their people back in preparation for war to confiscate more Amerindian lands.[16]

The perennial problem of European squatters on Amerindian lands also re-emerged with special intensity after 1760. American settlers, some of whom had been paid for Virginia military service with entitlement to Ohio Valley lands, began farming around the English military posts, creating clearings elsewhere at their convenience, and hunting deer in competition with Amerindians. These farms were in violation of the Treaty of Easton (1758) and ignored Amerindian occupancy as well as the lack of any formal Anglo-French peace to relinquish French claims. Amerindian complaints prompted Colonel Bouquet, with approval of his military superior, General Monckton, to issue a proclamation in October 1761 prohibiting all European hunting and settlement west of the mountains, with violators to be tried by court-martial at Fort Pitt. It is noteworthy that the military assumed this responsibility, even though enforcement proved impossible beyond the occasional burning of cabins and the confiscating of horses and deerskins.[17]

American traders were initially welcome in the Ohio after the fall of Fort Duquesne, though their prices were high and the range of their goods, dominated by whiskey and rum, was narrow. Amerindians responded to exorbitant prices by stealing, quarreling, and occasionally killing a trader. The commander at Fort Pitt reported as early as January 1759 that he had bought much of the excess whiskey that dominated trader's cargoes, ostensibly to reduce the amount traded to Amerindians. A ban on trading rum was a complete failure, only aggravating both the traders and the customers. In attempting to control English hunters, traders, and settlers, the British army was quickly assuming a policing role between Amerindians and Americans. This position was taken for military reasons, in country that was not yet at peace, but it made few friends among Americans or Amerindians.

Although these issues might have encouraged Amerindians to notice and exploit the differences between the British and the Americans, they did not yet do so because of a major grievance against the British army.[18] General Amherst's ban on presents for Amerindians is rightly regarded as a major cause of the ensuing war. The British government had strained its resources in pursuing the Seven Years' War, and attempts to limit costs prompted policies that provoked the resistance of Amerindians long before that of Americans. The regular distribution of presents had been part of French diplomacy in the *pays d'en haut*, and these gifts may have been regarded by Amerindians as ground rent for forts, payment for permission to trade, tokens to sustain the alliance, or even as tribute. Favored "medal" chiefs had reinforced their own and the donor's standing in village and tribal politics by distributing impressive gifts to warriors, followers, and allies. Johnson, as superintendent of Indian affairs, intended to preserve and control this system, but had no budget independent of Amherst. Amherst saw the British simply as military conquerors, and the Amerindians as subjects whose good behavior should not have to be bought and whose bad behavior would be punished. Amherst intended open trade and the security of Amerindian hunting lands; the former did not develop quickly enough, and the latter was sabotaged by many, including Johnson and Croghan. Unheeded warnings from Johnson and his assistant, George Croghan, were sensible, if self-interested, pleas to postpone this policy, introduce it gradually, or reconsider it completely. What proved a very false economy on presents was imposed at a time when the regular flow of trade goods had not been restored, European hunters and settlers were reducing the deer population, and hungry Amerindians were particularly short of gunpowder. Not only had Amherst eliminated gunpowder along with the other gifts, but he also ordered that the trade in gunpowder to Amerindians be clandestinely restricted.[19]

The Amerindians of the Great Lakes and the Ohio Valley, victorious against both the British and the Americans in the recent war, were also encouraged to resistance by intertribal exchanges of diplomats and war belts. When Detroit was formally ceded to a British garrison in November 1760, local Ottawa, Potawatomi, Huron, and Ojibwa had invited the Six Nations to discuss ousting the British. Dissident Seneca had sent a war belt west in the spring of 1761, urging attacks on Detroit, Niagara, Fort Pitt, Presqu'île, and Venango, and this belt continued to circulate despite its denunciation by Six Nation and Ottawa chiefs at a Detroit conference the following spring. By 1763, this belt was accompanied by another from the missions at Montréal, a third from the Illinois, and a fourth from Pontiac at Detroit. Although intertribal rivalries were also intensifying in these uncertain times and being actively fomented by Johnson, the breadth of the wish to resist the English was impressive.[20]

The trigger for the Amerindian War was not the grievances, but how Pontiac and his associates reacted to the news that these problems would continue. News of the preliminary terms of the Peace of Paris, including transfer to the British of all French claims east of the Mississippi, had reached Detroit and the Ohio Valley by the spring of 1763. Amerindians, as well as French traders and *habitants*, were reluctant to accept the disturbing news that these terms were final, and the rumor that the French would return became a persistent part of Pontiac's vision. Although Amerindian motives were various, their apparent purpose was not a race war. The French were not hated for giving away a country that was not theirs to give; both Neolin and Pontiac expressed high regard for the French. Pontiac appropriated the ritual role of preserver of French influence, appointed a renegade drummer from the French regulars as interim "commandant" of Detroit, used the white flag of the Bourbons on occasion, and carried a bogus letter from the French government. No wonder the British mistook the French as the instigators of a conspiracy.[21] Whether or not Pontiac believed in the return of the French, he found that it inspired his supporters, frightened the British, and lured some French to his cause. The actions of Amerindians who followed or imitated Pontiac suggest that their purpose was not to return to ancient days. Captured forts were not all burned as centers of iniquity; their power was more often appropriated. Amerindian actions suggest that the world they initially sought to restore was not the pristine one of their ancestors and not quite the independent one that Neolin envisaged, but the best of the world they had just lost.

Pontiac's siege of Detroit, commencing on May 9, signaled the beginning of an Amerindian protest that would, within two months, become loosely linked attacks on all British forts west of Niagara. Pontiac failed to take Detroit with a ruse very similar to that tried on Fort Prince George by the Cherokee three years earlier. However, the same method of concealing weapons to surprise unsuspecting garrisons gained various Amerindian forces a total of seven forts in little more than a month. Forts Sandusky (May 16), St. Joseph (May 25), Miami (May 27), and Venango (ca. June 16) each had fifteen-man garrisons that, suspecting nothing, were tricked and killed. Michilimackinac (June 2) was the largest of these garrisons; fifteen of its thirty-five men were killed in the now-famous ruse by Ojibwa pursuing an errant lacrosse ball into the fort. The small garrison at Green Bay (ca. June 15) and the survivors from Michilimackinac were smuggled to Montréal by sympathetic Ottawa. The twenty soldiers in Fort Ouiatenon (June 1) were all taken as prisoners of war to the commander of the only remaining French post at Fort de Chartres. This initial explosion of violence involved a dozen tribes who had been allies of the French, but did not involve the predicted centers of trouble, Seneca country and the upper Ohio.[22]

The Chenussio band of Seneca, who resented Amherst's unauthorized land grants to soldiers around Fort Niagara and who had advocated the destruction of the British since early 1761, conducted a particularly effective campaign. They tricked the garrison at Venango and forced Lieutenant Francis Gordon to write down their grievances against too many British forts threatening their country, and gunpowder that was too scarce and too expensive. Gordon was then slowly burned to death in his fort, and the rest of the garrison were killed. These Seneca then proceeded to attack English-held Fort Le Boeuf (June 18) with musket fire, and the fourteen-man garrison escaped to Fort Pitt during the night. These same warriors joined Ottawa, Huron, and Ojibwa from Detroit to attack Presqu'île (June 19–21), laying siege by building breastworks, digging approach trenches, and shooting musket balls and flaming arrows. After two days, the thirty-man garrison surrendered and were divided among the four tribes as prisoners, despite a promise that they could go to Fort Pitt.

After this swift and easy retribution against isolated and unsuspecting British outposts, Amerindians focused on besieging Fort Detroit, Fort Pitt, and Fort Niagara. Success had, ironically, forced Amerindians into precisely the type of campaign for which they were least inclined or equipped. These forts had not fallen to trickery and had wary and substantial garrisons, adequate supplies, and good roads or water access to reinforcements.

Without the French cannon that had broken the resistance at Fort Oswego and Fort William Henry, and without much prospect of starving the garrisons into surrender, as at Fort Loudoun, the best opportunities for Amerindian besiegers were attacks on relief and supply columns. The easiest targets at Detroit were ten bateaux of provisions from Niagara, escorted by Lieutenant Abraham Cuyler and ninety-six Queen's Rangers. Unaware that war had begun, these rangers were attacked while making camp on Point Pelee on May 28. Cuyler escaped back to Niagara with fewer than half his men and less than a tenth of the provisions. Pontiac's forces, numbering about 500 Ottawa, Huron, Potawatomi, and Ojibwa, had less success against the two armed sloops that supplied Detroit or against a relief force of 261 that tripled the garrison at the end of July. The ambitious leader of that reinforcement, Captain James Dalyell, even won permission from the cautious Major Henry Gladwin to undertake a night attack on Pontiac's camp. Dalyell's force was expertly ambushed and was given a "damn'd drubbing" in which at least nineteen, including Dalyell, were killed and thirty-seven wounded.[23]

For the Delaware, receipt of the news that fighting had begun at Detroit coincided with a fresh grievance of their own. On the night of

April 19, 1763, the entire twenty dwellings of Delaware "King" Teed-yuscung's village of Wyoming had mysteriously burned to the ground. Teedyuscung, a prominent chief who had been developing Delaware tribal unity for a decade, died in a fire that proved extremely convenient to a Connecticut-based land company.[24] Delaware and Mingo warriors, led by the Delaware–Wyandot chief, Wolf, sold pelts to English traders for powder and ammunition, then attacked a particularly resented English frontier settlement in the Monongahela Valley before beginning a siege of Fort Pitt. The garrison of 250 regulars and Pennsylvania volunteers under Captain Simeon Ecuyer accepted English refugees within a fort that was considerably stronger than Detroit. Ecuyer rebuffed an invitation to surrender, sending food and liquor out to the besiegers to nourish them "on their way home" and indicate that he was well supplied. Subsequent attempts failed to take this fort by ruse or by storm.[25]

Colonel Bouquet gained Amherst's permission to relieve Fort Pitt with a force of 460 regulars, from Highland regiments, his Royal Americans, and ranger companies. Amherst and Bouquet exchanged angry denunciations of Amerindians as "vermin," and this contempt was reinforced both by Amherst's suggestion that Bouquet take no prisoners and by his infamous proposal, carried out at least once, that smallpox be spread by infected gift blankets. Except for understandable difficulty recruiting wagoners to drive teams into a war zone, Bouquet's contingent proceeded without incident up Forbes's road, from Carlisle through the fortified posts crowded with refugee settlers and traders.

On August 5, about twenty-six miles east of Fort Pitt, Bouquet's force and 340 packhorses laden with flour were attacked by a comparable force of Delaware, Mingo, Shawnee, and Wyandot (Figure 12). The surrounded convoy exchanged heavy fire until nightfall allowed Bouquet's force to retreat, camp on a hilltop, and arrange a central ring of stacked bags of flour to protect the wounded. At the height of renewed fighting the next day, Bouquet ordered two companies to retreat toward the central circle, while two others were deployed to create a battlefield ambush, then bayonet charge, against those warriors who rushed what appeared to be a collapsing section of the British defense. Taking heavy losses, including Wolf and the leading Delaware negotiator, the Amerindians retreated. Fifty of Bouquet's force were killed, sixty wounded, and five captured. This Battle of Bushy Run allowed Bouquet to relieve Fort Pitt and showed that regulars could cope with Amerindian attack, but it was far from a conquest. Bouquet felt it was still unsafe to follow Amherst's suggestion and proceed to the forts taken by the Seneca. This British victory was unusual and celebrated, but it was no more decisive than Pontiac's victory over Dalyell at Detroit.[26]

Although stone Fort Niagara, Captain Pouchot's engineering feat,

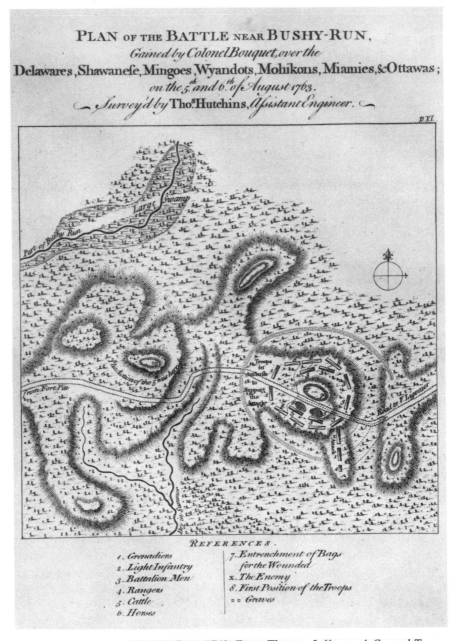

Figure 12. Battle of Bushy Run, 1763. From Thomas Jefferys, *A General Topography of North America* (London, 1768). (Courtesy of the Trustees of the Boston Public Library)

was even less susceptible to Amerindian assault than were Fort Detroit and Fort Pitt, the road from the fort to Lake Erie was very vulnerable to attack. During the French regime, the Seneca had monopolized the transport of cargoes between Lakes Ontario and Erie because the treacherous trail through their territory was impassable without their consent. By 1763 British military cargoes for the *pays d'en haut* were unloaded and carried by wagon up this winding nine-mile trail to the top of the falls for loading aboard the armed sloops bound for Detroit. On September 14, at least three hundred Chenussio Seneca and allies from Detroit prepared a devastating ambush at Devil's Hole, where this trail skirted the Niagara whirlpool. They first attacked a convoy of twenty-five wagons escorted by thirty-one soldiers, only two of whom escaped alive. The musket fire alerted about eighty regulars who rushed into a second ambush, from which only twenty-nine escaped to the fort. By the time the entire garrison reached the site, the Seneca and all the supplies for Detroit were gone; the seventy-two scalped and stripped bodies, and eight badly wounded survivors, made this the heaviest British military loss of the war.[27]

This Amerindian War was not only against British garrisons; it was also an even more deadly war on American settlers and traders, reminiscent of 1755 to 1758. An estimated two thousand American traders and settlers were killed or taken captive, and thousands more were driven from farms in the mountain valleys that the Amerindians again reclaimed from the frontiers of Pennsylvania, Maryland, and Virginia. Small companies of colonial rangers operated with uneven success, and the forts along Forbes's road provided refuge, but fear and anger remained strong throughout the year. American settlers' anger and frustration could erupt against innocent Amerindians far from the frontier, as it did in Pennsylvania in December 1763. A group that came to be called the Paxton Boys attacked several families of peaceful Conestoga, a remnant of the Susquehannock tribe, killing and scalping six men, women, and children. Governor John Penn's proclamation for the arrest of the murderers brought no results, and when the magistrates of Lancaster gathered the survivors in jail for their own protection, the Paxton Boys attacked the jail, killing and mutilating all fourteen Amerindians. Determined to kill all Amerindians, some 500 rioters marched on Philadelphia, where 140 Amerindian converts were protected in the army barracks. This bloodthirsty mob was finally deterred by forces equipped with cannon, but they were allowed to disperse without punishment. Fifty-six of the Amerindians died of smallpox contracted while in the barracks.[28]

The siege of Detroit ended in October, as some supporters of Pontiac lost interest in what was becoming a stalemate. At mid-month, the influential Mississauga chief, Wabbicommicot, who was friendly to the British even though some of his tribe were with Pontiac, began talks with Major Gladwin that soon involved some Ojibwa and Ottawa. Others who had supported Pontiac drifted away for their winter hunt. The French community at Detroit, which had been divided throughout the siege, now separated into those who made their peace with the British and those active supporters of Pontiac who began leaving for the west. On October 29, Pontiac received a letter from the commander of Fort de Chartres formally notifying Amerindians allied with France that French and English would now "smoke the same pipe, and eat out of the same spoon." The courier's letters for French inhabitants and for Gladwin confirmed the situation, and Pontiac ended the siege and accompanied the messenger back to Fort de Chartres.[29]

In planning for the next year, Amherst should have listened to Gladwin, a tough officer who had been wounded with Braddock and again at Ticonderoga, had commanded his regiment on that front during the successes of 1759, and had just withstood Pontiac's five-month siege. Gladwin advised Amherst to make examples of a few local French collaborators, but to negotiate a settlement with the Amerindians in the spring, when their supply of gunpowder would be very low. Gladwin regarded continued fighting as costly to the army and bound to fail against so fragmented, dispersed, and mobile an enemy. At best, the hostile Amerindians would only be driven west to turn other tribes against the British. Gladwin added, as though talking past Amherst to the politicians, that continuing the war would also ruin the fur trade and destroy markets for British goods.[30] Predictably, Amherst remained determined to crush the Amerindians, planning one attack by Bradstreet into the Lake Erie region and another by Bouquet into the Ohio Valley. General Amherst sailed for England in November, having failed to prevent, or contain, the Amerindian War, and his plans for the next year were inherited by General Thomas Gage.

The Royal Proclamation of 1763 promised to change the atmosphere from punishment to conciliation by indicating that Amerindian and colonial settlement would be separated by a clear line. When Gage received copies of the proclamation, on the last day of November, he hurriedly sent some westward, "as I imagine these Arrangements must be very satisfactory to the Indians."[31] This idea of a line dividing English colonies from Amerindian country had already gained some currency in North America; Ohio Amerindian leaders had spoken of it since 1749, and inter-colonial delegates who met for the Albany Congress of 1754 had endorsed the concept. In 1759 William Johnson had urged the British government to initiate "Treaties of Limitations" to determine the line between colonies and Amerindian country.[32] Parts of such a line had been agreed to at the Treaty of Easton (1758), the Treaty of Lancaster (1760), and the South Carolina treaty of peace with the Cherokee (1761). Bouquet had also proclaimed and attempted to enforce a line in October 1761. Although affected by the proclamation line, the outbreak of the Amerindian War had not prompted this policy. British administrators had begun discussing such a line as soon as formal peace with France was concluded early in February 1763, presuming that they had won sovereignty over the western lands by defeating France, and that they would reserve part of that British territory for Amerindians. This proclamation would cause much more discontent among British colonials, who regarded the line as a temporary, and unwarranted, infringement on their access to western lands, than it did among Amerindians, who were convinced that the land was still theirs and that the line was permanent.[33]

Although General Gage reiterated the belligerent nature of Amherst's planned attacks against the Amerindians, the 1764 expeditions, following William Johnson's conciliatory lead, became heavily armed truce legations. The Amerindians did not reassemble to fight after the winter hunt; they may have been tired of fighting, short of gunpowder, or satisfied with the proclamation of 1763 as vindication and proof of their victory. Bradstreet's expedition, only half the intended size at fourteen hundred men, left Albany in June 1764. Johnson accompanied this force as far as Niagara for a major Amerindian conference attended by two thousand representatives of nineteen tribes, not all of whom had been involved in the previous fighting. They learned that the Seneca had already made peace with the English, given hostages for the return of "all ye Prisoners, Deserters, Frenchmen & Negroes," and ceded lands around Fort Niagara.[34] The Iroquois Confederacy had never supported the Amerindian War, and the Seneca, in attempting to compensate the British for the attacks by the Chenussio band, had sent a war party of two hundred against a Susquehanna Delaware village accused of prominence in the raids on the Pennsylvania and Virginia frontiers.

In addition to learning how leniently the British had dealt with the Chenussio Seneca, the assembled heard Johnson's general terms for peace: an immediate return of all prisoners, compensation to traders for stolen property and freedom for the English to travel in the region, an end to all contacts with enemies of the British, and submission of all future grievances to the commander at Detroit or to Johnson himself. The proclamation of 1763 and Johnson's announced schedule of fixed prices for trade goods were also offered as remedies for the presumed causes of the war.

Bradstreet observed these proceedings, then sailed west in August with an army that was smaller and less disciplined than he had anticipated, now including about five hundred warriors from the Six Nations, Caughnawaga, and Ojibwa. General Gage's instructions were to attack the Wyandot of Sandusky and the Delaware and Shawnee of the Muskingum and Scioto rivers and, if the Detroit Amerindians resumed hostilities, to "use your best endeavours to destroy and extirpate them, by every means in your power."[35] Bradstreet promptly ignored the clear and central purpose of his expedition, and his instructions to leave all peacemaking to Johnson. At the burned site of Presqu'île, Bradstreet, who claimed to represent the British, negotiated a preliminary peace with ten Amerindians, claiming to represent the warring Shawnee, Delaware, Wyandot, and Mingo. This "treaty" of August 12 called for a return of all prisoners to Sandusky within twenty-five days, an immediate exchange of hostages, and a scheme for Amerindian enforcement of the peace. Bradstreet even agreed to have Bouquet's force restrained in the meantime. Bradstreet then proceeded directly to Detroit, where he negotiated a treaty that Johnson denounced as interfering with agreements just made at Niagara. Bradstreet then sailed to Sandusky Bay to find neither the promised prisoners nor Amerindian negotiators. Instead, he received an angry letter from Gage, who repudiated his Presqu'île treaty because it included no punishment for "the many horrid murders committed by those Barbarians," and because frontier raids against the colonies continued. Gage again ordered Bradstreet to attack the Shawnee of the Scioto River region, but, with the season advancing, supplies running low, and morale even lower, Bradstreet decided to return to Niagara. On his way back from this ineffective campaign, Bradstreet lost half his boats and a few of his men in a series of Lake Erie storms.[36]

Although Bouquet's expedition started even later and also fought no one, it fulfilled Gage's intentions. Delayed by difficulty recruiting the Pennsylvania regiment that was to accompany his regulars, the fifteen hundred men did not leave Fort Pitt until October. After marching through several evacuated Delaware towns, apparently without destroying them, Bouquet was approached by six Delaware, Shawnee, and Mingo chiefs. They were told to bring all their European prisoners to Bouquet within twelve days if they wanted to hear his peace terms. Bouquet's forces marched farther into what is now south-central Ohio, establishing a fortified camp within a day's march of several substantial Shawnee and Delaware towns. These threatened tribes knew they could not flee the area without encroaching on the hunting lands of other tribes; unwilling to challenge Bouquet's army, they brought more than two hundred prisoners before mid-November and promised another hundred in the spring. Bouquet did not negotiate a peace, but withdrew his army, together with the fourteen Shawnee and Delaware hostages whom he had demanded to support a promise that these tribes would negotiate with Johnson in the spring.[37] Bouquet obtained a truce, the release of English prisoners, and held Amerindian hostages. Neither Bouquet nor Bradstreet had conquered or punished anyone, and peace was still to be negotiated.

Making peace after several simultaneous outbreaks of war was bound to be complex, but the peace with the Ohio Delaware became the model for the others. The Delaware returned a hundred more English prisoners to Johnson's extensive Mohawk Valley estate in the spring of 1765 and made peace in the presence of the Six Nations. In return for a royal pardon "for what hath passed," the Delaware agreed to give the English free passage through their lands, to help them take control of the Illinios country from the French, and to return any remaining English prisoners. "As the Indians have no Established Lawes for punishing the guilty," Delaware who committed crimes against British subjects were to be turned over to the English for trial in a colonial court. The Ohio Delaware were also made subject to the Six Nations by this treaty. English traders wronged in the recent war were to be compensated with land grants, assigned with royal and Six Nations approval. The Delaware were to accept whatever boundary line was established between the English and the Six Nations, but this was a clause the Delaware would soon regret. The granting of lands within cannon-shot of British western forts, for the soldiers to plant gardens, was arranged directly between the British and the Six Nations.[38]

The Shawnee were beginning their own accommodation with the British. On May 10, 1765, beating drums and singing their song of peace, the Shawnee arrived at Fort Pitt in a flotilla of canoes to return their prisoners. This meeting with Bouquet was the first time the Shawnee spoke of the English as "father," a title previously offered only to the French.[39] Two months later, the Shawnee, Mingo, and a few Delaware came down the Mohawk River to "Fort Johnson" to make peace. Here they formally subscribed to the same peace terms as the Delaware, as well as recording their desire to be formally regarded as children of the British king. As with the Delaware peace, Johnson's settlement with the Shawnee gave the Six Nations special power. Chief Warrior Deiaquande of the Onondaga, representing the Six Nations, explained that the paper they had just signed kept a much more precise accounting of what had been agreed than did wampum belts, which "when we come to forget the subject matter of the Contents, the Belts can be of no further use." The recorded portion of the proceedings ended with Deiaquande sounding like Johnson's enforcer, reminding the assembled that, being resolved to follow the treaty carefully, "we hope, expect & we insist on the same from you, as making together but one same spirit & body politick."[40]

Beyond these significant beginnings, achieving peace was more complicated. Johnson tried to enlist the Shawnee to carry the peace to other tribes still at war, but three Shawnee chiefs who had already joined an escort for George Croghan, Johnson's assistant, from Fort Pitt to Illinois country were among those killed by a Mascouten and Kickapoo war party at the end of May 1765. Ironically, this attack helped solve the British problem of making peace with a wide variety of hostile western tribes and villages. The attackers soon realized that their Wabash Valley towns could be raided by British-supported Shawnee, Delaware, and Six Nations. In seeking a mediator, they turned to Pontiac, the Ottawa chief who had been so prominent in the early stages of the war.

The British, anxious to complete the peace without more campaigning, were already prepared to consider Pontiac as an intertribal leader whose agreement might have enough influence to end the war. Croghan first met Pontiac, along with Illinois, Shawnee, Delaware, and Six Nations representatives, at Fort Ouiatenon in mid-June and met him again at Detroit in August, when Ottawa, Wyandot, Potawatomi, Ojibwa, Miami, Kickapoo, and Mascouten were among those attending. The submission to the British "father" was universal, with Pontiac prominent in the conferences. There was one frequent and ominous note amid the general enthusiam:

> [W]e tell you now the French never conquered us neither did they purchase a foot of our Country, nor have they a right to give it to you, we gave them liberty to settle for which they always rewarded us & treated us with great Civility while they had it in their power, but as they are become now your people, if you expect to keep these Posts, we will expect to have proper returns from you.

A belt accompanied this point, in what proved a vain effort to fix it in English memory.[41]

What had never been Pontiac's war was becoming Pontiac's peace. The chief warmed to the assignment, speaking presumptuously "in the name of all the Nations to the Westward whom I command." When Johnson met Pontiac and other Ottawa, Potawatomi, Huron, and Ojibwa chiefs at Oswego in July 1766, he could confirm that there was peace; the raids on the English colonies had ceased for an entire year. The accommodation completed, Johnson could dismiss the recent Amerindian War as "the time you were drunk" and distribute the expected presents.[42]

An unprecedented balance of power had been achieved; the war had become a stalemate, and the peace was an accommodation. Amerindians realized that the major British forts could not be taken and that their own need for gunpowder became debilitating once the Anglo-French peace ended an alternative source of supply. Also, the Amerindians had to buy peace by returning all their prisoners. The British insisted that their victory over the French gave them sovereignty over the west, though that subject was not included in the treaties, unless it was implied in the carefully documented Amerindian acceptance of the British king as "father."

A diverse group of tribes, without the coherence of the successful Six Nation, Cherokee, or Creek confederations, had not been conquered, however. Amerindians had inflicted as many as two thousand casualties without any effective retaliation, a coup reminiscent of earlier massacres. The British army could not hope to conquer the Amerindians, given fiscal restraints and a peacetime army of only seventy-five hundred men. In the peace settlement, Amerindians appeared to recover the world they had lost; their presents were resumed, their lands were protected by the proclamation of their new British "father," and Johnson issued a schedule of fair trade prices.

Admittedly, the treaties did not indicate how these protections against American traders and settlers were to be enforced. Amerindians were now outnumbered by the English in eastern North America in 1765, as the Canadians had been in 1687, by odds of twenty to one. It was clear that Johnson's schemes for an elaborate government department to manage "Indian country" could not be funded by taxing colonists who had just won the repeal of the Stamp Act. The British army had not been able to enforce settlement restrictions five years earlier and would be distracted by troubles on the American seaboard even before 1768, when the British government would abandon all attempts to control western trade, and the proclamation line would be moved westward by the treacherous Treaty of Fort Stanwix.[43]

The Amerindian War of 1763 to 1765, like the Seven Years' War in North America, was revolutionary. Before 1755, English invaders and colonists had been much more relentless in fighting Amerindians than they had been in fighting New France. After 1755, the British military proved more relentless than the Americans in the conquest of New France, and more limited in its objectives against the Amerindians. This was the first major multitribal war against the European invaders that ended in accommodation rather than complete Amerindian defeat. It was a notable and unprecedented achievement, though the Anglo-Amerindian peace of 1765 soon unraveled, as did Britain's complete victory over European rivals for eastern North America.

NOTES

Abbreviations

AHR	*American Historical Review*
CHR	*Canadian Historical Review*
CSPC	*Calendar of State Papers, Colonial Series, America and the West Indies*
DAB	*Dictionary of American Biography*, ed. Allen Johnson and Dumas Malone, 22 vols. (New York, 1928–1944)
DCB	*Dictionary of Canadian Biography*, ed. Frances Halpenny et al., 12 vols. to date (Toronto, 1966–)
Historical Statistics	U.S. Bureau of the Census, *Historical Statistics of the United States*, 2nd ed., 2 vols. (Washington, D.C., 1975)
HL	Huntington Library and Art Gallery, San Marino, California
JAH	*Journal of American History*
JICH	*Journal of Imperial and Commonwealth History*
Johnson Papers	*The Papers of Sir William Johnson*, ed. James Sullivan, 14 vols. (Albany, N.Y., 1921–1965)
NAC	National Archives of Canada (formerly Public Archives of Canada), Ottawa
NEQ	*New England Quarterly*
NYCD	*Documents Relative to the Colonial History of the State of New York*, ed. Edmund B. O'Callaghan and Berthold Fernow, 15 vols. (Albany, N.Y., 1856–1887)
RAPQ	*Rapport de l'Archiviste de la Province de Québec*
RHAF	*Revue d'histoire de l'Amérique Française*
VMHB	*Virginia Magazine of History and Biography*
W&MQ	*William & Mary Quarterly*

1. Arms in Arcadia, 1513–1565

1. For an analysis of the arguments, see John D. Daniels, "The Indian Population of North America in 1492," *W&MQ* 49 (1992): 298–320.

2. Robert F. Berkofer, Jr., *The White Man's Indian* (New York, 1978), 1–31.

3. Felipe Fernández-Armesto, *The Canary Islands after the Conquest: The Making of a Colonial Society in the Early Sixteenth Century* (New York, 1982).

4. Carl Ortwin Sauer, *Sixteenth Century North America* (Berkeley, 1971), 26–28.

5. D. B. Quinn, ed., *New American World: A Documentary History of North America to 1612*, 5 vols. (New York, 1979), 1:243; Sauer, *Sixteenth Century*, 30–31.

6. The use of crossbows against Christians was outlawed by the Second Lateran Council of 1139.

7. Paul E. Hoffman, *A New Andalucia and a Way to the Orient* (Baton Rouge, 1990), 3–33.

8. Hoffman, *New Andalucia*, 53–59.

9. Quinn, *New American World*, 1:248–71; Paul Quattlebaum, *The Land Called Chicora* (Gainesville, Fla., 1956), 3–41; Sauer, *Sixteenth Century*, 70–76; Hoffman, *New Andalucia*, 60–83.

10. Sauer, *Sixteenth Century*, 36–46; for the terms of the grant, see Quinn, *New American World*, 2:4–10.

11. Jerald T. Milanich, "The Western Timucua: Patterns of Acculturation and Change," in Jerald T. Milanich and Samuel Proctor, eds., *Tacachale: Essays on the Indians of Florida and Southeastern Georgia during the Historic Period* (Gainesville, Fla., 1978), 59–88; David Henige, "If Pigs Could Fly: Timucuan Population and Native American Historical Demography," *Journal of Interdisciplinary History* 16 (1986): 701–20.

12. A good translation of the memoirs of Cabeza de Vaca is by Cyclone Covey, *Adventures in the Unknown Interior of America* (New York, 1961).

13. Cabeza de Vaca, *Adventures*, 31.

14. Cabeza de Vaca, *Adventures*, 37.

15. Cabeza de Vaca, *Adventures*, 42.

16. Cabeza de Vaca, *Adventures*, 45–47. On Spanish armor and its adaptation in the New World, see Thomas Flickema, "The Siege of Cuzco," *Revista de historia de América* 92 (1981): 17–47, and Lyle N. McAlister, *Spain and Portugal in the New World, 1492–1700* (Minneapolis, 1984), 96–99.

17. Quinn, *New American World*, 2:93–96.

18. M. L. Brown, *Firearms in Colonial America: The Impact on History and Technology, 1492–1792* (Washington, D.C., 1980), 38–41. Spanish infantry had earlier used massed matchlock musket fire effectively in the Italian wars, but the invincible Spanish *tercio*, an infantry unit that would dominate European warfare for 150 years, was formally introduced into the Spanish army only in 1534, when the age of the *conquistadores* was nearly over in America. The *tercio* consisted of three thousand men, half of whom carried pikes, one-quarter used short swords and javelins, and one-sixth had arquebuses. American silver paid for the *tercios*, but the *tercios* did not conquer America (J. H. Elliott, *Imperial Spain, 1469–1716* [London, 1963]; Henry Kamen, *Spain, 1469–1714: A Society in*

Conflict [London, 1983]; John Lynch, *Spain, 1516–1598: From Nation State to World Empire* [Oxford, 1991], 211–50).

19. *Memoir of Do. d'Escalante Fonteneda Respecting Florida [c. 1575]*, ed. David O. True (Coral Gables, Fla., 1945), 31, 55n34; Flickema, "Siege of Cuzco," 17–47; McAlister, *Spain and Portugal*, 98–99. Reliable translations of the major narratives of the expedition are conveniently reprinted in Quinn, *New American World*, 2:90–188. See also Sauer, *Sixteenth Century*, 157–85.

20. Alfred W. Crosby, *The Columbian Exchange: Biological and Cultural Consequences of 1492* (Newport, Conn., 1972), 75–79.

21. Quinn, *New American World*, 2:123; James M. Crawford, *The Mobilian Trade Language* (Knoxville, Tenn., 1978).

22. Quinn, *New American World*, 2:121–24, 176–77; Sauer, *Sixteenth Century*, 170–72; John R. Swanton et al., *Final Report of the United States De Soto Expedition Commission* (Washington, D.C., 1939), 211–13; Robert L. Blakely, ed., *The King Site: Continuity and Contact in Sixteenth-Century Georgia* (Athens, Ga., 1988), esp. 101–34.

23. Quoted in Jerald T. Milanich and Susan Milbrath, eds., *First Encounters: Spanish Explorations in the Caribbean and the United States, 1492 1570* (Gainesville, Fla., 1989), 98; Swanton, *Final Report*, 52, 272.

24. Quinn, *New American World*, 2:189–98; Hoffman, *New Andalucia*, 99–101.

25. Philip Wayne Powell, *Soldiers, Indians & Silver: The Northward Advance of New Spain, 1550–1600* (Berkeley, 1969).

26. A. P. Newton, *The European Nations in the West Indies, 1493–1688* (London, 1933), 47–60.

27. Brown, *Firearms in Colonial America*, 43–44.

28. Marvin T. Smith, "Indian Responses to European Contact: The Coosa Example," in Milanich and Milbrath, *First Encounters*, 135–49.

29. On the de Luna expedition, see Charles Hudson et al., "The Tristán de Luna Expedition, 1559–1561," in Milanich and Milbrath, *First Encounters*, 119–34; Sauer, *Sixteenth Century*, 189 95; Herbert I. Priestley, *The Luna Papers*, 2 vols. (Deland, Fla., 1928); and Hoffman, *New Andalucia*, 169–202.

Part I. Bases for Invasion, 1565–1684

1. Bruce I. Watson, "Fortification and the 'Idea' of Force in Early English East India Company Relations with India," *Past & Present*, no. 88 (August 1980): 70–87.

2. Bruce G. Trigger, "Early Native North American Responses to European Contact: Romantic versus Rationalistic Interpretations," *JAH* 77 (1990–1991): 1195–1215.

3. John D. Daniels discusses the literature in "The Indian Population of North America in 1492," *W&MQ* 49 (1992): 298–320; Peter H. Wood, "The Changing Population of the Colonial South: An Overview by Race and Region, 1685–1790," in Peter H. Wood, Gregory A. Waselkov, and M. Thomas Hatley, eds., *Powhatan's Mantle: Indians in the Colonial Southeast* (Lincoln, Neb., 1989), 35–103.

2. Spanish San Agustín, 1565–1672

1. D. B. Quinn, ed., *New American World: A Documentary History of North America to 1612*, 5 vols. (New York, 1979), 2:314; Paul E. Hoffman, *A New Andalucia and a Way to the Orient* (Baton Rouge, 1990), 209, 216.

2. Report of Hernando Manrique de Tojas, in Quinn, *New American World*, 2:308–16. See also Paul Quattlebaum, *The Land Called Chicora: The Carolinas under Spanish Rule with French Intrusions, 1520–1670* (Gainesville, Fla., 1956), 45–53; René Laudonnière, *Three Voyages*, trans. Charles E. Bennett (Gainesville, Fla., 1975); and Lewis H. Larson, Jr., "Historic Guale Indians of the Georgia Coast and the Impact of the Spanish Mission Effort," in Jerald T. Milanich and Samuel Proctor, eds., *Tacachale: Essays on the Indians of Florida and Southeastern Georgia during the Historic Period* (Gainesville, Fla., 1978), 120–40.

3. Eugene Lyon, *The Enterprise of Florida: Pedro Menéndez de Avilés and the Spanish Conquest of 1565–1568* (Gainesville, Fla., 1976), 19–70; Paul E. Hoffman, *The Spanish Crown and the Defense of the Caribbean, 1565–1585: Precedent, Patrimonialism, and Royal Parsimony* (Baton Rouge, 1980), 218–28.

4. Lyon, *Enterprise of Florida*, 100–130; Hoffman, *New Andalucia*, 205–30; Quattlebaum, *Land Called Chicora*, 42–59.

5. Quattlebaum, *Land Called Chicora*, 65.

6. Kathleen A. Deagan, "Cultures in Transition: Fusion and Assimilation among the Eastern Timucua," in Milanich and Proctor, *Tacachale*, 100–104.

7. Quattlebaum, *Land Called Chicora*, 65.

8. Quattlebaum, *Land Called Chicora*, 65–69; Hoffman, *New Andalucia*, 256; Charles Hudson, *The Juan Pardo Expeditions: Exploration of the Carolinas and Tennessee, 1566–1568* (Washington, D.C., 1990).

9. Quattlebaum, *Land Called Chicora*, 73.

10. Quattlebaum, *Land Called Chicora*, 72–76; Hoffman, *New Andalucia*, 278–80.

11. Quattlebaum, *Land Called Chicora*, 65.

12. Hoffman, *New Andalucia*, 183–87, 244–45, 261–66; Clifford M. Lewis and Albert J. Loomie, *The Spanish Jesuit Mission in Virginia, 1570–1572* (Chapel Hill, N.C., 1972); Charlotte M. Gradie, "Spanish Jesuits in Virginia: The Mission that Failed," *VMHB* 96 (1988): 131–56.

13. Milanich and Proctor, *Tacachale*; John Tate Lanning, *The Spanish Missions of Georgia* (Chapel Hill, N.C., 1935).

14. John H. Hann, *Apalachee: The Land between the Rivers* (Gainesville, Fla., 1988), 9–12.

15. Amy Turner Bushnell, "Ruling 'the Republic of Indians' in Seventeenth-Century Florida," in Peter H. Wood, Gregory A. Waselkov, and M. Thomas Hatley, eds., *Powhatan's Mantle: Indians in the Colonial Southeast* (Lincoln, Neb., 1989), 134–50.

16. Hann, *Apalachee*, 16–23.

17. Peter H. Wood, "The Changing Population of the Colonial South: An Overview by Race and Region, 1685–1790," in Wood, Waselkov, and Hatley, *Powhatan's Mantle*, 52; David J. Weber, *The Spanish Frontier in North America, 1513–1821* (New Haven, 1992), 100–106.

18. Robert Allen Matter, "Missions in the Defense of Spanish Florida," *Florida Historical Quarterly* 54 (1975): 18–38.

19. Between 1594 and 1763, only 8 of 1705 women marrying in San Agustín

were not native to the town (Kathleen A. Deagan, "Spanish–Indian Interaction in Sixteenth-Century Florida and Hispaniola," in William W. Fitzhugh, ed., *Cultures in Contact: The Impact of European Contacts on Native American Cultural Institutions, A.D. 1000–1800* [Washington, D.C., 1985], 305–6; Deagan, *Spanish St. Augustine: The Archeology of a Colonial Creole Community* [New York, 1983]).

20. Verne E. Chatelain, *The Defenses of Spanish Florida, 1565 to 1763* (Washington, D.C., 1941), 41–48; Edward Chaney and Kathleen Deagan, "St. Augustine and La Florida Colony: New Life-Styles in a New Land," in Jerald T. Milanich and Susan Milbrath, eds., *First Encounters: Spanish Explorations in the Caribbean and the United States, 1492–1570* (Gainesville, Fla., 1989), 166–82.

21. Chatelain, *Defenses of Spanish Florida*, 48–54; *Sir Francis Drake's West Indian Voyage, 1585–1586*, ed. Mary Frear Keeler (London, 1981), 9, 39, 205–8, 264–69.

22. Chatelain, *Defenses of Spanish Florida*, 54–55; Charles W. Arnade, *Florida on Trial, 1593–1602* (Coral Gables, Fla., 1959).

23. M. L. Brown, *Firearms in Colonial America: The Impact on History and Technology, 1492–1792* (Washington, D.C., 1980), 115.

24. Chatelain, *Defenses of Spanish Florida*, 60–64; Deagan, *Spanish St. Augustine*, 40–42.

25. Brown, *Firearms in Colonial America*, 118.

26. Chatelain, *Defenses of Spanish Florida*, 64–94.

3. English Jamestown and the Powhatan, 1607–1677

1. Helen C. Rountree, *The Powhatan Indians of Virginia: Their Traditional Culture* (Norman, Okla., 1989); James Axtell, "The Rise and Fall of the Powhatan Empire," in his *After Columbus* (New York, 1988), 182–221; Stephen R. Potter, "Early English Effects on Virginia Algonquian Exchange and Tribute in the Tidewater Potomac," in Peter H. Wood, Gregory A. Waselkov, and M. Thomas Hatley, eds., *Powhatan's Mantle: Indians in the Colonial Southeast* (Lincoln, Neb., 1989), 152–57; Helen C. Rountree, *Pocahontas's People: The Powhatan Indians of Virginia Through Four Centuries* (Norman, Okla., 1990), 7.

2. D. B. Quinn, *Set Fair for Roanoke: Voyages and Colonies, 1584–1606* (Chapel Hill, N.C., 1985), esp. 341–78; Christian F. Feest, "Virginia Algonquians," in *The Handbook of North American Indians*, vol. 15, *The Northeast*, ed. Bruce Trigger (Washington, D.C., 1978), 253–70; Rountree, *Pocahontas's People*, 20–24.

3. John Smith, *Travels and Works*, ed. E. Arbor, 2 vols. (Edinburgh, 1910), 1: xxxiii–xxxvii.

4. Ester Boserup, *The Conditions of Agricultural Growth: The Economics of Agrarian Change under Population Pressure* (Chicago, 1965), is seminal in this connection.

5. Rountree, *Pocahontas's People*, 62; Karen O. Kupperman, *Settling with the Indians: The Meeting of English and Indian Cultures in America, 1580–1640* (Totowa, N.J., 1981), 169–88.

6. Darrett B. Rutman and Anita H. Rutman, "Of Agues and Fevers: Malaria in the Early Chesapeake," *W&MQ* 33 (1976): 31–60; Carville V. Earle, "Environment, Disease, and Mortality in Early Virginia," in Thad Tate and David Ammerman, eds., *The Chesapeake in the Seventeenth Century* (Chapel Hill, N.C., 1979), 96–125; Rountree, *Pocahontas's People*, 7.

7. Quoted in Rountree, *Pocahontas's People*, 30; Allen Mardis, Jr., "Visions of James Fort," *VMHB* 97 (1989): 463–98.

8. J. Frederick Fausz, "An 'Abundance of Blood Shed on Both Sides': England's First Indian War, 1609–1614," *VMHB* 98 (1990): 9–16; William L. Shea, *The Virginia Militia in the Seventeenth Century* (Baton Rouge, 1983), 8.

9. Rountree, *Powhatan Indians*, 119, 121–22, 148; Rountree, *Pocahontas's People*, 38–39.

10. *The Complete Works of Captain John Smith (1580–1631)*, ed. Philip L. Barbour, 3 vols. (Chapel Hill, N.C., 1986), 1:5–117; Fausz, "Abundance of Blood," 16–18; Rountree, *Powhatan Indians*, 125.

11. S. M. Kingsbury, ed., *The Records of the Virginia Company of London*, 4 vols. (Washington, D.C., 1906–1935), 3:672.

12. *Smith's Works*, 2:103, 236; Rountree, *Pocahontas's People*, 54–55.

13. The best account of this war is Fausz, "Abundance of Blood." Darrett B. Rutman, "The Virginia Company and Its Military Regime," in his *The Old Dominion: Essays for Thomas Perkins Abernethy* (Charlottesville, Va., 1964), 1–20; Rountree, *Pocahontas's People*, 49–60.

14. Rountree, *Pocahontas's People*, 59–60.

15. Rountree, *Pocahontas's People*, 61.

16. "Minutes of the Council and Great Court, 1622–1624," *VMHB* 20 (1912): 157; J. Frederick Fausz, "Opechancanough: Indian Resistance Leader," in David G. Sweet and Gary B. Nash, eds., *Struggle and Survival in Colonial America* (Berkeley, 1981), 21–37.

17. *Historical Statistics*, series Z, 457; L. G. Carr et al., *Robert Cole's World* (Chapel Hill, N.C., 1991), 40–42. See also Rountree, *Pocahontas's People*, 66–67.

18. Kingsbury, *Virginia Company Records*, 4:9, 117–18; Fausz, "Opechancanough," 28.

19. "Minutes of the Council and Great Court," 157.

20. Alden T. Vaughan, " 'Expulsion of the Salvages': English Policy and the Virginia Massacre of 1622," *W&MQ* 35 (1978): 57–84; J. Frederick Fausz, "The 'Barbarous Massacre' Reconsidered: The Powhatan Uprising of 1622 and the Historians," *Explorations in Ethnic Studies* 1 (1978): 16–36; Axtell, "Rise and Fall," 208; Rountree, *Pocahontas's People*, 71–75, 302n45.

21. Rountree, *Powhatan Indians*, 121; Rountree, *Pocahontas's People*, 19–20.

22. Shea, *Virginia Militia*, 27–34.

23. J. Frederick Fausz, "Fighting Fire with Firearms: The Anglo-Powhatan Arms Race in Early Virginia," *American Indian Culture and Research Journal* 3 (1979): 43.

24. John Bennett Bodie, "Edward Bennett of London and Virginia," *W&MQ*, 2nd ser., 13 (1933): 121–23; Potter, "Early English Effects on Virginia Algonquian Exchange," 152–57; Vaughan, "Expulsion," 77–78; Axtell, "Rise and Fall," 218–19; Shea, *Virginia Militia*, 34–38.

25. James H. Merrell, "Cultural Continuity among the Piscataway Indians of Colonial Maryland," *W&MQ* 36 (1979): 548–70.

26. Fausz, "Fighting Fire with Firearms," 44.

27. Shea, *Virginia Militia*, 41–42; Fausz, "Fighting Fire with Firearms," 44; Kingsbury, *Virginia Company Records*, 4:508.

28. Shea, *Virginia Militia*, 43–55; Edmund S. Morgan, *American Slavery, American Freedom: The Ordeal of Colonial Virginia* (New York, 1975), 99–100; Bernard

Sheehan, *Savagism and Civility: Indians and Englishmen in Colonial Virginia* (Cambridge, 1980), 177–81.

29. William W. Hening, ed., *The Statutes at Large . . . of Virginia . . .* , 13 vols. (New York, 1809–1823), 1:255–56; Rountree, *Pocahontas's People*, 82–83.

30. *Historical Statistics*, series Z, 13, 14, 457–59.

31. Rountree, *Pocahontas's People*, 85–86.

32. *Historical Statistics*, series Z, 13, 14, 457–59.

33. Shea, *Virginia Militia*, 89–96.

34. Shea, *Virginia Militia*, 51–72, 78–80; Rountree, *Pocahontas's People*, 91–93; J. Leitch Wright, Jr., *The Only Land They Knew: The Tragic Story of the American Indians in the Old South* (New York, 1981), 87–88; Richard L. Morton, *Colonial Virginia*, 2 vols. (Chapel Hill, N.C., 1960), 1:156; Nancy O. Lurie, "Indian Cultural Adjustment to European Civilization," in James M. Smith, ed., *Seventeenth Century America* (Chapel Hill, N.C., 1959), 54; Martha W. McCartney, "Cockacoeske, Queen of Pamunkey: Diplomat and Suzeraine," in Wood, Waselkov, and Hatley, *Powhatan's Mantle*, 174.

35. Verner W. Crane, *The Southern Frontier, 1670–1732* (Ann Arbor, 1929), 12–21; Wright, *Only Land They Knew*, 105–7; James H. Merrell, *The Indians' New World: Catawbas and Their Neighbors from European Contact through the Era of Removal* (Chapel Hill, N.C., 1989), 40–41; Marvin T. Smith, "Aboriginal Population Movements in the Early Historic Period Interior Southeast," in Wood, Waselkov, and Hatley, *Powhatan's Mantle*, 30.

36. Francis Jennings, *The Ambiguous Iroquois Empire* (New York, 1984), 18–22, 127–30; Francis Jennings, "Susquehannocks," in Trigger, *Handbook of North American Indians*, 15: 362–67; Merrell, "Cultural Continuity," 548–70; George T. Hunt, *Wars of the Iroquois* (Madison, Wis., 1960), 137–42; Stephen S. Webb, *1676: The End of American Independence* (New York, 1984), 290–95.

37. Hunt, *Wars of the Iroquois*, 137–42; Francis Jennings, "Glory, Death, and Transfiguration: The Susquehannock Indians in the Seventeenth Century," *Proceedings of the American Philosophical Society* 112 (1968): 15–53, vs. Elisabeth Tooker, "The Demise of the Susquehannocks: A 17th Century Mystery," *Pennsylvania Archeologist* 54 (1984): 1–10.

38. Wilcomb E. Washburn, *The Governor and the Rebel: A History of Bacon's Rebellion in Virginia* (Chapel Hill, N.C., 1957), 20–21; Jennings, *Ambiguous Iroquois Empire*, 145–46.

39. Shea, *Virginia Militia*, 97–99; Washburn, *Governor and Rebel*, 24–25; Jennings, *Ambiguous Iroquois Empire*, 146–47.

40. Washburn, *Governor and Rebel*, 24–25.

41. Longleat Ms. LXXVII, fol. 145, quoted in Washburn, *Governor and Rebel*, vi.

42. Washburn, *Governor and Rebel*, 40–48; Shea, *Virginia Militia*, 103–4; Morgan, *American Slavery*, 259–60, 328–29.

43. Morgan, *American Slavery*, 262–65; Washburn, *Governor and Rebel*, 49–67.

44. Shea, *Virginia Militia*, 111–14; Washburn, *Governor and Rebel*, 81–83.

45. Morgan, *American Slavery*, 328–29; Hening, *Statutes . . . of Virginia*, 2:341–52; Rountree, *Pocahontas's People*, 139.

46. Webb, *1676*, 374–78; McCartney, "Cockacoeske, Queen of Pamunkey," 178–95.

47. Shea, *Virginia Militia*, 122–35.

48. Stephen S. Webb, *The Governors-General: The English Army and the Defi-*

nition of Empire, 1569–1681 (Chapel Hill, N.C., 1979), 378–83; Webb, *1676*, 124–63.

4. French Québec, 1608–1682

1. Marcel Trudel, *The Beginnings of New France, 1524–1663* (Toronto, 1973), 11–19; *DCB*, 1:275–76; Neal Salisbury, *Manitou and Providence: Indians, Europeans, and the Making of New England, 1500–1643* (New York, 1982), 54.
2. Trudel, *Beginnings of New France*, 34–53.
3. Trudel, *Beginnings of New France*, 63–70; W. J. Eccles, *France in America*, 2nd ed. (Markham, Ont., 1990), 8–14.
4. Salisbury, *Manitou and Providence*, 56–72; *DCB*, 1:500–501.
5. *DCB*, 1:291–94, 529–30; Trudel, *Beginnings of New France*, 71–92, 107–17; Eccles, *France in America*, 14–17.
6. Bruce G. Trigger, *The Children of Aataentsic*, 2 vols. (Montreal, 1976), 1: 214–24; Trudel, *Beginnings of New France*, 71–81.
7. *The Works of Samuel de Champlain*, ed. H. P. Biggar, 6 vols. (Toronto, 1922–1936), 2:82–107; Trigger, *Children of Aataentsic*, 1:246–56.
8. *Champlain's Works*, 1:122–34.
9. Trigger, *Children of Aataentsic*, 1:256–61.
10. Trigger, *Children of Aataentsic*, 1:308–15; cf. Trudel, *Beginnings of New France*, 119–21.
11. Robert A. Goldstein, *French–Iroquois Diplomatic and Military Relations 1609–1701* (The Hague, 1969), 59–61.
12. Eccles, *France in America*, 28–29.
13. Eccles, *France in America*, 26–29; Trigger, *Children of Aataentsic*, 2:456–62; Trudel, *Beginnings of New France*, 172–78.
14. Bruce G. Trigger, *Natives and Newcomers: Canada's "Heroic Age" Reconsidered* (Kingston, Ont., and Montreal, 1985), 204.
15. Calvin Martin, *Keepers of the Game: Indian–Animal Relationships and the Fur Trade* (Berkeley, 1978), pioneered this subject, provoking Shepard Krech, III, ed., *Indians, Animals, and the Fur Trade: A Critique of Keepers of the Game* (Athens, Ga., 1981). See also Arthur J. Ray, *Indians in the Fur Trade: Their Role as Trappers, Hunters, and Middlemen in the Lands Southwest of Hudson Bay, 1660–1870* (Toronto, 1974); Arthur J. Ray and Donald Freeman, *"Give Us Good Measure": An Economic Analysis of Relations between the Indians and the Hudson's Bay Company before 1763* (Toronto, 1978); Daniel H. Usner, Jr., *Indians, Settlers, & Slaves in a Frontier Exchange Economy: The Lower Mississippi Valley before 1783* (Chapel Hill, N.C., 1992); and Richard White, *The Middle Ground: Indians, Empires, and Republics in the Great Lakes Region, 1650–1815* (Cambridge, 1991), 94–141.
16. Trigger, *Children of Aataentsic*, 2:463–67.
17. Trigger, *Children of Aataentsic*, 2:546–51, 699–740, esp. 739; Susan Johnston, "Epidemics, the Forgotten Factor in Seventeenth-Century Native Warfare in the St. Lawrence Region," in Bruce A. Cox, ed., *Native People, Native Lands* (Ottawa, 1988), 14–31.
18. Brian J. Given, "The Iroquois Wars and Native Firearms," in Cox, *Native People*, 1–13; Trigger, *Children of Aataentsic*, 2:754–55.

19. Trigger, *Children of Aataentsic*, 2:789–840.

20. Converted Mohawk women were prominent in the migration (William N. Fenton and Elisabeth Tooker, "Mohawk," in *The Handbook of North American Indians*, vol. 15, *The Northeast*, ed. Bruce Trigger [Washington, D.C., 1978], 466–80).

21. Gordon M. Day and Bruce G. Trigger, "Algonkins," in Trigger, *Handbook of North American Indians*, 15:792–97.

22. George T. Hunt, *The Wars of the Iroquois* (Madison, Wis., 1960), 66–104; White, *Middle Ground*.

23. Trigger, *Children of Aataentsic*, 2:794–97, 806–15.

24. *DCB*, 1:64–65, 266–75; J. A. Dickinson, "Annaotaha et Dollard vus de l'autre côté de la palissade," *RHAF* 35 (1981): 163–78.

25. John A. Dickinson, "La Guerre iroquoise et la mortalité en Nouvelle-France, 1608–1666," *RHAF* 36 (1982–1983): 31–54; Daniel Dessert and Jean-Louis Journet, "Le Lobby Colbert: un royaume, ou une affaire de famille?" *Annales. Economies, Sociétés, Civilisations* 30 (1975): 1303–37; Eccles, *France in America*, 30–62.

26. Jack Verney, *The Good Regiment: The Carignan-Salières Regiment in Canada, 1665–1668* (Montreal, 1991), 37–53; W. J. Eccles, *Canada under Louis XIV, 1663–1701* (Toronto, 1964), 39–41; *NYCD*, 3:118–19.

27. Verney, *Good Regiment*, 71–84; *DCB*, 1:554–57; Eccles, *Canada under Louis XIV*, 41–44.

28. Verney, *Good Regiment*, 110, 116–17; W. J. Eccles, *Essays on New France* (Toronto, 1987), 110–24; Eccles, *France in America*, 73–74, 116–18.

29. Eccles, *France in America*, 63–88.

30. Eccles, *France in America*, 88–90; White, *Middle Ground*, 108.

31. M. L. Brown, *Firearms in Colonial America: The Impact on History and Technology, 1492–1792* (Washington, D.C., 1980), 157.

32. *DCB*, 1:172–84; Patricia K. Galloway, ed., *La Salle and His Legacy: Frenchmen and Indians in the Lower Mississippi Valley* (Jackson, Miss., 1982); Carl O. Sauer, *Seventeenth Century North America* (Berkeley, 1980), 127–216; David J. Weber, *The Spanish Frontier in North America* (New Haven, 1992), 148–52.

5. Plymouth, New England, and the Wampanoag, 1620–1677

1. *The Voyages of Giovanni da Verrazzano, 1524–1528*, ed. Lawrence C. Wroth (New Haven, 1970), 134–41.

2. William Cronon, *Changes in the Land: Indians, Colonists, and the Ecology of New England* (New York, 1983), 34–53.

3. Catherine Marten, "The Wampanoags in the Seventeenth Century: An Ethnological Study," *Occasional Papers in Old Colony Studies* 2 (1970): 3–40; Neal Salisbury, *Manitou and Providence: Indians, Europeans, and the Making of New England, 1500–1643* (New York, 1982), 13–49.

4. J. F. Jameson, ed., *Narratives of New Netherlands* (New York, 1919), 41; Salisbury, *Manitou and Providence*, 50–84.

5. David B. Quinn, *England and the Discovery of America, 1481–1620* (London, 1974), 419–31; Salisbury, *Manitou and Providence*, 86–93; Richard A. Preston, *Gorges of Plymouth Fort* (Toronto, 1953), 137–51.

6. Charles McLean Andrews, *The Colonial Period of American History*, 4 vols. (New Haven, 1934–1938), 1:90–97.

7. Salisbury, *Manitou and Providence*, 92–94.

8. *The Complete Works of Captain John Smith (1580–1631)*, ed. Philip L. Barbour, 3 vols. (Chapel Hill, N.C., 1986), 1:293–94, 433; 2:399, 403, 441; Salisbury, *Manitou and Providence*, 96–97.

9. Salisbury, *Manitou and Providence*, 96–101; Preston, *Gorges*, 154–64.

10. Dean R. Snow and Kim M. Lanphear, "European Contact and Indian Depopulation in the Northeast: The Timing of the First Epidemics," *Ethnohistory* 35 (1988): 15–33; Salisbury, *Manitou and Providence*, 101–9.

11. Salisbury, *Manitou and Providence*, 107–8; Andrews, *Colonial Period*, 1:322–29.

12. William Bradford, *Of Plymouth Plantation, 1620–1647*, ed. Samuel E. Morison (New York, 1952), 50.

13. H. L. Peterson, "The Military Equipment of the Plymouth and Bay Colonies: 1620–1690," *NEQ* 20 (1947):197–208; Peterson, *Arms and Armor in Colonial America* (New York, 1956), 44–46, 79–81.

14. Salisbury, *Manitou and Providence*, 111–14; George D. Langdon, Jr., *Pilgrim Colony: A History of New Plymouth, 1620–1691* (New Haven, 1966), 12–14; George F. Willison, *Saints and Strangers* (New York, 1945), 146–57.

15. Willison, *Saints*, 158–68; Bradford, *Of Plymouth Plantation*, 52n; Douglas E. Leach, "The Military System of Plymouth Colony," *NEQ* 24 (1951): 342–64.

16. Salisbury, *Manitou and Providence*, 114–21; Willison, *Saints*, 171–77.

17. Bradford, *Of Plymouth Plantation*, 108–10, 113–19; Salisbury, *Manitou and Providence*, 125–39; Willison, *Saints*, 214–30.

18. Lynn Ceci, "Native Wampum as a Peripheral Resource in the Seventeenth-Century World-System," in Laurence M. Hauptman and James D. Wherry, eds., *The Pequots in Southern New England: The Fall and Rise of an American Indian Nation* (Norman, Okla., 1990), 48–63; Salisbury, *Manitou and Providence*, 144–52.

19. Bradford, *Of Plymouth Plantation*, 204–10, 216–17; Bernard Bailyn, *The New England Merchants in the Seventeenth Century* (Cambridge, Mass., 1955), 23–26.

20. William A. Starna, "The Pequots in the Early Seventeenth Century," in Hauptman and Wherry, *Pequots in Southern New England*, 45–46.

21. Darrett B. Rutman, *Husbandmen of Plymouth: Farms and Villages in the Old Colony, 1620–1692* (Boston, 1967); Cronon, *Changes in the Land*.

22. Alfred A. Cave, "Who Killed John Stone? A Note on the Origins of the Pequot War," *W&MQ* 49 (1992): 509–21; Francis Jennings, *The Invasion of America: Indians, Colonialism, and the Cant of Conquest* (Chapel Hill, N.C., 1975), 188–209; Salisbury, *Manitou and Providence*, 203–15.

23. Adam J. Hirsch, "The Collision of Military Cultures in Seventeenth Century New England," *JAH* 74 (1987–1988): 1187–1212; Jennings, *Invasion of America*, 209–12; Salisbury, *Manitou and Providence*, 214.

24. J. Franklin Jameson, ed., *Johnson's Wonder-Working Providence, 1628–1651* (New York, 1910), 148–50.

25. Karen Ordahl Kupperman, *Settling with the Indians: The Meeting of English and Indian Cultures in America, 1580–1640* (Totowa, N.J., 1980), 184–85.

26. Bradford, *Of Plymouth Plantation*, 294–97, 394–98; Jennings, *Invasion of America*, 215–26; Salisbury, *Manitou and Providence*, 218–25; J. Underhill, *Newes from America* (London, 1638); Steven T. Katz, "The Pequot War Reconsidered," *NEQ* 64 (1991): 206–24; Patrick M. Malone, "Changing Military Technology Among the Indians of Southern New England, 1600–1677," *American Quarterly* 25 (1973): 61; Hirsch, "Collision of Military Cultures."

27. Quoted in Willison, *Saints*, 392.

28. Quoted in Salisbury, *Manitou and Providence*, 13, 231.

29. Salisbury, *Manitou and Providence*, 228–35; Jennings, *Invasion of America*, 258–81; Harry M. Ward, *The United Colonies of New England, 1643–1690* (New York, 1961).

30. David Cressy, *Coming Over: Migration and Communication between England and New England in the Seventeenth Century* (Cambridge, 1987), esp. 199–205; *Historical Statistics*, series Z, 2–8.

31. George A. Rawlyk, *Nova Scotia's Massachusetts: A Study of Massachusetts–Nova Scotia Relations, 1630 to 1784* (Montreal, 1973), 23–27; *DCB*, 1:604–5; Jennings, *Invasion of America*, 254–81; Neal Salisbury, "Indians and Colonists in Southern New England after the Pequot War: An Uneasy Balance," in Hauptman and Wherry, *Pequots in Southern New England*, 81–95.

32. Langdon, *Pilgrim Colony*, 55–57, 157; Salisbury, "Indians and Colonists," 81–95.

33. Neal Salisbury, "Towards the Covenant Chain: Iroquois and Southern New England Algonkians, 1637–1684," in Daniel K. Richter and James H. Merrell, eds., *Beyond the Covenant Chain: The Iroquois and Their Neighbors in Indian North America, 1600–1800* (Syracuse, N.Y., 1987), 61–73; Salisbury, "Indians and Colonists," 81–95; Jennings, *Invasion of America*, 282–97.

34. Twelve square miles were sold for £143 (Langdon, *Pilgrim Colony*, 155).

35. Jennings, *Invasion of America*, 228–53; Alden T. Vaughan, *New England Frontier: Puritans and Indians, 1620–1675* (Boston, 1965), 235–308; Langdon, *Pilgrim Colony*, 158.

36. Jennings, *Invasion of America*, 292–97; Philip Ranlet, "Another Look at the Causes of King Philip's War," *NEQ* 61 (1988): 79–100; Douglas Edward Leach, *Flintlock and Tomahawk: New England in King Philip's War* (New York, 1958), 30–36.

37. Nathaniel B. Shurtleff, ed., *The Records of the Governor and Company of the Massachusetts Bay in New England*, 5 vols. (Boston, 1853–1854), 5:47; Leach, *Flintlock and Tomahawk*, 1; *Historical Statistics*, series Z, 5, 6, 8.

38. For the details of the war, see Leach, *Flintlock and Tomahawk*, passim, and Jennings, *Invasion of America*, 298–326. On Plymouth, see Langdon, *Pilgrim Colony*, 164–87.

39. Jennings, *Invasion of America*, 304, makes this claim, which goes beyond available evidence.

40. Jennings, *Invasion of America*, 312n.

41. *The Soveraignty & Goodness of God, Together, with the Faithfulness of His Promises Displayed . . .* (Cambridge, Mass., 1682).

42. Arthur J. Worrall, "Persecution, Politics and War: Roger Williams, Quakers and King Philip's War," *Quaker History* 66 (1977): 73–86.

43. Charles H. Lincoln, ed., *Narratives of the Indian Wars, 1675–1699* (New York, 1913), 95–96; Leach, *Flintlock and Tomahawk*, 200–204.

44. Jenny West, *Gunpowder, Government and War in the Mid-Eighteenth Century* (London, 1991), 1–22, 64–66.

45. Mary Rowlandson, "The Sovereignty and Goodness of God," in Alden T. Vaughan and Edward W. Clark, eds., *Puritans among the Indians* (Cambridge, Mass., 1981), 34, 39, 45, 47–49, 54, 62, 68–69; Jennings, *Invasion of America*, 319–21; Leach, *Flintlock and Tomahawk*, 211–12.

46. Quoted in Langdon, *Pilgrim Colony, 180.*

47. James Axtell, ed., "The Vengeful Women of Marblehead: Robert Roule's Deposition of 1677," *W&MQ* 31 (1974): 647–52.

48. Leach, *Flintlock and Tomahawk*, 226; Jennings, *Invasion of America*, 324.

49. Langdon, *Pilgrim Colony*, 181–83; Leach, *Flintlock and Tomahawk*, 109–11; Willison, *Saints*, 401–2; T. H. Breen, "War, Taxes, and Political Brokers: The Ordeal of Massachusetts Bay, 1675–1692," in his *Puritans and Adventurers* (New York, 1980), 81–105.

50. Colin G. Calloway, *The Western Abenaki of Vermont, 1600–1800: War, Migration, and the Survival of an Indian People* (Norman, Okla., 1991), 76–89; William A. Haviland and Marjory W. Power, *The Original Vermonters: Native Inhabitants Past and Present* (Hanover, N.H., 1981), 216–34; Alfred Goldsworthy Bailey, *The Conflict of European and Eastern Algonkian Cultures, 1504–1700*, 2nd ed. (Toronto, 1969), 30–31.

6. Dutch Fort Orange (Albany) and the Five Nations, 1624–1684

1. Simon Schama, *The Embarrassment of Riches: An Interpretation of Dutch Culture in the Golden Age* (Berkeley, 1988); K.H.D. Haley, *The Dutch in the Seventeenth Century* (London, 1972).

2. Schama, *Embarrassment of Riches*, 289–372; Violet Barbour, *Capitalism in Amsterdam in the Seventeenth Century* (Baltimore, 1950).

3. C. R. Boxer, *The Dutch Seaborne Empire, 1600–1800* (London, 1965); Maurice Aymard, ed., *Dutch Capitalism, World Capitalism* (Cambridge, 1981); Jonathan I. Israel, *Dutch Primacy in World Trade, 1585–1740* (Oxford, 1989).

4. Denys Delâge, *Le Pays renversé: Amérindiens et Européens en Amérique du Nord-Est, 1600–1664* (Québec, 1990), 41–45.

5. Daniel K. Richter, *The Ordeal of the Longhouse: The Peoples of the Iroquois League in the Era of European Colonization* (Chapel Hill, N.C., 1992), 87–89; Allen W. Trelease, *Indian Affairs in Colonial New York: The Seventeenth Century* (Ithaca, N.Y., 1960), 25–34; Francis Jennings, *The Ambiguous Iroquois Empire* (New York, 1984), 48.

6. Richter, *Ordeal of the Longhouse*, 1–49.

7. Trelease, *Indian Affairs*, 46–48; Jennings, *Ambiguous Iroquois Empire*, 49, 53, 71; Bruce G. Trigger, "The Mohawk–Mahican War (1624–28): The Establishment of a Pattern," *CHR* 52 (1971): 276–86.

8. George T. Hunt, *The Wars of the Iroquois: A Study in Intertribal Trade Relations* (Madison, Wis., 1960), 32–34, 165–72; Richter, *Ordeal of the Longhouse*, 55–57, 84–85; Trelease, *Indian Affairs*, 43, 48; Jennings, *Ambiguous Iroquois Empire*, 51, 71–73, 78.

9. Dean R. Snow and Kim M. Lanphear, "European Contact and Indian Depopulation in the Northeast: The Timing of the First Epidemics," *Ethnohistory* 35 (1988): 15–33.

10. Richter, *Ordeal of the Longhouse*, 58–74; Susan Johnston, "Epidemics: The Forgotten Factor in Seventeenth Century Native Warfare in the St. Lawrence Region," in Bruce A. Cox, ed., *Native People, Native Lands* (Ottawa, 1988), 14–31.

11. Jennings, *Ambiguous Iroquois Empire*, 53–57; Richter, *Ordeal of the Longhouse*, 62–64; cf. Hunt, *Wars of the Iroquois*, 165–72; Brian J. Given, "The Iroquois Wars and Native Arms," in Cox, *Native People*, 3–13.

12. Trelease, *Indian Affairs*, 60–84.

13. Trelease, *Indian Affairs*, 79–80.

14. Jennings, *Ambiguous Iroquois Empire*, 53–57; Trelease, *Indian Affairs*, 81–85.

15. Trelease, *Indian Affairs*, 131; Richter, *Ordeal of the Longhouse*, 87.

16. Jennings, *Ambiguous Iroquois Empire*, 113–21.

17. Jennings, *Ambiguous Iroquois Empire*, 108–11; Trelease, *Indian Affairs*, 138–68.

18. Richard I. Melvoin, *New England Outpost: War and Society in Colonial Deerfield* (New York, 1989), 280–81.

19. Richter, *Ordeal of the Longhouse*, 50–74; Jennings, *Ambiguous Iroquois Empire*, 84–112, 128–29; Gordon M. Day, "The Ouragie War: A Case History in Iroquois–New England Indian Relations," in Michael K. Foster, Jack Campisi, and Marianne Mithun, eds., *Extending the Rafters: Interdisciplinary Approaches to Iroquoian Studies* (Albany, N.Y., 1984), 35–50.

20. Richter, *Ordeal of the Longhouse*, 50–74; Jennings, *Ambiguous Iroquois Empire*, 84–112.

21. Trelease, *Indian Affairs*, 107–8; *Historical Statistics*, series Z, 1–9.

22. *NYCD*, 3:67–68; Robert C. Ritchie, *The Duke's Province: A Study of New York Politics and Society, 1664–1691* (Chapel Hill, N.C., 1977), 9–24.

23. Ritchie, *Duke's Province*, 23–24; C. A. Weslager, *The English on the Delaware, 1610–1682* (New Brunswick, N.J., 1967), 176–96.

24. Richter, *Ordeal of the Longhouse*, passim.

25. *DCB*, 1:322–23, 650–51; Richter, *Ordeal of the Longhouse*, 105–32.

26. Victor Konrad, "An Iroquois Frontier: The North Shore of Lake Ontario During the Late Seventeenth Century," *Journal of Historical Geography* 7 (1981): 129–44.

27. Richter, *Ordeal of the Longhouse*, 105–32.

28. Stephen S. Webb, *1676: The End of American Independence* (New York, 1984), 328–54, 413; Richard L. Haan, "Covenant and Consensus: Iroquois and English, 1676–1760," in Daniel K. Richter and James H. Merrell, eds., *Beyond the Covenant Chain: The Iroquois and Their Neighbors in Indian North America, 1600–1800* (Syracuse, N.Y., 1987), 41–57.

29. Francis Jennings, *The Invasion of America: Indians, Colonialism, and the Cant of Conquest* (Chapel Hill, N.C., 1975), 298–326; Jennings, *Ambiguous Iroquois Empire*, 148–71; Webb, *1676*, 355–74; Richter, *Ordeal of the Longhouse*, 133–61.

30. Jennings, *Ambiguous Iroquois Empire*, 154–71; Richter, *Ordeal of the Longhouse*, 145.

31. Hunt, *Wars of the Iroquois*, 135–39; Jennings, *Ambiguous Iroquois Empire*, 172–75; Richard White, *The Middle Ground: Indians, Empires, and Republics in the Great Lakes Region, 1650–1815* (Cambridge, 1991), 29–34, 107; Russell Thornton, *American Indian Holocaust and Survival: A Population History Since 1492* (Norman, Okla., 1987), 86–87.

32. Hunt, *Wars of the Iroquois*, 150–57; Jennings, *Ambiguous Iroquois Empire*,

175–76; Richter, *Ordeal of the Longhouse*, 144–49; W. J. Eccles, *The Canadian Frontier, 1534–1760* (New York, 1969), 114–16.

33. Trelease, *Indian Affairs*, 258–65; Richter, *Ordeal of the Longhouse*, 150–53; Jennings, *Ambiguous Iroquois Empire*, 180–83.

34. *DCB*, 1:525–26; Eccles, *Canadian Frontier*, 116–17; Richter, *Ordeal of the Longhouse*, 151–55; Jennings, *Ambiguous Iroquois Empire*, 183–86.

35. Robert V. Wells, *The Population of the British Colonies in America before 1776: A Survey of Census Data* (Princeton, 1975), 123–29; *Historical Statistics*, series Z, 9; Ritchie, *Duke's Province*, 128–29; Donna Merwick, *Possessing Albany, 1630–1710: The Dutch and English Experiences* (Cambridge, 1990), 188–219; Merwick, "Dutch Townsmen and Land Use: A Spatial Perspective on Seventeenth-Century Albany, New York," *W&MQ* 37 (1980): 53–78.

36. Trelease, *Indian Affairs*, 215–25; Merwick, *Possessing Albany*, 212–15.

37. Trelease, *Indian Affairs*, 204–27.

38. *NYCD*, 3:260–62; Stephen S. Webb, *The Governors-General: The English Army and the Definition of Empire, 1569–1681* (Chapel Hill, N.C., 1979). For appraisals, see Ian K. Steele, "Thin Red Lines: Governors of England's Empire before 1681," *Reviews in American History* 8 (1980): 318–22; Richard R. Johnson, "The Imperial Webb: The Thesis of Garrison Government in Early America Considered," *W&MQ* 43 (1986): 408–30; and Stephen S. Webb, "The Data and Theory of Restoration Empire," *W&MQ* 43 (1986): 431–59.

Part II. Colonies and Tribes, 1687–1748

1. Richard R. Johnson, *Adjustment to Empire: The New England Colonies, 1675–1715* (New Brunswick, N.J., 1981), 242–421; William Pencak, *War, Politics, & Revolution in Provincial Massachusetts* (Boston, 1981), 1–60.

2. *Private Correspondence of Sarah, Duchess of Marlborough*, 2nd ed. (London, 1838), 2:419.

3. Gerald S. Graham, *Empire of the North Atlantic*, 2nd ed. (Toronto, 1958), 58–82.

4. Only the base at Plaisance, Newfoundland, and the Louisiana colony remained beyond his reach.

5. Fred Anderson, *A People's Army: Massachusetts Soldiers and Society in the Seven Years' War* (Chapel Hill, N.C., 1984); Gary Nash, *The Urban Crucible: Social Change, Political Consciousness, and the Origins of the American Revolution* (Cambridge, Mass., 1979), 55–65, 165–70, 173, 235–39; Sylvia R. Frey, *The British Soldier in America: A Social History of Military Life in the Revolutionary Period* (Austin, Tex., 1981), 3–21.

6. John W. Shy, "A New Look at Colonial Militia," in his *A People Numerous and Armed* (New York, 1976), 21–34; Lawrence D. Cress, *Citizens in Arms: The Army and Militia in American Society to the War of 1812* (Chapel Hill, N.C., 1982), 1–14; Harold E. Selesky, *War and Society in Colonial Connecticut* (New Haven, 1990).

7. For debates on this issue, see E. Wayne Carp, "Early American Military History: A Review of Recent Work," *VMHB* 94 (1986): 259–84.

8. Don Higginbotham, "Early American Way of War: Reconnaissance and Appraisal," *W&MQ* 44 (1987): 234.

7. Establishing Patterns, 1687–1701

1. W. J. Eccles, *Canada under Louis XIV, 1663–1701* (Toronto, 1964), 147–48; *DCB*, 1:653; 2:98–105.

2. *NYCD*, 9:331–33; Eccles, *Canada under Louis XIV*, 150–52.

3. Eccles, *Canada under Louis XIV*, 148–60; *DCB*, 2:98–105.

4. *Historical Statistics*, series Z, 1–11; David S. Lovejoy, *The Glorious Revolution in America* (New York, 1972).

5. *DCB*, 2:4–7; Viola Barnes, *The Dominion of New England* (New Haven, 1923), 212–30; Kenneth M. Morrison, *The Embattled Northeast: The Elusive Ideal of Alliance in Abenaki–Euramerican Relations* (Berkeley, 1984), 107–17.

6. *NYCD*, 3:581.

7. Quoted in Daniel K. Richter, *The Ordeal of the Longhouse: The Peoples of the Iroquois League in the Era of European Colonization* (Chapel Hill, N.C., 1992), 160–61.

8. Eccles, *Canada under Louis XIV*, 164–66.

9. Eccles, *Canada under Louis XIV*, 172–74; Thomas E. Burke, Jr., *Mohawk Frontier: The Dutch Community of Schenectady, New York, 1661–1710* (Ithaca, N.Y., 1991), 68–110, 123.

10. *NYCD*, 3:390, 394; Richter, *Ordeal of the Longhouse*, 173.

11. *NYCD*, 3:708, 717, 727, 751–54; 4:193–96; Richard S. Dunn, *Puritans and Yankees: The Winthrop Dynasty of New England, 1630–1717* (Princeton, 1962), 177–79, 195–98, 208.

12. Eccles, *Canada under Louis XIV*, 186–87.

13. Thomas Church, *The History of the Great Indian War of 1675 and 1676 . . .* (Boston, 1825), 192–93, 210; Barnes, *Dominion*, 218–19.

14. Mark van Doren, Preface to *The Life of Sir William Phips*, a eulogy by Cotton Mather (New York, 1929), ix; *The Diary of Samuel Sewall, 1674–1729*, ed. M. Halsey Thomas, 2 vols. (New York, 1973), 1:454n.

15. Cotton Mather, *Decennium Luctuosum*, in C. H. Lincoln, ed., *Narratives of the Indian Wars* (New York, 1913), 214.

16. The flagship *Six Friends* carried forty-four guns (Mather, *Life of Phips*, 68–69).

17. Major Walley's journal, in Ernest Myrand, ed., *Sir William Phips devant Québec* (Québec, 1893), 38.

18. Francis Parkman, *Count Frontenac and New France under Louis XIV* (Boston, 1905), 290.

19. Major Thomas Savage, quoted in Myrand, *William Phips*, 50.

20. Myrand, *William Phips*, 46–47.

21. *Plymouth Church Records, 1620–1859*, 2 vols. (Baltimore, 1975), 1:167.

22. Ian K. Steele, *The English Atlantic, 1675–1740* (New York, 1986), 257–58.

23. *The Travels of John Heckewelder in Frontier America*, ed. Paul A. W. Wallace (Pittsburgh, 1958), 91–92.

24. Alden T. Vaughan and Edward W. Clark, eds., *Puritans among the Indians: Accounts of Captivity and Redemption, 1676–1724* (Cambridge, Mass., 1981), 161–64; Laurel Thatcher Ulrich, *Good Wives: Image and Reality in the Lives of Women in Northern New England, 1650–1750* (New York, 1982), 167–72, 234–35.

25. Morrison, *Embattled Northeast*, 117–59; Kenneth M. Morrison, "The Bias of Colonial Law: English Paranoia and the Abenaki Arena of King Philip's War," *NEQ* 53 (1980): 363–87.

26. *NYCD*, 9:145, 539; Richter, *Ordeal of the Longhouse*, 173.

27. Richter, *Ordeal of the Longhouse*, 185; *NYCD*, 9:679–81.

28. Richter, *Ordeal of the Longhouse*, 162–213; Dale Miquelon, *New France, 1701–1744: "A Supplement to Europe"* (Toronto, 1987), 18–25: Eccles, *Canada under Louis XIV*, 185–206, 242–44.

29. *CSPC, 1696–1697*, 165.

8. Recurring Patterns, 1702–1748

1. Benbow's instructions of October 23, 1701, Southwell Papers, 5:315–17, National Maritime Museum, Greenwich, England; *The Marlborough–Godolphin Correspondence*, ed. H. L. Snyder, 3 vols. (London, 1973), 1:15, 19.

2. David H. Corkran, *The Creek Frontier, 1540–1783* (Norman, Okla., 1967), 1–55; James Leitch Wright, Jr., *Anglo-Spanish Rivalry in North America* (Athens, Ga., 1971), 46–59; M. L. Brown, *Firearms in Colonial America: The Impact on History and Technology, 1492–1792* (Washington, D.C., 1980), 167.

3. Quoted in Verner W. Crane, *The Southern Frontier, 1670–1732* (Ann Arbor, 1929), 74–75; Peter H. Wood, "The Changing Population of the Colonial South: An Overview by Race and Region, 1685–1790," in Peter H. Wood, Gregory A. Waselkov, and M. Thomas Hatley, eds., *Powhatan's Mantle: Indians in the Colonial Southeast* (Lincoln, Neb., 1989), 38; *DAB*, 7:127–28.

4. Theda Perdue, *Slavery and the Evolution of Cherokee Society, 1540–1866* (Knoxville, Tenn., 1979), 25.

5. Charles W. Arnade, *The Siege of St. Augustine in 1702* (Gainesville, Fla., 1959); John Jay TePaske, *The Governorship of Spanish Florida, 1700–1763* (Durham, N.C., 1964), 110–13.

6. John H. Hann, *Apalachee: The Land between the Rivers* (Gainesville, Fla., 1988), 264–83; Corkran, *Creek Frontier*, 55–57; Wright, *Anglo-Spanish Rivalry*, 60–68.

7. Kenneth M. Morrison, *The Embattled Northeast: The Elusive Ideal of Alliance in Abenaki–Euramerican Relations* (Berkeley, 1984), 156–64; Richard I. Melvoin, *New England Outpost: War and Society in Colonial Deerfield* (New York, 1989), 209–48.

8. Philip S. Haffenden, *New England in the English Nation, 1689–1713* (Oxford, 1974), 255–59.

9. Henry St. John to Robert Hunter, February 6, 1710/1711, in Gerald S. Graham, ed., *The Walker Expedition to Quebec, 1711* (Toronto, 1953), 277.

10. Tentative estimates are offered by Howard H. Peckham, *The Colonial Wars, 1689–1762* (Chicago, 1964), 74–75.

11. *CSPC, 1716–1717*, 34–40.

12. Quoted in Yves F. Zoltvany, "The Problem of Western Policy under Philippe de Rigaud de Vaudreuil, 1703–1725," in *CHA Report for 1964* (Ottawa, 1965), 16.

13. Wood, "Changing Population of the Colonial South," 43–46; James H. Merrell, "'Their Very Bones Shall Fight': The Catawba–Iroquois Wars," and Douglas W. Boyce, "'As the Wind Scatters the Smoke': The Tuscarora in the Eighteenth Century," both in Daniel K. Richter and James H. Merrell, eds., *Beyond the Covenant Chain: The Iroquois and Their Neighbors in Indian North Amer-*

ica, 1600–1800 (Syracuse, N.Y., 1987), 115–33, 151–63; J. Leitch Wright, Jr., *The Only Land They Knew: The Tragic Story of the American Indians in the Old South* (New York, 1981), 117–21; Crane, *Southern Frontier*, 156–61.

14. Quoted in A. M. Wilson, *French Foreign Policy during the Administration of Cardinal Fleury, 1726–1743* (Cambridge, Mass., 1936), 65.

15. See, for instance, *CSPC, 1719–1720*, 32–41; *CSPC, 1720–1721*, 408–49; *RAPQ, 1947–1948*, 272–88, 291–95.

16. Colin G. Calloway, *The Western Abenaki of Vermont, 1600–1800* (Norman Okla., 1991), 113–31; Douglas Edward Leach, *Arms for Empire: A Military History of the British Colonies in North America, 1607–1763* (New York, 1973), 181–86; Dale Miquelon, *New France, 1701–1744: "A Supplement to Europe"* (Toronto, 1987), 106–8; *DCB*, 2:542–45.

17. John Robert McNeill, *Atlantic Empires of France and Spain: Louisbourg and Havana, 1700–1763* (Chapel Hill, N.C., 1985), 182, 201.

18. *DCB*, 2:346, 562–63; F.-E. Audet, *Les Premiers Établissement français au pays des Illinois: la guerre de Renards* (Paris, 1938); Richard White, *The Middle Ground: Indians, Empires, and Republics in the Great Lakes Region, 1650–1815* (Cambridge, 1991), 149–66.

19. Joseph L. Peyser, *Letters from New France: The Upper Country, 1686–1783* (Urbana, Ill., 1992), 123–34; White, *Middle Ground*, 168–73; Miquelon, *New France*, 44–47, 166–68, 176–79.

20. Quoted in Patricia D. Woods, "The French and the Natchez Indians in Louisiana, 1700–1731," *Louisiana History* 19 (1978): 432.

21. Woods, "French and the Natchez," 413–35; Patricia D. Woods, *French–Indian Relations on the Southern Frontier, 1699–1762* (Ann Arbor, 1980), 23–32, 55–64, 95–110. For Bienville, see *DCB*, 3:379–84.

22. Daniel H. Usner, Jr., *Indians, Settlers, & Slaves in a Frontier Exchange Economy: The Lower Mississippi Valley before 1783* (Chapel Hill, N.C., 1992), 81–87; Woods, *French–Indian Relations*, 13–22, 45–54, 111–46; Arrell Morgan Gibson, *The Chickasaws* (Norman, Okla., 1971), 31–57.

23. Corkran, *Creek Frontier*, 59–81; Wright, *Anglo-Spanish Rivalry*, 60–74; James H. Merrell, "Our Bond of Peace: Patterns of Intercultural Exchange in the Carolina Piedmont, 1650–1750," in Wood, Waselkov, and Hatley, *Powhatan's Mantle*, 208–10; Wright, *Only Land They Knew*, 121–25; W. Stitt Robinson, *The Southern Colonial Frontier, 1607–1763* (Albuquerque, N.M., 1979), 110–15, 119, 185–86; John Phillip Reid, *A Better Kind of Hatchet* (University Park, Pa., 1976), 190–96.

24. Merrell, "Their Very Bones"; Theda Perdue, "Cherokee Relations with the Iroquois in the Eighteenth Century," in Richter and Merrell, *Beyond the Covenant Chain*, 135–49.

25. M. Eugene Sirmans, *Colonial South Carolina, a Political History, 1663–1763* (Chapel Hill, N.C., 1966), 157, 161.

26. Wright, *Anglo-Spanish Rivalry*, 90–91; Douglas Edward Leach, *Roots of Conflict: British Armed Forces and Colonial Americans, 1677–1763* (Chapel Hill, N.C., 1986), 42–44; Peter H. Wood, *Black Majority: Negroes in Colonial South Carolina from 1670 through the Stono Rebellion* (New York, 1974), 314–23; Larry E. Ivers, *British Drums on the Southern Frontier: The Military Colonization of Georgia, 1733–1749* (Chapel Hill, N.C., 1974).

27. Julian Gwyn, *The Enterprising Admiral: The Personal Fortune of Admiral Sir Peter Warren* (Montreal, 1974), 12; TePaske, *Governorship of Spanish Florida*, 142–45.

28. TePaske, *Governorship of Spanish Florida*, 146–54; Leach, *Arms for Empire*, 220–23; Wright, *Anglo-Spanish Rivalry*, 87–100.

29. G. M. Wrong, ed., "Lettre d'un habitant de Louisbourg," *University of Toronto Studies in History and Economics* 1 (1897): 15.

30. John A. Schutz, *William Shirley, King's Governor of Massachusetts* (Chapel Hill, N.C., 1961), 80–103.

31. G. A. Rawlyk, *Yankees at Louisbourg* (Orono, Maine, 1967); Robert E. Wall,"Louisbourg, 1745," *NEQ* 37 (1964): 64–83.

32. Wrong, "Lettre d'un habitant," 37–38.

33. Edward J. Cashin, *Lachlan McGillivray, Indian Trader: The Shaping of the Southern Colonial Frontier* (Athens, Ga., 1992), 81–103.

34. Calloway, *Western Abenaki*, 143–59.

35. John Lax and William Pencak, "The Knowles Riot and the Crisis of the 1740s in Massachusetts," *Perspectives in American History* 10 (1976): 161–214; Leach, *Roots of Conflict*, 146–56; N.A.M. Rodger, *The Wooden World: An Anatomy of the Georgian Navy* (Annapolis, Md., 1986), 174–76, 181–82.

36. *The Correspondence of William Shirley*, ed. Charles Henry Lincoln, 2 vols. (New York, 1912), 2:13. For a comparable French position, see *NYCD*, 10:270.

37. Guy Frégault, *Le Grand Marquis: Pierre de Rigaud de Vaudreuil et la Louisiane* (Montreal, 1952); Woods, *French–Indian Relations*, 147–59.

Part III. Empires, Colonies, and Tribes, 1748–1765

1. Richard White, *The Middle Ground: Indians, Empires, and Republics in the Great Lakes Region, 1650–1815* (Cambridge, 1991), 223–68.

2. *Pennsylvania Archives*, 4th ser., 2:373.

3. William Pencak, "Warfare and Political Change in Mid-Eighteenth-Century Massachusetts," *JICH* 8 (1980): 51–73.

9. Invading the Ohio, 1748–1755

1. W. J. Eccles, *The Canadian Frontier, 1534–1760* (New York, 1969), 151–54; David H. Corkran, *The Creek Frontier, 1540–1783* (Norman, Okla., 1967), 116–30; *NYCD*, 6:740; 10:140, 156.

2. Richard White, *Middle Ground: Indians, Empires, and Republics in the Great Lakes Region, 1650–1815* (Cambridge, 1991), 202–8; *DCB*, 3:99–101.

3. Lawrence Henry Gipson, *The British Empire before the American Revolution*, 15 vols. (Caldwell, Idaho, and New York, 1936–1970), 4:222–24; David Edmunds, "Pickawillany: French Military Power versus British Economics," *Western Pennsylvania Historical Magazine* 58 (1975): 169–84; Gregory Evans Dowd, *A Spirited Resistance: The North American Indian Struggle for Unity, 1745–1815* (Baltimore, 1992), 23–24; White, *Middle Ground*, 220–34.

4. *NYCD*, 6:778–79; Paul A. W. Wallace, *Conrad Weiser: Friend of Colonist and Mohawk* (Philadelphia, 1945), 530; Francis Jennings, *Empire of Fortune:*

Crowns, Colonies & Tribes in the Seven Years' War in America (New York, 1988), 54–57.

5. Quoted in James Titus, *The Old Dominion at War: Society, Politics, and Warfare in Late Colonial Virginia* (Columbia, S.C., 1991), 55.

6. Hugh Cleland, *George Washington in the Ohio Valley* (Pittsburgh, 1955), 97–98; Charles Morse Stotz, *Outposts of the War for Empire* (Pittsburgh, 1985), 95–97.

7. Quoted in Reed Browning, *The Duke of Newcastle* (New Haven, 1975), 207.

8. Quoted in L. H. Gipson, "A French Project for Victory Short of a Declaration of War, 1755," *CHR* 26 (1945): 362.

9. T. Roy Clayton, "The Duke of Newcastle, the Earl of Halifax, and the American Origins of the Seven Years' War," *Historical Journal* 24 (1981): 571–603.

10. *NYCD*, 10:265, 270.

11. James Pritchard, *Louis XV's Navy, 1748–1762: A Study of Organization and Administration* (Kingston, Ont., 1987), 137, 140; A. T. Mahan, *The Influence of Sea Power upon History, 1660–1783* (Boston, 1890), 291.

12. Quoted in Gipson, *British Empire*, 6:109.

13. Guy Frégault,"La Guerre de Sept Ans et la civilisation canadienne-française," *RHAF* 7 (1953–1954): 186, 194.

14. *NYCD*, 6:901–3, 915–16, 920–22; *The Correspondence of William Shirley*, ed. Charles Henry Lincoln, 2 vols. (New York, 1912), 2:98–101; Stanley M. Pargellis, ed., *Military Affairs in North America, 1748–1765* (New York, 1936), 36–39; Clayton, "American Origins," 571–603; Lee McCardell, *Ill-Starred General: Braddock of the Coldstream Guards* (Pittsburgh, 1958), 124–25.

15. Gipson, *British Empire*, 6:64–65, 77.

16. Augustin Grignon, "Seventy-Two Years' Recollections of Wisconsin," *Wisconsin Historical Society Collections* 3 (1857): 214; Paul E. Kopperman, *Braddock at the Monongahela* (Pittsburgh, 1977), 9, 24, 26; Jennings, *Empire of Fortune*, 153–57; *DCB*, 3:400–402; Guy Frégault, *La Guerre de la conquête* (Montreal, 1955), 140; Hew Strachan, *European Armies and the Conduct of War* (London, 1983), 28.

17. Leroy V. Eid, " 'A Kind of Running Fight': Indian Battlefield Tactics in the Late Eighteenth Century," *Western Pennsylvania Historical Magazine* 71 (1988): 147–71.

18. Peter F. Russell, "Redcoats in the Wilderness: British Officers and Irregular Warfare in Europe and America, 1740 to 1760," *W&MQ* 35 (1978): 629–52.

19. Gipson, *British Empire*, 6:62–98; Stanley M. Pargellis, "Braddock's Defeat," *AHR* 41 (1936): 253–69.

20. Ian K. Steele, *Betrayals: Fort William Henry and the "Massacre,"* rev. ed. (New York, 1993), 33–35; Jennings, *Empire of Fortune*, 162–63.

21. Leroy V. Eid, " 'National' War among Indians of Northeastern North America," *Canadian Review of American Studies* 16 (1985): 125–54; Willis E. Wright, *Colonel Ephraim Williams, a Documentary Life* (Pittsfield, Mass., 1970).

22. *NYCD*, 6:1005.

23. Steele, *Betrayals*, 28–56.

24. *Report of the Canadian Archives for 1905*, 2: Appendix C: 56.

25. *DCB*, 4:540–42, 630–32.

26. Stanley M. Pargellis, *Lord Loudoun in North America* (New Haven, 1933), 37–41.

27. Pargellis, *Military Affairs*, 134; Pargellis, *Loudoun*, 45–82.

28. Pargellis, *Military Affairs*, 141.

10. Vaudreuil's Offensive, 1756–1757

1. *DCB*, 4:662–74; Guy Frégault, *Le Grand Marquis, Pierre de Rigaud de Vaudreuil et la Louisiane*, 2nd ed. (Montreal, 1964).

2. *NYCD*, 10:269.

3. Quoted in Richard White, *The Middle Ground: Indians, Empires, and Republics in the Great Lakes Region, 1650–1815* (Cambridge, 1991), 245.

4. *NYCD*, 10:423–24, 484.

5. R.L.D. Davidson, *War Comes to Quaker Pennsylvania, 1682–1756* (New York, 1957), 91–198.

6. James Titus, *The Old Dominion at War: Society, Politics, and Warfare in Late Colonial Virginia* (Columbia, S.C., 1991), 94–95, 100–101; Hayes Baker-Crothers, *Virginia and the French and Indian War* (Chicago, 1928), 82–105.

7. Stanley M. Pargellis, *Lord Loudoun in North America* (New Haven, 1933), 148–62.

8. HL, LO 977; *NYCD*, 10:396–97, 403–5, 481, 529.

9. NAC, MG 17, A7–1, 4:2797; *Adventure in the Wilderness: The American Journals of Louis Antoine de Bougainville, 1756–1760*, ed. Edward P. Hamilton (Norman, Okla., 1964), 5, 8–10.

10. *NYCD*, 10:462.

11. *NYCD*, 10:490–93, 499, 538.

12. *NYCD*, 10:523–26.

13. The following discussion is derived from Ian K. Steele, *Betrayals: Fort William Henry and the "Massacre,"* rev. ed. (New York, 1993).

14. *NYCD*, 10:542–55; Steele, *Betrayals*, 75–77.

15. James Smith's narrative, in Samuel G. Drake, *Indian Captivities* (Buffalo, N.Y., 1854), 220; John Duffy, *Epidemics in Colonial America* (Baton Rouge, 1953), 86–91.

16. *Bougainville's Journals*, 118, 120–21, 151.

17. Abbé Picquet, "Réduction du fort Georges," NAC, MG 17, A7–1, 4:2823.

18. *NYCD*, 10:659–66.

19. R. Michalon, "Vaudreuil et Montcalm," in J. Delmas, ed., *Conflits des sociétés au Canada français pendant la Guerre de Sept Ans et leur influence sur les opérations* (Vincennes, France, 1978), 41–175; *NYCD*, 10:868, 874.

11. The British Imperial Victory, 1758–1763

1. Stanley M. Pargellis, *Lord Loudoun in North America* (New Haven, 1933), 337–65.

2. For recent correctives, see especially Richard Middleton, *The Bells of Victory: The Pitt–Newcastle Ministry and the Conduct of the Seven Years' War, 1757–1762* (Cambridge, 1985); Marie Peters, *Pitt and Popularity: The Patriot Minister*

and London Opinion during the Seven Years' War (Oxford, 1980); and Peters, ''The Myth of William Pitt, Earl of Chatham, Great Imperialist. Part I: Pitt and Imperial Expansion, 1738–1763,'' *JICH* 21 (1993): 31–74.

3. Horace Walpole, quoted in Lawrence Henry Gipson, *The British Empire before the American Revolution*, 15 vols. (Caldwell, Idaho, and New York, 1936–1970), 7:12.

4. Rex Whitworth, *Field Marshal Lord Ligonier* (Oxford, 1958).

5. Middleton, *Bells of Victory*, 88; John Brewer, *The Sinews of Power: War, Money and the English State, 1688–1783* (New York, 1989), 29–63, 88–134, 191–217.

6. Julian Gwyn, ''British Government Spending and the North American Colonies,'' *JICH* 8 (1980): 74–84; Pargellis, *Loudoun*, 351–55; Middleton, *Bells of Victory*, 55.

7. Daniel J. Beattie, ''The Adaptation of the British Army to Wilderness Warfare, 1755–1763,'' in Maarten Ultee, ed., *Adapting to Conditions: War and Society in the Eighteenth Century* (University, Ala., 1986), 73.

8. Don Higginbotham, ''Early American Way of War: Reconnaissance and Appraisal,'' *W&MQ* 44 (1987): 235; James Titus, *The Old Dominion at War: Society, Politics, and Warfare in Late Colonial Virginia* (Columbia, S.C., 1991); Fred Anderson, ''Why Did Colonial New Englanders Make Bad Soldiers? Contractual Principles and Military Conduct during the Seven Years' War,'' *W&MQ* 38 (1981): 395–417; Anderson, *A People's Army: Massachusetts Soldiers and Society in the Seven Years' War* (Chapel Hill, N.C., 1984); Harold E. Selesky, *War and Society in Colonial Connecticut* (New Haven, 1990).

9. Middleton, *Bells of Victory*, 24–25; James Pritchard, *Louis XV's Navy, 1748–1762: A Study of Organization and Administration* (Kingston, Ont., 1987), 136–37; G. Modelski and W. B. Thompson, *Seapower in Global Politics, 1494–1993* (London, 1988), 221–24, 259–62, 280–82; John Robert McNeill, *Atlantic Empires of France and Spain: Louisbourg and Havana* (Chapel Hill, N.C., 1985), 75.

10. Gipson, *British Empire*, 7:103–5; Stanley M. Pargellis, ed., *Military Affairs in North America, 1748–1765* (New York, 1936), 391–94.

11 J Mackay Hitsman and C.C.J. Bond, ''The Assault Landing at Louisbourg, 1758,'' *CHR* 35 (1954): 323–24.

12. Ian K. Steele, *Betrayals: Fort William Henry and the ''Massacre,''* rev. ed. (New York, 1993), 109–28; Roger Michalon, ''Vaudreuil et Montcalm, les hommes, leurs relations, influence de ces relations sur la conduite de la guerre, 1756–1759,'' in Jean Delmas, ed., *Conflits des sociétés au Canada français pendant la Guerre de Sept Ans et leur influence sur les opérations* (Vincennes, France, 1978), 41–176.

13. *NYCD*, 10:720.

14. *Adventure in the Wilderness: The American Journals of Louis Antoine de Bougainville, 1756–1760*, ed. E. P. Hamilton (Norman, Okla., 1964), 252–53.

15. Quoted in Gipson, *British Empire*, 7:227.

16. Guy Frégault, *La Guerre de la conquête* (Montreal, 1955), 305; Gipson, *British Empire*, 7:208–46.

17. William G. Godfrey, *Pursuit of Profit and Preferment: John Bradstreet's Quest* (Waterloo, Ont., 1982), 115–41; W. J. Eccles, *France in America*, 2nd ed. (Markham, Ont., 1990), 207.

18. *NYCD*, 10:831.

19. Anthony F. C. Wallace, *King of the Delawares: Teedyuscung, 1700–1763* (Philadelphia, 1949), 192–207; Gipson, *British Empire*, 7:278–79; Francis Jen-

nings, *Empire of Fortune: Crowns, Colonies & Tribes in the Seven Years' War in America* (New York, 1988), 405–14; Richard White, *The Middle Ground: Indians, Empires, and Republics in the Great Lakes Region, 1650–1815* (Cambridge, 1991), 248–56.

20. Gipson, *British Empire*, 7:247–86; *DCB*, 3:218–19, 378–79.

21. *NYCD*, 10:934; G. S. Graham, *Empire of the North Atlantic*, 2nd ed. (Toronto, 1958), 150–51, 170–71.

22. Guy Frégault, "La Guerre de Sept Ans et la civilisation canadienne-française," *RHAF* 7 (1953–1954): 190–91.

23. *NYCD*, 10:926, 952–58, 960; Frégault, *La Guerre*, 283.

24. *NYCD*, 7:375–94, quote on 386.

25. *NYCD*, 7:402–3; Gipson, *British Empire*, 7:344–56; Brian Leigh Dunnigan, *Siege 1759: The Campaign against Niagara* (Youngstown, N.Y., 1986).

26. Eccles, *France in America*, 210–18; Gipson, *British Empire*, 7:377–427; C. P. Stacey, *Quebec 1759: The Siege and the Battle* (Toronto, 1959), 120–55.

27. Gipson, *British Empire*, 7:335, 338–39.

28. Stacey, *Quebec 1759*, 164.

29. Stacey, *Quebec 1759*, 165; George F. G. Stanley, *New France, the Last Phase, 1744–1760* (Toronto, 1968), 259–61; Gilles Proulx, "Le Dernier Effort de la France au Canada—secours ou fraude?" *RHAF* 36 (1982): 413–26.

30. Stanley, *New France*, 81–94.

31. *Journal des campagnes du Chevalier de Lévis en Canada de 1756 à 1760*, ed. H. R. Casgrain (Montreal, 1889), 315.

32. *DCB*, 4:481.

33. David Syrett, "American Provincials and the Havana Campaign of 1762," *New York History* 49 (1968): 375–90.

34. Higginbotham, "Early American Way of War," 235.

35. Benjamin Franklin to Lord Kames, 1760, in *The Papers of Benjamin Franklin*, ed. Leonard Woods Labaree, 29 vols. (New Haven, 1959–1992), 9:6–7.

36. Jack P. Greene, "The Seven Years' War and the American Revolution: The Causal Relationship Reconsidered," *JICH* 8 (1980): 85–105; John M. Murrin, "The French and Indian War, the American Revolution, and the Counterfactual Hypothesis: Reflections on Lawrence Henry Gipson and John Shy," *Reviews in American History* 1 (1973): 307–18; Paul A. Varg, "The Advent of Nationalism," *American Quarterly* 16 (1964): 169–81; Bruce Bliven, Jr., *Under the Guns: New York, 1775–1776* (New York, 1972), 222, 353–54.

37. W. L. Grant, "Canada Versus Guadeloupe, an Episode of the Seven Years' War," *AHR* 17 (1911–1912): 735–43; Marjorie G. Reid, "Pitt's Decision to Keep Canada in 1761," *CHA Report for 1926* (Ottawa, 1927), 21.

38. *A Sermon Preached before His Excellency Francis Bernard, Esq. . . .* (Boston, 1763), 44.

39. William Pencak, *War, Politics, & Revolution in Provincial Massachusetts* (Boston, 1981), 135, 154.

12. Different Drummers, 1759–1765

1. Quoted in Richard White, *The Middle Ground: Indians, Empires, and Republics in the Great Lakes Region, 1650–1815* (Cambridge, 1991), 252.

2. White, *Middle Ground*, 252–55; Francis Jennings, *Empire of Fortune: Crowns, Colonies & Tribes in the Seven Years' War in America* (Chapel Hill, N.C., 1988), 431–32; Stephen F. Auth, *The Ten Years' War: Indian–White Relations in Pennsylvania, 1755–1765* (New York, 1989), 111–12.

3. Colin G. Calloway, *The Western Abenaki of Vermont, 1600–1800: War, Migration, and the Survival of an Indian People* (Norman, Okla., 1991), 175–81, 193; Thomas-Marie Charland, *Histoire des Abénakis d'Odanak* (Montreal, 1964), 107–18; Gordon M. Day, "Rogers' Raid in Indian Tradition," *Historical New Hampshire* 17 (1962): 3–17.

4. John R. Cuneo, *Robert Rogers of the Rangers* (New York, 1959), 129–41.

5. Discussion based on David H. Corkran, *The Cherokee Frontier: Conflict and Survival, 1740–1762* (Norman, Okla., 1962), 142–272; Lawrence Henry Gipson, *The British Empire before the American Revolution*, 15 vols. (Caldwell, Idaho, and New York, 1936–1970), 9:55–87; Gary C. Goodwin, *Cherokees in Transition: A Study of Changing Culture and Environment prior to 1775* (Chicago, 1977); and Russell Thornton, *The Cherokees: A Population History* (Lincoln, Neb., 1990), 1–37.

6. Corkran, *Cherokee Frontier*, 174.

7. Corkran, *Cherokee Frontier*, 163–99; Gipson, *British Empire*, 9:63–69.

8. Corkran, *Cherokee Frontier*, 207–15; Gipson, *British Empire*, 9:68–75.

9. Corkran, *Cherokee Frontier*, 216–22; John R. Alden, *John Stuart and the Southern Colonial Frontier* (Ann Arbor, 1944), 101–22.

10. Corkran, *Cherokee Frontier*, 230–72.

11. *Johnson Papers*, 3:336–37, 346.

12. *Johnson Papers*, 3:336–37, 449, 496, 498; Corkran, *Cherokee Frontier*, 157, 160, 165, 196, 203–5, 232–33, 243, 255; Alden, *John Stuart*, 109, 120–21, 129.

13. *Johnson Papers*, 3:517.

14. Alden, *John Stuart*, 117n.

15. Gregory Evans Dowd, *A Spirited Resistance: The North American Indian Struggle for Unity, 1745–1815* (Baltimore, 1992), 27–37; Dowd, "Thinking and Believing: Nativism and Unity in the Ages of Pontiac and Tecumseh," *American Indian Quarterly* 16 (1992): 309–35; Duane Champagne, "The Delaware Revitalization Movement of the Early 1760s: A Suggested Reinterpretation," *American Indian Quarterly* 12 (1988): 107–26; White, *Middle Ground*, 279–85.

16. White, *Middle Ground*, 261–63.

17. Randolph C. Downes, *Council Fires on the Upper Ohio* (Pittsburgh, 1940), 113–14.

18. White, *Middle Ground*, 263–65.

19. White, *Middle Ground*, 256–60; Jennings, *Empire of Fortune*, 441–42; Auth, *Ten Years' War*, 111–20, 134–36.

20. White, *Middle Ground*, 271–76; Gregory Evans Dowd, "The French King Wakes Up in Detroit: 'Pontiac's War' in Rumor and History," *Ethnohistory* 37 (1990): 254–78; *Johnson Papers*, 3:662, 698, 732–33.

21. White, *Middle Ground*, 277–79; Dowd, "French King Wakes Up."

22. Gipson, *British Empire*, 9:99–105; Howard H. Peckham, *Pontiac and the Indian Uprising* (Princeton, 1947), 156–70.

23. Peckham, *Pontiac*, 201–9; on casualties, compare his edition of *Narratives of Colonial America* (Chicago, 1971), 219, with Cuneo, *Robert Rogers*, 164–67.

24. Anthony F. C. Wallace, *King of the Delawares: Teedyuscung, 1700–1763* (Philadelphia, 1949), 258–61.

25. "William Trent's Journal at Fort Pitt, 1763," ed. A. T. Volwiler, *Mississippi Valley Historical Review* 11 (1924): 408–10.

26. Peckham, *Pontiac*, 210–13; Gipson, *British Empire*, 9:108–12; White, *Middle Ground*, 288–89; Jennings, *Empire of Fortune*, 447–49.

27. *NYCD*, 7:562; Peckham, *Pontiac*, 221–25.

28. *The Travels of John Heckewelder in Frontier America*, ed. Paul A. W. Wallace (Pittsburgh, 1958), 71–84; *Pennsylvania Gazette*, January 5, 1764; Alden T. Vaughan, "Frontier Banditti and the Indians: The Paxton Boys' Legacy, 1763–1775," *Pennsylvania History* 51 (1984): 1–29.

29. Peckham, *Pontiac*, 229–42, quote on 236; *DCB*, 3:525–31, 651–52.

30. Peckham, *Pontiac*, 238–40; *DCB*, 4:297.

31. *The Correspondence of General Thomas Gage with the Secretaries of State, 1763–1775*, ed. Clarence Edwin Carter, 2 vols. (New Haven, 1931, 1933), 1:2.

32. *NYCD*, 7:377.

33. Gipson, *British Empire*, 9:41–54; Jack M. Sosin, *Whitehall and the Wilderness: The Middle West in British Colonial Policy, 1760–1775* (Lincoln, Neb., 1961), 52–73; Jennings, *Empire of Fortune*, 461–63; Jack Stagg, *Anglo-Indian Relations in North America to 1763 and an Analysis of the Royal Proclamation of 7 October 1763* (Ottawa, 1981).

34. *NYCD*, 7:621–22, 718.

35. William G. Godfrey, *Pursuit of Profit and Preferment in Colonial North America: John Bradstreet's Quest* (Waterloo, Ont., 1982), 186.

36. *Johnson Papers*, 4:521–23; *NYCD*, 7:469–501; *DCB*, 4:83–87; Godfrey, *Pursuit of Profit*, 196–232; Gipson, *British Empire*, 9:117–23; Thomas Mante, *The History of the Late War in North America* (London, 1772), 535.

37. Gipson, *British Empire*, 9:114–16, 123–26.

38. *NYCD*, 7:718–41, quote on 739; Downes, *Council Fires*, 121–22.

39. Quoted in Downes, *Council Fires*, 122.

40. *NYCD*, 7:750–58, quotes on 757; Downes, *Council Fires*, 122.

41. *NYCD*, 7:765–67, 779–88, quote on 784; White, *Middle Ground*, 296–97, 302–14.

42. *NYCD*, 7:854–67, quotes on 858, 861.

43. Peter Marshall, "Colonial Protest and Imperial Retrenchment: Indian Policy, 1764–1768," *Journal of American Studies* 5 (1971): 1–17.

INDEX

Index

Index

Index

Index

Index

Index

Index

Index

TUTU

Born 1931

TUTU

VOICE OF THE VOICELESS

SHIRLEY DU BOULAY

WILLIAM B. EERDMANS PUBLISHING COMPANY
GRAND RAPIDS, MICHIGAN

Copyright © 1988 by Shirley du Boulay

First published 1988 by Hodder and Stoughton Limited, London.
This edition published 1988 through special arrangement with
Hodder and Stoughton by Wm. B. Eerdmans Publishing Co.,
255 Jefferson Ave. SE, Grand Rapids, MI 49503.

ISBN 0-8028-3649-6

/

To all who seek peace and justice
in South Africa

Contents

List of Illustrations

Acknowledgments

1 Desmond Tutu
2 Anglican Consultative Council
3 Press Association
4 Wendy Schwetmann
5 Ben Maclennan
6 Selwyn Tait/Time magazine
7 Rex Features
8 The Photo Source Ltd
9 Associated Press
10 Camera Press

Acknowledgments

I would like to thank all those whose help made this book possible, especially: Malcolm and Helene Alexander, Bishop Timothy Bavin, The Rev. Dr Allan Boesak, Professor David Bosch, The Rev. Brian Brown, Canon and Mrs Ronald Brownrigg, Bishop Duncan Buchanan, Canon M. and Dr E. Carmichael, William Carmichael, The Rev. Charles Cartwright, The Rev. Michael Cassidy, Brother Charles CR, The Rev. Frank Chikane, The Rev. Richard Coggins, Margaret Comber, Martin Conway, Michael Corke, Gregory E. Craig, Margaret Davies, Christopher Doherty, Sheena Duncan, Brother Edward SSF, Jose Emery, The Rev. Christopher Evans, The Rev. Dr Sydney Evans, John Ewington, The Rev. James Fenhagen, Frank Ferrari, The Rev. Bill Fosbrook, Kevin Garcia, Brother Geoffrey SSF, Tim and Sarah Goad, Rev. Simon Gqubule, Professor John de Gruchy, Bishop Richard Harries, Mr and Mrs Havemeyer, Moira Henderson, Dr William Howard, Archbishop Trevor Huddleston CR, Anne Hughes, Archbishop Denis Hurley, The Rev. Jesse Jackson, Lady Johnston, Vernon E. Jordan, Helen Joseph, Sister Josephine SPB, Mother Julian SPB, Sydney Kentridge, Martin Kenyon, B. M. Khaketla, The Very Rev. E. L. King, Dean of Cape Town, Anne Kingsley, Father Kingston CR, Dr Wolfram Kistner, J. L. R. Kotsokoane, Arthur Krim, Christa Kuljian, Melanie Lambert, Ian Linden, Rev. Gerrie Lubbe, Ruth Lundie, Canon Norman Luyt, Caroline Macomber, Father Sipho Masemola, Sophie Mazibuko, Professor J. M. Mohapeloa, Father Zakes Mohutsioa, Justice Moloto, Murphy Morobe, Stanley Motjuwadi, Dr Ntatho Motlana, Sally Motlana, Shirley Moulder, Mr and Mrs Mqotsi, Dr Margaret Nash, The Rev. Dr C. F. Beyers Naudé, Bishop Donald Nestor, Bishop Simeon Nkoane CR, Archdeacon David Nkwe, Canon Paul Oestreicher, Godfrey Pitje, The Rev. Barney Pityana, Bernice Powell, Dr Mamphela Ramphele, Bridget Rees, Dr and Mrs Rockwell, Dr Robert Runcie, Archbishop of Canterbury, Archbishop Philip Russell, Marjorie Sandle, Judith Scott, Father Sebidi, Father Sekgaphane, Thembi Sekgaphane, Joe Seremane, Professor Gabriel Setiloane, Joe Sibiya, Dr Michael Sovern, Bishop J. S. Spong, Father Tom Stanton CR, The Rev. Peter Storey, Barry Streek, Father Aelred Stubbs CR, Helen Suzman MP, Bishop John Taylor, Bishop Selby Taylor, Daphne Terry, Leah Tutu, Professor Charles Villa-Vicencio, Bishop John Walker, Mrs Betty Ward, Father Dale White, Canon Boyd Williams, Professor Francis Wilson, Dr Tim Wilson, The British Council of Churches, The Catholic Institute for International Relations, The South African Council of Churches,

Acknowledgments

Manuscripts and Archives Department – University of Cape Town Libraries.

I must single out Elizabeth Storey, for typing many of the interviews and for her support, Dan Vaughan, who read the entire manuscript and made valuable suggestions but who bears no responsibility for any errors remaining, to my editor Louise Tulip, and my husband John, whose encouragement sustained me through thick and thin.

Also thanks for hospitality to Dr and Mrs Rockwell, the Sisters of St Benedict's, Margaret Davies, Megan and Doug Walker, and Shirley Moulder.

There are others who, because of the political situation in South Africa, cannot be named.

Lastly, I must thank Archbishop Tutu for allowing me to write about him and for refusing to be canonised.

S. du B.

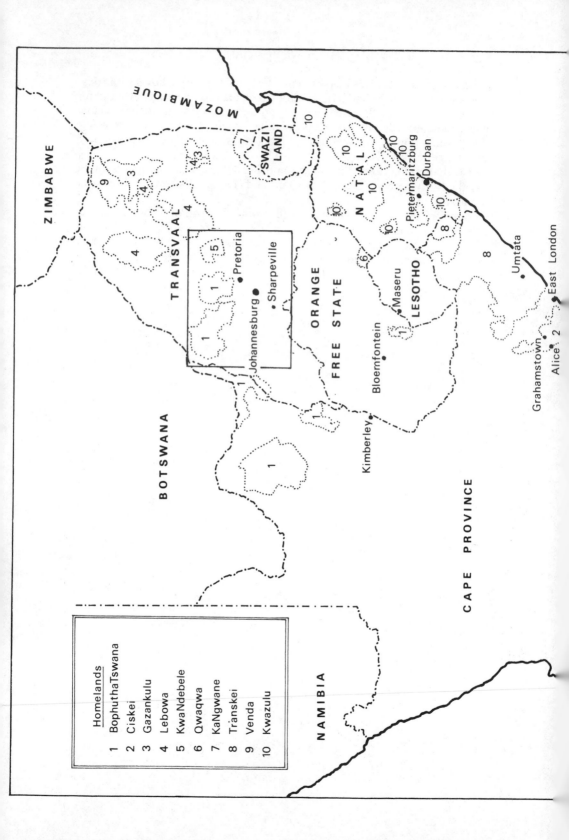

MOZAMBIQUE

ZIMBABWE

SWAZI LAND

TRANSVAAL

9
3
4
4
43
7
10

10
10
10
10
10
10
10
10

NATAL

Pietermaritzburg
Durban

● Pretoria
5
1
1
● Sharpeville
Johannesburg ●
1

ORANGE FREE STATE

6

Maseru ●
LESOTHO
1

Umtata
●

East London
●

Grahamstown ●
Alice ● 2

8

8

BOTSWANA

Bloemfontein ●

Kimberley ●

1

1

1

CAPE PROVINCE

NAMIBIA

Homelands
1 BophuthaTswana
2 Ciskei
3 Gazankulu
4 Lebowa
5 KwaNdebele
6 Qwaqwa
7 KaNgwane
8 Transkei
9 Venda
10 Kwazulu

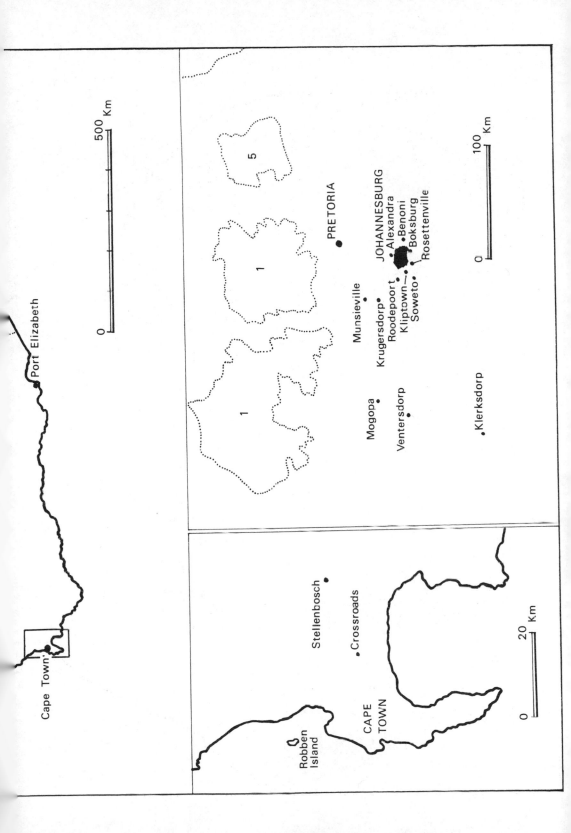

HAIL STICK OF REDEMPTION

(A praise song in the traditional mould, composed by Mzilikazi-ka-Khumalo and Temba Msimang and sung at Desmond Tutu's enthronement as Archbishop of Cape Town.)

Sing, here comes the misimbithi stick
Sing, here comes the redemption stick
Which grew from barren soil
Grow, Mpilo kaTutu
It was weak as it grew
It kept bending as it grew
Here is the misimbithi stick
Which sprang from barren soil
Grow, Mpilo kaTutu
It was weak as it grew
Sing

PRAISE: The msimbithi plant
Which grew and shone
And attracted scholars
They say what kind of plant is this
Which attracts while on barren land?
They rush to the Anglicans
Saying this comes from fertile soil
Soil from the mission
At home in Sofaya [Sophiatown]
It shone at Christ the King
And it bore fruit
All my life
I'd never seen a msimbithi bear fruit
It was the fruit of the saviour
I had never seen a msimbithi plant
Bear spiritual fruit

CHOIR: Sing

PRAISE: The msimbithi stick
Plucked by Trevor Huddleston
One of the Anglican bishops
He plucked it, and smoothed it
He plucked it, and sharpened it
And made it a weapon
To protect the believers

PRAISE (by a few men): Go on!

POET: The stick hits fighting veterans
By hitting those in power

Who say it will hit its own people
Because they are the wrongdoers
But a black skin
Doesn't mean darkness
And a white skin
Doesn't mean brightness
This stick hits those who rule it
And leaves those who are ruled
Because it hits those in power

CHOIR: Sing

POET: Even overseas in England
They saw the stick
They were drawn by its sharpness
They started fishing for it
They fished for it by air
It crossed the seas on the air
When it came, they anointed it

CHOIR: Sing

POET: Even overseas in America
They clap hands for it
Its weight was felt at Harvard
And all of Boston agreed
Norway also felt its weight
And gave it Nobel honours
This man rates with Luthuli
Among black heroes
He rates with King
Among black heroes

CHOIR: Sing

POET: Hail spiritual stick
Your people congratulate you
Hail stick of protection
Today you protect everyone
A black man you protect
And a white man you protect

ULULATION: li-li-li-li-li-iiiiiiiiii

Tutu: Voice of the Voiceless

POET: The stick for feeling water
Crossed the Johannesburg stream
Today it has crossed the sea
To pave the way in Cape Town
At the top of the believers
Go on mysterious stick
Collect your sheep and lead them
These sheep were given to you
They were given to you by blacks
They were given to you by whites
They were given to you by ancestors
They were given to you by those above
Let the sheep graze
Take them from the kraals of oppression
Take them from the kraals of darkness
And lead them to green pastures
Lead them to pastures of freedom
Lead them to spiritual pastures
Where they'll feed
with no consideration of colour
Then the msimbithi stick
Will become the stick of redemption

CHOIR: Sing, here is the msimbithi stick
Sing the song of redemption
HalalaHalalaHalalaHalalaHalala

Prologue

It is October 18th, 1984. While in America Bishop Desmond Tutu has learnt that he has been awarded the Nobel Peace Prize. He flies back to Johannesburg to be with his family, friends and colleagues. The mood is jubilant. People of all races sing, dance, laugh, cry and embrace one another in joy. The Bishop stands and leads them in an African hymn; then he speaks. He is, he says, merely 'a little focus' of the stalwarts of the struggle for freedom. He thanks God for those who have gone into exile, those who have been banned or detained without trial, those who have died. This award is for them and for all the people who suffer daily under apartheid:

This award is for you – Mothers, who sit near railway stations trying to eke out an existence, selling potatoes, selling meali, selling pigs' trotters.

This award is for you – Fathers, sitting in a single-sex hostel, separated from your children for eleven months of the year.

This award is for you – Mothers in the squatter camps, whose shelters are destroyed callously every day and who have to sit on soaking mattresses in the winter rain, holding whimpering babies and whose crime in this country is that you want to be with your husbands.

This award is for you – three and a half million of our people who have been uprooted and dumped as if they were rubbish. The world says we recognise you, we recognise that you are people who love peace.

This award is for you – dear children, who despite receiving a poisonous gruel, designed to make you believe that you are inferior, have said 'there is something that God put into us which will not be manipulated by man, which tells us that we are your children.' This award is for you – and I am proud to accept it on your behalf as you spurn a travesty of an education.

This award is for you, who down the ages have said we seek to change this evil system peacefully. The world recognises that we are agents of peace, of reconciliation, of love, of justice, of caring, of compassion. I have the great honour of receiving this award on your behalf. It is our prize. It is not Desmond Tutu's prize. The world recognises that and thank God that our God is God. Thank God that our God is in charge.

17

With these words, Desmond Tutu is, as always, identifying himself firmly with the oppressed people of South Africa, the 'non-whites', for years victims of a regime which has legislated the subservience of the many to the few, a people whose peaceful resistance has been continually countered by yet more repression, for the most part a people who, astonishingly, remain loving in a world of hate and fear. In accepting this award, he has stepped decisively on to the world stage – a black South African, a Christian, a reconciler, a fearless critic of apartheid, who has become a spokesman for his people, a voice of the voiceless.

Desmond Tutu's rise from his birth and childhood in the barren black townships of the Transvaal to international spokesman for his countrymen and holder of the highest Anglican office in South Africa, Archbishop of Cape Town, was against all the odds. In any success story there is an element of luck and Tutu constantly admits his debt to the people he was fortunate enough to meet, but it takes more than luck and kindness to turn a small black boy into an Archbishop. The road from township to Bishop's Palace is paved by more than good intentions.

The extraordinary attempts to discredit him made by the South African Broadcasting Corporation, much of the white press and even the government itself, have made it hard to know the man himself, difficult to discern the true from the false. Many of the judgments made of him are based on ignorance and misinformation. Is he pastor or self-publicist, churchman or politician, reconciler or rabble-rouser, peace-maker or agitator?

He is a man of many layers; his small frame embraces many contradictory tensions. He has a deep need to be loved, yet he inspires as much hate as any man could tolerate. Very much his own man, he is also a man of the people, all too familiar with the humiliation of living in an apartheid society and still as at home with the youth of Soweto as with the dignitaries with whom he now associates. His desire for peace is matched by such indignation at the injustice of apartheid that his remarks – outspoken, articulate, witty, courageous and sometimes naïve in their spontaneity – fuel flames of outrage. Though he was slow to take an active part in the maze of South African politics, since becoming Dean of Johannesburg in 1975 he has shown, in both words and deeds, that religion and politics cannot be separated. If his attempts to stand above division and to reconcile opposing parties have left him isolated and subject to criticism from all sides, so too has it given him a freedom to speak what he feels is God's will. For above all he is a man with a deep spiritual life, whose conviction stems from long hours of prayer and meditation.

Prologue

Though he now has the ear of Presidents and Prime Ministers, though he is so well-known a symbol of his country that a New York cab-driver talking to a journalist on his way to South Africa simply reacted by saying 'Ah yes – Tutu', he is a son of the soil of Africa and it is in the dusty ghettos of Johannesburg that his story must begin.

I

'Hertzog is my shepherd'

Black children born into the South Africa of the thirties did not think it strange that they lived in corrugated-iron shacks while whites sunned themselves in the pleasant gardens of rich homes; they did not wonder why there were places they could not go, even seats on which they could not sit; they were humiliated, but not surprised, when their middle-aged parents were addressed as 'Boy' and 'Girl'; they took it for granted that they walked on dirt tracks in unlit streets, that there was no sewage or electricity, that they were lucky if they were not hungry. That was how God had made the world – there were the 'haves' and the 'have-nots', and whether you were one or the other was determined by the colour of your skin.

Racial discrimination had not yet been fully enshrined into the apartheid laws, so life for blacks then was marginally more tolerable than it was to become. That whites were superior to blacks was, however, quite simply an accepted fact of life. Whites assumed that they should rule, that they should enjoy the riches of the land and that the blacks were there to serve their white masters and then become invisible as quickly as possible.

In 1925 the Prime Minister, General Hertzog, made a speech in the Orange Free State outlining his political programme. Segregation, he said, would protect 'civilised labour' – that is, white and 'coloured' (mixed race) – from 'uncivilised labour', the cheap labour of blacks. He proceeded to implement these ideas in a series of laws which became known as the 'Hertzog Bills'; their effect was encapsulated in a parody of the 23rd Psalm by an African poet:[1]

> Hertzog is my shepherd; I am in want.
> He maketh me to lie down on park benches,
> He leadeth me beside still factories,
> He arouseth my doubt of his intention.
> He leadeth me in the path of destruction for his Party's sake.
> Yea, I walk in the valley of the shadow of destruction
> And I fear evil, for thou art with me.
> The Politicians and the Profiteers, they frighten me;
> Thou preparest a reduction in my salary before me

In the Presence of mine enemies.
Thou anointest mine income with taxes,
My expense runneth over.
Surely unemployment and poverty will follow me
All the days of this Administration,
And I shall dwell in a mortgaged house for ever.

It was into this world that, on October 7th, 1931, Desmond Mpilo Tutu was born. His father, Zachariah, had profited from a Mission School education and was at the time Headmaster of the Methodist Primary School in Klerksdorp, a small town in the Western Transvaal. Many people remember Zachariah as a tall, thin, gaunt man – proud and impressive, very concerned that his children should be healthy and properly educated; a few knew that he sometimes drank too much and would then treat his wife in a way that deeply upset the young Desmond. Aletha Matlhare was a domestic servant, only educated to primary school level and a gentle woman who had a deep and lasting effect on Desmond. She became known as 'Komotso', 'the comforter of the afflicted', as she always took the side of whoever she felt was being worsted in an argument, whether they were right or wrong. Their children were all given both European and African names, a common practice in those days when the influence of the missions was still strong, the European name being a concession to their Christian background. The eldest was Sylvia Funeka, then there was another girl who died young, Desmond Mpilo was next and finally Gloria Lindiwe, the youngest.

Zachariah was a Fingo, one of the Xhosa tribes from the Eastern Cape, Aletha a Motswana and Aletha's mother, Kuku, a Mosotho. So from an early age Desmond and his sisters spoke Xhosa, Tswana and Sotho. Were they, then, Xhosa or Motswana? Like many urban blacks they did not know or very much mind, though sometimes Zachariah would tease Aletha for being a Motswana. It is the Nationalist government who tried (and still tries) to force ethnicity upon the blacks; tribal origin was not interesting or important to the Tutus; certainly it was not considered a divisive matter. They were *Africans*, more precisely *South Africans*, and that was where their national pride lay.

But being black in South Africa is no way to be confident of your identity. One of the worst things about racial discrimination is that, as Desmond Tutu was to say years later,[2]

You are brainwashed into an acquiescence in your oppression and exploitation. You come to believe what others have determined about you, filling you with self-disgust, self-contempt and self-hatred, accepting a negative self-image ... and you need a lot of grace to have that

22

demon of self-hatred exorcised, when you accept that only white races really matter and you allow the white person to set your standards and provide your role models.

These black boys, shunted off to live in dusty ghettos, rejoiced in anything which affirmed their humanity, which proved that blacks can succeed. So it is not hard to share Desmond's delight when one day he picked up a tattered copy of the American magazine *Ebony* and read about the exploits of an American black, Jackie Robinson, who had broken into major league baseball. Desmond 'didn't know baseball from pingpong' but he vividly remembers his pride in this fellow black's achievement:[3]

> I grew inches that day and I puffed out my chest, even though I was alone lolling against a wall, as I drank in what was like nectar from the Gods – this account of how my soul brothers and sisters were making it against untold odds those many thousands of miles across the seas . . . They were black like me, like us and here they were achieving against tremendous odds.

So he and his friends were agog to learn of the victories of Jesse Owens at the 1936 Olympics – victories which took place before the eyes of no less a racist than Adolf Hitler himself; they listened with wildly beating hearts to the music of Nat King Cole, Louis Armstrong, Fats Waller and Marion Anderson; they were dazzled by the dancing of the Mills Brothers and intoxicated by the zoot-suits introduced into the black townships by the all-black musical *Stormy Weather*.[4]

> I don't suppose one made the connection explicitly, but deep down in our psyches the gnawing self-doubt, the self-hatred, that insidious poison was being drained out of our systems and we were being prepared to accept the exhilarating obligations of being free responsible persons.

When Desmond was about eight years old, Zachariah was transferred to Ventersdorp, to a school of Africans, so-called 'coloureds' and Indians, who lived in town in the white areas. Desmond was a pupil there, and this mixture (later to be lost in favour of segregation not only between black and white, but between all the different racial groups) did not seem strange to him or his friends: 'Nobody then thought it was a potent or explosive mixture, nor curious that Indians should live cheek by jowl with whites. The heavens did not seem to have fallen in.'[5] Nevertheless, here Desmond met racial discrimination. The black community spoke Setswana and Afrikaans, so he learned the language hated by blacks as 'the language of the oppressor' and was able to understand the white boys taunting him as he cycled into town to buy his father a newspaper. They jeered '*Pik*' as he passed, to which he, thinking they were referring to the garden implement would, when at a safe distance, retort with schoolboy humour, '*Jou graaf*' (You're a spade). Only later did he realise that they were deriding him for being 'Pitch black'.

Looking back from the 1980s, when relations between black and white had deteriorated even further, Tutu finds it incredible that he was able to spread his copy of the *Star* or the *Rand Daily Mail* on the pavement and kneel to read it. 'Nobody walked over the pavement or jostled me.'[6] He recalls too, that whereas today most black soldiers are thought to be traitors to the liberation struggle, during the Second World War they were regarded as heroes by their fellow blacks. It was a matter of great pride if someone in the family wore a uniform; indeed his own uncle was a sergeant in the Union Defence Force. Like small boys anywhere, he and his friends enjoyed playing soldiers and would rush to the side of the road to wave ecstatically to the troops going 'up North'. They did not know that many Afrikaners were opposed to South Africans joining the war effort; they did not mind that black soldiers were not trusted with guns, but faced the might of Rommel's Afrika Corps armed only with assegais.

What Desmond did mind was seeing his father humiliated. Sometimes when walking together they would be stopped and Zachariah would be asked to produce his 'passbook', that divisive and hated document which every 'non-white' was forced to carry and to produce on demand. If they could not, they faced heavy fines, imprisonment, being sent to badly paid work, or forcible removal to one of the poverty stricken 'tribal areas' officially reserved for blacks. The passbook (which with typical humour the blacks called the '*Dompas*' – the 'Stupid pass') was the key to racial segregation and economic exploitation; it controlled every movement black people made outside the reserves or the locations. It was the badge of division as surely as was the Star of David the Jews had to wear in Nazi Germany.

As he saw more of the white areas, Desmond came across other things he could not understand. He was used to the children from the black locations scavenging for food, but sometimes he would go to town during school hours and see black children picking out fresh fruit and sandwiches from the dustbins of the white schools. The white children, it turned out, had more than they needed and preferred the lunches their mothers had prepared for them to the school meals provided by the government. Despite the desperate need of the black children, there was no school-feeding for them; it had been stopped by Dr Verwoerd because the government decided that since they could not feed all black children they would feed none at all.

Occasionally, too, Desmond wondered at some of the things they were taught at school. Certainly the students were not at all politicised. In fact, Desmond feels they were thoroughly unsophisticated and naïve, hardly questioning what appeared to be the divine ordering of their segregated society. But even they were disturbed by one of their history textbooks, written by a Methodist missionary:[7]

> We found it distinctly odd that in virtually every encounter between the black Xhosa and the white settlers, Mr Whitehead invariably described the Xhosas as those who *stole* the settlers' cattle and of the settlers he would write that the settlers *captured* the cattle from the Xhosa. We did not press the point at all, or hardly at all, in class discussion; but when we were outside we would mutter that it was very funny. It certainly seemed to be stretching coincidence to breaking point. We often remarked that after all, these farmers had no cattle when they landed in South Africa, and all the cattle had to be procured from the indigenous peoples.

For the most part, Desmond was fortunate in his early contacts with whites. There was, for instance, the Greek who ran the only café in town and who always gave him sweets; but he was to make more significant friendships in his early teens, when Zachariah's job took him to another town in the Western Transvaal, Roodepoort.

Roodepoort location was a slum area, the houses separated by dirty, dusty lanes and the air filled with the stench of overflowing night soil buckets. Here Desmond's mother worked at Ezenzeleni Blind School, the first school for black blind people, which had been founded by the Reverend Arthur Blaxall and his wife. Forty five years later Arthur Blaxall still remembers a man called Radcliffe, blind, deaf and dumb, whom Mrs Blaxall, entering with incredible patience into his dark, silent world, taught to be more independent than anyone would have thought possible. Through her Radcliffe learnt to read and write English in Braille, to 'listen' to speech and music by placing his fingers where he could sense the vibrations, even to walk from his hostel to the Blaxalls' home. Young as he was, Desmond was deeply moved by her dedication; when she was an old lady he wrote to her:[8]

> I can still see Radcliffe, who was born blind, deaf and dumb, standing by the piano with a pipe in his mouth, stamping away with his foot to the rhythm that was coming from the piano. Or even seeing him dancing with you at some of the socials that we used to have. Or enjoying the music of a guitar and knowing that it had taken you many, many, many months of patient teaching to get him out of himself so that he could 'hear' the rhythm that went through the pulsations that went through

his fingers. And that you had helped him to become human whereas in normal African circumstances with that degree of handicap he would have been reduced to a twilight existence.

Mrs Blaxall had not only given meaning to Radcliffe's life, she had done something to ease the resentment black people felt for whites. Desmond's letter ends:

> We cannot compute your influence. Knowing you has made it virtually impossible, I think, for people to be embittered because of how they were treated in this country, because they would recall how you had treated them as if they were what they knew themselves to be, human beings made in the image of God. And so your contribution to this country is immeasurable. And thank you very much, Nomsa ['Mother of people'].

More significant still was a meeting that has become part of South African folk history. One day, in the early 1940s, Desmond was with his mother at Ezenzeleni when a white man wearing a cassock and a huge black hat passed them. As he passed, he raised his hat to Mrs Tutu in greeting. Desmond was overwhelmed. He simply couldn't believe it – a white man raising his hat to a simple black labouring woman. The white man was Bishop Trevor Huddleston, then a parish priest in the black Johannesburg location Sophiatown, who was to make such a massive contribution to the struggle for justice in South Africa.

In 1943, when Desmond was twelve, the Tutus moved yet again, this time to Munsieville, the black location in Krugersdorp. It was as sordid and run-down as most of the locations, its houses row upon row of identical boxes, but it had a certain vitality, was smaller than many of the townships, and people were fond of it. Being one of the original locations – black people had been living there since 1910 – it was nearer to the white areas than those built later, when black areas were designed to be out of sight of white eyes, so the Tutus led a less segregated life geographically and there was at least some relationship between blacks and whites.

The five of them lived in a typically crowded house. They had three rooms – Desmond's bedroom doubled as a sitting room and a dining room – there was no electricity, no sewage, and the dirt street in front of the house had rocky outcrops. Desmond's younger sister lives there now and it is still, forty years later, in the same deplorable condition. But they did have running water and a bathroom and Aletha was a skilful housewife; visitors remember it as a very sweet home, where they always received a warm welcome. In true African style, the Tutus shared what they had. Zachariah would always notice if one of his pupils was late for school because he had so far to walk and would

26

take him in to live with his family; many boys were rescued by the Tutus in this way.

Though the Tutus were better off than most, times were often hard. Desmond used to go to the white suburbs to collect and return laundry for his mother to wash; she would be paid two shillings, a princely sum, which went a long way in those days. Indeed, during the school holidays, when Zachariah was not working, it had to cover all their needs. They usually spent Christmas holidays with Aletha's mother Kuku, in Boksburg, where Zachariah would work in a bottle store as a delivery boy. Kuku was still taking in washing and the children would wait for her to return with the bread she had saved from the lunch her white 'madam' had given her. Sometimes there would be marmalade as well, but this strange jam, both sweet and bitter, was not popular.

Desmond remembers his childhood as quite a happy time. He was loved – and probably rather spoilt – by his sisters and, though there was no money to spare, fun was derived from very simple things. Nobody had toys, but when the house was being cleaned they would put all the chairs on to the stoep and soon they would become a train; they would make cars out of odd pieces of wire and play football with an old tennis ball. To earn a bit of pocket money Desmond would walk three miles to the market with his friend Joe Sibiya; they would bring back bags of oranges and sell them at a small profit. Later he sold peanuts at suburban railway stations and caddied at the Killarney golf course in Johannesburg. There was one occasion when another close friend, Stanley Motjuwadi (who later became editor of the African magazine *Drum*) found him 'bawling in the clutches of a towering cop who had mistaken him for a waif';[9] but for the most part he enjoyed these early money-making adventures and was quite a good businessman. He also joined the scouts, once walking nearly eight miles from Munsieville to Stirkfontein and earning both his 'Tenderfoot' and 'Second Class' badges; he was even awarded a Proficiency Badge in cooking.

One morning in 1945 a scrawny, spindly legged Desmond, wearing shorts but no shoes, reported for his first day at Western High, the government secondary school in the old Western Native Township, near Sophiatown. Black children had to go to different areas for different levels of education; at the time Western High was the only High School on the entire West Rand, serving several townships. It was a large school and pretty rough. There were about sixty pupils to a class and not enough desks to go round; in fact, for the first six months the younger children had to write on their laps or kneeling on the floor. However, under the headship of Mr Madibane, the doyen of black educationalists and a great Anglican churchman, it had become famous, turning out many black leaders and becoming known as 'Madibane High'.

Classes lasted from 8.30 a.m. until 5 p.m. Being a school for blacks, there were no school meals, but the children were given sixpence by their parents with which to find their own lunch and tea. Stanley and Desmond used to go to the soda fountain in Main Street, Sophiatown, and buy roasted peanuts, a slice of bread covered with fish crumbs and a glass of flavoured water. That cost them threepence, a 'tickey'; the other tickey went on a 'fat cake', which resembles a doughnut and which Desmond still enjoys, for the afternoon break.

Like any township urchin (as Desmond refers to himself in those days), the acquisition and spending of pocket money was a continuing challenge in their life of poverty. Stanley and Desmond used to travel the fifteen miles to school together on the train, where they became famous as card sharps. As Stanley explains:[10]

> We would take on workers commuting with us and never lost. A deft scratching of the heart was a hint to Des to call hearts. A scooping with the open hand was spades, and three outstretched fingers meant clubs. According to strict ethics this was cheating, but deprived boys have to survive, was our logic then. The workers we were fleecing did not seem to mind it. In fact they admired Des' prowess and nicknamed him 'Professor'.

Once a month, when Desmond's father gave him some money, they bought themselves a pack of fifty cigarettes, which soon disappeared. It was Desmond who discovered that by buying tobacco and papers and making 'zolls', they could smoke for the whole month.

Desmond was hard-working and bright, but he was not good at arithmetic, in fact failing arithmetic nearly prevented him passing Standard Six and qualifying for his first-year Junior Certificate. However, 'The Shark', as Mr Madibane was known to his pupils, did not live up to his nickname and allowed Desmond to move up. His trust was justified, for in the first half-yearly exams Desmond came top, on aggregate, of all 250 pupils in Form 1. In the next form there were desks, but Desmond, Stanley and another boy all had to share a desk meant for two. Desmond, being left-handed, somehow managed to sit crab-like, occupying three-quarters of the space and squeezing the other two to the end. This led to endless fights between the two friends and to Stanley dubbing him a 'selfish southpaw'.

That Desmond was unusually intelligent was willingly accepted by his contemporaries. Joe Sibiya recalls the speed of his thought: 'He was streets ahead of me. We would read something together and he would apply it in all sorts of ways. I couldn't follow him. I hobbled along, it was so strenuous trying to keep up with him.' Joe was also impressed at the way he would take nothing for granted: 'Let's read this verse,' he would say, 'and see what it really means.' His photographic memory enabled him to answer a classmate's question with 'Your answer is on page 179 of Duggan, three lines from the top of the page.'[11] And already his sense of humour was evident. For instance he was once asked by the zoology master for a definition of heredity. 'It is when your son looks like your neighbour or your best friend,' he retorted.[12] On another occasion he delighted a physical training instructor, more remarkable for his bulk than his brains, by telling him about what he called 'Einstein's Law of Common Sense' – that when a body is immersed in liquid it experiences an apparent loss of weight.

Though in many ways Desmond was an ordinary, if exceptionally gifted, township boy – 'no angel' according to Stanley, and not above taunting white officials on the trains – he was already showing impressive moral courage. Joe Sibiya remembers him as 'a very honest guy who used to put us to shame. For instance if we went off to rob a peach tree he wouldn't come.' He was slow to anger, would not harbour grudges and would rather discuss than engage in fisticuffs. He has inherited his mother's gentle, caring temperament and would have nothing to do with anything that hurt others; when his friends joked and laughed at one another Desmond would say they should laugh *with* them, not *at* them. It has been suggested that his unwillingness to take part in the fights that were an inevitable part of township life could have been because he was physically frail – his grandmother gave him the name 'Mpilo', meaning life, as he was not a strong baby – but from the impression he made on his contemporaries it is hard to believe that, had he been the toughest boy in class, he would ever have been an aggressive child.

When Desmond was fourteen – though according to Father Huddleston he was so small he looked about twelve – his studies were interrupted for nearly two years by a serious illness. At the time he was staying at a new hostel run by the Fathers of the Community of the Resurrection in Sophiatown, as commuting from Munsieville was proving too expensive. (Even finding the fare home for weekends was often difficult; when there was no cash for him, he would walk into town and collect the two shillings his mother earned from her white 'madam'.) He hadn't been eating well, but that had not seemed particularly unusual, as the students in the hostel prepared their own food, tending to live on a diet of fish and chips and bread. However, one day Desmond was driving through Sophiatown with one of the Fathers, when he had a very bad headache and needed to sit by the window to breathe. He was taken to Rietfontein Hospital, where tuberculosis was diagnosed. He was there for twenty months, receiving the treatment usually given in those days, pneumothorax. At regular intervals air was introduced into the pleural cavity in the chest, allowing the lung to collapse; Desmond describes it as rather like immobilising a broken arm by putting it in plaster. At the same time he was given a new drug, PAS, which killed off the tubercular organisms.

It was an unpleasant treatment and Rietfontein Hospital, a state-run TB sanatorium, was a depressing place, full of burnt-out cases of TB and syphilis, but for Desmond this illness turned out to be a cloud with several silver linings.

First, it was in hospital that his lifelong friendship with Father Huddleston developed. Every week, for all those eighty odd weeks, he would visit Desmond, not in any official capacity – he was not the hospital chaplain – but because they took such pleasure in each other's company. Father Huddleston found Desmond quite exceptionally bright, interested in everything and a marvellously optimistic patient. He in turn was the greatest single influence in the life of the young Desmond, who still wonders at Father Huddleston's pastoral care and love: 'Who was I? – just another black boy – that he should visit me.'

Though he was a cheerful patient, never sliding into depression, the one thing that really distressed Desmond was the fear that he might drop behind at school; it was a particularly bad time for him, as he was due to take his first public exam, the Junior Certificate. He was always anxious to know what he was missing, so Father Huddleston brought books – *Treasure Island*, *Oliver Twist*, whatever they were currently reading in class and more besides – while Stanley, apart from keeping him abreast with what was happening in the world of sport, would bring his school notes. Zachariah had always encouraged Desmond to read and he had a huge collection of comics – *Superman*, *Batman*, whatever he could get hold of – which were the rather surprising source of his love of English. In hospital he had time to read prodigiously, so far from falling behind, though admittedly he missed his Junior Certificate, Desmond became the best-read pupil at the school.

It was in hospital, too, that Desmond's Christianity became firmly embedded. The Tutus were a devout Christian family, more concerned with the essential message than with any particular denomination. Zachariah's father had been a minister of the Ethiopian Church of South Africa, Desmond was baptised a Methodist, while they were living at Ventersdorp they followed Sylvia's lead into the African Methodist Episcopal Church, then finally, in 1943, they all became

Anglicans. He even had a spell with an Independent African Church, as a relative of his father's was a minister of an obscure sect. Desmond used to carry the banner round Roodepoort location singing '*Simon Peter, Ndicedise*' – 'Simon Peter, help me', becoming known by the location children as 'Simon Peter's son'. His ecumenism started early.

In hospital everything seemed to come together. The devout background was there, the long weeks lying still gave time for reflection and Father Huddleston acted as the catalyst. Desmond did not then understand the white priest's political views, but was convinced that everything he did stemmed from his prayers and his faith:[13]

> He was full of laughter and caring. He made you feel special. He was a wonderful man (he is a wonderful man), a white man who made you feel you mattered. And he was so genuine, caring passionately about his parishioners in Sophiatown. His white cassock became grubby quickly as he walked around its streets, because he attracted children so naturally and they all wanted to grab him crying all the while, 'Hello Fada, hello Fada'. At one time his office would be filled with urchins playing marbles on the floor and the very next moment it held some very important personage, an ambassador or an influential businessman.

So in hospital he made a great friend, he laid the foundation on which his wide-ranging knowledge was to be built and he found a faith which quite surprised him by its intensity. He remembers on one occasion when he was very ill, haemorrhaging badly and coughing up a lot of blood, being overcome by a profound sense of calm and saying to God, 'Well, if I have to die – okay.' His Christianity had moved from outward observance to the depths of his soul.

When he left hospital he began the disciplined spiritual life that was to intensify as the years went by. He made his 'first really good confession' to Father Huddleston in the Church of Christ the King in Sophiatown; he became a server at his parish church of St Paul's in Munsieville – later training other boys to be servers; he would often, to the surprise of his friends, slip quietly off to church and pray for an hour at a time.

If Father Huddleston was the greatest single influence in Desmond's life, there were many others and he never tires of acknowledging his debt to them. While the Tutus were attending the African Methodist Episcopal Church, Desmond was very impressed by Pastor Makhene, a very gentle man with a quiet authority that nobody ever thought to challenge. Desmond, aged about eight at the time, felt very flattered that he was allowed to play with the Makhene teenage children and loved being in their calm, peaceful home. Then there was Father Sekgaphane, an African priest who, after a long and serious interview, admitted the Tutus to the Anglican Church. He never scolded the boys, he too was a gentle man – Desmond is always impressed by gentleness – and the boys sometimes accompanied him to 'outstations'. 'At the end of the service people would be dancing attendance on him, ushering him into a private room to eat the special meals they had prepared and leaving us nonentities outside. But he would never sit down to eat until he was sure that we had been fed.'[14] That simple action left an indelible impression on at least one of the boys. 'Maybe at the back of my mind I was saying "I'd like to be like him".'

At Ventersdorp there were the Blaxalls, whose names, says Desmond, 'should be inscribed in letters of gold when a proper history of South Africa is written'[15] and Ezekiel Mphahlele, who was to become a well-known writer and a Professor at the University of the Witwatersrand. He was then a clerk and driver to Arthur Blaxall, quietly studying for a degree in his spare time and becoming the first person of any race to obtain an MA in English with distinction at UNISA, the University of South Africa. Desmond feels that Mphahlele too probably owes much to the Blaxalls. Ezekiel encouraged the children to read, telling them 'to make a book your friend'; he also encouraged Desmond in physical activities. He had taken up running and physical training to overcome a physical ailment and Desmond, admiring his grit and determination, used to join him on long runs. In order to give Desmond more confidence to face up to the township bullies, Ezekiel also taught Desmond boxing.

When Desmond came out of hospital he was for a while isolated in his parents' bedroom and his friends had to talk to him through the window – Joe Sibiya was mystified at Aletha's wrath when she once found them sharing an orange. But eventually, apart from an atrophied right hand, he seemed to return to normal health. Certainly he had plenty of energy and would join in anything that was going. 'Find children playing ball – he'd join them. Find children playing hide and seek – he'd be there,' recalls Sally Motlana, to whom he was like a brother. He loved everybody, even the thugs, the 'tsotsis'; the younger boys, no doubt sensing this, would 'follow him round like little puppies'. His leadership qualities were beginning to show.

Back at school he was very put out to find he had fallen behind Stanley. Again 'The Shark' had pity on him and allowed him to join the 'Matric' class; again he was justified as Desmond continued to come top of his class. At the end of 1950, once more commuting from Munsieville and studying long hours after dark by candlelight, he passed the Joint Matriculation Board of the University of South Africa; his subjects were English, Afrikaans, Mathematics, Zoology, History and Zulu. His schooldays were over. Now he had to decide what to do.

2

Forbidden pastures

While Desmond was in his last two years at school the political face of South Africa was changing; life for the blacks was to become worse, far worse.

In 1948, at a time when racial segregation was being challenged by the United Nations and in America the black voice was beginning to be heard, in South Africa the National Party won the General Election by promising apartheid to the white electorate. Apartheid, the Afrikaans word for 'apartness', was explicitly designed to preserve white supremacy or *baaskap* (boss-ship) by separating blacks from whites in every sphere of life. It aimed to produce a black community with no rights, no political power, no defence; it extinguished any possibility of black majority rule. The white government was mortally afraid of African unity and, taking refuge in the policy of 'divide and rule', they sought to keep the huge majority of Africans, estimated at the time at 8½ million (not to mention 1 million 'coloureds' and ½ million Indians), under the control of about 2½ million whites.[1]

The apartheid system gave the existing racial segregation the support and protection of the law, backed up by police powers of imprisonment and arrest. The first legislation to be drafted was the Prohibition of Mixed Marriages Act. Marriage between white and black had been banned since 1923; this was now extended to include marriage between whites and 'coloureds' or Indians. A year later the Immorality Act was passed, making illegal any form of sexual contact between whites and 'non-whites'.

Though these laws led to countless individual tragedies – there were over 10,000 convictions under the Immorality Act before it was repealed in 1986 – their national significance was slight in comparison with another piece of legislation passed in 1950, the Population Registration Act, in which every individual South African was classified by race – white, 'coloured', Indian or Native, as the majority community was called at the time. (At various times the black population have been referred to as Kaffirs, a word which means 'heathen', though many were in fact Christians; Natives, a claim the whites were anxious to disprove; and Bantu, an African word for people. The renaming of the Department of Bantu Affairs as the Department of Plural Affairs opened the door to endless ridicule from blacks. Desmond still jokes that presumably a black from the country is 'a rural Plural' and there was even a suggestion that a primitive drawing might be 'a rural Plural's mural'. Except when deliberately insulted, they are now generally referred to as blacks, and are content to be so-called.)

Whites, despite consisting of a mixed bag of Dutch, English, Portuguese, French, Germans, Greeks and others, were regarded as one unit, as were Indians; but Africans were split into linguistically based 'national units', regardless of whether they even knew the language of the group into which they were put. This cold-blooded division of people was carried out with far less feeling than the botanist Linnaeus showed for the classification of plants. Skin colour in South Africa varies from the richest black to 'European' white, with an infinity of shades in between. Nor can a definition always be confirmed by lips and hair; appearance alone was often not enough to determine ethnicity. Instructions as to where to look for the signs that would denote a particular race (fingernails, the whites of the eye) were issued to clerks in the government departments responsible and in cases of doubt crude tests were devised. Perhaps the most laughable and the most humiliating was 'the pencil in the hair' test. If the pencil stayed firmly in the tight curls, then the verdict was 'African'; if it fell through straighter locks, then it was 'coloured'. So families could be divided, sometimes with brothers and sisters being given different groupings, on the strength of the gravitational weight of a pencil.

Parliament was busy in 1950. In that same year it also passed the Group Areas Act, known by some as the Ghetto Act, by Prime Minister Dr Malan as 'The Kernel of Apartheid'. This Act created the machinery whereby racial segregation could be not only legally perpetuated, but extended. Every section of the population, as classified in the Population Registration Act, was allocated separate residential and trading areas. Traditional property rights were disregarded and commercial life was disrupted as thousands of blacks, 'coloureds' and Indians were uprooted; every 'non-white' was haunted with anxiety as they waited to hear if they would be moved, when it would happen and where they would be sent. This legislation was necessary, according to the Minister of the Interior, so that there should be the least possible contact between the various communities. It was, he was convinced, in the interests of the material, cultural and spiritual development of all races that the white man and Western civilisation should be supreme.

The African, says the policy of apartheid, must not be a burden to the white man; he is only allowed into the 'white' areas to work. So the system of 'reserves' became, in the Bantu Authorities Act of 1951, the basis of the bantustans – the 'homelands' or 'reserves'. There are ten bantustans, some, like Bophuthatswana, consisting of several different geographical areas separated by corridors of choice land allocated to whites. Here, in what Tutu calls 'these dumping grounds', irrespective of where they were born or spent their lives, is where blacks officially belong, where their only political rights are exercised and where they return if they fall sick, become redundant or grow old. The black community was being, in effect, retribalised under the aegis of the white rulers. An African writer compared this compartmentalisation to some racial Messiah let loose in London, 'shuffling the population according to their original tribal or clan groupings, putting English, Welsh, Irish, Scots, Jews into separate locations. Then further dividing the men of Sussex, Wessex and so on – or your Macdonalds, Mactavishes or Mac-what-nots . . .'[2]

It was in any case hardly a fair division of a vast, beautiful and rich country. The Africans, comprising about 73 per cent of the population, were allotted 13 per cent of the land; it was for the most part the poorest land, with no major towns or cities and generally lacking the natural resources with which South Africa is so abundantly blessed. There was hardly any work to be had in the homelands, but the inhabitants of the bantustans provided cheap labour for the mines, the white farms and industry. Often black people had (and still have) to travel miles every day, leaving home as early as 4 a.m. and returning late at night. They were, as this African writer clearly thought, being treated like animals:[3]

> Like game reserves, the Homelands have always been regarded as places where the African could be seen in his 'natural, unspoilt surroundings'. Like game reserves, 'strangers' may not be admitted without a permit and residents may not leave the reserve without a permit. Animals in game reserves cannot make decisions for themselves as they do not have the power of rational thinking. In the African reserves decisions about development are taken by the white government and their officials. All animals belong to a game reserve and the fact that they are sometimes brought out of the reserve for entertainment and other uses will never change their status. When the animals are no longer of use to humans outside the game reserve they have to be sent back to it – by force.

So how, in the increasingly restricted life of the 1950s, was Tutu going to earn his living? He was exceptionally intelligent, reasonably ambitious and one of the ½ per cent of black Africans who had qualified for university entrance by passing the examination of the

Joint Matriculation Board of the University of South Africa; it was natural that he should aspire to one of the top professions open to him. The peak of black aspirations at the time was to become a medical doctor, exemplified in Tutu's youth by Dr Xuma, who lived in Sophiatown and had been President of the African National Congress (ANC) while Tutu was an impressionable schoolboy. Dr Xuma was admired to the point of envy. He had a qualification no one could deny, he had studied in America, England and Europe and he could earn quite a respectable salary. With this example and with his own recent experience of illness, Tutu's first ambition was to become a doctor and to do research into TB. He gained a place at the Witwatersrand Medical School, but he could not get a bursary. There was no other source of finance, so that avenue was closed before he had even taken the first steps down it. He decided to follow in his father's footsteps and become a teacher, so in 1951 he went to the new government college outside Pretoria, the Bantu Normal College, to study for a Teacher's Diploma.

It was one of the first Bantu Education institutions, all the lecturers being appointed by the Nationalist government. The standard of teaching was quite good, but it was impossible to escape the persistent reminders of racial segregation. The students even had to live in rondavels – small round thatched huts – so that they should 'develop along their own lines'; conventional rectangular buildings were, as Desmond recalled years later, 'somehow harmful to our Bantu psyches'.[4] They endured endless insults, especially as the college was in white Pretoria. Stanley Motjuwadi, who went on to train as a teacher with Tutu, recalls how he was once going through a park when he saw some white boys sitting on the grass and realised he would have to pass them. Instinctively he scented trouble and was prepared to sprint off. As he neared the group one of them stood up and threw a stone at him, so he started running. A second stone was on its way when the white boy's friend stopped him. Was there, perhaps, a civilised white boy in the park? There was not. As Stanley ran, he heard the boy say, in Afrikaans, 'What the hell, why do you dirty that stone?' Another incident shows black wit in the face of white boorishness. A friend of Tutu's was walking along Paul Kruger Street, the main street in Pretoria, when he saw three burly Afrikaners coming towards him. 'I don't give way to monkeys,' said one of them, pushing his way through. The black boy let him pass, bowing gracefully and saying, 'I usually do.'

Racial prejudice even found its way into the classroom. There was a biology lecturer who showed the students a specimen of human skin under a microscope. One of the boys enquired about the spots he could see on the enlarged fragment. 'Never mind about them,' he was told, 'the skin comes from a native I killed in the bush. I tried to wash it off in acid, but it wouldn't go white.' Another occasion Desmond remembers was during the oral examination for his Finals, when the examiner pointed to some ink that had been spilled on a desk and said scornfully, '*Kaffirwerk*'.

The students do not seem to have minded this loutish behaviour too much – they were used to it, brought up to it, they had never known anything else. But Tutu's tolerance was stretched when a black priest, Canon John Tsebe, was at the receiving end of this sort of treatment. It was at a meeting of the college debating society at which Tutu, as chairman of the society, had invited Father Trevor Huddleston to speak. After the address – on the relevance of religion to the problems of everyday life – the Afrikaner Principal, a member of the Dutch Reformed Church (DRC), asked Father Huddleston to his house for a cup of tea. Huddleston's request that he might bring an African priest with him was greeted with embarrassed silence and the three men walked across the veld to the Principal's house, where Father Huddleston was entertained in the sitting room, while Canon Tsebe was shown into the office. Huddleston recalls: 'We all had tea – was it from the same pot? – and were treated courteously, but separately. Only the light of the moon and the sounds of the veld we shared as South Africans that night.'[5]

Tutu, like most of his friends and contemporaries, was not politicised and did not think in terms of boycotts or strikes, or even of peaceful demonstrations, but he was deeply aware of the unjust society in which they lived. Iron was beginning to enter the souls of these black students. When they listened to the news and heard that, for instance, a white had been killed in a car accident, the whole place would erupt as they cheered and shouted 'One oppressor less'. Desmond remembers even then feeling that this degree of bitterness, in people who were going to become teachers and mould the minds of children, was very frightening.

In 1954 Tutu passed the Transvaal Bantu Teacher's Diploma and taught for a year at his old school, Madibane High, living with his parents and commuting from Krugersdorp, as in his High School days. He used the time on the train to mark students' essays, leaving the evenings free to study for a postal degree. The following year, he obtained his BA from the University of South Africa; his subjects were Zulu, Sociology, English, History of Education, Biology and History.

Again he was fortunate in the people he met – maybe something in him drew these people to him. He was helped in his studies by one of the great South Africans who were active in the non-violent protest campaigns of the 1950s – Robert Mangaliso Sobukwe. Sobukwe, who a few years later was to become the first President of the Pan-Africanist Congress (PAC) and whose declared aim was government 'of the African, by the African, for the African', was the first major political figure that Desmond came to know personally. Sobukwe was someone to whom students often turned and though Tutu did not join in his political activities, the qualities he admired in 'The Prof', as Sobukwe was known at the University of the Witwatersrand, give a clue as to the way he himself was developing:[6]

> He had an outstanding intellect and yet walked with the humblest, who felt at home in his company. He was too great to have a base or mean thought, and so quite amazingly he was untouched by bitterness, despite the unjust and cruel experiences he underwent for what he believed with all the fibre of his being. Even his most determined opponents had to admit that his was an attractive and magnetic personality. All who met him fell under the spell of his irresistible smile and charm. Even the Security Police ate out of his hand. They could not help it. He had the gentleness of a dove and yet he had the unshaken firmness of the person of principle.

On July 2nd, 1955, Desmond Tutu, with a year's teaching experience and a BA behind him, was married. His bride was Leah Shenxane, who had been one of his father's brightest pupils. She lived with one of her elder brothers in a rented backyard in Munsieville, while their mother worked as a domestic servant in Springs. Leah was a close friend of Desmond's younger sister Gloria, so she had known the Tutu family for years and was frequently in and out of their home. As a giggling, noisy primary schoolgirl she had made no impression on the studious Desmond. 'He was a stuck-up Headmaster's son. All I could say to him was "Hi". I never got to talking to him as he was always hoity-toity, reading. I liked him the first time I saw him, but he was too stuck-up to notice.' By the time she was at teacher training college, a beautiful as well as a highly intelligent girl, he did, with Gloria's encouragement, notice her. It was not long before he asked her to marry him.

Despite the richness of their married life, despite over thirty years' close and happy reliance on this strong woman, it was not inevitable that Desmond should marry. The manner of his proposal shows that already he was drawn to a religious way of life. He made it clear to Leah that if she rejected him he would not ask anyone else; it was not a threat, he assured her, but he had been seriously contemplating joining the Community of the Resurrection (CR). He was to become even more deeply indebted to this admirable group of men, but already their influence, in particular that of Father Huddleston, was making an indelible mark on him.

However, any vocation he might have had was not put to the test; Leah accepted and they began to plan their wedding. Despite their poverty, African love of ritual and ceremony ensured that somehow it would be a great occasion. Desmond could not afford a new suit, so his sister Sylvia promised to buy him one; she was to bring it on the day of the wedding and there were some anxious moments when the celebrations were about to begin and there was no Sylvia, no wedding suit. She arrived with minutes to spare, to the relief of everyone, especially the best man, Stanley Motjuwadi, who having no suit of his own, was wearing Desmond's (which was too large, so had to have the sleeves tucked in) and would, presumably, have had to return it to the groom. African and European customs combined, with Leah in a white dress, bridesmaids, cars and a reception in the community hall together with the ritual slaughtering of beasts, without which no African ceremony would be complete.

After their marriage, Desmond changed jobs as well as status, and began teaching at Munsieville High School, newly built next to the Anglican school where his father was still Headmaster. There are many who remember being taught at primary level by the father, at High School by the son.

Teaching conditions at Munsieville High School were not easy. There were often as many as 60 to a class, with an age range from 14 to 27. This long span was because people would attend school for a year or two, then go out to work for a few years to earn some money – perhaps to support younger members of their families, perhaps to pay their own fees as there was no free education – then return to complete their education.

To say Tutu was a popular and successful teacher would be an understatement – he was a sensation. He was inspiring, even when teaching mathematics, a subject at which he had not himself excelled; he could keep order; he was loved; he fired his pupils with a new vision of life.

Three languages were used at Munsieville High School: English, Afrikaans and the appropriate mother tongue. Language has always been an emotive issue in South Africa. The pupils resented Afrikaans, the language of the oppressor; they even disliked their mother tongue, Xhosa, Tswana or Sotho, as Bantu education sought to force it on them, thereby excluding them from the mainstream of South African life; English was favoured, as on the whole the black students related better to the English, perceiving them as more liberal, more understanding, more subtle. But Tutu transcended these attitudes. For him language was a means of communication, a tool. If you have a number of tools at your disposal, why deprive yourself? He taught without prejudice, trying to encourage his pupils to use any language imaginatively and well. His Xhosa-speaking pupils were 'raving mad' over his classes, he even succeeded in arousing interest in Afrikaans classes, and his teaching of English remains to this day a bright memory in his pupils of thirty years ago.

Joe Seremane was one such pupil. As a student he won prizes in a student publication called *Young Opinion*, primarily for Englishspeaking students; once, talking about Charles Dickens, he so impressed a woman in charge of a book exhibition in Johannesburg that she called the white students together to listen to him. He still feels indebted to Tutu's inspiration:

> The dream I have is that when I retire I want to sit down and write. He planted in me that desire. I found through his teaching that it is through writing that you can make a contribution towards improving the lot of humanity. I owe that dream to Desmond, who fired me. People often say 'Oh Joe, you write so well' and I always respond 'It's not me, it's Desmond who taught me all those things.'

It was his ability to arouse interest that enabled Tutu to keep order. Where other teachers used a system of repetition and the rod, having to force the students to work, Tutu encouraged and inspired, so that they would work willingly and on their own. He never used corporal punishment or needed to. Though well aware of truancy and tricks and able to deal with them, when the boys teased and distracted the girls Tutu had only to say, 'Talk to them, tell them to go away, tell them we are working.'

An incident that took place when Tutu was teaching at Munsieville High School shows that he already possessed the courage that was to be tested so often in later life. Munsieville was a rough area, the gangsters tougher than anywhere else on the Reef, even in those days carrying guns. One day a group of them came to the school looking for girls. There was panic. The Headmaster hid in his office, the teachers locked the classroom doors and in Tutu's class the girls were crying, the boys rushing to secure their doors. Paying no attention to their cries of 'Don't go out, they'll kill you', Tutu threw open the door and confronted the gangsters, who were as surprised as the students were frightened. For a while he talked to them, eventually managing to take the gun. Soon the terrified pupils heard the sound of laughter as their teacher sent the gangsters packing.

He was more like a friend than a teacher to many of the pupils, who would often read in their spare time and discuss the books with him. Their affection was shown in their manner of address. His colourful rendering of *The Three Musketeers* of Dumas led to the nickname 'D'Artagnan'; he introduced them to the French Revolution with an insight that earned him the title 'Monsieur'; others, knowing that his pet name at home was 'Boy', called him *'Braboy'* – lovable boy, charming boy.

Like all good teachers, his influence went beyond the subjects that he taught; for instance in discussing Christopher Marlowe's *Faust*, he would reflect on the nature of ambition. Joe Seremane still remembers the soft, chilling tones of Tutu delivering Marlowe's lines when Faustus realises the commitment he has made – that he has given up his soul:

> Ah, Faustus, now hast thou but one bare hour to live,
> And then thou must be damned perpetually;
> Stand still you ever-moving spheres of heaven,
> That time may cease, and midnight never come . . .
> O lente, lente currite noctis equi:
> The stars stand still, time runs, the clock will strike,
> The devil will come, and Faustus must be damned.

The dramatic rendering and the quality of the thought that accompanied his teaching of the play had a permanent effect on Joe's attitude to ambition: 'Through that type of presentation he was telling us we should be masters of our aspirations and ambitions. Don't sell your soul for anything. Every time you have an ambition you've got to reflect seriously and see what the implications are for you and for society as a whole. You must not be self-centred.'

Tutu the teacher could control because he could inspire, he could pass on his vision of life because he was loved and respected. The total man was emerging in all his richness.

Desmond Tutu had barely begun teaching when the government struck again: On March 31st, 1955, the Bantu Education Act was implemented. It was the most deliberately vicious of all the legislation of the 1950s, seeking, as it did, to ensure that black people remained for ever in a position of servitude. The declared aim of the Act was to produce Africans who would aspire to nothing higher than 'certain forms of labour'.

That the Nationalist Government found such an Act necessary was a back-handed tribute to the mission schools. It is easy to criticise the missions as being an arm of Western imperialism, to claim that they invaded African soil armed with a Bible in one hand and a gun in the other; probably it has more truth than many Christians would wish to recognise. However, there is no doubting the contribution they made in the field of education.

It was the missions who started educating Africans in the 1850s. They erected the buildings, paid the teachers and supervised the running of the schools. After three-quarters of a century the State gave small Grants-in-Aid, inevitably tied to corresponding State control, but as late as 1945, when Tutu was a fourteen-year-old schoolboy, there were only 230 government schools against 4,360 mission schools. Even so, it was not enough, and the Africans struggled to contribute to their children's education themselves. Father Huddleston remembers how:[7]

> Empty garages, disused church halls, the backyards of private houses became private schools . . . Many times I have gone round to the school in Tucker Street, an old, crumbling red-brick chapel; its windows broken, its wooden floor curving and cracking under the weight of children sitting there, a hundred, two hundred perhaps, their slates in their hands, no desks, no benches, no blackboards, no books . . . Just the teacher sitting at a rickety wooden table, trying to hold their attention . . . 'Say after me . . . C A T . . . say it . . .'

The Africans' avidity for education is boundless, not least because, in the words of Chief Albert Luthuli, 'The riches of the land and the material opulence of the city are not for Africans. All the more, then, did we regard education as a thirsty wayfarer yearns for a water-hole.'[8]

But at least, under the mission schools, there were some Africans who were receiving a reasonable education. For the lucky ones, there were high standards and a broad range of subjects, corresponding to the British syllabus; the two cultures met and married, each enriching the other. Occasionally people claimed that schools like Edendale and St Peter's, Rosettenville, produced 'Black Englishmen' – claims that angered Chief Albert Luthuli: 'I am aware of a profound gratitude for what I have learned. I remain an African. I think as an African, I speak as an African, I act as an African, and as an African I worship the God whose children we all are. I do not see why it should be otherwise.'[9]

The government, however, did think it should be otherwise. Seeing black Africans becoming educated, realising just how able they were, that there was no reason, intellectually, why they should not occupy the highest positions, was not at all what it intended. Educated Africans might spread liberal ideas, they could even threaten white domination.

Politicians wanting to manipulate the social order must deal with the system and content of education.

The Bantu Education Act was based on the findings of the Eiselen Commission of 1949. Its lengthy report included research into the relative brainpower of Africans and Europeans and concluded that the African child differed from the European so slightly, both physically and psychologically, that there was no reason why they should not profit from a similar education. Despite these findings, the government devised a system of 'Bantu Education' which was to be taken away from the Department of Education and put under the Department of Native Affairs, whose Minister was, at the time, Dr Verwoerd. Soon South Africa would be able to boast of having the only educational system in the world deliberately designed to render its pupils unable to participate in the running of their country.

The Nationalists felt no shame in what they were doing; speakers debating the issue in Parliament as early as 1945 rivalled one another in their mutual assurances. J. N. le Roux asserted: 'We should not give the Natives an academic education, as some people are prone to do. If we do this we shall later be burdened with a number of academically trained Europeans and non-Europeans, and who is going to do the manual work in the country?'[10] 'The Natives should learn to be good natives as tribal natives and should not be imitators of the white man,' cried C. R. Swart.[11] Another speaker, Captain Strydom, was adamant that the African must not be allowed to develop, particularly in education: 'We say the African must live in his hut and we must live in the house. He must remain separate and in his place.'[12] When the Bill was eventually tabled in 1953, most fervent of all was Dr Verwoerd, himself a product of German universities and a Nazi sympathiser:[13]

> My department's policy is that Bantu education should stand with both its feet in the reserves. What is the use of teaching the Bantu child mathematics when it cannot use it in practice? . . . It is of no avail to him to receive a training which has as its aim absorption in the European community. Until now he has been subject to a school system which drew him away from his own community and misled him by showing him the green pastures of European society in which he is not allowed to graze.

The whole basis of apartheid was exposed as he said: 'I just want to remind honourable members that if the Native in South Africa today is being taught to expect that he will live his adult life under a policy of equal rights, he is making a big mistake.'

Gone were the days when blacks could hope to receive the same education as whites. Now they were to be fed what Tutu accurately calls 'a thin gruel'. Apart from studying their mother tongues, gaining a rudimentary knowledge of Afrikaans and English and long hours devoted to religious activities, there was little intellectual sustenance. The three Rs gave way to manual, even menial, work: 'Broom, pick and shovel are the tools he must be familiar with. It sometimes happens that children spend as much as a whole week in the brickyard making bricks for school buildings. Or they have to stop school work to go road-making.'[14] Heavy penalties were imposed on anyone teaching without the Minister's permission. A retired African teacher gathered some children together, partly to keep them off the streets; he was found teaching them under the trees, arrested and fined £75.

The old textbooks were banished, to be replaced by hastily written books considered suitable for Bantu schools; teachers were retrained, deprived of professional status and owned, body and soul, by the Department of Native Affairs. Their morale was lowered by deplorable service conditions, loss of security of tenure and low pay. The salaries which European teachers enjoyed were considered in no way a fit or permissible criterion for paying Bantu teachers, who were, in effect, forced to become collaborators in apartheid.

It is not hard to imagine the effect these changes had on Desmond Tutu. He who wanted his pupils to become free, independent adults, able to think for themselves, was being told deliberately to limit their knowledge. Years later he addressed the students of the University of the Witwatersrand on freedom and education. With an exuberant string of metaphors he accused the educational system of teaching people what to think rather than how to think: 'It is designed to produce docile unquestioning creatures who could not say "boo" to a goose. They are taught that the best way to survive is by toeing the line, not rocking the boat and keeping in with the herd – totally at variance with the ideals of true liberalism (which, do note, is close to liberation).'[15] His anger mounted as he decried a system of education that stuffed people with 'predigested "facts" and readymade, shop-soiled, flyblown hackneyed responses'. Good education, for Tutu, is meant to make people realise their full potential, become more fully human. There is no reason to believe he did not think in the same way in 1955; how could he be party to this new dispensation?

It was a hard decision. He had only just qualified as a teacher, he had no other job to go to. He loved the children, he loved teaching and he excelled at it. The Act was implemented first at the junior level, so he stayed for three years to follow through the children he had started to teach, and then he left.

3

Growing into priesthood

The anguishing decision to leave the work he so enjoyed caused Desmond Tutu to ask himself some very radical questions about what he should do with his life. During his time at Munsieville High School he thought long and hard and made his decision: he offered himself to the Bishop of Johannesburg to train for the priesthood and was accepted.

He had no illusions about his vocation, freely admitting he 'didn't have very high, noble, reasons for going to theological college'. There was, however, a sound basis for his choice. He was a deeply committed Christian, actively involved in the life of the Church. In 1955, along with his old scoutmaster Zakes Mohutsioa, he had been admitted as a sub-Deacon at Krugersdorp, so he was regularly administering the chalice during Holy Communion, reading the Epistle, even conducting Matins; he had for a while been choirmaster. He had fallen under the spell of people like Father Sekgaphane, Pastor Makhene and Father Trevor Huddleston, whose influence had inspired him to consider following in their footsteps. In any case, he needed a job, one which gave some direction to his life. But these various pulls do not amount to the mysterious magnetism of a vocation; it is quite probable that had it not been for the Bantu Education Act, he might have lived out his life as a brilliant, but relatively obscure, teacher.

It cannot have been an easy decision. Desmond Tutu knew his abilities – how could he not? – and the ministry was, in those days, a less significant job than teaching for an ambitious black person. Black priests were respected by their own community, but they occupied a lowly place in white eyes – remember Canon John Tsebe, who was not allowed to drink tea in the white man's sitting room. They were, according to another friend of Tutu's, Godfrey Pitje, 'doomed to be shepherded and controlled by white priests, able only to eat the crumbs from their tables'. Though the gap was narrowing, there had been a gross disparity between the stipends of black and white priests; nor could black priests realistically aspire to high positions on the clerical ladder – the first black Bishop, Alpheus Zulu, was not consecrated until 1960. On a personal level, Tutu's father was deeply depressed

45

that this gifted young man, whom he had educated to university degree standard and had hoped might become headmaster of a High School, should make a move that was, at least in his eyes, a step down the professional ladder. Even some of Desmond's friends disapproved. Joe Seremane, who was in prison on Robben Island for political offences at the time, remembers how he and his companions, many of whom were Christians, were devastated at the news that their brilliant teacher was becoming a priest – from their experience of the way he taught, they had been expecting him 'to produce many Einsteins'. In any case, they felt cheated by the Church, whose part in the struggle for liberation had disappointed them. 'What a waste,' they said, 'a wonderful brain like that going into the Church.'

Nor were candidates for ordination going to be free of apartheid; the government was tightening its grip even on the churches. The year that Desmond was accepted for training saw Dr Verwoerd's announcement of the Native Laws Amendment Bill, with its infamous Clause 29(c), known as 'the church clause', stipulating that no church in the 'white' areas could admit an African without the permission of the Minister of Native Affairs. Though defiance and protest from the churches caused this Bill to be amended and to have little effect, its very existence reveals that the Church, enjoined by Christ to teach all nations, could be threatened by racist legislation. The religious climate was one that saw individual churches observing their own forms of racism, for instance providing a special bench at the back of churches for blacks to occupy and preventing them making their Communion until the end, when all the whites in the congregation had been up to the altar. Might their black lips sully the cup?

However, Tutu's mind was made up – he later referred to 'God grabbing me by the scruff of my neck' – and in 1958, when he left Munsieville High School, he went to St Peter's, Rosettenville, the theological college run by the Fathers of the Community of the Resurrection. St Peter's College had grown from being a school for catechists and interpreters in the first decade of the century, to becoming a college for training Africans to the ordained ministry. In comparison to English theological colleges the standard had not been high, but by 1958 the Principal was Father Godfrey Pawson, honoured by his fellow monks as the most outstanding lecturer in their Community at the time. He was very much an English priest, a profoundly orthodox Anglo-Catholic. Though he was too old to empathise very well with the Africans and though many of them found him a formidable figure, under his leadership St Peter's reached new heights.

46

Desmond, not easily frightened of anyone, was well able to profit from his teaching.

There were two courses open to the students: the Certificate of Theology, examined internally, and the Licentiate of Theology, which fell under the auspices of the Church of the Province of South Africa. Desmond was one of only two students in his year who were doing the L.Th., which was considerably the higher of the two courses – the equivalent of the general ordination examination in the United Kingdom. The syllabus covered Old and New Testament studies, Church History, Doctrine, Greek, Morals, Ascetics and Worship.

Not many blacks offering themselves for ordination training were graduates. Desmond Tutu was unique in both having a degree and four years' teaching experience. He was a star from the moment he arrived at the college; the only student who came near him was Laurence Zulu, who was to become Bishop of Zululand. Father Aelred Stubbs, who succeeded Father Pawson as Principal and was in charge of St Peter's for Desmond's last two terms, remembers him well: 'My view of Desmond intellectually is that essentially he's an assimilator, rather than an original mind. He was very quick, very bright. He was also very acceptable from an English point of view, because of this great gift of assimilation, more than any other African I've known.' He was so quick, so advanced, that he found the lectures slow and dull, and Father Pawson would give him private tuition. He excelled in tests, his name usually coming top, with marks in the 80s and 90s. He did so brilliantly in the first part of his exams (his results surpassed those of any of the white students at St Paul's in Grahamstown) that he was expected to get a *summa cum laude* in his finals. So he did, in a tragi-comic way. The registrar for the examinations managed to lose all the students' exam papers. Father Stubbs was particularly upset for Desmond, who had been doing so well, and he insisted that his papers should be marked at the level of his previous exams. Such was the confidence of his teachers that he was given the benefit of the doubt and awarded his L.Th., with two distinctions.

His contemporaries were surprised to find him humble, more concerned to encourage them in their studies than to relish his own success. He would be embarrassed when he was congratulated on his high marks and would refer to his private tuition in a self-mocking way, saying that 'only educated people have extra tutorials'. Father Stubbs thought it 'greatly to his credit that he didn't become an intolerable little prig, which could easily have happened'. Though there were some who were jealous of him, a few who did not like his manner and called him 'a strutter' and one or two among the staff who felt he was too ready to accept gifts from liberal whites anxious to help the students, he was popular. Sipho Masemola, now a priest in the East Rand, delighted in his jocular, gregarious personality, 'bubbling with love for people'. David Nkwe, now an Archdeacon in the diocese of Johannesburg, remembers him 'oozing love, laughter and caring'.

It is impossible to exaggerate the importance of the Community of the Resurrection in Tutu's spiritual development – he regards his debt to them as incalculable. It is they who, in his words, 'enabled me to see very clearly something that I hope has stayed with me – the centrality of the spiritual.'[1] Every day there was compulsory meditation before breakfast, followed by Matins and Mass. There were frequent retreats and devotional addresses. He was continually impressed at the amount of time these men devoted to prayer; apart from the round of monastic hours, there was always someone on his knees in the Fathers' chapel. They taught by example rather than by precept; whole generations of black students were impressed at the way their spiritual life was demonstrated in their total identification with the oppressed and suffering – when the residents of Sophiatown were forcibly removed, they were there, when there were problems in the schools, it was they who would be speaking with the voice of sanity. Through their influence, Tutu's spirituality became rooted in the ordinary, the everyday, the down-to-earth:[2]

> It is from these remarkable men that I have learned that it is impossible for religion to be sealed off in a watertight compartment that has no connection with the hurly burly business of ordinary daily living, that our encounter with God in prayer, meditation, the sacraments and bible study is authenticated and expressed in our dealings with our neighbour, whose keeper we must be willy nilly.

His absorption of an incarnational spirituality, that sees God in everything and everyone, continues to constrain him not only to do whatever he can to help people in trouble, but to love his fellow man, whether or not that love is returned or even welcomed.

It was through the years at St Peter's that the Eucharist, prayer, meditation and retreats became so integral a part of Desmond's life. He used often to be found praying in the chapel at 5.30 in the morning and the habit of prayer has never left him. 'If I do not spend a reasonable amount of time in meditation early in the morning, then I feel a physical discomfort – it is worse than having forgotten to brush my teeth! . . . I would be completely rudderless and lost if I did not have these times with God.'[3]

Again there were individuals whose influence was to stay with him, again it was gentleness and selflessness that most impressed him. Father Timothy Stanton, a shy and reserved man who in his late sixties went to prison for six months rather than testify in a trial for subversion involving two Afrikaner students, is still his Father Confessor and spiritual director: 'He is quite undoubtedly a holy man, truly saintly. I remember how I was amazed that he, the Vice-Principal, and a white man to boot, would join us black students in doing some of the most menial chores in college.'[4]

In his third year Desmond was made senior student. It was the custom for the senior student to be appointed by the Fathers, though he had to represent the students – an absurd position that no one could accomplish very satisfactorily. David Nkwe, who was in his first year while Desmond held the office, was very impressed at the way he made all the first year students feel important, no one was allowed to feel insignificant. Most of them saw him as someone with a bright future; some saw him as a future lecturer, who might one day be Principal of the college, one or two claim to have seen him as a future Bishop, but they all remember him as someone who was already taking the lead. For instance in the way he encouraged the students to realise that a senior student must have their confidence and not merely be imposed on them by the Fathers; in turn he persuaded the Fathers that the college could be more democratically run. His role as a reconciler was beginning.

By 1960, when he had passed his L.Th. and was ordained Deacon, Tutu had discovered his vocation as a priest and his gift for reconciliation was emerging. However, he still did not think politically. He was not unusual. Black people in those days put up with conditions which twenty-five years later would be considered quite unthinkable. Like many of his contemporaries Desmond simply did not consider standing up to the government or becoming involved in organising resistance. But there were those who did; in fact looking back at the 1950s is to look back on a decade of protest.

It was in 1952, with the Defiance Campaign, that black South African protest first hit the world's headlines. The previous year had seen black freedom abused and eroded by more and more legislation against them and at their annual meeting in December the African National Congress, who had been trying to represent the interests of African, 'coloured' and Indian people since 1912, passed a resolution that the government should be asked to repeal 'six unjust laws'. If they did not, the ANC, together with the South African Indian Council, would organise a campaign of peaceful resistance. Anthony Sampson, then editor of the African magazine *Drum*, attended the

49

meeting and heard 300 people sing the hymn that had become the Congress anthem, '*Nkosi Sikele' iAfrika*'.[5]

> I watched the faces of the crowd, transformed by passion. A delicate little clergyman with a tiny goatee beard, straining his thin throat with singing; a ragged old man swinging his arms to the rhythm, gazing rapturously at the rafters; a bulging woman shouting the song with indignation in every syllable. I noticed, to my surprise, a meek-looking messenger who delivered packages to *Drum* singing earnestly among the crowd. He came up to me afterwards. 'Please, baas, don't tell my baas that you saw me here . . .'

At the end of the anthem Dr Moroka, then President of Congress, raised his hand in the ANC salute, calling *Mayibuye*; the crowd shouted back *Africa*. ('Come back, Africa' – the traditional ANC slogan. It refers to the old days of freedom before the white man came.)

The government's response was that it had no intention of repealing the laws, which in any case were protective, not degrading; it would quell any disturbances and deal with the leaders.

Mass protests – 'a warm-up' according to Chief Albert Luthuli, then President of the Natal Congress – were organised on April 6th, a date chosen with grim humour. It was the tercentenary of Jan van Riebeeck's arrival in the Cape;[6] a day when whites would celebrate 300 years of 'progress', while blacks could only look back on 300 years of exploitation. There were gatherings all over the country: in Cape Town, Pretoria, Port Elizabeth, East London and Durban. Crowds of up to 10,000 demonstrated their support, while in Johannesburg Dr Moroka called for 'a solemn oath that we will muster all our forces of mind, body and soul to see that this state of affairs, these crushing conditions under which we live, shall not continue any longer'.[7]

The campaign proper was launched on June 26th, known as Freedom Day since 1950, when demonstrations and strikes in opposition to the Suppression of Communism Act were held on that date. It spread like wildfire through the country and continued for months as volunteers deliberately defied the apartheid laws, intending to be arrested and to put such strain on the prisons and law courts that the system would break down:[8]

> The first day set the pattern for the campaign. In the next five months, eight thousand people went to jail for one to three weeks. They marched into locations, walked out after curfew, travelled in European railway coaches, entered stations by European entrances. Everywhere they marched quietly and did what they were told, singing hymns with their

thumbs up. They always informed the police beforehand, to make sure they would be arrested.

A new spirit was emerging as people learned to act politically – the country would never be quite the same again.

But that is to speak with hindsight. On Desmond and his fellow students, engrossed in their studies at the teacher-training course in Pretoria, the Defiance Campaign made little impact. There was the odd person who would raise his fist in the ANC salute during the singing of the National Anthem, they would read about people being arrested, but somehow it did not seem their business. Desmond admits that 'You would think "How wonderful", but you didn't think that this called on you to be particularly involved.'

By 1955, when the Freedom Charter was written, Desmond was, through Father Huddleston's involvement, a little closer to events, but he was still fairly remote. He was coping with the implementation of the Bantu Education Act and his decisions consequent on that; he was married a week after the Charter was proclaimed – there was plenty to occupy his attention. 'You just said, "Well, there's another landmark in our people's march to freedom", but you didn't think that there was any significant part for you to play.'

The Freedom Charter must be one of the most democratic documents ever written. A leaflet in several languages was sent out by the multi-racial National Action Council of the Congress of the People. In a poetic style, reminiscent of the Lebanese mystic Kahlil Gibran, it addressed farmers, miners, factory workers, teachers, housewives and mothers. Each group of people was separately invoked:

> WE CALL THE PEOPLE OF SOUTH AFRICA BLACK AND WHITE
> LET US SPEAK TOGETHER OF FREEDOM!
> We call the teachers, students and the preachers.
> Let us speak of the light that comes from learning,
> and the ways we are kept in darkness.
> Let us speak of great services we can render,
> and of narrow ways that are open to us.
> Let us speak of laws, and governments, and rights.
> LET US SPEAK OF FREEDOM.

The responses flooded in, sometimes drafted formally, sometimes scrawled on odd bits of paper. Their demands were discussed and drafted into a Charter at a meeting on the weekend of June 25th/26th; the site chosen was a football ground in Kliptown, near Johannesburg, where 3,000 delegates packed the enclosure, while another 2,000 watched from outside. By the Sunday evening the leaders were able to read the Preamble and the ten points that make up the Charter. As each section was read it was acclaimed by a show of hands and shouts of *Africa*. The ten sections are headed:

THE PEOPLE SHALL GOVERN.
ALL NATIONAL GROUPS SHALL HAVE EQUAL RIGHTS.
THE PEOPLE SHALL SHARE IN THE COUNTRY'S WEALTH.
THE LAND SHALL BE SHARED AMONG THOSE WHO WORK IN IT.
ALL SHALL BE EQUAL BEFORE THE LAW.
ALL SHALL ENJOY EQUAL HUMAN RIGHTS.
THERE SHALL BE WORK AND SECURITY.
THE DOORS OF LEARNING AND CULTURE SHALL BE OPENED.
THERE SHALL BE HOUSES, SECURITY AND COMFORT.
THERE SHALL BE PEACE AND FRIENDSHIP.

It ends, 'These freedoms we shall fight for, side by side, throughout our lives, until we have won our liberty.'

Hardly a revolutionary document – in fact it has been criticised for its declaration that 'South Africa belongs to all who live in it, *black and white*'. Nevertheless, as the great campaigner Helen Joseph gave her speech on houses, security and comfort, the police arrived, bearing a warrant to investigate for high treason. Until darkness fell, they searched the delegates and seized thousands of copies of the Charter. They were wasting their time; an idea cannot be destroyed. Over thirty years later the Freedom Charter lives in the hearts and minds of millions of black people in South Africa and Kliptown football stadium is revered as holy ground.

As the Congress Movement grew stronger and more unified, so it posed a greater threat to the government. At sunrise on December 5th, 1956, eighteen months after that great day at Kliptown, 156 leaders of the Movement were arrested and charged with high treason, a charge which carried the death penalty. The 'Treason Trials' dragged on for four long years, ending with the acquittal of all the defendants.

The young ordinands at St Peter's, Rosettenville, have one very special memory of the Treason Trialists. During the second year of the trial, charges were dropped against sixty-one of the accused. Two of the released men, Chief Albert Luthuli and Professor Z. K. Matthews (known as 'The Chief' and 'The Prof'), came over to the priory and met some of the students, who were becoming increasingly concerned about the fate of their country. David Nkwe was impressed by the way Tutu reacted to the visit of these two great statesmen, one a future Nobel Prize-winner, the other head of Fort Hare University until he was forced to leave. Tutu spoke for all when he said 'we need a dozen such people to demonstrate to our country that blacks are human beings'.

While Tutu was in his last year at St Peter's, South Africa hit the world's headlines again in one of the blackest days of its history – March 21st, 1960.

During the 1950s a few African countries had gained independence and 1960 saw no fewer than seventeen other States throw off the shackles of colonial rule: early in 1960 the British Prime Minister, Harold Macmillan, warned the South African government of the strength of African nationalism in his famous 'winds of change' speech. The spirit of freedom was in the air. The South African resistance movements, encouraged by the examples of their neighbours in the north, decided once again to voice their protest in organised, peaceful defiance. The ANC intended to hold demonstrations against the pass laws throughout the country on March 31st. In a clearly competitive move the recently formed Pan-Africanist Congress (the 'Africanist' element who had left the ANC, wanting government 'of the African, by the African, for the African' rather than believing, with the ANC, that South Africa belonged to both black and white) decided to launch its own campaign ten days earlier. The people were to leave their passes at home, assemble outside police stations and demand to be arrested.

Early in the morning of March 21st the PAC leaders surrendered themselves at Orlando police station. As the day drew on, people began to gather round the country; in Sharpeville the crowd swelled to some 10,000. They had been led to believe that a statement would be made announcing changes in the pass laws and they waited quietly. Suddenly, without any order being given, the police panicked and opened fire. Seven hundred shots were fired into the crowd: 180 people were wounded, 69 killed, many shot in the back as they turned to run away. At Langa township, 1,000 miles away, 2 were killed and 49 injured in a similar situation. That night the crowds went berserk, burning Bantu education schools and public buildings.

The ANC called for a national day of mourning, which was to take the form of a stay-at-home strike on March 28th, the day of the funerals. On the same day the government announced that both the ANC and the PAC were banned. Two days later a country-wide 'state of emergency' was declared.

News of the massacre flashed round the world. Like many others, Tutu heard of it on the radio. 'We were just stunned, we really were. You were benumbed and you didn't, you didn't quite believe. Again there wasn't a great deal that you could do. There you were feeling angry, impotent and not knowing what there was for us to do.' He felt great pride in the Bishop of Johannesburg, Ambrose Reeves, who became a thorn in the flesh of the authorities by drawing attention to the shame of Sharpeville. When the state of emergency was declared Bishop Reeves, fearing arrest, fled to Swaziland. On his return he was greeted by a protective demonstration of students of St Peter's, who felt the clear support of his flock would make it harder for the government to take action against him. Their gesture must have touched him, but did not affect the authorities. For a few days he stayed at St Benedict's House, the convent next to St Peter's, shadowed by a police car. The students were mystified by the comings and goings of the police car, shattered when their Bishop was eventually deported. They were seeing the brutality of the government from a new perspective.

Some people wonder at Tutu's lack of involvement in the political protest of this period – indeed he has been known to question it himself – but he does not feel there is much to be gained from self-recrimination; in any case it was only the minority who were politically active. His first concern was to learn to be a good priest. In December 1960 he was ordained Deacon in St Mary's Cathedral, Johannesburg, and took up his first curacy at St Alban's Church in Benoni location.

Here his Rector was Canon Mokoatla, a powerful and strict character, an impressive preacher – one of the old-style African priests. Godfrey Pitje didn't feel he treated Desmond very well: 'He was a typical black Englishman, exuding confidence. He seemed to be saying "I have arrived where I am by dint of hard work and effort. These young fellows will never get to the same position".' He tended to treat his new curate like a small boy, who should do menial tasks like washing his car; nor did he help to find reasonable accommodation for Desmond and Leah and the three children that had by now been born to them.

The Tutus' first two children, Trevor (after Father Trevor Huddleston) Thamsanqua and Thandeka Theresa, were born while Tutu was still teaching. The birth of his first child was, for the proud father, 'A very definitive kind of experience. I had a thing in the back of my mind about the perpetuation of my name. Having a son as firstborn says you have arrived, you have made it.' It was not only a proud moment, it was a humbling one. 'You have a little sense of what it must mean to be God. Here you and your wife are and this precious thing has come about through your creative attributes. You have a kind of religious experience when you see your child for the first time.'[9]

Unfortunately, while they were at St Peter's, which in those days was run rather like a monastic institution, he and Leah had not been able to live together and Leah had been so lonely without him that Desmond's mother had looked after the children during the day so that she could start training as a nurse. At Benoni the family, with the birth of Nontomdi Naomi in 1960 now five in number, could at least be together, but in conditions barely acceptable for animals. They were housed in a garage, one room serving as the main bedroom, the children's bedroom, the sitting room and dining room; they used the small second room as a kitchen. Father Stubbs says the Tutu family were living in the worst conditions, without exception, which he had seen any African priest endure. The garage was next to a stable, so in summer it was infested with flies; in winter it was cold, very cold – hardly suitable conditions for someone who was still under the shadow of TB. To the surprise of those who felt Tutu had materialistic ambitions, he never complained. In fact, he did not react in any way, accepting it as part of his vocation to the life of a priest. Canon Mokoatla, typical of the old guard, saw nothing wrong at all. 'These young men need to be put through it,' was his attitude, so, for Tutu's first year as Deacon, the garage was their home.

At the end of 1961, now thirty years old, Tutu was ordained priest. His ordination was not the joyous event it might have been. Bishop Reeves, who should have officiated, had already been deported, while the attitude of Canon Mokoatla left much to be desired. He made himself responsible for Desmond, but completely disregarded Leah and the children. Had it not been for Godfrey Pitje, who brought them to the ceremony, they might not have been present. Godfrey remembers how painful this was for him, seeing them so excluded, let alone for Leah.

Soon after he became a priest Tutu was moved to Thokoza, to a new church in a recently built township – a result of the Group Areas Act. Strictly speaking, he was not yet ready for a church of his own, but here, though he was responsible to the Rector at Natalspruit, he was effectively priest-in-charge and had a fairly free hand. He was also given better accommodation – a four-roomed municipal house. It was a matchbox, with few facilities, but an improvement on a garage.

In these first two years in the ministry Tutu acquired valuable experience. Despite the way Canon Mokoatla treated his curate, Tutu respected and admired him. He is, in fact, greatly indebted to the old priest, for it was through him that Desmond acquired the rudiments of preaching. He learned to take preaching seriously, he learned how powerful a good sermon can be. The foundations of his oratorical style were laid at Benoni.

He also discovered the privilege of priesthood. 'There is the joy of being welcomed into a home as you go round visiting the parishioners. And people share some of their deepest secrets with you; that always leaves me feeling very humble.'[10] His easy, loving way with people endeared him to the parishioners, who were so fond of him that it has even been suggested that Canon Mokoatla was a bit jealous. Tutu, in turn, was deeply impressed by the people he met,[11]

> staggered at the strength of their attachment to Our Lord and amazed by the strange kind of joy they have in the midst of their poverty and suffering. They sometimes brought tears to my eyes. I was infinitely more well off than they were, but when I was grousing they were able to thank God for something good that had happened to them.

Years later Desmond spoke of pastoral visiting to a group of Deacons about to be ordained as priests:[12]

> You can sit all day in your house and not visit your people, not take communion to the sick, to the aged, and nobody will usually complain to you, but your church will grow emptier. You can't love people and not visit them. You can't love them unless you know them, and you can't know them unless you visit them regularly. A good shepherd knows his sheep by name.

Tutu was becoming a pastor, the best sort of pastor who cares, really cares, about his parishioners. Already he felt keen pleasure in visiting their homes, in taking Holy Communion to the sick and the dying. He remembers pain and guilt at the memory of a sick woman who died without a visit from him; he knew he should have called on her and had not.

If initially his vocation had not been overwhelmingly strong, there was no doubting it now.

4

No passbook required

While Tutu was still a curate in Benoni he became the subject of a long correspondence between Father Stubbs and the Reverend Sydney Evans, the Dean of King's College in the University of London. Father Stubbs was becoming increasingly aware of the need for St Peter's to have an African member of staff who could hold his own academically; he was sure that the most suitable man known to him was Desmond Tutu. It was unusual to send someone overseas so soon after his ordination – normally the young priests would serve three years in their first curacy – but Tutu was an older man who had already held a responsible job as a teacher. Father Stubbs was keen that his star pupil should come over to England to read for a degree in theology, then, when he returned to South Africa, that he should join the staff of St Peter's.

Between them, Father Stubbs and Dean Evans made the practical arrangements. In order to sit for a degree at the University of London a 'Statement of Eligibility' was necessary; papers had to be submitted to show the candidate's attainments up to that point. In the case of students from the United Kingdom this is routine, but the papers of overseas students are scrutinised rather more closely. However, soon a delighted Tutu was able to tell the Dean that he had this essential piece of paper, though 'his bank balance was nil'.[1] Money was found from several different sources, including the diocese of Johannesburg and the Community of the Resurrection; he was also given bursaries by King's College and awarded a scholarship by the World Council of Churches' Theological Education Fund. South African politics made this a delicate matter: Tutu advised the Dean that it should be referred to as a 'Church Bursary', as anything to do with the WCC, given its support of revolutionary movements, would be 'hardly acceptable to our government'.[2] Eventually the path was clear; on September 14th, 1962, Tutu arrived in England.

For a while, living in lodgings without his family, he was lonely and homesick, but after a couple of months one of the college tutors found him a curate's flat at St Alban's Church in Golders Green. Desmond wrote ecstatically to the Dean: 'Father Trueman has brought off a coup! The flat is a pleasant modern one with two bedrooms, a bathroom, a kitchenette, a larder, a living room-cum-dining room and a study.' He could have it rent-free in exchange for 'a modest amount of Sunday duty'.[3] Soon Leah arrived with the two older children, Trevor and Theresa, for the moment leaving the youngest, Naomi, with Desmond's mother in Johannesburg. 'It was obviously quite another world to which we had been transported. For one thing we had splendid accommodation in salubrious quarters. There was a park, a ubiquitous and pleasant feature of London, just round the corner from our flat, with penned animals, a further delight to our children.'[4]

It is hard for those who have not been the victims of an oppressive regime to appreciate quite the revelation that living in England was for the Tutus; racism in the United Kingdom is not in the same league as in South Africa. The Tutus hardly realised themselves how conditioned they had become by living under apartheid:[5]

> You didn't know that gnawing away at you was this worm which was sowing a horrible kind of self-doubt in you. You wondered when they called you non-this, non-the-other – you are a non-European coming from non-Europe – whether in fact they weren't perhaps right . . . The most horrible aspect of apartheid, a blasphemous aspect, is it can make a child of God doubt that they are a child of God, when you ask yourself in the middle of the night 'God, am I your step-child?'

So imagine the delight with which they experienced the extraordinary novelty of walking freely, without having to look nervously for signs saying whether or not they were permitted to be where they were; the surprise in seeing mixed couples walking hand-in-hand – for a long time Desmond instinctively worried that their arrest could be imminent; the joy with which they put away their passbooks. 'To be able to just walk around and use any exit, I mean it's almost ineffable. It's difficult to express the sense of exhilaration, of liberation, of being made to feel human.'[6] Desmond and Leah would walk in Trafalgar Square, late at night or in the early hours of the morning, just to savour the freedom of knowing they would not be accosted by a policeman asking for a piece of paper, knowing they would not be told there was a curfew and that black people should not be there. They sometimes asked for directions, even knowing perfectly well where they were going, simply for the pleasure of being addressed courteously by a white unarmed policeman. Once Tutu was waiting in a bank, due to be served next, when a white man rushed past him in a great hurry and tried to jump the queue. 'As a well-behaved Bantu, I was ready to let this happen when the lady bank clerk told him firmly but politely that *I* was next. You could have knocked me down with a feather.'[7] He went back later to thank her and tell her she was now his 'pin-up'. He was even more impressed when she told him she would have done it for anybody.

A familiar tradition of English life, wonderfully pleasing to Tutu, was Speakers' Corner. There he witnessed people 'sometimes spewing forth the most outlandish sentiments' in the presence of a policeman, there not to silence the oratory but to protect freedom of speech. Similarly he was amazed, after the bland lies broadcast by the South African Broadcasting Corporation, to hear the irreverence and abrasiveness with which politicians were interviewed on television; impressed that the Prime Minister, when responding to the weekly challenge of 'Question Time' in Parliament, was treated with such scant respect. There was, he thought, 'a proper iconoclasm about. Sacred cows were for the slaughter. It was exhilarating.'[8]

Overseas students do not necessarily find life in the United Kingdom easy, but Tutu was one of the lucky ones, his passage smoothed by the small but highly developed network of the Community of the Resurrection. It was through Father Stubbs that he was greeted at Heathrow Airport by the writer Nicholas Mosley, through him too that he met Martin Kenyon, who was to become a lifelong friend of the whole Tutu family.

Martin Kenyon, a man of many friends and at the time an energetic bachelor, introduced Desmond to aspects of British life that elude many native-born Britons. Within weeks of his arrival he took him to the Travellers' Club in Pall Mall, where Tutu, in a manner not typical of London clubs in the early 1960s, was warmly welcomed and addressed by the porter as 'Sir'. After the treatment he was accustomed to receiving in his own country, this reception must have been a gratifying experience; his most vivid memory of the occasion, however, is eating grouse and picking the shot out of his teeth. With Martin he indulged his passion for cricket at no less a mecca than Lord's, where they sat in the stand reserved for friends of MCC members. They went together to a residential conference on 'Nationalism, Neutralism and Neo-colonialism', where Tutu was one of the tutors; the speakers included the President of the African National Congress, Oliver Tambo, exiled since 1960 from South Africa and Tutu's old hero, Bishop Ambrose Reeves. A free afternoon was spent visiting Haddon Hall, home of the Duke of Rutland; on another Tutu played in that traditional cricketing event 'England v. the World'. One summer holiday they all went to stay in a cottage next to Martin Kenyon's parents in Lydbury North, a remote Shropshire village on the Welsh borders, where the Tutus' black skins were as much a novelty to the villagers as the young calves were to the Tutu children.

People are often amazed by Tutu's lack of bitterness, and he is quite ready to admit how much this is due to his time in England. He is quite certain that had they not had this experience they could have had enormous chips on their shoulders.[9]

> Now, because we have met white people and suddenly seem to have made a tremendous scientific discovery, that actually white people aren't so bad, we have been able to go back to South Africa, and even when we have encountered horribleness we have known that no, you can't have stereotypes, because that's exactly what they have been doing to us. That they are ordinary human beings, some of them good human beings and some bad human beings. And so we can walk tall.

So, too, his delight in the academic education spilled over. After the stultifying restrictions of education for blacks in South Africa, he marvelled at the 'bewildering array of options', delighted in the lack of dogmatism, typified by the lecturer who invariably used the phrase 'It is not unreasonable to suppose . . .', and was overcome by sitting at the feet of people who were, at least in his discipline, household names. 'Mind boggling! Well, I couldn't contain myself. And here they were, I mean you could really touch them!'[10]

He had indeed been well guided. King's is a fully constituted college of the University of London, taking London degrees. Though in the early 1960s it was less radical, less critical, less exciting than it was to become towards the end of the decade, it had a sound academic reputation and was the one college in London that specialised in teaching theology both to those who went on for a fourth-year ordination course, and those who, like Tutu, were already ordained. Being a multi-faculty college where students had contact with other disciplines, it was more alive to the outside world than many universities, becoming a magnet for overseas students and boasting teaching staff of the calibre of Professor Ulrich Simon and Professor Geoffrey Parrinder. Not least, it was ahead of many universities in its disregard of colour.

The college had experienced the embarrassment of overseas students coming half across the world only to find they were unable to settle in England, could not stand the climate or, most humiliating, could not cope with the academic standards. Tutu gave the lie to anyone who thought, as some still did, that blacks were of a lower intellectual calibre; his tutors still remember him as a pleasure to teach. The Dean found him 'A joy to have around. He was so vivid, pulsating with life.' Richard Coggins, for a while his tutor in Old Testament studies, experienced him as 'hungry and thirsty for knowledge and well able to absorb and digest it'. He threw himself into the life, determined, as Canon Ronald Brownrigg said, 'to be baked on both sides academically'. He did so well in the Preliminary exams at the end of his first year that the College authorities decided he should change from the ordinary Pass course to the far tougher Honours course, which included Hebrew and the History and Philosophy of Religion.

Liberation theology was not yet a force in the Christian Church; the Jesus of the theological colleges of the early 1960s was no social revolutionary. Tutu was being trained as a traditional Anglican theologian, in a settled atmosphere which gave no hint of the tests to which his thinking was to be put. It did, however, give him a background of knowledge and insight against which his personal faith and inner commitment deepened. It formed the sound hull of a ship which was going to take the buffeting of violent storms.

When it came to the Final BD examinations there were high hopes that he would get a First. He found it an exhausting ordeal and was not pleased with his own performance, but happily his fears were misplaced; he did so well that he was viva'ed for a First. It was the only year that the University Examiners for the BD had vivas and, surprisingly for someone so articulate, Tutu failed on this oral examination. He was, however, awarded a good Second.

It was the custom for graduates who were about to be awarded their degrees to be wined and dined by the Principal or the Dean. In 1965 it was the Dean who took the chair, so it was for him to select one of the students to reply to the toast. He chose Tutu and never forgot his words:

> It was the most moving thing. Desmond said something like this: 'When I was in Africa I thought that perhaps I was no less important than anyone else, though I didn't have any reason to believe this might be true, until I came to England, to King's, where I was treated like everyone else. And this was the turning point. So my gratitude to England and my gratitude to King's is that I have discovered who I am.'

The next day Tutu went to the Royal Albert Hall, a spectacular event attended by hundreds of people, where he was awarded his degree by the Chancellor of the University, the Queen Mother.

Though the intention had been that when he graduated Tutu should return to St Peter's to teach, Father Stubbs, hearing how well he had done, was willing to adjust his plans in order to give Tutu the opportunity of doing a postgraduate course. The tutors were enthusiastic; so was Tutu, in a way which shows how he was beginning to see his future role in South Africa. He wrote to the Dean:[11]

> I would, I think, want to have a shot at it. In a sense it is part of the struggle for our liberation. Please, I hope it does not sound big-headed or, worse, downright silly. But if I go back home as highly qualified as you can make me, the more ridiculous our Government's policy will appear to be to earnest and intelligent people. Away from home we do unfortunately bear the burden of representing our people, who are judged by our achievements or lack of them. I hope this does not sound like something out of Hyde Park Corner.

Previously it had been considered impossible to complete a Master's degree in theology in less than two years, but in 1965 a new higher degree was introduced, taking only one year. So, with the blessing of his tutors and a good Upper Second degree, Tutu was in a position to enrol for the course – the only remaining hurdle was financial.

Tutu, it has to be said, was not good with money. He has been accused of irresponsibility and extravagance, but the truth lies more in a kind of innocence. He had not been brought up with the idea of money as a familiar commodity. If South African blacks had money, they spent it, for the simple reason that they needed something. There was no question of saving – with scarcely enough to go round, the matter did not arise. Couple that background with Tutu's spontaneous, generous personality, add a wife and four children (Mpho, the youngest, was born in England in 1963), and the accusation has to be modified.

The Dean and Father Stubbs, who between them looked after the Tutus like a couple of caring uncles, took endless pains on their behalf, not least in seeing they had enough to live on, and Tutu was appreciative and grateful. On one occasion he had overspent and, in accepting a rebuke from the Dean, wrote back. 'I cannot explain how this happens, for I assure you I am not extravagant. You have been so generous to us. I have done nothing but get and get. I have not given at all.'[12] In his own way, he *would* give, and they knew it.

Eventually his various grants and scholarships were extended, leaving only the question of what subject he should take. At first Father Stubbs favoured Old Testament, but the Dean, doubting whether he had done enough Hebrew, suggested New Testament. In the end Desmond decided for himself. New Testament would be 'full of theological nit-picking', he told one of his tutors; the growing religious force in Africa, the one he needed to know more about, was Islam. It was a theme that had woven itself into his academic life since, as an ordinand, he had entered for the 'Archbishop's Essay Prize', whose subject had to be either Islam or Calvin. The prize had been instituted by Archbishop Joost de Blank, who was appalled at the ignorance of the Anglican clergy in the areas of Calvinism, crucial to an understanding of the Dutch Reformed Church, and Islam, a strong influence in the Western Cape and a growing force throughout Africa. Professor Monica Wilson, who was one of the examiners, found that St Peter's students were by far the best. Best of all was Tutu, who wrote on Islam and won the prize. Now this would be the subject of his Master's degree.

Alongside Desmond's social and academic life in London were his duties as a curate. In Golders Green he had his first experience of ministering to a white congregation, where – not quite knowing what to expect – he discovered his parishioners were ordinary human beings, with the strengths and weaknesses, resentments and triumphs, joys, foibles, sins and sorrows of any other group of people. That this was something of a revelation, surprising him enough for him to recall his reaction in a public statement years later, speaks yet again of the iniquity of apartheid, which leads its victims to believe that human emotions vary with skin colour. Though the churchmanship at St Alban's was a little low for Tutu, and despite the verger, who lived in the flat below the Tutus, protesting that the children made too much noise, both parishioners and curate were content. Even the cold – it snowed from their arrival on Boxing Day until well into February – did not reach them. They felt 'wonderfully insulated' by the warmth of the parishioners and of the priest, the late John Halsey and his wife. Soon the tiny flat became open house to the entire parish. Anyone with worries or problems or just wanting a bit of company was assured of a welcome.

After nearly three years in Golders Green, Tutu wrote to the Dean of King's College, saying he would welcome a change to a parish in a less well-to-do part of London. Wishes can be granted in strange ways: he was moved; but not to a working-class parish, not to another part of London, but to a village in Surrey's 'Gin and Jaguar' belt – Bletchingley. The Tutus were to be thrown into English life in all its variety.

In those days Bletchingley was a mixed parish. There was a council estate, built in the 1940s, but with several aristocratic families of the 'landed gentry', a peer of the realm, a chairman of Lloyds, a number of farmers and farmworkers, some of whom had lived in the village for generations, the tone was almost feudal. This encounter with the British class system was not at all what Tutu had in mind. 'The inhabitants of Bletchingley were divided as with a knife into those who lived on the housing estate and the landed and monied gentry who had the proper accents and had gone to the right public schools and to Oxford and Cambridge.'[13] Nor was a black South African curate quite what the Anglicans of the village had expected – it was rare to see a black skin at all in Bletchingley, least of all in the pulpit. Yet this surprising partnership was to be a resounding success.

That it was such a success was due as much to the parishioners as to Tutu. Though outwardly Bletchingley was a prototype commuter village of the 1960s, once inside the perfectly restored old cottages with their manicured gardens, the manorial houses and the fine old church with its Norman tower, a very different picture emerged. According to Canon Ronald Brownrigg, who was Rector during Desmond's time, this was due to half a dozen people who, by virtue of the way they lived, became leaders of the community. The church was so strong that Sunday, Holy Week and religious festivals were dedicated solely to religious activities – nothing else happened in the village. The spirit was such that the entire village had clubbed together to pay for an Arab ordinand to be trained in Bangalore; there was nothing unusual in finding the floor of the local geriatric asylum being cleaned by a lady of title. The churchmanship was high, which appealed to Desmond, who wrote approvingly to the Dean of King's College about his first impressions: 'The Parish is Catholic with regular confessions and Reservation and a general Intercession book that appears to be used quite conscientiously by the parishioners.'[14]

Outstanding amongst these local leaders was Uvedale Lambert, Guardian of the Shrine at Walsingham, Sheriff of Surrey, Master of Foxhounds and a member of the old Church Assembly before the Synod came into being. He was a successful gentleman farmer, a devout Christian, a brilliant theologian and a member of the Fraternity of the Community of the Resurrection, the lay wing of the order. His home, South Park, a manor house with its own chapel, was for many years a sort of spiritual salon, where twice a year he and his American wife, Melanie, would give 'Holy Parties'.

Never did the spiritual and the secular meet more graciously than at South Park. On arrival the 'retreatant' (if that is the word) would be greeted with an excellently mixed dry Martini, he would be fed on delicious food and could wander round the lovely house and gardens. Yet these weekends, known by some as 'Gin and God' parties, were predominantly serious, with regular prayer and worship and at least seven teaching sessions, taken by members of the Community of the Resurrection like Father Raynes, for whom South Park was almost a second home.

Martin Kenyon was a member of this circle, and one day he

happened to mention to Uvedale Lambert that he was trying to find a curacy for an exceptional black South African who was studying for his Master's degree in theology at King's College. 'I think,' ruminated Lambert, 'that Bletchingley is ready for an overseas curate.' And so it was; the acceptable face of paternalism brought Tutu to Bletchingley.

Uvedale Lambert was right; the parishioners responded enthusiastically to the idea. One August Sunday, at the eight o'clock service, the Rector put up a list in the church detailing the various things the Tutus would need – beds, chairs, cutlery, linen – and asking for those willing and able to give anything to sign against the appropriate item. By the end of the ten o'clock service the list was full and within twenty-four hours the cottage, loaned to the Tutus by a cousin of the Lamberts until the curate's house was vacant, was furnished. Early the next week Uvedale Lambert and the Rector went up to Golders Green in one of the farm Land-Rovers and brought Desmond and Leah, Trevor, Theresa, Naomi and Mpho, to their new home.

People still living in Bletchingley admit that initially there was, at least in some quarters, 'a certain reserve'; but it was soon overcome. John Ewington, the organist for many years, says 'Desmond just won them over as he wins everybody over, not only by his example – he was obviously a very prayerful man – but also by his great sense of humour. He's always laughing, this most infectious laugh.' His jokes, which he is not too proud to repeat, are ingenuous and do not translate easily to the page. Though he is a talented mimic – he and his great friend Walter Makhulu[15] could make their audience helpless with laughter as they imitated the South African police at a road block – his humour has none of the cool acerbity that makes for real wit. Teasing and jocularity are, in him, more a way of expressing the richness of his emotions; they show a desire to share and communicate, a spilling over of goodwill. He relishes jokes about his colour, responding to compliments with 'One of the great advantages of a black skin is that when you blush nobody notices', he is amused by the thought of being 'tickled pink' and was delighted that when he preached from the high pulpit, which is backed by a dark Jacobean screen, all the congregation could see of him were his teeth and the whites of his eyes. His friendship with Uvedale Lambert blossomed from the moment when they were moving his luggage and Uvedale, knowing Desmond had had TB, tried to save him from lifting heavy things. 'What's the matter, Uvedale,' Tutu said, 'don't you like to see me working like a nigger?'

The village were soon accustomed to seeing their new curate roaring round on his Vespa, often with one or two children aboard, or meeting him in the local fish and chip shop, buying the family's supper. People would drop in to the Clerk's House, a charming old cottage in the main street, to chat to Leah as she scrubbed the kitchen floor and snatch a word with Desmond as he took a break from studying for his Master's degree.

As the local people came to know the family, their instinctive kindness towards a newcomer became more specific, more focused; Bletchingley generosity towards the family, especially the children, was impressive. As the only black children in the village, they got more than their share of attention; all four were, in any case, alert, amusing and bright. (When Naomi joined the rest of the family in 1963, flying over with the Bishop of Pretoria, she had delighted the passengers by spending most of the flight dancing 'the twist' – the current rage – up and down the aisle.) A friend of Melanie Lambert's, whose kitchen window was by the bus stop, was amused to hear Trevor disciplining the other local children, as they arrived, helter-skelter and often late, to catch the school bus. 'This will not do,' he said, 'the way we meet this bus. We must do it in a much more orderly fashion. Now let's line up as each person arrives and we'll walk with dignity into the bus.' So from that moment, a punctual row of children walked in perfect order on to their bus.

Several people began to feel that Trevor needed more stimulation than he could have in the village school, so they clubbed together to send him to Hawthorn's, a private school, where he was one of the top three students the whole time he was there. It was a 'Tory blue' private school, turning Trevor temporarily into a rabid royalist; he and his friends wept when the Labour Party won the 1966 Election. Such is the power of conditioning.

The village gave most bounteously to the Tutus: when he went back to South Africa they put their hands in their pockets again to buy him a car; later, when he was in Lesotho, some of them gave him a horse. There are those – not, it should be said, from Bletchingley – who feel that Tutu accepts too readily, but this criticism shows a failure to understand African generosity. What Africans have, they share – ask anyone who has had the privilege of being entertained in an African home. The Tutus were moved and grateful, their gratitude was unbounded, but they did not find it odd; it was exactly what they would have done themselves. In any case, as Melanie Lambert says, however much they received materially, they gave more, far more: 'They were full of such love and such humour and joy, joy, triumphant joy.'

What then, did Tutu give to Bletchingley? While the abiding memory of him is his capacity for love and joy, he also, not surprisingly, woke them to the realities of life in South Africa. Bletchingley was not an active village politically; the generosity of its inhabitants was not motivated by any strong feelings about social injustice, it was more a combination of kind hearts and collective white guilt. Sarah and Tim Goad, who lived in the next village and knew Tutu well, say that, but for him, nobody would have thought much about South Africa. 'If pressed, the people of Bletchingley would hedge their bets on South Africa. Desmond pricked our consciences. Our view of South Africa now is 99 per cent Desmond.' He could, and did, tell them just what life was like for blacks in South Africa. John Ewington is not alone in feeling he cannot believe everything he reads in the newspapers:

> It is not until someone like Desmond, whom you know and trust implicitly, gives you a first hand account, that you know what it's like. That it is horrifying and that it's a police state. He told us how the police can knock at the door and take away the husband or the wife, and if a neighbour doesn't happen to see, that person has just gone and you have no idea where they've gone, they just disappear.

In a very small way Tutu had begun to speak for his people.

This awakening of white consciences was incidental, peripheral to his work as a curate – politics seldom came into his sermons. He and the Rector, Ronald Brownrigg, made a good team, sharing their duties, even sharing their days off. Since his time at Benoni Tutu has kept regular 'quiet days' and he would insist that once a month they went out of the parish, took a room in a local convent, and spent a day sleeping, eating, praying and reading. He was happy, too, with the ecumenical tradition that the Rector was establishing. The parish had strong links with the Roman Catholics and the Methodists; all three denominations used the Anglican church, with its better facilities, they all contributed to the parish magazine, joined forces on many committees, even sometimes prepared mixed couples for marriage together.

Tutu was not afraid to speak out. There were at St Mary the Virgin, as at many Anglican churches, two strains of churchmanship, whose wishes were met by slightly different services, one at eight o'clock, the other at ten. Tutu thought it scandalous that the parish should be separated for Holy Communion, and he said so. On another occasion he gave a talk in which he defended two people who were not popular in the village, vigorously reprimanding his audience for their behaviour. As a pastor, too, he trod where others might fear to go. A parishioner once went to church in a state of such anger with a neighbour that she did not feel able to make her Communion. She was no sooner home than the telephone rang. It was Tutu, asking her what the trouble was and did she want to see him.

However well Tutu fitted in to the Surrey scene – and he was as at home at South Park as in his garage in Benoni – he was an African, expressing himself with typical African warmth and a spontaneous lack of inhibition which, at first, came as a shock to the reticent English. In worship he would give himself totally, indifferent to whether the congregation approved or even noticed. When conducting the Veneration of the Cross on Good Friday he did not follow English custom and kneel, with head touching the ground. As he reached the Cross he would kick off his shoes and lie on his face in total prostration, flat on the floor with arms extended. After the Midnight Mass at Christmas, he was once seen dancing in the starlight, quite alone: he was just dancing round the churchyard with the joy of Christmas. How enriched Western Christianity could be by more such encounters.

The parishioners cannot speak too warmly of Tutu. 'Bletchingley fell in love with the Tutus,' says one. 'He just loved everybody; you can't help responding to that,' says another. A third, when they left, said, 'Everyone loved them so much it was an agony.' Twenty years later, when, as Bishop of Johannesburg, he returned to preach, he told the congregation how back in South Africa, surrounded by hate, the memory of their love had protected him 'like a ring of fire'. The press, expecting a political sermon but disappointed, were there in force, astounded at the way 'the parishioners of Bletchingley treated Desmond as one of their own. Time and again, arms clothed in Harris tweed enveloped him while women in quilted green anoraks smothered him with kisses.'[16]

When Desmond had obtained his Master's degree and the family prepared to leave, the whole village, including those who were not church-goers, turned out for the farewell party. The Tutus were presented with a large cheque and their luggage grew more and more unmanageable as everyone gave them presents; there were even four specially made vestments. By the end of the party everyone was in tears. Some of those tears were shed by people who understood something of the South Africa to which the Tutus were returning.

5

An oasis in the Eastern Cape

It was indeed hard for the Tutus once again to become second-class citizens. They had known what to expect, but found that no preparation could reconcile them to their racially divided country. Soon after they returned to South Africa Desmond wrote to Martin Kenyon:[1]

> I don't want to sound melodramatic, but it is extremely difficult being back here, having to ask permission from various white officials to visit my parents! Having to carry my heavy passbook and look out for entrances meant especially for us . . . It is as well that Our Lord expects us not to like but to love our enemies and neighbours. It will be extremely difficult to love the white man as it is. Awful sentiment isn't it?

It is easy to take Desmond's lack of bitterness for granted, to forget that it is something for which he has had to struggle, that he prays constantly for the strength to win this struggle, even pleading for help from friends. He wrote, again to Martin Kenyon, 'Pray for us that we may not succumb to the temptation to hate and become bitter.'[2] That his prayers have been answered is due to good fortune as well as good nature; as he was fortunate in his inter-racial contacts in England, so he was to find himself, in his first post as a qualified theologian in South Africa, in a non-racial, non-denominational institution that was determined to create a harmonious environment, as far as possible disregarding the government's petty restrictions. After only a few weeks in Johannesburg the Tutus moved down to the small town of Alice, in the Eastern Cape, where Tutu had been appointed a lecturer at St Peter's College, since 1961 part of the Federal Theological Seminary, known in South Africa as Fedsem.

St Peter's enforced trek from Rosettenville to Alice was caused by various manifestations of apartheid as, by 1960, the Anglicans, the Methodists, the Congregationalists and the Presbyterians all needed new premises for training 'non-European' candidates for the ordained ministry. The influence of the Christian missionaries may have been ambiguous – the missions have, after all, been dubbed 'the soft edge of imperialism' – but there has never been any doubting their dimension of real concern; they did, for the most part, strive for a non-racial society. That was something the Nationalist government could not tolerate. One by one, it picked them off.

The Congregationalists had been part of Adams College, one of the oldest and most famous institutions for African education in South Africa, whose illustrious sons included Chief Albert Luthuli; the College refused to register under the Bantu Education Act and was forced to close in 1956. The Methodists and Presbyterians had trained at the equally famous Fort Hare University since 1921. As part of its scheme to tribalise the universities, the government took over Fort Hare, reserving it for Xhosas only. Most of the lecturers, including Professor Z. K. Matthews, the African Vice-Principal, resigned in protest and two more denominations lost their theological base. The Anglicans at Rosettenville had been living for years under the Damoclean sword of the Urban Areas Act; it had been increasingly difficult to get permits for Africans not resident in Johannesburg to study there. Finally it became impossible and they too were homeless.

Out of the evil that, in a nominally Christian country, had deprived Christians of their theological training, came good; the Theological Education Fund, prospecting for sites for the four denominations, suggested that they should come together in a Federal Seminary. Relationships between the Churches were not close, so a commission was set up to investigate the viability of the idea. Eventually, agreement was reached, but the level of trust was so low that it was decided that each Church should remain autonomous within the union. The Bishops then decided that the Community of the Resurrection should be invited to run the Anglican department; they accepted and the name of St Peter's was retained.

After more deliberation, and much searching, a site was chosen at Alice, near Port Elizabeth. It was close to both Lovedale College and Fort Hare University, which before government intervention had earned formidable academic reputations and between them produced leaders like Nelson Mandela, Robert Sobukwe, James Moroka, Oliver Tambo, Steve Biko and Gatsha Buthelezi. St Peter's may in one sense have been moving from the sophisticated life of the city to a sleepy village, but it was making its home in an area with its roots deep in the Xhosa tradition as well as in a British colonial past, finding itself in the political heartland of African resistance.

The seminary was, in its proximity to Fort Hare, next to a political minefield. It should have been natural for the seminary and the university to work together, but Fort Hare, now run by the Bantu Education Department, was in a state of deep despair. In any case, how could a seminary devoted to educating and freeing South Africans collaborate with an institution run by a government dedicated to keeping them in a state of servitude? The question of their academic relationship was the cause of a long and bitter battle, with feelings so passionate that the seminary was brought to the verge of disintegration, but eventually a compromise was reached. The four denominations made independent decisions, the Anglicans agreeing, whenever possible, to make the possession of a non-theological degree the basis of entry into the seminary. Thus St Peter's made some use of Fort Hare without any sacrifice of autonomy or integrity.

The move from Johannesburg had taken place in the early 1960s, so when Tutu, trained at St Peter's, Rosettenville, arrived at St Peter's, Alice, the seminary had been in its new home for nearly four years. The four constituent colleges – Methodist, Congregationalist, Presbyterian and Anglican – retained their independence by living in separate colleges with their own Principal, their own staff, their own refectories, while worshipping together in the assembly hall at least once a week, sharing a central administrative block, the library – considered to be one of the best theological libraries in South Africa, if not the whole of Africa – and later, as they grew more confident in their ecumenical stance, the lectures. Each Principal took it in turn to be President for a two-year period and the students, together with those from St Paul's, Grahamstown and St Bede's, Umtata, took the same examinations, the Associate of the Federation of Theological Seminaries. The partnership was, eventually, a success. Church unity is crucially important in South Africa, with its numerous Independent Churches (formerly known as 'Separatist Churches'), and the creation and the forging into a unity of the four distinct traditions comprising the seminary was, according to Father Aelred Stubbs, the President from 1965 till 1967, the most significant ecumenical achievement in South Africa in the 1960s.

Particularly significant was the utter refusal of anyone at the seminary, staff or student, to bow to the pressures of a racial society – Alice stood proudly as an oasis in the desert of apartheid. Visitors arrived to feel they were in another land, where black and white could be together without causing any trouble and where, as one of them said, 'Even the air was different'. Simon Gqubule, the only other black on the staff in Tutu's time, points out a subtle but important indication of the depth of their non-racialism. 'As a community we paid no attention to colour. It was not something we did consciously, we *unconsciously* paid no attention to it.' The various permits necessary for Africans, 'coloureds', Indians and whites to live together had been obtained; the restrictions of 'petty apartheid', decreeing where men of different skin colour should sleep, eat and wash, were quite simply ignored. So, for instance, Father Stubbs and his Vice-Principal,

Father Mark Tweedy, had rooms in the same block as the students, who themselves mixed with total freedom, all sharing the bathroom, the showers, the lavatory – living, in short, as students anywhere. They somehow got away with it, though their activities were probably known to the Special Branch.

This non-racial climate was, of course, balm to the souls of the Tutus. Leah wrote: 'The Seminary is a marvellous place. The friendliness and cooperation is such that you would have to travel the far corners of the Republic and still be lucky if you found anything like it . . . What happens outside the Seminary is unprintable.'[3] Desmond found it 'exhilarating and great fun being here. We are so far getting on like a house on fire with the CR.'[4] Mpho, the only one of the children not at boarding school, was, at four years old and more fluent in English than Xhosa, slightly confused, telling someone she was 'a non-white European'. They were thrilled with the house, an L-shaped bungalow furnished for them by the CR Fathers, and filled it with people; the Tutus, in turn, were a roaring success. Canon Michael Carmichael, then Principal of St Bede's Theological College in Umtata, remembers the Tutus 'taking everyone by storm, throwing their immense friendliness and warmth around'; Elizabeth Crace, visiting them one Christmas, carried away a lasting impression:

> South Africa to me means singing and dancing and fun and happiness, not poverty and problems – that is what we are all missing when we think of South Africa. Africans have this marvellous capacity for happiness which we poor Europeans don't have to anything like the same extent and the Tutus are the best exponents of it. We all love talking about Desmond – even thinking about him is good, he gives you such hope.

Tutu came like a breath of fresh air to the students. As well as being a lecturer at the seminary, he was Anglican Chaplain to Fort Hare. The students, who found the university a claustrophobic place, full of rules and regulations, would take refuge in the friendliness of the seminary; particularly they felt at ease with the Tutus, flocking to their Sunday 'Coffee Evenings'. Tutu took an active part in the various plays and revues put on by Ruth Lundie, who taught English at the seminary. They would do sketches in which colour roles were reversed, yellow make-up put on black skins, black on white. On one occasion a Presbyterian minister who had agreed to sing 'Glasgow Belongs To Me', was overcome by scruples (the last line, 'When I am tight on a Saturday night', was too much for him) and withdrew. Tutu, dressed in kilt and sporran and entered as 'Father Desmond MacTutu', took his place, rendering the songs with 'great shrieks and howls' in an atrociously ham Glasgow accent.

Tutu was one of six lecturers, teaching mainly Doctrine and Greek. Surprisingly, in view of his academic record, he found the work very testing and wrote humbly: 'I am of course up to my neck in work, having to organise my little knowledge into notes that are readily assimilable.'[5] Leah went further: 'I can't say he is enjoying it, he is still trying to find his feet. He is so lacking in self-confidence that I said to him, in anger, that it would take him a century to find them.'[6]

He was, in fact, considered the most highly qualified black Anglican theologian in the country, better qualified, as Father Stubbs willingly admits, than either he or Father Mark Tweedy. Perhaps this was part of the problem. Tutu was already all too aware of his responsibility as a representative of black education and now the CR Fathers, previously his teachers and mentors, were his colleagues. But if he found it all a bit daunting, he did not show it and everyone believed the confident façade, one of the lecturers saying, 'he was, as you would expect, confident, but he was never aggressive in a nasty way'. Nor did the students have any inkling of the truth; Zakes Mohutsioa, his former scoutmaster, now at Fedsem as a mature student, found him 'Impressive, thorough, very fine, very strict'. Hardly a tribute to a nervous teacher.

Tutu was not going to be party to any teaching that made life easier for blacks because they were blacks. He had himself experienced the oppressive mental bondage under which blacks laboured, continually told they were not as intellectual as whites, suffering under the paternalistic assumption that blacks could not hope to equal whites in civilisation, though 'one day perhaps ... in a thousand years ...' He fought against any insularity, black or white, for example in his insistence that his students should read and understand the works of theologians like Paul Tillich and Karl Barth. They may have had little or no preparation for such work, there may even have been a feeling among the white staff that this was a little more than should be expected, but he refused to compromise or accept any difference in standards. Never can Tillich or Barth have been so popular as at Alice, where they were symbols of intellectual equality.

Alongside his duties as a lecturer, Tutu was also continuing his private studies in Islam, which, after taking his Master's degree at King's College, he had studied further during two months in the Holy Land on his way back from England to South Africa. At Alice he started to work for a doctorate with the University of South Africa; his thesis, combining his interests in Islam and the Old Testament, being on Moses and the Koran. Father Stubbs did his best to arrange his teaching schedule in such a way that he had time to study and Brother Charles, who had tutored him in Islam at Rosettenville, remembers him lying ill in bed romping through a paperback Arabic grammar as if it were a novel. Though Tutu did not complete the thesis, this does not lessen the respect in which he is held academically. In fact Father Stubbs suggests that

> He had the kind of academic excellence that made it a perfectly reasonable thing to do and I don't doubt that if other things of an ecclesiastical political nature had not intervened, he would have gone ahead and got it – he's certainly got the ability. It's one of the reasons one never minds Desmond getting all these Honorary Doctorates, because he could have become a Doctor in his own right if he hadn't been called to a more active part as a leader.

This leadership role was one into which Tutu grew slowly, almost unwillingly. His rise is reminiscent of Shakespeare's 'Some are born great, some achieve greatness, some have greatness thrust upon them'.[7] Desmond's achievements belong to the third of those categories, though greatness was not so much thrust upon him as emerging, with a remorseless inevitability, from his religious beliefs. His political role is inextricably entwined with his calling as a pastor.

It was at Alice that he first began to experience politics and religion as being indivisible. Since the days of his first curacy at Benoni, Tutu had been first and foremost a pastor, feeling that this was where his vocation lay. Though he enjoyed his teaching work at the seminary, he knew that ultimately what he said was less important than what he was, the values for which he stood: 'It was more exciting to see the students grow in their relationship to our Lord Jesus Christ than it was to see them acquire some of the academic and technical things which I taught. In fact it was, and still is, tremendously thrilling to see people grow in spiritual stature.'[8] It was largely as a pastor, specifically in his job as Chaplain to Fort Hare University, that he earned the love and respect of the students, perhaps by caring spiritual counselling, loving concern over personal problems or as a sometimes humorous reconciler. (He once diffused a potentially explosive situation when one of the Methodist students objected to invoking the name of the Virgin Mary – a tactless remark in this non-denominational setting. The ensuing silence was broken by a laugh from Tutu: 'You've done away with the whole theory of intercession!')

His pastoral care could also take the form of standing up for justice. He continuously affirmed the students' dignity as human beings, he wanted them to understand that they had a *right* to share the good

74

things of the world; the message was not new, but Tutu's ability to put it across was impressive. And the context was one of an oppression and injustice harsh even by South African standards.

The early 1960s had been a low point in black African resistance. After the Sharpeville Massacre the government banned both the African National Congress and the Pan-Africanist Congress, with penalties of up to ten years' imprisonment for anyone found to be furthering their aims; legislation grew increasingly repressive, detention without trial was given the spurious dignity of law and horrifying reports emerged about the conditions under which blacks were imprisoned, the torture they endured at the hands of the security police. After nearly fifty years with a policy of non-violence, the ANC, operating underground under the leadership of Nelson Mandela, formed an armed wing, Umkhonto we Sizwe (The Spear of the Nation), which, based in a house in a northern Johannesburg suburb called Rivonia, was to carry on the struggle in a new way, sabotaging installations and offices, but expressly not injuring or killing people. The Pan-Africanist Congress, not content with these limited targets, formed its own armed resistance wing, *Poqo* (meaning 'pure', 'standing alone'). The main national liberation movements had consistently refused to use any form of violence, but, as Umkhonto's manifesto points out, 'The time comes in the life of any nation when there remain only two choices: submit or fight. That time has now come in South Africa. We shall not submit and we have no choice but to hit back with all means within our power in defence of our people, our future and our freedom.'[9] Predictably the security police unleashed their power. Poqo was broken, in August 1962 Nelson Mandela was arrested, the following July the Rivonia headquarters were raided and most of the remaining leaders arrested. The subsequent 'Rivonia Trial' led to their imprisonment for life.

During these bleak years Tutu was in England. 'In one sense he didn't miss much,' says Father Stubbs, 'but in another he missed going through that experience of deep darkness, a deep kind of death in a way.' Tutu was, however, to be involved in the next stage of African resistance.

The late 1960s were a time of seething unrest in the Eastern Cape. Many of the students had brothers, fathers or uncles imprisoned on Robben Island, banned, gone into exile; there was the constant fear of informers. From this cauldron a new response to white oppression was beginning to emerge – black consciousness.

The Black Consciousness Movement started in 1968 at a conference of the University Christian Movement at Stutterheim, a white area not far from Alice. It was a multi-racial conference and most of the whites were in sympathy with black aspirations; nevertheless the black students were becoming more and more frustrated by their inability to have a voice in formulating policy.

There were at the time only three black universities in South Africa, as against nine white, so the blacks were outnumbered. Further, the leadership positions were being taken by whites, who, with the advantages of better school education and wider reading, were more articulate, more confident. Perhaps most crucially, the whites, not sharing the same problems as the black students, could not enter completely into the black predicament. For instance, while they were legally free to be present at the conference without special permission, the blacks had to apply for permits to be in a white area. Because of the stance they took against apartheid, the black students did not see why they needed permission to be anywhere in South Africa; they refused to apply, thereby risking arrest. They found the white response to this sort of situation naïve. The whites might, for instance, suggest that they should all lie in front of the vans when the police came to round up those blacks without permits, but the oppressed and per-secuted students knew all too well what the result of that would be. The whites would simply be removed, possibly reprimanded; the blacks would be arrested and would spend the conference in the police cells.

These differences – of numbers, education and legal status – led to the black students pulling out of the main conference and discussing their problems in their own caucus. They decided their needs were not being met in a multi-racial organisation and that the whites could never have a real appreciation of their problems; it was time they formed their own organisation. The aspirations of the blacks should be met by the blacks alone. Hence SASO, the South African Students Organisation, first of the Black Consciousness groupings, was born.

Steve Biko, the first President of SASO and known as 'The Father of Black Consciousness', defined this new ideology, whose emphasis was on the inner attitude of the black man to himself:[10]

> All in all the black man has become a shell, a shadow of a man, completely defeated, drowning in his own misery, a slave, an ox bearing the yoke of oppression with sheepish timidity. This is the first truth, bitter as it may seem, that we have to acknowledge before we can start on any programme designed to change the status quo. It becomes more necessary to see the truth as it is if you realise that the only vehicle for change are these people who have lost their personality. The first step therefore is to make the black man come to himself; to pump back life into his empty shell; to infuse him with pride and dignity, to remind him of his complicity in the crime of allowing himself to be misused

and therefore letting evil reign supreme in the country of his birth. This is what we mean by an inward-looking process. This is the definition of 'Black Consciousness'.

How then, did Tutu respond? Broadly he was, of course, in total sympathy with the aims of these radical young students. They were, after all, affirming the dignity of the black man in their way, just as he was in his. But there were differences. The students felt that Tutu's assumptions about the future of South Africa were too optimistic, they found his views too moderate, lacking the sense of urgency which coursed through their veins. After four years in England his attitude was so essentially non-racial that he was in a sense *above* race. While he longed for co-operation, sharing and harmony between black and white, while he wanted to call upon the white students and radicalise them, Black Consciousness was saying otherwise. In the words of Justice Moloto, a student at Fort Hare at the time, 'It was important for the black man to withdraw from the white man, consolidate himself, to learn leadership skills and only come back and meet the white man on an equal footing. And we must, therefore, come together and work out our strategies in such a way that when we do go out we are not going back to the white man cap-in-hand.' Despite this difference in stance, the students respected Tutu deeply, appreciating that he was operating first and foremost as a Christian priest and that, on the staff of a non-racial seminary and Chaplain to a backward, government-controlled university, he was in a very difficult position.

But if he was not as radical as the students, he was not afraid to stand up and be counted. For instance he refused to meet Sir Alec and Lady Douglas-Home when they visited the seminary to meet the staff. 'I stayed away because although the Homes are themselves probably attractive people, we thought the Conservatives had behaved abominably over issues which touched our hearts most nearly.'[11] He frequently spoke up, often in a way which has remained in the minds of those who heard him.

Barney Pityana, a student at Fort Hare and very active politically, remembers an occasion in 1967. The setting was the conference of the Anglican Students Federation at Michaelhouse in Natal, the subject under discussion was Bishop Crowther, the Bishop of Kimberley and an outspoken critic of apartheid – was the government right to deport him? Some of the white delegates, mostly from Stellenbosch and Cape Town Universities, spoke up on the side of the government, saying the Bishop's behaviour was 'unpatriotic and unSouth African' and that he deserved to be sent packing. As he listened, Barney's rage mounted at the white students' assumption that everyone shared their views on what was and was not patriotic; he weighed in, trying to overturn the motion. To his pleasant surprise Tutu, who, as a university chaplain, was present, supported Barney with a powerful speech in defence of all critics of apartheid. The respect in which he was held ensured that he was listened to with rapt attention – though it did not, of course, affect the fate of Bishop Crowther, who was soon on his way back to the USA.

Tutu would also make his views known from the pulpit. He used regularly to take his turn preaching in 'the travesty next door',[12] Fort Hare University, his congregation often the whole university, not just the Anglicans. One such occasion was in 1968, soon after that dreadful August night when Soviet troops marched into Czechoslovakia. Tutu spoke about human rights, comparing the position of the black South Africans under apartheid with the Czechs, trampled by the Russians. Afterwards the university buzzed with excitement, the students, knowing the mentality of the authorities all too well, fearing he would never be invited to preach at the university again. He was not.

These were two of many occasions which were, in a sense, paving the way to an experience which was to bring Tutu face-to-face with the savagery of apartheid and its perpetrators in a way he had not previously witnessed – the Fort Hare strike.

It was after the August vacation in 1968, the year when students all over Europe and America were making their voices heard. There was no formal student representation at Fort Hare, as that would be to condone the government-run university, with all that it implied; nevertheless there had been a series of strikes, as the students called for an end to racist education, demanded more competent academic staff or protested, for instance, at the presence on campus of the Deputy Minister of Bantu Education. A climax was reached when a new Rector, J. J. de Wet, was appointed and a group of active Christians, including Barney Pityana and Justice Moloto, asked to see him. They wanted 'to persuade him to treat them as responsible human beings, not as a lower form of human life'.[13] The Rector, far from listening to them, demanded that the graffiti and slogans should be removed and that they should put a stop to the insubordination reigning on campus; if this was not done, disciplinary action would follow. The group, seeing this as victimisation, refused to accept the mantle of formal leadership he was trying to throw on their shoulders, arguing that on these matters he should address the whole student body. The students backed this demand, the Rector insisted he would only talk to a small group: it looked as if stalemate had been reached. Eventually the students agreed to elect a delegation, at which point the Rector refused to see them.

At this the whole campus erupted into protest; 500 of the 550 students sat, defiantly but quite peacefully, on the lawn in front of the administration buildings. This continued for several days; demonstration simply took the place of work as, in an orderly and well-disciplined way, they clocked in, broke for lunch, sat it out for the rest of the day. Then one day, at eleven o'clock, there was an announcement on the loudspeaker that all the students were going to be expelled; they were to be off the campus by two o'clock. Nobody moved. At precisely two o'clock all hell was let loose as police screamed on to the campus in armoured cars, complete with dogs and guns and tear-gas. Before they knew what was happening, the petrified students were surrounded at gun point, wondering what was going to happen to them. Soon, with the indomitable spirit of black South Africans, they started singing freedom songs, while a small crowd gathered, helplessly watching. Nobody was allowed out, nor was anyone allowed through to talk to them – until, that is, Tutu came over from the seminary. The police tried to prevent him, but he simply said, 'Don't stop me, because if you are arresting the students you can count me, as their Chaplain, with them,' and elbowed his way through. For the rest of the day, as they were herded off to their rooms to pack their bags and put on to buses to take them to the railway station, he stayed with them, offering encouragement and support.

Tutu's total identification with their cause impressed the students deeply. He was, according to Justice Moloto, 'as visible by his presence as other people, the white lecturers from Fort Hare for instance, were by their absence. He has always been a leading light in the black man's struggle, whether in a very small way on a university campus or at national level.' For Barney Pityana, this incident actually changed his life: 'It was a deeply moving experience. The students flocked round him in relief and excitement, asking for his blessing. I knew then what I wanted to do. That was the first real experience of my feeling of what it means to be a priest. And I thought there was something in it for me.'

It changed Tutu too. 'I never felt so desolated,' he said years later. 'I was angry with God. I couldn't understand how he could let all that happen to those students.' He was, says Father Stubbs, 'completely bouleversed, bewildered, by the experience – he hadn't realised just how savagely the students could be dealt with by the authorities.' The next day, celebrating Mass in St Peter's Chapel, he completely broke down. Elizabeth Cracc was there: 'I remember so well in this lovely Chapel with its grey stone floor, kneeling at the Communion rail while Desmond came with the chalice and the tears pouring down his face and splashing on the grey floor. I remember thinking they looked like black tears, because they left these black marks on the grey floor.'

Tutu may have initially had reservations about the thinking that was to become the Black Consciousness Movement, but he never failed to listen to the students, talk and argue with them, and to show solidarity with them. By the end of his time at Fedsem he had come to identify with them very strongly.

It was a rich time, those two years in Alice. Tutu was bursting to communicate and he did so; he had opportunities to fulfil his deep need of a pastoral role; he entered the political arena in a new and more intense way. He also took part in the Churches' struggle to articulate the Christian response to apartheid by taking part in various commissions and sitting on committees of theological education. He could have stayed at Alice; he was in fact earmarked as a future Principal of the seminary and was already due to be Vice-Principal in January 1970. However, with mixed feelings, he decided to accept an invitation to be a lecturer in the University of Botswana, Lesotho and Swaziland, based at Roma in Lesotho. So once again he was to be away from the action in South Africa.

6

Out of South Africa

In moving from Alice to Roma Tutu was making the first of a series of difficult decisions: over the next ten years he was to change his job five times. Was he ambitious, restless, uncertain of exactly what he should be doing with his life? Was it that his gifts led to a constant stream of tempting offers which, with his inborn desire to please, he found hard to refuse? Was he, as one of his colleagues has suggested, 'in a hurry'? Though all these ingredients may well have been present, in every decision the mix was different. There was only one constant, that was his wish to do what he understood to be God's will; for that understanding he has, in every case, prayed long and hard.

The later decisions were to become more complex, more agonising; in 1969, when he was invited to Roma, the issues were relatively straightforward. Personal ambition was not the obvious motive – indeed there were those on the seminary staff who thought that to give up the opportunity to be Principal of the biggest theological college in South Africa was plain foolish – but it played its part: 'I enjoyed teaching and this was an opportunity to work in an institute of higher learning. Also teaching at a university had kudos and it was good for your CV.' The higher salary was welcome to a father of a growing family, and, further, having experienced life outside South Africa, the opportunity of a good job in a society free of apartheid was tempting. But his decision to accept a lectureship at Roma revolved less around his own wishes than the needs of his family, in particular the education of his four children. He had always been determined that they should not be educated under Bantu Education and at Roma the educational opportunities would be better.

Tutu is a loving and concerned father; his regular Christmas letters, circulated to an ever-growing group of friends around the world, are full of the hopes and achievements of his family. Though he has been criticised for sending his children overseas for their education – 'It's all very well for him,' poorer South Africans sometimes say, 'what about our children?' – he has refused to be moved. It is a very human response; most people wish to give their children the best they can and at the time there were no private schools in South Africa that would take black children. Neither were the Tutus unique; black South Africans who could manage to have their children educated overseas have been doing so since Professor Jabavu, the first South African graduate and a father figure of African education, qualified in London over fifty years ago.

While the Tutus were at Alice the three older children were at fee-paying schools in Swaziland: Trevor at Waterford, the famous multi-racial school in Mbabane, Theresa and Naomi at St Michael's, a convent school in Manzini, where they were soon to be joined by Mpho. Though Desmond and Leah's friends have made generous contributions towards the children's education (Trevor's fees were paid in full by Tutu's old parish of Bletchingley), and while the children were bright, much of their fees being covered by scholarships, there were still expenses which the Tutus often had difficulty in meeting. Even ferrying the children to and from school was, with six trips of over 800 miles every year, a substantial cost in petrol alone; living at Roma would halve the travelling distance. An even greater advantage was that the two younger children, Naomi and Mpho, could be educated at the primary school on the university campus, where there were special allowances for the children of staff.

Roma gets its name from a Roman Catholic Mission established there in 1862, though the university only dates from 1945. It began very humbly when four Roman Catholic priest-lecturers, with strictly limited resources, began teaching five students in a converted primary school, later to be extended with the help of the Paramount Chief of Basutoland and named Pius XII College. It was soon taken over by a religious order and by the early 1960s there were 175 students, accommodation for about twenty members of staff, a modern science block and the beginnings of a university campus. They were, however, having financial problems; worse, there were difficulties with the 'special relationship' they had entered into with the University of South Africa. It was becoming clear that the college could not continue to function in its existing form. At about the same time the governments of what were then the High Commission Territories of Basutoland, Bechuanaland Protectorate and Swaziland were exploring the possibilities of providing more higher education for their nationals. Could a partnership be arranged? Eventually it was agreed that an independent, secular university, serving principally the three countries of Bechuanaland, Basutoland and Swaziland, should be founded by taking over the grounds and buildings of Pius XII College.

On October 9th, 1964, the university was formally inaugurated as an autonomous institution, granting its own certificates, diplomas and degrees. By 1970, when Tutu started work, the three countries had been granted independence and the university had correspondingly changed its name to the University of Botswana, Lesotho and Swaziland. Though there were no racial or religious barriers to admission, the 400 students included only a few whites, mostly the children of members of staff. The only racial conflict on the campus concerned staffing – should they all be African or should whites be appointed? The majority feeling was that lecturers from the three countries the university was founded to serve were preferred over other Africans; whites, for the most part, accepted that they were only there for as long as they were needed.

Tutu had been to Lesotho on holiday, when he had climbed a mountain in his walking shoes and, according to Ruth Lundie, one of his companions, 'quite fallen in love with the place'. Lesotho, 'The Kingdom in the Sky', is a mountainous region surrounded on all sides by the Republic of South Africa, the only country in the world whose entire area is more than 1,000 metres above sea level. Bushman paintings, cannibal caves and fossil footprints of five-toed dinosaurs 180 million years old are reminders of old Africa, long before the white man came. Even today there is a timeless quality about the blanket-wrapped people riding the famous Basotho ponies – often the most reliable form of transport – across the spectacular mountains. Not least, it is out of South Africa, out of reach of apartheid.

It is not, however, free of political strife, nor was it free of South African interference. Lesotho politics were dominated by religion, with the government mainly Roman Catholic, the opposition mainly Protestant – a situation Tutu referred to as 'an Ulster in reverse'.[1] White South Africa backed the ruling Basuto National Party, a preference which was felt in the university by the constant fear of informers. The government was suspicious of a federal university; it liked to know what was going on, was always on the watch for 'subversives'.

In January 1970, soon after Desmond arrived, the Basuto National Party committed the ultimate sin in a democracy – it interfered with the elections. Half-way through the count it realised it was losing, so, with fewer than ten of the sixty seats unannounced, it accused the Opposition of thuggery and chicanery, stopped the elections and declared a State of Emergency. Under Chief Leabua Jonathan the Basuto National Government, initially anxious to keep on good terms with South Africa to whom it was an economic hostage, ruled until the coup of 1986 (brought off with the connivance and assistance of that same fickle South African government) removed it from office.

By the time he came to Roma Tutu was known to the ever-vigilant South African authorities, already unpopular with them and regarded as a potential subversive, though he was in no way actively involved in politics. He was working hard teaching theology to the degree-course students; he was still studying for his doctoral thesis on Moses and the Koran; as always he was fulfilling his pastoral role, both officially, as the Anglican Chaplain, and simply by being himself. And his desire to do something about the injustice in his country was beginning to find expression in his growing involvement with black theology.

The term 'Black Theology' reached South Africa around 1970. It originated in America, where it was largely a theological response to black power; in South Africa it is intimately related to black consciousness.

A major trend in modern theology claims that theology is not formed in a vacuum: it is a response to circumstances, it speaks from a specific situation. Black theology (which is liberation theology in South Africa) emerges from the pain of suffering and oppression; it is not occasioned by abstract problems of human suffering, it tries to meet the anguish and the questions of a specific people who suffer hunger, poverty, humiliation and fear at the hands of other human beings, whose lives are governed by literally hundreds of oppressive laws, whose rights and privileges are determined not by the fact of their humanity, but by their pigmentation – a people who had come to question their own identity. To conquer the humiliating self-doubt of the black man living under apartheid and to assert the value of every human being is something for which Tutu never ceases to strive:[2]

> Have you seen a symphony orchestra? They are all dolled up and beautiful, with their magnificent instruments, cellos, violins, etc. Sometimes, dolled up as the rest, there is a chap at the back carrying a triangle. Now and again the conductor will point to him and he will play 'ting'. That might seem so insignificant, but in the conception of the composer something irreplaceable would be lost to the total beauty of the symphony if that 'ting' did not happen. In the praise ascending to God's throne something totally irreplaceable of your unique way of loving God would be missing. We are each, says Jesus, of unique and inestimable value.

As God chose to come to earth as a man, not as a spirit or as an animal, then men are temples of the Holy Spirit. We must not only accept and affirm one another, but honour one another, because 'We are God-carriers and ought to genuflect to one another as we do to the reserved sacrament in the tabernacle'.[3] So to accord people different treatment by virtue of their race is as silly as to imagine a university where qualifications for entry 'were to be determined by whether one had a large nose or not, and if you did not possess such a proboscis then you had to obtain special permission to enter this institution of higher learning reserved only for those with large noses.'[4]

Tutu espoused the cause of black theology instantly and enthusiastically. Though his opposition to apartheid stems from a simple awareness of the dignity of man, he could not but be attracted by the opportunity of giving his instincts theological backing. Much of his time, both while he was at Roma and later, was spent going to black theology conferences, writing papers, giving talks. The violation of the humanity of the black man was, he wrote in one such paper, the reason for the emergence of black theology:[5]

> Black theology has occurred mainly in South Africa, where blacks have had their noses rubbed in the dust by white racism, depersonalising them to the extent that they have – blasphemy of blasphemies – come to doubt the reality of their own personhood and humanity. They have come to believe that the denigration of their humanity by those who oppress them is the truth about themselves . . . Liberation theology becomes part of a people's struggle for liberation; it tries to help victims of oppression to assert their humanity and so look the other chap in the eye and speak face to face without shuffling their feet and apologising for their black existence.

In writing that, Tutu could have been writing from the point of view of black consciousness: humanity stands central. The black man is important and he is important for what he *is*, not for what he does. It is a hair's breadth from a religious approach. Though there were many Christians behind the emergence of black consciousness, they did not have to concern themselves with theological issues; black theology, its theological counterpart, obviously does. It needs to justify the ways of God to Man, to seek to understand the exploitation of man by man. When every day the black man sees the ladder of privilege, with the exploiter on the top rung, the exploited on the bottom, he must ask 'Whose side is God on?' He must question whether Jesus was necessarily the Jew of history or the white man of Western Christianity. Why should he not have been black?

Black theology has little difficulty in arguing that the God of the Bible is on the side of the oppressed. Tutu's thinking on the subject of liberation as a theme of the Old Testament is one of his major contributions to understanding a black view of theology. He rejoices that the first book of Genesis – 'a magnificent hymn to creation, a paean of praise to God the Creator'[6] – should have been written at a tragic time in Jewish history, when the Israelites were exiled in Babylon, surrounded by strange gods, depressed and dejected. (Might one compare their response to the gallant spirit of the black South Africans, singing freedom songs when confronted by bullets, tear-gas and arrest?) In his own forthright style, Tutu explores the parallels between his fellow blacks and the rabble of Israelite slaves, working as builders for their taskmasters, chastised when they could not make bricks without straw. He points out that though the Israelites suffered for long years, though they must have thought that God did not care, even that he did not exist, history shows that eventually they were set free, that they did reach the promised land:[7]

> This God did not just talk – he acted. He showed himself to be a doing God. Perhaps we might add another point about God – He takes sides. He is not a neutral God. He took the side of the slaves, the oppressed, the victims. He is still the same even today, he sides with the poor, the hungry, the oppressed, the victims of injustice.

But though the Bible affirms that God is always on the side of the downtrodden, it is not because they are better or more deserving than their oppressors, but simply because they are oppressed, because that is the kind of God he is. 'So to the anguished cry, "God, on whose side are you?" we say emphatically, God is on your side, not as some jingoistic national deity who says "my people right or wrong," but as one who saves and yet ultimately judges those whom he saves.'[8]

God's compassion does not mean he ceases to judge, so Tutu warns that liberation is challenging, costly, demands a high sense of responsibility. He argues that the spirit of the Israelites was broken: they had been dehumanised by their bondage, acquired a slave mentality:[9]

> We know just what this sense of inferiority can do to people. We develop a self-hatred and despise one another as a result. And we treat one another as scum. Have you seen how we drive in town and how we drive in Soweto? In Soweto we stop our cars anywhere because we despise one another and treat one another as of little worth.

There is little use in casting off one form of oppression, only to put on the almost equally oppressive garments of bitterness and division.

The Jesus of the New Testament explicitly came to the poor, the broken-hearted, 'to preach deliverance to the captives, to set at liberty them that are bruised'.[10] There is no question whose side he is on. When Tutu writes on liberation in the New Testament he is most concerned with personal liberation, freedom from sin, sickness and hunger. 'People are set free *from* bondage to the world, the Devil and sin, in order to be free *for* God, and to be fully human because Christ came that they might have life in its abundant fullness.'[11] His constant plea is for a South Africa liberated from oppression and injustice so that it may be filled with reconciliation, caring and compassion.

Though books on black theology frequently include a chapter by Desmond Tutu and though he is one of its most eloquent and persuasive communicators, he is not a black theologian in the technical sense; he has not read, reflected or wrestled with the issues in sufficient depth – even if he felt the inclination he has not had the time. His thinking is expressed more in sermons, devotional talks and addresses than in serious theological writing. (Though it should be said that many theologians, like the distinguished Professor John de Gruchy, have no doubt he could make an important contribution – there is no question as to his theological ability.) Desmond Tutu's involvement with black theology is a natural consequence of his faith; it is part, not the whole, of his theological pilgrimage.

Tutu's theology is deeply incarnational, rooted in the fact that, in Jesus, God has entered fully into the human situation. (It is significant that he is very drawn to William Temple's statement that Christianity is the most materialistic of all religions.) 'The God whom we worship is wonderfully transcendent – St John in his Gospel sums it up by saying "God is Spirit". Yet when this God wanted to intervene decisively in the affairs of Man, he did not come as a spiritual being. He did not come as an angel. No, he came as a human being.'[12] While the centrality of the spiritual is never in question, the encounter with God forces Tutu to seek a spirituality relevant to his time and his situation. 'He is the transcendent one who fills us with awe – the *mysterium tremendum et fascinans*. But He does not allow those who worship Him to remain in an exclusive spiritual ghetto. Our encounter with Him launches us into the world, to work together with this God for the establishment of his kingdom.'[13]

So there can be no separation of the spiritual and the material, the religious and the political. There can be no 'pie in the sky when you die', no dodging the social responsibility the Christian shoulders when he is baptised. Tutu's involvement in black theology confirmed his growing instinct that, in South Africa, Christians must proclaim the injustice of apartheid and God's firm stand with the oppressed:[14]

> Liberation theology challenges churches everywhere to be true to their calling to exercise a prophetic ministry in speaking up for the dumb, the voiceless, for those too weak to speak up for themselves, to oppose oppression, injustice, corruption, and evil wherever these may be found. This could be a call to martyrdom, but if God is for us who can be against us?

In August 1971, after only eighteen months at Roma, temptation was once again put in Tutu's path. He was asked by Dr Walter Cason, the acting Director of the Theological Education Fund, to allow his name to be shortlisted for the post of Associate Director responsible for Africa. It was an attractive offer. The job was challenging and reasonably well-paid; he would be contributing to the very organisation which had made it possible for him to go to King's College; the idea of moving back to England, where the TEF was based, appealed to the rest of the family, not least because the children would once again have the educational advantages of the United Kingdom.

The Dean of King's College, whose name Tutu had given as a referee, wrote enthusiastically to the Director, Dr Shoki Coe. His opinion was that Desmond Tutu would be 'a fine worker in the field' and that both domestically and academically he felt it would be a wise appointment. But he did have reservations:[15]

> I have no hesitation at all in strongly recommending you to consider him as a candidate for this vacancy, though it is with the greatest regret that I do so because I have always hoped that Desmond would become a theological teaching power in South Africa, and bringing him to Europe seems almost to be undermining his influence there.

Further, he wondered just what his old pupil's motivation was in considering the post. Was there some element of social advancement? Was he considering the post primarily for the sake of his children?

Tutu was, however, offered the job and he accepted, reasoning on the same pragmatic lines as he had two years earlier: it was a wonderful opportunity, both for him and his family. 'I wouldn't want to make out I was idealistic or anything of that sort. I'm just trying to do what I can.' So in January 1972, on a bitter winter's day, all six Tutus arrived in England, tired and cold, to be met at Heathrow by Tutu's new secretary, Betty Ward, and her husband, together with Jim Bergquist, who was already working with the TEF. They all drove to a furnished house in South-East London, where the Tutus were to stay until they moved to a permanent home in Grove Park. The assumption was that after some sixteen hours' travel they would spend the day settling in; but, far from attending to his creature comforts, Tutu insisted on going straight away to the office in Bromley to meet his new colleagues.

The Theological Education Fund was founded to improve theological education in the third world. It was started in 1960 by Charles Ransom, an Irish Methodist missionary who had worked in India, where he had been appalled at the inefficiency of a system in which the denominations operated separately, so from the beginning the whole thrust was ecumenical. The aim was to help the churches of Africa, Asia and Latin America – the 'younger churches' as they were then called – to be free from dependence on Western missionary societies; the intention was to train indigenous teachers for the theological seminaries, indigenous pastors to lead the congregations. $4 million was provided by John D. Rockefeller Jr and eight American missionary societies, this money to be spent over five years, a period which became known as the 'First Mandate'.

It was an *ad hoc* organisation, only continuing if the mandate was renewed and financial support was available. The success of the first mandate led to a second and a third, and it was at the start of this third mandate that Tutu arrived to take up his post. The policy by then was that senior staff should come not from the West, but from the areas for which they were responsible. Thus the Taiwanese Director, Dr Shoki Coe, dealt with North-East Asia, supported by four Associate Directors: Aharon Sapsezian from Brazil was responsible for Latin America, Ivy Chou from Malaysia for South-East Asia, Jim Bergquist from the USA for the Pacific, with Africa under the aegis of Desmond Tutu.

Though Tutu was by then forty-one, he had never worked in an office before and, to start with, he had little idea what was expected of him. His job description was necessarily vague, involving 'working from this office, collaborating with our international team of directors and the TEF Committee, corresponding with theological colleges and others in Africa engaged in various forms of theological education, and spending quite a large part of the year travelling in order to visit these people.'[16]

Travel was indeed an important part of the work. Each Director would visit his area, possibly making as many as five trips a year. He would find out the needs of the theological colleges and encourage them to formulate projects that might be funded by the TEF; he would then suggest how the grants should be given to whom. The climax to the year's work came at the Annual General Meeting every July, when for a week the Directors would present their cases before the international committee and justify their requests – like Cabinet Ministers before a budget, each wanting the largest share of the financial cake.

For Tutu this side of the work was both difficult and exasperating. He would return from his trips to Africa bubbling over with excitement, determined to do something for everyone he had seen. He sometimes became so over-emotional that it was hard for him to be specific and business-like; he could barely control his understandable wish that as much as possible should be given to the people he was trying to help. He enjoyed spending, he longed especially to help Africa – so much that at first he seemed to find it hard to understand that, despite the huge budget, money was a limited commodity. It was an experience that, with his gift of assimilation, was to stand him in good stead. During his time at the TEF he learnt to manage money, he learnt to negotiate and he became an impressive administrator. Father Aelred Stubbs, who was present at the 1973 AGM, was amazed at the mastery with which the man he had first known as a young ordinand handled the situation. At about the same time he read a paper at a conference in Johannesburg on 'Theological Education by Extension': the extent to which he had developed and grown made a tremendous impact on people, some of whom had not heard him speak since he was a curate in Benoni.

In spending nearly half the year travelling to the Third World, he was seeing and experiencing more than most people do in a lifetime. He saw the violence and repression of Amin's Uganda, he was in Ethiopia just before the overthrow of Emperor Haile Selassie, he witnessed the terrible aftermath of the Biafran war. There was sometimes personal danger – he was detained in Kampala airport by Amin's security police, who held up the plane and went through his papers, somehow missing a report highly critical of the regime. At Salisbury airport he was searched by Ian Smith's security men, who found a draft of a paper he was writing on black theology. 'That's not theology,' they screamed at him. 'That's politics.' But they let him through.

He felt continually blessed by being a member of the Christian Church, delighting in experiences of fellowship – particularly by the way he was accepted into people's homes, even when he could not speak their language. 'The fact that we were Christians was enough to pull us towards each other and bind us together.'[17] On one occasion he was at a packed church service in Zaire, where most of the congregation were black but whose language he did not understand. He considered it a profound parable of what it means to belong to the body of Christ when he found himself next to a white missionary, an American Baptist, who acted as his interpreter.

During the first two years of the Third Mandate the Theological Education Fund dealt only with the most necessary projects, as it was deliberately taking time to reflect on and analyse the current situation in the Third World Churches. A key concept to emerge from this period was 'contextualisation', a term that was to become important in South African thinking with the formation, in 1981, of the Institute for Contextual Theology.

The term had been created in the Presbyterian Church in Taiwan. It means all that is implied in indigenisation, yet it seeks to press further. While indigenisation involves responding to Christianity in terms of the local traditional culture, contextualisation also embraces secular conditions, technology and, most particularly, the struggle for human justice. So in contextual Christianity the Church seeks to tie economic and socio-political change to its indigenous cultural roots. This thinking must appeal to anyone working for change in South Africa and Tutu was proud to have been associated with the early development of the concept.

There had been some concern as to whether a South African black would be acceptable to blacks in other parts of Africa. Given the suspicion surrounding blacks in official positions in South Africa, would they fear he was collaborating with the government? However, Tutu's engaging personality ensured that this hurdle was soon cleared. The doubt was rather whether his outspoken contributions to conferences would lead to his not being allowed back into his own country. Indeed at one stage there were rumours that agents provocateurs were being sent from South Africa; their brief – to incriminate him by tripping him into treasonable statements.

His colleagues found that, despite his ebullient nature, he could be moody if he was worried or angry. He has, to an impressive degree, stood above racial bitterness, but in the early 1970s he still carried the scars of living in an apartheid society; people found they had to be careful what they said, or rather how they expressed it. For instance he could be upset by the assumptions behind some phrases in the English language. English people do not think what they are saying when they use phrases like 'as black as sin'; they do not wonder at the way the term 'black magic' involves the devil, while 'white magic' is sorcery in which the devil is not invoked. Tutu could be hurt, sometimes with every justification; once he came into the office speechless with fury after someone had said, 'You bastard, get back to Uganda'. But he could also be quite simply touchy; nor did he bother to conceal his feelings. He was, for example, hurt and insulted for a very long time by an absent-minded member of the office who did not hear his 'Good Morning' greeting and failed to respond.

Once they had become accustomed to his combination of ebullience and sensitivity, his colleagues found him delightful company. For his part, he revelled in the lively mixture of nationalities, each person having his or her own distinctive idiosyncrasies and differing ideology. They were indeed a colourful group, who between them had seen much of the world's tragedies. Dr Coe had been banished from Taiwan, Ivy Chou, a cousin of the then Prime Minister Chou En-lai, though now Malaysian had been born in mainland China, Aharon Sapsezian was a Brazilian national of Armenian extraction and Jim Bergquist, the only Caucasian, was a North American Lutheran. Their ideological differences became the springboard for discussions that were noisy, friendly and sometimes constructive. They would, for instance, argue about the term 'the Third World', by then in general use, in relation to their own backgrounds. Desmond Tutu and Dr Coe claimed that their countries still had colonial status, that they were second-class citizens in their own countries, that in fact they did not, as Aharon Sapsezian claimed, come from the Third World at all, but the Fourth. These conversations, especially this first real encounter with Latin American liberation theology, were another milestone in the development of Tutu's political awareness.

Life in England was, for the Tutus, 'an almost paradisial existence'.[18] Tutu's horror of Bantu Education knows no bounds, so it is easy to imagine his delight in knowing that Trevor was attending Colfe's, a grammar school founded, ironically, in 1652, the very year when the feet of permanent white settlers first trod on South African soil. Theresa and Naomi went to Ravensbourne School for Girls in Bromley and Mpho to the local primary school. The Tutus were buying their own house, Desmond and Leah had the vote – Leah was so delighted at being canvassed by rival political parties that she used to promise her vote to every supplicant. Most important of all, they came to enjoy being what they are, black South Africans.[19]

> We learned to grow in self-confidence and self-acceptance, not needing to apologise for our blackness, indeed to take pride in that which it had seemed wise to God to create us. We did not always articulate this as black consciousness (though such it was). What we learned and were exhilarated by was the new knowledge that we should have a proper pride in ourselves and realise that we could be best only at who we had been created to be and not in striving fruitlessly at being someone else.

Never happy without a pastoral role, Tutu was licensed as an Honorary Curate at St Augustine's, Bromley; whenever he could, he would preach or celebrate the Eucharist. He made a deep impression on the parishioners and their Vicar, Charles Cartwright:[20]

> His message was of the love of God for all his children whatever and wherever they were. And it was God's love that shone from Desmond himself. We all felt – yes really felt – the love of God when Desmond was with us. The other commanding mark of his presence was joy. Whenever he came, to a Eucharist, to a meeting, to a party, to a meal –

the whole company bubbled over with the sheer joy of being together with him. It was always as though the very place was lit up by his presence and permeated by his infectious laughter.

This joy, felt by countless people who have been close to him, is the fruit of a life constantly fed by the richness of his spiritual life. Prayer, regular attendance at the Eucharist, meditation, retreats and the reading of devotional books are an essential part of every day of his life, no matter what the demands may be upon his time. He would urge his colleagues at the Theological Education Fund to make space for this spiritual nourishment. He appreciated the opportunities provided in the timetable for regular worship and prayer, but found it insufficient. He questioned whether the community was a supporting, prayerful fellowship; whether it set a good example; to what extent the Eucharist was the centre and powerhouse of the life of the college.[21]

> Because, as you know, for Christians God the Holy Spirit works through what we call the covenanted and uncovenanted means of grace, the sacraments being the former and other devotional means – meditation, prayer, retreats, Bible and devotional reading – being the latter. And there is no other way available to us to cultivate a real and deeply personal relationship with God our great lover in whose presence we want to luxuriate, falling into ever greater and deeper silence, the silence of love, the stillness of adoration and contemplation – the sort of stillness which is so eloquent when it happens between two who are in love.

Theological education was one of Tutu's great interests. He was doing well at the Theological Education Fund, there was even talk of him becoming the next Director. But once again he was to be swept on by the ineluctable tide of his advancement.

7

Dean of Johannesburg

In 1974 Leslie Stradling, for many years Bishop of Johannesburg, retired, so the search was on for his successor. Many people were realising that it was time the Church had another African Diocesan Bishop – the only one at the time was Bishop Alpheus Zulu, who was forced by white prejudice to wait long years for his bishopric. Father Aelred Stubbs and Father Leo Rakale, a much respected black priest, led a powerful lobby for Tutu, who was thought to be the only African competent to be a Diocesan Bishop, as opposed to a Suffragan or Assistant. Though he had spent so much time out of the country, he was well remembered from his time as a priest in the diocese. More recently he had impressed those who had met him when he had visited Africa on behalf of the Theological Education Fund. Indeed Father Stubbs was so keen that Tutu should become Bishop of Johannesburg that he decided not to accept nomination himself.

The Elective Assembly, consisting of about 150 clergy and laity, sat all day without reaching a conclusion. The proceedings of an elective assembly are confidential, but it is widely reported that Tutu's share of the vote increased steadily, indeed that he finally came within nineteen votes of being elected. However, when after six inconclusive ballots it was clear that an impasse had been reached, a group of whites lobbied the Dean, Timothy Bavin, feeling that he would be acceptable to a wide cross-section of people: the Dean, who had in the earlier ballots consistently voted for Tutu, eventually accepted nomination, 'With some confidence, because I didn't think there was the slightest likelihood of my being more than an ingredient in the pot'. His modesty was, however, misplaced. Despite continued pressure from the Tutu lobby, before the day was out Dean Bavin had been elected Bishop. As soon as he was consecrated he invited Tutu to become his Dean – an arrangement which even Tutu's supporters consider with hindsight to have been more appropriate than, at that stage, his election as Bishop of Johannesburg.

The Tutu family were thrown into turmoil. Leah quite simply did not want to go; she was very happy in England, where they had their own house, their own friends. The three girls were living at home and going to good schools. Trevor had just started a degree course in Zoology at Imperial College, London, and came home frequently. Returning to South Africa, once again to be enslaved under apartheid, would change all this.

For Tutu it was more complex. While from the personal and domestic point of view he was in total agreement with his wife – after all, he had said he found life in England 'a paradisial existence' – he needed to discover God's will for him, then to find the courage to do it. His instinct was to go on retreat, to have a few days to pray and reflect on this decision; in fact his duties and his inclination coincided, for he was booked to take a retreat in Woking.

It was a traumatic decision. Not only was there his own wish to stay in England and avoid disrupting his family, but he would have to break his contract with the Theological Education Fund, which still had three years to run. On the other hand he was under great pressure to accept. For instance, Canon Carmichael, who had been asked by Father Leo Rakale to use his powers of persuasion, wrote him a long letter, pointing out that the situation in South Africa was one that needed an articulate black person in a position of leadership, someone who could express to the Church and to white society just how the blacks felt. No doubt Tutu also remembered a conversation in Zambia the previous year, when several black colleagues attending the All Africa Conference of Churches Consultation had urged him to come home: his response, that he would come back when there were signs that conditions were changing, was met with 'There won't be change, until people like you come back and fight for it'. Even Dr Coe, who might have been expected to encourage him to complete his time with the TEF, took the longer view, saying, 'Either you go back now or you never go back', and promising to try to persuade Leah that the right decision would be for them to go back so that her husband could make his contribution to their country's struggle.

However much Tutu values advice from his friends, it is, in the end, the voice of God to which he listens. Few of the retreatants realised that during those few days in Woking he was himself at a watershed, agonising, though twelve years later they all remember noticing a special quality of inspiration and dynamism about him during those few days. Frankie Brownrigg, though she did not at the time appreciate the personal implications, was deeply moved at the way he talked about the courage needed to take a leap in the dark – 'the capacity to jump with confidence into the everlasting arms in the darkness of God'. In the course of the retreat he made his decision. Despite his enjoyment of life in England, despite the wishes of his wife, despite his contract and the annoyance that would be felt by some of his colleagues at the TEF, though with the support of his children – something their grateful father still remembers appreciatively – he would go back to South Africa as the first black Dean of Johannesburg and Rector of the St Mary's Cathedral Parish.

He was welcomed home with joy. For the first time in the history of the Anglican Church in South Africa a black man was to occupy high office in the large, wealthy and vibrant diocese of Johannesburg; better still, he was no token black, but someone eminently qualified to hold the position. He would be able to demonstrate that a black man is not inferior to anyone. The black community, especially the clergy, were ecstatic – vindicated, optimistic, injected with a new confidence. In Archdeacon Nkwe's words:

> In most cases in South Africa, when a black person in a position of authority succeeded it was thought 'He's an exception'; if he failed people said 'What did you expect?' In Desmond Tutu we were assured that history was being made by a black person becoming Dean of Johannesburg and demonstrating to all and sundry that God does not only choose white people to become Deans.

Those who knew Tutu were confident, too, that he would not allow racialism in reverse, but would show that the Church is above race.

There was barely standing room at his Installation, an ecumenical occasion witnessed by 3,000 people of all races, including most of South Africa's church leaders and Archbishop Sirkassian of the Armenian Orthodox Church, a member of the World Council of Churches who was representing the Theological Education Fund. At the end of the service the new Dean astonished everyone by his confidence, as he stood at the west door being hugged and kissed, even – unbelievably in the Johannesburg of the 1970s – by white women. A new era had, undoubtedly, begun.

The arrival of a black Dean was front-page news in many of the South African papers, itself a comment on the crazy society apartheid creates. One of the consequences of his appointment that drew considerable attention was the question of where the Tutus should live. As all the previous Deans had been white, the deanery was in a white suburb, the affluent area of Houghton. Despite the Group Areas Act, in which residential areas are determined by race, the Tutus were invited to move into the official residence, but they adamantly refused to become 'honorary whites', electing instead to share the conditions of their fellow blacks by living in Soweto. After owning his own house in a pleasant leafy suburb of London, Tutu was even more conscious than most black people of the poverty, dreariness and inadequacy of the conditions under which they were expected to live. One of his letters to England was written in St Mary's Cathedral, as he sat in the confessional 'waiting for "customers"'.[1]

> Large crowds are scurrying home past the Cathedral on their way to the main Johannesburg railway station; they seem like so many ants. In the morning it is the same story only the traffic is in the opposite direction. Because Blacks live more than 12 miles away, mainly in the twin city of Soweto (abbreviation for *So*uth *We*stern *To*wnships) with nearly a million black inhabitants. They start from home in the dark and return when the street lights (where they have them) are on. They hardly see their children except over the weekend and their transport is woefully inadequate, with dangerously overcrowded trams and buses.

It should be added that black South Africans are daily reminded of how they *could* live – if they were white. Daily they see the cars speed along fast, wide motorways, taking their owners the short distance to rich residential areas with smart houses, usually with their own swimming pools; they know that there the air is clear, the streets lit and the gardens bright with flowers. Daily, as they enter Soweto, which in 1975 still had no electricity, they pass the huge generator which feeds only the white areas; they return to unmade-up roads, dark streets, small back yards and the murky atmosphere which rises from several thousand coal stoves. There is a swimming pool – one, built at Father Huddleston's initiative and shared by 1 million people.

Having decided to live in Soweto, the Tutus had to be 'influxed' into Johannesburg, as apartheid declares that no black can live in the city without special permission from the authorities. If some people were disappointed that Tutu missed an opportunity to crack the Group Areas Act by living in Houghton, many more were delighted at this symbolic gesture of identification with his people. Neither Desmond nor Leah was, however, content to be housed in one of the monotonous boxes that are considered adequate for black people, so they spent some time and money improving it – an activity indulged in by people the world over, but the object of criticism when done by a black South African clergyman.

Outside St Mary's Cathedral there is a large notice, proclaiming in four languages (English, Afrikaans, Zulu and Sotho) that the church is open to all races. Of the five priests on Dean Tutu's staff, two others were black, three were white; the choir, servers' guild and team of sacristans were racially mixed, as were the congregation, the majority of whom, attracted by the multi-racial mix, came from outside the parish. For Tutu, who remembered when black people had to sit on a bench at the back of the church, not coming up to the Communion rail until after the whites, this was a microcosm of the South Africa that *could* be:[2]

> As I have knelt in the Dean's stall at the superb 9.30 High Mass, with incense, bells and everything, watching a multi-racial crowd file up to the altar rails to be communicated, the one bread and the one cup given by a mixed team of clergy and lay ministers, with a multi-racial choir, servers and sidesmen – all this in apartheid-mad South Africa – then tears sometimes streamed down my cheeks, tears of joy that it could be that indeed Jesus Christ had broken down the wall of partition and here were the first fruits of the eschatological community right in front of my eyes.

Yet despite the initial welcome, despite the extent to which black and white were integrated (previous Deans included people like Gonville ffrench-Beytagh, whose courageous non-racial stand had led to his being accused of treason), some of the congregation left, finding that taking non-racialism from a white mouth was one thing, somehow they could not tolerate it from a black. Though Tutu could take comfort from those, both black and white, who began to attend the cathedral precisely because they *wanted* the ministry of a black person, the defections were deeply hurtful to someone as sensitive as he, especially after the enthusiasm and love he had experienced at Bletchingley. The more so as some claimed to be put off even more by his manner than by his colour.

Wherever Desmond Tutu goes he makes his mark; it was not long before St Mary's Cathedral felt the impact of his personality. In worship, for instance. When he arrived St Mary's was still using the 1662 version of the Communion Service and was quite content with it; within weeks he introduced the new 'Liturgy '75'. He encouraged his congregation, many of them self-conscious Europeans, to move about the church, insisted on including the Kiss of Peace, and – horror of horrors – even wanted them to hug and kiss one another.

Half the congregation were up in arms, feeling he was riding roughshod over their feelings, that he was being too authoritarian. Even those broadly in sympathy with him felt that allowing the organist to speak against the new liturgy at the start of the service at which it was introduced was hardly giving the opposition sufficient voice. Surely, especially in such a conservative parish as St Mary's, a former teacher should realise the importance of preparation, should give some teaching of the theological significance of what they were doing?

He brought a liberal, world-wide perspective, allowing members of the congregation to put on experimental services, appealing to many by being in favour of the ordination of women and by making a point of using non-sexist language, always changing 'men' to 'people' – at the time one of the few priests in the country consistently to show this particular sensitivity. Intercessions had previously been concerned primarily with South Africa; Dean Tutu's prayers regularly embraced the whole world.

There were those who were pleased that complacency was being shown the door, excited by his ideas, stimulated by the larger horizons. Others, however, found it all a bit much. One honest parishioner complained ruefully, 'He was so enthusiastic and one doesn't always feel like being enthusiastic.' Bishop Bavin generously admits that the Dean sometimes ruffled his feathers; he found him 'very disturbing and challenging', not least because he was so often right. For instance Tutu was not content with the perfunctory five minutes prayer at the beginning of a staff meeting. Why could they not have a Eucharist, followed by a period of silence? And if that took forty minutes instead of five, what was wrong with that? He was concerned too, if they seemed to be speeding through an agenda too smoothly, lest efficiency meant glossing over pastoral problems.

The parish was going through a bad time financially and some provident members of the parish council dreaded finance meetings under Dean Tutu, never being quite sure 'what madcap scheme he would come up with next'. They were worried by the ease with which he spent money and disturbed by some of his impulsive ideas. For instance he was keen to link Soweto formally with the cathedral. While people from the townships had always been free to come, he wanted to ensure they received a warm welcome. He suggested that the cathedral should send a bus round Soweto to bring worshippers to St Mary's. He saw it as a way of saving them the long and awkward journey; the parish council was not only horrified at the expense but saw it as stealing sheep from other priests' pastures.

Expectations had been polarised, some people hoping Dean Tutu would be like Dean ffrench-Beytagh, some hoping he would be more conservative. So, too, were the reactions. For every person who found him irritating, scores felt, with Helen Joseph, 'He was a man of God. He really manages to bring God close to you.' For everyone who criticised his extravagance, several rejoiced in the activity he stimulated. But his greatest contribution as Dean was the confidence he gave to black members of the congregation, the way he involved them in the running of the cathedral. It was no longer the white man's church; for the first time black Christians had a sense of being at the heart of things. Bishop Bavin feels Tutu prepared the way for his successors by proving that if one is black one is not incompetent or insensitive. 'I think Desmond actually helped to give the cleaner or the cook, those who hadn't the education or the sophistication of the white members of the congregation, a sense of having a part to play in the councils of the cathedral and therefore being able to look fellow cathedral members in the eye – not to be cringing. The black members increasingly became not simply on the receiving end of decisions but part of making them.'

This was what Desmond Tutu passionately wanted to do – to affirm the black man's dignity; it was indeed one of the reasons why he had agreed to return to South Africa. He wanted to make his own contribution to the liberation struggle, to tell black people that they did not have to apologise for who they were, 'that they were of infinite value because they were created in the image of God'.[3] What amazed him was to discover that it was whites, more than blacks, who needed to hear the message, 'that they must not behave like bullies, who know that they are hollow inside and must have people take notice of them by throwing their weight around or by amassing material possessions, as if *that* was who they were'.[4]

Reconciliation is in every part of a man or it is nowhere; Dean Tutu showed himself as a reconciler in every dimension of his life – including humour. He could joke, for instance, about white fears of black retaliation. In 1975 there was still total apartheid on the beaches and Tutu would say 'The whites think the black people want to drive them into the sea. What they forget is, with apartheid on the beaches – we can't even *get* to the sea.' He could reduce people to helpless laughter by demonstrating his first principle of reconciliation. Soon after he became Dean, Helen Joseph remembers him at a party. He found the highest chair in the room, climbed on to it and stood as tall as his small frame allowed:

> If I am standing up here (voice high as he stretches even further upwards) and the fellow I am speaking to is down there on the ground (crouched low and pointing downwards) I cannot speak to him about reconciliation. I must pick him up by the shoulders and stand him on his feet. When we are face to face – *then* I'll talk to him about reconciliation.

In sermons, addresses, at conferences and in articles, he put his case. Reconciliation is only possible between equals. If society is ordered in such a way that one section of the community is denied its humanity, with all its obligations and responsibilities, then the other side is also enslaved – whites cannot be truly free until blacks are free. 'The freedom of the white man is bound up with that of the black man. So long as the black man is dehumanised and unfree, so long too will the white man remain dehumanised and unfree because he will be plagued by fear and anxiety.'[5] In a situation of injustice and oppression it is impossible to say that God does not take sides, or to speak about forgiveness without asking for repentance from the perpetrators of injustice. Small wonder if words like forgiveness and reconciliation tend to be dismissed, regarded by the oppressed as acquiescence in their oppression:[6]

> It is forgotten that reconciliation is no easy option, nor does it rule out confrontation. After all, it did cost God the death of His Son to effect reconciliation; the cross of Jesus was to expose the sinfulness of sin when he took on the powers of evil and routed them comprehensively. No, just as there can be no cheap grace, so there can be no cheap reconciliation, because we cannot cry, 'peace, peace' where there is no peace.

In taking this stance, in insisting that the problem belongs as much to the oppressor as to the oppressed and placing himself firmly in the role of a reconciler, he was taking the first step along the political tightrope on which he was to balance for the rest of his public life. And if it was a balance that sometimes, from the outside, might look slightly precarious, it is in reality a poise very firmly held, infused with an inner confidence, a 'centredness' that can only belong to someone deeply rooted in something beyond the changing world of outer events.

Tutu himself finds it hard to chart his political development: he is a man of instinct rather than analysis. But there are a few milestones which mark his journey from detached student to international spokesman. Though at the time of Sharpeville he felt helpless, when he was at King's College he was realising that any contribution he might make to South Africa's struggle for liberation would be strengthened if he could sharpen his intellectual tools to their keenest edge. The traumatic Fort Hare strike was the catalyst for a deeper emotional involvement; intellectual backing came from his involvement with black theology and his encounter with Latin American liberation theology at the TEF. By the time he became Dean of Johannesburg he knew that politics and theology, especially in South Africa, could not be separated. Further, he was aware that he had been given 'the privilege of a platform' and that now, thanks largely to his time at the TEF, he had 'a proper sense of self-confidence'. At last he had been remorselessly drawn into the political arena: from this time there was to be no question as to his involvement, only how his part could best be played.

Whether or not the Church should be involved in politics is a question that has been debated since the Prophet Amos urged the importance of social justice to the Israelites over 2,000 years ago. There are firmly held convictions on both sides of the argument.

Those who believe that the Church should concern itself exclusively with the things of the spirit, that religion is a private matter between man and his Creator, argue that the business of religion is to prepare its followers for eternal life. If this earthly preparation involves suffering, then that is part of God's plan and it is our duty to bear it with patience; in any case society will always contain injustice, it is only individuals who may, by the Grace of God, be converted. Nor, the argument might continue, is there anything intrinsically wrong with hierarchical systems; the master–servant relationship is an extension of divine lordship; after all the Bible itself says there must be hewers of wood and drawers of water. The Church's duty is to advocate peace and unity in the social system in which it finds itself; if in doing this it casts a blind eye to injustice – well, it is not its business anyway.

On the other side of the argument are those who insist on God's power to transform human life. It is therefore the Church's job to act as God's agent in improving the quality of life on earth. This work must be done through the structures of society; if these structures militate against justice, then they must be changed. It follows that the Church must be involved in that fight for change. Further, that the Church has a responsibility to 'remind the state that justice is the only basis for true order, and that the state exists for the good of *all* people under its authority'.[7]

When Desmond Tutu became Dean of Johannesburg he was, considering his forty-four years and his South African background, less politically aware than one might have expected. His contribution to the liberation of his people had been in becoming a good priest; he had, in any case, spent nine of his adult years out of the country. Now he was in a key position in the most politically aware city of South Africa. He lost no time in becoming involved in the struggle in all its dimensions.

Father Aelred Stubbs, while admiring the strength of Tutu's Christian faith and witness, felt strongly that now that his old pupil was in a leadership position he should be more in touch with the current political climate. He encouraged him to go and see a group of young activists centred round the Black Consciousness leader Steve Biko, including a remarkable young doctor, Mamphela Ramphele. With an eagerness and humility that impressed Father Stubbs, Tutu took up the suggestion, and though unfortunately Steve Biko was in detention at the time of his visit, he spent a couple of days with the group. Dr Ramphele realised that when Tutu left the country it was at a time when black people were trying to show that they too were human beings by *doing* things. Now, in the 1970s, the mood had changed. 'We are people because we are people, not because we are just as good as the Western cultured people, not because we can do just as well in this field or in that field. We also are people and now we are actually going to determine the pace of change.'

It was not difficult for Tutu to appreciate the new South African reality. Meeting Steve Biko's group, talking to respected leaders of the Soweto community like Dr Motlana and Tom Manthata, above all living in Soweto, where every day he was in touch with the people, sharing their lives, he soon filled in any gaps in his understanding caused by his time abroad.

Tutu did not find it hard to justify his stance theologically. Since his student days he had been studying the Scriptures, looking for what they had to say about liberation:[8]

> Do they say God is concerned only about individual salvation and has no interest in the redemption of the socio-political and economic matrix in which individuals live? Does it say the world is religiously and ethically neutral and of no consequence to salvation and the final consummation of all things, that what happens in the market place, in the courtroom, or in Parliament is of no particular religious significance, and all that matters to God is what is confined to the sacred sphere of the ecclesiastical? Does it say God is in fact not really interested too much in what happens from Monday to Friday but only in that which happens on Sunday, and that He does not much care about the plight of the hungry, the dispossessed, the voiceless, the powerless ones – that He does not take sides? When two persons are engaged in a conflict and one of them is considerably stronger than the other, to be neutral is not just and fair and impartisan because to be neutral is in fact to side with the powerful.

After five years out of South Africa he was shocked at the increasing tension he found in the black community, especially among the young; he was filled with a sense of foreboding and alarm. He warned a local synod that the Church must concern itself, immediately, with the needs of the youth: 'We are creating a monster for ourselves which we won't be able to handle unless we address the needs of the youth here and now.' In a letter to his English friends he wrote that[9]

> change, real change, must happen quickly if it is going to be peaceful. I am worried that many whites don't want to know just how deeply hurt and disillusioned blacks are; and change may come too late for it to be significant and peaceful. The Church must be prophetic, speaking hope and judgement and love and reconciliation and repentance.

Those who did not take him seriously were soon to regret it.

Again and again he appealed to people's humanity. In January 1976, in an address to one of the regional groups of the South African Institute of Race Relations, he pleaded with his audience to come out of their fool's paradise and listen to one another; to face reality and resist the temptation to say only what people wanted to hear. He reminded his audience that whites are human beings: 'They laugh, they love, they cuddle babies, they weep, they eat, they sleep – they are human. But if they are human, why, oh why can't they see that we laugh too, we love too, we weep too, we cuddle babies too, we eat, we sleep – why can't they see that it is impossible for things to go on like this?'[10]

But he found grounds for hope. He wondered – as does anyone who knows them – at black people's capacity to forgive, admitting that the seeds of bitterness and hatred are sown early in a black person's life, yet, after all he has endured at the hands of whites, he is still ready to extend the hand of friendship. He found hope in the Black Consciousness Movement, that was giving blacks a sense of their own worth. Hope that the Afrikaner, who had braved dangers in the pursuit of his own freedom, would understand that others shared this need. He had hope of the English, because they come from a tradition that affirms human freedom; hope because of the many in the white community who stood up for justice. Ultimately, he had hope because 'This is God's world and he is in charge. We were all created by the same God, redeemed by the same Jesus Christ and are sanctified by the same Holy Spirit. We belong together. The survival of the white man depends on the survival of the black man and vice versa, and this includes so-called Coloured people and Indians.'[11]

There might be time for peaceful change, but the whites must listen, they must act before it was too late. 'Do you refuse to hear our anguished cries? . . . How loud and how long do we have to shout for you to hear?'[12] He warned that the people were desperate and would resort to desperate measures.

Desmond Tutu is a man of action, his theology needed to be incarnated. What he should do came to him a few weeks later, during a three-day clergy retreat in Johannesburg; on May 6th, 1976, in his first public political initiative, he sent an open letter to the Prime Minister, John Vorster.

It is a remarkable letter, heartfelt yet statesmanlike, direct yet never failing to be tactful and courteous, eloquent, informed and precise in its suggestions. He writes as the Anglican Dean of Johannesburg and spokesman for his people; he is writing to the highest political figure in the land, but he appeals to him first in the context of their shared humanity:[13]

> I am writing to you, Sir, as one who is passionately devoted to a happy and stable family life as the indispensable foundation of a sound and healthy society. You have flung out your arms to embrace and hug your children and your grandchildren, to smother them with your kisses, you have loved, you have wept, you have watched by the bed of a sick one whom you loved, you have watched by the deathbed of a beloved relative, you have been a proud father at the wedding of your children, you have shed tears by the graveside of one for whom your heart has been broken.

Tutu also appealed to the Prime Minister as an Afrikaner, whose forebears had known the humiliation of being a subject people, who knew that 'absolutely nothing will stop a people from attaining their freedom to be a people who can hold their heads high, whose dignity to be human persons is respected, who can assume the responsibilities and obligations that are necessary concomitants of the freedom they yearn for with all their being.'[14] He pointed out that blacks could not attain this freedom in the 'homelands', because they felt they had contributed to the prosperity of an undivided South Africa. In any case they could not understand why whites, comprised of Greeks, Italians, Portuguese, Afrikaners, French, Germans and English, should be said to form one nation, while blacks, most of whom are much closer to one another ethnically, are said to form several and split up accordingly. He did not make any accusations concerning the 'divide and rule' thinking which he knew very well lay behind the development of the 'homelands', but simply pleaded that everyone, black and white, should be fellow South Africans.

He went on to admit that he had seen little evidence of the move against discrimination based on race which had been announced by 'Pik' Botha, who was at the time the Ambassador to the United Nations – he was not impressed by cosmetic changes such as the removal of signs from park benches. Though he gave the Prime Minister credit for his efforts to promote détente and dialogue, it had to be qualified approval:[15]

> In these efforts many of us here wanted to support you eagerly, but we feel we cannot in honesty do this, when external détente is not paralleled by equally vigorous efforts at internal détente. Blacks are grateful for all that has been done for them, but now they claim *an inalienable right to do things for themselves,* in co-operation with their fellow South Africans of all races.

With great restraint and politeness, Tutu objected to the power given to the army and the security police without making them accountable to the courts; he appealed for the detainees – that they should be released or punished if found guilty of indictable offences; he reminded the Prime Minister that freedom is indivisible and that the whites would not be free until the whole community was free; most crucially, he warned that there was a limit to the blatant injustice and suffering that a people can take. 'I have a growing and nightmarish fear that unless something drastic is done very soon then bloodshed and violence are going to happen in South Africa almost inevitably.'[16]

The letter suggests three ways in which the government could demonstrate that it was sincere in saying it wanted peaceful change. First it must accept the urban black as a permanent inhabitant of 'white' South Africa, with consequent freehold rights – he would then have a stake in the land and would not easily join any who wished to destroy his country. Second, it must repeal the pass laws. Third, it must call a National Convention, made up of leaders recognised as such by the community.

Three weeks later, at the beginning of June, the Prime Minister answered, questioning Dean Tutu's motives in writing and suggesting he was merely trying to put out political propaganda. When the Dean asked for permission to publish the reply he received a curt rejection.

Tutu's nightmare was to become reality, sooner and more tragically than even he had feared. On June 16th, 15,000 children from Soweto organised themselves into a mass protest, objecting to separate Bantu education and in particular to the use of Afrikaans, the language of the hated oppressor, as a medium of instruction. Singing, they marched from school to school, determined but peaceful, armed only with their placards; they were met with police gunfire. Hector Peterson, just twelve years old, was the first of over 600 people to die in the next few weeks, most of them schoolchildren and students.

At the time Tutu was Vicar-General, as Bishop Bavin was overseas, and he was in the cathedral when someone telephoned to say they were shooting children in Soweto. His horrified, disbelieving enquiries to the authorities were met with assurances that everything was under control and that the brigadier to whom he eventually spoke was not going to answer questions from anyone. The Dean replied that he was not anyone, he was Vicar-General of the diocese and he was very concerned and wanted to know what had happened – at which the brigadier hung up on him.

Tutu spent most of the day in Soweto, talking to children and parents, trying not to show anger, trying less successfully to conceal his tears. It was a day of such pain and trauma that he remembers very little, but he does recall the next Sunday saying to his largely white congregation, 'We have been really shattered by the deafening silence from the white community. You will say, what could you do? And all I would say to you is, what would you have done had they been white children? And that is all we would have wanted you to have done.'

As trouble flared all over the country and the toll of deaths and injuries mounted, Tutu was suffering a particular personal anguish. Earlier in the year, even before he wrote to John Vorster, he had agreed to become Bishop of Lesotho. With the anger and frustration in the townships reaching fever pitch he had, once again, to leave the country.

8

The mountain kingdom

Despite the fact that those who work for the Church are not supposed to show ambition and are in fact criticised if they aspire to its highest offices, Desmond Tutu has never denied that he was ambitious. Nevertheless, the invitation to allow his name to go forward for election to the bishopric of Lesotho threw him into a turmoil of indecision and anguish.

It was too soon. He had only been Dean for a few months, he was barely settling down, beginning to feel accepted, growing to love the people of St Mary's. 'It had seemed to be work that God wanted me to do. I thought that I had turned the corner in terms of hostility. I mean people began to think that perhaps I *might* be a Pastor.'

It was too soon and he decided to refuse. But he was put under tremendous pressure to accept, in fact he was quite literally pursued. The diocese of Lesotho even went to the unusual lengths of sending a delegation to Soweto; they were waiting as he left a meeting at the church of Regina Mundi and came home with him, using all their powers of persuasion to urge him to change his mind. They argued that he was the only man available and that he must stand.

He asked advice from Leah, from the parish council, from friends and colleagues. Leah, only just coming to terms with leaving England, was almost indifferent to being uprooted yet again. With a commendable lack of self-interest, she pointed out that when the delegates had made such an effort it would look very arrogant if he disregarded their pleas. The parish council, on the other hand, urged him not to consider it. They did not all see eye to eye with him, but they did not want yet another change. The last few years had been very traumatic, with a long interregnum after Dean ffrench-Beytagh's trial and deportation, then the swift elevation of Timothy Bavin after only eighteen months as Dean. They needed some stability and felt that his duty lay with them. On the other hand, there were those who felt that as leadership in the Anglican Church is vested in the bench of Bishops, the sooner Dean Tutu joined them, the sooner he would be able to play his part as a leader. The argument closest to Tutu's heart came from Phillip Russell, at the time Bishop of Natal. If God is active in an elective assembly, he reasoned, then it is wrong to refuse to stand because if it was not God's will that he should be Bishop of Lesotho then he would not be elected anyway. Yet the pendulum of indecision swung again as Father Aelred Stubbs advised him very strongly against accepting nomination – he had not been Dean for long enough.

There were a few people in the parish who felt that in even considering nomination their Dean was guilty of culpable ambition; there were even suggestions that he was using his position in Johannesburg as a stepping stone to higher things. However Bishop Bavin, who knew him better than most, is confident that Tutu was not thinking about himself or what the move would mean for him; he believes that his concern was for the people he would be leaving and the people to whom he would be going. There is no doubt that for Tutu it was sheer agony. 'There have been very few occasions when I have felt so torn apart. Which way should I go? What is God's will for me?'[1]

On the day of the elective assembly Tutu was in Pietermaritzburg, attending a meeting of the Federal Theological Seminary Council.[2] He was lunching with the Principal, rejoicing that the election must be over and that as he had heard nothing they must have chosen someone else, when he was called to the telephone. He had been elected Bishop of Lesotho. His reaction, 'Oh *no*', cannot have been very encouraging to the bearer of the news. As if in a nightmare, he went home to Leah and wept; he felt God was being unfair to demand this of him. He had wanted to be a Bishop, but never less so than at the time of his election.

On July 11th, 1976, Desmond Tutu was consecrated Bishop of Lesotho in St Mary's Cathedral, Johannesburg, where less than a year before he had been installed Dean. The next month, in a snow-covered Maseru, he was enthroned at St James's Cathedral. The eager crowds, delighted to have won the Tutu tug-of-war, packed the cathedral to overflowing, many grateful to listen to the service on loudspeakers and catch the smallest glimpse of the proceedings. Among the first to embrace the new Bishop were King Moshoeshoe II, Queen Mamohato and the Prime Minister Chief Leabua Jonathan.

It was only three weeks after the Soweto riots and by then Tutu's distress at leaving Johannesburg was even more intense. It was agonising for him to leave then, when there was so much to do in his own country; there was also the fear – justified by the remarks of a few of the enemies he was beginning to acquire – that people would say that he was running away. However, Tutu is a resilient man, who throws himself wholeheartedly into whatever he is doing. The sadness of leaving South Africa was never completely assuaged, but once the anguish of indecision and the immediate pain of parting were behind him he found a deep satisfaction in being a Bishop. It suited him on many levels, from the superficial to the profound. At one end of the scale was his delight in ritual and ceremony with its attendant pageantry and dress – a pleasure he shares with many Africans; he admitted to an English friend that he still enjoys seeing himself in photographs, 'especially if I'm coped and mitred'. But the real significance was that he had become 'pastor of pastors'.

From the very beginning he made it clear how he wanted to be regarded; at his enthronement sermon he appealed to the diocese to call him 'Father' or 'Bishop', not 'My Lord', saying, 'I want to be your father in God, not an ecclesiastical bureaucrat.' He knew that there were those who would enjoy addressing a fellow black with due formality and might feel disappointed that their first black diocesan Bishop should refuse to be thus honoured, but he knew who his model should be. 'The pattern of my lordship was determined by our Lord himself and it is spelt out in terms of one who tied a towel round his waist to wash the disciples' feet.'[3]

In this sermon he also asked that callers should use the front door of the Bishop's House. This might seem an odd request – surely the front door is the one visitors normally use? In fact Bishop Tutu was showing great sensitivity to the Basotho.[4]

> When most of your diocese are simple country folk, who are very humble, it is so easy for the Bishop to be seen to accept the sophisticated and the educated and the high and the mighty through the front door and that these good people, the people of the land, are made to go to the back like servants in South Africa.[5]

He went further; if anyone came to the back door, he promised that his wife would greet them with a bucket of cold water.

Tutu had seen too much of separation, of people being compartmentalised, divided and deprived of dignity, so he was careful about giving too much time to the social duties that fall to a Bishop's lot and can set him apart from his people. He was living in Maseru, the capital of the kingdom and the headquarters of all its official bodies like the Diplomatic Corps; he was a personal friend of the King and Queen. (He once had to stay at a party at the Palace until 3 a.m.; the King was enjoying his company so much that he was refused permission to go home at a time more suitable for a busy Bishop.) The Tutus could easily have been caught up in a round of cocktail parties and official functions, but both he and Leah tried to restrict themselves to the minimum. He also relinquished the chairmanship of many diocesan committees, retaining this role only with the least developed school that he felt most needed his attention.

By freeing himself as much as possible from bureaucracy and the peripheral concerns that can consume the time of people in senior positions, he was trying to give himself space for real involvement at a pastoral level. He wanted the Bishop's presence to be a familiar event, not a rare occurrence; to be seen as a shepherd of his people, not a purple-clad bureaucrat. In order to keep in touch with as many people as possible he celebrated the Eucharist at different churches in Maseru each day of the week; once a month he went with one of the Cathedral staff to take communion to the sick and elderly; occasionally – usually at Christmas – he went to the Central Prison in Maseru.

Visiting the country districts was more complicated. The twenty-three parishes, some with as many as twenty 'outstations', were spread over an area about the size of Belgium, and while by African standards the diocese was not geographically or numerically large, the mountainous nature of the region – the Maluti Mountains occupied three-quarters of the country – meant that communication presented a very real problem. There were few roads or telephones and the main method of transport was on horseback; travellers could meet thunderstorms or find themselves on a road made impassable by erosion or, in winter, by snow. Even under good conditions it could take days, walking and riding, to cross one parish. So conducting two confirmation services, for instance, could take a Bishop three days. He would probably go by air into the country, spend a couple of hours riding to a remote village on horseback, then spend a night in a hut and conduct a confirmation service the next morning. Several hours' riding would bring him to his next destination, where he would hold a second service and ride to the nearest airstrip, where there would almost certainly be a long wait before he could catch a flight back to Maseru.

The essentially urban Bishop Tutu was not at all accustomed to this sort of thing, but he took to it with good humour, trekking for as long as eight hours on horseback, collapsing exhausted into bed and tackling another five hours the next day. He complained wistfully, 'I did not know the ground was so far. There was no rapport between me and the horse – when I go up, he goes down with rather unpleasant consequences for certain unmentionable parts of my anatomy.'[6] However, he was exhilarated the first time he persuaded his mount to gallop.

He would use the long journeys on horseback as a chance to get to know the priest who was travelling with him. Though he was criticised for being out of the country too much (largely honouring previous commitments), his pastoral concern for his priests was very real. It was in Lesotho that he began a practice he was to continue all his life. He put details of his staff – a Suffragan Bishop, a Dean and about forty priests – in his intercession book, noting their birthdays, wedding anniversaries, the names of wives and children and any particular problems in their personal or professional lives. Every day he prayed for each one by name. 'Like the high priest of Israel, I saw my Pectoral Cross in a sense as being like the breastplate with the 12 precious stones reminding me that I had to be carrying specially the clergy in my heart regularly.'[7]

Donald Nestor, then a priest in the diocese, now Suffragan Bishop of Lesotho, was one man who deeply valued Bishop Tutu's personal concern:

> He trusted me in my work and upheld and encouraged me. He knew me as a person quite deeply and wanted to build me up. He would give pertinent spiritual advice, not necessarily when asked. He could penetrate to what was essential about me and tell me things about myself which other people had not seen – for instance he would tell me not to apologise so much. He could see where I would be most useful and was concerned for me to grow.

In a surprisingly short time, Tutu managed to meet most of his parishioners, even the most far-flung. For them his visits would be a great event, eagerly awaited, joyously celebrated. He would be met by a posse of horsemen wearing their colourful Basotho hats, the church would be crowded with people, many of whom had walked for miles, and the service – in Sotho and English – with the speeches, meals and festivities, could last as long as five hours. He loved it. He revelled in the warmth, generosity and love of the Basotho:[8]

> When I arrived as their Bishop, the people said *ke ntate*, this is our father. And they really meant it. That was something that shattered me. It was not just a convention or a polite title; they believed I was their father in God, that was what I was challenged to become. Every time it happened I was filled with awe and a great sense of responsibility as well as joy.

This sense of responsibility came as something of a shock; he discovered not only the loneliness of high office, but the problem of power. Though he tried very hard to exercise a participatory ministry, he could not escape the Church's hierarchical element. All the various committees and bodies in a diocese are advisory to the Bishop and every decision is ultimately his; in diocesan synods a Bishop can ignore all the advice he is given and veto their decisions. He found that he was quite unprepared for the exercise of this power; the only way he could learn to handle the demon was to draw on his experience as a pastor and a priest.

Ultimately he was convinced that the only thing that really mattered was love – both people and clergy must know that they are loved. At his consecration a Bishop is given a ring, symbolic of the sense in which he is married to his diocese; this is something very real to Bishop Tutu. When his great friend Walter Makhulu became Bishop of Botswana Tutu wrote him a long and moving letter, sharing the joy and the pain of being a Christian Bishop:[9]

> You will look splendid in cope and mitre. But I know too, that many times you will weep tears because God has given you the gift of tears. You will weep tears of joy; you will weep tears at being overwhelmed by God's grace; you will weep tears at the love of God's people because Walter, all they want is that you should love them. And then you can do virtually anything with them. They will eat out of your hand. You can scold them. You can be strict. And they will know when you love them. You can never bluff love.

As South Africa was part of the British Empire for 100 years, there is a very real sense in which all South Africans, from far-right Afrikaner to far-left black radical, feel comfortable with British culture. Tutu, like all educated South Africans of his generation a product of the British mission schools, is at home in any culture: it is easy to forget that he is first and foremost an African, with his roots firmly in South African soil. He can straddle cultures so comfortably that his old scoutmaster Zakes Mohutsioa can say 'when he's among Europeans he's a European, when he's among Africans he's an African'.

During his time as Bishop of Lesotho he was more regularly and more predominantly close to African thinking than, as his life became more and more cosmopolitan, he was ever to be again. There were people in Lesotho untouched by Christianity, who held to their old beliefs, giving great significance to dreams, making sacrifices to their ancestors. There were still witch doctors, who were recognised by the government and had their own association. At the extreme, one of the problems that the clergy had to tackle was the question of initiation schools to prepare teenagers for manhood and womanhood. Though attempts had been made to stop these customs since the time of King Moshoeshoe I, they were still held in secret, sometimes leading to people being ritually killed so that their organs could be used for medicine. It was the Bishop who had to conduct acts of exorcism after these practices had taken place.

Some people who only know Tutu superficially feel he has lost contact with his African roots – for instance, when he was at the seminary in Alice he was criticised for bringing up his children in too Western a way, particularly for sending them to multi-racial schools. However, people close to him, like Barney Pityana, appreciate that he is deeply African, from his ability to speak several African languages – Zulu, Sotho, Tswana, Xhosa – to his taste for ting and tripe,[10] the instinctive way he moves round the altar in a slow, dancing rhythm, and his enjoyment of African hymns and festivals.

Most profoundly, most pertinently, is the extent to which his spirituality is African. The African theologian Professor Gabriel Setiloane suggests that when Tutu is speaking at his best it is the African in him who is speaking, because he is filled with that mysterious quality known as 'ubuntu'. Ubuntu is often translated as humanity, but it is deeper than humaneness, deeper than generosity of spirit or understanding; it is the very essence of that mysterious quality which makes a person a person in African understanding. The worst thing that can be said about anyone is that he has not got ubuntu – he is not a person.

This quality of ubuntu is the springboard of Tutu's thinking; it is deep in his being, it shines from him, irradiating his words and actions. He is fond of quoting a Xhosa saying that penetrates to the heart of African thinking: 'A person is a person through other persons.' Though he himself is very punctual, he feels the world could learn something from that aspect of Africa which can infuriate Europeans – 'African time'. He claims that behind this concept lies the conviction that people are more important than punctuality. Being in tune with the rhythm of the universe and with life – which includes the ancestors and those not yet born as well as those living in the world at any particular moment – is of greater value than rigid adherence to the clock. Related to this idea is the way he frequently refers to himself as 'we'; he points out that when a Xhosa is asked how he is and says 'We are well', he is not using the 'royal we', he is reflecting his membership of the family of mankind.

He sometimes illustrates the interdependence of people with a parable:[11]

Light bulb used to shine and glow wonderfully. Everybody was attracted to brilliant light bulb until light bulb grew with pride and arrogance. He thought his brilliance was self-generated. He disdained the flexes hidden away in the ceiling which connected him to the dynamo, the source of his energy. Then one day someone unscrewed light bulb from the socket and laid him on the table. Try as he would, light bulb just remained black and cold and people passed him by without paying him the slightest attention.

Africans have always been a deeply religious people, with a world view, Tutu argues, more consistent with that of the Bible than the world view emanating from the West. This essential difference between black and white attitudes can rarely have been better put than by Nelson Mandela:[12]

> In South Africa, the conflict has emerged as one of race on the one side and one of ideals on the other. The White man regards the Universe as a gigantic machine hurtling through space and time to its final destruction: individuals in it are but tiny organisms with private lives that lead to private deaths: personal power, success and fame are the absolute measure of values; the things to live for. This outlook on life divides the Universe into a host of individual little entities which cannot help being in constant conflict thereby hastening the approach of the hour of their final destruction.
>
> The African, on his side, regards the Universe as one composite whole; an organic entity, progressively driving towards greater harmony and unity whose individual parts exist merely as interdependent aspects of one whole realising their fullest life in the corporate life where communal contentment is the absolute measure of values. His philosophy of life strives towards unity and aggregation; towards greater social responsibility.

Christianity in South Africa cannot but be associated with the white missionaries, who brought their culture as well as their religion. Consequently, there has been a movement to develop an indigenous African theology. African theology is an attempt to relate African culture and spirituality to Christian faith and is sometimes seen in opposition to black theology, a theology of political protest. The theologian John Mbiti, who sees a clear distinction between the two, writes that African theology 'grows out of our joy and experience of the Christian faith, whereas black theology emerges from the pain of oppression'.[13] However, in an article published just before he came to Lesotho, Tutu, who is an exponent of both theologies, prefers to emphasise the similarities between the two. He writes movingly about the unity between black people, whether they have crossed the Atlantic or remained in the continent of their ancestors:[14]

> All of us are bound to Mother Africa by invisible but tenacious bonds. She has nurtured the deepest things in us blacks. All of us have roots

that go deep in the warm soil of Africa; so that no matter how long and traumatic our separation from our ancestral home has been, there are things we are often unable to articulate, but which we feel in our very bones, things which make us . . . different from others who have not suckled the breasts of our mother, Africa. Don't most of us, for instance, find the classical arguments for the existence of God just an interesting cerebral game because Africa taught us long ago that life without belief in a supreme being was just too absurd to contemplate? And don't most of us thrill as we approach the awesomeness of the transcendent when many other of our contemporaries find even the word God an embarrassment? How do you explain our shared sense of the corporate-ness of life, of our rejection of hellenistic dichotomies in our insistence that life, material and spiritual, secular and sacred, that it is all of a piece?

He goes on to claim that there cannot be one, universal theology; that theology can only be relevant if it has 'the humility to accept the scandal of its particularity as well as its transience'. Both African and black theology have arisen as reactions against a situation in which black humanity has been defined in the terms of the white man; in which 'to be really human he had to see himself and be seen as a chocolate coloured white man'. They both assert that if the Incarnation is taken seriously, then Christianity for the African must be incarnated in Africa, speaking to the African from an African context. Both repudiate the tacit claims of the supremacy of Western values.

Yet he admits there are also differences. He is critical of African theology for failing to produce a sufficiently sharp cutting edge or to address contemporary problems satisfactorily; he believes it can learn from the more abrasive black theology. Blacks must stop testing their theology against the value systems of the West and develop their own insights. 'It is only when African theology is true to itself that it will go on to speak relevantly to the contemporary African – surely its primary task – and also, incidentally, make its valuable contribution to the rich Christian heritage which belongs to all of us.'

Immersed as he was in fulfilling his episcopal duties, Bishop Tutu, by now part of the political scene, did not evade the further responsi-bilities this laid on him. He found no difficulty in accepting that the Church had a role as watchdog, that it should keep abreast of what was happening in government. In fact in his first sermon in Maseru he pointed out that the South African government was always looking for examples of mismanagement in countries run by Africans; that South Africa was watching Lesotho, so Lesotho must set an example.

Unfortunately Lesotho was not setting a good example and Tutu did not take kindly to the unelected government, still in power as a result of the 1970 coup. The Anglican, Catholic and Lesotho Evangelical Churches worked not only for reconciliation between themselves, but between the government and the opposition. Bishop Tutu, a driving force in ecumenical relations, did not hesitate to criticise the government, or, with other church leaders, to issue statements about 'the sad state of affairs in Lesotho, warning against infringement of the standards set by the Gospel of Jesus Christ, for injustice is injustice whoever it is who perpetrates it'.[15] While his courage was applauded by people like the ecumenical Christian Council of Lesotho, the government, not surprisingly, resented it bitterly. They must have been fearful of his influence, because they not only attacked him through the Press, but the Minister of Information even went to the lengths of organising a campaign against him.

As far as South Africa was concerned Tutu could not do much more than keep in touch with events, but it is a measure of the respect in which he was now held in his own country that in September 1977, when Steve Biko was buried in Kingwilliamstown, it was Tutu who was invited to give the funeral oration.

Steve Biko is honoured not only as the founder of the South African Students Organisation and Black People's Convention, not only as a student leader and political activist, but as a thinker whose views have made an ineradicable mark wherever human rights are taken seriously. 'Selfless revolutionary', a phrase he used of others, has been applied to him. The question has even been raised as to whether he should be regarded as a Christian martyr. His arrest, detention and brutal death at the hands of the South African security police was one of the most violent acts of a violent regime. The shock waves reverberated far beyond South Africa; the free world was outraged that a young man of such noble ideals should no longer be able to play his part in creating the free South Africa for which he had given so much – indeed for which he died.

Biko was only thirty when he was killed, so one can only guess how he would have developed, but during his lifetime there was a difference not so much in content as in emphasis, between his thinking and Bishop Tutu's. Both shared the common ideals of trying to give the black man back the dignity of which apartheid had tried to rob him, both were adamant that they were fighting for the liberation not only of the oppressed but also of the oppressor. However, Biko was not only more overtly political, but also more single-mindedly dedicated to the uplifting of the African spirit, while Tutu aspires to a climate where the colour of the skin is irrelevant. So successful has black consciousness been that there are many who claim that it has done its work and that had Biko still been alive he would have by now moved to a more universalist position, closer to Tutu's. One of the tragedies of his death is that we will never know.

The funeral was a huge occasion; some 30,000 people came from all over South Africa to honour him. Tutu had not known Steve Biko personally, but he did identify at a very deep level with the ideals for which Biko stood and his presence was warmly welcomed by Biko's friends like Justice Moloto and Dr Mamphela Ramphele.

In his oration Tutu emphasised one aspect of Biko's thinking especially near to his own:[16]

> Steve saw, more than most of us, how injustice and oppression can dehumanise and make us all, black and white, victim and perpetrator alike, less than God intended us to be. Now it has always sounded like sloganeering when people have said 'Oppression dehumanises the oppressor as well as the oppressed.' But have we not had an unbelievably shocking example of this, if he has been quoted correctly, in Mr Kruger's[17] heartless remark that Steve's death 'leaves him cold'? Of all human beings he is the most to be pitied. What has happened to him as a human being when the death of a fellow human being can leave him cold? And I bid you pray for the rulers of this land, for the police – especially the security police and those in the prison service – that they may realise that they are human beings too. I bid you pray for whites in South Africa.

While Steve Biko would have agreed with this sentiment, probably not everyone present felt like praying for their rulers at such a time. But it was typical of Tutu to make such a demand.

Tutu had not been in Lesotho for long before he noticed the number of women in the congregations – sometimes there would hardly be a man in the church. The reason was not hard to find. Over 100,000 Basotho men were in South Africa, working in the mines as migrant labourers.

The Nationalist government's declared aim was that Africans might only be in 'white' South Africa on a casual basis to sell their labour. They could own no land, have no political rights, they could not even bring their wives and children with them. As early as 1922 a government commission put it baldly: 'Natives should only be allowed to enter the urban areas to minister to the needs of the white man and should depart therefrom when he ceases so to minister.'[18] By 1970 the government still did not feel it had achieved its aims. The Minister of Bantu Education expressed his hopes thus: 'As far as I am concerned the ideal condition would be if we could succeed in due course in having all Bantu present in the white areas on a basis of migratory labour only.'[19]

So thousands of labourers, desperate for work, are herded together in conditions that would be condemned in many countries if they were inflicted on animals. For eleven months of the year up to 300 men live in dreary, barrack-like single-sex hostels, with as many as ten hostels in a compound. There is no heating, just one common room for entertaining and, as Helen Suzman told Parliament, 'an electronically controlled steel door that can be slid down to seal off any section of the building in case of riot or trouble ... installed on the instructions of the former Commissioner of Police'.[20] There could be forty-eight people in a room, sleeping on concrete slabs just long enough and just wide enough to accommodate a man's body. Not much larger than a coffin. Once a year they go to the bantustan to which they had been allocated to see, for a few short weeks, their parents, wives and children, known in government-speak as 'superfluous appendages'.

Tutu, who regards any insult to people's dignity as, in the final analysis, an act of blasphemy, pointed out that while the system of migrant labour is not peculiar to South Africa, and cannot be abolished entirely 'while there are depressed areas contiguous with more prosperous and developed ones', for it to be standard practice, as it is for the South African labourer, is contrary to the Gospel. In 1968, while he was still teaching at the Federal Theological Seminary in Alice, he had written about the theology of migrant labour for *South African Outlook*. His argument was not concerned so much with the appalling conditions under which these men were forced to live as with the effect on family life. He adapted Shylock's lines from Shakespeare's *The Merchant of Venice* to emphasise that these men were of flesh and blood: 'Hath not an African eyes? hath not an African hands, organs, dimensions, senses, affections, passions? fed with the same food, hurt with the same weapons, subject to the same diseases, heal'd by the same means, warm'd and cool'd by the same winter and summer as a White man is?'[21] So why, in a country that observes Family Day as a national holiday, should the majority of its population be made to live in conditions where a healthy family life was impossible. Was it surprising if there was homosexuality, prostitution and illegitimacy?

He argues that, far from accepting the charge of interfering in matters that do not concern the Church, she cannot be true to her calling if she acquiesces in conditions that are subversive of a healthy family life. Further, the Dutch Reformed Church itself, not usually eager to disagree with the government, pleaded at a Synod in 1965 that the State should change, or at least adapt, a system which it admitted could have disastrous results for the Church in the republic.

The system also leads to specific problems for the priest. For instance, a migrant labourer, deprived of his wife for eleven months of the year, often takes a town wife; strictly speaking he is then excluded from Holy Communion. Should the priest risk offending members of his Church by giving such persons the Sacraments? On the other hand,[22]

> are we discharging our pastoral responsibilities to the victims of a callous system, since it means their exclusion from the Sacraments for virtually all their life, when by law they may not live with their families at or near a place of work? Is it realistic, let alone fair, to expect a married man to remain continent in the highly charged atmosphere of an urban township, when through no fault of his own, he has been separated from his wife and family?

Children whose fathers are constantly absent from home are known to have problems; Tutu points out that this absence can colour their ideas about God. Children base their conceptions of the fatherhood of God on their relationship with their earthly fathers. 'And can we blame the children of the migrant labourer when their conception of God is the heretical one of a deistic absentee landlord who visits his creation only occasionally?'[23]

Conscious that eventually the Basotho should have one of their own people as their spiritual leader, one of the first things Bishop Tutu did was to groom Philip Mokuku, whom he had appointed as his Dean, to succeed him. The previous Bishop, John Maund, had never allowed the clergy to travel, so Mokuku, who had grown up as a country boy in the mountains of Lesotho, had seen nothing of the world and had little idea of what a cathedral could be. Tutu asked the Department of Mission at the South African Council of Churches (SACC) to organise a world tour of cathedrals, to broaden Mokuku's horizons and expose him to what was going on in places like Singapore, Washington and Coventry.

Tutu had not expected to remain in Lesotho for more than five years, but he cannot have expected the next invitation to come quite so soon. After only a few months in his new diocese he was invited to become General Secretary of SACC. He consulted his fellow bishops, who not surprisingly, said he should not accept. After three months the person appointed to the post resigned; again Bishop Tutu was approached and again, uncertain of God's will in the matter, he placed himself in the hands of the Bishops. This time, to Tutu's surprise, the Episcopal Synod unanimously urged him to accept.

Though he had been in the diocese for such a short time it was not a hard decision. True, he had come to love the mountains and the people, but now he knew that his place was in South Africa: 'There was the uncomfortable feeling of being a renegade; of being away from South Africa where people were being hurt as they struggled for freedom.'[24] There were also personal reasons for leaving. The children did not affect the decision either way; Trevor was at King's College in London, Theresa was studying to be a doctor in Botswana and Naomi and Mpho were at school in Swaziland. But for Leah returning to the republic held many attractions. She was spending a week of every month working in Johannesburg, where she was National Director of the Domestic Workers and Employers Project, a body set up to try to ensure better working conditions and salaries for domestic workers, who are nearly all black. Living 300 miles from the office is hardly commuting distance and she was happy to return to Johannesburg.

Though there were many who were sad at Bishop Tutu leaving Lesotho, some who were angry and felt let down, even some who accused him of acting irresponsibly and of deserting his flock, most people who knew him well felt he was right to move on. 'Lesotho was too small for him,' said one. 'He couldn't have stood it much longer,' admitted another. Though he had been criticised for travelling too much, he had managed to spend a lot of time with the people, a man of the people mixing with them and earning their love in a way no white man could have done. He had infused the diocese with hope, he had let in a breath of fresh air – most of all, he had prepared Philip Mokuku to succeed him.

Father Aelred Stubbs, at the time in Lesotho himself, wrote to Tutu easing any doubts he may have had:[25]

> Some of us had been reconciled to the thought of your leaving Johannesburg by considering that a spell of five or six years as Diocesan here would fit you for Cape Town. But what *He* had in mind was that you should make it possible for a Mosotho of the Basotho to be made ready for the office and work of a Bishop in the Church of God here! So I hope you feel you can say Nunc Dimittis, as far as Lesotho is concerned, in great peace and thankfulness.

9

The Church wakes up

By returning to South Africa to be General Secretary of the South African Council of Churches, Bishop Tutu was to spearhead a body that had become a brave voice in the Churches' struggle against apartheid; it was a struggle they had been slow to join.

If the Christian conscience was pricked by apartheid's violation of human dignity it had not been very evident. There were a few notable exceptions like Archbishop Geoffrey Clayton, Bishop Ambrose Reeves, the Reverend Michael Scott, Father Trevor Huddleston and Dean Gonville ffrench-Beytagh among the Anglicans, the Roman Catholic Archbishop Denis Hurley, and Methodists such as C. K. Storey and the Reverend Douglas Thompson, but for years there were few signs of resistance within the Churches. This apathy was encouraged by the very success of apartheid. The ring of rough land that encircles each township, keeping it well out of sight of white eyes, is more than a symbol of separation; few of the privileged minority knew or cared how the majority lived or the extent of their humiliation and suffering.

Since first coming to South Africa in 1943, Father Huddleston had fought apartheid tirelessly; in 1954 his exasperation with the Church reached boiling point. In a powerful and prophetic article for the *Observer*, which he entitled 'The Church Sleeps On', he castigated the Churches' indifference, pleading: 'In God's name, cannot the Church bestir itself all over the world and act? Cannot Christians everywhere show their distress in practical ways by so isolating South Africa from contact with all civilised communities that she realises her position and feels some pain in it?'[1]

Trevor Huddleston was going to have to wait many years for the international community to become seriously involved, but six years later the tragic events of Sharpeville did at last stir the Christian community into action. In late 1960 the World Council of Churches convened the Cottesloe Consultation to discuss Christian responsibility in race relations. At the end of the week-long conference the WCC's eight South African member Churches – five English-speaking and three Afrikaans-speaking – issued a statement urging racial reforms. They demanded, for instance, that all racial groups should be regarded as indigenous, they called for freedom of worship on a multi-racial basis and encouraged consultation between the Churches.

Though it was a moderate statement, too moderate for many of the delegates, since it left the principles of separate development intact, it was not acceptable to the reactionary *Voortrekker* Church, the Nederduitse Hervormde Kerk (NHK), who rejected it outright. However, the marginally less conservative Dutch Reformed Church, who had in any case prepared the discussion documents, did agree to sign. But it reckoned without Prime Minister Verwoerd, who, like most of his government, was a member of the DRC. He called it to order, reminded it of the high purpose of apartheid and urged it to recant. The majority of the DRC delegates did as they were told. In fact they went further: the two DRC synods who had attended the Consultation withdrew from the World Council of Churches.

The Cottesloe Consultation had been a high point in the relations between the Afrikaans- and English-speaking Churches; the rejection of its concluding statement was a bitter disappointment. If the Afrikaans Churches were to continue to give support and biblical justification to apartheid, concerted action was necessary by those who were beginning to realise that they could not. A new initiative, independent of Church structures, must be taken.

The child of this marriage between need and defeat was the Christian Institute, founded by that charismatic man who had been one of the key figures in the DRC delegation at the Cottesloe Consultation, Beyers Naudé. The Institute was explicit in its determination not to be answerable to the Churches; it was a fellowship of individuals answerable only to itself. This independence, while it avoided the denominational problems encountered at Cottesloe, involved the 180 individuals concerned in anguishing decisions and great personal suffering. Prof. A. G. Geyser of the NHK was tried for heresy; most notably Beyers Naudé, who was in line to be Moderator of the General Synod of the DRC, a post second only to the Prime Minister in influence, was forced to choose between his Church and the Institute. At the time he was acting as Moderator, and in choosing the Christian Institute he was compelled to resign from that position, part from his congregation and leave the Broederbond[2] after twenty-two years of membership. His passport was withdrawn, he was harassed, vilified in the South African press, sent to gaol and finally subjected for seven years to a banning order.

Those who live in a free society would find it hard to fault the Christian Institute's aims. Firmly committed to peace and to non-violent change, it sought, through study groups and the Institute's journal *Pro Veritate*, to rediscover the original message of the Bible; it tried to identify with the poor and seek a redistribution of power; it encouraged a wider perspective by helping young clergy to study and travel overseas and by sponsoring visits to South Africa by eminent Church leaders and theologians.

But its activities infuriated the government. However much the government might wish it to be otherwise, theology and politics are not separately defined areas in South Africa; they are closely related, constantly interacting with each other. Nevertheless, given the government's need to justify apartheid biblically, the Institute was treading a dangerous path. Beyers Naudé's vision of forming a confessing Church movement, on the lines of that which arose in the 1930s in response to Hitler's Germany, made the parallels between apartheid and Nazism uncomfortably public; the Institute's encouragement of black initiatives like the Black Consciousness Movement was hardly likely to appeal to those who preferred to satisfy the demands of Afrikaner consciousness. Nor was the Institute's avowed aim to show Christians in South Africa that 'southern Africa is a sick society because of its alienation, and doomed to die unless it is healed'[3] likely to appeal to a government seeking to convince the world that separate development was for the good of all.

The Christian Institute did succeed in some of its aims. It not only helped to articulate an indigenous South African liberation theology, but, according to Peter Walshe, 'it functioned as a vital matrix for the dissemination of ideas at a time when African political organisations had been systematically repressed'.[4] It was also instrumental in forging bonds between the African Independent Churches (which have a total membership of about 3½ million) and in helping them relate to the wider Church. To this end it supported the establishment of the African Independent Churches Association.

The Institute was the subject of continual harassment by the government. In 1972, together with the National Union of South African Students (NUSAS), the University Christian Movement and the South African Institute of Race Relations, it was summoned to appear before the Schlebusch Commission. As a result of the Commission's findings the Institute was declared an 'affected organisation', which prevented it from receiving funds from overseas, thus effectively cutting off most of its financial support. This was not going to throttle these courageous people and shortly after the Soweto riots they defiantly published an account of political trials, detentions and bannings called *Is South Africa a Police State?*. The next year excerpts from another publication, *Torture in South Africa?*, reached both the local and the foreign press.

The end came on October 19th, 1977. The Christian Institute was declared illegal, *Pro Veritate* was ordered to cease publication and Beyers Naudé's banning order meant he was no longer allowed to speak in public, to be quoted in the press, to meet more than one person at a time or to travel beyond the magisterial area of Johannesburg. Many of the Institute's black workers were detained by the police, several of its senior staff like Theo Kotzé and Brian Brown went into exile. On that same day seventeen other groups were banned, including the Black People's Convention, Black Community Programme and the South African Students Organisation; so was the black newspaper *The World* and its editor Percy Qoboza; so was Donald Woods, the editor of the East London *Daily Dispatch*. It was one of the darkest days in the history of resistance to white domination in South Africa.

For the last nine years of its life the Christian Institute had been an active member of the South African Council of Churches, whose roots can be traced through the Christian Council back to the early years of the century with the founding, by both Dutch Reformed and English-speaking Churches, of the General Missionary Conference. In 1934 a visit from the American missionary Dr Mott inspired an attempt to form a stronger and more closely knit organisation, with the emphasis on the established Churches rather than on the missions, and in 1936 the Christian Council of South Africa (CCSA) was born.

The CCSA had an initial membership of twenty-nine Churches and missionary organisations, including the Cape and Transvaal Synods of the DRC. It was not long, however, before the inevitable conflict over racial policies, abetted by Afrikaner resistance to the use of English as the medium of communication, led to the DRC's withdrawal. Tentatively the CCSA began to speak against racial discrimination. In 1948, when the Nationalists came to power and began to institutionalise apartheid, the CCSA responded by, once again, searching the Bible. At a conference held in Rosettenville in 1949 it concluded that its work could not confine itself to the purely spiritual, it must extend to the search for unity. Further, in direct criticism of apartheid, it affirmed that the franchise should be accorded to all those capable of exercising it, that every child deserved the best available education and every man had the right to work to his highest ability.

In 1968, in keeping with the world-wide trend set in motion by the founding of the World Council of Churches, the Christian Council decided to become the South African Council of Churches, a change of name that not only reflected the end of its missionary phase, but the growing importance of the indigenous Churches. It also heralded a new phase in the Church's struggle against apartheid.

*   *   *

Within months the SACC was launched into the national headlines. It published and disseminated a six-page document, prepared in collaboration with the Christian Institute, called *Message to the People of South Africa*. Its thrust was simple. It declared apartheid and separate development to be contrary to the Gospel of Jesus Christ; it was 'a false faith, a novel Gospel, which holds out to men a security built not on Christ but on the theory of separation and the preservation of their racial identity.'[5] The Prime Minister, now John Vorster, reacted as violently as had his predecessor, Dr Verwoerd, to the Cottesloe Statement. He warned any clerics planning 'to do the kind of thing here in South Africa that Martin Luther King did in America' to 'cut it out, cut it out immediately, for the cloak you carry will not protect you if you try to do this in South Africa'.[6] An exchange of letters followed, in which the Church leaders assured the Prime Minister that 'as long as attempts are made to justify the policy of apartheid by appeal to God's word, we will persist in denying their validity'.[7] Vorster replied that it was 'with the utmost despisal [sic], however, that I reject the insolence you display in attacking my Church as you do.'[8] One message, two such different interpretations; it is hard to believe they shared the same Bible.

The *Message* ended with a challenge:[9]

> And so we wish to put to every Christian person in this country the question which we ourselves are bound to face each day, to whom, or to what, are you truly giving your first loyalty, your primary commitment? Is it to a subsection of mankind, an ethnic group, a human tradition, a political idea; or to Christ?

By now the Churches had taken the bit between their teeth. Far from being warned off, the Christian Institute and the SACC established SPRO-CAS – the Study Project on Christianity in Apartheid Society.

SPRO-CAS, the SACC's first venture into the socio-political scene, aimed, in the words of its Director Peter Randall, 'to help the church move from a mere denunciation of apartheid, no matter how eloquent and even passionate, to a more meaningful and concrete involvement in the hard issues facing those church members who opposed the policy.'[10] The project attracted a galaxy of talent – theologians, economists, lawyers and political thinkers. The novelist André Brink, Professor Fatima Meer, Chief Gatsha Buthelezi, Dr van Zyl Slabbert, Steve Biko and Desmond Tutu, at that time teaching at the Federal Theological Seminary at Alice, were all involved in its work.

The SPRO-CAS brief was to seek a social system in which racism would have no part and its first phase was directed towards finding viable alternatives to apartheid. SPRO-CAS II took the next and logical step: action. It sought, for instance, better wages and greater social security for black workers, to change white attitudes, to develop black awareness and black leadership. If the absence of a clear multi-racial attitude and the separation of black and white programmes seems curious today, it must be remembered that this was 1969, soon after the birth of black consciousness. SPRO-CAS was a child of its time, a time when the twin needs, to raise white awareness and to develop black community programmes, could best be served separately.

At the same time as SPRO-CAS was moving from theory to action, so too was the World Council of Churches. Founded, ironically, in 1948 (the year that the Nationalists came to power in South Africa) the WCC had for twenty years consistently opposed racism in resolutions, conferences and statements. In 1969 it felt impelled to move towards a more direct involvement with racism, wherever it might occur, and the Program to Combat Racism was established. The next year it announced that grants were to be made to anti-racist liberation movements such as the Patriotic Front in Rhodesia, Frelimo in Mozambique, Swapo in Namibia, the African National Congress and the Pan-Africanist Congress in South Africa.

The SACC, who had not been consulted by the WCC and who first heard this startling news through the daily newspapers, was caught unprepared for the threats that ricocheted back from Mr Vorster – the SACC must leave the World Council of Churches or face government action. The fact that the grants were made for humanitarian purposes and that the WCC was not commending violence, but only making it clear where its support lay – an important point of emphasis – was not conveyed to the South African public. Faced with a choice between its loyalty to the WCC and its own convictions, the SACC decided that while it supported most of the work done by the Program to Combat Racism, and while it would retain its membership of the WCC, it was committed to non-violence; on that issue it could not give its support.

It was not an easy decision. With hindsight it is easy to see that the WCC realised, ahead of the South African Church leadership, that the days when black hopes, aspirations and anger could be contained in non-violent protest were numbered; but at the time the SACC stood to be accused on the one hand of condoning violence by its continuing relationship with the WCC, on the other of failing to support the radical groups. Nor did its compromise decision please the government, who not only made it illegal for funds to be sent from South Africa to the WCC, but did its best to prevent anyone associated with the WCC from visiting South Africa. The SACC and the South African government were on a collision course.

In 1970 John Rees, a white Methodist layman, took over from Bishop Bill Burnett as General Secretary of the SACC. Under his leadership the Council grew rapidly – the staff quadrupled and the budget expanded. Raising money has special problems in South Africa, where the vast majority of Christians are black and poor, barely able to contribute to their own churches, let alone ecumenical organisations. Support from overseas churches and foundations was, and still is, essential; raising funds was something at which John Rees excelled.

During those early years the SACC grappled with many of the problems that were to tax Tutu in his years as General Secretary. Apart from the uproar which greeted the publication of the *Message* and the confusion following the WCC's decision to give grants to liberation movements, there were crucial questions concerning the Churches' attitude to issues like disinvestment and violence, which began to take on a significance that was eventually to lead to direct confrontation between Church and State.

One such issue was conscientious objection, which by 1974 was beginning to polarise opinion more sharply than ever before. Frelimo had recently won power in Mozambique, there was guerrilla warfare in Rhodesia and Namibia, civil war in Angola. In South Africa on the one hand young blacks were feeling that their time, too, might be at hand; on the other, the government was pouring money into military training and arms. The SACC needed to state its position on violence and military service.

At its annual national conference the delegates, some of whom had relatives in the militant arm of liberation movements, discussed the role of the Christian in war. While the Christian tradition regards the fighting of a 'just war' as acceptable, could it be right for a Christian to participate in a military force defending an unjust and discriminatory society? If the use of violence between Afrikaner and British in the Boer War was considered acceptable, why should the same not apply to the blacks, in their struggle for freedom? If violence is condemned when perpetrated by liberation movements, how can it be condoned when practised with the apparent respectability of government backing? Does military service become a duty simply because it is demanded by the State? Is not the Christian responsible to a higher authority?

After hours of heated debate, the resolution was finally passed. Its fifteen clauses included a refusal to accept that the Christian has an automatic duty to engage in war at the demand of the State; it pointed

Right: Desmond and Leah Tutu on their wedding day, July 2, 1955.

Below: The Tutu family in London, 1964. From left to right the children are Trevor, Theresa, Naomi and Mpho.

Desmond Tutu after his consecration as Bishop of Lesotho.

Desmond and Leah celebrate their 25th wedding anniversary with their mothers. Mrs Aletta Tutu is on the left.

Bishop Tutu in discussion with Dr Robert Runcie, the Archbishop of Canterbury.

Receiving the Nobel Peace Prize from Egil Aarvik, Chairman of the Nobel Committee.

Desmond Tutu holding a vigil with some of the residents of Mogopa shortly before they were forcibly removed from their homes.

A hostel for migrant workers. Behind the communal stove are the concrete bunks used for sleeping.

Bishop Tutu coming to the rescue of a suspected police informer under attack from an angry mob.

Imploring mourners at a township funeral to avoid bloodshed.

Part of Soweto, home to over a million blacks, including the Tutus.

Mayor Andrew Young, Coretta Scott King, Bishop Desmond Tutu and Martin Luther King III leading a march through Atlanta in honour of Dr Martin Luther King.

Above: Bishop Tutu and President P. W. Botha in Pretoria after their second meeting, 1986.

Left: Joining in festivities at a UDF rally in Soweto.

Desmond Tutu outside St George's Cathedral after his enthronement as Archbishop of Cape Town.

H M Queen Elizabeth II greeting Archbishop Tutu at a Commonwealth Day reception in London. In the centre is Sir Shridath Ramphal, Secretary-General of the Commonwealth.

The Church wakes up

out that the primary violence was institutionalised apartheid and that the South African military forces were being prepared to defend this unjust system. It deplored the use of violence and requested that a task force should study methods of non-violent action for change and called on the member Churches who had chaplains in the armed forces to reconsider the basis on which they were appointed. In short it concluded that conscientious objection was a valid Christian option.

The resolution was supported by blacks and strengthened the standing of the SACC; predictably, it was also met by a barrage of criticism. Critics conveniently failed to notice that violence was explicitly deplored and the government introduced a Bill providing heavy penalties – up to ten years' imprisonment – for anyone trying to persuade another person to avoid military service. This Bill aroused so much opposition in Parliament that it was modified and, in fact, never invoked. The government also began a campaign of formal harassment of the SACC by funding the Christian League, a group headed by a Methodist minister, Fred Shaw, whose explicit purpose was to ward off the perceived threat of Communism and to persuade South African Churches to withdraw from the WCC.

One of John Rees's most significant contributions to the SACC was the determination with which he ousted apartheid from life in the office. Though blacks made up at least 80 per cent of the membership, when Rees took over as General Secretary authority was vested almost exclusively in whites and signs of 'petty apartheid' – different salaries, separate toilets – still belied the Council's stand on racial discrimination. Rees was not going to stand for that: 'We must increasingly make plans, not only within the Church structures, but also within the structure of the Council itself for the voice of our black brethren to be heard . . .'[11] He was as good as his word, paying black and white staff equal salaries for equal work, desegregating toilets, moving blacks into senior positions and giving every white administrator a black secretary and every black administrator a white secretary. At his first national conference a black President was elected.

Likewise in the matter of membership. As churches that had originated as missions were handed over to indigenous leadership, so they joined the Council. By 1971, with the added membership of the African Independent Churches' Association, hundreds of black-led churches were related to the SACC. In 1975 the admission of the Nederduitse Gereformeerde Kerk in Afrika (NGA), the black 'daughter' Church of the DRC (the DRC – the 'mother' Church – has three 'daughter' Churches, one each for blacks, 'coloureds' and Indians) was celebrated. By the time Tutu arrived in March 1978 the SACC was beginning to be a microcosm of a future, non-racial South Africa.

10

A parish without frontiers

On March 1st, 1978, when Bishop Tutu started work as the General Secretary of the South African Council of Churches, he was taking on a formidable task, demanding formidable qualities. The work was to involve him at many levels, in concentric circles of concern. Inside the Council itself there was the delicate matter of keeping a harmonious balance between the sixteen departments and judging the relative claims of long-range and short-term programmes; he would also have to involve himself in the often emotional relationships with the constituent Churches. At a national level he knew that there would be many people, from committed Christians to those with no claims to religious belief, who would question his integrity. Most crucially, there was the question of the increasing polarisation between Church and State and the harassment both the Council and Tutu personally were to endure from the government. Finally, he was soon to become an international spokesman for millions of black South Africans. What were the qualities that informed his actions in this exposed position? It is time to consider the nature of the man who for six years occupied a post known as 'the hottest ecclesiastical seat in the country'.

He immediately brought his own style to bear on the Council. Despite the tensions inherent in any such disparate body of people – there were over thirty different members and groups affiliated to the Council and the racial mix was accompanied by inevitable diversities of temperament – and despite the national issues that tend to pre-occupy South Africans, he insisted on seeing the Council's problems from a world perspective, resisting insularity, whether black or white. This global vision was one of the first things to impress his new colleagues, particularly the Methodist Minister Peter Storey, who was one of the two Vice-Presidents at the time: 'Here was a man who had been liberated from the paranoia and the almost psychotic obsessions that South Africa produces in us if we are concerned at all. He had experienced the broad vistas of human thought and behaviour across the world and he brought that global consciousness into our thinking.' Tutu's reports, whether at the national conferences or the quarterly executive meetings, were masterly surveys of contemporary world affairs. Peter Storey would tease him for taking them on 'Cook's Tours' as he castigated the puppet regime established in Afghanistan by the Russians or condemned United States support of the Contras in Nicaragua, spelt out the broad outlines of international debt, reacted to a recent change of government, lamented the unresolved strife in Ulster, or internecine war in the Middle East or urban terrorism in Italy. Smaller fish were caught in his net as he worried that Belgium might split up over the issue of language or wondered how the latest Springbok Rugby Tour was going to affect the meeting of Commonwealth Finance Ministers. He would welcome good news, praising the Peace Movement, rejoicing in the exchange of Ambassadors between Israel and Egypt or in the liberation of Zimbabwe from white minority rule and the extraordinary news that on Independence Night former Rhodesian soldiers paraded with former guerrillas.

Sometimes, undeterred by the limited value of such communications, Tutu's concern took the form of letters, statements and telegrams. In 1982, for instance, he cabled the Prime Minister of Israel, appealing to him to stop bombing Beirut: 'Be true to great Jewish tradition and don't let Jews be cause of untold suffering for others.' A simultaneous telegram to Mr Arafat called for 'greater realism about Israel's existence'. A third assured the people of Lebanon of 'our fervent prayers and God's strength in these horrible days'. On behalf of the SACC he wrote to the Prime Ministers of Zimbabwe, Lesotho and Swaziland and the Presidents of Botswana and Mozambique, thanking them for giving hospitality to South African refugees and appealing to them not to send any refugee back to South Africa against his or her will. Occasionally his intervention brought success; his appeal to the President of the Seychelles for the release of Martin Dolinschek, one of five South Africans who had been sentenced to death, brought him a grateful letter saying that he was the only person of stature to intercede – most of the letters sent to the President were appeals to save the turtles. And always Tutu remembered the international community in prayer, both private and public. Dr Margaret Nash, the ecumenical officer with the SACC, will never forget 'the sense in which he was, so to speak, taking the world in his hands and holding it up to God, place by place, situation by situation, person by person'. At the SACC he was a Bishop without a diocese, but now the world was his parish.

It was a parish with no boundaries, but it had a centre, a beating heart – the offices of the SACC. From the day he arrived his relationship with the staff was encapsulated in his response to the question greeting any new boss, 'What shall we call you?'. 'Father,' he replied and, apart from formal occasions when he was addressed as Bishop and a few close friends who called him Desmond, 'Father' or '*Baba*' (the African equivalent) he remained.

As the SACC is an ecumenical body, there were those from Nonconformist traditions who were not easy with this title, others who were resentful, feeling that addressing him as 'Father' prevented them being on equal terms. Yet the appellation suited his style and his temperament. Sophie Mazibuko, a colleague at the SACC and a close friend of Leah's, knows him in many roles: 'He can be a child, he can be an adult, he can be a father, he can be a strict husband, he can be a very good friend.' Versatile though he is, his instincts are paternal. Many of the staff tended to relate to him as a father and he encouraged them to do so; he seemed to think of them as 'his children' and would often address the younger members of his staff as 'My child'.

This paternal attitude was at its strongest in his relationship with his two secretaries, Thembi Segkaphane and Peter Storey's wife Elizabeth. Thembi is black and a Seventh-Day Adventist, Elizabeth white and a Methodist. Religious and racial barriers presented no problem and their friendship gave Tutu deep pleasure – it was how he wanted everyone to live. They were his daughters, one black, one white, each given appropriate duties but both part of his family, sharing each others' joys and sorrows. If they failed to greet him with a kiss on Monday morning, or kiss him goodbye on Friday afternoon there would be trouble. He could even be jealous of their husbands – in the office they were *his* family.

Thembi and Elizabeth were very sensitive to his moods, sometimes saying 'Now he's black' or 'Now he's white' and together working out the things peculiar to each culture. For instance, he is methodical, meticulous and punctual, something more easily understood by Elizabeth than by Thembi. On the other hand there were things from his culture that were foreign to Elizabeth. For instance if, in a European context, one is offered a biscuit, there is no offence in declining; Tutu (presumably on a day when he was black), would be furious, saying, 'You never say "no thank you" to food, it is food given to you and your family, so if you don't want it you take it home to your family.' To Elizabeth this would have felt hypocritical so eventually she plucked up her courage, stuck to her own culture and said 'No thank you'. His anger, considering how long he had spent in England, surprised even Elizabeth, who knows him so well.

Like any father, he could be strict. When a member of staff who had been on sabbatical leave failed to return in time for the national conference, as she had promised, she received a memo saying: 'I will have to come back and discuss this matter with you sternly, because this is not how I want to operate.' And even his greatest admirers were critical of him in his role of authoritarian Bishop; some were curious that he donned full episcopal regalia for the office Mass, others felt threatened by his insistence that they all went on yearly retreats, whether or not it was in their tradition.

He was loved, feared, respected, indulged, occasionally resented and to a great extent understood. They came to know his tastes – his love of 'fat cakes', samosas, dates, marshmallows and Yogi Sip, his passion for cricket and music, his habit of early-morning jogging and midday naps, his loathing of bad language. More importantly they learnt to cope with his sensitivity, to realise how very easily he could be hurt. This vulnerability is something he manages to conceal from the world at large, but it did not escape the notice of Elizabeth: 'He is very human and life isn't easy for him. He has great ups and great downs as well and sometimes they are very obvious. He can't cover things up, like his hurt – he gets tremendously hurt and he has this craving to be loved. He is a very ordinary person who has ordinary feelings.'

Tutu makes no secret of his wish to be loved, something he regards as 'a horrible weakness'; he is perhaps less aware of his vulnerability, which can cause trouble out of all proportion to the cause. Anyone failing to acknowledge an increment, or who is late for prayers and does not come up to his office to apologise, anyone who does not thank him, even for a small thing, risks giving him offence. Dan Vaughan, a senior and much respected colleague, once questioned the wisdom of one of his public statements. Tutu swung on him saying, 'I make my own decisions – no one is going to tell me what to say.' Though they were travelling together, it was not until the next day that a smile and a hand on the shoulder indicated that Dan was forgiven. Another colleague who had the temerity to disagree with him was told: 'You're a silly child. Get out of my office. I'm not going to talk to you again until you've come to your senses.' And for three weeks Tutu was as good as his word. While for the most part he shows the sensitivity to others that he would wish them to show to him, he can fall short of his own ideals. There was a period when he hurt Thembi because of her allegiance to the Seventh-Day Adventists. Ecumenist though he is, it took him some years to accept that one of his beloved children should belong to this particular sect.

Just as he is easily hurt, so both laughter and tears are as close as breathing. He is a man of passionate emotions, sometimes laughing when the only alternative would be to cry. He can make a joke even of such obscenities as the migrant labour system – 'This is the only country in the world where it is illegal to sleep with your own wife'; or of the white man's rape of his country – 'We had the land and they had the Bible. Then they said "Let us pray" and we closed our eyes. When we opened them again, they had the land and we had the Bible. Maybe we had the better of the deal.' His wit peppers every speech and sermon and his entry into a room is usually surrounded by an aura of good humour that is almost tangible. So, too, do his tears flow easily. Once, in the formal context of an executive meeting, he became so aware of white resistance to what he was saying that he burst out, 'Good people I am here to work with you, to serve the people of God. I am here as a brother and I love you so much', and burst into tears.

Like most honest people – and he is honest to a fault – he trusts his staff not only in their work, but in their integrity. In South Africa the possibility of informers is something that has always to be taken into account, but when there were convincing rumours that an informer was in their midst, on the staff of the SACC, he called a meeting, saying he could not and would not operate on a basis of suspicion, he would rather be deceived. It was eight years before he discovered that the rumours had been true. On another occasion he found that a junior secretary had for months been stashing away letters, cheques and receipts instead of posting or filing them. When he eventually became aware of what was going on he did not discipline her, he was not even angry; he said that his heart bled for her, that he could not 'throw her to the wolves' and simply moved her to another department. There were to be times when this refusal to be suspicious was to lead him into very deep waters indeed.

The essence of fatherhood, paternalism at its best, is found in the role of Pastor, the Shepherd of the Flock. It is in this sphere that Tutu feels most at home, most sure that he is doing God's will. His concept of priesthood demands faithfulness rather than success, a faithfulness that should be manifested in a disciplined rule of life with regular saying of the office, study of the Scriptures, prayer, meditation and – too often neglected – pastoral visiting. 'You can't love people and not visit them. You can't love them unless you know them, and you can't know them unless you visit them regularly. And the good shepherd knows his sheep by name.'[1] He values courteousness and humility in a priest as in a layman, and is eloquent in extolling the need for gentleness:[2]

Let us watch our tongues. We can hurt, we can extinguish a weak flickering light by harsh words . . . It is easy to discourage, it is far too easy, all too easy to criticize, to complain, to rebuke. Let us try instead to be more quick to see even a small amount of good in a person and concentrate on that. Let us be more quick to praise than to find fault. Let us be more quick to thank others than to complain – 'Thank you' and 'Please' are small words, but they are oh, so powerful. My dear Brothers, please be gentle with God's people.

Valuing priesthood so highly, rejoicing in his calling, it is no surprise that as soon as he had agreed to resign his see and take a secular job, he wrote to the Bishop of Johannesburg, Timothy Bavin, asking if he could help in a parish. Bishop Bavin suggested that until the demands on his time were known he should be content to work as a member of the relieving staff, so it was not until the beginning of 1981 that, in addition to his work at the SACC, Tutu became Rector of a church in Soweto – St Augustine's, Orlando West. It was in an area poor even by Soweto standards and the parish had been full of argument and quarrelling, but St Augustine's and Tutu gave each other life. He, far from finding yet more work the last straw after a busy week, was excited by the challenge. The parishioners were given a new dignity, a new peace. He persuaded them to paint the church, found a carpet to replace the worn old lino, took Bible Study classes and encouraged them to visit one another, street by street. Soon the children who came to Sunday school were getting scholarships to study and St Augustine's, from being a gossiping, defeated congregation, became a new living community. As their Rector became more and more widely known, so the television cameras came to film him preaching and the church became famous.

But his pastoral role is not confined to parish or congregation, its mantle embraces everyone he meets. His own need for affirmation is mirrored in his ability to affirm others; people feel better just for being with him. The tributes are endless: 'He has this amazing capacity to make people relax and help them to be freer.'[3] 'He really manages to bring God so close to you.'[4] 'I come away from quick and relatively casual meetings with a tremendous feeling of encouragement. My obedience is strengthened and I feel I am more of a Christian for being with him for three minutes.'[5] His conviction that every human being is made in the image of God, that we are all 'God-carriers', is so deep-rooted that he feels one should mentally genuflect to everyone one meets in the street. So when he meets a secretary at the British Council of Churches, he does not just smile and pass through to her boss's office, he spends ten minutes in animated conversation with her. And when she moves to another job, she receives a personal letter from him saying, 'I am devastated, you have forsaken me.' Sophie Mazibuko experienced his care in tragedy, when her son became a quadriplegic:

Fortunately Desmond was in the country then and I could phone him anytime and he would talk to me for fifteen or twenty minutes, trying to be a spiritual base. I dare not tell him if, for instance, I am trying to get my son into hospital in Cape Town because he would move the stars – so I don't tell him unless I have an insurmountable problem.

Nor is this sensitive attention only given when it is convenient. He was so determined to support the Anglican priest, David Russell, when he was on trial for breaking his banning order to attend a Synod, that he cancelled an important meeting and went back to Cape Town, from where, incidentally, he had just returned. Similarly he found time to be present for a few minutes at the funeral of a friend's father on, of all days, June 16th, 1976, the day of the Soweto killings. Neither is his care confined to those who are fond of him. He amazed an elderly man, who had made no secret of his dislike, by visiting him regularly while he was recovering from an operation. Similarly, he went to the funeral of a woman who had frankly hated him.

This concern for people, whether in matters great or small, also finds regular expression in his correspondence. Given the weight of his commitments he is prompt in answering his letters, at length if the occasion demands, nearly always with charity and gentleness.

Among the official letters, the stream of requests that he should recommend people for posts or vice versa, the requests to preach, speak at conferences, sit on commissions, attend ambassadorial functions, dine with businessmen, the occasional brush with authority – a traffic offence or an unpaid bill – his postbag reveals a glorious cross-section of humanity in all its richness. A browse through his files reveals, for instance, an invitation from the Kwazakhele Rugby Union to attend the opening of the Dan Qeqe Stadium, where he was to kick off the match, a letter asking him to speak at the Ikageng Women's Club, a card from a small boy, sick in bed, thanking him for the cartons of Pear Liqui Fruit. There are letters seeking help from people who see hope for all black South Africans in Bishop Tutu's own rise from location urchin to episcopal purple. To an ambitious correspondent who writes 'I would like to be world Bishop – I have passed Form Four', he suggests 'Shouldn't you pass Matric first and then study for ordination?' Equally practical advice is given to a fifty-one-year-old Principal of a primary school asking for financial assistance in his 'forlorn, FORLORN desire to learn music.' As he was a member of the Moravian Church, Tutu suggested he should ask his Church for help.

There are greetings from overseas admirers, like an Italian priest who has decided to make Tutu's name known in Europe: 'We never met, but it is almost the same for me as if I had. I feel I do know you as if I were your closest friend. I am not here to flatter you, but I feel today you are a real hope for the church in South Africa.' There is even a series of letters from a man for whom Tutu figured in visionary dreams: 'The Lord has laid it upon my heart to send the attached prophecies ... I saw the Prophet lying sick, suffering from severe poisoning. The prophet was a VIP ... Bishop Tutu was by the sea. There were two pillars named faith and prayer. Three times Jesus asked him "Desmond, do you love me?"'

Some people are filled with a generalised love for mankind; others are able to translate this love into practical care. Tutu belongs to the second category. His attention to the detail of people's lives is remarkable. The Mqotsis, African friends of the Tutus living in London, wanted one of the striped blazers worn at the University of the Witwatersrand. They had not been made for twelve years, Tutu told them, but would they like a Wits badge on a navy blue blazer? If so, he would bring it when he next came to England. He might write to the bank or the post office, commending a member of their staff who had been particularly courteous, send flowers to cheer a sick secretary or greet someone just released from prison. Often the morning starts with little notes being written to people he knows are going through a difficult time; when he is overseas, every member of the staff receives a postcard. He is meticulous in remembering birthdays and anniversaries, whether wedding, profession, or consecration. Perhaps this scrupulous attention owes something to the fact that he himself can be hurt if the dates significant in his own life are not remembered.

To the bereaved he writes with a sensitivity which must bring the recipient as near to hope as is possible at such a time:[6]

> I know that it may be true that it is easy on a full stomach to praise fasting and so for someone who has not been touched personally by a bereavement to speak about the consoling powers of God's Holy Spirit. I know that there is a void in your life which nothing and no one will be able to fill and that there are many moments when it seems like it is a dream or maybe a nightmare and that Tom will walk through the door with his pipe in his mouth. Or that you will hear his familiar tones as he tells a joke and chuckles away. But then it dawns on you that in fact, no, he won't physically, he is away. But in another sense he isn't. He has given you himself. He has helped to make you what you are just as much as you helped to make him what he was. And there are things that no one will ever be able to take away from you which you treasure. And then of course, we know, we believe, we belong to the resurrected body of our Lord Jesus Christ and that in Jesus we are always together.

That there is no separation. There is no farewell. There is no departure.
There is only returning and finding one another.

From his first months at the SACC Tutu began to receive critical
letters. When they were couched in reasonable, positive terms he
would invite the writer to come and talk to him; when they were
offensive – and they frequently were – he was capable of retaliating.
A letter accusing him of 'bearing false witness' and ending 'look to
your conscience if you have such a thing' received a stern reply: 'I
expect a full apology forthwith for your scurrilous attack and if not
given within a week I will place your letter in the hands of our
solicitors.' (He duly received an apology.) Mostly, though, his reaction
was to ignore them, taking St Paul's advice to 'rejoice, inasmuch as
ye are partakers of Christ's sufferings'. Significantly, one of his
favourite texts is, 'If God is for us, who can be against us?'

Any public figure attracts criticism, yet surely Tutu has had to
endure more than his share? It is particularly painful for such a man,
with so deep a need for love and affirmation, to know that he is not
merely criticised, but is, for many, an object of hatred.

There are many possible reasons why Tutu should attract such
venom; strong people evoke strong emotions. Though he has his
critics amongst the black community – the radicals who find him too
moderate, a few who, uncomfortable because they are not playing
their part in working for justice and peace in their country, are irritated
by his constant calls for change – those who dislike him are mostly
white and politically conservative. Tutu not only threatens their way
of life, but disturbs them; in their hearts they know that apartheid is
abhorrent, that he is right to resist it. He also attracts a particular sort
of racism, as Helen Suzman admits:

> There's a natural antagonism among the majority of white South Afri-
> cans at having to pay obeisance to a black man, be he a Bishop or not.
> And it is very hard for many of them who are not real, practising
> Christians but are Anglican members, or DRC or Roman Catholic or
> whatever, to get used to the idea of having a black man in command of
> a very important section of their lives. That, of course, is pure racist,
> but you can't ignore it in this country.

Tutu had experienced this attitude before he was a Bishop, when he
preached at a white girls' school near Alice. After the service one of
the girls said to the headmistress that it was one of the best sermons
she had ever heard, adding: 'but I still think a black man should not
come into our chapel'.

So from all sides the arrows flew. Within months of his return to

Johannesburg the *Sunday Express* was dismissing him as 'Tutu of the trendy specs and trendier hair-do, so sure that justice will be done'; headlines screamed 'BELT UP, TUTU'; a statement was greeted as 'the latest Tutu-muchism'; he was referred to as 'that insect in dark glasses' and accused of 'boring people with his particular mixture of syrupy promises and petty politicking'. Letters demanded 'Why, oh why do you spike Jesus' guns? Do you see what is wrong in our country more than Jesus does?'; asked 'Why do you promote Marxist goals? Many people grow sick of what you say'; informed him that 'One thing a Bishop should not suffer from is Foot in Mouth disease'. Death threats became commonplace and he has had to learn to live with constant physical fear. He was once walking through the concourse of Jan Smuts Airport when a white woman said, quite loud enough for him to hear, 'Isn't that that bastard Tutu – if I had a gun I would shoot him now.'

It is hard to believe that these angry people, many of whom did not even have the courage to sign their letters, are talking about the same man; the real person bears so little relation to the public image, as people who hear him for themselves find out. A young Afrikaner wrote to him in amazement after listening to him speak: 'How the newspapers must have distorted you – or how you must have changed! . . . it was the Spirit of Love, Patience and Reconciliation more than anything else that stirred my heart. Even more so because of the image I have of you which made me expect something quite different.'[7] Anyone who actually listens to what he is saying, anyone who talks to him face-to-face, has to revise their opinion. Even those opposed to him politically cannot but warm to him at a personal level. Peter Storey has found that 'time and again I have seen people introduced to Desmond with ice in their eyes and I have seen them melt as they discovered the real person'.

When the real Desmond Tutu is met he is loved, and one of the reasons he is loved is because of the love he feels – *really* feels, it is not just some priestly role he dons – for every man, woman and child; he sees and honours what the Quakers call 'that of God in every man'. He constantly reminds people, black and white alike, of their value as human beings, telling audiences they are 'princes and princesses' or 'masterpieces' – sometimes making hundreds of people say with him 'We are masterpieces'. Even his criticism is couched in these terms; talking to an audience which included the head of the Broederbond, ultra-conservative theologians and students he told them:[8]

I don't think many of you really believe that you are people of infinite worth. Because you don't realise this you tend to behave like bullies.

Bullies throw their weight about to make their mark. Whites amass material wealth to prove their worth. But you have infinite worth because God has created you in his image. If you would only believe it of yourselves, you would believe it of others.

One of Tutu's great contributions to the SACC, something he gave from the very centre of his being, was his emphasis on the spiritual foundation of its work. On a formal level he introduced daily prayers, insisting that the entire staff come together as a community from 8.30 to 9.30 a.m. every morning; once a month there was a Eucharist, taken by the various denominations in rotation. During these periods everything, from staff birthdays to the most recent national or international event, was considered in the light of the Gospel, prayed about, placed before God. In keeping with Gospel teaching this included a concern for people who might be considered enemies. Despite continual pressure – even from fellow Christians – he steadfastly refuses to stop praying for P. W. Botha; when praying for friends in prison he prays also for the jailors and the police 'because they are God's children too'.

Sometimes he would recall with gratitude other people's prayers; for him the concept of the world-wide Church community is rich in meaning. He once wrote of this to an Australian priest who was showing his support in prayer:[9]

> It is a great comfort to know that one need only throw oneself into this current and be borne by it and upheld by it . . . It is wonderful to belong to the Church of God and I know for myself that I would have collapsed long ago were it not for the fact that I know and experience myself as being upheld and buoyed by the sense of all those who love us and pray for us.

When the SACC staff felt despondent because of government harassment, 'so low we could crawl under a snake', he would be cheered by remembering the prayers of a Lutheran Pastor from Alaska, or an anchorite in Arizona who prayed for them at 3 a.m. every morning. 'What hope have the government got of defeating us when we are being prayed for every day in Arizona?'

He also helped individual members of the staff with their prayer life, not only insisting on the importance of regular prayer but encouraging them to relate to God as to a human being – to scold as well as to petition, to express disappointment as well as reverence. Even, if God seemed silent, to cry out 'What kind of God are you? Are you God only for white people?' For many, brought up to a self-abasing and penitential attitude to prayer, this brought profound relief. Sophie

Mazibuko is one of many who rejoiced in this approach: 'We were all brought up with the idea that God is the person with the big eye in the middle and that he is always looking at you. You never saw God as a friend, you never saw him as your creator and the best person to talk to when you are in trouble. Prayer is now something I can go along with.'

Extravert though Tutu is, he has also a deeply private, introvert side. Anyone who has spent even a short time alone with him will have sensed an indefinable quality, an undercurrent throbbing beneath the quick responses and easy jokes. Centredness? Peace? Communion with God? Whatever one calls it, there is no doubt that it is the fruit of his inner life. It is as if whatever he is doing, part of him, like a Russian *staretz*, prays without ceasing.

His life is shot through with prayer. He rises early in the morning, sometimes as early as 3.30, to be sure of a full hour's prayer before his daily jog; then, after a quick breakfast, he goes to Mass or, if it is not possible to go to church, he celebrates it at home, with Leah as his single congregant. During the working day every interview and meeting is preceded by a short prayer. However busy he is, whatever his current concerns, once a month he goes to a nearby convent for a 'quiet day' and occasionally he fasts and holds vigils; at least once a year he goes on a retreat of three days or longer. The importance of these longer periods of prayer and reflection in Tutu's life, especially before any crucial event or decision, can hardly be overemphasised. In that space he is strengthened, in that space he listens to what God is saying to him, finding answers to apparently insoluble problems. Peter Storey, whose first meeting with Tutu was waking one morning in a shared hotel room thinking he had seen a ghost – it was the small, sheet-covered figure of Desmond Tutu on hands and knees – found that when he came back from a retreat 'there was a new steel core to his resolution and a new initiative'. Dan Vaughan remembers one occasion when Tutu came into the office at a particularly tense time saying, 'I am going to fast for a week, this is what God has said to me.' So he spent all day in the chapel, his secretary brought him a cup of Milo at midday, and he went home at night.

His prayer life is not only disciplined and regular, it spills over into every activity – even driving the car. Regular passengers have learnt not to be surprised if he tells them to 'shut up' while he combines driving and praying; even so, Peter Storey remembers an occasion when he might have preferred prudence to prayer. They had driven together to Vendaland, where some Lutheran clergy were being ill-treated in prison. They went to the police station (Tutu with no passport – his way of showing that he does not recognise the 'homelands') saying they would like to pray with the prisoners. The police felt they needed to seek higher authority for this dangerous activity. The higher authority forbade it, adding that they were prohibited immigrants and would be deported. Escorted by two Land-Rovers, they were taken into the bush, where the police began to rough them up, threatening to kill them. Eventually they were released and drove thankfully away with Tutu at the wheel. As they crossed the border he joked about 'prisoners of Venda', saying, 'We could have been killed. We need to thank God for keeping us safe,' and as they sped along he firmly shut his eyes to pray.

This pattern of prayer evolved over many years, but during his time as Bishop of Lesotho another element was added when a Franciscan monk, Brother Geoffrey, came to his house in Maseru to hold a meeting about the Third Order of the Franciscans. Tutu was captivated, saying that this was what he had been searching for and asking if he might test his vocation as a Tertiary.

While the First Order of the Society of St Francis consists of men and women living an active life under the traditional vows of poverty, chastity and obedience and the Second Order of women leading an enclosed life of contemplative prayer, the Third Order is open to men and women, ordained and lay, married or single, who feel called to live out a Franciscan vocation in the world. Aspirants to this way of life undergo six months as postulants, followed by a novitiate of two years. Once professed, the intention is life-long adherence to the personal rule of life they will have drawn up with a spiritual counsellor, though to safeguard against merely nominal membership their vows are renewed annually.

Tutu's devotion to the Community of the Resurrection is such that one might have expected him to join *their* Third Order, rather than the Franciscans. What drew him away from his old family?

Perhaps the answer lies partially in the very closeness of this tie; the CR were his spiritual parents, their influence was, and still is, immeasurable. In taking this new step he needed to go forward rather than back, to be independent of these treasured parents. There is, too, much that is Franciscan in his spirituality. In the CR he found a toughness and a courage that appealed to him, he met men who were not sitting on the fence, but whose Christianity constrained them to join the fight for a just South Africa. This strengthened and inspired him, eventually encouraging and confirming his political commitment, but there was something else he needed. Bishop John Taylor suggests that 'He wanted his lightheartedness endorsed, that peculiar thing in Desmond that is carefree, a kind of troubadour fighter'. He found it with the Franciscans.

His counsellor used to hold him up as a model novice, meticulous in reporting every three months; since he was professed he has continued to renew his vows every year, though he rarely has the time to attend the Third Order meetings. The firm background given him by the Community of the Resurrection, combined with his own disciplined prayer life and the simplicity and joy of Franciscan spirituality, gave him an unassailable strength to tackle the problems ahead. In 1980 he wrote to a nun friend,[10]

> Recently I have been discovering again the tingling joy of the gospel that I have to do nothing to gain acceptance by God. That it is his acceptance of me which enables there to be me and for there to be acts and for there to be thoughts and words by me. One ought to have a semi-cartesian dictum, 'I am loved therefore I am'.

The hottest ecclesiastical seat

The South Africa to which Tutu returned in 1978 was as split as ever by the axe of apartheid; nothing much had changed in the two years he had been away. In fact apartheid was so successful that whites could still sip their exquisite wines, watch the sun set over the valley and thank their white racist God for so tranquil an existence. Though the more perceptive recognised 'a pall of despondency and helplessness hanging over South Africa,[1] there was a surface calm. Few whites knew (or if they suspected, they hastily repressed their suspicions) the conditions under which the majority of the population lived and the anger that seethed in the townships. Still fewer appreciated the extent to which the Black Consciousness Movement had restored black dignity; or that after the Soweto killings of 1976 a new generation of young blacks, fearless and determined, was emerging, young people who would not submit, as they felt their parents had, to the barbaric system of apartheid.

Though petty apartheid was slowly being abolished (some public parks were desegregated, blacks who could afford to were allowed to attend selected theatres and concerts, to eat in some of the same restaurants as whites and go into a few of the international hotels), the black community were still victims of an edifice of social engineering manifested in literally hundreds of laws and implemented with ruthless brutality. Forced removals were regular occurrences; during the preceding year nearly 300,000 people had been arrested under the Pass Laws; the murder of Steve Biko had been followed by the mysterious deaths of others held in police custody; people were still being reclassified under the Population Registration Act – blacks becoming 'coloured', 'coloured' becoming 'white' at the stroke of a pen. A tenuous peace was maintained by arresting, banning or killing any who dared oppose the system, but South Africans were living on top of a volcano.

Nor was the outward serenity of the National Party more than skin deep. 1978 was the year in which South Africa reeled from the political explosion caused by news breaking that a secret fund was being used by the South African Department of Information for clandestine counter-propaganda exercises. The 'Information Affair', as it came to be called, led to the resignation of Dr Connie Mulder, the Minister of Information, and many believe it played its part in the resignation of John Vorster himself. In September 1978 his place was taken by P. W. Botha.

The SACC, at least to all outward appearances, was riding high and Tutu was typically generous in his praise of John Rees. The new General Secretary felt he had inherited a very good team of colleagues and an impressive outfit: 'I could not possibly try to emulate my predecessor and so I can only do and be what I know best and that is to be myself. We have come to this job with considerable trepidation.'[2]

This trepidation was well-placed. He was taking on a job which would have been exacting and demanding at any time, never more so than at this period of South African history. With the banning of all the Black Consciousness organisations and several black newspapers in 1977, the SACC was one of the few organisations in the country able to articulate the aspirations of the oppressed majority. Tutu's wish was that the Council should play an effective part in the struggle for liberation by being the conscience of the community, pointing out how the apartheid system is inconsistent with the teaching of Jesus Christ. 'At the risk of sounding like a cliché-ridden creature, I hope that God will be able to use us as one of his instruments for justice and reconciliation; to be like those who demonstrated their solidarity with the poor and down-trodden and, as far as possible, to be a voice for the voiceless ones.'[3] Despite this overt commitment, from the very beginning he made it clear that the SACC was not a political body, but that everything it did was constrained by Christian imperatives. For instance in response to the Gospel demand to visit those in prison, he argued that while it was not the SACC's wish or intention to encourage subversive activities, it *was* its business to look after those who had been convicted of political crimes.

He had also taken on a huge and complicated administrative job. Though the Dutch Reformed Church was conspicuous by its absence and the Roman Catholics only had observer status, most of the other mainline Churches in South Africa, from the African Orthodox Church to the Student Christian Movement, from the Society of Friends to the Bantu Methodist Church, were members of the SACC. In terms of individual people, the number represented was around 12 million[4] and the annual budget about R4 million. The SACC ran sixteen divisions, each with its own Director, covering between them a huge spectrum of human concerns; it also published periodicals like *Ecunews* and *Kairos*.

But under the prosperous surface, all was not well. The SACC

Tutu inherited has been described as a huge circus tent, large and effective, but the whole edifice depending on the pole that had held it up – John Rees. With one young secretary, Rees had been responsible for all the administration and fund-raising, while finance came under the care of an outside agency. The other fifty-eight members of staff ran the sixteen divisions creatively and well, but less as a team than as a group of individuals, whose work programmes John Rees had little time to oversee. The Council had also become distanced from its thirty-odd member Churches, who felt so out of touch that they did not feel it necessary to pay their subscriptions; nor was payment even demanded. The Council had grown too big, too quickly.

Tutu had envisaged his role as that of a visionary, speaking up against evil and trying to exercise a prophetic ministry. In fact the first phase of his work was preoccupied with the need to scotch rumours of financial mismanagement that flew around once the surface of the administration had been scratched, then dealing with some extremely unpleasant irregularities that were uncovered. Far from carrying out a visionary role, the idealistic General Secretary found he was forced to wash his predecessor's dirty linen in public. Worse, he got much criticism and little thanks for his pains.

The fact that during John Rees's term of office financial control had been in the hands of an outside agency, the South African Council of Churches Accounting Services (SACCAS), was a cause of considerable tension. The firm was well-intentioned and tolerably efficient, though they were sometimes found to be slow in responding to requests, but its role in the Council's affairs was part of a deep and continually erupting resentment – why should financial control not lie in the heart of the Council? Resentment coupled with rumour hardly made for efficiency and in June 1980, with the approval of the Executive Committee, Tutu dismantled SACCAS and commissioned Tim Potter to investigate the SACC's affairs. In the light of the suspicions and distrust that were to follow it is worth pointing out that Tim Potter was a senior partner in a well-respected firm of chartered accountants and the immediate past-President of the Transvaal Society of Chartered Accountants. Tutu's worldly wisdom showed in his choice of so prestigious a man.

In August 1980 Tim Potter presented a preliminary report. Though he found the financial administration and record keeping between 1976 and 1978 'generally unsatisfactory', he had found no evidence of improper payments or self-enrichment in the Council. He gave it a clean bill of health.

However, Tutu asked Tim Potter to continue his investigations and, as layer after layer of the Council's affairs was uncovered, irregularities were disclosed. In the course of his investigations Tim Potter found that a junior member of staff had been cashing cheques intended to replenish the franking machine. While Tutu was able to dispose of this affair pastorally rather than through the courts, and the employee was simply dismissed as quietly as possible, another matter was more serious. Elphas Mbatha, the Chief Accountant of SACCAS, had, it seemed, taken advantage of the weakness in the controls of the company to embezzle substantial sums by falsifying invoices. As soon as he discovered this, Tim Potter prepared a separate report and placed it in the hands of the police. Mbatha was taken to trial, but was acquitted on the grounds that his guilt could not be established beyond reasonable doubt. The Magistrate suggested that the poor state of records at the SACC and SACCAS made adequate proof impossible and raised the possibility that 'the charges against the accused were laid in order to find a scapegoat and divert attention from the unsatisfactory state of the SACC's affairs'.[5]

Just as Mbatha's alleged fraud was uncovered by the SACC's determination to run a clean ship, in a similar way another offence was uncovered, this one more serious still. During 1978 it was found that St Ansgar's Mission, a property owned by the SACC and used as a theological school for Independent Church leaders, was being badly mismanaged, so a professional ombudsman, Eugene Roelofse, was appointed as Acting Manager to rescue the property. In the course of his duties he heard rumours of misdemeanours involving a senior member of the SACC, Bishop Isaac Mokoena, who was Chairman of the board of the South African Theological College for Independent Churches (SATCIC) and ran the college. Roelofse submitted reports to the General Secretary containing photographic evidence of forgeries committed by Mokoena in the signing of SATCIC cheques and at a meeting of the Praesidium of the SACC (which consisted of the President, the two Vice-Presidents and the General Secretary) Mokoena admitted to the forgeries already uncovered, confessed that there had been many more and offered to pay back what he had taken.

To Roelofse's dismay the SACC, partly because it recognised the sensitive situation that exists between the Independent Churches to which Mokoena belonged and the historic churches represented by the SACC, again decided not to prefer criminal charges but to deal with the matter pastorally; in fact, as Mokoena had already been dismissed, they even asked the ombudsman to discontinue his investigations. This was an offence to his professional pride and at his insistence enquiries were resumed. Further evidence was unearthed, Tutu was persuaded to lay charges and Mokoena was brought to trial. Despite his earlier confession in front of four people and the photographic evidence, he was, at two separate trials, found not guilty. Once again the state of the Council's books was blamed for the inability to prove fraud; once again the SACC was accused of trying to find a scapegoat – on this occasion being reprimanded for being 'slow to take protective steps in this matter'.[6]

The Mokoena affair hit Tutu where it hurt most poignantly: on several occasions and in several ways his integrity was questioned. For a man who claimed to be trying to be transparent in his dealings, who was doing his best to clean up the messy situation he had inherited, for someone to whom honesty and good repute were as natural as breathing, it was a deeply disturbing experience and one to which for months and months he continued to refer.

One of the first people to criticise him was Eugene Roelofse, who accused Tutu of having a blind eye in putting pastoral concerns before the clear issues of right and wrong. Just before Mokoena's second trial, in a confused and emotional interview held in Bishop Tutu's office at the SACC and attended by both human and electronic witnesses, the Bishop admitted to finding the whole situation intolerable. He could not understand why he and Peter Storey, to whom Mokoena had confessed, had not been called as witnesses; he needed to justify his wish to handle the matter pastorally; he wanted to know on what grounds he had been charged with using the case as a cover-up for the unsatisfactory state of SACC affairs; he urged Roelofse to explain why he had repeated a rumour that the General Secretary had shared Mokoena's ill-gotten gains; most of all he was concerned about the deteriorating relationship between himself and Roelofse.

This interview shows to an almost pathetic degree how deeply Tutu can be hurt and the innocent and almost childlike way in which he reacts to emotional pain. Time and again unguarded, emotional phrases burst out of him: 'I cannot accept to be thought of as having no integrity.' 'I will not accept being vilified even by innuendo.' 'I feel a deep hurt that you think I am trying to cover up.' 'I want to know what you think of me.'[7]

At Mokoena's second trial it was even worse as, in open court, the Magistrate accused Tutu of being 'vague, evasive and contradictory', of concealing evidence from the court, of wanting to place Mokoena in a bad light. Mokoena, who had been overheard saying 'I aim to smash the SACC, I'm going to grind them to dust' (or words to that effect), told the court that Tutu had offered him R1,500 'to skip the country' and that the SACC wanted to get rid of him 'because he knew too much'.[8] All this was of course reported in the press, with consequent humiliation and suffering for Tutu. A decade of exposure to jibes, innuendo and accusation has taught him to hide his feelings, but his reaction to this affair shows that underneath the mature, competent, assured man there is, as with half humanity, a vulnerable child.

Apart from dealing with these offences and clearing up the financial affairs of the Council, Tutu also found that structural changes had to be made: the weight of the tent had to be better distributed, the space inside it more equally shared. His determination that as a Council they should never forget the spiritual basis of their work provided the springboard; by talking with the senior staff and visiting the leaders of the member Churches he found the way. Soon a greater degree of consultation was established, given structural shape by the institution of monthly executive staff meetings at which the Directors thrashed out their problems together. They came to realise that they had been acting and thinking in too individualistic a way; under Tutu's leadership and with the help of structural devices, such as compartmentalising the divisions into three 'clusters', they began to work as a team.

Tutu's quick mind and skill as a delegator enabled these changes to happen surprisingly quickly and smoothly. If it seems curious that moves towards greater sharing, greater democracy, should have been initiated by one who is himself so very much a star, it should be remembered that one of Tutu's great gifts is his ability to create working conditions that are both efficient and happy; he is an individualist who thrives on working in a team. Dan Vaughan, who was at the time Director of the Division of Mission and Evangelism, feels that Tutu is 'not the grand planner, not the strategist, but he is intuitively brilliant. In a way he left us to do what we could do, supporting and encouraging us. Things happened because he was around.'

And despite these legal and administrative preoccupations, which must have seemed trivial and frustrating diversions from his real work, Tutu did indeed prove to be a catalyst, both in the support and encouragement he gave his staff and through his own creative initiative.

The heart of the Council's work is its programmes, run by the three 'clusters' known as *Church and Mission*, *Development and Service* and *Justice and Society*. The vitally important *Church and Mission* cluster dealt with the theological basis of the SACC's work and included the divisions of Theological Education, Mission and Evangelism, Ecumenical Resources and the smaller Choir Resources Project, which tried to encourage the use of indigenous music and instruments.

The *Development and Service* cluster was concerned to affirm that everyone, black and white, is made in the image of Christ and that the role of the Church is to help people towards a better society for all people. Its divisions included Inter-Church Aid, which tried to alleviate poverty, disease and unemployment by promoting self-help and self-reliance, a separate Unemployment Project and a Women's Desk, working mostly with the black domestic servants employed by white 'madams', women who not only have few facilities and little to do in their spare time, but who are very often unaware of their rights.

The cluster of *Justice and Society* provided most of the theological thinking on issues such as investments and violence, dealt with the bursary and scholarship programmes and included the Dependants' Conference, so-called because as well as providing legal aid for anyone in need of it, it looked after the dependants of those who had been found guilty of political crimes and were serving sentences in maximum security prisons like Robben Island. Many of its projects were financed by the Asingeni Relief Fund, a large fund in the control of the General Secretary.

One of Tutu's great virtues as a leader, and one of the ways in which he is able to cope with a vast workload, is his ability to delegate. He not only encouraged initiative in people running the various divisions, but once he had given a project his blessing he allowed them to develop it in their own way, sometimes so completely that, wanting to test out their ideas with him, they felt mildly neglected. This supportive trust earned him the gratitude of countless people, from senior members of staff like the wise and influential Dr Kistner, who had been Director of the Division of Justice and Reconciliation since before Tutu's arrival, to junior secretaries. Dr Margaret Nash, the ecumenical officer, feels it was Tutu's encouragement which launched her into a cycle of writing, both stretching and enriching her and leading to a significant contribution to the literature on forced removals and settlements.

He also showed imagination in projects he was responsible for initiating. One of the first things he did was to ask Sheena Duncan, at the time President of the Black Sash (the women's protest organisation and political pressure group started in 1955), to start advice centres. His idea was that volunteers should be trained to do in centres around the country what the Black Sash does in Johannesburg – namely, help black people find their way through the maze of pass laws, trying to ensure that they enjoy at least those few rights to which they are entitled. Mrs Duncan feels that this showed brilliant foresight, for though at first nobody was interested, now the centres cannot keep up with the demand. He also developed the Education Opportunities Council, whose objectives include encouraging South Africans to be educated overseas and to return and provide much-needed leadership in their own country.

His greatest single contribution to the programmes run by the SACC, the stand he took over forced removals, resulted directly from a conversation which seared into his imagination and which he resolved to repeat whenever the occasion offered. In June 1979 he visited Zweledinga, a resettlement camp near Queenstown. There he met a small girl coming out of a shack in which she lived with her widowed mother and sister. The Bishop spoke to her.

'Does your mother receive a pension or grant or something?'

'No,' she replied.

'Then what do you do for food?'

'We borrow food,' she answered.

'Have you ever returned any of the food you have borrowed?'

'No.'

'What do you do when you can't borrow food?'

'We drink water to fill our stomachs.'

This little family were among the three million Africans who, between 1960 and 1980, were forcibly removed to the so-called 'homelands' for no other reason than that it suited the white minority. This policy has its roots in the 1913 Land Act, which forced Africans to settle in special 'reserves' to supply the mines with cheap and plentiful labour. The situation remained fairly static until the early 1950s, when legislation was introduced to set up the 'Bantustans' or 'Homelands', a massive social engineering project which segregated millions of Africans along strictly ethnic lines. In 1976 the Transkei was the first of the 'homelands' to become an independent national State, thus forcing its mostly unwilling inhabitants to give up any claim to South African citizenship and forswear any hope of political rights in the Republic. It was in order to implement this policy that black people living on land now allocated to white people were forcibly removed and 'resettled' in the 'homelands'.

These removals were perfectly legal, as the Prime Minister pointed out in response to a letter from Tutu on the subject, but legal and morally right are not the same thing. It was legal because a minority government had made it so in order to ensure that the whites lived separately on the best of the land, while enjoying the benefit of a large black workforce, prepared to settle for the poor pay and working conditions because they had no alternative employment. This exclusion of the black population from 'white' South Africa was quite deliberate and open. In 1976 the Minister of Bantu Administration and Development wrote:[9]

> All Bantu persons in the white areas, whether they were born there or not, remain members of their respective nations. In other words, the fact that they work here does not make them members of the white nation – they remain Zulu, Tswana, Venda and so on. The basis on which the Bantu is present in the white area is to sell their labour here and for nothing else . . .

The suffering endured by Africans uprooted from their homes and, in Tutu's words, 'dumped like a sack of potatoes' in remote, arid areas is incalculable. In a huge country, rich in resources, the vast majority (over 70 per cent) were allocated 13 per cent of the land, most of it too poor for extensive cultivation. For those who were not migrant labourers there was little work that did not involve lengthy journeys – it was not uncommon for six hours a day to be spent travelling. People were torn away from their homes, where sometimes they had lived for generations. 'What hurts is being driven like an animal out of your own home town. I was born in Johannesburg and proud of it. Now they tell me I'm a citizen of an up-country state called Qwa-Qwa – I've never ever seen the bloody place.'[10]

In the resettlement camps people were (and still are) starving. Tutu has seen this for himself:[11]

> They are starving not because of an accident or a misfortune. No, they are starving because of deliberate Government policy made in the name of White Christian civilisation . . . Many can't work, not because they won't work but because there is no work available . . . They are there as a reservoir, deliberately created, of cheap labour.

And they were starving to a point of serious malnutrition, which it was recognised could lead to irreversible brain damage. The *Financial Mail* admitted that 'humanitarian considerations apart, the present neglect is false economy which costs the country millions of pounds annually in hospitalisation'.[12]

Forced removals were not only a national scandal, they were a direct concern of the Church. Dr Margaret Nash points out that[13]

> Whole congregations have been dispossessed and dispersed; or removed and weakened in the process. Buildings representing the love, labour, sacrifice and devotion of two or three generations have been demolished or left as empty shells, to be ravaged by wind, weather and vandals. Clergy have been summoned by ethnic leaders and told quite bluntly what the religious policy of the new 'government' is to be. And

the message has been plain: if you do not like it, get out; because if you criticise or fail to conform, we shall not hesitate to act against you.

Tutu, however, was not going to be prevented from criticising; he declared he was prepared to give his life to be rid of this evil. He brought cases of threatened removals to the attention of Church leaders, involving himself in the plight of the residents of Driefontein, for instance, whose pleas to the Minister of Co-operation and Development were met with responses like 'only the terms under which the move will take place are negotiable'.[14] He also heightened the political cost of the removals policy by giving publicity to what was happening in statements and speeches, in specially made films and in pamphlets. While he recognised that in the long term the solution had to be political, he also operated through the normal channels of the SACC, who held its national conference the month after Tutu had been to Zwedelinga. Resolutions were passed to put the whole issue of forced removals and resettlement high on the agenda and a four-fold programme was worked out: to gather more information, to call the Church to a more effective ministry to people who were victims of the process, to give more financial assistance and to show solidarity with communities threatened with removal.

Tutu was so deeply shocked by the obscenity of forced removals that he was determined to show solidarity personally. In 1983 the people of Mogopa, a small village in the western Transvaal, were told they were to be moved from land they had tilled for generations and sent to the independent 'homeland' of Bophuthatswana. (Mogopa was on good land and the envy of white eyes, so it had been designated a 'black spot' – an area in which Africans own land, but which the apartheid regime has decided belongs to another group, usually white.) The lovingly built stone houses were demolished, bulldozers tore through the churches and schools, water pumps were taken away and the buses stopped. In the face of this brutal show of State strength the people refused to move: they simply began to rebuild their houses. Tutu telephoned other Church leaders and arranged an all-night vigil to protest against the removals. Dr Allan Boesak and Tutu were among those able to be present and it is easy to imagine what their presence meant to the villagers, whose community and way of life were threatened with destruction; equally, it is no surprise that their peaceful protest made not the smallest dent in the government's resolve. On February 14th, 1984, Mogopa was surrounded by armed police with dogs and loud-hailers. The villagers were informed that they were to be moved and the whole population was forcibly loaded on to lorries and buses and taken away, while white farmers bought up their livestock at a tenth of its value.

For the SACC to implement its programmes clearly involved considerable, potentially almost limitless, expense. Raising and spending money was one of the General Secretary's most pressing preoccupations.

Theoretically the member Churches were expected to contribute on a regular basis, but until 1984, when donations were regularised, this somehow did not happen. In his report to the executive committee in May 1980 Tutu appealed to them to step up their giving, pointing out that if 1,000 congregations gave as little as R50 a year it would amount to R50,000.[15] Yet by the following year nothing had changed. At the national conference an Indian delegate asked why the member Churches did not contribute more and how long ago had the minimum subscription of R50 a year been fixed? It turned out that no letter had ever been sent requesting the money and that such money as did come was entirely haphazard.

Nor did Tutu have much luck with the private sector. Some firms he approached did not even bother to answer, most sent their regrets. While he was grateful to the few businesses that did give funds, making a habit of telling them just how their money was spent, he also pointed out, with typical directness, that the private sector would be judged according to whether it assisted or sought to retard the liberation struggle.

Where Tutu, like John Rees, had phenomenal success was in raising funds from overseas donors. Though he was criticised for the amount of time he spent travelling, no one was less than grateful for the way these trips not only led to the building of strong links with overseas Church bodies, but filled the coffers of the SACC. As to the source of the funds, his approach, though strictly moral, was pragmatic. He did not mind, for instance, accepting money from institutions being boycotted by anti-apartheid groups overseas and would justify his stand. He felt that South Africans had to live with compromise (though he would never travel overseas with South African Airways, inside the country there was no alternative), so it was pointless to worry too much. This argument, coupled with the belief that the destination of the money and the urgent need for it justified its origins, did not have universal support.

Each division of the SACC drew up its own budgets to present to donors, who decided which projects they wished to finance; the allocation was then arranged through the finance committee under Matt Stevenson, whom Tutu had brought in to head the section.

The only discretionary money, and as such a cause of considerable controversy, was the Asingeni Fund.

The Asingeni Fund was set up after the Soweto killings, initially to help with the immediate needs of food, clothing and funeral expenses, later to help with bail and legal aid for people who were arrested. Feelings erupted soon after Tutu's arrival, when there were rumours that the finance department was considering tightening up on the General Secretary's discretion. Many of the staff, especially the blacks, were furious; it was openly pointed out that when the General Secretary was a white man he was given total discretion, so why should the goalposts be moved now that a black man was in charge? Although the balance of staff favoured blacks rather than whites, the power – and what is a more telling symbol of power than money? – was held mainly by whites. The overriding feeling in the Council was that Tutu should be firmly in control and seen to be so. When, therefore, finance was brought firmly into the Council, steps were also taken to ensure that Tutu retained his discretionary control over this large fund.

In practice nearly 80 per cent of the money went on legal expenses, only the remaining 20 per cent being used in a wholly discretionary way. The fact that there were some who criticised Tutu's use of the fund, suggesting that the bees drawn to his financial honey pot tended to include too many rice-Christian followers, underlines the difficulty of administering discretionary money. One man's discretion can so easily be another man's folly. A glance through the payments made from the Asingeni Fund tell much about the state of South Africa as well as reflecting something of Tutu's vision. There are frequent payments to help meet educational expenses and to relieve workers on strike; funds were made to the 'Release Mandela' campaign and for mourners to attend the funerals of Robert Sobukwe and Steve Biko; a substantial sum was spent on the making of a film about the SACC and there are sad entries which tell their own tale: 'Blankets for the needy', 'Crossroads rental arrears', 'Grant for working against eviction of Indians and Coloureds', 'Bill for food to Modderbee Prison'.

Virtually everyone who worked at the SACC during Tutu's time as General Secretary vouches for his qualities as a leader and praises the way he transformed the Council into a major institution on the South African political/religious scene. They stress the contribution he made through his insistence that the basis of the whole operation must be spiritual, finding great confidence in the way his words and actions clearly sprang from convictions so deeply rooted in a strong theology. He also contributed towards forming closer ties with the other Councils of Churches of Southern Africa – Swaziland,

Mozambique, Zambia, Zimbabwe, Angola, Namibia, Lesotho and Botswana.

But his influence extended beyond the Church. By raising the SACC's profile both nationally and internationally, by sharing in the distress of the people and by identifying with the struggle for liberation, he gave it greater credibility than it had ever had before. Though the Council had become larger and more bureaucratised, the black community were in no doubt whose side both it and its leader were on. This was due not only to the sense of direction he gave, but to his gifts as a spokesman and his courage in speaking and acting for human justice and against apartheid. The SACC's first black General Secretary had become the most articulate voice free to speak in South Africa.

12

Crying in the wilderness

From 1978, when Tutu returned to South Africa, he began to wear the lonely mantle of the prophet. The popular image of the prophet as one who foretells the future is only part of the biblical concept; the prophetic role is pre-eminently to communicate the word of God to the people, to act as God's spokesman. Prophets were messengers rather than soothsayers, or, as Tutu himself said in a lecture on the subject, 'forthtellers rather than foretellers'.

Though his detractors felt it inconceivable that Bishop Tutu was hearing the word of God and others found the prophetic role inappropriate to twentieth-century South Africa, he has been compared to the prophet Amos, whose message was delivered at a time when the few were accumulating wealth at the expense of the many. Amos recognised how much was wrong with the society in which he was living, how complacent were the leaders of that society. So strong were his indictments of Israel's social injustice that he was accused of sedition.

Tutu's stand on apartheid is unequivocal and, like the prophets, he speaks out courageously, with insight as much as with foresight; like the prophets, his utterances are disturbing to the advantaged, pleasing to the disadvantaged; like the prophets, he believes he is communicating the word of God and is adamant that he will speak as and when he sees fit and not as he is told, or even advised. He has declared that, whatever the cost to him, he will do all in his power to destroy apartheid; Leah, with typical wry humour, is sure that even if his tongue were cut off, he would not be prevented from speaking.

Since the publication of the *Message to the People of South Africa* in 1968 the SACC had been concerned with communication and by 1977 it had considerable expertise in the field; with the arrival of Bishop Tutu it had acquired a leader who excelled in the art. Not only is he fearless in speaking out, but his possession of that elusive gift, star quality, enables him to hold an audience spellbound – an American priest remarked that when he takes the podium 'everyone feels the electricity as if a 220 volt wire had suddenly been plugged in'. He is also able to handle tricky situations in a way that is little short of miraculous. He has what a colleague has called 'a good share of Holy Guile' and when uncertain what to do he simply plays the clown, frequently diffusing tense situations by scrapping his prepared text and amusing his audience until they are ready to hear what he has to say. On one such occasion, when he was Bishop of Lesotho, he strode on to the platform in an Afro-style shirt and mimicked Dorothy Lamour until the audience had relaxed into fits of laughter. But the quality that informs his every word and action rests deep in his spirituality. What he *is* shines through his words, whether they are serious or amusing, gentle or forceful. In him being and doing go hand-in-hand – the idea of Tutu being insincere or in any way untrue to himself is simply inconceivable.

Soon his voice was heard from Cape Town to Pietersburg, from Durban to Springbok. He spoke both personally and through the SACC. In addresses, sermons, press interviews and statements he said that the apartheid system, and all the suffering that follows in its wake, is not only unjust, but immoral and unChristian; that to claim that God created human beings to be separate and divided is totally alien to the traditional aim of an undivided Christendom. If, as members of the government sometimes claimed, apartheid was dead, then they 'would like to see the corpse first'.

Many of these statements were made in his role as General Secretary of the SACC, receiving its full support. For instance at the end of his first full year in office, in his report to the executive committee, Tutu warned that unless the attitude of whites changed significantly there could be a split in the Churches along racial lines. He went on to ask why there had been no public outcry at the recent eviction of 'coloured' and Indian families from their homes and to voice his disquiet at the way the press were being hammered by the government, while people like Dr Rhoodie and Dr Connie Mulder, key figures in the 'Information Scandal', were being treated so lightly.

In that same report the SACC expressed its concern at the increase of arrests under the pass laws (272,887 in 1978); it called on the West Rand Administration Board not to implement its 'black spots removal policy' by moving families from Alexandra township (at the time the only area in Johannesburg where blacks could still enjoy freehold rights) to live in single-sex hostels; it expressed alarm that thousands of children in Soweto had not been placed in schools; it called for a ceasefire in Namibia, 'in the name of God and of humanity'.

Speaking as it did, for God and humanity, there was no area of life that was not its concern, so in August 1981 the SACC's offices served as the venue for a meeting of black trades unions and representatives of the Azanian People's Organisation (AZAPO).[1] Black and multi-racial trades unions had been legalised only the previous year and new labour legislation was being debated in Parliament; as these measures would affect basic human rights the Council had no doubt that the Churches' involvement was justified.

At the meeting Tutu claimed that the government wished to control the trades unions as much as possible and that the Church should be in the forefront of those protesting at legislation directed against the workers. Further, the Church should play its part in the education of the black worker. The next month he wrote that the trades unions were the most significant force for reasonably peaceful change and that the government, recognising this, aimed to emasculate them.[7]

> The outside world is hoodwinked if it thinks that by recognising black trade unions, Government has begun to liberalise apartheid. It has done nothing of the sort. It realised that with the interest of multi-national corporations in the work situation it had to do something. Legislation will attempt to undermine the unions and curb them. The Black Unions have said that they will defy any laws that intend to turn them into toothless bulldogs and the SACC has said that it will want to be supportive.

While the SACC's involvement with the trades unions was not likely to please the government, an earlier resolution had worried it even more. During the 1979 national conference, where the theme was 'The Church and the Alternative Society', Dr Allan Bocsak proposed that the Church, since the banning of most of the black organisations now more important than ever as a vehicle for the expression of black aspirations, should initiate and support programmes of civil disobedience on a massive scale. The proposal was enthusiastically received and a resolution was passed, saying:

> This Conference believes that the South African Churches are under an obligation to withdraw, as far as that is possible, from co-operation with the State in all those areas in the ordering of our society where the law violates the justice of God. We call upon all Christian people to examine their lives and to seek to identify the ways in which each one reinforces the policy and props up the system.

Tutu's backing of this proposal was untypically cautious, though soon after the conference he gave an example of civil disobedience on a BBC programme. He suggested that a white, coming into Soweto and wishing to accompany him to church, should flout the law demanding that he have a permit – from such small beginnings a process of disobeying unjust laws on a large scale could be built.

The conference did not suggest that acts of disobedience should be performed by the Council itself, nevertheless it was a significant move. The SACC had accepted the principle of civil disobedience, thus giving moral justification to any of its members who felt their cause could be furthered by refusing to co-operate with laws they considered unjust. This was significant enough for the *Cape Times* to report that 'A broadly representative gathering of South African Christians (excluding the DRC) have resolved that Christianity and apartheid cannot co-exist.'[3] The authorities were sufficiently frightened by the resolution to summon Bishop Tutu and warn the SACC and 'leftist ministers and spiritual leaders' to 'cease and desist from irresponsible action and encouraging people to break the law'.[4] Tutu's response was to challenge the government to take action against them.

Prophets tend to cause trouble, both for themselves and for those around them; Tutu was no exception. In September 1979, on a trip to Denmark, he was interviewed on Danish television. To the question 'Why is it that the Council is against foreign investment in South Africa?' he responded that the SACC was critical because it believed that foreign investment supported the system. Further, that efforts made by some businesses investing in South Africa to improve conditions for blacks only served 'to shift the furniture around the room, instead of changing the furniture'. When he was asked if he would advise Denmark to stop buying South African coal, the following exchange took place.

'Well,' said Tutu, 'I find it rather disgraceful that Denmark is buying South African coal and increasing a dependence on South Africa, whereas one would hope that we could get South Africa to having a weaker position in bargaining, so that we could get this change as soon as possible.' The interviewer replied, 'But if we do not buy coal, for instance, a lot of blacks are going to be unemployed.' Tutu responded, 'They would be unemployed and suffer temporarily. It would be a suffering with a purpose. We would not be doing what is happening now, where blacks are suffering and it seems to be a suffering that is going to go on and on and on.'[5]

He knew what he was doing. By simply speaking of the withdrawal of foreign investments he was risking prosecution under Section 6 of the Terrorism Act; he might also anger blacks whose jobs would be threatened by boycotts. He returned to South Africa to find the country split. On the one hand he was supported by prominent black spokesmen such as Dr Nthato Motlana, and by numerous letters to the black press; he was cheered to the echo when he told a meeting of the Soweto Civic Association: 'We want political participation, not petty dispensation. We want a completely integrated society'.[6] On the other hand his mandate to speak for black miners was questioned and he was greeted with fury and resentment by most of the white community. The government-controlled television and radio produced black leaders working within the system to refute his stand and he was called to Pretoria, reminded that his remarks were economic sabotage and told to retract his statement and apologise.

In view of his position at the SACC and the furore that had been generated by his remarks, a meeting was arranged between Tutu, the executive committee and leaders of several of the Churches. The subject: should the General Secretary be allowed to speak on his own behalf without reference to the Council? Tutu explained that he had been trying to make a sober contribution to his country's problems, arguing that it was essential to search for strategies of reasonably non-violent change and that these strategies must involve international economic pressure. Not everyone agreed with the statement he had made in Denmark, but they all supported his right to make it and resolved to stand by him. They noted that the significant constituency who agreed with him were inhibited by law from discussing the subject and unanimously agreed that for him to retract or apologise would be 'a denial of his prophetic calling'.

He had been given a green light. Had he previously felt any constraints on his freedom to speak, now he was licensed by his colleagues to follow his instinct. There was no holding him. At home and overseas, on radio and television, after dinners, at conferences, before audiences ranging from the United Nations Special Committee against Apartheid to groups of university students, he lived up to his own promise to do everything in his power to rid the country of the system he variously referred to as 'diabolical', 'this pernicious evil', 'one of the most vicious systems since Nazism'.

He constantly reminded his audiences that he was committed to black liberation because he was committed to white liberation and that whites could never be truly free until blacks were free. He urged them, in the name of morality and justice, to take sides, to express their commitment to a just redistribution of wealth and resources and to make friends with blacks before it was too late. A typical example was in 1980, when he ended a speech to the students at the University of the Witwatersrand with this rousing peroration:[7]

> So join the liberation struggle. Throw off your lethargy and the apathy of affluence. Work for a better South Africa for yourselves and ourselves and for your children. Uproot all evil and oppression and injustice of which Blacks are victims and you whites are beneficiaries, so that you won't reap the whirlwind. Join the winning side. Oppression, injustice, exploitation – all these have lost, for God is on our side – on the side

of Justice, of Peace, of Reconciliation, of Laughter and Joy, of Sharing
and Compassion and Goodness and Righteousness.

So, too, he showed his support for those who were involved in the
struggle. Shocked at the detention and banning of members of AZAPO
within days of its formation, he issued a statement questioning the
authorities' refusal to listen to the authentic spokesmen of the black
community, criticising them for acting against the new group before
it had even drawn up its constitution. He asked, as he asked so often
in similar situations, why, if the activities of the detained men were
illegal, they were not charged in a court of law? Was it perhaps that
there was no evidence that could stand up to legal scrutiny? Similarly,
when Dr Motlana, the Chairman of the Soweto Civic Association,
was banned from speaking at public gatherings, Tutu again appealed
to the authorities, not least in their own interests, to heed the voices
of those the black community considered its leaders. He insisted that
there could be no real peace or security until black views were taken
seriously and that Dr Motlana was only articulating those views, not
advocating violence or subversion.

Often he warned of what could happen if the present order did
not change. If the government continued to treat the black community
with contempt and brutality, if it continued to uproot people from
their homes and dump them in some arid 'homeland', if it were
determined to balkanise South Africa and to deprive blacks of citizen-
ship, 'then there won't be a peaceful solution, then they are declaring
war on us. What are Blacks then expected to do in such a situation.
Fold our hands?'[8] He warned that, patient though blacks were, they
could be provoked beyond endurance. The time might come when
they would find it difficult to forgive the suffering that whites had
inflicted on them. Quoting Alan Paton's fearful cry, 'Oh God help us
that when the whites have turned to loving the blacks will not have
turned to hating',[9] he warned of the bloodbath to which present
policies could lead.

There is a thin line between a warning and a threat, but Tutu has
been careful, often even explicit, in acknowledging the distinction. (In
voicing these fears he was, in any case, in the company of such as
Vorster, who warned of 'the alternative too ghastly to contemplate'
and P. W. Botha, who urged his countrymen to 'adapt or die'.) In
encouraging people to play their part in the liberation struggle Tutu
frequently reminded them that a post-liberation South Africa will
never forget who were their friends and who were not. 'Make no
mistake about it, if you go over to the other side, then the day of
reckoning will come. This is not a threat, it is just the plain truth. Blacks

will never forget that you were traitors to the liberation struggle.'[10]

He warned his own people that liberation would be costly. In 1982, preaching at the funeral of Mlungiso Mxenge, a Durban lawyer believed to have been killed by agents of the authorities, he ended his oration, 'Many more will be detained. Many more will be banned. Many more will be deported and killed. Yes, it will be costly. But we shall be free. Nothing will stop us becoming free – no police bullets, dogs, tear-gas, prison, death, no, nothing will stop us because God is on our side.'[11]

And always he spoke with hope. He would quote from the book of Exodus, showing how God rescued the Israelites from slavery. He told a group of Anglican students that the Old Testament God did not just talk – he acted: 'He showed himself to be a doing God. Perhaps we might add another point about God – He takes sides. He is not a neutral God. He took the side of the slaves, the oppressed, the victims.' He assured his audience that God was still the same in twentieth-century South Africa: 'He does not sleep or go on holiday or take a day off. He is always there. So don't despair.'[12] Eager always to stress the good, he would marvel that the majority of blacks still wanted a non-racial South Africa, still wanted black and white to live and share together.

Later he was to be accused by those anxious to discredit him of making inflammatory speeches, of seldom expressing himself publicly 'on matters other than socio-political and economic issues',[13] so it is important to remember not only that most of his sermons were of a purely spiritual or theological nature, but that even his pronouncements against the system were desperate appeals for peace and justice, wherever possible couched in reconciliatory terms. Time and again he would declare that both he and the SACC were committed to finding and using peaceful means to bring about change. In lamenting the refusal of the Afrikaans Churches to attend a consultation on racism he asked their forgiveness for any way in which the SACC's attitude had hurt them. Often he agreed it was difficult for the whites to give up so much privilege, even admitting he would need a lot of grace to do it himself, were he in their position.

Whenever he could find reason to praise or show gratitude, he was keen to do so. He frequently commended P. W. Botha on his grasp of reality and his courage; he sent a telegram to Louis le Grange congratulating him for allowing political prisoners to do post-Matriculation studies; when calling for an end to the provocative use of army personnel he also pointed out that the police had a duty to maintain law and order and needed co-operation from the public; he commended Dr Koornhof for showing compassion to the people of

Crossroads and Alexandra. Are these the actions of a man seeking to inflame or to reconcile?

Tutu is adamant that he is not a politician. When accused of having political ambitions he frequently responds by saying that there are three very good reasons why religious leaders should not become politicians in the party political sense – the Ayatollah Khomeini, Bishop Muzerewa and Archbishop Makarios. Even when encouraged to consider himself a politician he declines. He once received a charming letter from a schoolboy headed 'Application for a share in your political experience' which said, 'As a political amateur, I wish to grow under your guidance'. Tutu's response was: 'I would like to explain to you that I really am not a politician as I work on the basis of the Christian Gospel.'

And that is the point. Tutu's politics spring directly and inevitably from his Christianity. He has often said that he is puzzled which Bible people read when they suggest that religion and politics don't mix. In Old Testament Israel no one would know what you meant if you tried to separate them, and, in any case, in South Africa *everything* is politics. The most innocent action – where you sit on a train, where you drink your morning coffee – can be interpreted as a political gesture. Tutu argues that a political conscience does not disappear with ordination and that Christians must always test political systems against the Gospel, asking if they are usurping the place of God. As a law-abiding citizen, he is in no doubt that the State should be obeyed when its authority is clearly legitimate, but if its laws conflict with the Gospel, then Christians not only have the right but the duty to agitate peacefully for their repeal. In a situation of injustice it is not possible to be neutral; not to oppose the system is in fact to support it.

He also points out that governments only object to clerics having political views when they criticise the status quo; those who uphold the system are applauded. It hardly befits the South African National Party, most of whose members belong to the DRC, who for many years sought to find biblical justification for apartheid, and one of whose Prime Ministers, D. F. Malan, was in fact a Dominee, to say that religion and politics do not mix.

So Tutu had no qualms about speaking against matters that could strictly be said to belong to the political arena. He refused to join the Buthelezi Commission on the constitutional and economic relations between Natal and KwaZulu 'Because of my total abhorrence of the Bantustan policy and my fear that this Commission could appear to give credibility to that policy.'[14] For the same reasons he opposed the Quail Commission on political options for the Ciskei: 'Such a

Commission should not have been allowed to happen. It assumes the premise that South Africa can be broken up, whereas we claim that until all the people of South Africa say "Yes" to such a proposition, South Africa must remain the unitary state that it is.'[15]

He pierced to the nerve centre of South African politics by predicting (in 1980) that there would be a black Prime Minister in South Africa within the next five to ten years. In the same week he called on parents to support a school boycott and warned the government that if it continued to detain and arrest protesters there could be a repetition of the 1976 riots. He told an audience of Stellenbosch students that the blacks did not want 'crumbs of concession from a generous master, they wanted to be at the table, planning the menu with him . . . the name of the game is political power-sharing'.

He did not hesitate to oppose government reforms that he, together with most of the black community, regarded as purely cosmetic or even dangerous. Most conspicuously he roundly condemned the report presented in May 1982 by the multi-racial President's Council, in which proposals were outlined for an electoral college consisting of white, 'coloured' and Indian members. Tutu conceded that the inclusion of non-white representatives on the council was a significant, indeed a revolutionary, departure from normal practice in South Africa, but drew attention to the report's fatal flaws. He pointed out that membership of the council was by nomination rather than by election; that, being only an advisory body, there was no guarantee that its suggestions would ever leave the realm of theory; third, and most seriously, that the African community was totally excluded, both from the council and from the proposed new constitution. The country was being encouraged to take the report seriously, to discuss and criticise it, but 'Why should we try to discuss its recommendations when we know we are not being listened to? Why shout into a void merely to hear your own echo?'[16] A few days later he told a meeting of the Natal Indian Congress why 'coloureds' and Indians were being co-opted into the system – because the whites could not defend the country on their own. If they joined the whites under the proposed new political dispensation the Africans would regard them as traitors in the liberation struggle and 'the day of reckoning would come'.

While the proposals were being debated in Parliament the following year, Tutu issued a statement in accordance with a resolution taken by the SACC. It drew attention to the fact that the new Bill not only permanently excluded 73 per cent of the population from sharing political power and legitimatised their exclusion, but that it also entrenched racial discrimination, ensured that the whites would retain their parliamentary majority and would make fundamental change by relatively peaceful means virtually impossible. He urged the member Churches to reject the proposed new constitution.

Tutu is by nature a reconciler; his wish is to build bridges rather than destroy them. In June 1980, during a period of sustained popular resistance, with school and university boycotts against apartheid education, bus boycotts, protests against rent increases, open support for the ANC and a campaign for the release of Nelson Mandela, he encouraged senior members of the SACC to seek a meeting with the Prime Minister to discuss the rapidly deteriorating situation.

It was not an easy decision to make. He was well aware of the danger of giving credibility to someone so distrusted in the eyes of the black community as P. W. Botha; he knew too how slim were the chances that he would be taken seriously. He admitted to the Pretoria Press Club that many whites regarded him as 'an irresponsible, radical fire-eater, who should have been locked up long ago'. He knew that others felt he was really a politician trying hard to be a Bishop, with 'horns under my funny bishop's hat, and my tail tucked away under my trailing cape'.[17] His conviction that the Gospel can change men's hearts and that as Christians they must try to communicate, even to deaf ears, was not shared by all his colleagues, but eventually they were persuaded and the letter requesting a meeting was sent.

Mr Botha prevaricated. He replied that he would grant the SACC delegation an interview on certain conditions: they must openly reject Communism for South Africa, guarantee not to undermine National Service, reject all organisations which supported violence and denounce the efforts of the ANC to overthrow orderly government. To this undignified sparring the SACC replied that, though it would have preferred to meet the Prime Minister unconditionally, it felt the need for dialogue was so great it would reiterate its standpoint on these issues. It wrote that it had never supported Communism, or indeed any other ideology, that though it insisted on the right of every citizen to conscientious objection it did not wish to undermine national service, it rejected violence to overthrow the system as much as it abhorred institutionalised violence and that as the SACC had never aligned itself with the ANC it was superfluous to dissociate itself from it.

So, on August 7th, 1980, Bishop Tutu, with representatives of the member Churches and the senior executives of the SACC, went to Pretoria to meet the Prime Minister, six Cabinet Ministers and two Deputy Ministers.

If ever a meeting demonstrated the differences between the two sides, it was this. The delegation was politely welcomed, the proceedings were civil, the name of Jesus Christ was invoked to guide the discussions; yet it was as if their words were no sooner uttered than they disappeared into the gulf between them. They quite simply could not hear each other.

The Prime Minister set the scene by saying that the State and the Church were two independent and autonomous bodies, who should not meddle in each other's affairs. Politics were not the function of the Church, nor was theology the affair of the State. In any case, with whom should he negotiate when the Church was itself divided? But as he aspired to rule by Christian principles, his door was open to Church leaders; he would give them two hours that morning, with the possibility of another meeting later in the year.

When it was Tutu's turn to speak he assured the Prime Minister that he had no political axe to grind, but that the Christian Gospel compelled him to reject apartheid. He urged the calling of a National Convention, to be attended by all the acknowledged leaders from every section of the population, including political leaders in prison or in detention. He then repeated his warning that though there was still much goodwill among the black community, patience was running out and anger and bitterness would continue to grow unless the government demonstrated clearly that it intended to bring about changes sufficiently fundamental to lead to political power-sharing. The nub of his presentation was a four-point prescription for change. First, that the government should commit itself to a common citizen-ship for all South Africans in an undivided South Africa; second, would it please abolish the pass laws; third, would it put an immediate stop to population removals; forth, it should set up a uniform education system. 'If these four things were done I would be the first to declare out loud "Please give the Government a chance, they seem in our view now to have embarked on the course of real change." I certainly would be one of the first to shout this out from the roof tops.'[18]

He might never have spoken. In his summing-up the Prime Minister made no reference to Tutu's suggestions, preferring to talk about fighting on the South African borders and to claim that South Africa's problem was a problem of minorities. He ended by saying he was prepared to lead his people on the road towards creating new dispen-sations, but he was not prepared to lead them on the road of a government of one man one vote. He warned the delegation that if they made 'provocative, negative statements' no further meeting would take place.

It was a historic meeting – never before had a black leader with no formal position inside the system talked with a white Prime Minister. Yet it did nothing to defuse the conflict, nor was Tutu's reputation as a negotiator enhanced. His approach was seen as politically naïve and soon afterwards leading South African theologians warned that further meetings could be met with resistance from radical black churchmen. Tutu could not share this view; his paradigms are biblical – Moses went to see Pharaoh not once, but several times. Whether or not Mr Botha, like Pharaoh, had hardened his heart, whether or not his actions received popular backing, Tutu would try again.

Though Desmond Tutu's instincts to negotiate rather than to confront, to reconcile rather than to attack, have received criticism, there has never been any doubting the courage of both his words and his actions, nor any wavering in his determination to stand with his people. From pinpricks like calling the Minister of Police 'an insufferable bore who needs a course in logic' for trying to depict the SACC as unpatriotic, to physically putting his own life in danger, he has shown the sort of courage that can only come from a deep sense of the rightness of his cause.

On one occasion in Soweto, seeing two large white policemen beating an elderly black man, he put his small frame between them, holding up his Bishop's cross until they stopped. On another he risked his life at a political funeral in the Ciskei by flinging himself across the body of a black security policeman being stoned by a large and angry mob. Thinking the crowd had desisted, he returned to the rostrum, his clothes soaked with the policeman's blood. They were, however, merely waiting for him to turn his back; later they dragged the policeman away and beat him to death. Though Tutu was prepared to protect this man in the government's employ, he was equally ready to attack the 'homeland' leaders working within the system: 'These leaders are largely corrupt men looking after their own interests, lining their pockets. South Africa consequently has a hold on them because they are almost without exception lacking integrity.'[19] Perhaps to make this statement needed even more courage.

There were numerous occasions when he spoke out in situations where many would have taken refuge in caution. On June 16th, 1982, he was taking a service in the Regina Mundi Church to commemorate the Soweto killings. In an effort to suppress press coverage of the event journalists were taken to the police station and the church was surrounded by hundreds of armed policemen. Inside the church Tutu was addressing 5,000 blacks in what Joseph Lelyveld, who later heard a tape recording, called 'an emotionally charged political litany'; '"Is there anyone here who doubts that apartheid is doomed to failure?" he cried. "No" the crowd shouted back. "Is there anyone who doubts we are going to be free?" "No" came the reply. Then Tutu made the crowd chant "We are going to be free!" [20] At the end of the service he went out to speak to the rioting crowd who were infuriated by the detention of the journalists, and persuaded them to stop throwing stones. It was on that occasion that he made the famous promise that on the day he was proved wrong about apartheid he would burn his Bible.

Several times he has spoken through peaceful protest. The first was in 1980 when he took part in a march organised by the General Secretary of the Congregationalists, the Reverend Joe Wing. Tutu, together with Leah, Bishop Timothy Bavin and fifty-one other church-men including the SACC Praesidium, marched to the Johannesburg police headquarters singing hymns and distributing pink and yellow pamphlets calling for the release of John Thorne, a Congregationalist minister whose attempts to diffuse a difficult situation arising from a schools boycott had led to his detention. The clergymen were stopped by policemen with automatic rifles and attack dogs, charged with contravening the Riotous Assemblies Act (carrying a maximum jail sentence of six months or a fine of R100) and held overnight in racially segregated cells. Tutu spent his first – and so far his only – night in jail praying, singing hymns and swapping stories with his fellow clerics. In 1981, in a show of passive resistance, he refused to celebrate the fortieth anniversary of South Africa becoming a Republic, asking what was there for blacks, second-class citizens in the land of their birth, to celebrate?

By the early 1980s Tutu had become an international figure; as early as 1979 his visits overseas were greeted with such publicity that he was finding it impossible to make a private visit. Honours were showered upon him: in 1978 he was elected a Fellow of his old college, King's College, London, accepting with pleasure but 'in a representative and corporate capacity'; by the end of the following year he had been awarded three Honorary Doctorates – from the General Theological Seminary in New York, from the universities of Kent in England and Harvard in the States. But while being honoured overseas, he was, for much of white South Africa, an object of hatred.

He was the recipient of a remorseless stream of death threats, obscene telephone calls and bomb scares. One evening he was speaking to 5,000 people at a meeting held by the South African Christian Leadership Assembly when the tyres of over 100 cars were deflated. Anonymous pamphlets, purporting to come from 'The United Trade Union Council' (a body which no one could trace) were distributed throughout the country to defame him, rumours and innuendoes about the financial administration of the SACC were encouraged to spread and the government-sponsored radio and television lost no opportunity to use the air-waves to stigmatise him. Puerile jokes were circulated – one even sank to the level of pointing out that in New Zealand a '*tutu*' is a poisonous plant. One day eight members of the National Front wearing crash helmets elbowed their way towards his office. They shouted abuse, then threw thirty pieces of silver into the outer office where his secretary was working, 'to pay you in the traditional way that all traitors are paid'.

There is something virtually unique about the vilification endured by Desmond Tutu. The hatred alone is bad enough; worse still was that much of it was organised by the government of the country to which, whether they would admit it or not, he belonged. Since 1974 the government had used a body called the Christian League as a front organisation to counter the influence of the World Council of Churches, infiltrate the SACC and break its influence. In the year 1979–80 it paid the Christian League R340,000 in return for its written undertaking to 'pursue an uninterrupted campaign against the SACC'.[21] At the very time that the Churches were, in good faith, holding talks with the government, that same government was doing its best to undermine the SACC.

So, simultaneously loved and hated, honoured and vilified, Tutu became a key figure in one of the most notorious confrontations between Church and State in the history of Christianity.

13

David and Goliath

The uniqueness of the confrontation between Church and State in South Africa, climaxing in the Eloff Commission, lay in the fact that it was not a case of an atheistic regime seeking to suppress Christianity, or even of a Christian government attacking a particular denomination. Here was a State, declared in its constitution to be Christian, taking on an ecumenical Christian body representing 12 million of its own people.

The government and the SACC had been on a collision course for years, in fact since 1949 when the Rosettenville Conference had opposed the government's new apartheid policies. A watershed was reached in 1968, with the publication of the *Message to the People of South Africa*; another in 1979, when Dr Allan Boesak challenged the Churches to adopt a programme of civil disobedience and actively to defy the apartheid laws. The government had been infuriated by the way the Church had spoken out on conscientious objection, on the South African Defence Force's raids into the frontline States and the unlawful occupation of Namibia, on bannings and detentions without trial; also by its support of the Free Mandela Campaign and by its boycott of the Republican Day festivals. In short the government were exasperated by the stance the Churches had taken against the whole apparatus of apartheid. The discord between Church and State is as easily defined as it has proved impossible to resolve. The Churches held a deep belief that the apartheid policy and its laws were evil, immoral and consequently unChristian; the government had passed those laws and intended to uphold them.

Against this backcloth of sustained disagreement, erupting into frequent open antagonism, appeared veiled threats and innuendoes directed against the SACC. There were rumours about past financial mismanagement, the press were probing, Christian right-wingers were pressing for an investigation. In 1981 the Prime Minister entered the fray personally, accusing the SACC of receiving more than R2½ million from abroad and channelling it into bodies and projects in order to further unrest. Tutu responded by saying that Mr Botha was lying and that he knew he was lying. Again, as he had after the resolution on civil disobedience in 1979, Tutu challenged the Prime Minister to charge the SACC in open court.

Mr Botha did not quite pick up the gauntlet which had been thrown down. Instead, on November 20th, 1981, he appointed a Commission of Enquiry to investigate the Council. The honourable Mr Justice C. F. Eloff, Judge of the Transvaal Provincial Division of the Supreme Court of South Africa, was the Chairman; his fellow commissioners, representing an entirely white perspective, were a chartered accountant, a Regional Court Magistrate, the Vice-Principal of the University of Pretoria and a senior civil servant. On March 1st of the following year the Commission began work and the SACC, still reeling from the report of the Steyn Commission on the press which had made a virulent attack on the World Council of Churches, the SACC and Bishop Tutu, was fighting for its life.

The government wanted to show that the SACC was subversive because its activities threatened the security of the State. Further that the Council's legitimate work, propagating the Gospel, had been abandoned in favour of matters beyond its competence. In its terms of reference the Commission was asked to enquire into the history and activities of the SACC and to report on all aspects of its finances and assets; there was also a catch-all clause covering 'any other matter pertaining to the SACC', including personnel, both past and present, so that a report could be made 'in the public interest'. As the limits of this phrase were determined by the government, clearly there were to be no inhibitions on the scope of the Commission's inquiries.

Behind these overt instructions there was little doubt that what the government hoped to do was to discredit both the SACC and Bishop Tutu. It was to attempt this on two fronts: on the one hand by trying to prove financial mismanagement; on the other by showing that the SACC was fomenting an unpatriotic revolution. Thus it could cause the Council to become an embarrassment to its member Churches and overseas donors, eroding support where it was most crucial. It also hoped to show that the Council was a microcosm of what it saw as an international conspiracy against the South African government. In the SACC the evils of internationalism – an aspect of the Council's work running counter to the insularity of Afrikanerdom and which had for years been an irritant – were encapsulated.

The Commission sat in a small rectangular room in a government building in Pretoria with the auspicious name 'Veritas'. Judge Eloff, flanked on each side by two commissioners, sat facing the witness and the two Counsels: the chief investigating officer Advocate K. S. P. O. von Lieres SC for the government and Sydney Kentridge SC, one of

South Africa's best-known advocates, who had represented the Biko family at the inquest into the death of Steve Biko, for the SACC. There were seats for a few visitors, and a handful of the press were usually present. It was, at least on the face of it, a quiet, civilised affair, with some special visitors being invited to take tea with Judge Eloff.

The SACC had decided to co-operate fully with the authorities; all the material they wanted was made available, nothing was concealed or ignored. Confident that it had nothing to hide, it wanted the world to know it. So every file requested was photocopied, catalogued and handed over. Extra help was brought in to trace the history of the Council, describe the developments of the various divisions and put all the papers together chronologically as a formal submission to the Commission. Dan Vaughan, in addition to his work as Planning Officer, was responsible for co-ordinating the preparation of the material. Not only did this cost the Council over R200,000, but its day-to-day work was constantly disrupted as staff were questioned and their papers searched.

The public hearings began in September with Tutu's evidence. Allistair Sparks was in the courtroom to hear what he suggested was probably 'the greatest sermon of the Bishop's life':[1]

> He sat bouncing and twisting in a carver chair, his hands shaping the outlines of his ideas with vivid gestures. It was like a mime show with voice accompaniment, when he spoke of the resurrection of the body, his arms folded around his own body in a hug.
>
> The voice was the other instrument in this concert performance. Sometimes it would be sonorous, playing with the cadences of his African accent, and sometimes it would break into a high-pitched chuckle as he would hit on some pertinent new insight. It would be sombre, joyful, impatient, humorous, reflective, switching rapidly in response to a quicksilver spirit.
>
> And all the while, the white Commissioners watched, expressionless.

Typically, Tutu began by expressing his appreciation to the officers of the Commission for examining the SACC's records in such a way as to dislocate its work as little as possible. Even more typically, he then went straight to the heart of the matter, stating that it was not the finances or any other activities of the SACC that were being investigated, but the Christian faith itself that was on trial. Quoting from an old leather-bound Bible, and showing that the SACC regarded the proceedings as a court case rather than an inquiry by resolutely addressing the Judge as 'My Lord', he demonstrated that all that the SACC did and said, indeed everything it was, was determined not by politics but by the Gospels, which not only licensed it to be actively involved with social justice but carried a divine obligation that it should be. The central issue was profoundly theological.

He argued that Jesus Christ was the Lord of *all* life, spiritual and secular. Though spirituality was central to the life of the Council, it knew that 'God does not permit us to dwell in a kind of spiritual ghetto, insulated from real life . . . He [Jesus] refused to remain on the Mount of Transfiguration, but descended to the valley beneath to be involved with healing the possessed boy.' Christ was on the side of the oppressed and his central work was to effect reconciliation between God and Man and between man and man. Apartheid is evil, he claimed, because it claims mankind was made for separateness, thus repudiating this central, reconciling truth of the Christian faith. Further, apartheid denies the unique value of each human being and its consequences are evil. In trying to defend it the government could only fail, 'for it is ranging itself on the side of evil, injustice and oppression'. It was also flying in the face of the recent declaration of the World Alliance of Reformed Churches (already rejected by the Afrikaner churches, whose membership of the Alliance had been suspended) that the theological justification of apartheid is a heresy.

Tutu was determined to show that the SACC and its member Churches were not 'a tuppenny halfpenny fly by night organisation' but they belonged to the Church of God, expressing their oneness in prayer, in giving and receiving and in suffering with one another. The only separation acknowledged by the Bible was the separation between believers on the one hand and unbelievers on the other.

He submitted 'with due respect' but with an impressive authority that no secular power, no Commission, had any competence whatsoever to determine the nature of the Gospel of Jesus Christ and that in trying to do so it was 'usurping divine prerogatives and the prerogatives of the church itself'. If the SACC had contravened the laws of the land, then there was an array of draconian measures at the disposal of the government. The Inquiry was 'totally superfluous' and the SACC had only agreed to appear before the Commission because it had nothing to hide. Nor did he fear the government:

> I want to say that there is nothing the government can do to me that will stop me from being involved in what I believe is what God wants me to do. I do not do it because I like doing it. I do it because I am under what I believe to be the influence of God's hand. I cannot help it. I cannot help it when I see injustice. I cannot keep quiet. I will not keep quiet, for, as Jeremiah says, when I try to keep quiet God's word

burns like a fire in my breast. But what is it that they can ultimately do? The most awful thing that they can do is to kill me, and death is not the worst thing that can happen to a Christian.

There were many milestones in the long journey of evidence and cross-examination that was the Eloff Commission. One was the suggestion of General Johan Coetzee, then Chief of the Security Police, that the SACC was the puppet of overseas organisations and that its financial help went to organisations that were in reality liberation movements. He said the SACC should be declared an affected organisation and subjected to the provisions of the Fund Raising Act. Such a step would cut off all overseas finance (96 per cent of its income) and bring such money as its member Churches could provide under direct government control and scrutiny. Another key moment was the appearance of Mr E. Cain, the Baptist editor of *Encounter*, an official mouthpiece of the government-sponsored Christian League and dedicated to the downfall of the SACC. He claimed that ministers of religion should have nothing to do with politics, except in the sense of attacking Communism and supporting the South African government; he even suggested that Jesus Christ had no concern for righting injustice. So ugly was the exchange, so nearly blasphemous, that the SACC defence stopped the cross-examination; even the Prosecuting Counsel felt unable to pursue it.

It is a curious fact that the Prosecution did not produce a right-wing theologian to support their case. Perhaps the experience of Mr Cain had discouraged them; perhaps it was the hesitancy of Afrikaner theologians, unaccustomed to being challenged, to go on record in justification of so dubious a cause. They might have hoped that the distinguished DRC theologian Professor David Bosch would have sided with them. In fact he only agreed to give evidence in order to introduce a slightly different perspective and was outstanding in his defence of the SACC's position. He gave it a strong theological legitimacy, addressing himself primarily to arguing that in attacking the SACC the Commission were attacking all the member Churches, who gave their total support to what the SACC was doing.

In November 1982, a year after the appointment of the Commission, came a turning point resulting from one of the most unpleasant episodes of the whole Inquiry. An anonymous letter, purporting to come from 'unhappy staff at the SACC', was sent to all its overseas donors and member Churches. It claimed that there was a rift between the SACC and its member Churches, alleged that the funds were disbursed for 'semi-political rather than evangelical or other strictly religious activities' and said they wished to express their 'distinct unhappiness over the extent to which this organisation has disintegrated and deteriorated under the control of Bishop Desmond Tutu'. The writers claimed to be sending the letter anonymously 'since we face the very real possibility of retribution if we speak out openly against the real situation in the SACC'. The letter (whose source was never confirmed) was strongly repudiated by the staff, who expressed their fullest trust and confidence in their General Secretary. In keeping with his policy of total transparency, Tutu promptly forwarded a copy of the letter to the Eloff Commission.

He also decided to invite the overseas donors to testify. The authorities, anxious to show that they too were playing fair, allowed entry visas to representatives from Norway, Denmark, Holland and Germany, so the worldwide Church, already kept informed of the situation by weekly telexes, was alerted to the gravity of the situation. Significantly, the Archbishop of Canterbury, Dr Robert Runcie, took the unusual step of showing the international support of the Anglican Church by sending out a five-person delegation consisting of Terry Waite, the lay assistant to the Archbishop of Canterbury on Anglican communion affairs, the Primus of the Scottish Episcopal Church, a member of the executive council of the Episcopal Church of the United States, the Prolocutor of the General Synod of the Anglican Church of Canada and the Primate of the Church of the Province of New Zealand. The press, asking if the SACC had paid the fares, were told by a delighted Bishop Tutu that they had not even paid the hotel bills:[2]

> The South African government has not yet recovered from the shock administered to it by that ecumenical and worldwide presence and I will not be over-anxious to help them recover too soon. They had hoped that they would have succeeded in vilifying us and discrediting us to such an extent that our friends would not want to touch us with the proverbial bargepole. It seems that they have been hoisted by their own petard.

It was the first time Archbishop Runcie had done such a thing (though he has done it twice since). 'It was to make the point that you are not simply dealing with a domestic matter. If you touch Desmond Tutu you touch a world family of Christians and there was a sense of Anglican identity there, which was visible and effective and not just a notional paper theory which crumbles when people see the autonomy of provinces.' Though the Anglican Church in South Africa expresses itself through its own culture and customs, it is historically tied to Canterbury and Canterbury was proud to support it. For his part Tutu's gratitude knew no bounds. This action by Runcie set the seal on the admiration and affection the two men have for each other.

The evidence taken by the Commission ran to eighty-two volumes; its final report, submitted to the State President at the end of 1983, ran to 450 pages. In February 1984 the report was tabled and the findings published.

The Commission, heedless of the testimony of the SACC and its member Churches, concluded that the SACC had changed from being a body principally concerned with spiritual matters 'into one concerned with political, social and economic interests, and having specific objectives in these fields'. It had 'opted for a revolutionary rather than an evolutionary process' to effect change and had become increasingly identified with the struggle for liberation. To this end it had campaigned for civil disobedience and non-cooperation with the State, supported disinvestment and conscientious objection – none of which actions were, in the opinion of the Commission, in the national interest. It accused the SACC of trying to conceal the origin and disbursement of its funds and engaging in 'secret and covert operations'. Finally it criticised the Council's financial administration.

In its recommendations the Commission questioned the capability of the law to counter calls for disinvestment and urged that existing legislation be reconsidered; it suggested that the SACC should be brought under the discipline of the Fund-raising Act of 1978 (though this was in fact never done). However, it decided against declaring the Council an affected organisation – a curious *non-sequitur* in the light of the case being built up in those 450 pages. The Commission's explanation was that such action would be viewed as a restraint on religious freedom and that in any case it would not prevent the flow of funds from overseas. It had to admit that it had found no evidence of the SACC being manipulated by its overseas donors, but claimed that though 'the money spent by the SACC to help the needy and deserving can only be described as meagre compared to that used for political purposes, innocent people would suffer if the organisation were to be rendered largely ineffective.'

All that evidence, all those cross-examinations, all that paper, had achieved virtually nothing; none of the allegations had been made to stick, the Commission had certainly not succeeded in undermining the moral credibility of the Council. The publication of the Eloff Report was even described as 'an almost non-event'. Disappointed government officials took refuge in issuing warnings. Louis le Grange, the Minister of Law and Order, said that if the SACC continued its 'tendency towards confrontation' the State might be forced to act against it – it must remember it was not above the law: 'I warn him [Tutu] and the SACC that . . . I will not allow any wicked acts to be committed under the cloak of religion.'

Nevertheless, neither the SACC, nor its supporters and General Secretary, were going to let the accusations that had been levelled at them go unchallenged. Within hours the SACC Praesidium issued a strong statement denying that there had been a campaign of civil disobedience, rejecting the use of the word 'revolutionary' in relation to its work and stating, 'It is intolerable that the Church be denied the right to determine and interpret the Gospel mandate in terms of the challenges of its environment'. The Southern African Catholic Bishops' Conference commented on the inability of the Commission to find anything deserving legal action and stated, 'In the black milieu the topics referred to sound like very moderate Christian reactions to a situation of unbearable privation and frustration'.

Two Progressive Federal Party MPs also spoke out in their defence. Dr Alex Boraine said that while the SACC must accept the consequences if it defied the State, the Church had the right to be involved in political, social and economic issues. David Dalling said that his party believed the government had no business probing the SACC's financial affairs, that there was no doubting that the Commission was inspired by political motives and that the SACC was a private organisation, dealing with private money and comparable to the South African Bureau of Racial Affairs and the Institute of Racial Relations.

Of all the responses to the Commission's findings, none were so forceful as Tutu's. He could only find one point of agreement with the Commission – that they had little understanding of theology, so how could they be expected to make a fair judgment? 'It really was like asking (speaking respectfully) a group of blind men to judge the Chelsea Flower Show.' He repeated that no secular authority was entitled to tell the Church how to go about its work and that if the Council had contravened the law, then it should have been charged in open court. The Commission not only had no theological expertise, it had not included one black person. What did it know of the anguish and humiliation endured by the black community? How could it understand how blacks regarded the SACC?

Heeding the old adage that 'the essence of defence is offence', Tutu reminded the Commission of the high-powered delegations from all over the world that had shown their support for the SACC, and challenged it to 'point to any self-respecting overseas Church that supports the White Dutch Reformed Church?' He met accusations of fomenting unrest by pointing out occasions when he had acted as a mediator. He told it to stop trying to bribe the SACC staff to spy for them – if it wanted to know anything, it had only to ask. He warned that

> if they take on the SACC then they must know that they are taking on the Church of God and other tyrants before them have tried to destroy the Church – Nero, Amin, Hitler, Bokassa, etc. . . . Where are they today? They have bitten the dust ignominiously. I warn the South African government again – they are not Gods, they are mere mortals, who will end up as mere marks on the pages of history, part of its flotsam and jetsam. I am not afraid of them.

The one issue on which the SACC was vulnerable concerned its financial management. Though the Commission were never able to show that money was mishandled or used for purposes other than that for which it was given, there was still evidence of poor accounting. This came as no surprise to the Council, which was the first to admit it; indeed, Tutu was well on the way towards bringing things under control before the Commission began to sit.

One reason for the poor book-keeping was the confidential nature of some of the donations, for instance when assistance was given to people who did not wish their names to be officially recorded. Another was that in trying to use their money as much as possible for the beneficiaries, the staff of the SACC kept their own salaries, from Bishop Tutu's downwards, as low as possible. The salary for a first-class accountant, qualified to handle its turnover of R4 million a year, would have been two or three times as high as that earned by the General Secretary. With hindsight it is clear that the Council's idealism led, in this respect, to an error of judgment.

The inadequacy of the accounting did, however, reveal a situation that was to cause much personal anguish inside the SACC. One of the State witnesses, Warrant-Officer A. J. Mills, found in the course of his investigations that the former General Secretary, John Rees, had deposited more than R250,000 from the Asingeni Fund in fifty-one bank accounts in his own name. The Council, knowing and admiring John Rees, were reluctant to prefer charges, but in the middle of their 1982 national conference news came that the former General Secretary had been arrested and charged with fraud. He was tried, found guilty and sentenced to ten years' imprisonment, suspended conditionally for five years. He was also fined R30,000.

This affair split the SACC. That John Rees's use of the money was unauthorised was not in question, but opinions were divided as to his motivation. Some felt he was playing Robin Hood, using the funds he had appropriated from the SACC to benefit the poor and needy; others saw his actions in various shades of grey, one person even suggesting he was 'a giant con-man buying power from the black community'. Nowhere was this division more personal or more painful than between Tutu and the SACC's distinguished President, Peter Storey.

Tutu, though unwilling to charge his predecessor and slow to believe in his guilt, was angry that the SACC should be brought into disrepute through events which had taken place before his time. He was also incensed by allegations that his reluctance to lay charges or to witness at the trial was due to John Rees having given him R14,000 towards buying a house – money which he had accepted, perhaps naïvely but certainly in good faith, as having been donated by a German Bishop but which turned out to have come from the funds misappropriated by the former General Secretary.[3] He felt, however, forced by the evidence to accept the guilty verdict.

Peter Storey's reactions were even more complicated. He was not only John Rees's friend, he was his pastor. His insistence on giving evidence in mitigation of John Rees was hard for Tutu to take, not least because of the ever-present suspicion of a racial dimension – was it a case of white supporting white (though too many blacks were devoted to John Rees for that charge to stick)? Eventually Peter Storey resigned as President of the SACC, an action which also lost Tutu Elizabeth, his devoted and able secretary who, as Peter Storey's wife, felt unable to work in the situation that had arisen between her husband and her boss. Peter Storey accepted that John Rees had been foolish, he had also to accept the verdict; but he felt he could not escape pastoral responsibility for a broken parishioner. Tutu, a pastor through and through himself, did not question this. What he *did* question was Peter Storey's refusal to admit John Rees's guilt. His final wistful comment on the matter was 'I only wish I had a friend like that'.

The John Rees affair, the one aspect of the Eloff Commission to hurt both the SACC and Tutu, emerged accidentally from the investigations. The Commission had not succeeded in proving any of its original accusations nor in discrediting the Council or its General Secretary. What had gone wrong for Pretoria?

They seem to have miscalculated the significance of the SACC on a number of levels. To start with they had not expected the Commission to become a world forum. The visible and vocal way in which the international community, particularly the Churches, rallied to the Council's support was a source of deep embarrassment. Impervious to world opinion though the South African government usually appears to be, it knew that to act against a body that had not been found guilty would be a judgment that could – and probably would – redound against it. Second, despite its own experience of Afrikaner unity under siege, it had not reckoned on the Council's capacity to draw closer against a common threat or taken account of the huge black membership of the SACC. Every assault against the Council, every accusation of involvement in the liberation struggle, was in fact a legitimatising of its role in the black community. With every attack the Council's credibility was increased rather than diminished.

Nor can the Commission have appreciated the extent to which it had entered the theological arena. This dimension proved to be its Achilles' heel, as a government claiming to be Christian could hardly be seen to behave, on so public a platform, in a way that was clearly unChristian. It was also caught out in a serious inconsistency. The Church was continually being told it must not be involved in politics (which meant the Church must not disagree with the government – those who agreed were not considered to be acting politically), yet the government had found itself involved in a debate that was, by its own implied admission, on the Church's territory. And in this matter it was a united Church; the State found that it was acting not just against a limb, but against the whole body. The Afrikaner Churches had been dismembered so long, had become so isolated from the body of the Christian Church, that memories of such unity were long forgotten. The Eloff Commission saw the ecumenical family at its best, taking one another's pain seriously, regarding a wound to one as a wound to all.

Most of all, it had reckoned without Desmond Tutu, in the whole affair the single most important person, both *ex officio* and through the charisma of his personality. Most Afrikaners are in thrall to an image of the black man as ignorant, slow, unsophisticated and gauche. The commissioners must have been perplexed to be faced with a profoundly spiritual man, who could run rings round them theologically and was at once widely travelled, witty and courteous, with a quicksilver mind and a disarming honesty.

As a result of some of the more damaging and vicious things that had been said and done in the course of the hearings, Tutu had elected to give evidence a second time. In this statement he not only illustrated the lives he and his countrymen led by giving a lengthy autobiographical sketch, he also drew attention to the way the police had 'sought to present a particular image of the SACC by a clever choice of words, by innuendo and by a kind of guilt by association' and, most relevantly, he brought the debate firmly back on to theological ground. As we have seen, Tutu's theology is, above all, incarnational. He is not much interested in the contemporary equivalent of medieval speculations as to how many angels could dance on the point of a needle; his theology is to do with the concerns of ordinary people in a particular place and time. So when the chief investigating officer asked him if the liberation struggle was part of the Church's role in South Africa, he responded by saying:

> You do not want biblical exegesis every time you ask me a question, but I think I have to indicate to you that liberation, setting free, is a key concept of the Bible. The paradigmatic event in the Bible is the Exodus, the setting free of a rabble of slaves . . . we are participating in God's glorious movement of setting his people free.

Nor should the light touch he brought to the proceedings be forgotten. For instance, when asked if he had indeed made a certain pronouncement about apartheid, he responded ruefully that they ought to have discovered by now 'that I sound like a cracked record, I am so repetitive'. On another occasion, for once slow to answer as he was engrossed in his written evidence, he apologised for not replying, explaining that 'I was reading. Sometimes I am surprised at the thin gs I say.' His humour and honesty made him a powerful and persuasive witness. He was open to accusations made against his administration, willing to take the skeletons on board, a response foreign to government ethos and in contrast to the way the truth had to be dragged out, piece by piece, in the recent Information Affair.

His personal success was won in the face of the media's efforts to discredit him. His youthful tuberculosis has left him with an atrophied hand, which he has a habit of rubbing. During a particularly unpleasant piece of evidence the cameras of the South African Broadcasting Corporation would focus on his wringing hands, as if to indicate his discomfort and guilt. This was something that upset him deeply and to which he still refers. Again during the Eloff Commission, the press misleadingly ran a 'Fingers in the Till' headline next to a picture of Tutu.

The Eloff Commission was emotionally a most testing and frustrating time for both the SACC and Desmond Tutu. For months and months every aspect of his private and public life was laid bare, questioned, scrutinised, criticised and often condemned. His time and energy were consumed and his work crippled by the constant onslaught of the hearings, his administration came under fire, he was not even given credit for the work he had done in dealing with the administrative and financial problems he had inherited.

But there were pearls among the grit. Despite attempts to drive wedges between the staff, it was, said Peter Storey (whose rift with

Bishop Tutu over the John Rees affair was soon healed), 'A magnificent witness to our togetherness. Through it all ran a serene confidence in the righteousness of our cause, the knowledge that God would triumph.' The Council was forced to examine and re-evaluate itself, the solidarity of the world Church was reaffirmed. In Dan Vaughan's words, 'Eloff turned the Council around. Eloff was, under God, the best thing that could have happened.' There were, in a sense, no winners. The State had not been able to prove its case against the SACC; for the SACC the Inquiry had been costly and time-consuming and had led to the trial and conviction of John Rees, deeply distressing for the staff of the SACC, many of whom had known and admired him. But at last the SACC and Tutu were vindicated and free to continue their work. David's small stone of truth had prevailed against the Goliath of the State.

14

Voice of the voiceless

One reason behind the Eloff Commission's inability to discredit the SACC was the international standing of its General Secretary. Ironically, the publicity surrounding the Inquiry attracted more attention to both Tutu and the SACC, leading to yet more invitations to speak. By the time the Commission's findings were published Tutu had become an even wider-travelled spokesman for his people. All over the world he articulated the plight of the blacks of South Africa, becoming a voice for his voiceless people as he showed, with a passionate conviction which brooked no disagreement, that apartheid is evil, immoral and vicious and inconsistent with the Gospel of Jesus Christ. As he became known and respected, not only in the Church but in the United Nations, in universities and in government circles, and as his statements gained prominence in the press of every country he visited, so he became an increasing irritant to the South African government.

His emergence on to the international scene was gradual. He made countless friends during his student days at King's College, London, and yet more as he travelled to the countries of the Third World for the Theological Education Fund. While he was Dean of Johannesburg and Bishop of Lesotho he went overseas occasionally – for instance in 1976 acting as Theological Consultant at a meeting of the Anglican Consultative Council in Port of Spain, Trinidad, and the following year addressing a convocation at Saskatoon.

His first appearance before the world-wide Anglican community was when he attended the 1978 Lambeth Conference, where he was on the steering committee and where, as chairman of a section entitled 'What Is the Church For?', he was responsible for a document on social issues, including the potentially explosive subject of the ordination of women. It was a measured, irenic debate, opposing factions agreeing to disagree and declaring that the Church's unity as a family transcended their differences. The resulting document recognised that in some provinces the ordination of women was already an accomplished fact and urged sensitivity from those on all sides of the debate. Tutu, himself – after long deliberation – in favour of women priests, felt it was really 'a permissive resolution', enabling Churches who wished to ordain women to do so. In fact he felt able to respond to a letter from an English Deaconess by telling her that if she were to apply for ordination in five years' time, she might well be accepted. 'But I hope very much that you will not wear a dog-collar. Nothing puts me off women in the ministry more than that and I am sure they can find something more feminine and attractive!'[1] History has shown that this was an optimistic judgment, but at least he was among those refusing to sit on the fence on this controversial subject.

He also made a dramatic personal impact. The Ugandan Bishops present at the conference knew that President Idi Amin had sent spies after them and their understandable tension found great relief in a smiling, joking Desmond, coming in like a hurricane as he greeted old friends and made new ones. Suddenly he became the spokesman, the symbol, of the Church in Africa. He even enlivened the restrained Anglican worship by leading them, African-style, in singing, dancing and hand-clapping. 'How often your smiling face and bright eyes come to mind when reflecting on Lambeth,' wrote the Bishop of Nevada. 'Your presence, your joy, your faith, but above all you – was one of the great benefits of that gathering.'[2]

For Tutu it was 'the experience of a lifetime'. Deeply Anglican as he is, he was fascinated by this gathering of the leaders of the Anglican communion – 'fat bishops, lean bishops, white bishops, jogging bishops' – awed by experiencing the continuity of history as they met on the modern campus of the University of Kent overlooking Canterbury Cathedral. When he returned to South Africa he reflected on the strange phenomenon that is the Anglican community. Twenty-seven self-governing provinces consisting of nearly 400 dioceses stretching from the Arctic to Australia, from the South Pacific to the North Sea; a community embracing nearly 70 million people of all tongues, complexions and cultures yet having no central authority but reaching their decisions through a process of consultation:[3]

> It really has no reason to exist in a world that is so fissiparous, yet it continues . . . The Anglican Communion continues to baffle all out-siders, because it is a family with all the tensions and differences, loves and hates, squabbles and agreements that characterize a family. Yes, we have the peculiar Anglican genius for accommodating all kinds of views in this extraordinary attribute called our comprehensiveness.

While he was in England Tutu gave an address to the Royal Commonwealth Society in which he said many of the things he was to repeat again and again all over the world. He urged the international community to apply diplomatic and economic pressures on South

Africa to avert the impending holocaust. He assured them that the blacks were on the winning side and that there was a new breed of young blacks who feared neither the police nor death. There was no doubt that the oppressed people were going to be free and when that day came the black community would remember who their friends were. The blacks had no wish to drive white South Africans into the sea, but if they were frustrated for too long, then white fears could become self-fulfilling prophecies. He said he feared that only a miracle could avert 'the alternative too ghastly to contemplate' but if the international community were alive to the situation and took action there was still time to effect a reasonably peaceful change. If these words have a familiar ring today, it must be remembered that this was 1978, only two years after the Soweto disturbances and long before the role of the international community in South African affairs had become something the newspaper reading public took in with their morning coffee.

In May 1979, Desmond and Leah visited the United States at the invitation of Bishop Jack Spong, one of the Bishops who had assisted at Desmond's own consecration. For a month Tutu worked as assistant Bishop in the Diocese of Newark, sharing in the pastoral work that he loves, taking confirmations and preaching, happy in an ethnically mixed diocese whose permanent staff included Koreans and Japanese priests and where Bishops from the Third World were encouraged to come and share their insights and experience. Inevitably he found himself asked to speak about the political situation in South Africa and though he would raise the question of the apartheid system being upheld by foreign investment, he refrained from calling explicitly for sanctions, knowing that such a call could have brought a charge of economic sabotage and the possibility of a five-year prison sentence. Similarly, in Boston, though he spoke on migrant labour and deplored the way the South African economy was built on the destruction of black family life, he was careful to avoid openly advocating disinvestment, simply telling his audience the consequences of apartheid policy. It was, however, later that year that he visited Copenhagen, where he made the much publicised remark about his disappointment that Denmark was still importing South African coal. Early in 1980 his passport was withdrawn.

The convoluted story of Tutu's passport, with its overtones of the school playground and the 'ya-boo' element of a child taking away his playmate's football, reflects poorly on the way the South African government has sought to control its turbulent priest. The government holds that it does not have to give reasons for issuing or refusing a passport – it is a privilege, not a right. Tutu, by making public statements that were, in South African law, only just on the right side of treason, had forsworn that privilege.

The first time his passport was seized was on March 4th, 1980. He was about to begin a service of thanksgiving for Robert Mugabe's election as Prime Minister of Zimbabwe, when two men, one a security policeman, arrived with an order withdrawing his passport. The reaction was immediate and world-wide. In seeking to silence Tutu the government had only succeeded in giving him yet more publicity. It even ran the risk of turning him into a martyr. Black leaders, in the company of the United Nations, condemned the action; messages of support came from American Church leaders and politicians; children from St James's Church in Madison Avenue sent 'passports of love'; the Archbishop of Canterbury, Dr Robert Runcie, led twenty-four Anglican Primates from all round the world in a statement deploring the action. It even caused comment in the South African House of Assembly, where Helen Suzman asked, 'Why infuriate blacks throughout South Africa by confiscating Bishop Tutu's passport? That was a petty, spiteful action and it did the government no good with thinking people in South Africa and with democratically minded people overseas.'[4]

She was right. It did not do the government much good with anyone, nor did it daunt Tutu. He pointed out that his speeches at home were so widely reported in the foreign press that his physical absence overseas would not silence his voice. Perhaps, he suggested, the government's real purpose was to test the measure of overseas reaction?

He has never feared authority. In 1978, when his passport was taken away at Maseru Bridge and he found his name was on the police files, he wrote to the security police demanding to know why he was on that blacklist, since at the time he travelled through other border posts in southern Africa without difficulty. He also protested at the discourteous way he was treated by a police constable who had said to him in Afrikaans: 'Desmond, is jy stout?' (Desmond, are you naughty?):[5]

> I am a Bishop of the Church and a leader of the churches in this country and would expect that every member of the public would be treated courteously by civil servants whatever his status. I want to point out that unless I get a satisfactory response from you on both these counts that I am going to take this matter up at the highest level in the Government.

It would have been interesting to see the expression on the faces of the police as they read these commanding words from someone they were accustomed to consider as merely 'a cheeky Kaffir'. His reaction to the seizure of his passport was equally dignified. He informed the authorities that he would be going on with the work God had given him and if they were trying to intimidate him they were wasting their time.

Clearly, however, it was extremely frustrating. The intermittent withdrawals of his passport, the refusals of his applications for its renewal, forced Tutu to turn down countless invitations to overseas conferences, synods and assemblies. It also prevented him from receiving personally the awards that were beginning to be heaped upon him.

The first was from his old college, King's College, London, which elected him an Honorary Fellow in March 1978. Honorary doctorates from the General Theological Seminary of New York and the University of Kent in England followed swiftly. Whether or not he could receive these awards personally depended, in each case, on the whim of the South African government. One of the highlights of his 1979 visit to the United States was when he was able to receive an Hon. LL.D from Harvard University, who recognised him as 'a Churchman of great faith and courage willing to risk his life on behalf of freedom and dignity for all people in South Africa'.[6] He found the occasion both touching – he was given a standing ovation by the 20,000 people present – and awesome, the ten others being honoured including the conductor Sir George Solti, Jean Jacques Cousteau ('who does funny things under water'),[7] the Nobel Prize-winning economist Milton Friedman and Helmut Schmidt, who was guarded by a phalanx from the secret service. On the other hand, though he had hoped to receive his honorary doctorate from Aberdeen University in person – indeed he had wired cheerfully 'Have passport, can travel' – his telegram had barely reached Scotland before he was once again without a passport. He was the first person ever to be awarded an honorary doctorate by the Ruhr University in West Germany, but again he could not be there; nor – most notably – could he attend the commencement exercises at Columbia University, where he was to have been awarded an honorary doctorate of Sacred Theology in May 1982.

In a moving address the university's President, Michael I. Sovern, explained that the empty chair on the platform would be left vacant until Tutu could fill it. Their absent guest was 'a beacon of hope and decency in a dark land and we want to help keep that light burning. We want him to know that we care. We want the government of South Africa to know that the world is watching. And we want to reaffirm our own humanity by presuming to claim that he and we are brothers.' Columbia University does not award degrees *in absentia*, so, for only the third time in its 228-year history (the other two people thus honoured were Abraham Lincoln, whose movements were restricted by the Civil War and a Judge of the Supreme Court, unable to travel through ill-health), they decided to award the degree off campus: 'To express our respect, with the highest honour in the gift of the University, we would go to the ends of the earth.'

So Dr Sovern and a small group of his colleagues applied for visas to South Africa, openly stating that their reason for visiting the country was 'to confer an award on Bishop Tutu'. They arranged to borrow the great hall of the University of the Witwatersrand, packed their academic caps and gowns and flew to Johannesburg. The hall was filled to overflowing when, on August 3rd, 1982, in a ceremony combining European academic splendour with African music from his favourite trio[8] (who sang in Xhosa a song which included the words 'How long, dear God, are we going to slave? How long this enslavement, this oppression?'), Bishop Tutu was awarded his fifth honorary doctorate.

Despite the restrictions on his movements overseas, whenever Tutu was granted the 'privilege' of a passport he used it well; apart from Pope John Paul II, he must be the most travelled churchman of his time. Of the numerous trips he made while he was General Secretary of the South African Council of Churches, three deserve special mention.

First there was the extensive tour of cities in Europe and America he made in 1981. In January of that year, when for ten months he had been unable to leave South Africa, his passport was returned and he was in a position to consider some of the invitations he had been forced to refuse. Peter Storey, at the time President of the SACC, encouraged him not just to respond to requests, but to set up a major itinerary across the world. Though in many ways the staff of the SACC had been relieved to have their General Secretary in one place for a while, there was a need for him to re-establish face-to-face contacts with their overseas partners. Equally both Tutu and the Council wanted to alert leaders in Church and State to the deteriorating situation in their country and to enlist their support in persuading the South African government to negotiate a settlement of the national crisis.

He left South Africa on March 4th, going first to Switzerland, where, in an hour long meeting at the Foreign Ministry, he stressed the need for the international community to apply political, diplomatic and above all economic pressures to bring the South African government to the negotiating table. He also suggested that the Swiss government show its disapproval of apartheid by demanding visas from South African nationals entering Switzerland, a suggestion that led to a long discussion of the meaning of neutrality and the inability of a neutral country to involve itself directly in the affairs of another State. He spent several days each in West Germany, Sweden, Norway and Denmark, and by March 20th he was in America, where he had a long meeting with Dr Waldheim, the Secretary-General of the United Nations, met Mrs Jeane Kirkpatrick, the United States Ambassador to the United Nations, and addressed the United Nations Special Committee Against Apartheid. At this meeting he is reported to have described the racial society of South Africa as 'one of the most vicious systems since Nazism' and to have again appealed for international economic pressure on the South African government on behalf of his 'voiceless' black compatriots. On to London, where he met the Lord Privy Seal, Sir Ian Gilmour, was interviewed by BBC Television's *Panorama* and, in a sermon in Westminster Abbey, accused certain Western countries and big business of 'a conspiracy to keep South African blacks in bondage'. He also admitted, in a public address, that he had 'decreased enthusiasm for another meeting between the SACC and the government because the government has not shown itself ready to move from its intransigence'. On his way back to South Africa he stopped off in Rome, where he met the Pope for the first time. Though on this occasion he just had a privileged place at a general audience in St Peter's Square, in 1983 he had a private audience, when he was able to discuss personally with the Pope the current situation in South Africa. In those days, before he had become accustomed to moving amongst eminent luminaries, he would come out of such meetings amazed that they had taken place, saying 'Pinch me, is it true?' Dan Vaughan, who was with him in Rome, remembers that Tutu was untypically nervous, delighted at the medals given to commemorate the occasion and highly amused that Dan, a Baptist, should meet the Supreme Pontiff.

On April 9th, 1981, Tutu arrived back in South Africa to a hero's welcome. Among the joyful crowd welcoming him was Peter Storey, who sensed that having met world statesmen and held his own had given him a new confidence. He also appreciated the 'weight on those very little shoulders' and the knowledge that as they walked out of the airport, through the jostling crowd, there could so easily be someone who wished him dead. 'One also sensed on that return that here was someone who knew – perhaps he had always known – that he came back as someone with destiny on his shoulders. A sense of having to be the instrument of his people's liberation, to be their spokesman.'

Prime Minister P. W. Botha must have had the same feeling. In a political rally in the Orange Free State he repeated his conviction that a passport was 'a favour from the State' and that Tutu had exploited it. 'As far as I am concerned, when he returns, his passport will be taken away.' It was. This came as no surprise to Tutu, who had thought it probable that he would also be banned or put under house arrest. The day after his return, on the eve of Good Friday, his passport was withdrawn for the second time in just over a year. It was as well he had used it with so much energy and courage.

One September afternoon in 1982, this time after nearly eighteen months without a passport, Tutu was attending the afternoon session of the Eloff Commission hearings in Pretoria when the proceedings were interrupted by officials bearing a limited 'travel document' for himself and Leah. It was more a letter of identity than a passport, it did not say where he had been born and opposite 'Nationality' it bore the offensive words 'Undeterminable at present', but at least it allowed him to attend the Triennial Convention of the Episcopal Church, USA, in New Orleans. Before the week was out the Tutus were on their way to the States.

Many people had been working for the return of Tutu's passport, this partial success being eventually achieved by none less than George Bush, the Vice-President of the United States and himself, along with many members of the United States government, an Episcopalian and one of the speakers at the 1982 Convention.

On this trip Tutu refrained from calling for economic pressure against Pretoria, but in no other way did he appear to be inhibited by fear of reprisal. He assured his audience that though South Africa's white rulers were powerful, they were scared, so busy protecting their privileged position that they could no longer enjoy it; that apartheid was not being dismantled, in fact in trying to co-opt the so-called 'coloureds' into Parliament the government was trying to reduce the proportional strength held by the Africans. Yet 'the people who are perpetrators of injury in our land are not sprouting horns or tails. They're just ordinary people like you and me. We are talking about ordinary people who are scared. Wouldn't you be scared if you were outnumbered five to one?'[9]

He made his audience laugh, suggesting that the Almighty himself must laugh at man's wilful, wayward behaviour – in South Africa an eighteen-year-old pimply white policeman, barely able to read or write, could, by virtue of his colour, exercise a vote while he, over fifty years old, a Bishop of the Church of God and the recipient of numerous academic degrees, could not. Among those present was

John Walker, the Bishop of Washington, who admits that at first the laughter was uncomfortable; soon, however, the audience realised that humour was being used to make a very real point about the problems of blacks in South Africa. Once Tutu knew they were on his side he became serious. 'He is *par excellence* a dramatist when he's speaking,' says Bishop Walker, 'and when he gets serious he takes you to the top of the mountain and you weep with him. He plays every emotional chord there is in the human body.'

The convention was electrified. They laughed, wept, clapped and roared their approval, constantly interrupting his address with bouts of spontaneous applause. When, after a fifteen-minute standing ovation, he left the hall, they could talk of nothing but this remarkable South African. For his part Tutu knew that the Episcopal Church of the United States was firmly on his side; he could say anything, do anything, and they would support him.

The travel document allowed the Tutus to be out of the country for nineteen days, so when the convention had ended they went to Kentucky to spend the weekend with their daughter Naomi and her American husband; it was not, however, an entirely domestic weekend. In a widely syndicated press interview Tutu said that apartheid in South Africa was far worse now than five years ago, when Steve Biko had died in jail. He feared that the authorities were resisting peaceful change, citing signs such as the recent death of two government opponents in jail and the limitations imposed on black activists by the extension of banning orders. Once again he deplored the provocative exclusion of the black majority from the limited power-sharing proposed for Asians and 'coloureds'. He feared that 'unless something happens quickly, we may be faced with Armageddon'. Before he returned to South Africa he met Dr Chester Crocker, the Assistant Secretary of State for African Affairs, and gave a major news conference. He loves America and the American people, but he has frequently criticised the Reagan administration. On this occasion he reminded the press that though the administration might have won him travel papers, its policy of 'constructive engagement' had not stopped banning orders or detention without trial. He also repeated his criticism of the proposed (but eventually withdrawn) Orderly Movement and Settlement of Black Persons Bill. He said it was the National Party's final solution for blacks, rather as the Nazis had a final solution for Jews.

Every time Tutu wanted to travel during the early 1980s he had to apply to the Department of Internal Affairs for permission, each case being 'considered on its merits' and most of them refused. He was, for instance, unable to accept an invitation to preach at St Paul's Cathedral. Even a formal protest to the South African Ambassador in London by the Dean of St Paul's, together with the Principal, Vice-Principal and Dean of King's College and seventeen of its Fellows, was met with a further refusal. But suddenly, while Tutu was in hospital having minor surgery on his nose, he received permission to attend the Sixth Assembly of the World Council of Churches in Vancouver. The Assembly had already begun, so Tutu took the next plane to Vancouver, where he was met by the Archbishop of Canterbury.

The Sixth Assembly was a huge affair. A thousand delegates from all over the world celebrated both their unity and their diversity as they sang Orthodox *Kyrie Eleisons* and Zimbabwean *Hallelujah's* in the great yellow-and-white striped tent that was the focus of the conference and met in groups, formulating the World Council of Churches' policy for the next seven years. Bishop Tutu arrived on the evening of the Feast of the Transfiguration, during a vigil for peace and justice linked with the anniversary of the dropping of the atomic bomb on Hiroshima and to which the whole of Vancouver had been invited. After a few hours' sleep he addressed the assembly. It was one of those events which no one present will ever forget.

It was five minutes to midnight. For nearly six hours there had been singing and dancing and worship. The procession, holding balloons and pigeons, had arrived at the tent, where they had held a solemn service of dedication and commitment to peace. They knew of the problems the delegate from the South African Council of Churches had been facing; they knew he had suddenly been given permission to come. There was, as Martin Conway, one of the British delegates, found, 'a tremendous sense of expectation and hero worship. You can just imagine the lionising we were all ready for.' It was a delicate moment to handle, in fact there were those who wondered whether the organisers had made the right decision in putting one of the delegates in this critical and exposed position. They need not have feared. 'I really cannot exaggerate how astonishingly right it was,' Martin Conway remembers:

> Every touch in it was simply marvellous. It was brief, people were tired and if he'd gone on even a few minutes longer it would have been too much after that long day. It was absolutely right in terms of this world-wide assembly. It was deeply prayerful. It was completely aware both of South Africa and of the rest of the world. I recall that as a moment of the most deeply winning Christian charm, of which no one else in the world would have been capable.

It was Desmond Tutu at his best. Sensing the mood of his audience and responding to it, humorous (even in that setting he drew a laugh by referring to the 'few local problems' they had had in South Africa), God-centred, fully aware of dramatic effect and, as so often, grateful. He reminded his audience of Zachariah speaking about Yahweh as a wall of fire around Jerusalem: 'It's been almost like a physical sensation, sometimes, when the powers of evil seem to be on the rampage, then we have experienced Yahweh in your prayers, like a wall of fire, keeping away the evil.' He ended by repeating the word 'Amen' until it was so soft that you could have heard an angel pass.

When Tutu first came to the States in the early 1970s he was an unknown black South African Bishop, relieved to be given a break from the claustrophobic atmosphere of his own country, hoping to raise money from wealthy and generous bodies such as the Ford Foundation and the National Council of Churches; if not exactly 'cap-in-hand' (he has too much dignity for that epithet ever to fit), he was certainly petitioner rather than petitioned. He stayed with the Rockwells in their New York apartment, sleeping in the room their young daughter Martha was happy to vacate for him. Hays Rockwell noticed how, after the award of the Harvard honorary doctorate, his friend became increasingly in demand; by the time of the commencement day ceremonies at Columbia University and the symbolic empty chair, he was a well-known figure receiving regular press coverage.

Typically of this small man, whose heart and mind span so vast a spectrum of human characteristics, the effect he has on Americans ranges from awed reverence to accusations of demagoguery. What is the nature of this impact? How much did he change American perceptions of the South African situation?

In America, as everywhere, Bishop Tutu is first and foremost a preacher and a pastor. Not only because he was initially invited as a churchman, carrying the credibility of the institution before he made his personal reputation, but because he is so infused by his priesthood that the man and the role cannot be disentangled. America's glittering, voracious variety is reflected in the three New York churches with which he is most closely connected. There is the suburban parish of St Simon's with its congregation of upper middle-class black professionals; then the wealthy, white parish of St James's in Madison Avenue, whose Rector, Hays Rockwell, had met Tutu in 1976; and thirdly the Church of the Intercession, a huge parish adjacent to a mixed-race community in upper Harlem. Here the congregation is almost entirely black, two-thirds speaking English and a third Spanish;

they also host a Marthoma community – about 300 Tamil-speaking Indians under the protection of the Bishop of New York. Tutu is equally at home in all three parishes.

Much of the impact he has on the macrocosm of the country can be seen in his effect on the microcosm of these parishes. Their congregations responded eagerly to his enthusiastic, rousing sermons, to the eucharistic nature of his ministry, to his insistence that Christians are 'prisoners of hope'. 'He is transparently a vehicle of God's grace,' says Canon Williams of Intercession Church. 'Our people see that and they respond to his authenticity and his integrity.' Joan Campbell, a priest in the Church of the Disciples of Christ, goes even further: 'Bishop Tutu helps me to understand what a saint is, if you believe that a saint is someone that the light shines through, even for a brief period. He illumines the truth for us.' So, too, his pastoral attention is constantly appreciated – from remembering someone's heavy cold four months earlier to sharing a friend's grief at the death of her elderly mother. Hays Rockwell is still touched at the memory of Bishop Tutu telephoning him after he had stood, unsuccessfully, for election as Bishop. 'In some part of you there is disappointment and I am calling to speak to that little part.'

His wider role in America was as a vehicle of information. Though America was waking up to the situation in South Africa and though organisations like Trans-Africa played an important part in this slow process, Tutu's contribution is significant enough to earn the praise of those in sympathy with him and infuriate some of those who are not. In America's complex society a distinction must be made between his effect on the black and the white community.

Of course white Americans had heard of apartheid, but South Africa is a long way from the United States and conditions there seemed very remote; in any case, unlike the English, Americans have no blood ties with South Africa. There was too, a certain resistance to the issue; their own civil rights movement was too recent, guilt over their involvement in slavery too pervasive.

Many Americans tended to equate their own civil rights movement with black South Africans' struggle against apartheid. They did not all realise that in South Africa it is the law itself which is against the majority of its citizens. Tutu, speaking to an American audience, expressed the difference:[10]

Ours is of course not a civil rights movement. You here were claiming what was guaranteed to you under your Constitution. The law was at least theoretically on your side. At home we are struggling for fundamen-

195

tal human rights and we are excluded by the Constitution from any meaningful participation in decision making. The law of the land is against us.

There was also ignorance of a kind bound to affect their reaction to any black coming from South Africa. Most Americans believed, as they were encouraged by Pretoria to believe, that blacks in opposition to white government were terrorists; they knew nothing of Oliver Tambo and only a few had heard of Nelson Mandela. Through Desmond Tutu they saw black opposition in a different light. He was able to make apartheid real, to bring home to them just how black South Africans live, how long they have suffered and what patience they have showed. 'He was just extraordinary,' says Caroline Macomber, a member of St James's congregation. 'None of us had had any contact with this issue. It was a revelation – he was the ideal spokesman. Not everyone believed him at first, but slowly and surely they were converted.' They were not only converted, they were proud, especially the Church leaders. A Methodist minister admits that 'For once a Christian was at the face front, not just sucked in and following'. American Christians had found a spokesman who could address them on one of the most crucial issues of the day.

Tutu has his critics in the United States, though few of them know the Bishop personally and most are unwilling to go on record as to the exact reason for their criticisms. The largest contingent is among fundamentalist Christians, many of whom are suspicious of a priest who seeks to change the social order, fearful that their theological beliefs will be subverted by his radical stand, threatened by his role as a leader both in and outside the Church. Slinging his arrows with the greatest venom was the television evangelist Jerry Falwell, the leader of the so-called Moral Majority; his accusations that the Bishop is 'a phoney' were widely criticised and Falwell himself somewhat discredited by making them. Tutu has a predictable and more formidable critic in the South African Ambassador, Herbert Beukes. Ambassador Beukes claims that the South African government is willing to negotiate and that Tutu knows very well that it is. In the company of other white leaders, he criticises Tutu for not condemning the exiled African National Congress and complains that 'he has caused greater division than healing'.[11] A few feel that he is facilitating a takeover by radical blacks; others complain at his temperance, urging him to endorse the revolution. His oratorical skill and his ability to sway the emotions of his audience opens him to accusations of demagoguery, notably from Elliot Abrams, an Under-Secretary in the State Department, and Patrick Buchanan, President Reagan's chief media adviser, who charged that 'whatever his moral splendour, the Bishop is a political ignoramus'.[12]

Though Tutu's stand on sanctions attracts criticism from white American businessmen, who consider his statements irresponsible and say that the consequences of what he is advocating would be the destruction of the country, few black leaders of any significance disagree with him. Even those not in total agreement with him remain convinced that he has the welfare of his people at heart and that he would not recommend economic measures if he could see any alternative. He is also considered a valuable counterweight to the Sullivan Principles, whose admirable concern for providing better working conditions for black South Africans does little to overthrow the actual structures of apartheid; in fact Leon Sullivan himself (who has since given up on 'Constructive Engagement'and backed the call for United States withdrawal from South Africa) is said to have a high personal regard for him. While extravagant claims have been made for Tutu's contribution to the sanctions debate in America – there have been suggestions, for instance, that he has done more than any other single person to influence the American people, and thus Congress, to favour sanctions – it is hard to overestimate his influence. The decision of the labour unions to back sanctions was more weighty, more crucial, but the eminent black Washington lawyer Vernon Jordan is probably right in saying that though Tutu alone has not swayed the American people, it could not have been done without him.

The black American community does not accept uncritically those who speak for it or for black people overseas. According to Dr William Howard, the Executive Director of the Black Council of the Reformed Church in America:

> The black community sits in constant evaluation and judgment of people like Desmond who emerge. They have seen leaders emerge and be overtaken by events and they constantly review, because for them leaders are not static. They have a sense that the outcome of the South African situation is directly related to their own destiny, so Desmond is one of their champions, because he is advancing a cause of which they are an integral part.

American blacks, better informed about apartheid and identifying with South African blacks in a way impossible for American whites, look back at their own long history of oppression, back to slavery, back to their struggle for civil rights, and they are in solidarity with Tutu. 'We recognise the cadences of oppression, he strikes a responsive chord because we recognise him as one of our own. He has incarnated the South African struggle for us, so that it has become our struggle,' says Canon Williams. Further, the Church is the strongest organised base of black Americans, automatically giving its spokesmen stature. But Tutu's high standing in the black community was earned, not given.

It was earned by the way he personalised the South African situation in a way equalled only by Dr Allan Boesak, through his ability to speak with theological authority and challenge apartheid as morally indefensible. It was earned by his ability to transcend all divisions and reach the broader community. Most of all it was earned by his determination to seek justice through peaceful means and his courage in speaking out in full knowledge of the risks. To Vernon Jordan he is 'A voice of conscience, a voice of reason, a voice of moderation, a voice of daring, fearlessly fighting against the oppressive system of apartheid and willing to put his life on the line to save other lives.'

To his own embarrassment and to the irritation of many of his friends (who see it as irrelevant), Tutu finds himself being likened to the civil rights leader Martin Luther King. Though King was a Baptist, Tutu an Anglican, though King's reserve is in contrast to Tutu's sparkle and wit, with both men being black ministers, both speaking out of a sense of moral outrage, both passionately affirming the humanity of every individual person, both advocates of non-violence – the comparison is inevitable. The minister and politician Jesse Jackson, who feels Desmond Tutu's stature is such that he should be seen in the prophetic tradition with Jesus Christ and Mahatma Gandhi, came back from a visit to South Africa in 1979 claiming to have met 'the Martin Luther King of South Africa ... his manner, his steadfastness, his blend of the infrastructure of the Church on the one hand and his calling beyond the Church on the other' recalling the civil rights leader. The journalist Allistair Sparks pointed out that both men were Christians with a mission, rather than politicians with a strategy, both have a streak of militancy within their moderation, both have a way with words, though Tutu's 'in a style with more of a cutting edge than King's rolling rhetoric'.[13] Dr Howard feels that Tutu has Martin Luther King's ability 'to hew a stone of hope from a mountain of despair'.

It is Tutu's outspoken remarks about apartheid and his calls for support from the international community that bring him into the headlines, but his role as a fund-raiser, though less visible, is a constant undercurrent to his trips. His charisma acts as a magnet to money; it is drawn from every source – individuals, churches, foundations – sometimes even before he asks. Hays Rockwell was one of the first to form a bond between his rich parish and the poor diocese of Lesotho (of which Tutu was then Bishop) when he became

Rector of St James's Church, so twice Tutu was the beneficiary of a portion (about one-third) of the annual spring festival, an event which brings in as much as $60,000 dollars a year. Smaller amounts come in from the most surprising sources. Mary Barbour is a retired and very poor seamstress who used to make costumes for the Dance Theatre of Harlem and attends Intercession Church. Though her hands are stiff and painful with rheumatoid arthritis, she took small sewing jobs, talked to her friends and eventually told her priest, Canon Williams, that she had collected some money. He suggested that she should come to a party being given for the Bishop and present the money to him herself. Timidly, she eventually agreed and, with the words 'So that our people can be free', she handed him an envelope. To everyone's amazement it contained $1,000. Then, feeling around in her pocket and saying 'I don't think that's enough for all the fine work you've done', she handed him a second envelope, containing another $1,000.

Some members of the professional funding community feel that Tutu oversimplifies the sanctions issue and that he is an unsubtle analyst of power structures; they notice too, that his name is too often used to underwrite projects, sometimes even without his knowledge. However, these reservations do not affect their willingness to finance him, though they do influence the causes to which they are prepared to give money. In fund-raising the proof of the pudding is in the eating, and the amount he has raised (in one way or another he was responsible for raising the entire SACC budget, which rose to R4 million in 1984) shows what success he had. William Carmichael of the Ford Foundation found him not only articulate, engaging and endearingly grateful, but a good correspondent, who keeps in touch and knows how to respond to queries. And if his reports are sometimes late, they are by no means the latest.

Desmond Tutu's trips to America resulted in funds for numerous projects to help his people and led to millions of people knowing something about the reality of the conditions under which South Africans were living. With every trip his friends grew more numerous and his fame increased. Soon he was to become a household name.

15

A kind of sacrament

At nine o'clock on October 15th, 1984, a limousine pulled up at the General Theological Seminary on New York's Ninth Avenue and the Norwegian Ambassador to the United Nations emerged carrying a huge bunch of yellow lilies, blue irises and red zinnias. He was shown up to the Tutus' flat, where he told the nervously awaiting couple that Desmond Tutu had been awarded the Nobel Peace Prize.

It did not come as a complete surprise. It was widely known that Tutu had, for the third time, been nominated for the prestigious award and the world's press had been gathering on Ninth Avenue since six o'clock; indeed, the night before the Ambassador had telephoned the Dean, James Fenhagen, to ensure that the Bishop would be free to see him. Dean Fenhagen had had the pleasurable task of giving the Tutus the news, at the same time alerting everyone at the seminary, who had been praying that the Ambassador's call really meant that their visiting lecturer (he was in the middle of a three-month sabbatical, taking a course in Contemporary Ecclesiology) had indeed been chosen. Within minutes of their hopes being confirmed the chapel bells were pealing and the entire staff – students and lecturers, cooks and maintenance men, along with various friends and neighbours – had assembled in the chapel. The campus was deserted and silent as the Dean, the Ambassador and the Tutus walked across to join them. After the thunderous applause which greeted their arrival there was a joyful rendition of 'Now Thank We All Our God', prayers of gratitude and a short address from the emotional and overcome Bishop.

Then the seminary gates were opened, the press poured in and Desmond Tutu became the property of the world. He was interviewed and photographed, he was on television morning, noon and night, he received telephone calls, telegrams and letters by the hundred, he was fêted daily, recognised wherever he went. The seminary had never seen anything like it. Calls came from all over the world as Prime Ministers, Kings and film stars, old friends and colleagues, rang to send their congratulations until the overworked switchboard broke down; a student was assigned to help with the mail but it soon became clear that a full-time secretary was needed. The staff tried to protect the man at the centre of it all, but he seemed tireless as, with shy delight and a humility and gratitude that was universally recognised as genuine, he responded to the endless demands.

His own reaction was to stress the corporate nature of the award. He saw it as a recognition of the patient suffering of his people, a tribute to the significance of the Church's contribution to their struggle, an affirmation of the justness of their case, a 'tremendous political statement', and 'a kind of sacrament, a wonderful symbol'. He knew that the award was a tremendous boost to the morale of the South African blacks. 'Hey, we are winning,' he declared. 'Justice is going to win.' And he knew that his place at this time was with his own people. After two hectic days in New York he and Leah, together with Naomi and Mpho, who were both in the United States at the time, flew to Johannesburg.

At Heathrow, where they stopped to change planes, they were greeted by the Archbishop of Canterbury and a group of distinguished churchmen. Terry Waite caused much amusement by welcoming the passengers disembarking from the British Airways Concorde with, 'The Archbishop greets all passengers, it's part of the deal', until eventually the Tutus, last off the plane, could accept the welcome themselves. There was just time for embraces, laughter and a vivacious news conference – at which he said most of the £160,000 prize money would go into a trust to help young blacks to study, but he and his family might enjoy a little of it themselves – and he was on the next plane.

A security police officer at Jan Smuts Airport had tried to prevent the waiting crowd from singing – singing was not allowed in the hall, he declared – but as soon as the Tutus appeared the jubilant crowd ignored his instructions and exploded into a rapturous welcome. Several hundred people, members of the South African Council of Churches, fellow clergymen, familiar friends and unknown supporters, surged round him, waving banners saying 'Welcome Baba' and 'Apartheid Goodbye', cheering, singing, dancing. Every time the police managed to quieten one section of the crowd another simply took up the refrain; in despair one policeman said to Dan Vaughan, at the time Acting General Secretary of the SACC, that if the crowd did not disperse immediately they would set the dogs on them. At which Dan, secure in the knowledge that the television cameras would let the whole world see if such a thing were done, laughed and said, 'Please feel free!' Order was only imposed when the crowd wished it, as everyone stood still, Desmond and Leah with heads bowed, to sing 'Nkosi Sikele' iAfrika'. It took the travellers almost an hour to make their way out of the airport; then the Tutus were taken to a hotel to have a rest before the celebratory lunch at the South African Council of Churches.

At Khotso House, the heart of Desmond Tutu's work, there was more embracing, laughing and singing as a gyrating, ululating human chain danced through the SACC's corridors and offices. Allan Boesak, who had flown up from Cape Town for the occasion, spoke about the great honour that had been bestowed on the General Secretary and on all the people of South Africa who had struggled so long against racism. The courageous Afrikaner Beyers Naudé, his voice breaking and on the edge of tears, said, 'I pray the day may come when my own people will understand something of the message you bring to black and white.'

There was an expectant hush when it came to Tutu's turn to speak, but typically he started singing a hymn in the Sotho language, 'Let Us All Give Praise To the Lord'. Only after giving thanks did he speak, and then it was to thank again: 'What does one say on an occasion such as this, except feebly, inadequately, thank you.' He went on to say how the award was for those 'whose noses are rubbed in the dust every day', the banned, the exiled, the detained; the mothers trying to support their families, the fathers living in single-sex hostels, the 3½ million people who had been forcibly resettled – 'uprooted and dumped as if they were rubbish', the children who refuse an education designed to make them inferior, for all who seek to change the evil system of apartheid peacefully.[1]

There were many celebrations in those few days. One especially near to his heart was a Thanksgiving service held at St Augustine's Church in Orlando West. A reporter for the *Sowetan* newspaper noted that as the Bishop warned 'Even if our enemies seek to destroy us, God will give us victory in the end', 'the heavens were ripped apart by a loud thunderclap, releasing a shower of rain. Elderly women wept. The heavens themselves were blessing Bishop Tutu as he stood at the altar thanking God for the award he had received.'[2] Then there was a feast, with a beast killed and the Sowetan choir Imilonji ka Ntu singing Xhosa and Sotho songs so movingly that Tutu removed the garland round his neck and placed it on the conductor, George Mxadana.

In choosing to celebrate the award with his own people Tutu had also to face a cruel barrage of criticism. The tragic divide between blacks (with a handful of whites) and the vast majority of white South Africa, was starkly revealed.

Amid all the rejoicing in the black community there was a deafening silence from Pretoria, just as there had been twenty-four years earlier when Chief Albert Luthuli won the prize. Whenever possible the government did not return calls from journalists; if caught on the telephone, for the most part they refused to make any official comment. President P. W. Botha and Foreign Minister 'Pik' Botha remained resolutely silent; the leader of the Conservative Party, Dr Andries Treurnicht, accused the Bishop of having threatened violence if government policy was not changed; the Minister of Internal Affairs, Mr F. W. de Klerk, pointed out that as Bishop Tutu had no passport he would have to apply for a travel document 'in the normal way' to receive the award in Norway. The South African Broadcasting Corporation (showing a curious news sense in view of the world-wide publicity) omitted all reference to the award in its afternoon news radio broadcast, but in the following *News Focus* programme subjected the Bishop to a ten-minute diatribe. It was suggested that the exuberant reaction to the award 'throws suspicion on the event' and that the Peace Prize had 'degenerated into an international political instrument'. Earlier awards to Albert Luthuli and Lech Wałesa were cited in a manner intended to throw doubt on the selection committee and Tutu's recent plea to a London audience, 'Do not abandon us, even – perhaps especially – if our struggle becomes violent', was used to show that his contribution to peace 'is neither remarkable nor consistent'.

The television news did cover the story; in the early evening it was placed sixth and given fifteen seconds, later it rose to fourth place and one minute's coverage. Needless to say there was no mention of the world-wide congratulations, no sight of the jubilant celebrations. The Afrikaans television service, attempting to show that while speaking of peaceful change, the Bishop in fact encouraged and promoted violence, showed footage of Tutu talking with his characteristic gesticulations, but soundless and apparently aggressive under the commentator's voice, until a phrase about a possible bloodbath was heard, out of context (a fate to which he has had to become accustomed) and shorn of the qualifying words with which he always surrounds such a statement.

Though some of the Afrikaans papers condemned the government's childish refusal to offer Tutu formal congratulations (notably *Die Vaderland*, whose editorial asserted that the Bishop was indeed advocating non-violent means for change), there were some vicious comments. *Beeld* referred to Tutu as 'the strangest recipient yet' and accused him of standing for anything but peace; *Die Transvaler* said Alfred Nobel could never have intended the prize to go to a man who, 'under the banner of the church, moves among the world's radicals and revolutionaries, and advocates violence as an option for our country's problems'.[3]

There were unenthusiastic, if predictable, reactions from people like the Reverend Fred Shaw, chairman of the Christian League, and from the conservative group, United Christian Action, who organised a protest and translated it into seven languages for world-wide distribution. Most surprising was an open letter in the *Sunday Times*, written by none other than Alan Paton, the author of *Cry the Beloved Country*, respected critic of apartheid and supporter of white protest. He objected to the award as a sign of world interference and criticised Tutu's views on sanctions, saying his morality was 'confused just as was the morality of the church in the Inquisition, or the morality of Dr Verwoerd in his utopian dreams'. With an extraordinary failure to understand Tutu's love and concern for his fellow blacks, he wrote: 'I do not understand how you can put a man out of work for a high moral principle.'[4] The following week Professor Charles Villa-Vicencio sprang to Tutu's defence, justifying the case for disinvestment as a strategy for reform and politely accusing Paton of being simplistic.[5]

The mixed reactions buffeted Tutu up and down, as he sought to maintain his equilibrium on a see-saw of venom and jubilation, assumed indifference and enthusiastic pride, resentment and delight. As at the General Seminary, the SACC's telex machine and switchboard worked overtime to keep up with the endless messages, even the local post office reeled under the weight of mail. Congratulations came from unexpected quarters – from a senior security policeman, a teenager living in a Pretoria suburb and the Coca-Cola company; also from university Professors, Ambassadors, Church leaders and heads of State; from Chief Gatsha Buthelezi and Oliver Tambo; from Dr Frederik van Zyl Slabbert and Mrs Helen Suzman; from Pope John Paul II, the Archbishop of Cape Town and a pastor of a small Winburg parish; from Lech Wałesa and Coretta Scott King; from Breyten Breytenbach and Nadine Gordimer; from Ronald Reagan, Walter Mondale, Neil Kinnock, Willy Brandt, Bob Hawke and Indira Gandhi. It was heady stuff.

The churlish critics were right in one thing, the Nobel Committee was indeed making a political statement – it made no bones about it. The text stated clearly that

> It is the Committee's wish that the Peace Prize now awarded to Desmond Tutu should be regarded not only as a gesture of support to him and to the South African Council of Churches of which he is leader, but

also to all individuals and groups in South Africa who, with their concern for human dignity, fraternity and democracy, incite the admiration of the world.

Later, when asked whether the choice of Bishop Tutu was meant to effect change in South Africa, the chairman of the committee agreed that it was. The argument against the award – shorn of bitterness and lies – was that political activism should not qualify for a peace prize. But the question went deeper. The Nobel Committee regarded apartheid itself as a threat to peace and argued that Tutu's continual resistance to racial oppression and his determination to oppose it peacefully unquestionably qualified him to receive the award.

Four of Tutu's pronouncements, considered unwise even by some of his supporters, had particularly fuelled white protest in South Africa: his references to economic pressures and disinvestment; his comparison of the apartheid system with the Nazi regime; his statement that the Russians would be welcome as liberators if they came to South Africa (made on the assumption that anything would be better than what the blacks were enduring); and his warning that a bloodbath was awaiting South Africa. He was criticised in particular for making these statements overseas, though, as he continually reminds his critics, he has said nothing abroad that he does not say at home. Whatever the rights and wrongs of his colourful way of speaking, he had succeeded in both stimulating and inspiring initiatives against apartheid and enraging the white community, who found the endorsement of his words and actions in so distinguished and public a way more than they could bear. Beyers Naudé, writing about the award, remarked that 'For the first time it seems as if a concerted action of disinvestment may get under way overseas and this creates a wave of uncertainty in the hearts of many whites who are concerned above all to hold on to their wealth, their privilege, and their power to the very last.'[6]

The significance of the award is immeasurable – the critics would not have been so vocal were it not so. It acknowledged both Tutu's role as a living symbol of the fight against apartheid and his success in communicating, with such passion and conviction, the agony, the humiliation and the aspirations of millions of his oppressed countrymen. Through the media exposure surrounding the award his message reached an even larger audience, focusing attention as never before on the problems of South Africa. The unacceptability of the new South African constitution, the inhumanity of forced removals, the indignity of the pass laws and the deep anger seething beneath the township unrest were brought to the attention of the world. Tutu was confirmed as a man of peace and his credibility increased, especially among his own people. Now he was an international figure, with access to heads of Church and State all over the world. It became harder for the government to harass or arrest him, virtually impossible for them to ignore him. It also placed an even greater responsibility on his small shoulders.

Desmond and Leah returned to America exhausted and content, but hurt by the official silence with which they had been greeted in South Africa. Tutu longed for the whites to 'stop treating me like an ogre'. His reception was, he said, 'as if I had raped a white woman'. But he does not easily harbour grudges and his first concern was to use the numerous opportunities he now had to spread awareness of the South African situation. Though he had hoped to find a little quiet during his three months on sabbatical at the General Seminary, the remainder of his time there was a whirlwind of interviews, addresses and meetings, not to mention his duties at the seminary which still had to be fulfilled. Dean Fenhagen was deeply impressed that through it all, even when in November his mother died and he and Leah had to return to South Africa for another short visit, he never missed a class or a seminary function.

That Tutu should have been in the United States when the award was made was a gift to the American media. His friend Frank Ferrari, the Senior Vice-President of the African–American Institute, remembers how 'He saturated the news. He got more space, more coverage, more copy than anything to do with South Africa ever had in the States. Whether Americans liked him or not, they saw him when they got up on the morning talk shows, they saw him on the evening talk shows and they went to bed with him on the late evening news.' Trans-Africa, a black-led anti-apartheid group that had come into being shortly after the Soweto killings in 1976, sprang into new life with a long series of picketings before the South African Embassy and daily demonstrations at which people put themselves forward for arrest. Jesse Jackson pointed out how the timing of the award, coming as it did just before the second Reagan–Mondale debate in the American election campaign, ensured that apartheid would be on the political agenda, just as the civil rights movement had come to the fore twenty years before, when Martin Luther King won the award. America was on the move, a growing majority of its people determined to make their government act against apartheid.

Two events stand out in this short and hectic period, the first being an invitation to Desmond Tutu to address the United Nations Security Council. Anyone seeking to use this address to prove their accusations against Tutu would have a hard time. It was gentle and reasoned, seeking to inform rather than inflame. He told them of an old lady he had met in one of the townships who looked after her grandchildren and the children of neighbours who were at work. One day her daughter burst in to the kitchen, calling for her. 'A grandson had fallen just inside the door, dead. The police had shot him in the back. He was six years old.' He commended President Botha for his courage in declaring that the future of South Africa could no longer be determined by whites only, but pointed out the inherent racism in the new constitutional proposals – that the first qualification for membership was racial and that this 'instrument in the politics of exclusion' was overwhelmingly rejected not only by the Africans who were denied a place (73 per cent of the population) but by a huge majority of the so-called 'coloureds' and Indians, who recognised it as perpetuating minority rule. He acknowledged the non-aggression treaty with Mozambique, the Nkomati Accord, but asked, 'Why is détente by the South African government only for export? Why is State aggression reserved for the black civilian population?' His statement contained no call for economic pressure, simply saying,[7]

> We ask you, please help us; urge the South African authorities to go to the conference table with the authentic sections of our community . . . Help us, that this freedom comes for all of us in South Africa, black and white, but that it comes with the least possible violence, that it comes peacefully, that it comes soon.

Since 1981, when Frank Ferrari introduced him to Senator Mark Hatfield, Tutu had been meeting Senators and Congressmen and had good contacts with the Congressional Black Caucus and the Africa Sub-Committee in the House and the Senate. In December, every door now open to him, Tutu found himself in the White House, politely disagreeing with the most powerful man in the world. Only three days earlier he had received a standing ovation from members of the House of Representatives Foreign Affairs Sub-Committee on Africa for the passion with which he had castigated the Reagan administration. However, on this occasion (which he referred to as friendly, but leaving them as far apart as ever), he restricted himself to telling the President that the situation was worsening. In support of this claim he quoted a recent report accusing the South African security forces of violence against civilians and asked the administration to act more forcefully to protest against South African policies. The President knew better. At a news conference after the meeting he claimed that those who criticised American companies for doing business in South Africa were ignorant: 'The simple truth is that most black tribal leaders there have openly expressed their support in American business investment there.' Nor did he agree that the situation had worsened: 'It has not. We have made sizeable progress there in expressing our repugnance for apartheid and in persuading the South African government to make changes. And we're going to continue with that policy.'[8] It was not surprising his position had remained unchanged: he would not listen to his own Congress; he was not likely to listen to a black Bishop.

The day after this meeting Desmond Tutu was on his way to Norway to receive the Nobel Peace Prize and enjoy four more days of feasting and celebration with the people of Oslo. Many friends were with him: Tom Manthata, Dan Vaughan, Joe Seremane and the trio of singers were among the dozen representing the SACC; the Rockwells, the Fenhagens and the Ferraris came from America; and the British group included Terry Waite, representing the Archbishop of Canterbury. The central event, the presentation of the award, was accompanied by a cornucopia of happenings. There was a magnificent torchlight parade of thousands of students; the labour unions – the first time they had ever done such a thing – organised a great celebration of folk music with the churches in the Trade Union Hall; there was a formal state dinner with music from the Norway Symphony Orchestra; the SACC contingent addressed meetings all over Norway.

The actual award took place in the aula of the University of Oslo on December 10th, when he was presented with the Gold Medal and Diploma (the cheque was given to him informally). But controversy is never far from Tutu. Half way through the dinner someone went up to the King's table and whispered in his ear – there was a bomb scare. With slow dignity the King left, followed by the orchestra; then everyone else was told to leave. They all clustered together on the steps of the university as Tutu led them in singing 'We Shall Overcome' and the security policy checked the hall. An hour later it was declared safe and the King returned, followed by most of the guests. However, the orchestra had other ideas and was never seen again, so the SACC group, joined by ex-patriate South Africans living in Norway, went on the stage to take their place. The evening continued with South African songs, including 'Nkosi Sikele' iAfrika', instead of Greig.

In a sermon in Oslo cathedral Tutu gave thanks for the demonstrations against apartheid that were mushrooming in the United States; in the traditional Nobel Lecture he was careful to refrain from any provocative utterances. It was, in the words of the *New York Times* reporter, 'more an invitation to believe than an incitement to action'.[9]

A kind of sacrament

His account of the effects of apartheid was restrained, calls for pressure on the South African government giving way to observing that the injustice to be found in his country was a microcosm of conditions found, in different degrees, all over the world. Peace and justice are inseparable, so 'If we want peace . . . let us work for justice. Let us beat our swords into ploughshares.'

It was Desmond Tutu's humility and gratitude that most impressed those who shared this great experience with him. It is an honest humility, that enables him to recognise his strengths as well as his weaknesses and which allowed him to take huge pride in receiving the award, at the same time never forgetting that he was doing so on behalf of his people. His manner was best expressed by Frank Ferrari: 'Desmond is a walking example to me of gratitude. He was so grateful that the gratitude that emanated from Desmond Tutu was all over Oslo.'

16

'Everybody's Bishop'

The award of the Nobel Peace Prize kept Tutu's name in both international and domestic news headlines for weeks; in fact since that day in October he has rarely been far from the limelight. On November 13th, in the middle of the hectic period between the announcement of the award and the celebrations in Oslo, fuel was added to the media flames by his election as Bishop of Johannesburg. It was the first time that a black man had occupied this post, after the archbishopric of Cape Town the most influential position in the Anglican Church in South Africa.

His appointment was surrounded by controversy. Together with several others, including the Reverend Peter Lee, Bishop Michael Nuttall of Natal and Bishop Bruce Evans of Port Elizabeth, he had been nominated in August, when it was announced that the present Bishop of Johannesburg, Timothy Bavin, was to return to England. On October 23rd the electoral assembly of the Johannesburg diocese (214 delegates consisting of all the clergy and one layman from each congregation) tried for two days to reach a decision. Although these proceedings are always held in secret, the *Sowetan* reported that after several rounds of voting Tutu was supported by 89 delegates, Peter Lee by 60, the remaining votes going to other candidates. Whether or not these figures were accurate, there is no doubt that the assembly could not reach the necessary two-thirds majority and that it was deadlocked.

Nobody doubted Tutu's ability to fill the post, few questioned his qualities as a Christian leader, but his supporters had to fight his case against fierce arguments from his opponents. There were suggestions that his international responsibilities would lead to his spending more time outside the diocese than in it, accusations of ambition, hints that he only wanted to be Bishop of Johannesburg as a stepping stone to the top job, Archbishop of Cape Town. Among the whites there was resentment at the thought of appointing a black Bishop in a diocese where, though 60 per cent of the diocese were black, the financial brunt was born by the remaining (and of course infinitely wealthier) 40 per cent; doubts from many who disapproved of Tutu's 'political' statements and, conversely, others who feared that occupying such a high ecclesiastical post would have a muzzling effect on him. Most of all there was concern that his appointment would divide the diocese. The assembly felt that the Church was in an invidious position. 'If it appoints Bishop Tutu as Bishop of Johannesburg, this will be seen as a political appointment,' said one clergyman. 'If it doesn't appoint him, it will be seen as a political disappointment.'[1]

It was largely a racial divide, with conservative, mostly white, priests blocking Tutu, while an equal weight of black priests prevented a white candidate from being chosen. So, amid a general feeling that Tutu would not be elected and that a compromise candidate would be chosen, and with the press reporting that the election had thrust the Church to the brink of its greatest crisis in years, the matter was referred to the synod of Bishops. It was these twenty-three men who, three weeks later, took the courageous decision to promote the controversial Bishop.

The appointment received, predictably, a mixed reaction. The black clergy were jubilant – the Johannesburg diocese was now, with its Suffragan Bishops Simeon Nkoane, based in KwaThema, and Sigisbert Ndwande on the West Rand, entirely run by Africans. Was the era of black Church leadership in the Christian community in sight? The Archdeacon of Johannesburg West, the Reverend David Nkwe, said that Tutu's appointment was the 'greatest thing to happen to the Church of God. In Desmond we have a caring pastor, a reconciler, who is always clear in what he wants to say and the direction he will guide the church into.'[2] The Roman Catholic Church and the Methodists welcomed the appointment and the Reverend T. M. Swart, General Secretary of the Baptist Union, said, 'This new posting can only be for the ultimate good of the Church as there are so few black church leaders in this country.'[3]

Opinions were not entirely divided by race. Many whites supported Tutu, including the outgoing Bishop Bavin, his fellow nominee Peter Lee, the Most Reverend Philip Russell, Archbishop of Cape Town, and Dan Vaughan, who, despite losing him as General Secretary of the South African Council of Churches, said he was 'a true man of God . . . definitely the right man for the position'.[4] The Reverend Dr Francis Cull expressed himself as 'three times delighted'. Surprisingly, some conservative congregations, like Turffontein and Nigel, were happy with the decision, though other parishes reported phone calls from disgruntled parishioners. On the other hand Chief Lennon Sebe, President of the Ciskei, said Tutu did not speak on behalf of blacks and asked 'how this man, preaching blood and starvation, can call himself a Bishop in the Christian Church?'[5]

Once again the white press was less than enthusiastic; once again there were harsh statements from right-wing religious organisations. United Christian Action declared that Tutu's appointment was a potential cause of further division and criticised the Bishops for succumbing to world pressure; Father Arthur Lewis of the Rhodesia Christian Group forecast that in a few years the Bishop would be 'no more than a forgotten demagogue';[6] the Gospel Defence League stated that Tutu gave 'open support for those who are involved in violence, promotion of the anti-biblical liberation theology and blasphemous statements concerning Jesus Christ'.[7] There were also letters to the press from angry Anglicans. One, who signed himself 'Toti Anglican' (it is interesting how seldom Tutu's critics are prepared to be named), asked what he had done for peace in South Africa? 'His only remarks and sentiments have been vicious, appallingly ill chosen, bitter, resentful and anything but peaceful.'[8]

The ability of the electoral assembly to reach a consensus and the referral to the synod of Bishops was distressing and mildly humiliating for Tutu. He was further hurt by the official silence and by the lack of any formal welcome from the City Council – a hurt that was to persist throughout his time in Johannesburg and beyond. However, he had for some time wanted to return to the pastoral ministry and his ebullient nature rose to the occasion as he welcomed the challenge of the new post and rejoiced at the honour of following in the footsteps of previous Bishops of Johannesburg, great Christians such as Geoffrey Clayton, Ambrose Reeves, Lesley Stradling and his immediate predecessor Timothy Bavin.

In his charge, delivered at his enthronement on February 3rd, 1985, he sympathised with those who felt he had been 'foisted on an unwilling diocese' and admitted he would have loved to have been chosen by the elective assembly. He allowed himself to indulge in a little self-justification, citing occasions where he had initiated moves towards reconciliation or congratulated government Ministers when he felt they deserved credit. Keen to allay worries exacerbated by the debate surrounding his election, he affirmed that in order that his new flock could get to know him better he had turned down virtually all invitations that would take him away from the diocese – perhaps he might turn out to be 'not quite such a horrid ogre as they thought'. He also assured them that unless it became abundantly clear that God had other ideas for him, he hoped to end his active ministry in Johannesburg. He went on to gratify his critics by calling for apartheid to be dismantled – remarking on the obscenity of the police van, frequently parked outside the cathedral ready to pick up worshippers without correct passes – and by promising to call for punitive economic sanctions (something he had so far stopped short of doing) if there were not signs that this was being done within eighteen to twenty-four months. He would do this whatever the legal consequences for him might be.

For the most part, however, his charge was a theological dissertation on the nature of the Church and of his intentions for the diocese. He questioned whether the Church was a cosy club, a mystical ivory tower, a spiritual ghetto or a centre of good works. No, it existed primarily for the worship of God. In the Old Testament language he is fond of using, he declared:

> The Church is the fellowship whence adoration, worship and praise ascend to the heavenly throne and in company with the angels and archangels and with the whole host of heaven we sing as did the cherubic choir in Isaiah's vision and as we shall soon be bidden to do in his glorious service: 'Holy, Holy, Holy, Lord God of Hosts, Heaven and earth are full of thy glory.'

In order to enrich the diocesan life of worship and to ensure the centrality of the spiritual, he made various suggestions. He urged the daily celebration of the Eucharist, encouraged penitence and intercession and the offering to God not only of time and talent, but of money. He would like the diocese to tithe its income to help in development programmes at home and abroad and he set a target of an Endowment Fund of R5 million. He expressed his hope that the diocese would become more and more non-racial, to this end promising more non-racial appointments, encouraging people to learn one another's languages and suggesting that it might be important to have white priests in black townships 'to dispel any erroneous notions which people may have picked up in having unfortunate dealings only with the police, the army and a phalanx of bureaucrats who have the unenviable task of applying evil and unChristian policies'. Finally he assured them that he loved them deeply and asked for a chance to show his love. Even if they did not give him that chance he would still love them.

Johannesburg is a large, cumbersome diocese, stretching 400 miles from Christiana to the Swaziland border, taking in a vast swathe of the southern Transvaal. It is the home of nearly a third of South Africa's Anglicans, including many of extreme right-wing political persuasion. Like most South African dioceses, it is rarely without some financial embarrassment, though there was one gratifying problem: so many men were applying for the priesthood that there was never enough money or enough places in the theological colleges to train them.

The eighteen months Desmond Tutu spent as Bishop of Johannesburg were not enough for him to see the wishes he expressed in his charge fulfilled or to make any structural changes, though he made a start. Previous Bishops had tried to make non-racial appointments and he already had two African Suffragan Bishops and a 'coloured' Dean, Mervyn Castle; he asked his old friend Godfrey Pitje to become Deputy Registrar of the diocese and a black woman, Connie Nkosi, to be Deputy Bursar. Soon after he took office he appointed two white Fathers from the Community of the Resurrection to Holy Cross Church in Soweto's Orlando district, but his efforts to make black appointments in white parishes, and vice versa, met with resistance from both sides. He inherited a white secretary, Margaret Davies, and brought Thembi Sekgaphane, who had been one of his secretaries at the SACC, as his personal assistant. Painfully aware that he had not been chosen by the electoral assembly and that there were many who resented his appointment, he made a point of visiting the white parishes as soon as he could, hoping that his image, so distorted by the media, could be balanced against the reality. Most of them soon came to realise he was not the political revolutionary they had been led to expect, though there was always the hard core whose resistance went too deep for change. Some white parents would not let him confirm their children – the thought of his black hands being laid on their white heads was too much for them.

As they have climbed the clerical ladder, the Tutus have had to endure many taunts about personal extravagance. In fact becoming a Bishop did not mean an increase in salary, far from it: Tutu took a considerable drop, though of course there was an allowance for official duties. Previous white Bishops had their own furniture, while what little the Tutus owned was to remain in their Soweto house (they were determined to keep a base in the townships), so the diocese had to cover the expenses involved in furnishing and redecorating the Bishop's official residence at Westcliff. However, the man who should know best, the Diocesan Secretary, considered that Tutu was not extravagant and had not cost the diocese very much. Though the Tutus like to live comfortably and perhaps feel a certain duty towards the black community to prove that blacks can succeed and be seen to succeed, and while they have a certain casualness in their attitude to money, they give as freely as they receive and many who know them well will vouch for their generosity in matters great and small. After trips overseas Tutu would, for instance, give small presents to all fifteen members of the diocesan office; once they were all given orchids on St Valentine's day. He would constantly give money to people in need, or send flowers to celebrate a special occasion. As far as Africans are concerned money is a commodity to be used; it should be circulated, not hoarded.

The way he dealt with the diocesan financial problems is typical of this abundance of nature. There were some white parishes who withdrew their diocesan quota in protest at his appointment and this, in addition to the ongoing financial hardship of the diocese, led to fears of bankruptcy. In fact it was a small, if vociferous, minority who acted in this way and Tutu actually left the Johannesburg diocese considerably better off than he found it, not by financial caution – in fact staff accustomed to thrifty Bishops were at first alarmed by his easy spending – but because he himself brought in so much money from his overseas travels. Questions were continually being asked about who paid his travelling expenses, questions which were easily answered – it was those who invited him who bore the cost. On these trips he would raise huge sums of money (R50,000 resulted from one visit to California) for black education, clergy training, or his own discretionary fund. He was thus able to insist, for instance, that a plan to reduce clergy stipends (they only got R532 a month in any case) was not implemented – he gave money from his discretionary fund to make up the difference. During his episcopate money moved freely; he both spent more and brought more into the diocese.

He is an exceptional administrator, able to place his trust in those to whom he has delegated responsibility. He also has an astonishing memory for detail. His successor Bishop Buchanan, who says Tutu was one of the most remarkable Bishops he has ever come across, once acted as his Vicar-General while he was abroad and remembers his briefing:

> For an hour and a half, without one note, he gave me a run down on every parish and every priest in the diocese. He knew their names, where they were, what their good points and their bad points were; he knew most of their family situations, though probably not all the children. He knew the wives and their problems, he knew the parishes themselves, very frequently he was also able to name the church wardens.

At the time there were, incidentally, 102 parishes.

It was not only an astonishing memory that made this feat possible, it is a reflection of his concern as 'pastor of pastors'. His informal style of leadership, continually accompanied by laughter, gave the clergy a sense of being loved and cared for in a deeply personal way. Though a few people complained that he was not sufficiently accessible, they were a minority. Father Sipho Masemola felt Tutu had more time for his priests than any other Bishop he had worked under and was impressed that he never had to wait more than a week for an interview. (Tutu tried to keep every Wednesday as an open day for clergy.) And if calls on his time prevented him from seeing them personally, he had what Bishop Bavin calls 'a great ministry on the telephone'. Stories abound of his loving attention to people, even to those who did not count themselves among his admirers. Like one sick priest, openly against his new Bishop, who was astonished that Tutu rang him every day for the two weeks he was in hospital. A less attractive side of Tutu's personality was revealed by another priest, who recalled an occasion when the Bishop was visiting him in hospital and was not recognised by the nurses. Tutu was so affronted that he complained audibly.

One very public example of his attitude to his priests was when Mervyn Castle, the Dean, was arrested on a charge of public indecency. Tutu wrote in *The Watchman* (the Diocesan newspaper) pleading that the Dean should be surrounded by love and care while he was passing through this traumatic time. He pointed out that the prosecutor had refused to accept the Dean's admission-of-guilt fine and noted how the newspapers had been tipped off three days before the court appearance, clearly indicating that someone was keen to extract the maximum benefit from the adverse publicity attracted by the case to the Anglican Church. He assured his readers that he would not think any less highly of the Dean, whatever the outcome of the case: 'The Dean is a greatly loved Pastor who has endeared himself to many by his quiet strength and compassionate caring ... we in the Church must demonstrate that we belong to the forgiving Koinonia of the forgiven and the reconciling fellowship of the reconciled.'[9]

It is part of a Bishop's job to give direction and focus to the people in his charge. Duncan Buchanan, whom Tutu had appointed Dean after Mervyn Castle's resignation, found Bishop Tutu was giving the diocese

> an air of freshness which stood the diocese on its head. He cut through a lot of encrustation, going right to the heart of things. Going into committees you discovered that people were thinking differently as a result of his being involved. That their eyes had been opened, their perceptions and vision were bigger than they were before.

While giving a special boost to the morale of the black people, he somehow managed to belong to everybody. When he visited a parish, every denomination claimed him as its own, recognising him as a Christian, rather than simply an Anglican, leader. It was that quality which led Bishop Jim Thompson, the Bishop of Stepney, to dub him 'Everybody's Bishop'.

Tutu tried to live up to his promise to cut down on overseas travel; indeed he was, by his own peripatetic standards, restrained. There were official visits in his ecclesiastical role which attracted no criticism. He attended the planning session for the 1988 Lambeth Conference in England and he accepted invitations from the Welsh Council of Churches, the World Council of Churches, the Churches of China and Japan and the Church of the West Indies. Although he did succumb to pressure from the United States, the American trips during his time as Bishop of Johannesburg only took him out of the country for a total of four weeks. His presence is so visible that he somehow gives the impression of travelling even more than he does.

However, of all his meetings with national and international figures, the one which was to have the most significant repercussions, which indeed was regarded by Tutu as a watershed, took place in his own country in January 1985, just a month before he was enthroned as Bishop of Johannesburg. It was the visit of Senator Edward Kennedy.

The Kennedy family had been concerned with South Africa for a long time. They had known a number of young, mostly white, anti-apartheid activists associated with the National Union of South African Students and Robert Kennedy had visited the country in 1966. Throughout his twenty-five years in the Senate, Edward Kennedy has focused on abuses of human rights wherever they have occurred and in October 1984, distressed that American policy towards South Africa had played so little part in the presidential campaign, he tried to organise a forum to draw attention to the subject. An important debate on nuclear arms control forced the cancellation of this meeting, but it so happened that both Tutu and Dr Allan Boesak, the President of the World Alliance of Reformed Churches, were in the United States at the time and on October 4th a lunch was organised with the two South Africans, Senator Kennedy, Frank Ferrari and Gregory Craig, Senator Kennedy's National Security Advisor.

Both Tutu and Boesak spoke powerfully about the suffering of the blacks and about how the level of deprivation was increasing both politically and economically. At the end of the lunch, when Senator Kennedy asked what he could do to help, they asked him to come to South Africa. He had never been there before, he wanted to be able to speak in the Senate from experience and he was keen to see South Africa through the eyes of black people, to witness for himself the conditions under which black South Africans lived rather than to rely on Pretoria's promises of reform. He accepted.

The invitation was, by pure chance, well timed. Only days later the Nobel Peace Prize was announced and the whole of America learned something of what Senator Kennedy had been told. Soon after Gregory Craig went to the South African Embassy to file applications for visas the first demonstration outside the Embassy, organised by Randall Robinson and the Free South Africa Movement, began. So the Kennedy trip was conceived in the early days of the wave of American revulsion to apartheid.

It was an invitation extended and accepted in goodwill. However, a section of black South Africans, including members of the Azanian People's Organisation, thought otherwise. When Senator Kennedy and his entourage arrived at Jan Smuts Airport on January 5th, they were welcomed by Bishop Tutu, Dr Allan Boesak and the Reverend Beyers Naudé, but jeered by some forty AZAPO demonstrators. On his way to Brandfort to see Winnie Mandela, Kennedy passed graffiti bearing the words 'Kennedy go home – and take Tutu with you'. As he flew to Durban to see Archbishop Hurley, there were demonstrators from AZAPO at the airport. Nevertheless, though there were conflicting reports about Kennedy's handling of the delicate situations with which he was faced, much of the visit was, at least in the opinion of his aides, a spectacular success. It included a candle-lit reception from 500 chanting Soweto residents, where he defied the Group Areas Act by spending the night with the Tutus, challenging speeches in Cape Town and Johannesburg and a visit to a resettlement camp in the Orange Free State. He received a rousing welcome at Crossroads and courageously reprimanded Chief Buthelezi for his attacks on Tutu and Boesak. Most telling of all was a letter from Winnie Mandela assuring him of the good wishes of 30 million of her people:[10]

> The memory of your visit to Brandfort, your profound concern about the tragic suffering inflicted upon the oppressed people of my country and your enduring campaign against the crime of apartheid *inter alia* has given me strength to carry on when the cross was at times too heavy for my tired shoulders ... We attribute the escalation of the campaign from the American public against apartheid directly to your visit.

This letter must have afforded the Senator much comfort, for his visit ended in chaos, when, on his last day, he was due to make a major speech at Regina Mundi Cathedral in Soweto. It was to have been the climax of his visit and up to 4,000 people were assembled to hear him. However, among the crowds were about 100 AZAPO supporters, bearing placards saying 'SOCIALIST AZAPO VS CAPITALIST KENNEDY' and 'AWAY WITH CIA, KENNEDY, OPPRESSION AND CAPITALISM'. They marched towards the altar shouting, 'No more Kennedy', creating such disturbance that a distressed Bishop Tutu had to intervene. He told the crowds that Senator Kennedy was his guest, that he had invited him to the country not as a liberator, but to help expose the evil system of apartheid. He warned them too, that 'the system knows how to turn us against ourselves'. (Senator Kennedy's aides are in no doubt that the government helped AZAPO create division by telling them where Kennedy was going to be, even helping to transport them to places on his schedule.) When Tutu asked the audience if they wanted Senator Kennedy to address the meeting, there was a great cry of 'Yes' from well over 3,000 people, challenged by 'No' from the vociferous minority of AZAPO supporters. It was clear that the overwhelming majority wished to hear what the Senator had to say, but the situation was tense and armed riot police and troops were only a few hundred yards away. The risk of a serious confrontation was great and eventually, on Tutu's recommendation, the Kennedy aides decided that the visit must be cancelled. The text of his prepared speech was issued and Senator Kennedy's motorcade, waiting some way from the cathedral while a decision was made, turned round and took him to the airport.

Tutu was humiliated and angry. He had not foreseen the political implications of the invitation and his hopes of bringing people together had ended in disaster. From its beginning he had supported AZAPO, publicly registering a protest when two AZAPO men were detained within days of its foundation. In 1983 he had been invited to the launch of the National Forum, a heterogeneous umbrella group bringing together AZAPO, ex-PAC members and other Black Consciousness groups, none of whom subscribed to the Freedom Charter. Two months later, despite its disagreements with AZAPO, he had become a patron of the non racial United Democratic Front (UDF). He had tried to avoid identifying too much with any political ideology, to hold on to a vision of peace and justice above man-made divisions. This incident underlined the differences he had sought to reconcile; there was a complete breakdown of communication between Tutu and AZAPO.

AZAPO had taken its stand against Kennedy before it knew of Tutu and Dr Boesak's involvement. Its members opposed, to the depths of their being, America's role in Cuba, Vietnam, Nicaragua and Granada and, however unjustly, regarded the Senator, who at the time was standing for President, as a symbol of United States imperialism. Further, they were convinced that he was using South Africa's suffering to help his election chances. Even though he represented the Democrats, to them he was part of the system; they felt it was impossible that a Kennedy could be welcomed by black people.

Though AZAPO says it was prepared to meet the Senator privately, it was unable to accept the high profile he was being given. The fact that it had not been consulted over his invitation to South Africa compounded the situation. South African blacks are among the most democratic people in the world, acutely aware of whether or not anyone is mandated to speak on their behalf. That Tutu should have invited Kennedy to visit South Africa without reference to them was, in the eyes of many adherents to Black Consciousness, intolerable. Tutu could not be a voice in isolation; he only carried weight to the extent that he was supported by the community. AZAPO considered that by acting in this unilateral fashion he was placing himself above the people.

The UDF had mixed feelings. It understood Tutu's reasons for wishing Senator Kennedy to visit the country and was prepared to listen to him; in fact, many of its members felt the Bishop's role in the affair was not inconsistent with his spiritual calling. Though some were critical of Tutu for failing to consult them, any resentment they felt was overridden by their personal loyalty to him.

AZAPO's stand against Tutu proved to be ill-advised tactically; it had underestimated the support he had amongst the mass of the people. Though efforts at reconciliation were made, relations between AZAPO and Tutu have never quite recovered and from that time Tutu began to distance himself from the Black Consciousness movement and identify more with the UDF.

Desmond Tutu has never sought a position of leadership in the secular world, insisting that he is only 'a leader by default', due to the actions taken by the government against black leaders like Nelson Mandela. Still less does he seek a political role. Nevertheless, in August 1985 a poll declared that 24 per cent of the black population considered him the best potential President of South Africa and he is never out of the political limelight, his every word and deed acquiring political overtones.

His short time as Bishop of Johannesburg was crammed with examples of his defiance and courage. Often these took place in a firmly ecclesiastical context, as in April 1985, a month after the police massacre of nineteen blacks in Uitenhage had shocked South Africa and the world, when he defended the Rector of Sharpeville, the Reverend Geoff Moselane. This shining Anglican priest had been detained for six months, a period which, in Tutu's estimation, was ample time for the authorities to have preferred charges against him. He decided to demonstrate his abhorrence of detention without trial and his support of this particular priest in a public act of witness. In full episcopal regalia and with his two Suffragan Bishops, Simeon Nkoane and Sigisbert Ndwande, he led a march of about forty clergymen from the Anglican Cathedral in Johannesburg to the local police headquarters at John Vorster Square. They presented a petition demanding Moselane's release, then held a short prayer service. Afterwards they were told by the head of the security police, Colonel Hennie Muller, and the Acting Divisional Commissioner, Brigadier Dries van den Heever, that the case was now with the Attorney-General and that the matter was no longer in police hands.

Though the names and addresses of everyone present, including journalists, were taken, there were no arrests. This came as a surprise to several of the clergy, who had feared the protest would be seen as a provocative act. Indeed the Diocesan Secretary was so sure it would lead to trouble that he had withdrawn R10,000 as bail for arrested clergy. On this occasion Tutu showed respect and tact in his dealings with the other clergy, many of whom had tried to persuade him not to go. He compromised by leaving the decision to individual judgment; he made it clear that he was determined to march, even if he had to march alone, but that those who chose not to accompany him would not be judged.

By 1985 there was virtually a state of war between the police and the people. In the first nine months of the year an estimated total of 700 were killed in township unrest; there were mysterious and unexplained deaths in detention. Children were now in the front line, venting their feelings by boycotting school, with the slogan 'Liberation now, education later'. In their frustration and anger the blacks, provoked by a mysterious force thought to be instigated by the government, began to turn on one another, inflicting on those they regarded as collaborators with the government the horrific 'necklace' killings (a rubber tyre placed round the neck of the victim, drenched with petrol and set on fire). One of the clergy's constant and tragic duties was to conduct the funerals of those who had died, funerals which became occasions not only of mourning, but of political demonstration. They also became occasions where Tutu made some of his most outspoken and publicised statements and where his courage took the form of risking his life.

One such was in Duduza, a township on Johannesburg's East Rand. Duduza is scarred by ruined houses – the homes of black policemen and community councillors burned by blacks who regard them as collaborators, the homes of activists allegedly burnt by the police. As in many townships, corrugated iron shacks are attached to houses to provide scant accommodation for homeless friends and relatives. Children urinate on the dirt-track roads, there is no sewage disposal, no running water (just stand pipes every ten houses or so), no recreational facilities save for one barren sports field, few shops, no gardens. Nothing alive, nothing beautiful or even pleasant to look at except its 40,000 inhabitants, who somehow manage to emerge fresh and clean from their squalid dwellings. Duduza had become a centre of dissent and in that week of July 1985 ten blacks had been shot dead by police.

During the funeral of four young men who had died in an explosion, Tutu had urged the mourners to forgo violence and to change apartheid by peaceful means. The young men were barely in their graves when the crowd turned on a black onlooker, accusing him of being a police spy. Crying 'Let the dog die', enraged youths attacked the man, overturned his car and set it alight 'to provide his funeral pyre'. Tutu tried arguing with them. 'Why don't we use methods of which we will be proud when our liberation is attained? This undermines the struggle.' 'No, it encourages the struggle,' was the unheeding reply. Words were no use. Bishop Simeon Nkoane and Bishop Kenneth Oram, a senior white Anglican cleric, somehow created a diversion and Tutu dragged the terrified, bleeding man into a car.

The wish for peaceful reconciliation had met, head-on, the passionate anger and frustration of the blacks, one of whom asked Tutu, 'Why don't you allow us to deal with these dogs in the same fashion that they treat us?' Tutu argued that no one should kill another person, whatever the provocation, and asked the questioner if he accepted the Bishops present as their leaders. He received grudging assent and managed to persuade the crowd to disperse quietly.

Only ten days later Duduza was the scene of one of South Africa's most horrific killings. Maki Shosana, a young woman living with her mother and five-year-old son, was suspected of collaborating with the police. At another funeral, in full view of the television cameras, a screaming crowd turned on her shouting, 'Informer'. David Beresford was there.[11]

> They chased her across the veld, they beat her, they stoned her, they tore her clothes off, they set her on fire, they put a huge rock on her so that she couldn't get up and they rammed a broken bottle into her vagina. Her mother was crying uncontrollably. The two black clergymen with me couldn't take any more and one of them lumbered to his feet and said 'Let us pray'. And so we stood there with heads bowed, around a plain kitchen table in the township of Duduza in the middle of the Transvaal. And her mother wept on and there were tears in all our eyes: tears for Maki, tears for the beloved country.

222

A few days later Tutu was conducting yet another funeral, attended by the Bishop of Lichfield, the Right Reverend Keith Sutton, who had been sent by the Archbishop of Canterbury to represent the Anglican Church and support both Bishop Tutu and Bishop Nkoane, who had been receiving death threats and whose house had twice been attacked. Addressing a crowd of 30,000 people in the sports stadium of KwaThema township, Tutu denounced violence and brutality, whether it came from the government or the black people; he implored the mourners to avoid bloodshed. His small purple figure stood high above his audience, arms and voice striving to express his feelings about the death of Maki Shosana:[12]

> If you do that kind of thing again I will find it difficult to speak for the cause of liberation. If the violence continues, I will pack my bags, collect my family and leave this beautiful country that I love so passionately . . . I say to you that I condemn in the strongest possible terms what happened in Duduza. Our cause is just and noble. That is why it will prevail and bring victory to us. You cannot use methods to attain the goal of liberation that our enemy will use against us.

Though a few taunted him for his moderation, most of the crowd supported him. The meeting ended with Tutu leading them in singing 'We dedicate ourselves to the freedom struggle, for all of us black and white. We shall be free.'

There may have been a certain arrogance in his assumption that his threat of leaving the country could influence the passionate rage with which black anger was turning against itself, indeed within hours he had qualified his statement, admitting that he spoke under extreme emotional pressure and hoping that he would not be put to the test. But no one there doubted his courage in standing so firmly against violence, nor the risks he was running in alienating both the government – by his insistence that theirs was the primary violence – and the militant blacks, too oppressed for too long, no longer able to hear the message of peace.

On July 20th, 1985 – just ten days after Tutu had rescued the police informer in Duduza and on the same day that Maki Shosana was so brutally murdered – the government declared a state of emergency in thirty-six magisterial districts. It was a serious move, the first time such a thing had been done since 1960, when a state of emergency was declared in the wake of the Sharpeville massacre. The authorities were empowered to detain any person, without warrant and indefinitely; they could use force, 'including force resulting in death', if anyone refused to heed instructions; they could use these powers in the knowledge that, by means of an indemnity clause, they had complete freedom, while the victims had no legal redress – indeed they could only consult a lawyer with ministerial permission. Further, restrictions on press coverage enabled the police and the army to operate as they wished, uninhibited by the presence of reporters or camera crews. (Though the state of emergency was suspended after nine months, its reimposition on June 12th, 1986, brought even tighter controls.)

Tutu, along with many others, was surprised that the government felt it necessary to add to its already draconian powers; he warned that any calm to which it might lead would only be a surface calm and that there could be 'an almighty explosion'. Within days restrictions were imposed on funerals of 'unrest victims' in areas where the state of emergency was in force. Only one person could be buried at a time, only ordained ministers of religion could speak and they could not 'defend, attack, criticise, propagate or discuss any form of government, any principle or policy of government'.[13] Nor could they comment on the state of emergency or the actions of the security forces. Mourners could not travel on foot, use loudspeakers or display banners and their route would be designated by the local police commander.

All eyes were on Tutu. How would he react to this latest crackdown? There should not have been much doubt. During a funeral service at Tumahole (which was not one of the thirty-six districts under the state of emergency), he called on the Minister of Law and Order to reconsider these regulations and announced that he would defy them, saying, 'I will not be told by any secular authorities what gospel I must preach.' (He was to take a similar line the following June, when he defied the ban on meetings to commemorate the Soweto killings by instructing the clergy to organise services and himself led prayers for justice and peace.)

He seldom missed an opportunity to let the outside world know what was happening in South Africa. When he was in London in October 1985 to discuss the forthcoming Lambeth Conference, he had a fruitless, if civilised, meeting with the intransigent Margaret Thatcher; he was one of the key people to talk to the Eminent Persons Group, though his refusal to see Geoffrey Howe was yet another blow to the British Foreign Secretary's ill-fated mission to South Africa; he was among those who met the British trades union delegation when it visited South Africa. In a talk to the International Press Institute in Vienna he reminded his audience that the South African media were constantly serving sectional interests and that the South African Broadcasting Corporation was 'really an extension of the Nationalist Party'. They had an 'Esau complex', he said; they had 'sold their birthright for a mess of potage'. He frequently castigated President

Reagan, Margaret Thatcher and Chancellor Helmut Kohl for doing so little to bring about reform in South Africa.

He even entered the arena of financial affairs. On October 22nd, 1985, he, the Reverend Beyers Naudé and Allan Boesak wrote to South Africa's creditor banks, asking them to make the rescheduling of South Africa's debt 'conditional on the resignation of the present regime and its replacement by an interim government responsive to the needs of all South Africa's people'. News that South Africa had reached agreement with its major foreign creditors led to an angry Desmond Tutu appearing on ITV's Channel 4, saying that South African blacks would see this as 'whites clubbing together against them' and that the West was 'good at rhetoric but develops cold feet when it comes to translating it into action'.

His outspoken defiance overseas reached a climax when he went to the United States for two weeks in January 1986 under the auspices of the Adelphia Foundation and Mrs Lia Belli. Even by his standards it was a hectic trip. He made as many as four or five speeches a day, covering twelve cities including New York, Washington, Baltimore, Detroit and Atlanta, where he received the Martin Luther King Peace Prize. Its organisation left much to be desired. He was constantly late – on one occasion the Mayor of Philadelphia had to wait two hours for him to arrive – and many criticised his judgment in allowing himself to be whisked across the country in sleek black limousines. However, from his point of view the trip was a resounding success. His purpose was to thank the Americans for their support, to raise funds and, in the light of the press clampdown, to keep the world informed of the state of affairs in South Africa. Apart from the fact that he also received four more honorary degrees, three gold medallions and the freedom of the city of Baltimore, he was ecstatically received by capacity crowds, eminent people queued up to meet him and he was entertained at endless prayer breakfasts, civic functions, small private meetings and huge formal banquets. His fund-raising for political prisoners, refugees and the Anglican Church was rewarded by donations and pledges amounting to R1 million. But predictably his statements about living under an apartheid society incurred the wrath of white South Africa.

The South African press covered these remarks widely, selectively and largely out of context. They reported that Tutu had warned that black servants could poison their employers' coffee, that the blacks might start picking up stones and fighting, that white school buses might be attacked; that he had predicted that the government would use nuclear weapons against the blacks in a 'scorched earth' policy; that he had again promised to call for sanctions unless reforms were started by the end of March; that he had said that under certain circumstances violence could be justified and that he had, most provocatively of all, called on Western governments to support the banned African National Congress.

On his return home Tutu was met by a chaotic reception of journalists, plainclothed and uniformed police and placards reading 'Tutu – no jobs, no food' and 'Tutu – down with the ANC'. He was ashamed of nothing and made no denials, but such had been the attacks on him in his absence that he called a press conference in which he stood by everything he had said. Unrepentant, he wished the 'lickspittle sycophants' of the South African press and television would prepare whites for the inevitable, as the country was not going to be run by a minority for ever. He repeated his determination to call for sanctions if there was no significant change before the end of March and reaffirmed his support for the ANC and his wish that Western leaders would side with them. He pointed out that his remarks on this matter had been directed to the US Vice-President, George Bush, who was on the platform at the time, and that he was questioning a foreign policy that could back the Contra guerrillas against the Sandinistas in Nicaragua, yet refuse to support the ANC against the South African government. Why was it justifiable to back one guerrilla movement seeking to overthrow a government by force and not another? He reminded the press that the Church teaches that there can be times when it is justifiable to overthrow an unjust government by violence, though that situation had not yet been reached. He challenged the government to show that he had been lying when he said that fourteen-year-olds had been in detention for five months, that children 'die by deliberate government policy', when they were dumped in places where the government knew there was no food.

While many doubted the wisdom of his remarks about 'soft targets', such as the possibility of black servants poisoning their employers' coffee, in fact such ideas had been in circulation in South Africa for years. In mentioning such things he was trying to avert them, not commend them; he was issuing warnings, not threats. As he said at his news conference, 'You tell people, "Look at that pile of cups on the edge, it is going to fall". You are warning them and the pile of cups falls and you are blamed for letting it fall.'

The following Sunday many white Anglicans stayed away from church in protest, threatening to withdraw their financial support. The Dean of Cape Town, the Reverend E. L. King, admitted that the Church was involved in 'the biggest and broadest controversy that's faced us to date', but he rejoiced in prophetic voices like

Desmond Tutu's making challenging and uncomfortable statements, adding with typical courage: 'The more people take their money out, the better the church – the kind of religion they're paying for is going off the market.'[14] The Bishop found support, too, in the liberal wing of the Progressive Federal Party, though the party was split and he was denounced by some Transvaal MPs. A Cabinet Minister declared his American speeches 'unworthy of a man of the cloth' and the right-wing conservatives went further, arguing that he should be prosecuted under the Internal Security Act for supporting a banned organisation. However, the government was apparently delighted that he was antagonising white liberals. Certainly it took no action against him, even when, on April 2nd, 1986, in a symbolic action courting arrest, he fulfilled his promise and called for immediate punitive sanctions against South Africa.

At the national level Bishop Tutu attempted, frequently and in vain, to relate to the State President, P. W. Botha. His reaction to the state of emergency was not only to condemn it and to defy its unreasonable restrictions, but to try to bring about some sort of reconciliation, so he offered himself as a broker to start negotiations with the President. The two men had not met since the unsatisfactory interview in 1980, just before the Eloff Commission was appointed. Nevertheless, Tutu made it clear that he would not be prejudiced by past events, though the talks must address the subject of the dismantling of apartheid. On July 29th, with the state of emergency just over a week old, with eighteen blacks killed and over 1,000 people arrested, he sent a telegram to Mr Botha asking for an urgent meeting to discuss the situation. The President's private secretary said he would arrange a meeting at the President's earliest possible convenience; but, in what the London *Times* called 'a calculated snub', Tutu received a telephone call informing him that President Botha refused to see him: he would not meet anyone who did not denounce violence (which Bishop Tutu had repeatedly done) and renounce civil disobedience (which he had not). The Bishop was told that President Botha had agreed to see Archbishop Russell and a small delegation on August 19th, but that his schedule made a separate meeting with Bishop Tutu quite impossible.

It is hard to justify this rebuff. The President found time that week to fit in a delegation of businessmen – his schedule seemed to be flexible when he wished it to be. A mediator was urgently needed and many people, including distinguished academics like Professor Adam Small, regarded the Bishop as the best person to fill the role. Tutu had risked his credibility among the blacks in requesting an interview;

Mr Botha had nothing to lose by extending a reconciling hand.

The refusal left Tutu with a difficult decision to make: should he join the other churchmen on August 19th? The Archbishop had said he would be welcome, a spokesman from the President's office had said it was possible he could be included. But to join this separate delegation might jeopardise the chances of the one-to-one meeting that Tutu felt would be more valuable; in any case he was not prepared to renounce civil disobedience. At the last minute, exposing himself to accusations of pique, he decided to pull out. This earned him a fresh stream of criticism, but in the event he had not missed much. The delegation had made four demands in a written memorandum. They asked that the government should announce its intention to dismantle apartheid, that a National Convention should be called, that the black people should have the right to select their own leaders for negotiation and that the state of emergency should be lifted. The nine clerics told a press conference that the President had addressed none of these issues.

Eventually, nearly a year later, Tutu and President Botha did meet. They had talks on June 13th, just after the reimposition of the state of emergency and again in July. Both meetings hurt Tutu politically and neither achieved very much. The first he described as 'frank and cordial' and of the second, which lasted for two hours, all the Bishop could say was 'We agreed that we are both Christians'.

Desmond Tutu is thought by some people to give too much time and attention to his national and international contacts at the expense of involvement at grassroots level. This accusation is not borne out by the facts. Though high office removed him, to some extent, from day-to-day contact with his fellow blacks, by keeping his house in Soweto he remained close to the feelings of the community. He sympathised with the rent boycott, part protest against apartheid in general, part a refusal to confer financial authority on the community councils imposed on the townships by the Botha government; he even showed his support by himself withholding his rent. He played an active, if controversial, part in the school boycott, taking a significant lead in the Soweto Parents Crisis Committee. He was also one of the most articulate voices in the Conference on Education held at the University of the Witwatersrand, when black educationalists agreed that if certain conditions were not met they would support the children boycotting school. He tried to reconcile warring factions at Crossroads – indeed he was among those who helped to bring about a ceasefire. Most conspicuously, he tried to diffuse an explosive situation in Alexandra.

Alexandra is one of the oldest townships on the Witwatersrand, its grimy square mile of shacks and potholed streets, home to 100,000 blacks, provocatively close to the fresh white municipality of Sandton. Mark Mathabane, who was born there in 1960, remembers living in constant fear, both of the police and of deportation to the tribal reserves: 'It meant hate, bitterness, hunger, pain, terror, violence, fear, dashed hopes and dreams . . . In the ghettos black children fight for survival from the moment they are born. They take to hating and fearing the police, soldiers and authorities as a baby takes to its mother's breast.'[15]

In February 1986 feelings were running high and the township was seeing its worst rioting in months. Shops were petrol-bombed, the streets were scarred with barricades and burnt-out cars, scores of people had been injured and twenty-two killed, sixteen of them by the police (other reports put the figure much higher). On February 18th, during an executive meeting of the SACC at which Tutu was present, news came that a large crowd had assembled in the football stadium. A group of senior churchmen, including the Reverend Beyers Naudé and Dr Boesak, went to Alexandra and tried to pass through the road blocks to speak to the people. At first they were refused entry, but Tutu, after arguing for more than an hour with heavily armed soldiers (an encounter filmed by courageous television crews, who were detained for breaking the new restrictions forbidding cameras or notebooks to be carried 'within telephone range' of the township), was eventually allowed through to the stadium.

He managed to diffuse the tension and bring some calm to the enraged residents. He told them not to discredit their cause by violent behaviour and promised that God saw what was happening to them. 'God will free you from oppression. There is no way in which you can be for ever oppressed. God says you are going to be free.' He undertook to put three of their demands to the local police chief: that the security forces should be withdrawn, that township residents should be released from detention and that the state of emergency should be lifted. The crowd dispersed and Tutu went to see the local Brigadier.

He did more. He and a small delegation of churchmen representing several denominations travelled to Cape Town to see P. W. Botha. Though once again he was snubbed by the State President, he was given an interview with Adriaan Vlok, the Deputy Minister of Law, Order and Defence. Tutu refused to tell the press what had passed between them. First he had to report back to Alexandra.

The expectant crowd gathered, over 40,000 of them; the public-address system was fixed. In a forty-minute address in Xhosa he told the residents that the government had granted none of their requests, only promised to 'look into them'. The crowd was sullen and angry, some of the younger people taunting and booing, others arguing with him and refusing to let him leave. He pleaded with them to be patient, to stop confronting the police. 'A man does not go up to a lion and say "Hullo lion" and jump into its mouth. We have to work at other ways of catching the lion.' But he could not communicate to the angry and disappointed crowd. They shouted that they were not going to put up with police harassment any longer and that they would not be prevented from responding in their own way. Eventually, sadly with head bowed, he managed to leave, admitting to Peter Storey, who was with him, 'They are not going to listen to me much longer.'

17

'Tutu can't swim'

Mention Desmond Tutu's name anywhere in South Africa and the odds are that the response will be a story – for instance, how President Botha gave up chess because he did not know how to move the black bishop. Tutu gleefully tells some of these legends himself, perhaps starting an address with 'Have you heard of Tutu fried chicken? It's got two left wings and a parson's nose!' Or he might recall the occasion on a flight from Durban when the stewardess asked if he would autograph a book for a group of of passengers. 'I was trying to look suitably modest, when she went on to say, "You are Bishop Muzerewa, aren't you?"' If he has more time to spare he will tell the story of how he died and took his turn in the queue at the pearly gates. Two men were in front of him. To the first St Peter said, 'For your sins you will be incarcerated with this lady', introducing him to a wizened old crone; to the second he said the same, but the lady was even more wrinkled, more bent. When Tutu's turn came St Peter produced Brigitte Bardot, saying to her, 'For *your* sins you will spend eternity with this little man.'

But the most frequently repeated Tutu story tells of an occasion when the Bishop and the President come together for talks, in search of privacy meeting in a small boat on Zoo Lake in northern Johannesburg. However, the ever-vigilant press hear of it and assemble round the lake armed with binoculars, telephoto lenses and radio microphones to record the historic event. As the two men talk the wind blows the President's hat into the water, so with a confident 'Don't worry', the Bishop gets out of the boat and walks across the water, retrieves the hat and returns it to the President. The next day the headlines read: 'Tutu kan nie swem nie' ('Tutu can't swim').

This story, whose archetypal nature is emphasised by its different locations (it is placed variously on the Vaal dam or in Cape Town harbour, with the press keeping watch from Table Mountain, as well as on Zoo Lake), illustrates how, whatever he does, Tutu attracts criticism from someone. He is on a tightrope, in his own words 'a marginal man between two forces'. It is time to disentangle the strands of this rope and discover how it is that he has not yet lost his balance.

Not only has fate placed Desmond Tutu in one of the most polarised situations of recent times, he has also had to come to terms with contradictions in his own temperament. His extravert nature conceals a private, introvert side that needs space and regular periods of quiet; his jocularity runs alongside a deep seriousness; his occasional bursts of apparent arrogance mask a genuine humility before God and his fellow men. He is a true son of Africa who can move easily in European and American circles, a man of the people who enjoys ritual and episcopal splendour, a member of an established Church, in some ways a traditionalist, who takes a radical, provocative and fearless stand against authority if he sees it to be unjust. It is usually the most spiritual who can rejoice in all created things and Tutu has no problem in reconciling the sacred and the secular, but critics note a conflict between his socialist ideology and his desire to live comfortably, dress well and lead a life that, while unexceptional in Europe or America, is considered affluent, tainted with capitalism, in the eyes of the deprived black community of South Africa.

His success and personal fame have led to other tensions, tensions which would have torn apart any but the most centred. He has to ride the see-saw of acclamation overseas, castigation at home. Even in the relative privacy of his office he might be reading a letter from a devoted admirer when the telephone rings, the see-saw tips, and he has to listen to tirades of abuse, even to hear threats on his life. (He lets the caller finish, blesses him and hangs up.) He loves the Americans but feels impelled to denounce Reagan's South African policies.

The sustained vilification and abuse by the South African media, the organised campaigns against him, often originating in the government itself, have ensured that the public image has no relation to the reality. When press and people indulge in 'Tutu-bashing' (one of South Africa's favourite sports) it is that public image they are abusing. It is an impressive fact that, apart from the conditioned and prejudiced, those who attack Tutu are invariably those who have not met him. Those who know the real man may fault him, but the feelings they have for him are deep affection, respect and – overwhelmingly – love.

It is in his passionate desire for reconciliation that Tutu finds himself so precariously balanced. He is, in the words of Professor Charles Villa-Vicencio, both 'the prophet who confronts the status quo on behalf of the people and at the same time the person who seeks to reconcile church and state. So he gets criticised from both sides.' In a country whose people are separated by law, whose aspirations are mutually exclusive, who are divided into oppressors and oppressed and where even members of the same Church are on opposite sides of the struggle, Desmond Tutu is a man of peace. And the peace he longs for is more than the absence of war; it is, to quote Professor Villa-Vicencio again, 'the active, positive exaltation of justice and social harmony, which Bishop Tutu has come to symbolize'.[1]

While it would be easy for him to keep quiet, time and again he speaks up and offers himself as a mediator between opposing forces. In initiating dialogue with the government, in insisting that 'Botha is my brother' and in refusing to believe that God's grace cannot operate on the President, by pleading with the Dutch Reformed Churches to join the SACC and to help find a solution to the country's problems, in his public speeches at universities and schools, in his contacts with the African National Congress, in his refusal to accept violence from anyone, black or white, he continually places himself in the firing line. His loving, reconciliatory approach even incurs disapproval from some of his black colleagues. One Roman Catholic priest has openly said that 'Bishop Tutu should learn to hate a little'.

Tutu's vision for South Africa was concisely expressed in 1979:[2]

> Basically I long and work for a South Africa that is more open and more just; where people count and where they will have equal access to the good things of life, with equal opportunity to live, work and learn. I long for a South Africa where there will be equal and untrammelled access to the courts of the land, where detention without trial will be a thing of the hoary past, where bannings and such arbitrary acts will no longer be even so much as mentioned, and where the rule of law will hold sway in the fullest sense. In addition, all adults will participate fully in political decision making, and in other decisions which affect their lives. Consequently they will have the vote and be eligible for election to all public offices. This South Africa will have integrity of territory with a common citizenship, and all the rights and privileges that go with such a citizenship, belonging to all its inhabitants.

This may read as no more than a claim for ordinary human rights, but for South African blacks it has a Utopian ring, while for the whites it poses an intolerable threat.

Tutu has sometimes caught glimpses of this vision and loves to recall them. For instance at a funeral in Uitenhage, when he saw two young women embracing each other – one white, one black. Or at another potentially explosive funeral, to which a young white couple came with their two-year-old child; the black people made way for the little family, patting the child on the head and smiling delightedly. He often recalls his young American friend, Martha Rockwell, who would regale him by the hour with stories of her wonderful teacher, Miss Morgan. Then one day all three met at a party. Eight-year-old Martha rushed up to the Bishop, saying, 'Bishop, Bishop, she's here, my teacher's here.' And he saw that Miss Morgan was black, something so unimportant to Martha that she had not thought to mention it.

Most vividly, most movingly, was the funeral of Molly Blackburn, that courageous white woman who campaigned fearlessly against apartheid. Ninety per cent of the 20,000 people there were black, people who, as Tutu said,[3]

> you would have thought by this time would be saying 'To hell with all white people'. They say 'Ah-ah, we don't hate white people, we hate apartheid, we hate injustice, we hate oppression and we are for goodness, for justice and for peace . . . We are going to stride into this great future, this new South Africa, this non-racial South Africa where people will count not because of the colour of their skins, but where people count because they have been made in the image of God.'

While Desmond Tutu long ago resolved any conflict in combining a political role with his Christian calling, summarising his attitude by expressing his wonder at which Bible people are reading when they suggest that religion and politics do not mix, inside the maze of South African politics his conciliatory role faces him with daunting problems. While some people are impressed at his skill in surviving at all in such a political minefield, even many of his admirers consider that he is a bad politician; that he is too good a Christian, too ready to believe in people's inherent goodness, too ready to prefer honesty to expediency and too politically naïve to indulge in the necessary tactical manoeuvring.

It is in his position between the militant blacks, who criticise him for being too moderate, and most of the whites, who consider him a supporter of radical black nationalists, even referring to him as a terrorist, that Tutu's position is at its most perilous. But there are many cleavages in South African politics apart from the racial separation; there are divisions inside both black and white communities, tensions between individuals, problems caused by the physical separation of those at home and those, like the ANC, forced into exile. Tutu relates to them all.

He does so in a dual role of infinite complexity, speaking both as a Bishop, where his duty to interpret the Gospel clearly does not stem from the democratic process, and as a political leader expressing the wishes of his people. Though he has no political ambition and steadfastly refuses to align himself exclusively with any particular political grouping, Tutu seems most at home with the United Democratic Front, an umbrella grouping of 600–700 grassroots organisations which, while not an explicit political party, embraces the broad demands of over 1 million people. In its aim to be a unifying force for national aspirations, in its adherence to the principles of the

Freedom Charter and in its desire for a non-racial South Africa achieved through non-violent means, it is totally in accord with Tutu's philosophy.

For its part the UDF appreciates his role. It recognises that as a priest he is first and foremost accountable to God and that it is quite proper for him to play a reconciliatory role, and understands that his refusal to take up an identifiable political position frees him to speak out and to fulfil his prophetic function. But while it sees the need for a negotiator, it is doubtful about his doctrine of reconciliation. His inclination is to equate political conflict with quarrels between individuals, capable of reconciliation by a change of heart, whereas the UDF feels that experience in other parts of the world shows that major changes have to be made to political structures before reconciliation can take place. In any case it has found that irenic moves from the black people are undermined by the violence of the State.

The various Black Consciousness organisations, which formed themselves into the National Forum Committee (NFC), are smaller and more sectarian. They represent an ultra-left political position, rejecting the Freedom Charter and talking in terms of the class struggle. While their position is pro-black rather than anti-white, they make a distinction between their racial attitude before and after liberation. They see no part for white people in the reshaping of South Africa, but are prepared to join hands in a post-apartheid society, whereas the UDF feels that a non-racial attitude should be part of the birth of a new South Africa.

Tutu, determined to talk to everybody and initially comfortable with the Black Consciousness Movement, was an executive member of the NFC, helping to prepare for its inauguration in 1983, even reading papers himself. He is a patron of the UDF, though he was not present at the Cape Town launch. This attempt to unify the forces against apartheid led to amazement – there would be laughter when he admitted at meetings 'I am a member of the NFC and a patron of the UDF'. In fact his dual commitment could not be maintained. After Senator Kennedy's visit was brought to its knees by the behaviour of AZAPO there was an attempt at reconciliation, when the UDF hosted a rally at Soweto to celebrate Tutu winning the Nobel Peace Prize, but it did not work. UDF and AZAPO went their separate ways and AZAPO, which valued his support even though it found his stance too moderate, was disappointed at Tutu's increasing sympathy with the UDF. It was inevitable and predictable. Many people felt that black consciousness had done its work in giving the black man back his dignity and that AZAPO's exclusion of whites was no longer necessary or even good strategy. Bishop Tutu's present stance implies that he is among those who feel that AZAPO's time is over.

Tutu's desire to unite the forces against apartheid is shared by the banned African National Congress, which appreciates the contribution the black consciousness movements have made to the struggle and has sought to relate to them and encourage them. However, like Tutu, it is worried by the racial element in their ideology. (As far back as 1973 the ANC had declared that 'the assertion of the national identity of the oppressed black peoples . . . is not an end in itself'.)[4] The ANC represents the views of the mass of the South African people and is seen to do so by most of the international community; it enjoys observer status at the United Nations and the Organisation of African Unity. Though membership of the ANC is forbidden in South Africa, even the possession of its literature being a treasonable offence, Tutu has never hidden his support. Whenever he is overseas he makes a point of meeting the Congress leaders and he frequently says that he agrees with their objectives of a non-racial, democratic and just society, but disagrees with their methods, particularly the use of violence by the armed wing, Umkhonto we Sizwe. They admire and respect him, amicably agreeing to differ on some matters and accepting what, in their eyes, are his limitations; in fact, Oliver Tambo, who once considered being a priest, has said that Tutu is doing exactly what he would have done, had he followed that early calling.

In his controversial trip to America in January 1986 Tutu moved even closer to the ANC, when he was publicly quoted as saying he hoped that the leaders of the Western world would side with the ANC, 'which sought to change an unjust system peacefully, non-violently and were only sent into the arms of the struggle through violence because the West abandoned us'.[5] He went on to express his inability to understand the logic of the United States government, which offered help to Unita in Angola and the Contras in Nicaragua, but would not support the ANC. This open siding with the ANC, who had welcomed the advent of the UDF and whose views coincided so closely with the UDF's, was too much for AZAPO. It claimed that the Bishop had destroyed his role as a neutral peacemaker in black politics and that his words would indirectly fan the flames of discord between AZAPO and the UDF.

Tutu's political ideology is, once again, in the centre. If pressed for a label he describes himself as a socialist, as someone looking for a sharing society. He abhors capitalism, which he regards as an ideology of the survival of the fittest, based on man's lowest instincts; he considers that Communism is too materialistic and atheistic an ideology to satisfy the deep spiritual aspirations of Africans. Predictably, he is denounced by whites as being a tool of the Communists and, though in fact he has read quite widely on the subject, criticised by radicals for having an ill-informed and unprogressive attitude to Communism and Marxism. But despite the ANC's long association with the South African Communist Party, his own attitude is quite unequivocal. After provoking howls of indignation when, preaching in England, he declared that most South Africans would welcome even the Russians as liberators, he justified the remark by saying: 'I hate communism with every fibre of my body, as I believe most blacks do – but when you are in a dungeon and a hand is stretched out to free you, you do not ask the pedigree of its owner.'[6]

For the trades unions Tutu's ability to unite people is his greatest strength. They find that his passionate pleas that radical elements should not destroy the struggle or lend credence to the theory that blacks cannot govern does succeed in having a calming effect; his insistence on the justice and dignity of their cause does inject a certain confidence. Though they wish the Church as an institution would provide stronger leadership, though they wish it could contribute more – for instance in giving more assistance during strikes by mobilising their communities at local level and by lending church facilities for community gatherings (the ecclesiastical authorities tend to bow to State pressure, such as the levies put on church buildings used for these purposes) – the feeling is that Tutu himself makes a significant contribution, though he could do more. A representative of the Council of the Unions of South Africa (CUSA) considers that 'He has this magnificent power and magnetism. If it was more coherently used, more logically used, it could take the struggle on to a whole new phase.'

In the opinion of those who have worked with Tutu at a political level his greatest weakness is that he tends to act without first consulting other concerned bodies. His solitary role, unidentified with any political grouping, coupled with his spontaneous temperament, lead him to draw his own conclusions and act on them unilaterally. 1985 saw two instances of this, both of which made him the object of much criticism.

The first was when he called for a day of prayer on October 9th. From the point of view of the unions this was ill-considered and impractical. October 10th was a public holiday, the 11th was a Friday, a day off for many workers; in effect it would mean three days without pay. The date also coincided with school examinations and the careers of thousands of pupils would be put in jeopardy.

In fact his call was not quite so high-handed as it appeared. The idea originated at a National Initiative for Reconciliation, organised by the evangelical organisation African Enterprise under the chairmanship of Michael Cassidy. Four hundred Christians from forty-seven denominations met in an effort to bring peace to a land increasingly torn by riots and bloodshed and at this meeting the delegates voted overwhelmingly to declare October 9th a day of prayer, fasting and mourning for 'those sinful aspects of our national life which have led us to this present crisis'.[7] It was a purely Church initiative, a stay-away rather than a strike, and Tutu, though it was his idea (in fact he originally wanted a full week's stay-away), was just one voice at the meeting, though it was his voice that was remembered, his call that featured in the press, he who spoke at a press conference, appealing to organisations not to hijack the day of prayer and explaining that it was called by the Churches and not trades unions or political organisations.

Nevertheless, there does seem to have been a lack of communication. Though letters were sent to industry and commerce and Barclays closed its banks countrywide, allowing employees to take leave if they wished to pray for the whole day, no one contacted the trades unions. At the least it was tactless, though it is unclear why it was Tutu who had to shoulder the entire blame.

The second instance concerned education, something that has deeply concerned Tutu since he decided to give up teaching rather than contribute to the humiliating system of Bantu education introduced by the government in 1955. Using one of the few weapons available to them to demonstrate against apartheid, students had been boycotting classes for a year when, on December 29th, a conference on the crisis in black education was convened by the Soweto Parents Crisis Committee in the Great Hall of the University of the Witwatersrand.

In his address to the 600-strong audience, Bishop Tutu praised the students for their uncompromising opposition to apartheid and the inferior education they were offered, but warned against an uneducated generation who would not be able to occupy skilled posts in a post-liberation South Africa. He then not only brought forward his deadline for sanctions, but called for a general strike of students, teachers, lecturers and Church leaders if their demands were not met by March 30th, 1986. His recommendations were unanimously adopted and there was no argument in the black community over the demands: that there should be freely elected student representative councils, that the Congress of South African Students should be unbanned, that student leaders in detention should be released, and that arrangements should be made for pupils to catch up with their lost studies. However, Tutu's call for a general strike without reference to the trades unions brought him such tirades of criticism that the occasion served as a turning point for him as he began to realise the necessity of proper consultation. Since then he has, on a number of occasions, acted in conjunction with someone like Allan Boesak when previously he might have gone ahead on his own; a month later when he attempted to negotiate with the government on behalf of the people of Alexandra, he went with their full knowledge and was careful to report back before he made any public statements. Even if it was over-optimistic to the point of naïveté, the fact that it ended in failure was no fault of his.

But actions such as this unmandated call for a general strike endanger his credibility. Ian Linden, the General Secretary of the Catholic Institute for International Relations, has said that:

> The degree to which he is able to act in a much more consensus fashion, with much more of a sense of participation in a popular movement, will be the degree to which his acceptability continues. The degree to which he speaks out off the top of his head will be the degree to which people reject him. Without any doubt.

It is curious that a man of such sensitivity and intelligence should have been so slow to realise that with a people as democratic as black South Africans he cannot act on his own. There have been suggestions that it is his background as an Anglican Bishop that distances him and leads him to act in this fashion, but there is a more profound explanation. He may disturb some colleagues by not talking things through with them sufficiently (though Bishop Buchanan is one of many who found he not only asked advice, but took it), but there is one person he consults regularly and humbly every day of his life, and that is God. There is something reminiscent of Moses – and deeply moving – in the image of Tutu going to the mountain top, seeking God's advice in prayer, then descending to tell the people what God has said to him. There is admittedly a contradiction between this prophetic model, implicitly announcing 'Thus saith the Lord', and the democratic process, which must always question whether the prophet truly represents the cry of the people; but it is neither arrogance nor insensitivity that leads him to these unilateral actions – it is an unshakeable conviction that he is doing the will of God.

Though his independence and his tendency to speak on behalf of the people without consulting other leaders land him in trouble with groups who have a political mandate, Tutu's ability to endear himself to virtually everyone who actually meets him – as opposed to those who absorb the media image – enables him to maintain affectionate relationships with individuals on a personal basis. There are of course exceptions – few members of the Nationalist government offer him more than the most superficial respect, black leaders co-operating with the system see him as a threat to their authenticity, Bishop Mokoena never misses an opportunity to sling stones in his direction – but by those working for a free South Africa he is accorded at the least grudging admiration, at the most something akin to reverence. Despite the government's attempt to create rifts between them, he and Allan Boesak have a good working relationship and his personal friends include people from all walks of life: the Church, the arts, the political world, the diplomatic corps. The one person with whom there are problems is Chief Gatsha Buthelezi.

Buthelezi, who now prefers to be known as Mangosuthu rather than Gatsha, is the Chief Minister of ZwaZulu, a self-governing, though not 'independent' 'homeland' in Natal, and founder of Inkatha, a Zulu cultural association which has become a political party boasting 1 million card-carrying members. His opposition to economic sanctions and his readiness to deal with Pretoria have led to his being portrayed by the media, both inside and outside South Africa, as the moderate man of peaceful change and many whites speak of him in glowing terms; but to the mass of the black people, including the ANC, the UDF and AZAPO, he is a 'Pretoria puppet' and Inkatha a Zulu version of Afrikaner nationalism. Further, he gives credibility to the government by enabling it to cite him as someone who opposes apartheid and yet has not accepted independence, which proves, it argues, that those who have accepted independence have done so freely.

Despite their real differences of strategy, Tutu would like to have amicable relations with Buthelezi. In fact, when the Tutus were living at the Federal Seminary in Alice and Buthelezi was a member of the college council, he was sometimes a guest in their house. The split in their personal relationship dates from 1978 and the funeral of the great Robert Sobukwe.

It took place in the rugby stadium at Graaf Reinet in Cape Province. Though it was well before the big funerals of the mid-1980s, it was at one level a political event and Chief Buthelezi's determination to be on the platform was not welcomed by thousands of the blacks who were present. In fact he was not just unwelcome, his presence was deeply resented and the atmosphere became more and more tense. Archdeacon David Nkwe still bears the scars from the kicks he received when he became part of the human wall that tried to protect the Chief from the increasingly violent young people. Eventually some of the priests persuaded Buthelezi that his life was in danger and that he must bow to these strong feelings. Led by Bishop Tutu, they managed to take him away to safety.

Since this humiliation Buthelezi has constantly attacked Tutu, whose refusal to respond must add salt to the wound. Though there have been many attempts to reconcile the two men, apart from one appearance on the same platform in 1982 and Buthelezi's formal congratulations on, for instance, the Nobel Peace Prize, the best that can be said of the relationship is that it has ceased to exist.

Of all the issues with which Tutu, along with all South Africans, has to grapple, the most crucial and the most complex are those of economic sanctions and the use of violence. Though no economist and unlettered in the detailed implications of economic measures, Tutu has long been in favour of sanctions, which he sees as the only peaceful option in the face of an intransigent government. Granted that there is no guarantee of their effectiveness, they are the last non-violent option left, the only alternative to taking up arms.

He argues that there are three ways in which change can be effected in a social dispensation: by the exercise of a democratic vote, something not available to blacks in South Africa; by violence, an option he rejects; or through the intervention of the international community. History shows that no one gives up power voluntarily and that pressure can be effective: the sports boycott led to some multi-racial sport in South Africa, the disinvestment campaign at least brought the Sullivan and EEC codes into being. And governments seem quite content to use sanctions when it suits them; for instance, America has acted against Poland and Nicaragua, and the United Kingdom, with arguable effect, against Rhodesia.

In taking this stand Tutu is speaking for the great majority of blacks. The ANC, recognising the extent to which apartheid is buttressed by overseas links, first called for sanctions twenty-five years ago. A poll taken in August 1985 showed that 77 per cent of urban blacks agreed with their imposition. They receive overwhelming support from the trades unions. Allan Boesak goes even further, suggesting that 99 per cent of the blacks feel Tutu is right on sanctions. Overseas members of the pro-sanctions lobby include Rajiv Gandhi, Kenneth Kaunda, Robert Mugabe, Bob Hawke, Sonny Ramphal and the British Labour Party. What, then, are the arguments against sanctions and why has Tutu's advocacy of economic pressure made him the object of such hatred? Why are there so many, notably Helen Suzman and Chief Buthelezi inside the country, and the American, United Kingdom and West German governments overseas, who vehemently oppose sanctions?

It is an infinitely complex subject and pitfalls of over-simplification yawn at the feet of every commentator, but there is no dodging the element of pure self-interest. White South Africans clearly have much to lose, as have a few blacks with a stake in the system; trading partners, such as Britain, with billions of pounds invested in the country, would not only be putting their financial interests in jeopardy, but have to consider the knock-on effects on jobs at home. There is, too, the obvious risk to all concerned of severe long-term damage to the South African economy and the certainty that, unless sanctions are comprehensively imposed, there will be sanction-busting from some opportunistic regime. Most tenuous, even hypocritical, is the argument that those who will be most hurt are the black South Africans themselves. Tutu has no problem dealing with this. In America he met the point by saying 'Blacks retort "When did you suddenly become so altruistic? Did you not benefit from black cheap and black migratory labour? Did you ever protest against these and other causes of black suffering?"'[8] In his own country, when accused by a government Minister of being indifferent to the suffering sanctions would bring to black people, he retorted 'His new found altruism is quite galling, when you realise that he is a member of a government whose policies have inflicted quite deliberately and of set purpose unnecessary and unacceptable suffering on our people . . . The Minister should spare us his crocodile tears.'[9]

The majority of blacks take a philosophical view on the harm sanctions would inflict on them. Representatives of the British Churches, visiting South Africa in 1985, found that the blacks felt that 'their present suffering was intolerable and they were prepared to accept whatever more the ending of apartheid would entail. "There is a difference," we were told, "between suffering in hope and suffering in hopelessness".'[10]

In his numerous statements on the subject, delivered all over the world in every available forum, Tutu has drawn a fine line between advocating diplomatic and economic pressure and calling for punitive sanctions; time and again he has skated close to making treasonable statements. Some think him wrong, some find his views naïve and ill-informed, but even those who do not agree with his thinking on the subject cannot but admire his courage when, on April 2nd, 1985, he fulfilled his promise and called for punitive economic sanctions. In doing this he not only faced the taunts of those who accuse him of commending fasting while himself enjoying a full stomach, but risked the real possibility of being charged with treason. Only his international fame has kept him out of prison.

Tutu's support of sanctions is a reflection of his abhorrence of violence, since 1984 endemic in the townships and certain to become worse if apartheid is not dismantled. (It must not be forgotten that the occasional periods of apparent calm are the result of brutal State suppression; true peace is a stranger in South Africa.) He has frequently said that he rejects all forms of violence, whether the primary violence of a repressive system or the violence of those who try to overthrow it. But, he usually adds, he is a peace-lover, not a pacifist.

The Church has traditionally defined the 'just war' by giving certain criteria which must be met by Christians before participating in an armed struggle: the cause must be worthy; the intention should be the advancement of good; the war must be waged by 'proper means'; there must be a reasonable chance of success; the good to be gained must be greater than the harm inflicted; all other methods of resolving the situation should have been attempted. How do these criteria apply in South Africa?

Apart from the right-wing minority there can be few people who do not appreciate the justice of the cause, nor can anyone who has studied the history of the ANC, or followed the fruitless attempts at peaceful protest made by opponents of apartheid, doubt that the blacks have not only shown extraordinary patience but are, as Tutu often says, 'peace-loving to a fault'. All methods of achieving a peaceful solution have been tried and failed. If exasperation has spilled over into unworthy means, such as the horrific 'necklace' killings, they have been repeatedly condemned, not only by Tutu, but by the majority of the people. The question of what might follow armed insurrection is obviously hypothetical, but Tutu is in no doubt of what his attitude would be if a black government came to power; if it perpetrated the same atrocities that are being perpetrated today he would be just as outspoken as he is in the face of the current white political dispensation. The hardest of these criteria for black Christians to meet is the question of the probable success of taking up arms. Given the huge power exercised by the whites – they proudly announce that they have not yet unleashed a fraction of their power – the chances are, to say the least of it, not high. The blacks have virtually no weapons to take up; all they have on their side are their numbers and the justice of their cause.

Tutu's tightrope is at its tautest and most precarious in his efforts to maintain a non-violent position in a situation of such hopelessness. To support violence is foreign to everything he stands for, yet the pressure to do so is overwhelming, both in terms of his own wish for justice and in his personal credibility, particularly with young blacks impatient of his moderation. Though he has never deviated from his wish for a non-violent solution, he argues that non-violence demands a certain minimum morality from the government if it is to be effective. As that is absent, he is increasingly expressing his sympathy with those for whom a violent response to a violent regime is the only answer, frequently saying, 'there may be a time when we have to take up arms and defend ourselves'. In June 1986 he went even further, saying at a rally in Toronto that if sanctions failed to persuade Pretoria to dismantle apartheid, 'The Church would have no alternative but to say it would be justifiable to use violence and force to overthrow an unjust regime'.[11]

There is an uncomfortable contradiction between, on the one hand, Tutu's condemnation of violence, on the other his readiness to admit that the Church itself teaches that there are times when it is justifiable to resort to arms. Though he has clarified his position on sanctions, on the even more crucial matter of violence his position is more ambivalent. While radical blacks think not only that he should come down on the side of the armed struggle, but that he will, Tutu insists that violence is evil, even when conditions make it justifiable. Most people agree that the conditions of the just war theory have been fulfilled in South Africa in the 1980s as surely as they were in Europe in 1914 and 1939. Many are aware that those who denounce blacks fighting for their freedom did not have any problems when countries defended themselves in two world wars. But the furthest Tutu will go is to say that the time is approaching when violence may be seen as a lesser evil than the continued oppression of the people. Even then, he says that people must decide for themselves – he could not pick up a gun and fight. It is hard to blame him.

Another strand of the tightrope Tutu walks, not least in the dilemma he faces over the issue of violence, is theological. He is firmly in the Anglican episcopal tradition, a custodian of a deposit of faith handed down through many generations, yet he lives in a country which is developing a strong modern contextual theology, rooted in the experience of people in South Africa and talking in terms of the oppressor and the oppressed. The problems for anyone living this duality were highlighted by the publication of one of the most significant theological statements to emerge from the crisis in South Africa, the *Kairos Document*.[12]

The *Kairos Document* (*Kairos* – the moment of truth), was released in September 1985 under the signatures of 151 South African theologians who had been meeting regularly to discuss the crisis into which South Africa has been plunged. It is a theological comment, not an official statement of the Church; a part of the on-going debate about the Christian response to the South African situation, not a final document. In pursuit of its goal – to articulate the experience of faith for the majority of South Africans – the document offers an analysis of how the Church, with its ill-matched bedfellows of both oppressor and oppressed, should respond to the situation in the country. It was intended to stimulate discussion and prayer and to lead to action.

It outspokenly condemns what it calls the 'State Theology' used to justify apartheid, saying it is not only heretical, but blasphemous; it is critical of 'Church theology', the response of the so-called 'English' Churches, saying it 'tends to make use of abstract principles like reconciliation, negotiation, non-violence and peaceful solutions and applies them indiscriminately and uncritically to all situations'. The authors insist that politics and political strategies cannot be bypassed and call for a 'prophetic theology'. The conflict, they state, is between the oppressor and the oppressed, between 'two irreconcilable causes or interests in which the one is just and the other unjust'. Reflecting on the question of whether the South African government should properly be termed tyrannical, they point out that a tyrant has traditionally been defined as an enemy of the common good and there is no doubt that the majority of people in South Africa think that apartheid is indeed that. If the State is tyrannical then 'the most loving thing we can do for both the oppressed and for our enemies who are oppressors is to eliminate the oppression'. God is undoubtedly on the side of the oppressed.

It ends with a message of hope and a challenge to action. The Church must take sides unequivocally, never doing anything that might appear 'to give legitimacy to a morally illegitimate regime'; further it must be prepared to be involved in civil disobedience, as 'a Church that takes its responsibilities seriously in these circumstances will sometimes have to confront and to disobey the State in order to obey God'.

Many senior churchmen of all denominations were disturbed by the *Kairos Document* and there has been much speculation as to why Bishop Tutu's name did not appear amongst the signatories to the document. Did it indicate his disapproval? Was he erring on the side of caution? Could he have been offended at the suggestion that it was aimed at people like him, who by virtue of their office represent the established Church? Had he perhaps not even been asked? The truth is simpler. The Kairos theologians were not campaigning for signatures; the document was signed only by those who had participated in the discussions and Tutu had not been amongst them. They did, however, keep him informed and made sure he had a copy of the draft, not least to prepare him for the inevitable questions from the press. The issue, in reality, was not whether he signed, but the nature of his reaction.

So part of the reason that he did not sign the document was that he had not been involved in it and had been too busy to read it closely.

But in the event he was glad he had not signed as, though he supported its broad outlines, he had reservations, which, had he been present at the discussions, he would have raised. He was distressed by 'the kind of blanket condemnation of what you would call white Church leadership', citing people like the Most Reverend Philip Russell, then Archbishop of Cape Town, and Peter Storey, then president of the Methodist Church of Southern Africa, who had risked so much in the struggle for freedom. He also felt the Kairos theologians had come close to justifying violence, something he simply could not do. He sympathised with its angry tone, reflecting that 'Prophets, I suppose, were not noted for their delicate language';[13] but, most crucially, he had real and deep-rooted problems over the question of reconciliation.

The Kairos theologians are adamant that repentance must precede reconciliation. They argue that there are conflicts – and South Africa's is one –

> where one side is a fully armed and violent oppressor while the other side is defenceless and oppressed. There are conflicts which can only be described as the struggle between justice and injustice, good and evil God and the devil. To speak of reconciling these two is not only a mistaken application of the Christian idea of reconciliation, it is a total betrayal of all that Christian faith has ever meant.

While Tutu may, intellectually, be persuaded by the logic of this argument, though there is no question whose side he is on, for him to stop seeking reconciliation goes directly against the grain of both his Christianity and his temperament; for him reconciliation is about people, not positions. As in the case of violence, he does not think less of those who are persuaded by such an argument; it is simply that he, in his heart, is not.

In the constantly changing situation in South Africa, Desmond Tutu holds determinedly to a central position. The things he says and does are radical, courageous and provocative, thus offending those with less determination to change the system; yet he comes over as a moderate man, too ready to negotiate to satisfy militant demands. So he is criticised from all sides, often by people who cannot hear what he is actually saying. It is not a comfortable position. He has to remember also that, in the words of Frank Chikane, 'There is no guarantee that because a group of people are oppressed they are saying what God is saying'. Though he listens ever more acutely to the voice of the community and is increasingly sensitive to the groundswell of popular feeling, he is an independent man, with ultimately one guide and counsellor, the God with whom he daily spends long hours in prayer.

18

Archbishop of Cape Town

In November 1985, when Philip Russell announced that he intended
to retire as Archbishop of Cape Town the following August, speculation as to who his successor would be began to mount. Tutu,
nominated when elections were last held in 1981, was an obvious
front-runner for the post, but there were predictable objections.

The months preceding the Elective Assembly had seen Tutu polar-
ising opinion even more than he had for the past decade. He was
constantly in the eye of the storm, reviled and loved, castigated and
admired, buffeted from every direction. Should so controversial a man
occupy the highest position in the Anglican Church in South Africa?
There were plenty of people who thought he should not. Though his
acts of courage in saving lives and his condemnation of violence,
whether from the police, the army, the ANC or the black community
themselves, had gained him some support in white eyes, it was
outweighed by his controversial American tour in January, in particular
by his call that the West should support the ANC. The balance tipped
further against him when, the shock-waves of that particular episode
still reverberating, he demanded punitive international sanctions
against South Africa. Among blacks he was, as ever, loved as a man
and honoured both as a religious leader and as a symbol of black
achievement, but some of his actions – his meetings with the President,
his threat to leave the country if the 'black-on-black' violence did
not stop, the confusion over his call for a day of prayer and his doomed
effort to negotiate with the government on behalf of the people of
Alexandra – had lessened his influence, particularly over the young
people, and diminished his credibility. He himself tells of a youth who
asked him what his efforts at reconciliation had actually achieved; he
even admitted, 'If I were a young black I wouldn't listen to Tutu any
more.' Poised on the threshold of high achievement in the Church,
as a political leader he was, according to a leading black journalist,
still a useful spokesman, 'but people will not follow him as they follow
the United Democratic Front or Cosatu' (the Congress of South
African Trade Unions.)[1]

He himself did not want the job. He has never denied being

247

ambitious – indeed when he was at the SACC he told a reporter with disarming candour that one day he would like to be Archbishop – but since becoming Bishop of Johannesburg he had assured the diocese that he was happy to retire in that job; indeed, after so short a time in the post, had he any right to subject the diocese of Johannesburg to another change? Also he knew that Leah, her considerable energy and talents harnessed to her work with the Domestic Workers Employment Project and with many friends in Johannesburg, was adamantly opposed to moving to Cape Town.

But this was not something to be decided by the country at large, it was a matter for the Anglican Church. Whatever his political standing, whether the graph of his credibility was moving up or down, there was no question in the minds of the majority of the clerics and lay people concerned that when they met to make their choice Bishop Tutu's name should be included among the nominees. Against his will and in spite of his wife's strong reservations, he was persuaded to stand. If it were God's will that he should stay in Johannesburg, he argued (as he had done a decade earlier before he became Bishop of Lesotho), then he would not be elected.

So on April 14th the Advisory Committee duly submitted the nominations and the 500-strong Elective Assembly, consisting of all the clergy of Cape Town Province, the elected lay representatives and one priest and one layman from every other diocese of the Province, met in Cape Town to consider each nominee in turn, put the arguments and vote for their choice. (The Bishops of the Province are present at the discussions but do not vote.) They were prepared to sit for many days, expecting the proceedings to run to the statutory maximum of five or six ballots before they could reach the necessary two-thirds majority; they might even reach deadlock and be forced to refer the decision to the Bishops, for it was a decision with far-reaching implications and a fierce battle was anticipated.

Though there were several strong contenders, notably the Right Reverend Michael Nuttall, Bishop of Natal, attention was concentrated on Bishop Tutu and there is a sense in which the questions the Assembly had to consider were the very same issues which had bedevilled Tutu for so long. What would the effect of Tutu's appointment be on the already worsening relations between Church and State? Though recent holders of the post – Archbishops Robert Selby-Taylor, Bill Burnett and Philip Russell – were all resolutely opposed to the government, none were so controversial, none so vociferous, none had so high a profile. If they chose Tutu would there be white defections from the Church, with all the resulting financial as well as spiritual consequences? Might there even be a split in the

Anglican Church? The choice of Bishop Tutu would most certainly indicate the Churches' support for his stand on sanctions, already the subject of a resolution by the SACC. And as always there was the racial issue, stirring up the same contradictory feelings as before he became Bishop of Johannesburg. This dilemma was summed up by Peter Collins, senior lecturer in political studies at the University of Cape Town: 'If Bishop Tutu is elected many whites will think the church has sold out to radicals. If he isn't elected many blacks will think the church is hypocritical in its commitment to non-racialism.'[2]

The very next day the press blazed out the news: TUTU CHOSEN. TUTU TO LEAD ANGLICANS. CHOICE OF TUTU IS HAILED. ELECTION OF TUTU WON'T PLEASE ALL. TUTU: 'CHOICE WILL RENEW CONTROVERSY'. Far from being a battle, the delegates had reached their conclusion in a matter of hours rather than days. Proceedings are held behind locked doors and are confidential, but it is widely thought that only two or three ballots were necessary; certainly they had achieved a clear two-thirds majority and the choice was unanimously approved by the Bishops.

The speed and unanimity of the decision baffled and, at least temporarily, muted his critics. Though the initial reaction among local white Anglicans was cool, a surprisingly large section of the press welcomed his appointment, recognising that it marked a historic moment in the history of the Anglican Church. They acknowledged the daunting task ahead of the Archbishop-Elect, asserting that he was 'an invaluable bridge across the racial gulf',[3] referring to him as 'a man of godliness and great courage'[4] and welcoming the even greater spiritual authority he would now have. The *Cape Times* even voiced the vain hope that perhaps there might be some mark of official recognition and goodwill.

The SACC expressed 'deep joy', the clergy of Cape Town were delighted, congratulations came from the Progressive Federal Party and the Azanian Students' Organisation, the Archbishop of Canterbury Dr Robert Runcie and Chief Buthelezi, from the DRC Minister Dr Nico Smit and Dr Alex Boraine, from Dr Allan Boesak, Bishop Michael Nuttall, the Dean of Cape Town, the Very Reverend E. L. King, Mary Burton of the Black Sash and many more. The black community rejoiced, as they had rejoiced when Tutu received the Nobel Peace Prize, feeling the election of a black man was a victory for all victims of apartheid.

Tutu's critics in the press mostly restrained themselves to admonishment, hoping that the new Archbishop would 'learn humility and greater understanding';[5] that he 'would moderate his political activities and viewpoints'[6] and that the responsibilities of high office would 'temper his impetuosity'.[7] The *Daily News*, in similar vein but with a lighter touch, hoped that his new responsibilities would have a restraining effect, reminding its readers of the Afrikaans proverb '*Maak die wolf die skaapwagter*' (Make the wolf the shepherd) and hoped that the new Archbishop would 'nurse his flock with tender care, not set fire to the pasturage'.[8] The *Daily Dispatch* used the occasion to point out that the apartheid system had been shown to be 'no barrier to his progress'.[9]

Many individual voices were raised in opposition to his election, in tones ranging from the tentative to the downright hostile. Alan Paton expressed his wish that Tutu would do well, but admitted that he would rather have seen the Bishop of Natal elected; the Deputy Minister of Information, Louis Nel, showing a curious ignorance of the Archbishop's views, urged him to reject violence as a means of change and to try to reconcile the different communities in the country; President Botha declined to comment. The rage of the right-wing knew no bounds. Dr Treurnicht, the leader of the Conservative Party, said that the election of Bishop Tutu did not bode well, as he had distinguished himself more as a political agitator than as a Church leader, and Louis Stofberg, the General Secretary of the Herstigste Nasionale Party, described the election as shocking, adding that it would further efforts to achieve a revolution in South Africa. Professor Ben Engelbrecht, head of the Department of Divinity at the University of the Witwatersrand, was the most hostile, calling the Bishop a 'theological impostor' and 'a prophet on a band-wagon'. 'Were it not for apartheid,' he wrote, 'it is almost certain that the name of "Tutu" would have remained in obscurity.'[10]

The man at the centre of it all had been nervous during the Assembly. He may not have wanted the job, but neither did he savour the idea of rejection, or even a repeat of the Johannesburg experience, when the inability of the delegates to agree caused the decision to be referred to the Bishops. He was so overcome by the news of his election that Moira Henderson, with whom he was staying, said, 'He was terribly subdued – all the bounce had gone out of him'. His first thought was to telephone Leah in Johannesburg; not expecting the decision for several days, she had gone out for the evening and he did not want her to hear from the press. He then celebrated with some of his future colleagues and – untypically – slept late the next morning.

Though Leah took a while to come to terms with yet another move, the shy delight on Tutu's face in the press photographs show that his doubts and misgivings had been dispelled by the unhesitating decision. 'I'm tongue-tied,' he told reporters; 'and some people hope it's permanent.' 'It's all like a dream. I am quite overcome by the awesomeness of it all, and of the tremendous responsibility that has been placed on my shoulders.' At a special thanksgiving Eucharist in the Chapel of Diocesan College, the Cape Town boys' school where the election proceedings had been held, his critics began turning into fans. The same boys who had been asking 'Why has a black wog been appointed Archbishop?' were, by the end of the service, queueing up to meet him. He had delighted them, not least by telling them that the reason the election was over so soon was that the delegates did not like the portable toilets that had been imported for the occasion and could not be done with it soon enough.

But he knew that not everyone would be won over so easily. In countless press interviews he asked people to remember that he would not be a one-man band, but would work with his fellow bishops. If people were angry over his appointment, 'they must not be angry with God and pull out of the Church. They must rather try to change my views.' He stressed that the Church has a mandate to speak out against oppression and that his intention was to show that the Church was one family, black and white together, and that it would continue to work for justice, peace and reconciliation. He was vindicated by the certainty of the decision, convinced that by changing from white leadership, with its traditional control of money and power, the Church 'was sending out a signal to the rest of the world and to the authorities here'. Refusing to apologise for his style of leadership, he asserted: 'I am me! I operate in the way Desmond Tutu operates. I don't sit down and work out strategies. I operate almost instinctively as I believe the Gospel demands.'

The five months between Tutu's election as Archbishop of Cape Town and his enthronement in September saw the situation in South Africa deteriorate yet further. There was not only the second state of emergency, with its ever-increasing expansion of police power and even fiercer restrictions on press freedom, but the accompanying detentions and the continual harassment and torture of blacks reached horrific proportions. The political divide widened even further with the upsurge of the right-wing, as Eugene Terre Blanche's followers, complete with Swastika-type flags and Nazi salutes, gained hysterical momentum; black despair reached a pitch which caused Oliver Tambo to call on South African blacks to 'steel themselves for war'. The government were losing control and death was a part of daily life.

Tutu was involved at every level, defiant and outspoken, constantly reacting. He greeted seemingly significant changes to apartheid, such as the dropping of the pass laws, with a warm welcome, but warned of the sting in the tail: 'One has to be very careful that they are not going to find another way of harassing blacks through "orderly urbanisation" or other means.'[11] (He was right. Though blacks were no longer liable to immediate arrest if found in white areas, there were still rigid controls over where they could live and work.) He repeated that he was not interested in incremental change – Frankenstein cannot be reformed, only destroyed; the name of the game was political power-sharing. He encouraged whites to be more involved in peaceful demonstrations and again urged Christians to be prepared to disobey unjust laws non-violently. He unequivocally condemned the recent spate of bomb attacks, praised the End Conscription Campaign as a sign of hope, expressed his admiration of people who boycotted the 1986 Olympics in their desire for sanctions against South Africa and his disappointment at the stubbornness of Margaret Thatcher. And he continued to say that there was still hope for South Africa – if the international community helped.

It was also during this period that his reaction to President Reagan's speech on July 22nd, 1986 caused people all over the world, even his admirers, to wonder if this time the Bishop had not gone too far. In this speech Reagan had, once again, declared his outright opposition to sanctions against South Africa and Tutu had responded by saying that the President, along with Britain's Margaret Thatcher and West Germany's Chancellor Helmut Kohl, were in effect saying to blacks 'You are utterly dispensable'. Reagan's speech he found 'nauseating', it was 'the pits' and for his part 'America and the West can go to hell'. Should a Bishop, even an admittedly angry Bishop, consign fellow human beings to hell?

He received so much flak for this remark that he did concede that his anger was unnecessary, because he should have known not to expect any better from President Reagan; and yes, perhaps he could have used 'less salty language'. But for the most part he was unapologetic. It was good for people to know how deeply blacks feel, he claimed, good for them to be reminded that South Africans were not just engaged in academic discussions. In any case, in speaking out so strongly he was following a distinguished biblical tradition:

> What do they make of what Our Lord said to the Pharisees? 'Generation of vipers' 'You whited sepulchres. You walk around looking smart outside when you are rotten bones inside.' And what about Paul? I mean, Paul says, 'I consign you to the devil.' He also said, 'He who Jesus says is not Lord, let him be accursed.' Well, saying the West can go to hell is no worse than that!

It was a good argument.

As so often, it was not so much the sentiment that outraged people, but its expression. Peter Storey has observed that

> He often says 'If you don't do such and such, then South Africa is for the birds' and the press always pick it up. If he had said 'South Africa will advance into deepening darkness', there would have been no problem. But this phrase 'for the birds' is the kind of thing that gets under whites' skins, they can't stand it.

Similarly, had he responded to Reagan's speech with a more considered phrase like 'We shall carry on our struggle without regard to America or the West' it would have annoyed fewer people, but equally it would probably have gone unnoticed. If his manner irritates, so does it draw attention to the enormity of the black predicament in South Africa. There are many such phrases in Tutu's verbal armoury. As when he said, again of Reagan, 'Your name is mud', or his tart response on being told that business companies were trying to improve working conditions for blacks – 'Baloney'. His remarks about the possibility of domestic workers poisoning their employers' coffee, which were intended as a warning, not a threat, or that the Russians would be received with open arms, struck many as flippant and irresponsible. How people respond depends partly on whether they enjoy his sense of humour, but even more on how well they understand the man and appreciate the sentiment behind the expression.

At the end of July, Tutu bade his formal farewell to the diocese of Johannesburg. (An occasion dubbed by one newspaper as 'Ta-ta for Tutu' – only one degree better than a cartoon captioned 'It Takes Tutu Tambo'. Such is the penalty of fame coupled with an unusual name.) Despite his rather equivocal election twenty months earlier, he had in fact succeeded in winning over a vast proportion of the community and, in the face of rumours of financial embarrassment, diocesan giving had actually gone up by 17 per cent in 1985. Suggestions that he had been appointed to Cape Town to remove him from Johannesburg were palpably untrue, not least because only two representatives of the Johannesburg diocese took part in the Elective Assembly.

So the farewell ceremony was an emotional occasion, as 2,000 members of the community gathered at the Ellis Park tennis stadium in a service for unity and peace. Tutu took the Christian family and the importance of sharing as his themes. Using one of his favourite sayings, 'A person is a person through other persons', he reminded his audience that Christians could not find salvation in isolation and that freedom was not something any person or group of people could have on their own. 'Freedom has to be shared, otherwise those who have it have no time to enjoy their separate freedom – they are too busy guarding it with guns and guard dogs and states of emergency. We all share in each other's glory – and equally in each other's shame.' Defying the government's ban on naming people in detention and warning once again that all that was legal was not necessarily moral, he urged people not to be intimidated, but to pray regularly for detainees by name. He also suggested that they devote one day a week to prayer and fasting for justice and peace and that they ring the church bells every day at noon until the state of emergency was lifted. By using the ways of the Church in the service of man, he had demonstrated yet again the close interrelation between religion and politics.

The parting words, delivered by Mr Henry Bennett, a lay member of the community, must have compensated for some of the hurt he had received as Bishop of his home city. After thanking Tutu for the 'outrageously long hours he worked and for listening to us with care', Mr Bennett said 'We admire you; we respect you; and we would like to emulate your steadfastness of purpose.'

Less personal, yet more poignant, was his last sermon in Soweto as Bishop of Johannesburg. During the previous week twenty-one people had been killed in riots in the White City area and Tutu had visited a mother who had lost a son in the shootings. All his optimism seemed drained out of him as, in a low anguished voice, he whispered,

> What do you say to these people? How do you tell them about the love of God? We suffer in a land that claims to be Christian and we suffer at the hands of those who say they are Christians. The price we have paid already is a heavy price. We will go on, paying yet more in lives.

In this service the pathos of South Africa's tragic divide was encapsulated. Not far away more than 100 police in armoured cars were preventing reporters from attending the funeral of a victim of the violence; inside the church hundreds of whites from northern Johannesburg, without the protection of permits, moved around the church in a multi-racial chain of worship carrying flowers and chanting 'Peace, Peace'.

As September 7th, the day of Tutu's enthronement as Archbishop of Cape Town, drew near, so did controversy mount. There were conflicting reports about disgruntled white conservatives leaving the Anglican Church. The Church of England in South Africa, from which the Church of the Province of South Africa had split in 1870, claimed that it was opening up new churches as defectors from the Church of the Province joined it; another breakaway Church, the Christian Fellowship, also boasted of growing congregations. A church in Natal found that so many supporters had withdrawn in the wake of Tutu's appointment to Cape Town that it was unable to pay its assessment to the diocese; conservative farming communities reported that their churches were 'virtually empty'. Yet most Anglican priests considered it was the casual attenders, not the regular churchgoers, who were leaving and the Very Reverend E. L. King, the Anglican Dean of Cape Town, felt that in Cape Town congregations had, if anything, increased. Bishop John Carter, the Anglican Church's provincial liaison officer, refused to be either surprised or concerned. He felt that black attendance could well be increasing and that more young people were joining the Church. 'We are just weathering the storm and are not depressed about it . . . The church will be here long after all this is over.'[12]

One issue that, however improbably, commanded international headlines was Tutu's guest list. Should he have invited members of the government? Should he be allowed to invite anyone he wished? Should so many leading black American entertainers and politicians have been included? Did he really know all these people, or was he merely trying to impress – and at the same time taunt the government?

The star-studded guest list, considered as Tutu's latest challenge to the government, even as a slap in the face for Pretoria, was published well in advance of the enthronement. The 165 invitations were issued to churchmen from all over the world, to politicians including Senator Edward Kennedy, Gary Hart and Congressman William Gray and to entertainers such as Harry Belafonte, Lionel Ritchie and Stevie Wonder. The former United Nations Ambassador Andrew Young was invited, as was the tennis star Arthur Ashe, the United Nations Secretary-General Javier Perez de Cuellar, Coretta Scott King, the widow of Martin Luther King and the Irish writer and fellow Nobel Peace Prize-winner Sean McBride.

Tutu asked the government for an assurance that his guests – who were in fact all personally known to him – would be granted visas, a request they predictably refused. The normal demands on the time of busy people saved them some embarrassment, as did the unwillingness of some of the more controversial figures to give the government the gratification of refusing them entry. Nevertheless, the sixty requests for visas that were received placed the authorities in an awkward predicament. Could they refuse visas to such distinguished guests? On the other hand how could they give their blessing to a major gathering of anti-apartheid campaigners? Political observers forecast that visas for churchmen and less controversial figures would be approved, while action on most requests would be delayed until after the ceremony. In fact, even some churchmen had difficulty obtaining entry. Some, like Bishop Ding, President of the China Christian Council, were refused visas. (When he rang Cape Town to express his disappointment Tutu said, 'It's outrageous, but let's pray for these people.') Some of the African Bishops were turned away at Jan Smuts Airport and some kept waiting for hours.

The day before the enthronement Cape Town's airport was throbbing with pressmen as the Tutus arrived to meet the Archbishop of Canterbury, Dr Robert Runcie, and his personal assistant Terry Waite. Even in the face of the government's restrictions many foreign dignitaries were in Cape Town that night. Among the Anglican primates were the Archbishops of Central Africa, Kampala, the Indian Ocean, Japan, Australia and New Zealand; Bishop John Walker of Washington and Bishop Edmond Browning, the Presiding Bishop of the Episcopal Church, had come from America, Bishop Amos Waiaru from the Solomon Isles. The Methodists, the Lutherans, the Baptists, the Churches of Norway and Sweden, the Roman Catholics, the Greek Orthodox Church, the Union Theological Seminary and the World Council of Churches were represented. Lay people included Mrs Coretta Scott King, the Mayor of Detroit, University Chancellors and Professors, a Congressman and a former Ambassador to the United Nations. From all over South Africa priests, colleagues and friends, including Winnie Mandela and Dr Ntatho Motlana, Dr Allan Boesak and Dr Beyers Naudé, Helen Joseph, Percy Qoboza and Allistair Sparks, were gathering.

While the Tutus' guests and friends were assembling in Cape Town, so too were their family. They were all there: the elder children – Trevor with his wife Zanele and daughter Palesa, a heavily pregnant Theresa and her husband Mthunzi – came from Johannesburg with Desmond's sister Gloria and Leah's blind mother; the Tutus' two younger daughters Naomi and Mpho flew over from the United States. They spent much of the time together at the home of Moira Henderson, where Desmond and Leah were staying, and Mrs Henderson remarked, as so many have done, on the closeness of the family and the way they welcome others into their circle: 'You all become Tutus, they absorb you into their family.' On the Saturday, with Helen Suzman, Martin Kenyon and various relations, they all went for a picnic; a few hours privacy before the next day's ceremonials.

* * *

On Sunday morning Tutu was up early, praying. For hours he prayed, then he had a glass of orange juice and he and Leah left for the cathedral.

Cape Town had known controversial Archbishops, indeed Tutu was inheriting a mantle worn by uncompromising critics of apartheid such as Geoffrey Clayton, Joost de Blank and Robert Selby Taylor, all thorns in the flesh of the various governments of their time. Politics and religion, symbolically close in the proximity of St George's Cathedral to the House of Assembly, were to be drawn even closer in the person of the Eleventh Archbishop of Cape Town; even with this heritage the enthronement of the provocative Bishop Tutu was an event that was creating world-wide interest. There were claims that 200 million people would be watching on television, even that as a television event it would come a close second to the recent royal wedding in Great Britain. The South African authorities ensured that this would not be so by forbidding any live transmission of the ceremony and barring all film crews, save a small independent production company, from the cathedral; the event was completely ignored in the South African Broadcasting Corporation's morning radio broadcasts. So, although press coverage the following day was lavish, with full pages of colour pictures, immediate appreciation of the event was limited to those fortunate enough to be present at the cathedral.

At this, the highest moment of Tutu's ecclesiastical career, the polarised reactions he provokes were in evidence on the very steps of St George's Cathedral. As he prepared to strike the great west door three times with his silver crook, a scuffle broke out: his supporters were trying to remove a wreath of white and purple flowers laid provocatively in his path by a white woman in black mourning dress acting in the name of United Christian Action and intended to mark 'the death of the Anglican Church'. The Gospel Defence League was distributing anti-Tutu tracts, in which his sayings (often inaccurately recorded) were set against quotations from the Bible. Another elderly white Anglican woman was standing with a placard bearing the legend 'TUTU STATEMENTS UN-CHRISTIAN. TUTU SANTIONS [sic] AGAINST BLACKS'.

Just as the ceremony took place in a context of conflicting praise and protest, so, inside the cathedral, some 1,700 people, including 150 Bishops, were gathered for a service which, in a curiously unerring way, reflected the rich diversity of the Archbishop's nature. It was both formal and informal, dignified and intimate. Deeply Anglican, it held African elements in an easy embrace; deeply spiritual, it was imbued with a spirit of festivity. Its high seriousness did not exclude humour.

It was a glittering affair, with the Tutu family in the front row, gaily dressed in bold African prints, the chancel a sea of priests wearing embroidered vestments in red, green, gold, silver, purple and white and the cathedral burnished and garlanded with flowers. The key points of the ancient ritual, from the three knocks on the door to the presentation of the diamond-studded Kimberley Cross and the shout of the people 'We welcome you in the name of the Lord', were firmly in the Anglican tradition, but an Anglican church has seldom resounded to such an uninhibited shout of 'VIVA TUTU'. No music could echo Anglican sentiments more truly than Sir Hubert Parry's 'I was glad when they said unto me', the hymn 'Praise to the holiest in the heights' or, by special request of Archbishop Tutu, 'Jesu Joy of Man's Desiring'. Yet for many people the musical high point was the singing of the eighty-strong group from Soweto, Imilonji ka Ntu, the black choir taking their turn with the cathedral choir. They had composed a traditional African praise-song for him, something that was a surprise to the Archbishop himself. 'Sing, here comes the msimbithi stick', it began, 'Sing, here comes the redemption stick'. In a glorious ten minutes of singing and ululating and interjections from Africans in the congregation, the praise-song traced the Archbishop's life from its roots 'in barren soil . . . it was weak as it grew' through overseas travel and international honours to that day: 'Go on mysterious stick, collect your sheep and lead them . . . Take them from the kraals of oppression . . . Lead them to spiritual pastures where they'll feed with no considerations of colour. Then the msimbithi stick will become the stick of redemption.'

Archbishop Tutu's charge ranged over God and Man, religion and politics, the spiritual and the secular, the humorous and the profoundly serious, while remaining rooted securely in its central unifying depths. He began by quoting a sermon given by Trevor Huddleston which started 'In the beginning, God' and finished 'In the end, God'; then, speaking in English, Sotho and Afrikaans, he spent some time in welcomes and thanks. More in the fashion of a good after-dinner speaker than a preacher, he amused his audience by greeting his 'brother . . . er . . . primates . . . a somewhat unfortunate name, that', his valued friend the Archbishop of Canterbury and 'the utterly inconspicuous Terry Waite'. He mentioned literally scores of people by name, ending with thanking his mother-in-law for providing Leah for him.

The central part of his address was vintage Tutu. Though it contained little that keen Tutu-watchers had not heard before, it was as complete a summary of his views as he has ever given at one hearing. In stressing the centrality of the spiritual he offered praise 'to God that our God is such a God' – a God for whom no one is a nonentity and whose existence makes all life religious. He compared the family of the Church with the human family, where disagreement does not destroy unity and whose members receive in relation to their need, not their contribution. Members of a family care for one another.

> How I pray that Our Lord would open our eyes so that we would see the real, the true identity of each one of us, that this is not a so-called 'coloured', or white, or black or Indian, but a brother, a sister – and treat each other as such. Would you let your brother live an unnatural life as a migrant worker in a single-sex hostel?

He reflected sadly that 'the fundamental attitude that "blacks are human, but . . ." has not changed' and that God wants to enlist us as his agents of transformation.

Typically, the sharp reminders of man's cruelty to man were followed by gratitude for the welling up of goodness. He praised the women of the Black Sash and the young people working with the End Conscription Campaign; he rejoiced that blacks could still forgive. Like a priest who, as he was being tortured, thought 'These are God's children and they are behaving like animals. They need us to help them recover the humanity they have lost'; and a former colleague who, after 230 days in solitary confinement and nearly a year in detention said on his release, 'Let us not be consumed by bitterness.'

While he offered the traditional prayers for President P. W. Botha 'and all in authority under him', he could not resist making a point that he knew would reach the absent government – but this time there was a difference. He said that he did not want sanctions and that if the government would lift the state of emergency, remove the troops from the townships, release political prisoners and detainees, unban political organisations and negotiate with the authentic representatives of the community for one undivided South Africa, 'then, for what it is worth, I would say to the world "put your sanction plans on hold". The onus must be on those who say no to sanctions – provide us with a viable non-violent strategy to force the dismantling of apartheid.'

As Archbishop Tutu left the cathedral to the tolling of bells, blessing the people and the city, the day was far from over: 10,000 people were already assembling at the Goodwood Stadium for a Eucharist, one of the largest ever held in South Africa. There were greetings to the new Archbishop from the UDF and, through Dr Allan Boesak, from forty-five heads of state and the exiled ANC President Oliver Tambo. There were massed choirs and marimba bands, the singing of Anglican and African hymns, including of course 'Nkosi Sikele' iAfrika'. The Archbishop of Canterbury gave a brave and impressive sermon, setting the tone of his call for peace with the sombre words, 'As I stand here, on the tip of Africa, I cannot escape the sense of history unfolding – the sense that here on what was once the Dark Continent, there is the threat of greater darkness still.' But even in the midst of this great celebration of unity, there were stirrings of unrest. Not from the police, who kept a discreet distance, but from young members of the UDF, wanting to use this vast gathering as a platform for their political views. So great was their excitement at seeing Winnie Mandela that she took the generous course and turned back, rather than let the service become a demonstration. Seeking another outlet, they started running rhythmically round the congregation – was this a good-humoured contribution to the proceedings or did it bode trouble? After a quick consultation it was agreed that Dr Allan Boesak and Mrs Albertina Sisulu, the wife of Walter Sisulu, in prison with Nelson Mandela, should take their turn amongst those speaking from the altar. Their words diffused the situation, though many were upset that a religious ceremony had come so close to becoming a political rally.

Tutu has never forgotten the way his election as Bishop of Johannesburg was ignored by that city, so the evening celebrations, when the Mayor of Cape Town hosted a reception in his honour in the Banqueting Hall, were balm to his soul. Though as he entered the City Hall he had to pass white youths bearing placards saying 'TUTU PREACHES SANCTIONS NOT THE GOSPEL' and 'OUR CHILDREN STARVE WHILE TUTUS EAT', once inside, he was among friends, not only those who had travelled to be with him for his enthronement, but his new friends in Cape Town. At last he had received an official welcome and, as he moved among the guests, at one stage climbing on to the stage to dance with the group who had come from Soweto, his delight shone from him.

It had been a great day, a day heralding a new era in the history of Christianity in South Africa. What lay ahead? The Dean of Cape Town, the Very Reverend E. L. King, summarised many people's feelings of excitement and apprehension as he said to the parish council at their first meeting after the enthronement, 'Hold on to your seat belts and enjoy the ride.'

Epilogue

After little more than a year as Archbishop of Cape Town it is too soon to assess Desmond Tutu's contribution to that high office. There are, however, clear indications as to the direction in which he seeks to steer the province.

His first wish, as always, is for reconciliation. 'I would think that I had been used effectively if the Anglican Church in South Africa were to recognise ourselves as family. If we were to recognise ourselves not as black, white, "coloured", Indian and so forth but that we were family. And that therefore we wanted to hold onto each other, despite all the centrifugal forces that are trying to pull us apart.' So he starts in his immediate domain, remembering the clergy in every dimension of their lives. His office is a centre of information and care for those who are sick, those who have problems; retired clergy and clergy widows are always included in diocesan functions and the entire staff troop to the funerals of clergy they thought long dead. He sends flowers to colleagues on their wedding anniversaries, flowers to celebrate their wives' birthdays, reprimands to clergy who don't send him photographs of themselves and their families. ('How can I pray for you if I can't *see* you?') He and Leah both want Bishopscourt to be a home for the diocese and one of the first things they did was to encourage the township children to come and swim and picnic in the extensive grounds. It is a microcosm of his hope of things to come, as hundreds of black children enjoy the benefits of what had hitherto been an exclusively white suburb, and where even the Tutus live illegally, if officially.

He wants the province to be enterprising, visionary and characterised by generosity. Rather than a penny-pinching approach, automatically fearing resources will not be available, he encourages people around him to dream, then see what money is needed and try to raise it. The province is not poor and Tutu feels it should be giving, not seeking assistance from overseas. 'If only we could manage somehow to respond to the divine generosity by an answering generosity on our part.'

But behind the sense of family, the hopes and visions, his passionate wish to affirm the centrality of the spiritual runs like a golden thread.

One practical outlet has been the appointment of Dr Francis Cull as Director of Spirituality, but the effect of Tutu's personal charisma and his own faith is incalculable. Dean Edward King writes that 'He just can't understand why so-called Christians cannot be aghast with "wonder, love and praise" as he is' and was deeply impressed by the simple fervour with which the Archbishop preached to a huge gathering of all the rectors and churchwardens in the diocese. 'It was just the outpouring of a man amazed at God's goodness . . . he spreads a spiritual contagion and you *know* he believes what he says.'[1]

1987 has seen little change for the better in South Africa. A glimmering of hope might be seen in the DRC's admission that its theology over apartheid was in error, but the admission soon led to a split in the DRC church and the formation of the dissident Afrikaanse Protestantse Kerk, an exclusive right-wing church for white Afrikaners. Spirits were temporarily raised in November, with the release of the ANC leader Govan Mbeki after twenty-three years in prison. But overall Tutu sees the situation as 'infinitely worse'. After the white elections in May, which saw the National Party strengthened and the Progressive Federal Party ousted by the right-wing Conservative Party as the official opposition, Tutu's reaction was unequivocal. He warned that South Africa was entering 'the dark ages of the history of this country' and that the stage was now set for further polarisation. On the one hand he foresaw 'an escalation in the intransigence of this government, an escalation in oppression and intolerance of any dissent'; on the other hand he felt 'the despondency in the air will deepen and so will the anger of the black community, where, even up to now, an amazing degree of goodwill still existed'.

As Archbishop, Tutu continues to speak out, enraging some, delighting others. Immediately after the election he was in Brazil, calling for all nations to break diplomatic relations with South Africa; the following month he joined radicals protesting against the government by urging Anglicans to wear black armbands and toll bells on the first anniversary of the state of emergency; on the eve of the Commonwealth Conference in Vancouver he renewed his call for sanctions; in December 1986, with an estimated 1,300 to 1,800 children held in detention, he called for their release, asking, 'What country detains eleven-year-olds because they are a threat to the security of the State?' With that informal directness which infuriates his critics, he said that the state of emergency had achieved nothing and warned the government that 'if you do not deal with the basic problems you are playing marbles'. And at a graduation ceremony at the University of the Western Cape he told the students, 'If Christ returned to South Africa today he would almost certainly be detained under the present security laws, because of his concern for the poor, the hungry and the oppressed.'

Though, like all South Africans, he is muzzled by press restrictions and though what has become known as 'sanctions fatigue' results in statements receiving less coverage than in the first half of the decade, in both words and actions he continues to defy Pretoria. By refusing to attend the State Opening of Parliament, by leading a group of religious leaders in talks with the ANC, by urging the government to return District Six to the coloured community and once again criticising them for 'moving people around like sacks of potatoes', by attacking the international banks for extending credit to South Africa without guarantees that apartheid would be eliminated. Most deliberately in April, by holding a service for detainees in St George's Cathedral. In doing this he was one of many clergymen putting to the test the latest government restrictions which made it illegal to sign petitions, to protest, to wear T-shirts calling for the release of detainees or – until the public outcry forced the government to back down – to pray publicly for detainees. (The government figures put the number of people detained between June 1986 and February 1987 at 13,244, but that figure excludes those held for less than thirty days. Other estimates put the figure as high as 25,000.)

Approval of these actions was shown in ways varying from the American jazz trumpeter Miles Davis naming his new album 'Tu Tu' to readers of the *Sowetan* newspaper placing him after Nelson Mandela and Oliver Tambo in their own poll for the leader of a post-apartheid government. He has also, in the first ten months of 1987, received three more honorary doctorates, the Freedom of the City of Durham, two awards from Brazil and the 'Pacem in Terris' award from Cleveland, Ohio. Criticism came, as usual, from all quarters, perhaps most dramatically from an Australian who referred to him as 'a modern-day witchdoctor dressed up in the garb of a clergyman'. And he continues to be misquoted. A pastoral visit to Mozambique became a political event as he was accused of saying, 'The time for violence has come.' What he had in fact said was, 'I will tell you the day I believe we must tell the world that we have now reached a point where we must use violence to overthrow an unjust system. I do not believe we are there yet.'

So much in the tragic situation in South Africa remains the same, it is not surprising that Tutu's responses do not, on the surface, seem to have changed. But, while he still feels it necessary to isolate South Africa through economic sanctions, he is also thinking towards that ever-receding horizon of a post-apartheid society. He is painfully aware that South Africans have never really belonged to their own continent and is convinced of the need for a wider vision. For too long apartheid has driven black South Africans into isolation, forced them into introspective agony on the one hand and reliance on America and the West on the other. They should be identifying with their own continent, their own people.

This stance is not only part of his personal development but is required by his role as Metropolitan of Southern African, a huge area including not only South Africa itself but Mozambique, Namibia, Lesotho, Swaziland, St Helena and Tristan da Cunha. Now that his official duties take him to these countries he has first-hand knowledge of what is going on and an ever-more prestigious platform from which to speak. His concern for South Africa's relationship to the continent, and his colleagues' welcome of that concern, is demonstrated by his election in September as President of the All-Africa Conference of Churches.

As businessmen and academics go to Lusaka to talk to the ANC, as the British and American governments swallow their prejudices and talk to Oliver Tambo, regent political leaders like Archbishop Tutu may return to the wings and leave the centre stage to the politicians. Brian Brown of the British Council of Churches sees Tutu's willingness to accept this role as 'an endorsement of the integrity of his person. His strength is that the ultimate liberation of his people is more important than his own prestige and power. It is like Moses reaching the mountain top and seeing the promised land, but saying "I am not here to do the leading, but to share the vision".' Once there is a commitment to justice the role of the prophet changes; demands for justice are replaced by demands for reconciliation. It needs just as much courage to say 'Pardon our enemies' as to say 'Let my people go'. When South Africa is free, Archbishop Tutu will continue to have a vital and precarious part to play. For the present, he continues to stand uncompromisingly for justice.

In a sermon in September 1987 Tutu said suffering was unavoidable, especially for the Christian who witnessed for Christ in a situation of injustice, oppression and exploitation. 'When we make the so-called preferential option for the poor; when we become the voice of the voiceless ones; when we stand in solidarity with the hungry and the homeless, the uprooted ones, the down-trodden, those that are marginalised, we must not be surprised that the world will hate us, and yet, another part of the world will love us.'[2]

He was speaking at a service to commemorate the tenth anniversary of the death of Phakamile Mabija in detention. He could have been speaking of himself.

NOVEMBER 1987

264

Awards

1978   Elected Fellow of King's College, London
Honorary Doctorate of Divinity, General Theological Seminary, USA
Honorary Doctorate of Civil Law, Kent University, UK

1979   Honorary Doctorate of Law, Harvard University, USA

1980   Prix d'Athene (Onassis Foundation)

1981   Honorary Doctorate of Theology, Ruhr University, Bochum, Germany

1982   Honorary Doctorate of Sacred Theology, Columbia University, USA

1983   Designated Member of International Social Prospects Academy
The Family of Man Gold Medal Award

1984   Honorary Doctorate of Humane Letters, St Paul's College, Lawrenceville, USA
Honorary Doctorate of Sacred Theology, Dickinson College, USA
Honorary Doctorate of Law, Claremont Graduate School, USA
Martin Luther King Jr Humanitarian Award of Annual Black American Heroes and Heroines Day, USA
Honorary Doctorate of Divinity, Aberdeen University, UK
Honorary Doctorate of Humane Letters, Howard University, USA
Nobel Peace Prize, Oslo, Norway

1985   Freedom of the City of Florence, Italy
Honorary LL.D, Temple University, Philadelphia, USA
Honorary Doctorate of Humanities, Wilberforce University, Ohio, USA
Honorary Doctorate of Divinity, Trinity Lutheran Seminary, Columbus, Ohio, USA
Honorary Doctorate of Divinity, Trinity College, Hartford, USA

1986   President's Award for Services of Distinction to Fellow-men, Glassboro State College, New Jersey, USA
Honorary Doctorate of Divinity, Chicago Theological Seminary, USA
Honorary Doctorate of Humane Letters, More House College, Atlanta, USA
Martin Luther King Jr Peace Award, Atlanta, USA
Honorary Doctorate of Humane Letters, Central University, Durham, North Carolina, USA
Honorary Doctorate of Humane Letters, Hunter College, University of New York, USA
Freedom of the City of Merthyr Tydfil, UK

1987   Freedom of the City of Durham, UK
       Order of the Southern Cross, Brazil
       Order of Merit of Brasilia, Brazil
       Honorary Doctorate, University of Rio, Rio de Janeiro, Brazil
       Honorary Doctorate of Divinity, University of the West Indies, Trinidad
       Honorary Doctorate of Divinity, Oberlin College, Davenport, Iowa, USA
       'Pacem in Terris' Peace and Freedom Award from the Quod Cities, Cleveland, Ohio, USA

Notes

1 'HERTZOG IS MY SHEPHERD'

1 Umteteli Wa Bantu, '"Civilized" labour policy' October 29th, 1932: quoted in Tim Couzens and Essop Patel, eds, *The Return of the Amasi Bird*.
2 'A Vision for Humanity', Address given on the award of the Martin Luther King Peace Prize, January 1986.
3 Ibid.
4 Ibid.
5 Evidence to the Eloff Commission, *Ecunews*, June 1983.
6 Ibid.
7 *New York Review of Books*, September 26th, 1985.
8 Letter from Desmond Tutu to Mrs Florence Blaxall, March 5th, 1979.
9 Stanley Motjuwadi in *Drum*, December 1984.
10 Ibid.
11 Ibid.
12 Ibid.
13 Evidence to the Eloff Commission, loc. cit.
14 Ibid.
15 Ibid.

2 FORBIDDEN PASTURES

1 Figures from Mary Benson, *The Struggle for a Birthright*.
2 I. B. Tabatha, *Education for Barbarism*.
3 M. B. Yengwa, source unknown.
4 Evidence to the Eloff Commission, *Ecunews*, June 1983.
5 Trevor Huddleston, *Naught For Your Comfort*.
6 Desmond Tutu, *Crying in the Wilderness*.
7 Trevor Huddleston, op. cit.
8 Albert Luthuli, *Let My People Go*.
9 Ibid.
10 *Hansard*, V, 11, 1945.
11 Ibid.
12 Ibid.
13 Ibid., V, 11, 1953.
14 I. B. Tabatha, op. cit.

15 Desmond Tutu, Nineteenth Feetham Lecture, Witwatersrand University, 1985.

3 GROWING INTO PRIESTHOOD

1 Interview with Shirley Moulder, *South African Outlook*, February 1982.
2 Evidence to the Eloff Commission, *Ecunews*, June 1983.
3 *South African Outlook*, February 1982.
4 Evidence to the Eloff Commission, loc. cit.
5 Anthony Sampson, *Drum*.
6 Jan van Riebeeck, the first government official at the Cape, is seen as the founding father of the nation by white South Africans.
7 Mary Benson, *The Struggle For a Birthright*.
8 Anthony Sampson, op. cit.
9 *Fair Lady*, May 1st, 1985.
10 *South African Outlook*, February 1982.
11 Ibid.
12 'Address to Deacons Lesotho, 1977', *Hope and Suffering*.

4 NO PASSBOOK REQUIRED

1 Letter from Desmond Tutu to the Dean of King's College, London, October 16th, 1961.
2 Ibid., February 1st, 1962.
3 Ibid., November 19th, 1962.
4 Evidence to the Eloff Commission, *Ecunews*, June 1983.
5 Comment, *King's College Newsletter*, December 1984.
6 Ibid.
7 Evidence to the Eloff Commission, loc. cit.
8 Ibid.
9 Comment, *King's College Newsletter*, December 1984.
10 Ibid.
11 Letter from Desmond Tutu to the Dean of King's College, October 27th, 1964.
12 Ibid., July 29th, 1964.
13 Evidence to the Eloff Commission, loc. cit.
14 Letter from Desmond Tutu to the Dean of King's College, August 23rd, 1965.
15 Walter Makhulu, later Bishop of Central Africa, was a curate in Battersea while Tutu was in England.
16 *Daily Mail*, October 7th, 1985.

5 AN OASIS IN THE EASTERN CAPE

1 Desmond Tutu to Martin Kenyon, December 19th, 1966.
2 Ibid., January 1st, 1967.
3 Leah Tutu to Mrs F. Brownrigg, March 9th, 1967.
4 Desmond Tutu to Martin Kenyon, February 24th, 1967.
5 Ibid.

6 Leah Tutu to Mrs F. Brownrigg, March 9th, 1967.
7 William Shakespeare, *Twelfth Night*, Act II, Scene V, 158.
8 Interview with Shirley Moulder, *South African Outlook*, February 1982.
9 Nelson Mandela, *The Struggle Is My Life*.
10 Steve Biko, *I Write What I Like*.
11 Desmond Tutu to Martin Kenyon, March 5th, 1968.
12 Ibid., February 24th, 1967.
13 Steve Biko, op. cit.

6 OUT OF SOUTH AFRICA

1 Evidence to the Eloff Commission, *Ecunews*, June 1983.
2 *Hope and Suffering*.
3 Ibid.
4 Ibid.
5 Kofi Appiah-Kubi and Sergio Torres, eds, *African Theology en route*.
6 Ibid.
7 *Hope and Suffering*.
8 Kofi Appiah-Kubi and Sergio Torres, op. cit.
9 *Hope and Suffering*.
10 St Luke, 4:18.
11 *Hope and Suffering*.
12 *Crying in the Wilderness*.
13 Charles Villa-Vicencio and John W. de Gruchy, eds, *Resistance and Hope: South African Essays in Honour of Beyers Naudé*.
14 Kofi Appiah-Kubi and Sergio Torres, op. cit.
15 Letter from Canon Sydney Evans to Dr Shoki Coe, August 25th, 1971.
16 Letter from Dr Shoki Coe to Canon Sydney Evans, August 5th, 1971
17 *South African Outlook*, February 1982.
18 *Concord Weekly*, October 26th–November 2nd, 1984.
19 Evidence to the Eloff Commission, loc. cit.
20 Letter from the Reverend Charles Cartwright to the author, July 21st, 1986.
21 From a taped talk given when Desmond Tutu was at the Theological Education Fund.

7 DEAN OF JOHANNESBURG

1 Christmas letter from Dean Tutu to friends, November 22nd, 1975.
2 *Hope and Suffering*.
3 *Concord Weekly*, October 26th–November 2nd, 1984.
4 Ibid.
5 *Pro Veritate*, 1975.
6 'Politics and Religion – The Seamless Garment', *Hope and Suffering*.
7 John W. de Gruchy, *The Church Struggle in South Africa*.
8 'Politics and Religion – The Seamless Garment'.
9 Circular letter to friends, September 16th, 1975.

10 *Race Relations News*, January 1976.
11 Ibid.
12 Ibid.
13 Open letter to Mr John Vorster, quoted in *Hope and Suffering*.
14 Ibid.
15 Ibid.
16 Ibid.

8   THE MOUNTAIN KINGDOM

1   *South African Outlook*, February 1982.
2   The Federal Theological Seminary moved to Pietermaritzburg in the mid-1970s.
3   Bishop Tutu to the Reverend Professor Hanson, November 14th, 1978.
4   Basotho: the people of Lesotho; Mosotho: singular.
5   Bishop Tutu to the Reverend Professor Hanson, op. cit.
6   Circular letter from Bishop Tutu to friends, December 3rd, 1976.
7   Bishop Tutu to the Reverend Professor Hanson, op. cit.
8   *South African Outlook*, February 1982.
9   Bishop Tutu to Bishop Walter Makhulu, February 21st, 1979.
10 Ting: corn meal made sour, like sour cream porridge.
11 The Inaugural Desmond Tutu Peace Lecture, September 1985. (This was to be held in Soweto, but was never delivered as the police banned the meeting.)
12 Nelson Mandela, *The Struggle is My Life*.
13 'An African Views American Black Theology', *Worldview*, vol. 17, no. 8, August 1974.
14 'Black Theology/African Theology – Soul Mates or Antagonists?', *Journal of Religious Thought*, 32, no. 2, Fall–Winter 1975.
15 Evidence to the Eloff Commission, *Ecunews*, June 1983.
16 Desmond Tutu, *Crying in the Wilderness*.
17 Mr Kruger was Minister of Justice at the time.
18 *Apartheid: The Facts*, International Defence and Aid Fund, 1983.
19 Allen Cook, *South Africa: The Imprisoned Society*.
20 Ibid.
21 'The Theology of Migrant Labour', *South African Outlook*, December 1968.
22 Ibid.
23 Ibid.
24 *South African Outlook*, February 1982.
25 Father Aelred Stubbs to Bishop Tutu, February 16th, 1978.

9   THE CHURCH WAKES UP

1   *Observer*, October 10th, 1954.
2   A secret Afrikaner society founded in 1918.

3 Marjorie Hope and James Young, *The South African Churches in a Revolutionary Situation*.
4 John de Gruchy, *The Church Struggle in South Africa*.
5 John de Gruchy and Charles Villa-Vicencio, eds, *Apartheid Is a Heresy*.
6 Councils in the Ecumenical Movement: South Africa 1904–1975 (Johannesburg: SACC, 1979), quoted in Hope and Young, op. cit.
7 'Pseudo-Gospels in South Africa', a report published in Johannesburg 1968, quoted in John de Gruchy, op. cit.
8 Ibid.
9 John de Gruchy and Charles Villa-Vicencio, op. cit.
10 John de Gruchy and Charles Villa-Vicencio, eds, *Resistance and Hope*.
11 Report of the Commission of Enquiry into the SACC (Republic of South Africa, 1983).

10 A PARISH WITHOUT FRONTIERS

1 *Hope and Suffering*.
2 Ibid.
3 Professor Francis Wilson in conversation with the author.
4 Helen Joseph in conversation with the author.
5 Martin Conway in conversation with the author.
6 Bishop Tutu to Mrs Campbell, November 5th, 1979.
7 David Botha to Bishop Tutu, June 29th, 1979.
8 *Argus*, March 5th, 1981.
9 Bishop Tutu to the Reverend V. Roberts, October 11th, 1982.
10 Bishop Tutu to Sister Pauline OHP, January 30th, 1980.

11 THE HOTTEST ECCLESIASTICAL SEAT

1 *Crucible*, July–September 1978.
2 Letter from Bishop Tutu to the Suffragan Bishop of Oregon, April 26th, 1978.
3 *South African Outlook*, February 1982.
4 Estimate based on 1970 statistics in the SACC report.
5 Report of the Commission of Enquiry into the SACC, 1983.
6 Ibid.
7 Transcript of taped interview between Bishop Tutu and Mr Eugene Roelofse, February 4th, 1980.
8 *Encounter*, April 1980.
9 *Apartheid: The Facts*, op. cit.
10 Ibid.
11 *Hope and Suffering*.
12 *Financial Mail*, March 1980.
13 Margaret Nash, *Black Uprooting from 'White' South Africa*.
14 Letter from the Minister of Co-Operation and Development to Mr Saul Mhkize, who was later shot dead by police during a removals protest.

15 At the time the South African Rand was equivalent to about 53p. sterling or 44 US cents.

12 CRYING IN THE WILDERNESS

1 'Azania' is a name used for South Africa by sections of the black consciousness movement. AZAPO was founded in the tradition of Black Consciousness after the banning of the black activist organisiations in 1977.
2 Report of the Commission of Inquiry into the SACC, 1983.
3 *Cape Times*, July 30th, 1979.
4 Marjorie Hope and James Young, *The South African Churches in a Revolutionary Situation*.
5 Report of the Commission of Inquiry into the SACC.
6 Hope and Young, op. cit.
7 Report of the Commission of Inquiry into the SACC.
8 Ibid.
9 Alan Paton, *Cry the Beloved Country*.
10 Report of the Commission of Inquiry into the SACC.
11 Ibid.
12 *Hope and Suffering*.
13 Report of the Commission of Enquiry into the SACC.
14 Letter from Bishop Tutu to A. J. Ardington, April 28th, 1981.
15 Letter from Bishop Tutu to R. Proctor Sims, July 19th, 1980.
16 *Star*, May 20th, 1982.
17 *Hope and Suffering*.
18 Transcript of the meeting between members of the SACC and P. W. Botha, August 27th, 1980.
19 *Citizen*, June 30th, 1982.
20 *New York Times*, June 17th, 1982.
21 *Ecunews*, vol. 9, 1979.

13 DAVID AND GOLIATH

1 *Observer*, September 5th, 1982.
2 The Drawbridge Lecture, November 19th, 1984, published by the Christian Institute Trustees.
3 On learning the true source of the money Bishop Tutu immediately refunded it.
   All other quotations in this chapter are from documents appertaining to the Eloff Commission in the possession of the SACC.

14 VOICE OF THE VOICELESS

1 Bishop Tutu to Deaconess Cooke, August 17th, 1978.
2 The Right Reverend Wesley Frensdorff to Bishop Tutu, October 17th, 1978.
3 *Parishioner*, September 1978.

4   *Rand Daily Mail*, April 17th, 1980.
5   Bishop Tutu to the Officer-in-Charge, December 22nd, 1978.
6   *Harvard Gazette*, June 7th, 1979.
7   Bishop Tutu to Betty Ward, July 17th, 1979.
8   Thembi Sekgaphane, Mary Mxadana and Lenki Khanyile from the SACC.
9   *Rand Daily Mail*, September 7th, 1982.
10 'A Vision for Humanity', Address on the award of the Martin Luther King Peace Prize, January 1986.
11 *Washington Post*, February 16th, 1986.
12 *Penthouse*, June 1986.
13 *Observer*, August 8th, 1982.

15   A KIND OF SACRAMENT

1   A longer section of this speech is quoted in the Prologue to this book.
2   *Sowetan*, October 22nd, 1984.
3   Quoted in the *Church of England Newspaper*, November 16th, 1984.
4   *Sunday Times*, October 21st, 1984.
5   Ibid., October 28th, 1984.
6   *Christianity and Crisis*, February 4th, 1985.
7   *Africa Report*, January–February 1985.
8   *New York Times*, December 8th, 1984.
9   Ibid., December 12th, 1984.

16   'EVERYBODY'S BISHOP'

1   *Sunday Times*, October 28th, 1984.
2   *Ecunews*, December 1984.
3   *Citizen*, November 15th, 1984.
4   Ibid.
5   *Sunday Star*, November 25th, 1984.
6   *Evening Post*, November 15th, 1984.
7   Ibid.
8   *South Coast Sun*, November 30th, 1984.
9   *Watchman*, November 1985.
10 Letter from Winnie Mandela to Senator Kennedy, January 24th, 1986.
11 *Guardian*, July 26th, 1985.
12 *Time*, August 5th, 1985.
13 *Guardian*, August 1st, 1985.
14 *Weekend Argus*, February 1st, 1986.
15 Mark Mathabane, *Kaffir Boy*.

17   'TUTU CAN'T SWIM'

1   Buti Tlhagale and Itumeleng Mosala, eds, *Hammering Swords Into Ploughshares*.

2 *Crying in the Wilderness.*
3 'Words for Penn', *Almanac*, March 4th, 1986.
4 *Second National Consultative Conference of the ANC* (ANC, 1985).
5 *Sunday Star*, January 26th, 1986.
6 Peter Godwin, *Sunday Times*, 1985.
7 *Seek*, October 1985.
8 Speech given in America 1986.
9 Press statement, August 1986.
10 'Whose Rubicon?', BCC and CIIR, 1986.
11 *Cape Times*, June 2nd, 1986.
12 Published by the Kairos Theologians, PO Box 3207, Braamfontein 2017; and in the UK by the Catholic Institute for International Relations and the British Council of Churches.
13 *Washington Post*, October 2nd, 1985.

18 ARCHBISHOP OF CAPE TOWN

1 *Observer*, September 7th, 1986.
2 *Weekend Argus*, April 12th, 1986.
3 *Star City*, May 15th, 1986.
4 *Natal Witness*, April 16th, 1986.
5 *Pretoria News*, April 15th, 1986.
6 *Citizen*, April 17th, 1986.
7 *Eastern Province Herald*, April 17th, 1986.
8 *Daily News*, April 15th, 1986.
9 *Daily Dispatch*, April 16th, 1986.
10 *Sunday Star*, April 20th, 1986.
11 *Cape Times*, April 19th, 1986.
12 *Star*, August 31st, 1986.

EPILOGUE

1 Letter to the author, September 29th, 1987.
2 *Seek*, September 1987.

Quotations used in the text and not listed above are from interviews with the author.

Select bibliography

Appiah-Kubi, Kofi, and Torres, Sergio, eds, *African Theology en route*, Orbis Books, 1983.
Austin, Dennis, *South Africa 1984*, Routledge & Kegan Paul, 1985.
Benson, Mary, *The Struggle for a Birthright*, International Defence and Aid Fund, 1985.
Benson, Mary, *Nelson Mandela*, Penguin Books, 1986.
Biko, Steve, *I Write What I Like*, The Bowerdean Press, 1978.
Boesak, Allan, *Black and Reformed*, Orbis Books, 1984.
British Council of Churches, *Whose Rubicon?*, 1986.
BCC & CIIR, *The Kairos Document*, 1986.
Calvocoressi, Peter, *Independent Africa & the World*, Longman, 1985.
Catholic Institute of International Relations, *South Africa in the 1980s*, CIIR, 1986.
CIIR, *Treason Against Apartheid*, CIIR, 1985.
Church Information Office, *The Report of the Lambeth Conference, 1978*, CIO Publishing, 1978.
Cole, Ernest, *House of Bondage*, Allen Lane/Penguin, 1968.
Commonwealth Report, *Mission to South Africa*, Penguin Books, 1986.
Cook, Allen, *South Africa: the Imprisoned Society*, IDAF, 1974.
Couzens, Tim, and Patel, Essop, eds, *The Return of the Amasi Bird*, Ravan Press, 1982.
Davidson, Basil, *Southern Africa, Progress or Disaster?*, IDAF, 1984.
Davies, J. G., *Christian Politics and Violent Revolution*, Orbis Books, 1976.
Davies, O'Meara and Dlamini, *The Struggle for South Africa*: Vols 1 and 2, Zed Books, 1984.
Desmond, Cosmas, *The Discarded People*, Christian Institute of South Africa, 1970.
Dube, David, *The Rise of Azania*, Daystar Publications Ltd, 1983.
Feinberg, Barry, ed., *Poets to the People*, George Allen & Unwin, 1974.
Fugard, Athol, *Tsotsi*, Penguin Books, 1980.
Gastrow, Shelagh, *Who's Who in South African Politics*, Ravan Press, 1985.
de Gruchy, John, *The Church Struggle in South Africa*, Eerdmans Publishing Co., 1979.
de Gruchy, John, *Cry Justice*, Collins, 1986.
de Gruchy John and Villa-Vicencio, Charles, eds, *Apartheid is a Heresy*, David Philip, 1983.

de Gruchy John and Villa-Vicencio, Charles, eds, *Resistance and Hope*, David Philip, 1985.

le Guma, Alex, *Apartheid – a collection of writings on SA Racism by South Africans*, Lawrence & Wishart, 1972.

Harrison, David, *The White Tribe of Africa*, Ariel/BBC, 1981.

Hinchcliff, Peter, *The Church in South Africa*, SPCK, 1968.

Hope, Marjorie, and Young, James, *The South African Churches in a Revolutionary Situation*, Orbis Books, 1981.

Huddleston, Trevor, *Naught For Your Comfort*, Collins, 1956.

International Defence and Aid Fund, *Apartheid: The Facts*, IDAF, 1983.

Joseph, Helen, *Side by Side*, Zed Books, 1986.

Kuzwayo, Ellen, *Call me Woman*, The Women's Press, 1985.

Leach, Graham, *South Africa*, Routledge & Kegan Paul, 1986.

Lelyveld, Joseph, *Move Your Shadow*, Michael Joseph, 1986.

Luthuli, Albert, *Let My People Go*, Fount Paperbacks, 1982.

Mandela, Nelson, *The Struggle Is My Life*, IDAF, 1978.

Mandela, Winnie, *Part of my Soul*, Penguin Books, 1985.

Mathabane, Mark, *Kaffir Boy*, Macmillan, 1986.

McConkey, E., *The Failure of Bantu Education*, Progressive Federal Party, South Africa, 1970.

Moore, Basil, *Black Theology*, C. Hurst & Co., 1973.

Mphalele, Ezekiel, *The African Image*, Faber & Faber, 1962.

Nash, Margaret, *Black Uprooting*, SACC, 1980.

Omond, Roger, *The Apartheid Handbook*, Penguin Books, 1985.

— Vols One and Two, Zed Books 1985.

Parsons, Neil, *A New History of Southern Africa*, Macmillan, 1982.

Paton, Alan, *Apartheid and the Archbishop*, David Philip, 1973.

Paton, Alan, *Cry the Beloved Country*, Penguin Books, 1958.

Paton, Alan, *Federation or Desolation*, South African Institute of Race Relations, 1985.

Pityana, Barney, *From South Africa to England*, Christian Concern for South Africa.

Sampson, Anthony, *Drum*, Hodder & Stoughton, 1956.

Sampson, Anthony, *Black and Gold*, Hodder & Stoughton, 1987.

SACC, *Relocations: The Churches' Report on Forced Removals in South Africa*, SACC, 1984.

Stanton, Hannah, *Go Well, Stay Well*, Hodder & Stoughton, 1961.

Tabatha, I. B., *Education for Barbarism*, Prometheus Durban, 1959.

Thlagale, Buti and Mosala, Itumeleng, eds, *Hammering Swords into Ploughshares*, Skotaville Publishers, 1986.

Tutu, Desmond, *Crying in the Wilderness*, Mowbray, 1982.

Tutu, Desmond, *Hope and Suffering*, Collins, 1983.

Uhlig, Mark, ed., *Apartheid in Crisis*, Penguin Books, 1986.

Villa-Vicencio, Charles, 'Southern Africa Today', *Journal of Theology for Southern Africa*, December 1984.

Woods, Donald, *Biko*, Penguin Books, 1978.

Ziemer, Gregor, *Education for Death*, Constable, 1942.

Index

Index

Index

Index